Command

Strategy: A History (OUP, 2013)

The Future of War: A History (Penguin, 2018)

Nuclear Deterrence (Michael Joseph, 2018)

Ukraine and the Art of Strategy (OUP, 2019)

with Jeffrey Michaels, *The Evolution of Nuclear Strategy*, 4th edn (Palgrave, 2019)

LAWRENCE FREEDMAN

Command

*The Politics of Military Operations
from Korea to Ukraine*

OXFORD
UNIVERSITY PRESS

OXFORD
UNIVERSITY PRESS

Oxford University Press is a department of the University of Oxford. It furthers
the University's objective of excellence in research, scholarship, and education
by publishing worldwide. Oxford is a registered trade mark of Oxford University
Press in the UK and in certain other countries.

Published in the United States of America by Oxford University Press
198 Madison Avenue, New York, NY 10016, United States of America.

First issued as an Oxford University Press paperback 2023

Library of Congress Control Number: 2022943047

ISBN 978–0–19–754067–1 (Hbk.)
ISBN 978–0–19–769457–2 (Pbk.)

Paperback printed by Sheridan Books, Inc., United States of America

For my grandchildren – Ava, Oscar, Gracie, Kit and Ida

Most of the arguments and clashes of opinion that precede a major operation are deliberately concealed because they touch political interests, or they are simply forgotten, being considered as scaffolding to be demolished when the building is complete.

Carl von Clausewitz, *On War*, I, 3

Contents

CONTENTS

List of Illustrations

Every effort has been made to contact all copyright holders. The publisher will be pleased to amend in future printings any errors or omissions brought to their attention. Numbers refer to plates.

capital of the Democratic Republic of the Congo remains tense as the fighting continues in the east of the country. Image ID: 2D55RGG. Photograph: Reuters / Alamy.

19. Russian President Boris Yeltsin (*right*) and Russian Defence Minister Pavel Grachev (*left*) visit Tula Airborne Division. Photograph: Springtime of Nations Blog.

20. Pre-strike and post-strike assessment photograph of the Pristina military installation airfield, Kosovo, Serbia, used by Joint Staff Vice Director for Strategic Plans and Policy Maj. Gen. Charles F. Wald, US Air Force, during a press briefing on NATO Operation Allied Force in the Pentagon on 16 April 1999. Photograph: US Department of Defense.

21. NATO supreme commander General Wesley Clark (*left*) with British KFOR commander Lieutenant General Mike Jackson at his side, said at Kosovo airport on 13 September 1999 that Serb forces will not be permitted to return in any significant strength to the province. Clark also said NATO and the former Kosovo Liberation Army (KLA) rebels were close to agreement on a civil defence-type of force that would include many of the former rebels. Image ID: 2D5EMP3. Photograph: Reuters / Alamy.

22. Self-proclaimed Prime Minister of the pro-Russian separatist 'Donetsk People's Republic', Alexander Borodai (*centre*), and 'Donetsk People's Republic' self-proclaimed Defence Minister, Igor Strelkov (*left*), deliver a press conference in Donetsk on 10 July 2014. Photograph: Dominique Faget / AFP via Getty Images.

23. Sloviansk city council under control of armed forces. Photograph: Yevgen Nasadyuk / Wikimedia Commons.

24. A Russian armoured vehicle burns after fighting in Kharkiv on 27 February 2022. Street fighting broke out as Russian troops entered Ukraine's second-largest city, and residents were urged to stay in shelters and not travel. Photograph: Marienko Andrew / AP.

25. General Tommy Franks, Commander of the US Central Command (*right*) gestures during a news conference as Secretary of Defense Donald Rumsfeld looks on at the Pentagon in Washington Friday 9 May 2003. Photograph: AP Photo / Charles Dharapak.

26. Anti-Taliban Afghan fighters walk past a huge bomb crater in the ruins of an al Qaeda camp in Tora Bora, Afghanistan, 18 December 2001. Image ID: 2D3GKCC. Photograph: Reuters / Alamy.

List of Maps

Acknowledgements

This was a book largely written during the enforced solitude of the Covid pandemic. Fortunately, these days it is possible to stay in touch with friends and colleagues, and that meant I was able to get valuable comments back on draft chapters, and in some cases early versions of the whole manuscript. I am truly grateful to Ben Barry, David Deptula, Toby Dodge, Sam Freedman Ofer Fridman, Jack Gill, Michel Goya, Sam Greene, Frank Hoffman, Anthony King, Ben Lambeth, Carter Malkasian, Ibrahim Al-Marashi, Dan Marston, Jeff Michaels, Srinath Rhagavan, Kori Schake, Ayesha Siddiqa, Bruno Tertrais and Tom Waldman. It has also been a pleasure to work again with two first-class editors – Stuart Proffitt at Penguin and David McBride at OUP. Both have been full of good ideas for improving the book. I also appreciate the contributions of the team at Penguin, including Alice Skinner and Sarah Waldram. I am very fortunate to be represented by my excellent agents, Catherine Clarke and George Lucas. My wife Judith continues to tolerate my curious enthusiasm for writing about war, despite us both supposedly being retired and the opportunities to spend time with our grandchildren. It is to our grandchildren that this book is dedicated, with thanks for the joy they bring us and the hope that they will live in more peaceful times.

Introduction: Command as Politics

MARK ANTONY *When Caesar says 'Do this', it is performed.*
William Shakespeare, *Julius Caesar*, Act 1, Scene 2

The word 'command' comes from the Latin *mandare*, meaning to commit or entrust, from which we also get 'mandate'. The verb sense led to the noun sense, which was from the start synonymous with an order, but one that came with special authority. Contemporary dictionary definitions still point to authoritative orders, to be obeyed without question. The British Army has defined command as 'the authority which an individual in military service lawfully exercises over subordinates by rank or assignment'. It 'embraces authority, responsibility and accountability', has 'a legal and constitutional status', and enables individuals 'to influence events and order subordinates to implement decisions'.[1]

In a chain of command, orders start at the top and then cascade down until they reach the lowliest individuals. Below the supreme command, those in the chain are always accountable to someone at a higher level for what they do with the orders they receive, and for the quality of the orders they issue. Those on the receiving end of orders may have inner doubts and uncertainties, or even make known their misgivings openly, but the orders must still be followed and followed well. Commands are therefore much more than requests or suggestions, and, when a command is challenged, it is not only the wisdom of a particular instruction that is questioned, but also, potentially, the whole hierarchical structure behind it. To disobey an order is insubordination; to walk away is desertion; to depose a commander is mutiny.

Military organizations need strong chains of command because they are about disciplined and purposive violence. Commanders put those serving under them into unnatural situations, where they might be killed as they seek to kill others. At times of war, the special challenge of military command lies in persuading people to act against their own survival instincts and overcome the normal prohibitions about murdering their fellow humans. The stakes can be extremely high. Commanders, especially at the senior levels, can feel the burden of responsibility for the fate of nations, deeply aware of the potential for national humiliation should they fail, as well as the glory if they succeed.

Disciplined, fighting organizations act on commands; but, however well crafted these commands might be, they are not necessarily followed automatically and as intended. Sometimes they are simply inappropriate, perhaps based on dated and incomplete intelligence, and could not be implemented even by the most diligent subordinate commander. In other cases, subordinates may feel that implementation is possible but unwise, or that there is a better way. Faced with orders they dislike or distrust, subordinates usually have alternatives to outright disobedience: They can procrastinate, follow orders half-heartedly, or interpret them in a way that fits better with the situation confronted. In some cases, commanders encourage those closer to the action to make the final decisions; others want to be consulted every step of the way.

Command, therefore, is not a simple matter. It is about much more than handing out orders and ensuring that they are enacted. The stresses of combat impose special demands on commanders at all levels and it is assumed to require people of special character. The qualities that contribute to effective command are often those that would be admirable in almost any setting: professional knowledge; efficient use of resources; communication skills; ability to get on with others; moral purpose; sense of responsibility and care for subordinates.[2] In 1948 the US Army developed '11 principles of leadership', which were published in an army field manual on leadership in 1951 and taught thereafter to new cadets at West Point. These included the need to ensure tasks are 'understood, supervised, and accomplished', that people are trained as a team, that decisions are 'sound and timely', and that units are employed 'in accordance with [their] capabilities'.[3] To motivate their subordinates without resorting to crude threats of punishment or dismissal, or equally crude promises of honours and promotions, appeals can be made to pride, patriotism and values, protection of families and solidarity with colleagues. Loyalty can be enhanced by showing care for those under one's command and not taking unwarranted risks. Trust can be built by sharing hardships and danger and acquiring a reputation for achieving victories against the odds.[4]

Being a fine leader may be a necessary condition for a fine general but is not sufficient. According to the military historian Basil Liddell Hart, 'the two qualities of mental initiative and strong personality, or determination, go a long way toward the power of command in war'. These are 'the hallmark of the Great Captains'.[5] Another historian, Andrew Roberts, highlights more strategic talents: 'a feel for the coup d'œil, the capacity for inspiring strangers, the ability to create surprise, a facility for public relations, the gift of interlocking strategy with tactics and vice versa, a faculty for predicting an opponent's likely behaviour, a capacity for retaining the initiative'. He quotes General George S. Patton, who stressed the importance of being able to tell 'somebody who thinks he is beaten that he is not beaten'.[6] That *coup d'œil* – 'look of the eye' – is a consistent theme. Napoleon famously looked for 'lucky' generals on whom good fortune smiled. He spoke of the *coup d'œil* as the 'gift of being able to see at a glance the possibilities offered by the terrain', a quality he himself possessed to an exceptional degree. The theme was picked up by Carl von Clausewitz, the great Prussian theorist of war:

> When all is said and done, it really is the commander's *coup d'œil*, his ability to see things simply, to identify the whole business of war completely with himself, that is the essence of good generalship. Only if the mind works in this comprehensive fashion can it achieve the freedom it needs to dominate events and not be dominated by them.[7]

Another historian, the American Barbara Tuchman, argues that senior command in battle is 'the only total human activity because it requires equal exercise of the physical, intellectual, and moral faculties at the same time'. Echoing Patton, one of the more pugnacious of American generals, she puts a premium on 'resolution' – the 'determination to win through, whether in the worst circumstance merely to survive or in a limited situation to complete the mission, but, whatever the circumstance, to prevail'. Sometimes working against resolve is judgement, the capacity to read situations informed by experience. Judgement can lead to boldness, but, Tuchman notes, it is more likely to counsel 'Cannot', even while resolve is saying 'Can'.[8] When resolve is combined with a keen strategic intelligence the effects can be impressive; when combined with stupidity they are likely to be catastrophic.

Another explanation for military calamities is offered by the psychologist, Norman Dixon. He developed the somewhat reductive thesis that Britain's regular failures in battle were the result of too many openings for upper-class men with authoritarian, anti-intellectual personalities, inclined to recruit and promote like-minded individuals, all bound by tradition and incapable of adjusting as a situation demanded.[9] Others have noted forms of inflexibility that lead to failure: excessive caution; fixation with certain tactics; insisting that all is going to plan when the results are evidently poor; underestimating the enemy, perhaps because of national or racial stereotypes.[10] But the problems faced may have causes that lie well beyond the control of the commander. Enemies come up with strategies that could not have been anticipated. Unexpected developments cause delay and diversion. The logistical system cannot cope. Orders do not get through in a timely fashion and weapons do not perform as advertised. The war has already effectively been lost before it started, because the aims can never be achieved. Successful operational command, therefore, is not just a function of having the right sort of character but of the situations in which commanders find themselves and the military tasks they must perform.

One figure who thought more than most about the requirements for senior command positions was General George C. Marshall. He took up his position as US Army chief of staff as Germany invaded Poland at the start of September 1939, well aware that in the not-too-distant future US forces could be committed to war. He had seen enough during the First World War to know the consequences of weak generals in key positions: slovenly planning, inappropriate tactics, deteriorating morale, lost lives and broken bodies. As the army grew in size, he looked to raise the quality of those moving into command positions by improving officer education and ensuring that the best people were selected for the top jobs.

In September 1941, just two months before the United States did join the war, he told the first graduating class from officer school about the special challenges of command they would face.

> When you are commanding, leading men under conditions where physical exhaustion and privations must be ignored, where the lives of men may be sacrificed, then, the efficiency of your leadership will depend only to a minor degree on your tactical ability.

It will primarily be determined by your character, your reputation, not much for courage – which will be accepted as a matter of course – but by the previous reputation you have established for fairness, for that high-minded patriotic purpose, that quality of unswerving determination to carry through any military task assigned you.[11]

For the most senior posts, he realized that all this would not be enough. To replace the generals he had removed, because they were too old or set in their ways, he promoted younger officers who better understood the demands of modern warfare. To be sure that they could cope, he gave them progressively more demanding jobs, checking that they could handle their responsibilities until he moved them on to the next level.[12] He chose well. As his generals began to work with the British in the fight against Nazi Germany, their inexperience showed, but they were quick learners.

Marshall needed an additional quality, and one not often mentioned in the lists of command qualities – a political sensibility. Having witnessed the friction between the American, British and French high commands in 1917–18,[13] he wanted commanders who could work with members of the government and their staffs, other senior figures with distinctive command responsibilities of their own, and those from Allied countries with similar responsibilities but answerable to their own governments. The sheer weight of resources the Americans brought to the war effort meant that they soon expected the top jobs in charge of the collective alliance effort. That is why Marshall chose General Dwight D. Eisenhower to be supreme allied commander in Europe.

Eisenhower made his name by being astute rather than heroic. He never had an opportunity to prove himself as a young officer by leading a company into battle and learning how to act decisively under fire or face the confusion and uncertainty of combat. While others got their chance in France during the First World War, he was stuck in the United States developing plans for tank warfare. Frustrated by this lack of combat command, he was dismayed when asked by Marshall to join his staff at the Pentagon after Pearl Harbor. Marshall wanted Eisenhower for his keen intelligence and administrative efficiency, but then promoted him because of his ability to get along with the great variety of characters, both military and civilian, required for coalition warfare. His man in Europe had to be naturally cooperative rather than competitive. Many on the British side, who would now be working under him, were at first unimpressed. The irascible British general Bernard Montgomery complained to a colleague that Eisenhower's 'ignorance as to how to run a war is absolute and complete'.[14] Yet Montgomery, whose first command was as a platoon commander in France in August 1914, when he led a charge brandishing his sword, could not have done Eisenhower's job. A 'brilliant commander in action and trainer of men', observed Field Marshal Sir Alan Brooke, Marshall's equivalent on the British side, of Montgomery, 'but liable to commit untold errors in lack of tact, lack of appreciation of other people's outlook'.[15]

Eisenhower's generalship was about preparing and directing large and complex military undertakings, involving various nationalities. He saw himself implementing policy rather than making it, and was clever and well versed in military history, but also careful to avoid making enemies by showing off. He was highly professional in his grasp of how military power should be developed and applied, but what made the difference was that he could work with the combined chiefs of staff of the United States and United Kingdom, maintain the confidence of President Franklin Roosevelt and Prime Minister Winston Churchill, and cope with egotistical generals, not just the British Montgomery but also the American Patton.

The greatest of Eisenhower's undertakings was Operation Overlord, the invasion of Normandy. This was months in preparation, involving demanding logistical preparations, intelligence gathering and efforts to deceive the enemy about when and where the landing would take place. The scale was extraordinary. By the start of June 1944, there were 2,876,000 Allied soldiers, sailors and airmen under Eisenhower's command. Four thousand American, British and Canadian ships were ready to sail, 1,200 aircraft were ready to fly, and some 175,000 men were contemplating storming onto or dropping behind the Normandy beaches. When the moment came, after all this preparation and mobilization, everything depended on the weather. Eisenhower had to decide, advised by his chief meteorological officer, first whether to delay for a day because of stormy conditions and then to take advantage of a temporary break to go ahead on 6 June. There was nobody else who could make the call. He did so, accepting responsibility for success or failure. A message was prepared in case the worst happened and he had to withdraw the landing force. 'The troops, the air and the Navy did all that bravery and devotion to duty could do. If any blame or fault attaches to the attempt it is mine alone.' At this critical moment, his leadership was not marked by physical courage, but it did depend on moral courage.

Had the landing failed, Eisenhower's many critics would then have 'painted him in unflattering terms as a chairman of the board, beholden to many and in command of none'. This single decision sealed his reputation.[16] Even so, Andrew Roberts considers that including Eisenhower in the book he edited *Great Commanders of the Modern World* was 'debate-able'. Other chapters were on 'hands-on tacticians and battlefield commanders, as opposed to chiefs of staff who decided grand strategy from behind the lines, or even in different countries altogether'.[17] Roberts's hesitation is understandable. The study of command naturally gravitates towards 'hands-on tacticians and battlefield commanders', the remarkable individuals who through a combination of ambition, talent, will, chance and circumstance find themselves with an opportunity to make history through battle. They provide the great dramas of command. Yet Eisen-hower's inclusion was entirely appropriate. He set up a template for supreme command that was followed into the post-war period. In 1951 he briefly reprised his war-time role when he became NATO's first supreme allied commander Europe (SACEUR). Eisenhower as diplomat-general was not the only model for a supreme commander. As we shall see in the first chapter, Douglas MacArthur provided another – aloof and overbearing – in the Pacific. Eisenhower's, however, is the model that other theatre commanders have tended to follow, making it their business to understand the political context in which they might be conducting future operations and to know the local leaders.

As Eisenhower knew, commanders judged to be 'political' are often compared unfavourably with those whose focus is entirely on preparing for and engaging in combat. It is still the case that to be called 'political' is 'almost universally considered a slur on one's character'.[18] The term is used to refer to officers who play a bureaucratic game, who manipulate situations to suit their self-interest, making sure they have been noticed by their superiors, taking credit for another's bravery, or looking out for their unit to make sure that it gets its chance of glory or is not pushed into a dire situation. Closely related to this, politics can be used to explain distortions in the promotions process and in the allocation of key commands, if they are handed out because of loyalty and prejudice, without regard for professional competence or experience. Politics acquires its most negative connotation when it refers to partisanship, backing a political party while still in uniform. In modern democracies, members of the armed forces are expected to show restraint when it comes to choosing a government, other than exercising their right to vote along with other citizens. Military power should be kept separate from political power.

Yet, as Hew Strachan has observed, to be political, often 'just means that officers have to be able to negotiate as well as to fight, to be sensitive to others' culture as well as to the morale of their own units'.[19] In practice, a political sensibility is an essential part of a professional competence, enabling officers to understand the contexts in which they operate, and how the way they act affects these contexts. This includes the 'high' politics of international relations, of security threats and border disputes, of ideological competition and alliance formation, of the United Nations and pressures for ceasefires. This is the arena in which vital interests, enemies and partners are identified, and out of which the objectives for military action emerge. But it also includes the 'low' politics of bureaucratic frictions, professional rivalries, personality clashes, and competition for scarce resources – of different organizational cultures and operational concepts. Success here requires navigating contentious relations with civilian policymakers, commanders of units of the same service working in parallel, other branches of the armed forces, awkward subordinates who are reluctant to do as they are told, or unreasonable superiors who hand down orders that are impossible to execute. This is the arena in which the sources of dysfunction within military organizations can be addressed, whether by reforming obsolete practices, getting new equipment, or making submissions to influence the higher levels of policy. Here, the stubborn aggression that might make a general formidable in battle may be less helpful than the qualities of coalition-building, shrewd management, bargaining and persuasion, although a ruthless streak might be helpful in both.

These two arenas overlap. In any organization, there can be a tension between those at the top of the hierarchy, who must pay attention to the big picture, and those lower down, who must try to make sense of the orders handed down from above. Because of the importance of civilian primacy in democratic systems, there must be a clear separation between the decision-making role of the government and the more advisory role of the generals and admirals when it comes to setting the objectives for the use of armed force. In practice, this advisory role is one of substantial influence, and is often exercised energetically.

The overlap between the civilian and military spheres may be very evident at times of peace, when there will be arguments about long-term planning, budgetary allocations, personnel policy and weapons procurement. It is also evident at times of war, despite assumptions about an 'operational level of war' where military decisions must be taken free from political interference.[20] The purposes set by the government should infuse all operational decisions, while the problems and opportunities encountered in the field should be fed back into the development of national strategy. When it comes to implementing policy, civilians may accept that they have no special competence. They expect their military colleagues to know how to address logistical, intelligence, equipment and tactical issues. But they will still have questions about the smooth functioning of the command system, the causes of any reverses, the likelihood of casualties and the prospects for success. And they will still be held accountable if things go wrong.

Because of the imperatives for integration in the development of policy for the use of armed force, the important divide may, at times, not be between the civilian and military spheres, but between those in the national capital and those in the field tasked with implementing the policy. The high command may acquire a keen appreciation of the challenges faced by a government as they seek to sustain public support, cope with financial pressures and engage in diplomatic negotiations, and so the logic behind the agreed strategy. Their subordinates may see only excuses and prevarications for a lack of resources and support. If these subordinates lose trust in the high command, finding them out of touch with the realities of their situation, then unwelcome orders may be ignored or reinterpreted, even leading to outright insubordination. At times of extreme pressure, core relationships may snap: the high command and political leadership blame each other for failures; key commanders are dismissed while others become mutinous.

The inherent tensions of war test political systems. Dictators may have the freedom to make bold decisions and implement them quickly, but that means the flaws in these decisions are less likely to be exposed and challenged. Dictators may also with good reason feel that they are vulnerable to coups and so be more concerned to ensure that the officer corps has proven loyalty and is trusted not to attempt a power grab of its their own, despite the effects on professional competence.

Studies of command are naturally drawn to the world wars of the twentieth century when vast armies met in one titanic clash after another. Their scale, intensity and complexity mean that there are always new aspects to explore. At some point in the future there may be another clash on a similar scale, perhaps between the United States and China, and for which these experiences might still provide some guidance. Yet there is also a reason to consider more recent conflicts. These could be as intense and vicious, with political twists and turns of their own. Rupert Smith, one of the most successful British generals of recent times, recalls how in the 1990s he came to recognize

> a dissonance between the organization of existing forces and their operational activity . . . The new situations were always a complex combination of political and military circumstances, though there appeared to be little comprehension as to how the two became intertwined – nor, far more seriously from the perspective of the military practitioner, how they constantly influenced each other as events unfolded.[21]

For the major powers, the politics of military operations since 1945 has been shaped first by their desire to avoid a third world war and second by the difficulties they have experienced with irregular forms of warfare. The desire to avoid yet another global confrontation would have been present even without nuclear weapons, but their arrival made the prospect even more terrifying. This meant that, instead of doing 'whatever it takes' in the drive to victory, some restraint would need to be shown in the methods used, with the result that the enemy's unconditional surrender was less likely to be achieved. Keeping a war limited meant accepting that all objectives might not be achieved, and that the enemy would live to fight another day. Once the nuclear age had begun, it just took a hint of impending confrontation for fears to be expressed that some unexpected or unintended event might trigger Armageddon.

The difficulties with irregular forms of warfare became apparent during the wars of national liberation against the colonial powers that began after the end of the Second World War. The problem for the colonial powers was that they had no obvious way of bringing these conflicts to a conclusion, because the enemy had a continuing source of recruits while the population at home could soon get impatient with futile campaigns. Occasional victories brought respite but not resolution. Even after the former colonies had achieved independence, whenever Western powers were drawn back in, perhaps to support a friendly government or to prevent a humanitarian disaster, there was a high risk of getting caught up in situations from which it was difficult to withdraw. A government that could only survive with external help early in a conflict rarely achieved self-sufficiency during its course, although, to avoid indefinite commitments, there were efforts to improve governance and the conditions of ordinary people, and to build up indigenous forces so they could cope without foreign armies.

In addition to the views of the belligerents, there was also international pressure to keep wars limited. This was normally expressed through the United Nations, where there would be active promotion of ceasefires and proposals to send peacekeepers to monitor and even enforce these ceasefires once agreed. Military operations were influenced by the desire to get as much achieved – or as little lost – as possible, before the pressure could no longer be resisted.

At the same time, new technologies have expanded the range of military options available – from mass destruction, with whole cities able to be obliterated by a single nuclear weapon, to single attacks of pin-point accuracy directed at terrorist leaders. In Western countries, apart from occasional terrorist outrages, war has become something that happens elsewhere. It makes little difference to the way of life of the bulk of the population. Young people are no longer conscripted to fight. The fighters are instead volunteers, accepting the risks of their chosen profession, though they are not considered expendable. Protecting them is often described as the priority for any new mission. Even when claiming grandiose objectives, governments seek to limit their liabilities. Tom Waldman describes these wars as 'vicarious'.[22]

As an alternative to combat, which, even if starting off limited, might escalate to something worse, there has been growing interest in non-violent forms of pressure, such as cyberattacks, information warfare and economic sanctions, separately or in combination. Resort to these methods has become so regular, as the major powers compete for advantage and try to undermine their rivals, that a 'grey area' between war and peace has been identified as a busy arena of constant struggle. Here the aim is more disruption than destruction, undermining rather than overthrowing an opponent's political system by spreading rumours and false news, triggering breakdowns in infrastructure, and adding to economic stress.

Although a third world war has been avoided, there has been no shortage of military engagements, coming in all shapes and sizes, and involving many countries, including the major powers. There have been set-piece battles comparable to those of the Second World War, but also rebellions and prolonged counter-insurgency campaigns. Conflicts have led to a range of coalitions being formed, from traditional alliance to outside powers working with indigenous forces to defeat a local enemy. Our world continues to be shaped by these conflicts and the form they take can often be both disturbing as well as surprising.

This book explores the issues raised by the interplay between these political and operational considerations by examining a series of command decisions taken in the period after 1945. The cases chosen capture the diversity of contemporary conflict. In addition to those involving the United States and the United Kingdom, such as Korea, the Cuban Missile Crisis, Vietnam, the Falklands, Kosovo, Iraq and Afghanistan, I have also included the French colonial wars in Indochina and Algeria, conflicts between Israel and Arab states, and between India and Pakistan, civil wars in the Congo and Russian interventions in Chechnya and Ukraine. The Ukraine chapter is largely about the events of 2014, but takes in the Russo-Ukrainian War of 2022, which was a direct consequence of those events. This was another war launched by an isolated autocrat, encouraged by sycophantic hardliners and unchallenged by prudent advisers, based on an unwarranted contempt for the enemy and exaggerated confidence in what force of arms could achieve. Because this was the most substantial land war fought between modern armies for some time, it also revealed some of the practical challenges that commanders in the field face once they are in a serious fight against a competent and determined enemy.

This is not a comprehensive account of warfare in the post-1945 world, but I have tried to provide the context necessary to understand these conflicts and hope to have thrown new light on some important moments in contemporary history. Through these moments we can appreciate some of the core issues surrounding the exercise of command. Very few command arrangements at times of war are friction-free. Those giving orders do not always succeed in communicating them effectively or getting them to be followed as required. Those receiving orders can find them foolish or dangerous, convinced that their superiors do not appreciate their predicament or alternatively the opportunities on offer if only they were allowed to take bold action. Some get close to outright insubordination; others retreat into sullen obedience. Allies rub up against each other, with the junior partners suspicious that they are being asked to take unreasonable risks. The conditions of command can ease these tensions. How easy is it for those in the chain of command to communicate with each other and explain their situation? How much latitude have subordinate commanders been given to take initiatives without having to check back continually? How well have the political purposes that should infuse all operations been explained and understood?

With so much at stake, it is not surprising that these are stories marked by high drama, with clashes of personalities, intense arguments and high emotions. They are about moments when human agency mattered, when the fates of whole societies as well as numerous people hung in the balance, and when quirks of character, a small hesitation, or a rush of hubris, could push momentous decisions one way or the other.

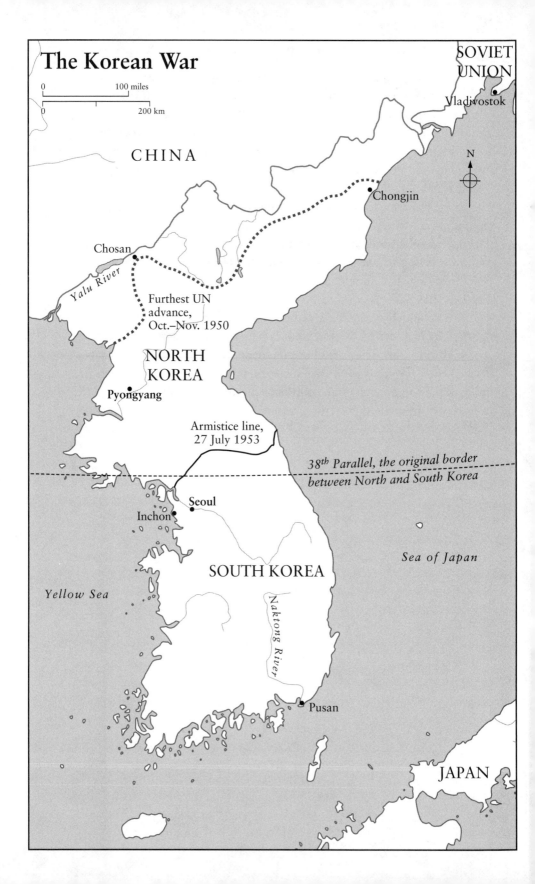

The Korean War

0   100 miles

0   200 km

SOVIET
UNION

Vladivostok

CHINA

N

Chongjin

Chosan

Yalu River

Furthest UN
advance,
Oct.–Nov. 1950

NORTH
KOREA

Pyongyang

Armistice line,
27 July 1953

*38th Parallel, the original border
between North and South Korea*

Seoul

Inchon

Sea of Japan

SOUTH KOREA

Yellow Sea

Naktong River

Pusan

JAPAN

I

Supreme Commander:
Truman and MacArthur

*I fired him because he wouldn't respect the authority of the Pres-
ident. I didn't fire him because he was a dumb son of a bitch,
although he was, but that's not against the law for generals. If it
was, half to three-quarters of them would be in jail.*
    Harry S. Truman, on why he dismissed Douglas MacArthur[1]

Democratic control of the armed forces requires that the military does
not get into a position where it can distort national priorities, pick and
choose the threats with which it wishes to deal, or else, and most seriously, take over the running of the country. The ideal situation is 'to
reconcile a military strong enough to do anything the civilians ask them
to do with a military subordinate enough to do only what civilians
authorize them to do'.[2] Civilians when in control are not invariably
right, and if the military voice becomes too muffled and hesitant then
national preparedness for war may suffer. For that reason, politicians
tend to be wary about gainsaying the military's professional advice.

  Samuel Huntington, in his 1957 book *The Soldier and the State*,
sets out a form of bargain by which civilians recognize 'autonomous
military professionalism', and in return get from the military political
neutrality and voluntary subordination. 'A highly professional officer
corps', Huntington observes, 'stands ready to carry out the wishes of
any civilian group which secures legitimate authority within the state.'[3]
This leads to distinct areas of responsibility. Soldiers should not run
states and politicians should not tell soldiers how to fight their battles.
In this way, the needs of both political accountability and operational
effectiveness are met.

This formula has been embraced by the military and taught at staff colleges. Governments provide political direction. Senior commanders offer advice on whether the objectives are too ambitious, not ambitious enough, misconceived or achievable. Once confirmed, the military must set about their implementation. Then the government must leave the operational decisions to the commanders. By this formula, the military are kept in their place: within that place their professional judgement prevails. For civilians, it is more problematic. It is good to have a military ethos that rules out coups, but short of coups there are still many ways in which civilian control can be undermined, while judgements presented by the military as being autonomous and professional can still seem to the lay observer to be poor and even dangerous. The formula cannot prevent the military influencing civilian decision-making, while civilians face strong resistance should they seek to challenge military decision-making.

At the same time, civilians are bound to have an interest in how wars are fought, not only because of the casualties incurred, but also because once a war starts there are always further strategic choices to be made. Where should the weight of force be best applied? Can specific objectives even be attained? How long can a society cope with an apparently never-ending war? Although it might not always be prudent for a politician to take an active interest in operational decisions, it is not improper. If they do not do so, generals and admirals may not be held to account and dismissed when they fail to deliver.[4] In practice, soldiers unavoidably influence the politics and civilians influence the operations.

The encounter that prompted Huntington, then a young Harvard political scientist, to embark on his study was that between President Harry Truman and General Douglas MacArthur, supreme commander in Korea.[5] In April 1951, Truman dismissed MacArthur. This clash gained headlines at the time and remained important because it captured in such an apparently pure form the tension between the civil and military spheres at the highest level of government. Truman saw the issue as a general challenging the president's political judgement; MacArthur framed it as a politician challenging a commander's military judgement. The clash went beyond civil–military relations, however. MacArthur had his supporters among Truman's political opponents, while MacArthur's judgement was questioned by senior military commanders. In this episode, all the sources of tension in command relationships came to the fore – issues of subordination, collegiality, character and competence, and political sensibility.

MacArthur was one of the most admired Americans of his time – far more so than Truman. He had acquired an unusual degree of autonomy from the constraints normally placed on serving officers. At 71, in 1951, he was well past the retirement age. While his flaws were well known, so were his strengths. The son of a military man who became governor-general of the Philippines, he had been in uniform since the start of the century. He gained his first star during the First World War and was US Army chief of staff in the 1930s. For nine years, through the Second World War and the subsequent occupation of Japan, he commanded US forces in the Pacific. From 1945, he was in charge of Japan, where he was treated with adulation and deference, with responsibilities that would normally have been assigned to a civilian. Clever and charismatic, but also vain, MacArthur was an active self-promoter with a keen appreciation of his own exceptional qualities. General Omar Bradley, chairman of the Joint Chiefs of Staff, described him as 'awesomely brilliant', yet with an 'obsession for self-glorification, almost no consideration for other men with whom he served, and a contempt for the judgement of his superiors'.[6]

George Marshall observed during the Second World War that MacArthur did not so much have a staff but a court, populated by sycophants, where he isolated himself from criticism and unwelcome advice.[7] This remained the pattern in Tokyo. Most of his staff had been with him since the 1930s and had perfected the arts of obsequiousness, reflecting his moods and prejudices, celebrating his achievements and blaming others, usually in Washington, for any setbacks. The columnist Joseph Alsop, visiting him in Tokyo, observed that his headquarters was 'proof of the basic rule of armies at war: the farther one gets from the front, the more laggards, toadies and fools one encounters'.[8] His boundless self-belief encouraged political ambitions; a long and close association with conservative Republicans gave him a strong base in the United States. He had been mooted as a possible contender for the Republican nomination in 1944 and his name reached the primaries in 1948. This did not get far, as he stayed both in uniform and in Japan.

Because of his long presence in a distant theatre, few in Washington knew MacArthur well personally. Even Secretary of Defense Marshall, previously chief of the army, had rarely met him. Secretary of State

Dean Acheson's low opinion of MacArthur was based on his behaviour and statements, not on any personal contact. This was all largely MacArthur's fault. From the start of the Korean War, he had refused all requests to come to Washington for consultations.[9]

This unfamiliarity was also true for Truman, who had made MacArthur effective viceroy of Japan in 1945, and put him in charge of the US and UN forces when North Korea invaded the South in June 1950. He could have appointed another general to take the lead in Korea, while leaving MacArthur in charge of the civilian administration in Japan. As it was, MacArthur held four separate commands: supreme commander for the Allied powers in Japan, commander-in-chief of UN forces, US commander-in-chief in the Far East and commanding general of US Army forces in the Far East, Despite the importance of his role, MacArthur would not deign to visit his commander-in-chief for consultations, a snub which confirmed Truman's view that he was a prima donna. For his part MacArthur had a low opinion of Truman, as he did of most politicians. Those who knew the president had come to admire the qualities that had enabled a man with little relevant experience to step into the job after Roosevelt's death and then address decisions of extraordinary significance over the next five years. By staying stubbornly in Tokyo, MacArthur had little appreciation of either the man or the issues with which his administration was grappling. When, after his dismissal, he was asked about how he ranked the risk of conflicts in Europe, he replied that he had never considered the matter as he was a theatre commander.

WAKE ISLAND

Because the general refused to move too far from the safe haven of his own headquarters, the president agreed to meet him on Wake Island in the Pacific on 15 October 1950. This was only an eight-hour flight away from Tokyo, although it required Truman to travel for three days. It is not clear what the president hoped for from the meeting. MacArthur suspected, with some justification, that Truman believed that it would help him in the forthcoming congressional elections. If he wanted a show of deference, he did not get it. Truman was greeted with a handshake rather than the salute due to him. The general was wearing an old hat and a baggy suit, with his trademark corn cob pipe. When the formal meeting was over, Truman invited him to stay for lunch. MacArthur pointedly declined, saying he had work to do in Tokyo.

The report of the formal meeting suggests a rather perfunctory conversation and contains no presidential assertion of authority. The only evidence of an attempt to do so comes from Truman's bodyguard, Floyd Boring. In an oral history, published decades later, he reported that as he drove the two men for a short car journey after the president arrived, Truman turned to MacArthur and said:

> Listen, you know I'm President, and you're the general, you're working for me ... You don't make any political decisions; I make the political decisions. You don't make any kind of a decision at all. Otherwise, I'm going to call you back, and get you out of there.[10]

If this conversation did take place, there is no indication that it made much of an impact on MacArthur. Secret Service agent Henry Nicholson, who was also in the car, recalled only that Truman asked anxious questions about possible Chinese intervention in Korea. Many accounts suggest that the meeting was generally cordial and positive. It would have been surprising if it had not been. The war had gone well up to this point and while Truman was apprehensive about the next stage he was impressed and reassured by MacArthur's confidence.[11] With his own ratings low and the general's high, the president was the needier. When MacArthur disregarded orders he disliked, or else interpreted them to suit his own preferences, the response in both the Pentagon and the White House tended to be cautious and tentative. MacArthur was not put on notice that his job was truly on the line until he was eventually dismissed.

In October 1950, MacArthur had good reason to feel confident. His prestige had never been higher. He had been thrust to the fore by the sudden extension of the Cold War from Europe into Asia. The previous year the communists took over China as the American-backed Nationalists retreated to the island of Formosa (now Taiwan). The 'loss' of China soon became a toxic issue in American politics, used by the Republican Party to attack Truman for his foreign policy weakness, with Senator Joseph McCarthy accusing him of harbouring active communists in his administration. The invasion of South Korea by the communist North in June 1950 was another unwelcome surprise. By means of some deft diplomacy at the United Nations, where the Soviet Union was absent from the Security Council in protest at the non-recognition of communist China, the administration was able to turn resistance to the communist advance into a UN cause. That is why MacArthur was the commander of UN forces as well as American. Once US troops reached Korea, they shored up South Korean resistance and then began to push the North Koreans back. In September, Mac-Arthur ordered a bold amphibious landing at Inchon, which many in the army saw as a reckless gamble. It caught the communists by surprise and turned out to be a brilliant manoeuvre. Truman sent his warmest congratulations for the victory: 'Well and nobly done.'[12]

Having prevented the unification of Korea under communist rule, the issue then became one of unifying it under anti-communist rule. There was no doubting MacArthur's preference about how to do this. Targets north of the 38th parallel (the dividing line between the two halves of Korea) had already been subjected to air strikes. If the North Korean army was allowed to retreat and then regroup, the original problem could return. Against this was the concern that if this led to China joining the war an even larger enemy would have to be fought.

On 27 September 1950, MacArthur was given his orders from the Joint Chiefs, approved by Truman. His 'military objective' was 'the destruction of the North Korean armed forces'. To achieve this, he was authorized to conduct operations, including the use of ground forces, north of the 38th parallel. The only proviso was that when he did so there were no 'major Soviet or Chinese Communist forces' in Korea or, should there be some present, they were not 'a threat to counter our operations militarily in North Korea'.

> Under no circumstances, however, will your forces cross the Manchurian or USSR borders of Korea and, as a matter of policy, no non-Korean ground forces will be used in the northeast provinces bordering the Soviet Union or in the area along the Manchurian border. Furthermore, support of your operations north or south of the 38° parallel will not include air or naval action against Manchuria or against USSR territory.[13]

Marshall sent a note adding: 'We want you to feel unhampered tactically and strategically to proceed north of 38th parallel', but also advising that he should make no public announcement of his intentions. This was because Moscow now appreciated its error in staying away from the Security Council and had returned. The Soviet Union could block a change in the UN mandate. Marshall urged that moves be justified on the basis of military necessity rather than a new political objective.[14]

Here we see how the military logic could push the political logic. The political objective, should the enemy army be destroyed, was, as agreed at the UN, to 'ensure conditions of stability throughout Korea', which implied unification. Although a clear limit was put on the extent of the permitted shift, as nothing must trigger war with China or the Soviet Union, the next move was framed in terms of military necessity. This left an inherent ambiguity. So long as the North Koreans still had an army, MacArthur's orders were to destroy it: if it were not destroyed, how could there be long-term stability? Yet, as the army retreated closer to the border, at some point the risk of a wider war would come into view. Exactly when this trigger point arrived would be a matter of judgement, best informed by intelligence assessments. There was also the question of whether MacArthur shared the concerns about the wider war, especially if he saw it as an opportunity to deal the Chinese communists a blow, as well as the North Koreans.

When Truman asked for reassurances at the Wake Island meeting, MacArthur told him that he believed 'formal resistance will end throughout North and South Korea by Thanksgiving.' He doubted that there would be Chinese or Soviet interference, but, should it occur, the US Air Force would inflict 'the greatest slaughter'.[15] Thus the trigger point was unlikely to be reached, but, if it were, his forces could cope. MacArthur was under no pressure from Truman to follow an alternative policy. The agreed communiqué referred to the 'very complete unanimity of views which prevailed', adding that this was why the meeting took so little time. On his return, Truman insisted that there was 'complete unity in the aims and conduct of our foreign policy.'[16] This unity, however, assumed that, under MacArthur, the UN forces would take what they wanted, but would also know when to stop.

CHINA INTERVENES

A few days later, MacArthur's forces captured the North Korean capital Pyongyang. Then hubris, a common affliction among successful and overconfident commanders, set in. On 24 October, in clear violation of his orders from the Joint Chiefs, he told his senior field commanders, 'to drive forward with all speed and with the full utilization of their force' to 'secure all of North Korea'. This meant going to the Yalu. Yet, in the face of this insubordination, the Chiefs hesitated. MacArthur's big moves taken in the past had turned out well. They confined themselves to asking him tentatively why he was departing from official policy. This was 'a matter of some concern here'.[17]

The risks were not hypothetical, as in early October there had already been some encounters with Chinese troops that had gone badly for US and Korean forces. Those risks were also confirmed by MacArthur's explanation – that Korean forces were unable to finish off the enemy on their own. Still, the Chiefs declared themselves satisfied.

A more ominous sign that matters were not as they should be came on 5 November. MacArthur again exceeded his orders, this time by bombing bridges across the Yalu River linking China to Korea without informing Washington of his intention. The Chiefs told MacArthur to stop. They found MacArthur's response stunning. He claimed an urgent military necessity. The Chinese threat was real.

> Men and material in large forces are pouring across all bridges over the Yalu from Manchuria. This movement not only jeopardizes but threatens the ultimate destruction of the forces under my command . . . Every hour that this is postponed will be paid for dearly in American and other United Nations blood.

He now wanted Truman to be asked specifically if he would countermand the Chiefs, lest their instructions 'result in a calamity of major proportion for which I cannot accept responsibility'. Bradley, as chairman, described himself 'dumbfounded' by this complete turnaround in the evaluation of the threat. Instead of being allowed latitude because he might bring victory, MacArthur now had to be given it to avoid defeat. At least he would have responsibility for whatever happened next. Perhaps, the Chiefs suggested in response, the objective of destroying all North Korean forces should now be reconsidered. Not at all, replied MacArthur, this still needed to be done.

Bombing the bridges was not enough to stop China's troops crossing into Korea. It was hard to hit them from the air, and, even if they were destroyed, the Chinese could put up pontoons. Soon the river froze, and bridges were not needed to get across. MacArthur now complained about being prohibited from attacking communist forces on Chinese territory, where they could enjoy sanctuary. He reported that he had three choices: go forward, remain immobile or withdraw. To do the second or third would mean giving up on victory, the definition of which he had recently expanded. So, he chose the first, hoping that the Chinese would still not intervene in numbers. On 24 November 1950, he announced the launch of a new offensive, which 'if successful' would

> for all practical purposes end the war, restore peace and unity to Korea, enable the prompt withdrawal of the United Nations military forces, and permit the complete assumption by the Korean people and nation of full sovereignty and international equality.

Without evidence, he claimed that Chinese supplies to the enemy had been interdicted. Reporters were told that he hoped 'to keep my promise to the G.I.'s to have them home by Christmas'.

At first the offensive went well. But the Chinese had gone to ground, not gone away. Instead of the around 25,000 enemy fighters MacArthur's HQ supposed, there were 200,000. UN forces were driven back in disarray with numerous casualties. Four days after he launched the 'end-the-war' offensive, the counterblow from the Chinese caught the Americans completely by surprise and inflicted heavy losses. The 2nd Infantry Division were mauled after marching into an ambush, while the 1st Marine Division struggled to escape after being surrounded at the Changjin Reservoir. Within a couple of weeks, the Eighth Army was back behind the 38th parallel preparing to defend Seoul, while X Corps was being pushed into a situation that could make evacuation unavoidable.

Now it was MacArthur's weakness rather than strength that kept him in place. Truman did not want to undermine his authority at a time of extreme pressure, while Marshall was opposed to giving tactical orders to a field commander from Washington. For his part, MacArthur had no compunction about blaming Washington for his predicament. He gave an interview to *US News & World Report* in which he complained that he was not allowed to pursue Chinese forces and attack their bases: 'An enormous handicap without precedent in military history'. At issue, he suggested, was his ability to 'safeguard the lives of his soldiers and safety of his army'.[18]

Truman was furious, but still hesitant, nervous about letting it appear that MacArthur was being fired because of his failures in command, although that was as good a reason as any. The attempt to rein him in was confined to an instruction of 6 December that all public statements on foreign policy must go through the State Department. No new orders were sent – neither those MacArthur wanted, allowing him more latitude, nor those he should have been given, which would have been more restrictive. General Matthew Ridgway, working for the Joint Chiefs at the time, asked General Hoyt Vandenberg, chief of the air staff, why MacArthur was not sent new orders. 'What good would it do?' replied Vandenberg. 'He wouldn't obey the orders. What can we do?' Ridgway asked: 'You can relieve any commander who won't obey orders, can't you?' Vandenberg's 'lips parted and he looked at me with an expression both puzzled and amazed'. He then walked away.[19]

DISMISSAL

It took until the spring for the issue to be resolved. In March, as the administration was beginning to explore a peace initiative, MacArthur released a statement demanding North Korea's surrender, in effect sabotaging the initiative. Congressman Joe Martin, the House Minority Leader, picked this up and observed in a speech that 'if we are not in Korea to win, then this Truman Administration should be indicted for the murder of thousands of American boys.' He sent MacArthur a copy of his speech. MacArthur wrote back to express his agreement, ending with the words, 'There is no substitute for victory.'[20]

After this letter was read on the floor of the House, Truman decided MacArthur had to go. Many of his advisers urged caution. The Speaker of the House of Representatives, Sam Rayburn, observed that MacArthur 'was something of a popular hero and any action would have political repercussions'. Even the chief justice of the Supreme Court was consulted. He urged care because 'the authority of the President of the United States was at stake and the constitutional questions involved.' Truman read up on past high-profile cases in which presidents had dismissed senior commanders, such as Lincoln's readiness to remove his top generals, until he found one that would fight the Civil War as it should be fought. Truman knew from the start that removing MacArthur was more than just an unusually tough personnel change.

Although Truman recalled Bradley as urging MacArthur's dismissal from the start, Bradley denied this. The general's own recollection was that he was uncertain about whether the insubordination case was strong enough. Past orders had perhaps been too vague, and then, when ignored, not enforced. With Marshall, Bradley proposed sending a message to MacArthur telling him to shut up. When they began to draft the message, they realized that it would lack sufficient bite. Aware that Truman wanted dismissal, Bradley came up with the formula that MacArthur would have to go because he was out of sympathy with the president's foreign policy. Thus, the official notice of 11 April 1951 stated that Mac-Arthur had been dismissed from his 'commands in the Far East' because he had been 'unable to give his wholehearted support to the policies of the United States Government and of the United Nations in matters pertaining to his official duties'.[21] This had the advantage of being true, but it had also been the case for some time. Furthermore, it had the disadvantage of pitting the general against the president, on the basis of their competing views on the communist menace and what to do about it.

Truman's own explanation was somewhat blunter. MacArthur was guilty of 'rank insubordination'.[22] In his memoir, the insubordination was linked to the policy differences:

> If there is one basic element in our Constitution, it is civilian control of the military. Policies are to be made by the elected political officials, not by generals or admirals. Yet time and again General MacArthur had shown that he was unwilling to accept the policies of the administration.[23]

What made the difference in April 1951, after months of insubordination, was that the aura surrounding MacArthur had been punctured by his failures in command, although the situation on the ground had helpfully stabilized sufficiently for this to be as good a time as any to dismiss him. His failures were more than not anticipating or preparing for a substantial Chinese intervention. Despite the material advantages enjoyed by US forces, there had been a succession of setbacks. Incompetent officers had been left in position; personal animosities allowed to fester; basic errors made in the disposition of the forces; inadequate support given to beleaguered front-line commanders; forces divided and unable to work together. There had been high casualties among units caught out by the Chinese attacks and stranded beyond reinforcement. Many wounded were left behind.

His senior intelligence officer, Major General Charles Willoughby, was dabbling extensively in right-wing politics, when he should have been attending to the Chinese. MacArthur called him his 'pet fascist'. (On retirement he worked for the Spanish dictator Francisco Franco.) Aware that his boss disliked the idea that the Chinese might enter the war, he had consistently dismissed evidence that this might happen, even when a talkative Chinese prisoner was captured (recast by Willoughby as a Korean resident of China who had volunteered to fight). Rather than preparing those in the field for what might come their way, the objective was to avoid giving Washington any excuse for taking too close an interest in MacArthur's plans.[24] General Edward Almond, another sycophant, in charge of X Corps, also played down the Chinese threat ('a bunch of Chinese laundrymen') and ordered units forward into disaster. After they became isolated and the Joint Chiefs became alarmed, MacArthur calmly told them that he had ordered Almond not to let this happen and not to worry as the enemy would not be able to take advantage of the fact that some of his elements had become over-extended.[25] Almond also fell out with, among others, the more talented General Walton Walker, commanding the Eighth Army. MacArthur, orchestrating the war from Tokyo, was unaware of the dysfunctional relations among his field commanders or indeed the state of the fighting.

When Walker was killed in a road accident in late December, he was replaced by Ridgway, an experienced and shrewd general, who was not under MacArthur's spell and understood the policy he was supposed to follow. Truman 'had made unmistakably clear that his primary concern was not to be responsible for initiating World War III'. In contrast, 'MacArthur had been proposing to attack China, to bring Nationalist troops onto the Korean peninsula, and to impose a blockade of the Chinese coast.'[26] Ridgway sorted out the Eighth Army and was soon ready to fight back against the enemy.[27] MacArthur did not appreciate what Ridgway had achieved, nor the importance of this demonstration that the war could be conducted without resorting to extreme remedies. Instead, he looked for opportunities to upstage Ridgway. But he was no longer held in awe. The Chiefs were disenchanted with MacArthur on military grounds. He had made some poor strategic and tactical decisions. As one of Bradley's staff observed:

What really counted was that MacArthur had lost confidence in himself and was beginning to lose the confidence of his field officers and troops. There is nothing in the book that more seriously undermines a commander's effectiveness than this.[28]

Truman wanted to dismiss MacArthur because of his insubordination. He was able to do so because MacArthur had revealed that he was flawed and had lost the support of the military leadership.

A more immediate issue was that MacArthur's core complaint was widely shared by many of his fellow officers. They were also bothered by an operational concept that accepted limitations on the use of force, described, somewhat unimaginatively, by MacArthur as appeasement. As Huntington notes, in terms of the senior military figures fighting the war in Korea, Ridgway was unusual. A congressional committee later reported 'a feeling of unease because victory was denied, a sense of frustration and a conviction that political considerations had overruled the military', and a desire to see these political restrictions removed.[29] The case for limited war in the nuclear age had been made, but in the military had not yet been accepted. The attritional strategy followed by Ridgway avoided defeat, although it also made it more difficult to bring the war to a satisfactory conclusion.

Once MacArthur had been dismissed, he returned to the United States, where he was a given a hero's welcome and feted by Republicans. He made stark his disagreement with the Truman administration, insisting that the issue was not about what policies to follow but how to fight a war. There was no 'alternative than to apply every available means to bring it to a swift end. War's very object is victory, not prolonged indecision. In war there can be no substitute for victory.'[30] His ability to mount a political challenge to Truman was hampered by his inability to present himself as the champion of a military position that had been ignored by cowardly politicians. The Joint Chiefs were clearly aligned with the president. Bradley famously warned that bombing China and blockading its ports 'would involve us in the wrong war, at the wrong place, at the wrong time, and with the wrong enemy'.[31] MacArthur was also showing his age. At the Republican convention in Chicago in July 1952, he was asked to give the keynote address, but he soon lost his audience. It was another former supreme commander who occupied centre stage at the convention. Dwight D. Eisenhower received his party's nomination and went on to become president.

CONCLUSION: OBEDIENCE TO THE COMMANDER-IN-CHIEF

MacArthur's dismissal is now taken as a vital assertion of the principle of military subordination to civilian authority. This was an important precedent but also an extreme case. The ability to dismiss a subordinate is an important feature of command at any level. There are three potential reasons for dismissal, each relevant in this case. The first, and most common, is for failure and incompetence. Even before disaster strikes, officers can be replaced because they lack the qualities for the job. Once disaster does strike, officers who have presided over a defeat, even if they have been unlucky and consider themselves scapegoats, are apt to be replaced. A second reason is insubordination. Insubordination comes in various forms, from occasionally disregarding orders to desperate attempts to change the course of a campaign. In any event, there can be no confidence that the subordinate will follow commands. Third, the subordinate does not accept the policy set by the government and so advocates alternative courses of action.

MacArthur had a career-long history of insubordination. Yet he created a legend around his own superior military judgement that enabled him to prosper despite his lack of regard for his superiors. In terms of the integrity of the command system, any insubordination should be intolerable. In practice, acts of apparent insubordination that have good results tend to be tolerated. This is what happened with MacArthur in Korea, at least up to late 1950. After playing down the possibility of an effective Chinese intervention, he made no apologies as UN forces were badly mauled and rushed to retreat. Instead, he raised the stakes by blaming the policy constraints under which he had to operate. When he was eventually sacked, this was put down to his policy differences with the government rather than command failures.

Why was this? In late 1950, Truman, though alarmed by the reverses, did not want to convey panic and desperation by sacking the top man. He also recognized MacArthur's special status as a revered figure, beyond criticism, and so unassailable. Truman had contributed to this by turning to him to respond to the North's invasion of the South in June 1950. To complicate matters further, he was a potential political rival as much as a subordinate commander, already discussed as presidential material and with a known Republican affiliation. So, despite his irritation with the supreme commander, the president held back. By the next spring, when the military situation was more stable, MacArthur had developed his critique of the administration's policy. Despite his dismissal being triggered because he disobeyed an order not to pronounce on policy matters, MacArthur was able to move the debate away from his performance as a commander and his insubordination, to his challenge to the supposed weakness of Truman's foreign policy and prosecution of the war. This was his preferred ground as it pushed the issue away from his professional competence to Truman's.

Once dismissed, MacArthur questioned whether he really was subordinate to Truman. He spoke of a

> new and heretofore unknown and dangerous concept, that members of our armed forces owe primary allegiance or loyalty to those who temporarily exercise the authority of the Executive Branch of the Government rather than to the country and its Constitution which they are sworn to defend. No proposition could be more dangerous.[32]

The proposition that military leaders can decide to be disloyal when they disagree with a particular president is normally considered to be far more dangerous than a president asserting authority over the military, for this is a logic that could lead to coups. At all levels of the chain of command, including the president, individuals have only temporary authority, but it is still sufficient to exercise command. Yet while in his case MacArthur's observation was disingenuous, behind it there was a perplexing question: what was an officer supposed to do when the chain of command demanded behaviour which was illegal, contradicted core values, or was otherwise unconscionable? It is a question to which we will return throughout this book.

2

The Fury of the Legions:
The French Army in Indochina
and Algeria

If it should be otherwise, if we should have to leave our bleached
bones on these desert sands in vain, then beware the fury of the
Legions.
Falsley attributed to Marcus Flavinius, second century CE

The question of whether the military's loyalty is to the government of the day or some higher notion of the interests of the state came up in an even starker form in the case of France's two great colonial wars in, respectively, Indochina and Algeria. The challenge presented itself most sharply in connection with the Algerian War, but the seeds were sown earlier in Indochina, as a weak government struggled to get a grip on the war and left soldiers trying to cope with inadequate resources and a confused political direction. The colonels and the captains, to the fore in the field and taking responsibility for the tactics on the ground, even when ethically distasteful, were the most prone to disaffection and a sense of distance from the political echelon. This led to a spiritual as well as physical separation.

This is powerfully covered in two novels by Jean Lartéguy – *The Centurions* and *The Praetorians*. Lartéguy had fought in the French resistance against the Nazis and then become a journalist and novelist, showing a particular affinity for the troops fighting thankless colonial wars. One of his leading characters was Lieutenant Colonel Pierre-Noel Raspéguy, a composite of the real individuals who had fought in these wars. He is a 'soldier's soldier', contemptuous of those who rise to the top through their political connections,

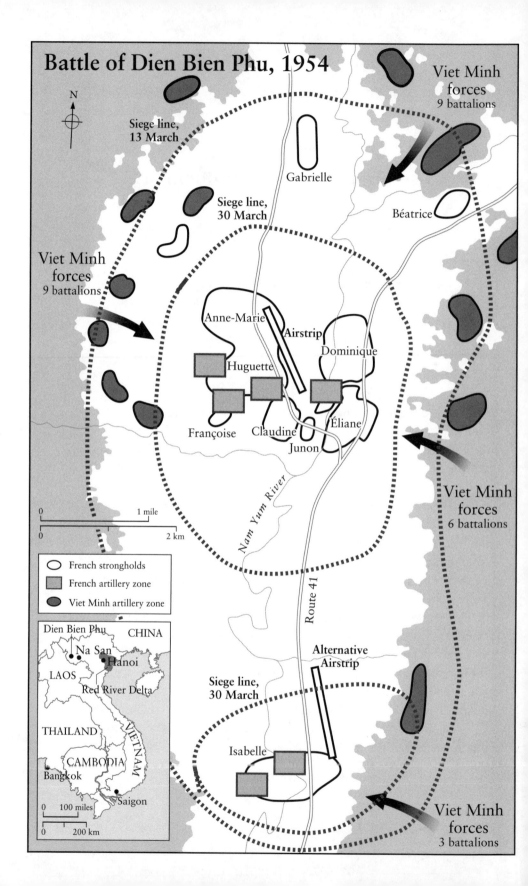

Battle of Dien Bien Phu, 1954

N

Viet Minh
forces
9 battalions

Siege line,
13 March

Siege line,
30 March

Gabrielle

Béatrice

Viet Minh
forces
9 battalions

Anne-Marie

Airstrip

Dominique

Huguette

Françoise

Claudine

Éliane

Junon

Viet Minh
forces
6 battalions

0   1 mile
0   2 km

French strongholds
French artillery zone
Viet Minh artillery zone

Nam Yum River

Route 41

Dien Bien Phu
CHINA
Na San
Hanoi
LAOS
Red River Delta
THAILAND
VIETNAM
CAMBODIA
Bangkok
Saigon

0   100 miles
0   200 km

Alternative
Airstrip

Siege line,
30 March

Isabelle

Viet Minh
forces
3 battalions

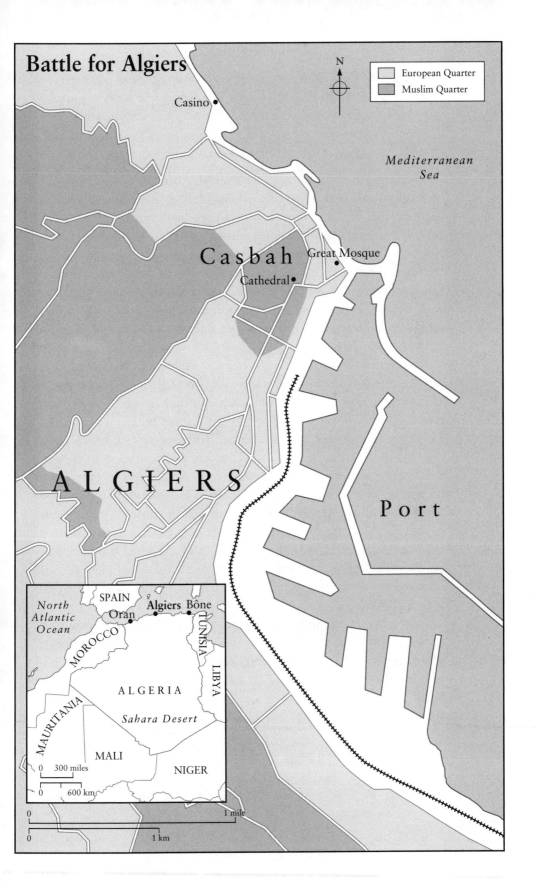

Battle for Algiers

N

European Quarter
Muslim Quarter

Casino

Mediterranean Sea

C a s b a h

Great Mosque

Cathedral

A L G I E R S

P o r t

North Atlantic Ocean

SPAIN

Oran   **Algiers**   Bône

MOROCCO

TUNISIA

LIBYA

MAURITANIA

ALGERIA

Sahara Desert

MALI

NIGER

0   300 miles

0   600 km

0   1 mile

0   1 km

who only do their fighting on paper, who draw up plans and believe that a battalion strength is eight hundred men, whereas in the line you're lucky if you have half that number; who believe that soldiers can go on forever, without being conscious of fatigue or despair, that they're nothing but machines with interchangeable gears.

The target of this contempt, General Meynier, has a higher opinion of Raspéguy. He is 'our best unit commander'. An engagement he led in Vietnam was a model of how to fight an 'infantryman's war', as he stayed in constant touch with his platoon commanders, inspiring them 'with his violence and strength and filling them with hope and zeal for the impending assault'. But, Meynier observes, he would never make a general, because he would lose the connection with his men. And there was another danger. Units like Raspéguy's are 'liable eventually to turn into sorts of sects which will no longer fight for a country or an ideal, but only themselves'.

Raspéguy is detached from the party squabbles of Paris politics, yet sees the outcomes of modern war as being determined by the strength of political convictions. When his men fight like the enemy he knows they can win. He gets the opportunity to prove his point in Algeria. Raspéguy uses the special bond he had with his men to demand that they follow only the rules he set. He tells his paratroopers 'to fight to the death, to keep my activity secret, to carry out every order I am given, no matter what it may be'. The war he is preparing to wage would be 'outside all regulations'.[1] He can see that the government in Paris is content to accept the results only so long as their tactics do not become public. In this way, the fighters become detached from the society they are supposed to serve, intolerant of those using them for the 'dirty work' who would be all too ready to push them aside when no longer of value.

Larteguy used the quotation, ostensibly from Marcus Flavinius, at the head of this chapter as a theme for *The Centurions*. It came from a letter apparently sent by the centurion to his cousin in Rome. Those who had sacrificed so much for the glory of Rome felt alarm when they heard that in the city

> factions and conspiracies are rife, that treachery flourishes, and that many people in their uncertainty and confusion lend a ready ear to the dire temptations of relinquishment and vilify our action.

34

Flavinius, it was suggested, had sought reassurance that they were supported. Otherwise 'beware the fury of the Legions'.

Only after using this letter in his book did Lartéguy discover that it was a fabrication, contrived by Roger Frey, a Gaullist politician associated with the hard-line faction in Algeria, who wished to encourage the French legions to push away a weak government in Paris.[2] This was the sentiment that led in May 1958 to the first 'revolt of the generals', which enabled General Charles de Gaulle to achieve power. There was a second revolt in April 1961, which President de Gaulle swatted away. In both cases, senior commanders in Algeria were at the heart of the revolts.

This was a time when military coups in West European countries were quite thinkable. Spain and Portugal were ruled by military dictatorships that had taken power before the Second World War. Later, from 1967 to 1974, Greece had a military government. Turkey suffered regularly from military coups. They tend to be justified as a response to the failures of civilian government, whether decadence, corruption or simple incompetence. The military claims to be loyal to the highest values of the state and more capable of their defence than whatever collection of politicians happens to be governing at the time. This is an issue that goes to the heart of civil–military relations, and one we have seen raised by MacArthur. Under what circumstances will – and should – senior commanders deny the legitimacy of the civil authority?

Behind this question is one of an army being asked to do a job away from home without popular understanding or approval. The Battle of Dien Bien Phu, the final act of French rule in Indochina, and then the conflict in Algeria, illustrate the challenge of sustaining colonial rule. In the first case, a struggling army was asked to continue to fight to hold a position in Indochina that was about to be abandoned in negotiations. In the second, the army considered what it had done enough to hold on to Algeria. The responsible commanders then became determined to ensure that the government in Paris did not betray their achievements.

An important part of the problem, aggravating questions of civil–military relations, is the lack of synchronization between the political and military strands of a nation's strategy. In Indochina, the meaning of the planned defence of Dien Bien Phu was transformed once the government agreed to a peace conference. In Algeria, the troops adopted harsh methods to meet what they believed to be the government's political objective of keeping Algeria French, only for the government to then abandon this objective.

FRENCH STRATEGY IN INDOCHINA

The communist-led insurgency against the French colonial position in Indochina began almost as soon as the Japanese left in 1945.[3] Ho Chi Minh had proclaimed the Democratic Republic of Vietnam (DRVN) in September 1945, with many nods in the direction of Western rhetoric on human rights. His people had fought with the Allies against the Japanese. He assumed that in turn the Allies would now be sympathetic to their self-determination. But General Charles de Gaulle, the head of the French provisional government, had no intention of abandoning his country's colonial possessions, and the Americans and British were not inclined to argue. At first the French suppressed the opposition. The component parts of Indochina – Vietnam, Laos and Cambodia – were given more autonomy, in the hope that local forces would then be able to defend themselves against anti-colonial forces. The results were unsatisfactory. In Vietnam, Bao Dai, a hereditary emperor, was granted power but enjoyed little popular support, not least because he spent more time on the Côte d'Azur instead of governing. One graduate of the military school questioned the sense of 'getting oneself killed in the jungle, for that man who comes up here to swear us in wearing a Riviera suit, a polka-dot tie, and inch-thick crepe soles'.[4]

Unsurprisingly, the DRVN were more successful at harnessing popular nationalism. It also became more overtly Marxist-Leninist and pushed aside non-communist nationalists. A major military boost to the DRVN, and its military arm, the Viet Minh, came when the communists seized control of China in 1949. Thereafter France was only able to cope thanks to American assistance, so, to keep Washington on side, the war was increasingly presented as one of resistance against communist advances, rather than simply an effort to hold on to colonies.

The war made increasing demands on both the local and the French armies. By 1954, it had cost more than 90,000 dead, wounded or missing. At its peak, the French Far East Expeditionary Corps (CEFEO) in Indochina consisted of about 175,000 troops, although less than a third of these were of French nationality; the others were from the Foreign

Legion and local units. By 1953, numbers were down and morale was low. Equipment and training were poor. As a result, men already enlisted failed to re-enlist, while French officers were exhausted, because they had to spend so much time in the field away from home.

The development of national strategy in Paris was not helped by cumbersome decision-making processes. Under the 1946 constitution, the president of the Fourth Republic was the commander-in-chief and the chairman of the National Defence Committee. The president of the Council (the upper house of the parliament) was in charge of the armed forces, though this task was delegated to the minister of national defence. This was a hapless position, which explains why there were 16 men in the post over a period of 12 years. They spent their time negotiating with separate ministers for the forces and two separate chiefs of staff committees, one advising the government and the other coordinating the staffs of the three services. The commander-in-chief of the forces in Indochina would receive directives from the minister, only after they had first been reviewed in Paris and then by the high commissioner in Saigon. This lack of policy drive and coordination disconnected Paris from events on the ground in Indochina. Only on 11 March 1954, as battle loomed at Dien Bien Phu, was a coordinating Restricted War Committee formed by the government. 'The whole tortuous web of responsibilities', notes Windrow, 'offered politicians and bureaucrats limitless opportunities to distance themselves from the consequences of their mistakes or indecision'.[5]

Successive French governments were worn down by the war, and public opinion became increasingly unenthusiastic. During the early 1950s, doubts grew about how long its stresses and costs could be sustained. The mood in Paris began to shift towards accepting the need for a negotiated settlement. After July 1953, when an armistice was agreed in Korea, interest in this option grew. The Americans did not see the two situations as analogous, and actively discouraged the French government from looking for a way out through talks. As their direct military assistance was vital to maintaining even the current level of effort, private pessimism had to be tempered with public optimism. Even if the way out was through negotiations it was still better to boost the military position to strengthen France's leverage in any talks.

In March 1953, Major General Henri Navarre was appointed commander-in-chief of all French forces in Indochina. Navarre, the son of a professor, had exemplary qualities: brilliant, authoritative, decisive, exacting but trusting, expecting his orders to be followed without constant checking. Not long after he was appointed in March 1953, just as he turned 55, he was the subject of a cover story in *Time* magazine, then on a mission to impress their readers with the promise of a revitalized French military effort. The phrases used to describe Navarre included 'icy reserve', 'cold and aloof', 'attractive to women' and, oddly, as having an '18th century fragrance' about him. The friend, so quoted, continued that 'one almost expects ruffles and a powdered wig', adding that he was still 'the hardest general I know, clever and ruthless. He believes in nothing but the army.'[6] The view that he was emotionally detached from the dramas swirling around him became a common theme.

Navarre projected, as new commanders are expected to do, confidence about the future, speaking of offensives, encouraging aggression in the troops under his command. In a metaphor that would now appear stunningly inappropriate, he described 'victory' as a 'woman who gives herself to those who know how to take her'.[7] Yet he did not know Indochina. In his first order of the day, as he assumed command, he explained how he was counting on those 'who are fighting on the front line, speedily to remedy my inexperience', which was hardly calculated to inspire. The briefings he received, including from his predecessor, described a grim situation. Moreover, nobody in Paris expected him to defeat the Viet Minh. His assigned task was to 'create the military conditions in Vietnam leading to a politically honourable solution'.[8]

In June 1953, the US Joint Chiefs sent General John O'Daniel, now commanding US Army forces in the Pacific, to assess but also stiffen the French strategy. Navarre explained that the matter of negotiations was one for Paris and not for him, but he aspired to more than just accepting a stalemate. The Americans provided their own ideas about how this could be done. Navarre had little choice but to take them seriously and incorporate them into his own plan, which depended on indigenous forces taking over the more static defensive and local security roles from the French. Counter-guerrilla operations would continue in the South, where the communists were generally weaker. The North was the most challenging theatre. This was where the Viet Minh were able to conduct large-scale operations as well as threaten Laos, and where offensive action was needed. When the plan was presented to the government in

July 1953, it was generally well received. O'Daniel reported enthusiastically back to Washington. Its execution would be another matter. Navarre had little spare capacity. However aggressive his own attitude, and that of his troops, it was unlikely to be matched in Paris. Any pretence otherwise was for the benefit of the Americans.

On 13 November, the National Defence Committee decided that Navarre could only have some of the reinforcements he had requested. French forces were just too stretched across Europe (with NATO commitments) and North Africa, as well as Indochina. Nor was he given much guidance on priorities. How much more effort should he devote to defending Laos, for example? Greater communist penetration there would create obvious political difficulties, without necessarily making a significant military difference. He regularly asked for more clarity. Marc Jacquet, secretary of state for relations with the associated states, passed the question back to Navarre.[9] Was the military balance yet good enough to make negotiations acceptable? No, said Navarre, better to wait until the winter campaigning season was over. His concern, which turned out to be correct, was that diplomatic approaches to the communists would lead them to step up their efforts and make the French position even more difficult. The risk was even greater if he could not count on significant reinforcements.

To make a military difference, Navarre decided to focus on the mountainous north-west Tonkin region. Here the French were almost the insurgents in an area largely controlled by the communists. In 1952, some French presence had been achieved by two 'air-land bases' – from where land offensives could be mounted so long as they could be supported from the air. When they no longer had value, they could be abandoned. The concept appeared to have been vindicated by a base established at Na San, against which the Viet Minh threw forces from late November to early December 1952. They were repulsed, taking some 3,000 casualties against France's 500. The French then abandoned the base. This comparatively rare success encouraged the French to believe that it was worth repeating the formula of a temporary base, hosting a substantial force of well-equipped troops, with its own airstrip. This would draw the enemy in and inflict heavy blows. The chosen spot for the next base was an open valley in north-west Vietnam, six miles from Dien Bien Phu (meaning nothing more exotic than 'seat of the border county prefecture'). The valley was close to the main communist supply route from Vietnam into Laos. It was just over five miles wide by ten miles long, surrounded by mountains. The French considered it eminently defensible because they would have superior artillery, and air power. Dien Bien Phu was therefore set up as a base with its own armour, artillery and close air support, from which offensive operations could be mounted. But it was also expected to be a redoubt that could be defended in all circumstances. This gave the commanders an opportunity to vary the mission of the garrison, but it also created an ambiguity about its main purpose.

THE BUILD-UP TO BATTLE

Navarre took the decision to move into Dien Bien Phu with Major General René Cogny, then 49 and the commander of land forces North Vietnam (FTNV). With a good academic record, handsome and well over six foot tall, he was also considered attractive to women (an attribute often mentioned in pen portraits of senior French officers at the time). After the French Army surrendered to the Germans in 1940, he had joined the resistance and ended up in Buchenwald concentration camp. He recovered but walked with a stick thereafter. Unlike Navarre, he knew Indochina well and had commanded a division there. He was said to be popular with his men as a gutsy commander. His main flaw was his concern with appearances. The use of motorcycle outriders earned him the nickname 'Coco the Siren'. He put a lot of effort into cultivating the press, at times giving away more than he should, while having a notoriously thin skin. He brooded on perceived slights. His combustible temperament contrasted with that of Navarre, whom Cogny described as being 'air-conditioned' and acting disconcertingly 'like an electronic computer'.[10]

Navarre was based in Saigon in the South; Cogny's headquarters were in Hanoi. He shared them with Brigadier General Jean Dechaux, commander of the French air force in Northern Indochina. Navarre exercised operational command largely though these two men, although neither was on the spot in Dien Bien Phu. Dechaux had concerns from the start about whether his transport aircraft could keep the garrison supplied, especially if the weather worked against regular flying. The main bases were some distance from Dien Bien Phu.

In charge of the actual garrison, and reporting to Cogny, was Colonel Christian de Castries. De Castries was from an aristocratic family and had been part of the national equestrian team. Yet he had worked his way up from the ranks. Logevall describes him as 'dashing and brave' and (perhaps inevitably) 'a notorious womanizer'. He had also been captured by the Germans in 1941. He escaped and made his way to the Free French forces in Africa, and was then wounded fighting in Germany and again in Indochina. Unlike Navarre and Cogny he had a good knowledge of armoured warfare. If the campaign required offensive operations, he had obvious advantages but no special aptitude for a defensive battle. Navarre knew him well from the Second World War. Cogny was less enamoured. He approved his appointment to get him away from his own HQ in Hanoi. This lack of trust, compounded by de Castries' relatively low rank as a colonel, had consequences later, when his pleas for reinforcements were taken insufficiently seriously.

The command was thus split between de Castries in Dien Bien Phu, Cogny and Dechaux in Hanoi and Navarre in Saigon. Navarre denied that this separation was ever a problem. He was in charge and visited Hanoi when necessary. To strengthen the chain of command he sent his deputy, Air Force General Pierre Bodet, to Hanoi to 'avoid any possible differences in viewpoints between the land and air commanders'. Bodet did not, however, impose himself on decision-making. With air power playing only a limited role, Cogny was the key figure at the Hanoi HQ.

Dien Bien Phu was occupied by paratroopers on 20 November 1953. From the start there was equivocation about the balance in its preparations for defensive and offensive operations. Cogny directed that at least half the available strength was to be kept for more offensive operations. As a result, insufficient effort was put into improving the base's fortifications and reducing its vulnerabilities to enemy fire. The two senior commanders also disagreed on the sort of offensive operations to be conducted. Navarre wanted them to be in the Tonkin region, where Dien Bien Phu was located, while Cogny was preoccupied with limiting communist influence around the Red River Delta. That is why he wanted the new base to be lighter, largely working with the local Tai people who were opposed to the communists and provided some military support to the French. Neither was tested: few offensive operations were ever mounted.

Almost as soon as the new base had been established, Cogny invited battle. He announced to the press, 'This is not a raid. We've taken the place and we shall stay there.' Paying close attention to these words was General Võ Nguyên Giáp, in sole charge of all Viet Minh forces. A former history teacher and self-taught general, he was tough and resourceful with a long and generally successful experience, first in fighting the Japanese and now the French. He had been given considerable latitude over all military strategy and tactics by the DRVN's political leader, Ho Chi Minh. Giáp built up his army from a disorganized guerrilla band into a formidable and professional army outnumbering the French by a ratio of some five to one. Having lost out at Na San, he planned to try again, having learned from his mistakes.[11] The sudden French evacuation of that base in July 1953, which was not spotted until too late, left Giáp and his party superiors unsure of his next move.

Now his strategy had been chosen for him in two respects. Paris's decision in October 1953 to seek an honourable exit from Indochina through negotiations was seen by Ho Chi Minh as an opportunity. He was worried about the risks associated with persisting with the armed struggle. It was taking its toll on the Vietnamese people and support for his party. He was also worried about the impact of direct US intervention. Not all his comrades shared his readiness to look for a negotiated outcome, so it was a relief when France took the initiative and Ho's response was immediate and positive. This set the next stage of his strategy, which was to improve the military situation on the ground as soon as possible. Dien Bien Phu was an excellent place to start. The DRVN leadership set the objective as one of annihilating the garrison in such a way as to coordinate with the coming diplomacy in Geneva. Ho told Giáp that this was to be a 'very important battle not only militarily, but also politically, not only domestically, but also internationally'.[12]

To this end a 'lightning battle' was planned for January, in line with the overall diplomatic strategy, but was then postponed because of Giáp's concern that his plan of attack had been discovered by the French. As a result, he shifted his strategy to one with less speed and more deliberation – 'steady attacks, steady advances'. He would not now rush into battle. He took the time to prepare carefully. The most important and demanding challenge was to neutralize the French advantages in firepower. This required moving his heavy equipment into place over long distances, kept concealed before the French realized what was going on. To this end, in a major feat of logistics, tens of thousands of civilian labourers kept roads open and camouflaged, even while they were being bombed and strafed. Artillery pieces and anti-aircraft guns were carried bit by bit, while disassembled trucks and howitzers, along with ammunition, were floated down the river. Giáp recalled how 'hundreds of thousands of Dan Cong, women as well as men, surmounted perils and difficulties and spent more than 3 million work days'.[13]

This was the starting point for the French failure. Neither Cogny nor Navarre could see how the Viet Minh could launch a successful attack on Dien Bien Phu. The choice of location, Navarre later admitted, was 'perhaps uninspired', but it was also 'very acceptable against the enemy that it was then reasonable to expect'.[14] Enemies, unfortunately, have a habit of not arriving in the reasonable form expected. Navarre and Cogny could not see how the Viet Minh could get their artillery to the high ground around Dien Bien Phu without being spotted and intercepted. Intelligence assessments discounted the possibility that Giáp could get a large enough force to the area.

Late in 1953, the base's potential vulnerability did begin to dawn on Navarre. After receiving information suggesting that the enemy might get into a better position than previously supposed, he even wondered whether it might be best to abandon the base. He asked Cogny on 29 December to examine in absolute secrecy whether the garrison could break out overland, should the need arise. 'One must face the fact that the battle may not go in our favour.' The defences might be 'dislocated by very powerful attacks mounted with modern resources employed for the first time'. A few days later he wrote to Jacquet in Paris:

> Two weeks ago I would have put the chances of victory at 100 per cent – Dien Bien Phu is a very good position . . . I have assembled there a strong force of infantry and artillery, equivalent to a heavy division. I have given command to a senior officer of whose energy I am certain . . . Battle has been accepted on terrain of our choosing and under the best conditions, against an enemy of whose resources we were aware up to about 15 December. But during the past two weeks serious intelligence informs us of the arrival of new resources (37mm AA guns, perhaps heavy artillery and motorized equipment); and if these really exist, and the enemy succeeds in getting them into action, then I can no longer guarantee success with certainty.[15]

This new analysis underlined the urgency of his request for reinforcements. The effect was limited. He was told by Jacquet that his letter was judged 'very pessimistic', even a 'sob story'. The case Navarre had made for extra aircraft had been accepted but this depended on negotiations with the Americans. Nothing could be achieved quickly. Eventually extra aircraft were made available, but too late to make a difference.[16]

Cogny considered the idea of a breakout, 'a solution of despair' and 'a quasi-impossibility'. Withdrawal would be a demanding, resourceheavy operation that risked providing attractive targets for the Viet Minh. He also remained optimistic about the garrison's ability to cope with a Viet Minh assault: 'Certainly, their artillery will be bothersome for a while, but we will silence it. Since Giáp is unable to move to Laos in force through fear of an obstacle rising up behind him, he finds himself forced to attack.'[17] De Castries later told the commission of inquiry that there was a 'general feeling' that

> Dien Bien Phu was very solid, that the Viet Minh knew it and would not dare unleash a general assault. Doubtless they would continue their harassments, sound out various strong points, even try to take them – but in the opinion of the troops there was no possibility of a general and sustained action.[18]

The main issue was the vulnerability of the airstrip. As it could not be built on mountain peaks, it had to be in the valley, along with the main base. This meant ceding the high ground. After the American General O'Daniel had visited the garrison, he reported back to the Joint Chiefs of Staff that 'a force with two or three battalions of medium artillery with air observation could make the area untenable'. 'When I asked about this,' he reported, 'the commander said that the fields of fire were better where they were.'[19] Charles Piroth, the artillery commander, insisted that Viet Minh batteries would be seen and then silenced by French aircraft and artillery. O'Daniel thus remained confident that the French were 'in no danger of suffering a military reverse'. On the contrary they were gaining in 'strength and confidence'.[20]

Giáp's more patient strategy, which required wearing the enemy down with artillery fire while eating away at the perimeter defences, was potentially jeopardized when, on 18 February, a sketch map was discovered on a Viet Minh prisoner showing the layout for a buried gun casement. But the French did not draw any new conclusions from the discovery. Piroth again insisted that the artillery could not be concealed. *Mon Général,*' he observed, 'no Viet Minh cannon will be able to fire three rounds before being destroyed by my artillery.' According to Fall, 'Navarre looked at him, looked back at the vista of the valley beyond and then said quietly: "Maybe so. But this won't be like Na San." '[21] By the end of the month, Piroth was starting to have his own doubts. What if the Viet Minh were in position with a stockpile of shells? If his guns were visible from the high ground, there was an inescapable problem. One of his officers recalled Piroth remarking:

> How can our batteries maintain their fire when the men have no cover? Only our artillery can save Dien Bien Phu, but we're in the open, firing blind, while the Viets have observers in forward positions. The situation may be irreversible. Not even God can help our cannoneers.

He told the officer that he must not share this view: 'Swear you won't breathe a word of this. It would be terrible for morale.' It was even worse for morale when his fears were realized.[22]

If he could not evacuate the base, Navarre now wondered whether the size of the garrison should be boosted. This might prompt Giáp to delay the battle to bring in more forces of his own, at which point the Viet Minh's preparations and operations might be hampered by the onset of the rainy season. He raised this issue on 4 March with Cogny and de Castries during a visit to Dien Bien Phu after two battalions had suffered losses when sent to dislodge enemy units discovered close to the perimeter. Navarre's idea was to add a defensive position on each side of the base. The two others convinced him that there were already too many people resident in the garrison. Any more would be an added logistical burden. At any rate, they lacked the materials to build additional strong points. Navarre later claimed that Cogny told him that the available forces would be sufficient to 'win a great defensive victory'. After the battle Cogny's somewhat lame justification was that he was trying to bolster de Castries' morale. This was another example of risks not being addressed honestly.

Relations between Navarre and Cogny were breaking down. They were communicating only 'in letters and dispatches scrupulously respecting the hierarchical formulas of military correspondence'.[23] If either of the two men had wanted a serious conversation, they had ample opportunity. Navarre also had the authority to replace Cogny with an officer he could fully trust, yet he kept him on, perhaps because of his experience in fighting in Indochina. He also had the authority to insist on extra forces, if he judged the numbers insufficient to cope with a siege. Hupe notes a 'strong pattern' of Navarre 'taking bad advice from his subordinates, frequently against his better judgment'.[24] He was reluctant to impose his views against contrary opinions.

BATTLE JOINED

By the time the main battle began on 13 March 1954, the French garrison had reached 10,814 troops. Later they were reinforced by another 4,291 men. By and large, these were from elite groups, including the Foreign Legion and parachute battalions. About a third of the original garrison were Vietnamese. There were six batteries of 105 mm guns, one of 155 mm howitzers and three companies of heavy mortars, along with ten American M24 tanks. One weakness was a lack of officers. Those available had already been overworked over a number of tours in harsh physical conditions. Instead of the normal complement of at least 18 officers and 60 to 80 NCOs, battalions were making do with 10 to 12 officers and about 40 NCOs.[25]

The French strongpoint known as Béatrice (all the hilltop defensive positions had been given a woman's name, reportedly those of de Castries' mistresses), the first to be attacked, was undermanned and depleted. Its officers were new to the battalion. A number were killed in the early artillery attacks. To the dismay of the defenders, Piroth's howitzers failed to make an impact as they tried to take out the Viet Minh batteries. The next day, no counter-attack was mounted to regain the lost position. One reason cited was the Viet Minh offer of a truce to evacuate the wounded, which the French accepted. But the main reason was the shock impact of the Viet Minh attack.

The timing did not catch the French by surprise. They knew it was coming. The problem was that, up to the moment it happened, the French troops had been confident in their position and relished the prospect of taking on the enemy. Now they suddenly realized that their position was not so strong after all. The effect on the garrison's senior command was devastating. De Castries 'had sunk into pessimism and inertia'. His chief of staff, Lieutenant Colonel René Keller, suffered a nervous breakdown. Another officer with long experience in Indochina, Lieutenant Colonel Pierre Langlais, in charge of the paratroopers, became de facto garrison commander. He was a bit younger than de Castries, and from a poor

Breton background. His reputation was of a hard man ready to take on tough assignments and with a temper to match.

As a paratrooper he was more suited to this role than de Castries the cavalryman, who knew all about bold manoeuvres but little about a positional defence.[26] At first Langlais struggled, caught between the offensive and defensive tasks, which had been at the heart of the garrison's problems from the start. Furious with the situation, on the morning of 15 March, he expressed his anger to Piroth about the failure of the artillery. Burdened by his responsibility for the calamitous advice he had given, the artillery colonel committed suicide by pulling the pin out of a hand grenade by his chest.

If Giáp had been able to press on immediately, the disarray at the senior levels of the garrison might have granted him an early victory, but he was nursing substantial losses of his own. Gradually Langlais restored order to the garrison, with the support of de Castries, who regained some of his authority. New officers were flown in to replace those that had been lost, notably Major Marcel Bigeard with his 6th Colonial Parachute Battalion, who provided calm and inspiring leadership. Also from a humble background, and a member of the war-time resistance against the Nazis, Bigeard had served in Indochina since 1946. Known as a fitness fanatic and brave leader, he was one of the models for Lartéguy's Pierre-Noel Raspéguy.

Langlais's role in the new command structure was confirmed. Ways were found to launch effective counter-attacks.[27] The battle was therefore not yet lost, even as the effects of constant fighting took their toll. NCOs were taking over command roles. On 16 March, personnel, equipment and stores were dropped in. De Castries told his men:

> We've taken some hard knocks and losses, but now we've received reinforcements and there are more where they came from; the artillery is intact, and when the weather lifts you'll see what the Air Force can do; everything depends on us, and in a few more days we'll have won, and avenged our comrades.[28]

He requested yet one more battalion from Cogny. At that time, it could have been inserted reasonably safely and made a major impact. But Cogny had been influenced by the garrison commander's earlier pessimism following the initial Viet Minh onslaught. He even told journalists 'Dien Bien Phu's carrots are cooked.' On this assumption, he was

nervous about sacrificing yet more troops, badly needed elsewhere, to a
futile cause. He radioed to de Castries:

> The only immediate possibility is to reinforce you by one battalion in
> order to compensate your losses suffered during the counterattacks; but
> even the dropping of that battalion can only be committed on the condi-
> tion that the integrity of the fortified camp can be guaranteed.[29]

De Castries replied: 'The situation will be difficult to restore without
reinforcements from outside. We are doing the impossible.' Before he
committed any more troops to Dien Bien Phu, Cogny wanted reinforcements from Navarre for his other operations in the North. Navarre was
also reluctant to change his priorities:

> I can only repeat what I have said many times before: that we are engaged
> in a general battle in which my absolute duty is to divide my forces
> between my senior subordinates in accordance with the missions which I
> have given them, and of which I must be the sole judge.[30]

The garrison had to make do with what they had. By the end of the
month, fighting hard, they were managing to repulse some Viet Minh
attacks and even mount occasional counter-attacks. Once again Langlais
and de Castries pushed for a reserve battalion, if possible before dawn
on 31 March.

As the request came in, Cogny was on a social engagement, while
Navarre was flying in from Saigon to Hanoi. On arrival, with Cogny
absent, Navarre drafted a message to de Castries. It was not encouraging. After urging him to tie down the Viet Minh, he was reminded that
'tanks, artillery and ammunition must not be allowed to fall into enemy
hands'. If he thought that was the issue, it is not surprising that he was
refusing to commit another battalion. Then Cogny turned up and gave
Navarre an out-of-date briefing. Navarre was furious. He later told
Roy, 'I exploded. I bawled him out. And he in return told me to my face
all that he had been telling others for some time.' Cogny told Navarre,
'If you weren't a four-star general, I'd slap you across the face.' Still
Navarre did not relieve Cogny.[31]

Though their relationship had already deteriorated to the point that
each was blaming the other, 'writing self-exculpatory memoranda in anticipation of a future commission of inquiry',[32] their views on next steps were
not that different. Cogny was also disinclined to risk much more in defence

of a garrison feared to be doomed. They did not offer much to de Castries and set strict conditions for any reinforcements. All that was on offer was 200 men, plus a surgical team and a recoilless rifle platoon, with possibly more to follow. But it had to be safe for them to land. This was backed by a firmer promise of air support, although this offer was soon negated by poor weather. At 11.50 on 31 March de Castries radioed Hanoi saying that they would do what they could to meet the 'security conditions demanded for parachuting but these drops must take place'. Again, bad weather made even limited drops impossible. They got some extra supplies but no reinforcements.[33] The next day, 1 April, reinforcements were still being discussed but nothing had arrived. Eventually some reinforcements arrived, just as the latest Viet Minh offensive was beaten back.

At this point the battle was not lost. Although he had still tens of thousands of troops available, Giáp's casualties were far higher than those of the French. He could not afford more direct assaults, so he was developing a trench system to get his men closer to the French positions. Cogny ordered de Castries to counter these trenches. De Castries grumbled that he lacked the personnel and the expertise. The fighting continued to be intense but inconclusive. With clear skies, French aircraft could cause immense damage to the Viet Minh infantry, but opportunities were few and far between. When the monsoon season came in mid-April air support declined, tanks became immobile and the battlefield became a quagmire. The lack of substantial reserves was still hampering the garrison and its losses were now affecting its ability to fight. By the end of April, the combat strength of most battalions was below 300 and all were exhausted. The tank squadron was at half strength. Morale was deteriorating, with some troops in a mutinous mood.

Only 783 replacements had been received. The local commanders felt let down. When Langlais demanded from headquarters another full battalion on 1 May, he added:

> We will win the battle without you and in spite of you. The message, copy of which I shall transmit to all airborne battalion commanders here, will be the last I shall address to you.

From de Castries:

> No more reserves left. Fatigue and wear and tear on units terrible. Supplies and ammunition insufficient. Quite difficult to resist one more such

push by Communists, at least without bringing in one brand-new battalion of excellent quality.[34]

Cogny had held back the reserve battalion when it might have made a difference. Perhaps because the angry communications from the garrison commanders may have left him feeling exposed to an eventual post-mortem, he now decided to drop it into what had become an almost hopeless situation. Another reason was an international conference on Indochina opening in Geneva. Its start date of 8 May had been announced on 18 February. Navarre only appreciated the significance of the announcement later. It was why Giáp was anxious to seal his victory quickly, but it should have been obvious. As it was, the French had imposed heavy losses on the Viet Minh – these might, if sustained, lead them to appear the weaker party going into the talks. Now Cogny may have hoped that, if the garrison could hang on a bit longer, it would be saved by diplomacy. Although a relief force had been sent from Hanoi by land, it was never likely to reach the garrison in time. By this time, it was also apparent that the Americans were not going to intervene to help out their allies, especially as the British would not commit any of their forces.

When 107 men were dropped into the base on 2 May, they brought newspapers that quoted a source in Hanoi (almost certainly Cogny) observing that Dien Bien Phu was unlikely to last for more than a few days. To try to boost morale, de Castries was promoted to brigadier and Langlais became a full colonel. Cogny 'had his own brigadier's stars parachuted to de Castries along with a bottle of champagne. They fell outside the French lines into Communist hands.'[35]

Determined to get the battle finished, Giáp reverted to human wave tactics to push the French out of their final positions in the face of cutting artillery fire. As the Viet Minh closed in on the French positions, resupply became ever more hazardous. Resistance continued until 7 May, at which point the following exchange took place:

De Castries: 'The Viets are everywhere. The situation is very grave. The combat is confused and goes on all about. I feel the end is approaching, but we will fight to the finish.'

Cogny: 'Well understood. You will fight to the end. It is out of the question to run up the white flag after your heroic resistance.'

And:

De Castries: 'I'm blowing up the installations. The ammunition dumps are already exploding. Au revoir.'

Cogny: 'Well, then, au revoir, mon vieux.'[36]

By nightfall, all French central positions had been captured and Dien Bien Phu had fallen.

At least 1,500 French soldiers died (some accounts put the number at over 2,200). The Viet Minh took 11,721 prisoners, of whom 4,436 were wounded. Probably more died from disease in the aftermath than were killed in the battle. The Viet Minh victory was therefore hard won. Giáp overwhelmed the French garrison with superior numbers but the cost was heavy. The Vietnamese reported their casualties as 4,020 dead and 9,118 wounded, and 792 missing, but it is likely that the actual numbers were twice as high.[37]

The fundamental mistake, common to most military defeats, was to underestimate the enemy, and especially in this case its ability to get its artillery onto the high ground overlooking the base. Yet after the shock of the initial Viet Minh attack the generals also underestimated the garrison. It is a common assumption that command posts caught by early blows and left reeling, shocked and disoriented will struggle to recover. This might have occurred at Dien Bien Phu if the Viet Minh had pushed forward in numbers immediately. Nonetheless, after the immediate paralysis, the garrison commanders pulled themselves together. Some of their tactical decisions can be criticized, but they fought back with conviction and determination. If this had been better appreciated in Hanoi and Saigon, reinforcements might have been found with more urgency.

While the failure to appreciate the risk from the Viet Minh was a shared command failure, it was aggravated by even more serious dysfunctions at the senior levels in Saigon and Hanoi. Navarre blamed the lack of political support from above and poor advice from below, notably Cogny's, for the defeat but the responsibility was still his. He had identified the weak points in the French position but then failed to act on his concerns. There were occasional visits to the front, but command was largely exercised from a distance and from two different centres by individuals whose personal relationship had broken down. The role of

THE FURY OF THE LEGIONS

the base and the purpose of the battle had not been thought through. Dien Bien Phu was marked by equivocation. The base was not optimized for defensive or offensive operations. It was also one of a number of commitments that the commanders were trying to balance, with the result that none got the necessary resources and attention. Dien Bien Phu was indispensable yet not made the top priority. Once the commitment had been made, it needed to be backed up with the full resources of the army. The big issue, a classic one for a theatre commander, was whether to send reserves. Again, there was equivocation, with the result that they were not sent when needed, but instead when it was too late to make a difference.

The constant equivocation by the high command in Indochina was more than matched in Paris. The North Vietnamese understood the implications of the move to negotiations and that shaped from the start their strategy, highlighting the importance of Dien Bien Phu, although this almost led them to commit too early, when the result would have been far worse for them. The diplomatic and the operational aspects of strategy were not coordinated between Paris and Saigon, and neither made the call that the situation required a far more determined effort in Dien Bien Phu. The responsibility was with the politicians. As they recognized the hopelessness of the situation and prepared to negotiate, they did not work out with the high command the implications for their strategy in Indochina. As the inquiry into the defeat, conducted by General George Catroux, noted, this was,

> in terms both of public opinion and of the military conduct of the war and operations, merely the end result of a long process of degradation of a faraway enterprise which, not having the assent of the nation, could not receive from the authorities the energetic impulse, and the size and continuity of effort, required for success.[38]

In his book *Agonie de l'Indochine*, Navarre accused Cogny of approving the operation in Dien Bien Phu and then losing his nerve once it appeared doomed. Cogny sued for libel. The conclusion was that he had not been defamed, although his 'high military qualities' were acknowledged.[39] As this judgement was confirmed, on 17 May 1958, France was consumed by the political crisis resulting from the Algerian campaign.

INSURGENCY AND TERRORISM
IN ALGERIA

As the 1954 Geneva conference, which left Vietnam divided, was getting down to business, this new theatre of conflict was opening up. The Algerian insurgency was led by the Front de Libération Nationale (FLN) and its military wing, the Armée de Libération Nationale (ALN).[40] They demanded independence for Algeria and the withdrawal of all French troops. Unlike Indochina, a distant colony, unsustainable over the long term, Algeria was constituted as part of France. The majority of the ten million population (a quarter the size of metropolitan France) was Muslim, effectively disenfranchised when the conflict began, and largely poor and uneducated. The European population, known as the *pieds noirs*, who had begun to move to Algeria from the start of French rule in 1830, were a million strong. They played a powerful role both locally and in the metropolis.

Algeria therefore mattered in French politics in a way that Indochina did not. It was not far away, on the other side of the Mediterranean, and not too difficult to supply and reinforce. If necessary, substantial forces could be applied to the counter-insurgency task. Because of Algeria's special status military operations could come under the heading of law enforcement. Given the battering the army had received in Indochina, there were insufficient volunteers, so, for the first time since 1895, conscripts were required for an overseas campaign. This was justified because Algeria was seen as national territory. For the veterans of Indochina it was welcome. They were no longer detached from the nation, and they could not be dismissed as mercenaries commanded by adventurers. Veterans such as Marcel Bigeard saw an opportunity to erase the humiliation of defeat. The most experienced generals were put in charge and, again unlike Indochina, the high command in Paris could follow operational developments closely.[41]

The conditions were therefore favourable for a counter-insurgency operation and by most measures, other than the final outcome, the French operation was successful. A whole theory of counter-insurgency developed around the Algerian experience. Its political logic lay in the assumption that the struggles of this time were essentially ideological.[42]

As in Indochina, it stressed the communist as much as the anti-colonial inspiration behind the liberation movements. The premise was that the insurgents were best defeated by turning their own methods against them. Instead of treating acts of terrorism as criminal, to be addressed by normal police and judicial processes, they were to be recognized as acts of war. Special measures were required. Civil society must accept the implications and toughen up. Those conducting the war in Algeria were convinced that they were struggling for all of France. 'If the tricolour is lowered in Algeria,' observed then Governor General Jacques Soustelle, 'the red flag will soon fly in Paris.'[43]

THE BATTLE OF ALGIERS

'Our duty is to win,' explains Colonel Philippe Mathieu, the tough paratrooper who seeks to crush the militants responsible for a spate of bombings and shootings in Gillo Pontecorvo's vivid 1967 film, *The Battle of Algiers*.[44] Mathieu is a character similar to Lartéguy's Raspéguy, a composite of the real characters who fought this battle. As when Mac-Arthur insisted that there was no alternative to 'victory', here is an affirmation of the soldier's conviction that success must mean the defeat of the enemy. Yet, while a military victory might be a precondition for meeting a campaign's political objective, it can never be sufficient. Soldiers have little say in what is done with their victories. That is up to the government.

Moreover, in an unconventional war, such as the one in Algeria, the meaning of victory can be elusive. Elsewhere in the film, Mathieu observes that what he really needs is 'political will, which is sometimes there and sometimes is not'. Pontecorvo's story is of the futility of occupation, even when backed with ruthless force. Another story of Algeria is that of the military's disenchantment. They had been tasked to preserve French colonial rule, but were let down by the politicians in Paris, who ended up negotiating with their enemies.

The origins of the war lay in the FLN's attempt to break the stalemate that had developed in the conflict and take advantage of France's stretched finances and discomfort after the 1956 Suez campaign.[45] The FLN wanted an 'Algerian Dien Bien Phu' to convince the government of the hopelessness of its position.[46] Terrorism would not only sow fear among the *pieds noirs* and lead them to doubt their long-term future in

Algeria, but also demonstrate that the FLN could operate as effectively in cities as it could in rural areas. At the same time, the message would be reinforced by non-violent means, such as general strikes. All this would gain international publicity for the FLN cause to enable it to influence such bodies as the UN General Assembly.

In October 1956, the FLN established a 'base area' in the Casbah District of Algiers, setting up an Autonomous Zone of Algiers (ZAA) as a shadow government. With around 4,500 members, it concentrated on raising recruits and funds, and pushing its political message. The ALN network operated separately, with approximately 1,400 members, organized into districts, each with three armed groups, headed by a leader and deputy and composed of three cells of three men each. There was also a separate 'bomb-throwing network' directly responsible to the ZAA. They kept in touch with the network chief using a system of letter boxes.[47] In January 1957, there were more than 100 terrorist incidents in Algiers, culminating in a general strike at the end of the month.

As this campaign was getting under way, at the start of the year, the socialist Governor General Robert Lacoste, brought two generals into his office. One was General Raoul Salan, recently appointed commander-in-chief, and the other was General Jacques Massu, recently returned with his elite 10ème Division Parachutiste from the abortive operation in Suez. The decision was that Massu's 4,600-man division must not only reinforce the 1,500-strong police force, which was struggling to cope with FLN violence and *pieds noirs* reactions, but take full responsibility for order in the city.

Salan was France's most decorated soldier. His career had begun during the First World War, and thereafter he had concentrated on colonial work, specializing in clandestine intelligence activities. He had been second-in-command and then commander in Indochina, eventually organizing the conclusion of the French presence. Horne describes him as having the appearance of a Roman proconsul, known to be prudent and politically astute, but with a complex personality. De Gaulle would later describe him as 'slippery and inscrutable'. He was at first viewed warily by the *pieds noirs*, largely because of Indochina, as a man likely to sell them out.[48] Horne was almost lyrical about Massu as a man exuding toughness, 'the stocky, vital figure' with 'the growling voice, the vigorous hair *en brosse* and the down-turned eyes . . . the square, set jaw and the aggressive, all-dominant nose, and the rugged features that altogether looked like they had been hewn, like a Swiss bear, from a block of wood'.

Massu did not relish taking police action ('a job for dustmen'). To his chief of staff he observed: 'I can tell you right away we're going to have some heaps of *emmerdements*!'[49] But he did not take long to work out his strategy. The city was divided into four zones, each controlled by a parachute regiment. Marcel Bigeard, was now commander of 3ème Régiment de Parachutistes Coloniaux and in charge of the Casbah.

There were also a series of parallel organizations, largely concerned with keeping the more dubious aspects of the operation secret. Lieutenant Colonel Roger Trinquier, Massu's deputy, had his own staff for intelligence gathering, with a network of informers. Paul Aussaresses had a unit for 'action implementation'. Aussaresses understood that his job was to do the 'dirty work', a 'safety net' in case someone in authority asked awkward questions, helping to spare the reputation of the division, unburdening 'the regiments of the most unpalatable tasks and...cover[ing] those they had to undertake on their own'.[50] There was yet another network of agents who penetrated the FLN leadership, while a Centre de Coordination Interarmées (CCI) also acted autonomously, picking up intelligence from various sources. The Détachement Opérationnel de Protection (DOP) was described by Massu as 'specialists in the investigation of suspects who wanted to say nothing'. Melnick describes them as commandos, placed by the special services under local military jurisdiction to work covertly. 'By using illegal methods, they could put into effect the most efficient (if not the most ethical) means to secure as rapidly as possible the necessary information during the interrogations' – and could also turn those arrested into double agents.[51] These parallel units made it harder – as intended – to assign individual responsibility for particular episodes.

Massu's focus was on the enemy organization rather than individuals and equipment. This required intelligence being acquired and applied quickly. In this, he was helped by the bureaucracy of the FLN, which had put too much down on paper, and by its internal divisions, which left them vulnerable to rumours designed to encourage internal strife. Massu's units had some core operational rules:

> Anyone who is a member of or helps a terrorist organization is guilty on pain of death.

Anyone who is captured will be interrogated immediately by the forces that captured him.

Anyone can be arrested and interrogated who is suspected of involvement.

Sentences for terrorists will be carried out within 48 hours.

Authority for these methods comes from the government.[52]

These unlimited powers of arrest were used to the full, so that, from the beginning of January to the end of September 1957, some 30 to 40 per cent of the male population of the Casbah were arrested and questioned. The ease with which individuals could be picked up meant that the system became overloaded. The pressure for urgent intelligence added to the reliance on torture. This went from beatings, to heads being held under water, to electric shocks to the genitals. Arrests were carried out at night shortly after curfew. Anyone seen after curfew was apt to be shot, their bodies left to be discovered in the morning. Bodies of tortured men were burned or dumped in the sea from a helicopter.

Trinquier offered both a moral and a pragmatic justification for the torture and killing. A terrorist, he argued, should be treated as neither a criminal nor a prisoner of war, but as a soldier with vital information about future attacks and the organization of which he is a part.

> If the prisoner gives the information requested, the examination is quickly terminated; if not, specialists must force his secret from him. Then, as a soldier, he must face the suffering, and perhaps the death, he has heretofore managed to avoid. The terrorist must accept this as a condition inherent in his trade and in the methods of warfare that, with full knowledge, his superiors and he himself have chosen.

It was hypocritical to permit 'artillery or aviation to bomb villages and slaughter women and children, while the real enemy usually escapes, and to refuse interrogation specialists the right to seize the truly guilty terrorist and spare the innocent'.[53] Moreover, he claimed, it worked. Without the action taken by the paratroopers, 'the entire city would have fallen into the hands of the F.L.N., the loss carrying with it the immediate abandonment of all Algeria'.[54] This rationale assumed that of the some 4,000 victims of extrajudicial executions, usually shot or strangled, most were members of the FLN and ready for terrorism.

Confidence in the appropriateness of the methods ran deep.

Aussaresses, a veteran of wartime special operations as well as Indo-china, had learned about 'extreme' interrogations in Algeria from the police at Philippeville. Before beatings or electric shocks began, he noted, prisoners usually provided all necessary information. He was nonetheless asked by his colonel, when he reported on this, whether the information could be obtained by more humane means. 'Even if I did agree with you, sir, to carry out the mission you've given me, I must avoid thinking in moral terms and only do what is most useful.' The colonel's alarm grew when Aussaresses explained what happened to the suspects after they had talked. 'If they're connected to the crimes per-petrated by the terrorists, I shoot them.' To the colonel, 'knocking off every member of the organization' was crazy. But, Aussaresses explained patiently that the courts could not handle the numbers – 'we can't just send hundreds of people to the guillotine'. He added: 'Since you gave me no orders I had to improvise. One thing is very clear: our mission demands results, requiring torture and summary executions, and as far as I can see it's only beginning.' To this he got the answer 'This is a dirty war and I don't like it.'[55]

The soldiers believed that they were rescuing a civilian administra-tion unable to cope, filling gaps beyond the police and judicial functions. One officer later complained: 'They never taught me in St Cyr [Military Academy] to arrange for a town's food supply, follow up a police inves-tigation, do the job of Prefect of Police, organize a polling station, or suspect my fellow officers.'[56] They also saw political leaders welcoming the results of the crackdown while distancing themselves from the methods. One general recalled a visit by ministers to Bigeard's head-quarters where statistics were produced, demonstrating that two-thirds of the rebel organization in his sector had been destroyed. When one congratulated Bigeard and encouraged him to finish the job, the colonel asked, 'Mr Minister, do you think that we arrive at such results with the procedures of a choir boy?' The reply was to 'be careful that too much mud did not stick'.[57] This appears to have been a ready metaphor for the army. When Massu told Aussaresses that 'we are going to knock them off very quickly and by every possible means', he added 'this is not an assignment for the choirboys'.[58] 'In time,' noted Trinquier, 'we climbed little by little to the summit of the pyramid.'[59]

By end of March, the terrorist network had effectively been crushed. In June, left isolated after many setbacks, the head of the ALN, Saadi

Yacef, instigated a final, desperate campaign, causing some large explosions, including one under the stage at a dance hall. By the end of July, this campaign too was over. In September, Yacef was captured. It took many years before the full extent of the torture and executions became known, but suspicions and rumours spread quickly, and condemnation was soon heard in France. Some officers asked to be transferred away from Algeria, because they could not follow their orders with good conscience. Prime Minister Guy Mollet acknowledged concerns though dismissed those about 'premeditated torture', which would be 'intolerable'. He placed the blame for all violence on 'terrorist atrocities'.[60]

Despite the government's efforts to deflect concerns, the criticisms grew. There were more general worries about whether the position in Algeria could be sustained over the long term. When a conservative government fell in mid-April 1958, the socialist Pierre Pflimlin prepared to form the next one. He not only favoured negotiations with the rebels, but was also thought likely to include communists in his government. In Algeria, the civil and military leadership, reflecting the increasingly hard-line *pieds noirs*, was alarmed. Governor Lacoste warned of a 'diplomatic Dien Bien Phu'. On 9 May, General Salan sent a telegram to General Paul Ély, chef d'état-major général des forces armées (CEMGFA), warning that the army could not accept the abandonment of Algeria.

> The army in Algeria is troubled by recognition of its responsibility towards the men who are fighting and risking a useless sacrifice if the representatives of the nation are not determined to maintain *Algérie française* . . .
>
> The French army, in its unanimity, would feel outraged by the abandonment of this national patrimony. One cannot predict how it would react in its despair.[61]

Rioting in Algiers on 13 May led officers to form a Committee of Public Safety, which Massu took over.

As the crisis deepened, supporters of Charles de Gaulle saw the opportunity to bring him back from his self-imposed exile and in so doing save the country.[62] De Gaulle knew all about insubordination for the sake of the higher interests of the state. His name had been made with a dramatic and consequential act of defiance, when he deliberately disobeyed the orders of the Vichy government to capitulate to Germany in 1940, an act now cited by the rebel officers in Algeria as a precedent.

In May 1951, the *New York Times* observed the similarities between de Gaulle and the recently dismissed Douglas MacArthur, reporting that the Frenchman had praised the American's 'audacity' and how this 'was now feared by those who had profited from it'. Each man, the newspaper noted, demonstrated 'supreme self-confidence' and was 'untroubled by concrete problems that fail to fit readily into his major thesis'. Both had seen their reputation grow while away from their country. While de Gaulle's self-imposed exile (in London) was shorter than MacArthur's, he was only really known to his compatriots after 1940 as the self-proclaimed leader of the Free French Forces, and a voice on the radio. He now looked with a 'cold disdain' on everyone, maintaining his mystery by speaking in a deliberately cryptic style. Like MacArthur, he had shown little interest in following orders with which he disagreed. This was not only in his refusal, unlike many others, to accept the authority of Vichy, but also in his disregard of Eisenhower's orders, when he was supposedly under his command, as France was liberated in 1944.[63]

He now seemed a natural leader, able to take over the country with the confidence of the military and ensure that war was backed effectively. On 15 May, addressing crowds from the governor general's balcony in Algiers, Salan ended with the cry of 'Vive la France, vive l'Algérie française', and then 'vive le général de Gaulle!' De Gaulle himself remained enigmatic as he met leading political figures, refusing explicitly to endorse actions that would threaten public order. The crisis deepened as the Committee of Public Safety became more prominent in Algeria. Another committee was set up in Corsica. As Pflimlin refused to concede, there was talk of a *coup d'état*.

The plan for 'Operation Resurrection', developed by Massu, involved 50,000 paratroopers flying in from south-west France and Algiers to seize key strategic sites in Paris, including the Eiffel Tower, the Ministry of the Interior and Communist Party offices. Massu and Trinquier would arrive early to meet up with General Miquel, commanding the Toulouse area, to set up an HQ in the Invalides. Once the capital was secure President René Coty would be escorted to de Gaulle's home in Colombey to present the general with a fait accompli.

De Gaulle himself preferred to obtain power by regular means, but he knew of the plan. If he had given the go ahead, it would have been implemented. On 29 May, there was uncertainty about whether he had actually done so. Salan's approval code was sent to trigger the operation ('the carrots are cooked'). Six aircraft set off from Le Bourget airport to Perpignan, where a parachute regiment was waiting to be taken to Paris. At this point, President Coty decided that with 'the country on the verge of civil war' he should ask de Gaulle to form a government. The insurrection plans were put on hold, and the planes turned back. The National Assembly accepted the recommendation. When de Gaulle took power on 1 June, the government he formed was broad-based. He had taken advantage of military hardliners while never becoming beholden to them. De Gaulle put forward a new constitution granting vastly expanded powers to the president, which he was to become. This was endorsed by a referendum on 28 September. Now he was in charge and determined to find a solution to the Algerian problem.

DE GAULLE IN POWER

On 4 June 1958, just after he had been propelled into power, de Gaulle flew to Algiers. He addressed cheering crowds, saying that he understood them, without explaining what it was that he understood. He continued with words of profound opacity. Only once in his trip did he utter the words 'Algérie française' and this he immediately regretted. He was increasingly seeing the Committee of Public Safety, and the army, as problems. 'The Generals hate me. And I feel the same about them. All idiots . . . Cretins preoccupied only by their promotions, their decorations, their comfort.' Salan he described as a 'drug addict' and Massu, a 'good sort but hardly a rocket scientist'.[64] He wrote to Massu, still presiding over the Committee of Public Safety, that to remain friends he should concentrate on being a soldier. Once his position was confirmed in the September 1958 referendum, de Gaulle told the army to cease participation in the Committee of Public Safety.

He decided to replace Salan, about whom he felt a growing contempt, with General Raul Challe. Challe was notable as an airman put in charge of a ground campaign, and trusted for having served for several years as chief of staff for General Ély. A 'calm, solid and tenacious pipe-smoker', as direct as Salan was cautious, he was tasked by de

Gaulle to take on the FLN. The president expected 'operations to take a dynamic turn which would result in our undisputed mastery of the field'. This would give him freedom of action. A new offensive had the additional advantage of keeping the army busy and away from political activism. To make sure that Challe did not follow Salan and start to act as de facto civil governor, Paul Delouvrier, a career civil servant, assumed the duties of delegate general. This was a humbler title than governor general and signalled that there would now be closer political control from Paris. Prime Minister Michel Debré explained the urgency at the start of 1959: 'We must be able to put out a victory bulletin in the month of July; for France is beginning to get bored with the war.'[65]

The situation Challe inherited gave him an opportunity to defeat the FLN on the ground. The French had begun the campaign with a force of around 50,000 in 1954 and had taken time to build up, but there were now some half a million fighting the insurgents, including 380,000 in the ground forces. At their peak, the FLN had perhaps 50,000 fighters in Algeria, and by 1959 they were severely weakened, with an estimated 18,000 combatants and only 13,800 weapons.[66] The ruthless tactics of 1957 had driven them out of the cities. The leadership had escaped to a sanctuary in Tunisia, but they were unable to get units back into Algeria. The construction of a defensive wall, with a mixture of barbed wire, mines and other obstacles, had begun in 1956. The French Navy were also preventing ships smuggling equipment into Algeria.

Challe brought new energy to the campaign. He judged that there was a lack of a 'general scheme', 'a guiding idea, an impetus from the top that shakes the habits, as methods obviously need to be replaced'.[67] He set out his views in two official documents. *Méthode de pacification générale* described the approach he wished to see followed, thereby precluding too much improvisation by local commanders. *Directive n° 1* detailed his instructions, which he stuck to through the rest of the campaign. His tenure was not troubled by strategic reappraisals.[68]

To clear the FLN out of rural areas, the *tache d'huile* (oil spot) technique was adopted, which required concentrating military, social and economic efforts over a designated area. Once this population had been secured, it was possible to move on, so that the area of control expanded like an oil spot. Initiatives were taken to draw the Muslim population more into the fight. Challe introduced Muslim troops in significant numbers (between 25 and 40 per cent) into regular units. They were not only cheaper to recruit, but, he argued, had better knowledge of local conditions and were a means of turning the local population against FLN.

The three military regions of Oran, Constantine and Algiers each had a corps commander responsible for both civil and military action. Challe replaced 35 of the 76 sector commanders in his first three months. He looked for subordinates with the qualities required for counter-insurgency work, which were not necessarily those of the orthodox soldier. According to Melnik, who worked closely with Prime Minister Michel Debré during the campaign, Challe sought young and dynamic leaders who could adjust to complex political–military situations. If such a leader were in charge of a sector, he would need the imagination and prestige to be 'simultaneously a military man, policeman, judge, admin-istrator, and political leader'. These 'innovating, impassioned, and dynamic' personalities achieved disparate results, noted Melnik. He also wondered whether these qualities meant that they felt betrayal more keenly, and so later became more inclined to turn against de Gaulle.[69]

Instead of having a ground forces commander managing the land battle, the post was eliminated. The corps commanders were under Challe's direct command, with a new unit established to investigate areas where implementation of orders was lax. The Reserve Générale was composed of elite units previously distributed piecemeal to deal with emergencies. It was now organized into larger components, becom-ing a highly mobile force, involved in large offensives and then used in the aftermath to prevent ALN elements hiding and regrouping. To keep up momentum by seizing new opportunities, Challe made regular trips to the front while trying not to get in the way of subordinate command-ers or dampen their initiatives.

The result was nine operations across Algeria credited with destroy-ing up to half of all armed groups in both personnel and materiel, with some 9,000 enemy casualties, and undermining the FLN's organization. As at the Battle of Algiers, the combat tactics were often brutal. The main constraint on more summary executions was concern that they might make the insurgents too desperate.[70] When Challe left Algiers on 23 April 1960, he could claim that the rebellion had been 'terminated in the interior . . . cut off from the population'. The 'military phase of the rebellion' was over.

There was an element of delusion in these claims. The victory was incomplete in three ways. First, the possibility of terrorist outrages could still not be precluded. The population might have been subdued, but it had not been won over. It remained on edge. Second, a key part of the campaign involved 'pacifying' rural areas with a Muslim resettlement programme. Salan's countryside offensive, concluding in December 1958, lacked Challe's successes but forced more than 1.3 million Algerians into overcrowded and unpleasant camps. The intention was to bring together otherwise vulnerable people into new villages. Challe lacked the funding and programmes to turn these into places where people might actually want to live. The camps caused misery and disruption to rural life. However many Muslims were disenchanted with the FLN, treatment of this sort led many to hate the French. This was an aspect of the war barely appreciated in France, at least until a reporter from *Figaro* visited one of the villages and reported on the hardships he saw. Third, while the ALN was weak and fragmented, the FLN leadership under Houari Boumedienne was now safe in Tunis. It realized that the game was up on the armed struggle and was concentrating instead on its international political profile. The Gouvernement Provisoire de la République Algérienne (GPRA) gained recognition from the international community.

De Gaulle had hoped that Challe would give him more options, but the essential problem was left unchanged. Large demonstrations on the streets showed that the majority of the population wanted the French out. The military gains appeared irrelevant because of the political successes of the GPRA. When he came to office, he had neither a prior record of public pronouncements on the matter nor a new plan. For a while, therefore, he could hide his dilemmas, and give the impression of being in control, with the sort of grandiose but gnomic pronouncements for which he had a unique talent. His ministers disagreed not only over what to do but also over the president's wishes. There were fervent proponents for the full integration of Algeria within France, but de Gaulle never considered that a serious option. The real choice came down to accepting independence under the FLN or developing the association with France, with more rights and prospects for the Muslims and more local autonomy. He may have hoped to find a more moderate Muslim opinion with which he could work. To this end, he ordered freeing internees, and getting Muslims elected to local councils. But Challe's campaign had weakened the Muslim middle ground. At first, he ignored feelers from the GPRA for talks because of Challe's military successes but he observed their continuing advances in international forums.

Above all he wanted to keep control. He wrote to General Ély in 1959: 'Whatever policy to be carried out regarding Algiers, it is completely my affair and I suspect of subordinates nothing other than this: that they execute it honestly.'[71] The politicization of the army bothered him. Instead of seeing himself as the beneficiary of military intervention in 1958, he argued that his actions had 'prevented the army, nolens volens, from taking over a governmental power that it would have been incapable of exercising'. Once the war was over, the army must be forbidden to have a political role.[72]

Delegate General Delouvrier tried to warn de Gaulle of the unrest among the soldiers. He had in mind Massu's colonels who were in close contact with the more excitable segments of the *pieds noirs*. One especially, Colonel Antoine Argoud, dismissed him as a 'political science professor' who did not understand the realities of Algeria. In an unguarded interview for a German paper published on 18 January 1960, Massu expressed his disappointment that de Gaulle had 'become a man of the Left', and wondered if the army had 'made a mistake' by putting him in power. He then made an incendiary remark: 'Myself, and the majority of officers in a position of command, will not execute unconditionally the orders of the Head of State.' Within days he was stripped of his command and transferred back to France, banned from returning to Algeria. Only the intervention of other senior commanders, who feared the reaction in Algeria, stopped him being dismissed from the army.[73]

Settler organizations immediately demanded his return and soon took to the streets, often showing small photos of Massu. When the gendarmerie was sent in to dismantle barricades, the demonstrators turned on them, killing 14 and wounding 123, while in turn 8 settlers were killed and 24 wounded. This added to the divide between the settlers and mainland France, especially as the barricades remained up, with banners proclaiming 'Vive Massu'. Some paratroopers showed sympathy, but the insurrection did not spread to the army. De Gaulle was unimpressed by the reluctance of Delouvrier and Challe to restore order, and now saw the need to assert his authority.

For a televised address on 29 January, he donned his uniform. As he explained in his broadcast, he did so 'in order to show that it is General de Gaulle who is speaking as much as the Head of State'. He defended his policy, insisting that only 'liars and conspirators' could suggest that he was going to abandon Algeria and hand it over to the rebellion. The army must 'liquidate the rebel force that wants to chase France out of Algeria', but it was also necessary to win over the 'hearts and minds' of the Muslim population. His core message was that he was 'the person responsible for the destiny of the nation. I must be obeyed by all French soldiers'.

> No soldier, under the penalty of being guilty of a serious offence, may associate himself, may associate himself at any time, even passively, with the insurrection. In the last analysis law and order must be re-established ... your duty is to bring this about. I have given, and am giving, this order.

He concluded with an appeal to patriotism: 'Well, my dear country, my old country, here we are together, once again, facing a harsh test.' He would not let France 'become but a poor broken toy adrift on the sea of hazard'. He was not bargaining but instead reminded everyone of their duty.[74] The broadcast had the desired effect. Those still on the barricades were left friendless, and also miserable as they were hit by heavy rain. Regardless, the anger that had prompted their actions was still there and morphed into active terrorism. In March 1961 the Organisation de l'Armée Secrète (OAS) began its campaign of bombings and attempted assassinations (including of de Gaulle) in Paris.

That month de Gaulle visited Algeria. He spoke to officers, off the record but soon reported, promising 'no diplomatic Dien Bien Phu' and that the army would stay in Algeria. The 'week of the barricades' had strengthened de Gaulle and weakened the hardliners. But the underlying problem had not been solved. By the end of 1960 pro-FLN demonstrations were large and impressive, sufficient for de Gaulle to realize that negotiations could not be avoided. The first steps towards direct talks with the FLN were taken.

On 11 April 1961, de Gaulle observed at a press conference that 'France has no interest in keeping Algeria under her laws or dependent on her ... Indeed the least one can say is that Algeria costs us more than it brings us ... that is why France would contemplate with the greatest sangfroid a solution by which Algeria would cease to belong to her.' Those who had been fighting to keep Algeria French were shocked.

Junior officers contrasted their sacrifices with de Gaulle's diplomacy. 'Among the elite formations that had borne the brunt of the fighting,' wrote Horne, 'the lieutenants were to be found working upon the captains, and captains upon the majors and colonels – though the colonels needed little enough pressurising.'[75]

Yet the most prominent figures from the past, such as Massu and Bigeard, now both away from Algeria, were not interested. Massu had concluded that independence was coming and that the rebels had no one to compare with de Gaulle. Instead, Salan came from Spain to join Challe and two other colleagues (Generals Jouhaud and Zeller) who had decided to stage a coup. Salan had been plotting for some time. The surprise was that Challe joined in. On 22 April, paratroopers and legionnaires seized key buildings in Algeria, and arrested de Gaulle's men – General Fernand Gambiez and Jean Morin, the new commander-in-chief and delegate general respectively. Challe told the population, 'The army has taken control of Algeria and the Sahara ... *Algérie française* is not dead ... There is not, and will never be, an independent Algeria.'[76] The initial moves succeeded without a shot being fired. The 400,000 troops of the Algerian-based army were twice as many as those in France.

But despite this potentially favourable balance of power, the organization was rushed, and the political objectives were unclear. French historian Maurice Vaïsse observes that the putsch almost succeeded, because it was improvised, and so caught the government by surprise, but also failed for the same reason, as the conspirators had not thought through either their objectives or their methods.[77] They were not of one mind. Challe intended to control of the war in Algeria until he could hand de Gaulle a perfect victory. Others wanted to topple the president. There was no developed plan to extend the coup to the mainland, and nobody there of any stature to take power. There was not even a plan to get the settlers to act. The actions were the result of frustration, dismay among the officer class that all their efforts and sacrifices might have been in vain, and a legitimate concern that all those Muslims that had worked with the French would be at risk if the FLN were allowed to take over the country. 'Do you want to renege on your promises, to abandon our European and Muslim brothers, to abandon our commanders, our soldiers, our Muslim supporters to the rebels' revenge?'[78]

The putsch was built on flimsy foundations. Challe and Salan disliked each other, and the other commanders in Algeria were either wavering or opposed. In Paris, the police were soon arresting officers inclined to extend the coup to the mainland. De Gaulle did not panic: 'Gentlemen, what is serious about this affair is that it isn't serious.' He professed himself shocked 'that an intelligent man like Challe can perpetrate such stupidity'. One additional piece of drama was provided by de Gaulle's order to bring forward a test of a nuclear device in southern Algeria, to avoid its getting into rebel hands but also to demonstrate that the government was still in charge.[79]

Soon he was back again in front of the television cameras, once more in full uniform. 'An insurrectional power has established itself in Algeria by a military pronunciamento.' He spoke of a 'group of fanatical, ambitious and partisan officers' with 'limited understanding' engaged in an enterprise that would lead to national disaster.

> In the name of France, I order that all means, I repeat all means, be employed everywhere to bar the road to these men until they have been defeated. I forbid any Frenchman, and in the first place any soldier, to execute any of their orders.[80]

There were rumours that soldiers were about to land from Algeria, leading to people being urged to occupy the airfields and on strike. But the speech had done the trick. The conscripts in Algeria (many of whom had transistor radios and so could listen to the president directly) had no interest in an insurrection. Only 25,000 soldiers out of 400,000 joined in. Challe and Zeller soon surrendered and were imprisoned. Salan and Jouhaud went into hiding to work with the OAS. On 18 March 1962, the Évian Agreements were signed granting Algeria independence and meeting the FLN goals. The Europeans in Algeria now saw no future and left en masse. Muslims who had supported France were left unprotected and were massacred.

There was a postscript. In May 1968, France once again faced disorder, as student demonstrations took over Paris followed by widespread strikes. Events appeared to be spiralling out of control, and for a while de Gaulle appeared at a loss what to do. On 29 May, he flew in secrecy to Baden-Baden. There he met Massu, with whom he had made up some time earlier, and who was now in charge of all French forces in Germany. According to Massu's account (the only one), the president arrived in despondent mood ('It's all over'), until he was convinced that he must fight on. Massu reported to one of the president's aides that he 'told the General, who wants to take refuge in Germany, that this is impossible. It is madness. He cannot do it.' Whether or not de Gaulle had gone for reassurance that the army was loyal or needed to be persuaded to hang on, that was now his decision. The next day he made one of his galvanizing speeches, this time on radio, that helped turn the crisis around. His supporters rallied and the revolution was defused.[81]

CONCLUSION:
DISENCHANTMENT AND DEFIANCE

The paratroopers who went to Algiers were prepared to test themselves against the enemy and the elements. Their shared experiences formed a bond that set them apart from careerists and compromisers, including those also in uniform. Yet while these warriors rejected being political in this self-serving sense, they did not deny the importance of a political mission. They took on the counter-terrorism campaign in Algeria so that France could avoid yet another humiliation. In the process, they developed theories of counter-insurgency that emphasized the importance of a political commitment. This built upon one of the lessons drawn by the veterans of Indochina from the success of the Viet Minh. In Algeria, it meant committing to the idea that this was an essential part of France, to 'Algérie française'.

In the pursuit of this idea, they were prepared to break the humanitarian rules on torture and then the constitutional rules on keeping out of politics. The paratroopers stepped into a desperate situation. The civil administration and police could not cope. To end the FLN's terror campaign, they resorted to brutal methods, including torture and murder. The target was the terrorist infrastructure. To subvert this required intelligence. The rationale was not to scare the opposition into submission but to extract intelligence, and their methods allowed this to be done with the required urgency. The methods of 'close interrogation' dehumanized the perpetrators as well as the victims. Individuals and even some whole units refused to participate.

Many of those who wanted to defend French Algeria believed that there were better alternatives – by making a more attractive offering to the Muslim community or still acting firmly but within the normal legal constraints. Even Massu sought counsel from his priest. Justifications of evil methods could be found in the need to overwhelm an even greater evil. These justifications were never tested in the courts. Actions were taken under the cover of special powers with no accountability. Every effort was made to hide what was going on, to admit to no more than pushing at the boundaries of law and ethics, denying that they were being exceeded.

When Lartéguy's fictional Raspéguy – a character similar to Mathieu in Pontecorvo's film, and a composite of the real characters who fought this battle such as Jacques Massu and Marcel Bigeard – is promoted to full colonel for what he has achieved in the Battle of Algiers, he remarks that it gives him no pleasure. He might have saved Algeria but he has lost his regiment. They have fallen into 'bad habits'. His men are drinking too much, because of what they have been forced to do. 'We've achieved better results than the others because we've wallowed in the shit more than others.' Sitting down around a campfire with some of his officers, he recalls how, when members of the government visited his HQ, he told them that they had done a disgusting job because the government had ordered it. 'Some of them pretended not to understand or think that I was making a huge joke. Others would answer with a sanctimonious little gesture . . . "It's for the sake of France".' Then they are threatened with court proceedings. 'Hold tight on to your guns, then no one will come and bother us.' This is the point at which one of his comrades declares, 'Beware of the anger of the legions.'[82]

The politicians go along with the extreme measures, preferring to be kept in the dark about the details, sufficient to feign ignorance about how far matters have been taken. The alienation of the officers in Algeria begins with contempt for the political class in Paris, who have let them down in Indochina and are now unable to grasp the nature of this uncompromising war, who willed the ends but not the means, and who then refused to accept responsibility for the means that brought success. The paratroopers do what they can to achieve victory, but victory is deceptive in such a conflict. These are political struggles that cannot be solved by military means. In Lartéguy's sequel, *The Praetorians*, he quotes a diary entry:

The government allowed the officers, when it did not actually encourage them, to give their word to the French Algerians as well as to the Moslems that they would never leave, and it proclaimed in all the papers, in every broadcast, that France would not come to terms with the F.L.N., although it knew these promises would not be kept. Therein lies the crime.[83]

Raspéguy, now aged and weary, is broken, putting on weight and not even doing his exercises. He dares not 'go back to his village, with my head hung in defeat and my old, tarnished colonel's badges of rank'.[84]

While the officers are full of self-pity about how they are being discarded, no longer deemed useful by those in Paris who had kept their consciences clean, a journalist who has discovered what they are up to observes that, while their real motive lies in their fear of being brought to justice for their crimes, the troops sought a positive motive for changing the government. They offered up as an ideology' a hotch-potch of conventional ideas in which Nationalism, Christianity and the West were all blended'. These 'haughty praetorians', she notes, tried to force de Gaulle to ratify their scheme but instead found that they were dealing with a man 'who was even more difficult and haughty than themselves'.[85] Not for the first or last time, soldiers who meddle in politics turn out not to be very good at it.

As in Lartéguy's novel, so in fact, the officers misread de Gaulle, perhaps because of his own record of insubordination. They helped him get to power, but he avoided making firm promises. Eventually he concluded that there was no choice but to negotiate with the FLN. But given the role of the army in helping him reach power, when the time came to face down the attempted coup of 1961, de Gaulle appreciated that he could not rely solely on his authority as president of the Republic. He put on his general's uniform, and framed the crisis as one in the chain of command. He ordered members of the army not to join the plotters as a general as much as a president.

This did not resolve the issue of the need for the military to obey the civil authorities. He encouraged Marshal Alphonse-Pierre Juin to write *Three Centuries of Military Obedience, 1650–1963*, which argued the importance of the military obeying the government without judging its legitimacy. The chief of staff of the army wrote in the preface that 'obedience remains constitutive of the soldier and this notion must be understood, accepted and internalized by each citizen who has made the choice to exercise the profession of arms.'[86] In 1966, a new code was introduced for the French Army. The previous version stated, 'Orders are executed literally without hesitation or grumbling. Protest by the subordinate is not allowed except when he has obeyed.' The new order stated, 'A subordinate faced with an order he believes illegal has the duty to protest it.'[87]

By this time the American army in Vietnam was starting to face its own crises, as young men refused to be drafted to fight what they considered to be not only an immoral but also a pointless war, and those in uniform were ordered to act in ways that they thought both illegal and unethical. The nuclear age had raised profound questions about whether an order to inflict mass death should be executed automatically, without query or dissent. The experience of Algeria argued for more questioning of orders to engage in torture and arbitrary killing even while insisting on the importance of subordination to civilian authorities.[88]

This did not completely eliminate the idea that there could be circumstances in which members of the armed forces could and should defy the civilian authorities. On 21 April 2021, 60 years after the attempted putsch against de Gaulle, a letter published in *Valeurs Actuelles*, a right-wing journal, signed by current and former officers, complained about the failure of the authorities to take action to stop the spread of radical Islamist ideas and warned of the possible need for our 'active comrades' to intervene 'in a perilous mission of protecting our civilisational values'.[89] In a second, anonymous letter in the same journal, younger officers who claimed to have served in Afghanistan, Mali and the Central African Republic, as well as domestic anti-terrorism operations, described themselves as having given 'their skin to destroy the Islamism to which you are giving concessions on our soil'. They warned of France becoming a failed state. 'If a civil war breaks out, the army will maintain order on its own soil.'[90] The letters were denounced, including by France's chief of staff of the armed forces, General François Lecointre. Some right-wing politicians commended the sentiments, for example Marine Le Pen of the National Rally. Her father, Jean-Marie Le Pen, from whom she was estranged, had his own links to these events. He served in Algeria in 1957 as a member of the Foreign Legion, even though he was an elected member of parliament for the right-wing Poujadiste Party.[91]

The likelihood of the sentiments expressed in these letters leading to a military coup was remote. The authors could claim that they were not promoting a coup but just pointing to a situation in which the army might plausibly feel compelled to act. Their significance lay in keeping alive the proposition that the first duty of the armed forces was to some essential, civilizational features of the country rather than the political leadership.

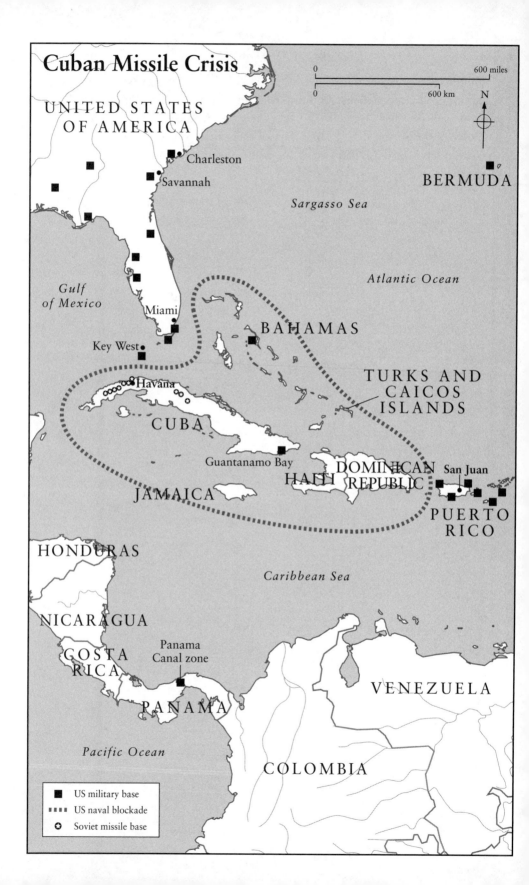

Cuban Missile Crisis

0   600 miles

0   600 km

N

UNITED STATES
OF AMERICA

Charleston

Savannah

BERMUDA

Sargasso Sea

Atlantic Ocean

*Gulf
of Mexico*

Miami

BAHAMAS

Key West

TURKS AND
CAICOS
ISLANDS

Havana

CUBA

Guantanamo Bay

HAITI   DOMINICAN
REPUBLIC   San Juan

JAMAICA

PUERTO
RICO

HONDURAS

Caribbean Sea

NICARAGUA

COSTA
RICA

Panama
Canal zone

VENEZUELA

PANAMA

Pacific Ocean

COLOMBIA

◼ US military base

▪▪▪▪ US naval blockade

✪ Soviet missile base

3

Keeping Control:
The Cuban Missile Crisis

There's always some son-of-a-bitch who doesn't get the word.
President John Kennedy, 27 October 1962[1]

The psychologist Erich Fromm observes that though human history began with Adam and Eve, a story of disobedience, it could well come to an end with an act of obedience. 'If mankind commits suicide,' he notes, 'it will be because people will obey those who command them to push the deadly buttons.' Certainly the most fateful command that could ever be sent or received would be to launch nuclear weapons. It would be an order to inflict mass death and would probably only be issued and executed as whole countries and their populations were being ripped to pieces. Societies might be spared if such orders were disobeyed, yet whole theories of deterrence depend on would-be aggressors assuming that they would be followed. They dare not assume that when it came to the crunch their victims would refrain from retaliating in the most devastating way available. These issues became more pressing as the scale of potential destruction grew. Following the introduction of atomic bombs at the end of the Second World War in August 1945, next came 'city-busting' thermonuclear weapons. During the 1950s, these were developed, tested, mass produced and deployed in large numbers and a variety of forms, carried by bombers and atop missiles.

Deterrence required orders to fire nuclear missiles being obeyed without questioning the morality of mass destruction. The only way to be sure of the automaticity of retaliation was to take human beings out of the loop. The potentially dire consequences of unthinking machines setting in motion Armageddon inspired movies, such as *Dr Strangelove* in

1964 and *WarGames* in 1983. The problem was not necessarily, as Fromm also feared, that the weapons would be unleashed out of obedience to 'the archaic passions of fear, hate, and greed' and the 'obsolete clichés of State sovereignty and national honour'.[2] The calamity could also be caused by a system failure, so that some technical malfunction or a manipulative, wayward officer led to the weapons being launched without an order from the commander-in-chief. Presidents might understand the need to ensure that, should the moment come, their orders to act would be followed without hesitation; but they would also want to ensure that there was no action without their orders. A variety of mechanisms were introduced to thwart rogue commanders and prevent accidental launches.

There were two problems with these mechanisms. The first was linked to the possibility of the national command authority being taken out in a surprise first strike. As there would then be nobody left to issue the order to retaliate, forms of 'pre-delegation' were enacted. These would allow commanders down the line to launch nuclear attacks if they feared that all those above them had been killed or were out of commission in some way. The second problem was that the more nuclear weapons that were produced and the more they were dispersed to field commanders, the greater the problems of control. During the 1950s, both sides developed so-called 'tactical' weapons – bombs, artillery, mines, depth charges and torpedoes – to be used in more conventional military situations, alongside the long-range bombers and intercontinental missiles that threatened the enemy homeland. The wide distribution of the weapons added to the opportunities for officers to start a nuclear war, not as acts of disobedience, but as responses to the exigencies of an intense battle or some calamitous misunderstanding at a time of crisis.

During the October 1962 Cuban Missile Crisis, this question of control weighed upon decision-makers in both the United States and the Soviet Union, although, as we shall see, it played out in different ways on the two sides. This is an episode to which scholars and practitioners return time and again, as a moment when there seemed to be a real and urgent possibility of nuclear war. There was both a quantitative and a qualitative arms race under way, with the move from long-range bombers to missiles and the introduction of nuclear submarines. Each side was unsure about the other's capabilities and intentions. Fortunately, the two leaders – John Kennedy in the United States and Nikita Khrushchev in the Soviet Union – found the right combination of resolve and creative diplomacy to agree on a peaceful conclusion to a crisis that appeared to be hurtling towards calamity. Kennedy moved away from preparing to order air strikes against Soviet missile bases in Cuba, potentially followed by an invasion, to opting for a limited blockade as his first move. For his part, Khrushchev was soon looking for a way out of the crisis he had triggered, without losing too much face. Yet both were concerned that they were not completely in control of events, and could be caught out by unexpected developments. Later historians of the crisis judged that they were right to be concerned.

This chapter does not consider all the dimensions of this crisis, and the issues of command and control they raise, including the use of surveillance aircraft and the planning for air strikes.[3] Instead, it focuses on maritime operations. The American side were concerned to implement the blockade and detect Soviet submarines, while the Soviet side sought to avoid a naval humiliation. Through this case we can explore the challenges facing policymakers who must delegate authority to those implementing their strategies. Unlike other cases in which the military was provided with insufficient guidance, the Cuban Missile Crisis is striking for the attempt to be specific and restrictive. In the United States, the chiefs of staff took their instinctive stance, objecting to any interference in their professional responsibilities, while tasking the local commanders to deal with any situation as they found it. The Soviet side provides a contrast, as Moscow sought to maintain control despite tenuous communications, although in the end they too depended upon the judgement of the officers on the spot.

There are a lot of 'what if's in the story of the Cuban Missile Crisis. Every moment has been scoured for an event that could have triggered a nuclear war, or almost did. Aircraft were shot down or veered off course and submarines feared they were under attack. The most important 'what if's concern who else might have been in charge or the different decisions that might have been taken. The president wanted to stay on top of the chain of command to ensure not that the missiles would be launched should it prove to be necessary, but that they were not launched when they should not be.

THE SOVIET GAMBLE

After Fidel Castro seized power in Cuba in January 1959, he first declared himself a Marxist-Leninist and then aligned his country with Moscow. In the face of intense hostility from the American government, including a failed landing by exiles at the Bay of Pigs in April 1961 and continuing reports of CIA plots, Soviet leader Nikita Khrushchev feared that the Kennedy administration might be tempted to embark on a full-scale invasion. In April 1962, having decided to build up Cuba's defences, first by sending systems for air and coastal defences, he decided on a much bolder step. He would deploy nuclear weapons on the island. One purpose was to deter attacks on Cuba. Another was to deter attacks on the Soviet Union. At the time, the US intercontinental ballistic missile (ICBM) programme was gathering pace, while the Russians lagged far behind. They only had 20 of their own. The Americans had recently been boasting about their superior position. The Soviets could do little to bridge the ICBM gap in the short term, but mobile medium- and intermediate-range missiles were not in short supply. If they could be put on Cuba, then there should be no difference in practice in the deterrent effect against American nuclear threats.

The plan was to deploy 60 R-12 and R-14 missiles, with respective ranges of 1,000 and 2,000 miles. They would be part of a major deployment of troops, aircraft, cruise missiles and submarines. This bold move required secrecy. Khrushchev did not want to announce the deployment until it was complete, and certainly not before the November 1962 congressional elections in the United States. He did not mind putting President Kennedy on the spot but was worried about his reaction if this happened on the eve of a major electoral test.

Over the summer, the Americans realized that something was up on Cuba. By late August, it was clear that a lot of construction work was under way and many ships were delivering military cargoes. The intent was assumed to be largely defensive but, just in case, Kennedy made it clear on 13 September that, if Cuba became 'an offensive military base of significant capacity for the Soviet Union, then this country will do whatever must be done to protect its own security and that of its allies'.[4] He thus set a red line that was already well on the way to being crossed. As it was too late to change his plans, the Soviet leader hoped that the missile deployment could be achieved without detection. The later sense of betrayal in Washington was not helped by private communications in which the Americans were reassured that no missiles were being sent to Cuba.

Indeed, aware of Kennedy's likely fury once the missiles were discovered, the Soviet leader doubled down. In addition to 80 nuclear-armed cruise missiles with 12-kiloton warheads, part of the original plan, Khrushchev decided to add six 'Luna' rocket launchers (known in the West as FROGs) with two 2-kiloton warheads each, along with six 12-kiloton nuclear bombs for the IL-28 aircraft already en route, and six nuclear depth charges. Khrushchev did not intend to disclose the existence of these 'tactical' systems. They were there in case of a major confrontation. The orders were that they could only be used with Moscow's explicit permission. Sent by sea, the missiles eventually arrived in Cuba in late September, soon followed by the first nuclear warheads.

Although the initial plan envisaged a new Soviet naval base on the island, which would have required many surface ships and submarines, the ambition was scaled back, leaving only the 69th Torpedo Submarine Brigade to be deployed into the most challenging area. The brigade was formed in August 1962. It was made up of the B-4, B-36, B-59 and B-130 Project 641 submarines, better known by their Western designation 'Foxtrot'.[5] They were powered by three electric motors and three diesel engines. The batteries enabled them to stay under the surface for days at a stretch, but then they could only travel slowly. The batteries also regularly needed to be repaired and recharged, which required getting to the surface. Because the batteries also took up a lot of space, the conditions on board for the 78 crew were cramped and unpleasant. There were 22 torpedoes for ten tubes. The unique feature of this deployment was that they also carried a single nuclear torpedo, with a maximum range of 15 kilometres and an explosive yield around 10 kilotons.

The brigade commander was Captain Vitalii Agafonov, and above him at the home port of Murmansk was the squadron commander, Admiral Leonid Rybalko. He reported to Admiral Vitalii A. Fokin, who was the deputy to Admiral Sergei Gorshkov, the commander-in-chief of the Soviet Navy. In principle Gorshkov was subordinate to Defence Minister Marshal Rodin Malinovsky, but he was unlikely to be overruled on naval matters. It was Gorshkov who gave Rybalko orders for the brigade. Their task was to get to the Cuban port of Mariel without detection, then reconnoitre the area around the port to establish what US ASW capabilities were present and await the arrival of the nuclear-powered Project 629 (known as Golf Class) submarines, which could carry a short-range ballistic missile with a nuclear warhead.[6] The brigade left for Cuba on 1 October.

MANAGING THE CRISIS

John Kennedy was bright, energetic and engaging, but he could not match the experience of Dwight Eisenhower, his predecessor. He was a war-time junior officer following a supreme commander. In his first year in office, he had been tested by Khrushchev over West Berlin, the non-communist enclave in the middle of communist East Germany, and struggled with conflicts in Laos and Vietnam. He did not trust his chiefs of staff, who were invariably hawkish, always coming up with maximalist options for the use of force, even when he was looking for minimalist ones. His closest advisers were his brother Robert, installed as attorney general; National Security Advisor McGeorge Bundy, a former dean at Harvard; and Secretary of Defense Robert McNamara, recruited from his post as president of the Ford Motor Company. McNamara was confident and analytically rigorous, although at times lacking in political nous. Secretary of State Dean Rusk was experienced and cautious, at times appearing uncomfortable with the disorderly decision-making that marked the Kennedy era.

On 14 October, an American U-2 reconnaissance aircraft took pictures of the first MRBM site. More information was gathered the next day, and by that evening the intelligence community had the evidence of the Soviet deception and developing capability on the island. Kennedy was informed the next morning. This set in motion intense debates within the administration, as Kennedy searched for a way to get Khrushchev to withdraw the missiles without triggering a nuclear war. He established a group that met regularly, almost like a rolling academic seminar, known as ExComm (for Executive Committee of the National Security Council). This included most of those with responsibilities for the conduct of the crisis and a few whose judgement Kennedy trusted. Although this helped the president explore and clarify his options, he did not expect this group to make his decisions for him.

Kennedy's initial reaction was to mount air strikes against the missile sites but he soon started to have second thoughts. ExComm remained divided on the issue. There were a number of arguments against air strikes: they would put the United States in the position of an aggressor mounting a surprise attack; some of the Soviet missiles were mobile and the Air Force could not guarantee their total destruction; it would be hard to avoid following this up without a full invasion of Cuba; the Soviets might retaliate by stepping up pressure on West Berlin. The president therefore opted for a less provocative first step – a narrow blockade of Cuba, described as a 'quarantine' (a blockade is normally considered an act of war). Although this option was politically more acceptable than air strikes, it was hard to be sure how effective it would be. Aircraft and submarines might get through with critical military items, including nuclear warheads, and it would have no effect on those capabilities already in place. As its advocates recognized it might be a temporary measure. Kennedy also wanted to keep the blockade limited. He rejected the Chiefs' proposal to include petroleum, oil and lubricants (POL), persuaded by Rusk that this would shift the objective to Castro's regime and away from the Soviet missiles. If necessary, POL could be added at a later date, should the initial pressure fail to work. It could be part of an escalating set of moves to intensify the pressure on Khrushchev. There could be a move from a partial to a complete blockade, and then to selective air strikes and on to an invasion, after which the options did not bear thinking about.

The world did not learn of the crisis until 19.00 on 22 October 1962, when Kennedy broadcast to the American people, announcing what had been discovered and what he proposed to do about it. He spoke about the Soviet missiles and the steps being taken to get them removed. First, there was to be a 'strict quarantine of all offensive military equipment under shipment to Cuba' which could be 'extended, if needed, to other types of cargo and carriers'. The necessities of life would not be denied. Second, he had directed continued close surveillance of Cuba and 'the Armed Forces to prepare for any eventualities'. Third, the president declared that any nuclear missile launched from Cuba against any nation in the Western hemisphere would be taken to be equivalent to a Soviet attack on the United States, and would prompt a 'full retaliatory response upon the Soviet Union'. Fourth, dependants of US personnel at the Guantanamo base were to be evacuated and additional military units placed on standby. Fifth and sixth, support was to be sought at the OAS (Organization of American States) and the United Nations. Lastly he called upon Khrushchev to eliminate this threat and to work with the United States for 'stable relations', so helping to 'move the world back from the abyss of destruction'. He warned of 'months of sacrifice and self-discipline'.[7] The warnings were clear: the quarantine might only be a first step of many in a crisis that could take months to resolve.

TENSIONS IN THE COMMAND STRUCTURE

Kennedy entered the crisis with civil–military relations in a poor state. From the moment he became secretary, McNamara had used a team of smart civilian analysts to take control of issues that the military considered to be uniquely theirs, including the procurement of new weapons systems. Nothing he had seen from his time in office had given him confidence in the advice coming from the Chiefs (who were often divided among themselves) and the staff work behind it. Kennedy had found military advice less than candid and often unrealistic, pushing policies that it was evident he would be unwilling to follow. When it came to deciding on the strategy, the military input was limited and largely disregarded. General Maxwell Taylor, chairman of the Joint Chiefs, was the only military member of ExComm, where he fairly, if not always forcefully, represented his colleagues. The Chiefs were unhappy with the civilians' cautious approach. They believed that the opportunity should be taken to deal with the Cuban problem once and for all through air strikes, and, if necessary, invasion. To this end, over the preceding months, they had been encouraged to develop plans, which were both detailed and advanced. Now there was a chance to implement them, the administration was shrinking away.

So, not for the first time, Kennedy found his Chiefs reckless in their proposals. They seemed to be incapable of modifying their advice to accommodate his expressed political concerns.[8] On 19 October, after they met with Kennedy, and with the tape still running, Marine General David Shoup exploded with a burst of profanity, complaining about Kennedy continually talking about 'escalation', which he saw to be all about doing the 'goddam thing piecemeal'. His recommendation was 'do this son of a bitch and do it right, and quit friggin' around.'[9] When the decision had been made to go for the quarantine, Taylor reported back to his colleagues that the president was aware of their unhappiness, but trusted that he would be supported in his decision. Taylor added: 'I assured him that we were against the decision but would back him completely.'[10]

In 1958, a few years before the crisis, President Eisenhower had introduced the Defense Reorganization Act to replace a command system considered 'cumbersome and unreliable in time of peace and not usable in time of war'. The new system would ensure that there were truly unified commands in the Pentagon separate from the military departments. The act also envisaged an expanded Joint Staff responsible for planning and drafting orders. The implementing directive described the chain of command as running 'from the President to the Secretary of Defense and through the Joint Chiefs of Staff to the commanders of the unified and specified commands'. It was not clear what 'through the Joint Chiefs of Staff' meant, as that was not actually in the new law.[11]

The new system was supposed to encourage delegation rather than centralization. The idea was that the operational commander would be allowed to get on with the job at hand. But not this time. The administration wanted tight control. The White House even had its own Situation Room, which had been set up the previous year, with the communications and facilities for managing crises. It was there that Kennedy was briefed during the crisis. Although there were later reports that he had spoken directly to ship captains during the crisis, he did not do so.[12] He largely exercised command through McNamara.

The need to enforce the quarantine of Cuba meant that the senior uniformed figure in the line of command was the chief of naval operations (CNO), Admiral George Anderson Jr. Anderson was an aviator who had graduated from the Naval Academy in 1927 and seen action during the Pacific War. Admired as a 'sailor's sailor' and considered a 'straight arrow' for his clean living, he looked as if he had been cast by Hollywood for the role.[13] His personal philosophy was: 'Keep a firm grasp on fundamentals. Leave details to the staff. Go for morale, which is of transcending importance. Don't bellyache and don't worry.' He saw his task as picking the right subordinates and then letting them get on with their jobs.[14] Along with his fellow Chiefs, Anderson had a low opinion of the civilian leadership, and the feeling was mutual. He did not attend ExComm, which meant that specialist naval advice was not always available when needed, and that he lacked a full appreciation of the operation's wider context and ramifications.

After he was asked by McNamara on 18 October to prepare plans for a limited blockade, rules of engagement were drafted by his staff over the next couple of days, largely adapting tactical naval publications. He then briefed Kennedy and McNamara on 21 October, and the rules were approved by McNamara that evening. After the briefing, Kennedy said to Anderson: 'Well, Admiral, it looks as though it is up to the Navy', to which he had responded 'The Navy will not let you down.'[15]

If the new command system had been applied during the Cuban crisis, orders would have been sent directly from McNamara to the unified commander, in this case Admiral Robert Dennison, commander-in-chief, Atlantic (CINCLANT). In practice, the Joint Chiefs reverted to the pre-1958 arrangements. Anderson was designated executive agent of the Joint Chiefs for the operation of the quarantine and the quarantine forces. He ran it through his operations control centre in the Pentagon, known as Flag Plot, rather than through the Joint Staff. He remarked to one of his staff at that time: 'This is a Navy show, we're going to show them how it's done.'[16]

Anderson wanted to be ready for escalation beyond the blockade. He told his commanders to prepare for the 'full spectrum' of military possibilities. He made a point of checking on the readiness of the Polaris ballistic missile carrying nuclear submarines, then based at Holy Loch in Scotland. He trusted that those boats alongside the tender at the base would 'be capable of getting underway with little or no notice in the event the Chiefs raised the defense condition of readiness or if you learn of any actions which would indicate such movements advisable'.

Later, after the president's announcement on 22 October, he urged units to beware submarine attacks:

> I cannot emphasize too strongly how smart we must be to keep our heavy ships, particularly carriers, from being hit by surprise attack from Soviet submarines. Use all available intelligence, deceptive tactics, and evasion during forthcoming days. Good luck.

He wanted a special intelligence effort on Soviet submarine activity, particularly in the Caribbean. He asked the British and Canadian navies for help 'giving us maximum intelligence support concerning potential undersea troublemakers. We have a big job to do and can use all the help we can get.'[17]

The procedures, as passed on to Dennison's ships, stressed minimum force. Interceptions were to take place in daylight hours. The first move would be for a destroyer to get sufficiently close to the targeted Soviet ship to be able to give a visual signal (but not so close that it might be rammed). It would then hoist a flag with the international signal 'K' ('You should stop at once') or 'ON' ('You should heave to at once'). All possible means of communication would be used 'including international code signals, flag hoists, blinking lights, radio, loud speakers, etc.'. If the ship failed to stop warning shots would be fired across the bow, and if it still carried on then the minimum necessary force could be used to 'damage non vital parts of the ship but to refrain if possible from personnel injury or loss of life'. Once the ship stopped, it would be boarded, with the party including Russian linguists. They would examine the manifest and inspect the cargo. If the captain of the ship refused, then it would be forcefully boarded and the ship taken into custody. If there was any resistance, the ship could be destroyed.[18]

A separate document was issued on use of force against merchant vessels. It concluded:

> If destruction of ship is necessary, ample warning and intentions should be given to permit sufficient time for debarkation by passengers and crew. Assistance to maximum extent permitted by operational conditions should be furnished.[19]

The quarantine proclamation issued by Kennedy on 23 October stated that

> force shall not be used except in case of failure or refusal to comply with directions, or with regulations or directives the Secretary of Defense issued hereunder, after reasonable efforts have been made to communicate them to the vessel or craft, or in case of self-defense.

Before he issued it, however, this quarantine proclamation was reviewed that evening by the president with ExComm. As he went through it, a variety of alarming eventualities occurred to Kennedy, raising his anxiety levels. All depended on the assumption that Soviets would be loath to back down. Their vessels would sail on regardless:

They're going to keep going. And we're going to try to shoot the rudder off, or the boiler. And then we're going to try to board it. And they're going to fire a gun, then machine guns. And we're going to have one hell of a time getting aboard that thing.

This would be a 'major military operation'. It might be best 'to sink it rather than just take it'. He appeared to imagine that Soviet vessels would have hundreds of armed men on board. McNamara pointed out that the crew would be small. Taylor suggested that all that was needed was a 'mission type of order' to use minimum force, and then leave it up to the local commander. Before he could finish, Kennedy interrupted:

I think this is the point. If he disables a ship and they're eight hundred miles out and they refuse to let us aboard, I don't think we ought, he ought to feel that he has to board that thing in order to carry out our orders.

Taylor replied: 'Well, he's to keep the ships from going into Cuba, that's his basic mission now.' Kennedy pressed on: 'I think at the beginning it would be better if this situation happened, to let that boat lie there disabled for a day or so, not to try and board it and have them [unclear] with machine gunning with thirty to forty people killed on each side.' McNamara came in urging that the local commander be given latitude: 'We don't believe we should give orders from here.'[20]

Then there was concern about the Soviet submarines, and the potential threat they posed to the carriers. At the end of the conversation, having shown his concerns about how matters could spiral out of control over the coming day, Kennedy turned to McNamara:

All right. Well, Mr Secretary. I think I'd like to make sure that you have reviewed these instructions that go out to the Navy, having in mind the conversation that we've just had.

McNamara: 'I have, and I will do so again tonight, Mr President.'[21]

This was what Anderson feared. As he had rubbed up against Mc-Namara a number of times, grumbling as the secretary and his staff interfered in his core responsibilities, he went to considerable lengths to prevent McNamara getting involved in operational decisions. Mc-Namara slept over at the Pentagon for the duration of the crisis, as did he. Anderson ensured that one of his deputies was always there, even while he was at meetings elsewhere, to prevent civilian meddling. 'We did not want, and I had it pretty well set up to prevent, any intrusion by McNamara or anybody else in the direct operations or any ship or squadron or anything of the sort.'[22]

Anderson held to the established US Navy philosophy of command which was to leave the key decisions up to the commander on the spot, and so he did not intend to second-guess Dennison. By contrast, McNamara believed second-guessing was essential. With the stakes so high, the navy could not be left alone. He intended to review orders on how individual encounters were to be handled before approving them. In a more complex situation, with many separate engagements to be managed, this level of engagement would not have been possible. In this case, a lot of American ships were in position to enforce the quarantine and not many vessels appeared ready to cross the line. In addition, any action would be taking place close to home, in an area of massive US superiority.

It was not only McNamara. Kennedy was anxious about any unnecessary risk-taking. Even after the earlier meeting, the president was still thinking about his discussion with Taylor about how well Soviet submarines could be tracked. He sent a message to the Pentagon directing that the navy 'put a hold on any depth charge attacks on submarines for 48 hours'. After having dinner with British Ambassador David Ormsby-Gore, he followed up the ambassador's suggestion that the quarantine line be moved back from 800 nautical miles to 500 to give the ships more time to turn.[23]

This was the background for the visit that McNamara paid that evening of 23 October to the navy Flag Plot, on the 4th floor of the Pentagon. As soon as he arrived with his deputy, Roswell Gilpatric, McNamara started to ask lots of questions of the admiral apparently in charge, who was reluctant to give answers. Anderson was soon in attendance. The conversation began with a question about a specific destroyer that was not on the quarantine line. The reason was that it was sitting on top of a Russian submarine. How the submarine position was known was highly classified.

As McNamara persisted, Anderson ushered McNamara and Gilpatric into a side room, known as the Intelligence Plot. There the conversation continued, with a discussion about how a submerged Soviet submarine would be given a signal to surface. The answer was that this would probably be a practice depth charge rather than an active one. Was it possible to have direct communications? It was not known 'whether or not our underwater telephone gear was compatible with Soviet underwater communications'.

Then the conversation, as recalled much later by McNamara, turned to enforcing the quarantine. A ship was moving towards the line. Anderson said it would be stopped. McNamara asked how. It would be hailed. McNamara asked in what language. Anderson presumed English. What if they did not understand English? International flags would be used.

'Suppose they don't stop?'

'We'll send a shot across the bow.'

'What if they don't stop then?'

'We'll put one through the rudder.'

'The damn thing may well blow up.'

'You've imposed a quarantine, and our job is to stop the vessels from passing the line.'

'Let me tell you something. There will be no firing of any kind at the Soviet ship without my personal authority, and I'm not going to give you permission until I discuss it with the President. We're trying to convey a political message, we're not trying to start a war.'

McNamara pointed out how little was known about the instructions from Khrushchev to the ship's captain and the risk of starting a war through a 'misunderstanding or lack of information'.

Anderson replied: 'Mr Secretary, the Navy has been carrying out quarantines or blockades since the time of John Paul Jones, and we have been doing it successfully. If you'll keep your fingers out of this situation, we'll carry out this successfully.'

McNamara concluded: 'George, there will be no firing on that ship without my permission.'[24]

Some care is needed in accepting this account. McNamara says that 'in effect' that is what Anderson said. Gilpatric's account, from much earlier, has Anderson using more profanities and telling McNamara to go back to his quarters, but with the same reference to John Paul Jones.[25] Some of the details in McNamara's recall are incorrect. He thought that it was 24 October rather than 23 October, and that the Soviet ship was a tanker. Anderson denies that he spoke of John Paul Jones or that the exchange was so heated. His recollection is that the conversation ended with something along the lines of a light-hearted, 'Well, Mr. Secretary, you go on back, and we'll take care of this blockade.'[26]

Another officer in a neighbouring room does not recall any raised voices, and reports a colleague's recollection that the argument was over McNamara's desire to shift the location of destroyers and the focus of air surveillance. This led to Anderson asking him what he wanted to achieve, so he could agree on what could be done with Dennison, whom he rang soon afterwards.[27] If McNamara did insist that there would be no firing on any ship without civilian authority, this was not actually the message that Kennedy had asked him to convey. The president realized that stopping Soviet ships might be necessary. It was boarding them that worried him, as he feared this would lead to a deadly exchange of fire.[28]

There is nonetheless no doubt that a conversation around these issues did take place. We also know that McNamara told Kennedy after the crisis was over about Anderson's 'insubordination' and saw to it that he was replaced as CNO.[29] Kennedy softened the blow by making Anderson ambassador to Portugal. The clash was the result of the determination by the civilians to assess the political sensitivity of every possible move and Anderson's determination to protect his operational prerogatives. Gilpatric claims that McNamara got his way, because soon after the conversation an emissary came from Anderson to McNamara asking for more information about his questions. The 'cooler heads and wiser counsel prevailed in that part of the Pentagon' as the navy submitted their plans for approval.[30] On the other hand, Anderson sent a memorandum to McNamara on the ships that they intended to intercept, noting that, because of the potential hazard from submarines, the interception would be made by a 'Hunter/Killer group'. 'From now on,' he added, 'I do not intend to interfere with Dennison or either of the admirals on scene unless we get some additional intelligence, as we are hoping for.'[31]

TO THE BRINK AND BACK

The sense of an imminent and dangerous crunch was reinforced by Strategic Air Command (SAC) moving to DEFCON (defence condition) 2 as the quarantine came into effect on 24 October. DEFCON 5 is the lowest, peaceful alert status; DEFCON 1 is the highest, meaning that hostilities have begun. From the start of the crisis, the strategic air commander, General Thomas Power, had wanted to move to DEFCON 2.[32] On the morning of 22 October, Air Force Chief General Curtis LeMay, on the advice of Power, proposed a variety of preparedness measures, geared to the possibilities of a major war. These included putting some of his aircraft on airborne alert, to move to DEFCON 3 at noon that day, and to DEFCON 2 the next day. After Taylor spoke with McNamara, it was agreed that the move to DEFCON 3 should be delayed until the president started speaking that evening, and that a move to DEFCON 2 would await a presidential decision.[33]

The Chiefs decided to move to DEFCON 2 at 14.00 on 23 October, when Anderson informed them that the quarantine would come into force at 10.00 the next day.[34] This was apparently approved by McNamara, presumably with Kennedy's knowledge.[35] The only available document is the instruction from the Joint Chiefs of Staff from late on 23 October to Power, directing SAC 'to generate its force toward a maximum readiness posture' to coincide with the start of the blockade. This meant moving to DEFCON 2. Both the White House and the Pentagon were copied in to the instruction.[36] What does appear to have surprised the White House was the message sent to Power's commanders, in a form that the Soviets would certainly pick up, emphasizing 'the seriousness of the situation this nation faces':

> we are in an advanced state of readiness to meet any emergencies and I feel that we are well prepared. I expect all of you to maintain strict security and use calm judgment during this tense period. Our plans are well prepared and are being executed smoothly.[37]

At once the Soviet Air Defence Command was brought up to the same alert status. After the crisis, a deputy foreign minister observed that when Khrushchev was told about the new alert status, he 'shat his pants'.[38] Power's move reinforced the narrative that alarmed the Soviet leader most – one in which the American president lost control of the crisis to hardline militarists.

ExComm, therefore, began its meeting at 10.00 on 24 October with the quarantine and the high alert status coming into effect. The first engagement was expected within a couple of hours. Nuclear forces were on their highest ever level of alert. To add to the anxiety, McNamara reported to the group on what he had learned about how a Soviet submarine would be signalled by sonar to surface and identify itself. If it refused, small explosive depth charges were to be used to force it to the surface. Kennedy asked what would happen if the submarine did not surface:

> If he doesn't surface or if he takes some action – takes some action to assist the merchant ship are we just going to attack him anyway? At what point are we going to attack him? I think we ought to wait on that today. We don't want to have the first thing we attack as a Soviet submarine.[39]

This was the prompt for what Robert Kennedy later described as the moment of 'greatest concern' for his brother:

> Was the world on the brink of a holocaust? Was it our error? A mistake? Was there something further that should have been done? Or not done? His hand went up to his face and covered his mouth. He opened and closed his fist. His face seemed drawn, his eyes pained, almost gray.

Robert worried about being 'on the edge of a precipice with no way off'.[40]

The crisis was far from over, but there was no need for the immediate level of anxiety, as no Soviet ships were actually approaching the 500-mile quarantine line.

The sudden reduction in the tension was the result of decisions taken by Khrushchev as soon as he realized the seriousness of the situation. Not long before Kennedy's broadcast on 22 October, the Soviet leadership had become aware that something was up, although they did not know whether the issue was Cuba or Berlin. Khrushchev arranged for a meeting of all members of the Presidium of the Central Committee of the Communist Party. He explained that by sending the missiles to Cuba he had wanted 'to cause a bit of a scare' and deter the Americans from attacking Cuba, but 'we don't want to unleash a war'. He also noted that the movement of missiles had been kept secret and was not yet complete. The medium-range R-12s had arrived, but the longer-range R-14s were still en route. The situation was potentially 'tragic', he stated, adding: 'they could attack, we would respond. This could spill out into a big war.' He saw the same menu of options for the Americans as had Kennedy, starting with a blockade and up to invasion of Cuba.

There was considerable discussion around the command and control of nuclear weapons. At first Khrushchev proposed to authorize, in the event of a US invasion, the use of tactical nuclear weapons, but only if there was a landing. When it came to strategic weapons, they must 'wait for orders'. In discussion, the Presidium considered whether it would be wise to allow Cubans any role in decisions to authorize nuclear use and decided that it would not. 'We'll leave the missiles as Soviet property,' Khrushchev concluded, 'subordinate only to us.' After this discussion, they thought it best to wait and hear what Kennedy had to say in his scheduled broadcast.

Once it became known, with relief, that Kennedy was starting with a blockade, the Presidium took steps to avoid an immediate confrontation. The *Aleksandrovsk*, the ship carrying 24 one-megaton warheads for the R-14 missiles, and 44 fourteen-kiloton warheads for tactical missiles, was close to Cuba, and so in a position to avoid being caught by the quarantine. It was ordered to make haste to the nearest port in Cuba, which it was able to do. Four other ships could also get to Cuba quickly, before the quarantine came into effect. and were instructed to do so. The other ships, including those carrying the R-14 missiles, which might be caught in a blockade were ordered to return home. One decision was taken, however, that could have led to trouble later in the week.[41]

The four diesel submarines were then still three days' sailing away, with the lead submarine approaching the Turks and Caicos Islands, at the entrance to the Caribbean. The first instinct, expressed by Khrushchev, was to order the Foxtrots to continue their journey, but his ally Anastas Mikoyan expressed concerns about the risks of a clash with US anti-submarine warfare (ASW) capabilities. Defence Minister Rodin Malinovsky pushed back, but Mikoyan was able to call in aid Gorshkov as commander-in-chief of the navy. He showed that the passages to Cuba were too narrow and how the boats would be tracked by the Americans. Once detected their presence would only increase the possibilities of confrontation. Instead, they were instructed to move to a holding position on the Sargasso Sea, which stretches from the Atlantic to Bermuda.[42] As we shall see, this did not do the submariners any favours.

Although the Soviet orders went out early in the morning (US time) on 23 October, when ExComm met that evening they were unaware of this critical development. A briefer informed them that the main Soviet vessel of interest was the *Kimovsk*. McNamara added that they 'know approximately what area of the ocean it's in', and that once found 'we have ample ability to tail them'. At different times both Robert Kennedy and McGeorge Bundy asked whether it was still on its way. McNamara replied: 'It's still coming. It has not yet turned around.'[43] *Kimovsk* and another vessel of interest, *Gagarin*, were expected to arrive at the quarantine line before noon on 24 October, while a third, the *Poltava*, would arrive a bit later.

The US Navy had limited knowledge of the positions of Soviet ships and submarines. They might be spotted by surveillance aircraft, but the main way that they gave themselves away was when they sent radio messages. These could be picked up by listening posts, which then reported the direction from which they came. If a number of posts picked up the same message, then the lines could be plotted to see where they intersected. Having got a fix at one time, and making assumptions about speed and direction of travel, estimates could be made about where ships were heading and when they might arrive, but if they changed path or slowed down, then they could soon be lost.

It was known on 23 October that an urgent message had been sent from Moscow to some Soviet merchant ships that morning, and that this had triggered a lot of further signalling to other ships, but the content was not known. Nor were the Americans trailing any individual vessels. The available information was getting old – the last fixes on the *Kimovsk* and *Poltava* had been at 03.00 and at 11.00 respectively that morning, with no known position for the *Gagarin*. Information did come in, however, during the day about the *Kimovsk*, suggesting that it had slowed or stopped, although it could still reach the line at the previously scheduled time the next day if it picked up speed. When McNamara had his encounter at the Flag Plot with Anderson that evening, had he asked for a briefing on the location of the ships, he would have been told that the *Kimovsk* and *Poltava* had slowed or stopped. But he did not ask, and so they did not tell.[44]

Soon there was more evidence from direction-finding radars that some Soviet vessels had stopped dead in the water while others had turned around. Before reporting this information, the Office of Naval Intelligence (ONI) wanted it to be verified, which would require aircraft looking for the ships in the morning. There was also some concern that this might have been a 'Soviet ploy' of some sort, and that deliberately misleading messages were being transmitted. The quarantine was not due to come into effect until 10.00, so there seemed to be no problem with waiting to be sure.[45] There are suggestions that both CIA Director John McCone and McNamara were told that some of the Soviet boats might be holding back in the early hours of the morning, but, if this was the case, it does not appear to have made much of an impression on them.

The briefing from the navy McNamara and Gilpatric received at 09.00 on 24 October was not updated with the new information, even though carrier aircraft had confirmed by this time that a number of vessels had stopped or reversed course. A US Navy history note: 'This information was inconclusive and Mr. McNamara was not informed.'[46] Nor apparently was Anderson, possibly because of the long delays then being experienced with the transmission of top secret naval communications.

From Gilpatric's notes, it is apparent that he and McNamara were still expecting the quarantine line to be tested at 10.30 by the *Kimovsk*. The navy could say that they had passed on what they had known when asked, and it was reasonable to wait for the surveillance flights to work out where the ships actually were. Yet, given the stress of the moment, it is fair to assume that those facing tough decisions that morning might have liked to have been at least alerted to the possibility that this stage of the crisis might turn out to be more manageable than feared.

At 10.25, while attending ExComm, McCone got a message reporting, as he told the assembled group, that some of the Soviet ships that had yet to reach the quarantine line 'had either stopped, or reversed course'. The impact of this potentially dramatic announcement was undermined by uncertainty over what it meant that they were in Cuban waters. As Kennedy observed, it made a difference whether they were coming or going, so McCone left the room to check. Even when he came back and confirmed that the ships that had stopped or reversed course were those that might otherwise have reached the quarantine line, there was still discussion of exactly which ships were affected. For a while, Kennedy was still assuming that the blockade might be challenged, until Taylor got back from talking to Anderson to confirm that this would not now be the case. So as to give the *Gagarin* and *Kimovsk* time to turn, the president ordered the *Essex* not to intervene.[47] Dean Rusk then uttered his famous line: 'We're eyeball to eyeball and I think the other fellow just blinked.'[48] This remained the perception of

American policymakers for some time. This had been like a game of chicken and the Soviets had veered away at the last moment.

As we have seen, Khrushchev had blinked 24 hours earlier. It gradually dawned on the Americans that the reason that a blockade was always likely to be effective was because Moscow would not want sensitive equipment to fall into American hands. When McNamara raised the question of whether to follow a ship carrying offensive arms that had turned away. Rusk, always keen to ensure that the administration focused on the main objective, advised against. From a Soviet perspective, they would be 'sensitive as a boil'.[49]

After hearing from Taylor, Anderson hurried to the Flag Plot. Orders were sent out to continue with maximum reconnaissance effort to be sure of the position of all Soviet ships. The USS *Essex* was sent a signal: 'Do not stop and board. Keep under surveillance.' Early interception was hardly an issue. At the time, the *Kimovsk* was some 800 miles away and the *Gagarin* about 500 miles.[50] The only other matter of note that morning was when one US ship reported a disappearing radar contact, leading to suspicions that this was a following submarine.

The operational issues concerning the quarantine now looked quite different. There was no reason to intercept other ships that were headed towards Cuba with cargoes that were almost certainly innocent, yet it would be odd to have a blockade and then make no interceptions. Although Moscow had ordered all ships carrying offensive arms to return home immediately, others had been told to wait for further instructions. Those with military cargoes were eventually told to return home. After a couple of days, ships with non-military cargoes, along with tankers, proceeded to Cuba. On the morning of 25 October, the CIA reported that 14 Soviet ships had turned back. Five tankers were still travelling towards Cuba along with three dry cargo ships, of which one, the *Belovodsk*, might have military equipment on board.[51]

Kennedy had announced: 'All ships of any kind bound for Cuba from whatever nation or port will, if found to contain cargoes of offensive weapons, be turned back.' Any ship sailing towards Cuba could be intercepted, but without problematic ships the quarantine was becoming 'a little flat', sending mixed signals because only the wrong sort of boats could be challenged.[52] The first tanker to appear, the *Bucharest*, was approached by USS *Gearing*, a destroyer from the *Essex* group, and asked for identification. It replied: 'My name is *Bucharest*, Russian ship from the Black Sea, bound for Cuba.' The destroyer pulled along-side. The *Bucharest* dipped her colours. The two ships exchanged 'good mornings'. Some photographs were taken showing that there was no deck cargo. As it was only carrying petroleum, the tanker was cleared for continued passage to port. Only after this did a message come from the White House, via Deputy Secretary of Defense Gilpatric, requesting that the *Bucharest* be trailed but not stopped or harassed. As questions were now being asked about the risks of confrontation, at 11.50 that morning, some 25 hours after ExComm had first received the news, the Pentagon announced that at least a dozen Soviet vessels had turned back, and that the *Bucharest* had been intercepted and allowed to pro-ceed towards Cuba without being boarded.

Kennedy preferred that the first ship to be boarded should be from anywhere other than the Soviet Union. He had initially been taken with the idea of stopping a British ship to make the point that he was pre-pared to stop friend and foe alike, but backed away from this after furious objections from the British ambassador.[53] The first suitable non-bloc ship identified was a Greek ship, *Sirus*, which had already identified herself, declared her cargo and requested permission to proceed to Cuba. A destroyer had been dispatched to meet *Sirus*, but then a Leba-nese freighter, *Marucla*, appeared to be a better candidate. It was Russian operated and had been loaded in Riga.

Two destroyers were dispatched to intercept and board her. One of them, the USS *John D Pierce*, closed in on what she thought was the *Marucla*. It turned out to be an East German cruise ship, *Völkerfreund-schaft*, with some 1,500 passengers on board. As any action could put passengers at risk and this would not look good, especially after just letting the *Bucharest* go, the ship was shadowed for a while and then let pass. Further confusion then resulted from a report that *Marucla* had turned around, which turned out not to be true. Eventually she was found again, although by this time the light was poor. Then the destroy-ers were ordered to board her whenever found, day or night, until this was amended so the boarding would take place at first light.

At 08.00 on 26 October, a boarding party reached the *Marucla* for the blockade's first actual interception. A copy of the cargo manifest was checked against the holdings. Although all holds were battened down and inaccessible, one was opened for inspection, since it con-tained questionable material listed as 'electro-measuring instruments'.

After half an hour the boarding party left the ship, and the *Marucla* was able to carry on with its journey to Cuba. Next came the Soviet tanker, *Groznyy*, bound from Odessa to Cuba. McNamara reported to ExComm that it was 'carrying a deck load which might be missile field tanks'. On the morning of the 27 October, a US destroyer pulled alongside the Soviet tanker. The ship showed no interest in stopping, presumably on the grounds that other tankers had already been allowed through. The destroyers however issued a warning and prepared to fire a warning shot. When the issue about what to do about the *Groznyy* was first raised that day McNamara argued it should be boarded. Increasingly the discussion about what to do about it became bound up with discussions around diplomatic efforts being made by U Thant, the UN secretary general, to defuse the crisis. Although few in the administration took these efforts seriously, Kennedy had suggested that Thant could use his good offices to appeal to Khrushchev to hold back Soviet ships, so that there would be no need to board them. Khrushchev had agreed. So, during a tense day, ExComm came to the view that perhaps *Groznyy* should not be boarded. If it did continue to Cuba this could be used as more evidence of Soviet bad faith.[54] The *Groznyy* stopped on the morning of 28 October.

ANTI-SUBMARINE OPERATIONS AND NUCLEAR TORPEDOES

The US Navy was aware of Soviet submarine activity in the Atlantic before they were aware of the Soviet missile sites on Cuba, and the readiness of its anti-submarine warfare (ASW) forces was already high. As the crisis developed, the presence of Soviet submarines so close to the United States provided, as Anderson later observed, 'perhaps the first opportunity since World War II for our anti-submarine warfare forces to exercise their trade, to perfect their skills, and to manifest their capability to detect and follow submarines of another nation'.[55] It was an opportunity embraced with enthusiasm. Kennedy was more worried. He saw that a tangle between these submarines and American anti-submarine forces could be a source of serious escalation. If he had known that the submarines were carrying nuclear torpedoes, he would have been even more worried. So, presumably, would have Anderson.[56]

By 24 October, the navy was aware of at least three Soviet Foxtrot submarines. As we noted earlier, at least one had already been detected when McNamara visited the Flag Plot late on 23 October. There were many other possible contacts, but, according to the navy's rules, they could only be counted with a visual sighting. The eventual conclusion was that five had been located and tracked, which meant that one was double counted. They were known to be Foxtrots, and so could not be carrying cruise or ballistic missiles. There was also no suggestion that they were carrying nuclear torpedoes. The major threat they potentially posed was to the American fleet imposing the quarantine. The administration stated publicly that they could be interdicted if they failed to surface when told to do so, and then potentially boarded.

Kennedy and McNamara saw a risk that submarines might use weapons when resisting attempts to force them to the surface. They wanted to find a way to ensure that they did not confuse a signal to surface with something more provocative or dangerous. The navy proposed to combine 'four or five harmless explosive sound devices' (practice depth charges) with the international code signal for 'rise to surface', which was still more aggressive than normal peacetime practice. This was published on 23 October as a notice to mariners ('Submarine Surfacing and Identification Procedures') and then communicated to Moscow. No acknowledgement was ever received from Moscow, so the Americans could not know if the Foxtrots knew what to expect.

Meanwhile the Foxtrots followed their new orders and moved to the Sargasso Sea. For personal, practical and patriotic reasons, they would have preferred to get to Cuba. While the journey to the port of Mariel would undoubtedly have been hazardous, being submerged in the Sargasso Sea invited attention from the whole range of US ASW assets. The long journey had already tested the boats. They had been buffeted by hurricanes that caused mass seasickness. Their cooling systems could not cope with the tropics, and the draining heat made the boats barely habitable. They had orders to avoid detection, but that was easier said than done. The boats were noisy and could be picked up by sonars. They had to surface to recharge their batteries. The optimum approach was to use the electric motors during the day and go to the surface at night, when they could use the three diesel engines while charging their batteries.

Maintaining communications with Moscow was the responsibility of radio intercept teams on each boat. They were also tasked with inter-cepting and decoding US radio transmissions. To pick up and receive messages, it was necessary to move to periscope depth or the surface, so this added to the risks of being caught by an enemy ship. The further away from Russia, the more difficult communications became. They were using low-power transmitters with antennae that had to be dried off before sending or receiving transmissions, which left little time to transmit. The same message would have to be retransmitted many times. Also, the communication sessions were scheduled in Moscow time, and as they moved to the west that was usually during daylight hours.

The nuclear torpedo required a special arrangement. Each had its own officer, responsible for maintenance, loading and assembly for use. As the captains of the four boats had been surprised to be taking nuclear weapons, they had asked during pre-deployment briefings about the circumstances in which they might be used. Fokin had advised that 'if they slap you on the left cheek, do not let them slap you on the right one.' Another senior officer suggested that they could be used if they were holed in the hull under the water, or were being shot at if forced to come to the surface, as well as 'when Moscow orders you to use these weapons'. As if encouraging them to take the initiative, there was a sug-gestion that 'you use the nuclear weapons first, and then you will figure out what to do after that'. According to Huchthausen, Rybalko was told something similar when getting his original orders from Gorsh-kov.[57] The formal orders, so secret that they could only be opened once at sea, instructed the boats to keep their weapons in a state of full com-bat readiness, but only to use them on the orders of higher authority – the commander-in-chief of the USSR Naval Forces, in the case of conven-tional weapons, and the defence minister in the case of the nuclear weapons.

For a naval officer, the contradiction between the formal and infor-mal guidance would not have seemed unusual. Captains at sea are always aware of possible situations in which their previous orders would be irrelevant and they would need to use their own initiative. One of the captains, Nikolai Shumkov of B-130, who was sceptical of claims that any use was ever seriously considered, wrote that the nuclear torpedo tube had a special lock which only the captain could open, with a key normally worn on a string around his neck. For the key to be used, an order would have needed to be received and then decrypted by the cipher officer, before being checked again by the political officer. If all was correct, it could lead to the launch of either a normal or a nuclear torpedo. Whether a commander would have managed to follow through these procedures when under an attack may be doubted. Although the commanders were not supposed to make such decisions independently, Shumkov acknowledged the technical possibility that they could. He queried, however, whether there would be any scenarios in which the nuclear torpedoes might be used. They were 'designed only to destroy coastal targets or large targets, for example, aircraft carriers'. As the firing range was no more than 15 kilometres, the US carriers were likely to be safely out of the way. Thus 'there was no point in removing the lock'.[58]

One indication that Moscow did not want captains to do too much on their own initiative was the requirement for a continuous communications channel with Moscow once they were in the Sargasso Sea, which could be used when the time came for a change in mission. They were also able to listen with relative ease to US Navy communications, which helped them get a sense of the extent of the ASW effort, and also the state of the crisis, about which they were told little by Moscow. They were aware that Kennedy had said that Russian submarines would not be allowed to operate in US coastal waters. They therefore knew that combat operations were a distinct possibility. The last orders they had were to hold and 'remain ready to deploy on command'. They expected to receive new orders to do so at any time from Moscow.[59]

They did actually know about the American advice about using practice decoys as a signal to surface. Their commander, Rybalko, only found out about it when visiting Moscow from Murmansk to discover what was happening to his submarines. Fokin told him that Gorshkov had forbidden communicating more than routine information on the scheduled submarine broadcasts, to avoid giving away anything operationally important to the Americans. As the brigade's orders were to stay covert, Rybalko thought they needed to know about American intentions. His view was that 'you owe absolute loyalty to the men under your command, just as they are loyal to follow your orders blindly'. He therefore went against his senior commanders and ensured that the message was inserted into the next broadcast.[60]

One problem was that, given the effects of even practice depth charges, it could be hard to distinguish between a signal and an attack.

It was assumed that the Americans wanted the Foxtrots to surface. The issue was what would happen if they continued to stay submerged. In the event no submarines surfaced because of the signals. When they did so, it was simply because they were unable to stay submerged any longer. They were thwarted because of failing equipment or batteries that needed charging.

Only the B-4 managed to avoid surfacing, although it *was* detected. It had sufficient battery power to stay under water and get away. The captain of the B-36 claimed that his boat was almost rammed by a US destroyer when attempting to surface. Although it was spotted when it eventually surfaced to recharge its batteries on 31 October (after being convinced that it had dodged a torpedo) it was able to submerge again and return home.

With the other two Foxtrots, there were issues with the nuclear torpedoes. The B-130 had only one working engine by the time it got its orders to take up its position in the Sargasso Sea. Captain Shumkov, who feared that they might be rammed or depth charged, instructed the officer guarding the 'special' torpedo to flood the torpedo tube. In some accounts, the political officer on board objected and he relented. Shumkov later insisted that he had no intention of firing the torpedo without a direct order, but he wanted to show that he was prepared to do so, to impress his senior officers in Moscow when he got back.[61] When the B-130's batteries gave up, on 30 October it surfaced in front of the US destroyer *Blandy*, but it did not seek American assistance. As it was unable to repair its engines, it had to wait for a tugboat to tow it back to Murmansk.

The most important incident involved the fourth submarine, the B-59. It is now highlighted as one of the most dangerous moments of the crisis, and by extension the Cold War.[62] This is in part because it took place on 27 October, one of the most fraught days of the crisis. A U-2 had been shot down over Cuba, and there were fears on the Soviet side that the United States was preparing to invade the island. In command of the B-59 was Captain Vitali Savitsky. Also on board was the 69th Brigade chief of staff, Captain Vasili Arkhipov.

The carrier USS *Randolph*'s group had detected the submarine and was determined to get it to the surface. The B-59 had spent many hours trying to avoid detection, by changes in diving depth, course and speed, as well as by using jamming devices. Just before 17.00 on 27 October, one of the destroyers attempted to signal the B-59 using practice depth charges and sonar. Half an hour later, another destroyer dropped five hand grenades. All this was disconcerting for a crew that had already been through a lot, coping with unbearably high temperatures on board, and, as far as they knew, possibly now at war. In one account, exhausted, unable to make contact with Moscow, and now at risk of being sunk by the Americans, Savitsky ordered the officer in charge of the torpedoes to get them to battle readiness.

> Maybe the war has already started up there, while we are doing summer-saults here . . . We're gonna blast them now! We will die, but we will sink them all – we will not become the shame of the fleet.

That was as far as it went. Savitsky contained himself, spoke with Arkhipov and the political officer on board, and decided not to take the matter further.

This account from Vadim Orlov has not been confirmed by another source.[63] There is, however, an alternative version. This has the issue arising after the B-59 had surfaced just before 21.00 on 27 October. The batteries were running low. As soon as it surfaced, the B-59 was immediately illuminated by searchlights from US destroyers. Savitsky, Arkhipov and the watchman went up to the bridge.

> And then it began. US PLO aircraft with the searchlights turned on entered at low level flight from the starboard side in a circle and, approaching the ship's side, opened fire from their weapons of such force that the voice communication was drowned out in the central post from the roar of cannonade. The submarine commander commands: 'Urgent dive! Prepare torpedo tubes # 1 and # 2 for firing!'

Tube 1 was for the nuclear torpedo. Before the dive could take place, however, the ship's signalman got stuck with his searchlight. At that moment, a message came from the closest US destroyer, USS *Cony*, calling for communication. Arkhipov ordered the dive to stop. To the question 'Whose ship?' went the reply 'The ship belongs to the USSR. Stop provocations!' After this message had been repeated the planes stopped flying and firing over the B-59.[64] Eventually, still on the surface, it turned east, charging its batteries as it went, followed by US ships. When one of the following frigates went to refuel, the B-59 took the opportunity to dive.

There is another account of the same incident from the American side. Ensign Gary Slaughter, responsible for communicating with the B-59, reported how a Navy P2V Neptune surveillance aircraft dropped incendiary devices to activate his photoelectric camera lenses. This is what the Soviets experienced as tracer bullets. As Slaughter saw the B-59 get into position to direct its torpedo tubes at *Cony*, his captain told him to apologize for the P2V's behaviour. In this account, Savitsky acknowledged the apology, closed his torpedo-tube doors and turned round to move in an easterly direction.

There is no confirmation that Savitsky intended at this point to use a nuclear torpedo. According to the commander of the torpedo squad, some of the crew were close to mutiny at the thought of getting into a fight at this stage, and it required some choice language to get the orders obeyed and the torpedo tubes filled with water and readied for action. But this account does not suggest that the nuclear torpedo was involved, and it would have been an odd choice of weapon to deal with a destroyer at close range.[65]

Cony's captain told Slaughter: 'Keep that Russian bastard happy.' Savitsky signalled that his crew could use some fresh bread and cigarettes after all. These were transferred to the submarine by high line. Thereafter the two men exchanged smiles until the American's watch was over.[66] There is no confirmation of this from the Soviet side, which is not necessarily surprising as accepting assistance from the Americans was not part of the narrative. While the B-59 was still on the surface, a navy band came out to play some jazz, which was a clue that perhaps war had not yet broken out. Savitsky ordered his men not to respond, and dismissed one from the bridge who was tapping his foot in time to the rhythm. After moving east on the surface, being circled by American ships, the B-59 managed to dive on 29 October and get away.

CONCLUSION: GETTING THE MESSAGE

Whatever actually happened on the B-59, and whether or not an outburst of frustration was given a retrospective, melodramatic significance, it was still the case, as Savranskaya notes, that a commander acting 'under acute time pressure and with limited information, under tremendous stress', was physically in a position to launch the torpedo without orders from Moscow.[67] Savitsky was not in a unique position. At this time, numerous field commanders, on both sides of the US–Soviet confrontation, had the capacity to fire nuclear weapons. Although Kennedy's team did not know that the Foxtrots were carrying the nuclear torpedoes, this sort of delegated power was one reason why they were anxious about escalation and about keeping close control of all military moves.

In this case, a large part of the problem, certainly for the crews of the Foxtrots, was the lack of a similar effort from Moscow. The submarines had been sent on their way at the start of the month in support of a mission that was effectively abandoned on 23 October, when ships were told to reverse course, and the other submarines were told no longer to proceed to the Caribbean. The Foxtrots were left alone. They were told only to move into a holding position, which had been chosen without much thought for the implications. In the Sargasso Sea they served as magnets for US ASW forces. This left the boats and their crews at the edge of their endurance. The high command in Moscow had little grasp of the conditions under which they were operating or their limited ability to stay out of trouble. When they eventually got home, they faced a furious Gorshkov. Their submarines had been detected against his express orders. He put this down to incompetence, rather than an unavoidable need to get to the surface to recharge batteries and communicate, a requirement that he appeared not to understand. He would not accept responsibility for putting the submariners in a terrible predicament, though he had ordered them into a hostile environment where they waited for new orders which never came. Communications from Moscow were so sparse that the captains had to rely on what they could understand from American news broadcasts to work out whether they were in a war or close to one. In the circumstances, it is remarkable that all boats managed to return home in one piece. This illustrates a crucial point that we will see elsewhere, that the problem was not so much civil–military interaction as with that between headquarters and the field commanders.

On the American side, exercising command and control was much easier, although they also had their problems with communications, notably the fleet radioteletype broadcast system. It was in the process of being converted into something faster and, as a result, could barely cope with the increased traffic generated by the crisis. The number of messages went up threefold. Many of them were too long for the system and had to be broken up. More than usual had the highest classification and had to be encrypted. Those attempting to send messages became frustrated with a painfully slow system, and so tried to jump the queue by giving their messages high precedence. This snarled up the system even more. At times, important orders did not get through, for example to a ship that was supposed to join the blockading force. A captain who needed to get ships to move to their patrol positions for the start of the quarantine found that it would take 38 hours to get instructions to a ship some 150 miles away. Instead, and in desperation, the vital message was taken by helicopter. As encounters at sea were few and far between, these communications problems did not make as much difference as they might have done. If the confrontation had become more intense, they could have seriously degraded the quality of crisis management.[68]

Senior military figures may have found the constant attention from civilians, and in particular McNamara, irritating, but no attempt was made to circumvent the established chain of command and the navy's operational proposals were largely approved. That a Soviet submarine might have assumed that it was under attack when it was being illuminated by a tracker aircraft was the sort of detail that worried the administration, but not one for which they could have legislated in advance. Its significance was appreciated by the commanders on the spot, and they acted quickly and appropriately. Again, the U-2 pilot who strayed into Soviet territory (the 'son-of-a-bitch' in the opening quote) did so not because of intent or incompetence, but because of the effects of the Aurora Borealis, which had made it difficult to get an accurate fix on his position.[69]

The crisis was resolved by a simple deal whereby Khrushchev agreed to withdraw the missiles and Kennedy agreed not to invade Cuba. He also informally agreed over time to remove US Jupiter missiles from Turkey. Kennedy has been given high marks for how he managed the crisis. This was in part because of the efforts of his aides to shape the initial historical record. Yet, he also consulted widely on his options, was clear on his political objectives – getting the missiles out of Cuba while avoiding nuclear war – and his strategy for meeting them. These were clearly communicated to the military and every effort was made to ensure that they were followed. There was also no public debate prior to his broadcast on 22 October, because the discovery of the Soviet missile bases was kept out of the public domain until the policy was agreed.

It is hard to believe that this sort of secrecy could be sustained now, although, for the same reason, a modern Khrushchev could not have any confidence in his original deception. Even in 1962, this was the big flaw in his plan.

Khrushchev moved quickly to end the crisis because he could see how events might get out of control. Whatever the prior instructions and attempts at communication, individuals on the front line would take decisions according to the circumstances as they perceived them, and it would not take too much for their perceptions to go awry, especially if they were egged on by Fidel Castro. Problems with communications and getting a full appreciation of the situation meant that attempts to give precise orders to address complex situations could well make matters worse. In this situation, where mistakes or unnecessary provocations could have had such dire consequences, Khrushchev's approach was not to try to control matters from a distance and through layers of command, but to resolve the crisis as soon as possible.

In 1962, Fletcher Knebel and Charles Bailey, two political reporters who knew how much the senior military despised Kennedy, published a book, *Seven Days in May*, describing an attempted military coup in the United States.[70] This was not long after the attempted coup in France. After reading the book, Kennedy observed 'it could happen' and that some generals 'might hanker to duplicate fiction'. He was keen to have the book made as a movie 'as a warning to the generals' and encouraged Kirk Douglas, who was already interested in the project, to do so. It was made and released to positive reviews ('provocatively topical') in February 1964, a few months after Kennedy's assassination.[71]

The plot in the story did not concern the Cuban Missile Crisis, but instead military opposition to an arms control treaty with the Soviet Union. President Jordan Lyman had a document in which the chairman of the Joint Chiefs, Air Force General James Scott, was reported to have said that should the president 'not be fulfilling his responsibility for the national security . . . it might be necessary for the good of the country to supersede him'. When reporting that he had sacked Scott, the president gave the MacArthur explanation: that he and the Joint Chiefs did not accept the settled policy of the administration and as they intended to continue in their opposition they had to resign.

In the real-life story of the crisis, the chiefs of staff did not directly challenge the president's authority though they were out of sympathy with his adopted policy. Kennedy was particularly dismayed by Air Force Chief Curtis LeMay, who effectively accused him of appeasement when they met as he was first working out his options, and then advocated attacking even after Khrushchev had agreed to withdraw the missiles, calling Kennedy's refusal to do so 'the gravest defeat in our history'. After the crisis was over, Kennedy observed that he would advise his successor 'to watch the generals, and to avoid feeling that just because they were military men their opinions on military matters were worth a damn'.[72]

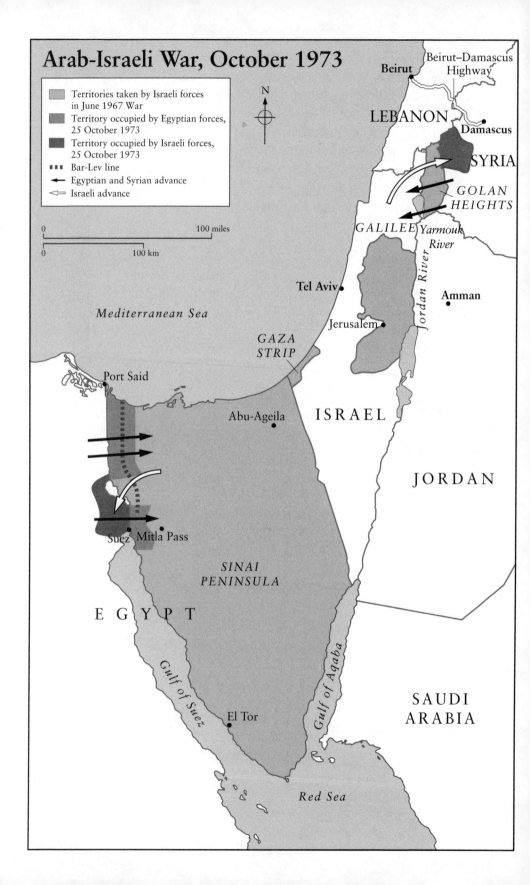

Arab-Israeli War, October 1973

Key:
- Territories taken by Israeli forces in June 1967 War
- Territory occupied by Egyptian forces, 25 October 1973
- Territory occupied by Israeli forces, 25 October 1973
- ▪▪▪ Bar-Lev line
- ◄— Egyptian and Syrian advance
- ⇐ Israeli advance

N

0   100 miles

0   100 km

Beirut

Beirut–Damascus Highway

LEBANON

Damascus

SYRIA

GOLAN HEIGHTS

GALILEE   Yarmouk River

Jordan River

Tel Aviv

Amman

Jerusalem

Mediterranean Sea

GAZA STRIP

Port Said

ISRAEL

Abu-Ageila

JORDAN

Suez   Mitla Pass

SINAI PENINSULA

E G Y P T

Gulf of Suez

Gulf of Aqaba

El Tor

SAUDI ARABIA

Red Sea

4

The Very Model of Insubordination: Ariel Sharon and Israel's Wars

For Arik, the report on the battle was part of the battle. You've got to fight your superiors too. They're men of little faith.

Shimon Peres, on Ariel Sharon[1]

In April 2005, as Prime Minister Ariel ('Arik') Sharon pledged to move Israeli troops and settlers from Gaza, Israeli historian Benny Morris asked whether Sharon might 'one day be remembered alongside Charles de Gaulle, who came to power committed to holding on to Algeria but swiftly moved to rid France of its colonial burden'. There were also reports that Sharon had read Alistair Horne's book about Algeria, *A Savage War of Peace*. Before he could follow up his move on Gaza with one on the West Bank, he had a stroke which left him comatose, leaving unanswered a series of questions about whether, as with de Gaulle, it would take a man associated with the right to achieve an aspiration of the left.[2] There were other points of comparison. Sharon had never been one for following orders with which he disagreed. He had made his name first as a general and then as a politician by refusing to compromise on matters of national security. Their political styles were nonetheless quite different. De Gaulle liked to keep an air of mystery around both his intent and his methods. Sharon's nickname was 'the Bulldozer'. Sharon fought in Israel's first four wars and led it into a fifth. This is the period, before he became prime minister, covered in this chapter. During this time, he clashed repeatedly with those above him in the chain of command, until eventually he could give the orders.

The Israeli case is distinctive. Israel is a relatively small country facing a range of security threats. For this reason, generals become

well-known figures, even celebrities, and when they retire they sometimes become politicians. Sharon was in the process of making this
transition when he was called back from the reserves to command a
division in the October War of 1973. He fought this war in both a military and a political capacity, antagonizing his fellow commanders as he
did so. In 1982, as minister of defence, he was directly involved in the
conduct of the Lebanon campaign. Like all democracies, Israel follows
the principle of military subordination to civilians, but when the civilian
and military elites are interchangeable the borderline between them can
become unclear. Sharon's military career therefore takes us back to the
perennial questions of obedience. How far should a commander go to
get the orders of his immediate superior overturned? And, if they cannot
be overturned, under what circumstances should they be disobeyed?

SHARON UNLEASHED: THE 1967 WAR

Sharon was an imposing, chunky figure, with tousled hair. Born in Palestine under the British mandate, he had fought aged 19 against the
Jordanian Army during the War of Independence in 1947–8, becoming
a platoon commander. His reputation was of a tough professional,
brave and audacious, but also reckless and hard to control. He enjoyed
patronage at the highest level, notably from Prime Minister David Ben-
Gurion, whose admiration he earned during the mid-1950s, when he
put together an elite force to conduct reprisal raids on Jordanian territory, following attacks against Israeli civilians. These were controversial
because of the many Arab civilians killed. In the 1956 War against
Egypt, he ignored orders to hold back from moving through the Mitla
Pass in the Sinai, which ended in a patrol being ambushed with heavy
casualties. This incident almost finished his career. The chief of staff
effectively froze Sharon's promotion until a more forgiving Yitzhak
Rabin took over. By May 1967, he was Major General Sharon commanding the 38th Division under the Southern Command.

Israel was facing its most serious crisis since it had gained independence 20 years earlier. At first it appeared that Egyptian President Gamal
Abdul Nasser's objective was no more than to deter an Israeli attack on
Syria, albeit one that Israel was not actually planning. (Nasser had been
fed false Soviet intelligence about Israeli troops massing on the Syrian

front.) But then one move followed another, and the crisis gathered pace. On 14 May, Egyptian forces were put on their highest state of readiness and ordered to move to 'designated assembly areas' in the Sinai Peninsula, preparing 'to bear the burden of the fighting on the Israeli front'.[3] Two days later the commander of the UN Emergency Force (UNEF) in the Sinai, deployed after the 1956 War to keep the peace, was told by Nasser to withdraw his forces. On 23 May, came the move that took Nasser's strategy beyond deterrence. He announced that Egypt would prevent Israeli shipping passing through the Straits of Tiran, blocking oil from Iran and exports to Africa and Southeast Asia. Soon he was speaking of 'confrontation' with Israel, and a 'general war' with the objective of destroying Israel.

Alarmed at this prospect, the major powers urged restraint on all sides but could not agree on action to prevent Israeli shipping being blockaded. Israel was also being urged not to act unilaterally even though it was unclear what diplomacy could achieve. When the cabinet met on 28 May, it was split on whether to act now or give diplomacy more time. Prime Minister Levi Eshkol was inclined to side with the hawks, but that afternoon he received a message from US President Lyndon Johnson, warning about possible Soviet intervention on Egypt's behalf if Israel initiated hostilities, adding that, should Israel pre-empt, 'it would make it impossible for the friends of Israel to stand by your side'.[4]

Torn by these conflicting pressures, he then gave an address to the nation on television. It went badly. Eshkol appeared hesitant and unsure, stumbling over a script that had been altered in ways he could not quite follow. This reinforced his image as a weak leader, when strength was demanded. Unfavourable comparisons were made with Ben-Gurion, his tough and charismatic predecessor. Eshkol could be sharp and witty in private; in public he came over as wooden. His pragmatic temperament appeared as indecisive, oscillating between war and diplomacy. He was not a natural war leader. His direct military experience was half a century old – brief service with the British in the First World War. His roles in government had largely been organizational, though vital in building up Israel's military capability.

That evening, following a difficult cabinet, diplomatic pressure and the unfortunate broadcast, he stepped into the new headquarters of the Israeli Defence Forces (IDF) in Tel Aviv. It was not a propitious moment to exert his political authority. He faced an outspoken and activist military leadership that because of the crisis was overwrought and borderline mutinous. The generals who met him were from a quite different generation, with reputations forged in the 1947–8 fight for independence and then the 1956 War with Egypt. They had been demanding action for days, warning with vehemence and urgency that the country's security was being jeopardized because the prime minister refused to unleash the country's air and land power. Morale was in decline, they warned, as the opportunity to deal the Egyptians a decisive blow passed. Continued passivity would embolden the enemy.

The strategic calculation was simple. Israel was surrounded by much larger enemies. It potentially faced a three-front war – with Syria and Jordan as well as Egypt. If war was inevitable, it had to take out Egypt, the largest and most substantial of its enemies, with a pre-emptive strike. The air force was primed and ready to go. The idea of an international operation to keep open the Straits of Tiran appeared to the IDF as a forlorn hope. 'The days dragged on,' IDF Chief of Staff Rabin later wrote, 'with their burden of nerve-racking meetings and consultations . . . Time and again, we assessed the situation, foresaw options, stationed units, formulated plans – while our political leaders remained captive to the illusory hope that war might be averted.'[5] Rabin had already taken time off through nervous exhaustion. He wanted the prime minister to explain the situation to his colleagues, as he had no desire to do so.

It was not the generals' responsibility to balance military with political considerations or receive demands from Washington for restraint. Inevitably, Eshkol's request for more patience made little headway. The soldiers' response was fierce. Uzi Narkiss, chief of the Central Front: the Arab forces were like 'soap bubbles – one pin will burst them'. Yeshayahu Gavish, chief of Southern Command: if this opportunity was not taken, 'more of our men will die'. The most forceful statement came from Sharon: 'Today we have removed with our own hand our most powerful weapon – the enemy's fear of us . . . We will have to pay a higher price in the future for something that we in any case had to do now.' At stake was 'the existence of the people of Israel . . . We present ourselves as a helpless nation. We have never degraded ourselves that much before.'[6]

These remarks took Sharon over the fuzzy line that separates military advice from political opinion. He went even further over the line, as he was now wondering about the desirability of a form of military coup. He mentioned it to Rabin the next day. It would not be about seizing power or a desire to rule, 'but in the sense of taking a decision, a fundamental decision'.[7] On 2 June, after yet another meeting with Eshkol, when his complaints about 'hesitation and foot-dragging' led the prime minister to object about this 'rearing up against the government', Sharon stayed to speak with Rabin. This is his account of what he said:

> I said that if we had got up at a certain point and said, 'Listen, you lot, your decisions are endangering the State of Israel. And since the situation is extremely serious, you are hereby requested to go into the adjoining room and stay there while the chief of staff goes to the national radio station and broadcasts an announcement.' In my judgement, if we did that, they would have accepted it with a sense of relief and liberation.[8]

Sharon's biographer wonders whether this was largely imagined, but the overall mood was rebellious. Eshkol's wife later spoke of a 'real putsch'.[9] No action was attempted. By this time, aware of the erosion of his personal authority, Eshkol had decided to hand the defence portfolio to Moshe Dayan, a dashing figure with his black eyepatch, an ally of Ben-Gurion's, and chief of staff during the 1956 War. His appointment signalled that the decision for war had effectively been made. On 5 June, it began, with the promised strike on Egypt's air bases coming early in the morning, taking out the Egyptian Air Force and, as the generals promised, effectively deciding the outcome of the campaign against Egypt.

On the eve of the war, Sharon faced yet more frustration. General Gavish, the southern commander, planned that Sharon's division should hold a defensive position, while two other divisions mounted the attack. When Gavish attended Sharon's briefing to his staff, it soon became clear that he had no intention of confining his division to defence. Gavish told him to stick to the original plan. Sharon took the issue to Rabin to get him to countermand Gavish. He was told: 'Obey Gavish's order or hand over your command.' Nonetheless, Sharon was given an offensive task for the first day of the war. This was to capture the road junction at Abu-Ageila – the 'Gateway to Sinai' – close to the border. He had been plotting how to take this for some time, and had even discussed it with Dayan, before the latter joined the government. It had taken Dayan three days to take this same objective in the 1956 War; Sharon wanted to take it in a night. Once it was seized, the central route into the Sinai Desert would be opened up. Sharon's plan was as elaborate as the Egyptian defences to be overcome, 'based on a highly centralized command that he intended to decentralize in the midst of battle'. He described it as the most complicated operation the army had ever carried out.[10]

Instead of concentrating his forces to punch his way through enemy defences, Sharon divided them up into discrete units, each with their own task. This put enormous demands on synchronizing the individual moves. Units would be isolated from each other and would be unable to provide mutual support. The plan depended on achieving maximum surprise, which required moving at night and in some cases on foot through the sand dunes to avoid alerting the enemy. There were feints to draw the Egyptian command's attention away from what was going on. Sharon pulled together all available artillery to batter Egyptian fortifications. 'Let everything tremble,' he ordered his artillery officer at 22.30. 'Tremble it shall,' came the reply.[11] Meanwhile, helicopters got a paratrooper brigade into position to attack the enemy artillery. The most challenging part of the plan was to move tanks through the Egyptian defences to their rear. At about midnight, two tank brigades moved forward, broke through Egyptian trenches and cleared a minefield. Then in the early hours the Egyptian tank battalions were attacked from two sides and largely destroyed. By 07.00 the road junction was in Israeli hands.

At one point, there was uncertainty about whether Sharon's plan was just too intricate and what would happen if Egyptian commanders began to respond more aggressively. Gavish was worried that the operation was going forward without air power. Not long before it began, he asked Sharon whether he should delay until the morning of 6 June, when he would have air support. Typically, Sharon, who was never one to hesitate, wanted to press on. Gavish decided to deploy an extra tank battalion in support, although by the time it had got into position it was no longer needed.

Enemy mistakes contributed to an impressive operational victory. The Egyptians had not anticipated their artillery and forward trenches being attacked from the north, and were unprepared for the assaults when they came. The loss of such an important position so early in the land war added to the demoralization of the Egyptian high command, and led them to pull back their forces towards the Canal. Forty Israelis had been killed in action and 19 tanks lost. The Egyptians had lost as many as 2,000 men and 60 tanks.

Israeli victory then followed Israeli victory in rapid succession. Jordan decided, despite entreaties from Israel, to join the war to support Egypt, without appreciating that Egypt had already been defeated. The result was that Israel occupied all of Jordan's territory west of the Jordan River. Then as the pressure for a ceasefire grew, it quickly moved to seize the high ground of the Golan Heights from Syria. In a few days, the map of the Middle East was redrawn. These military accomplishments did not end the conflict between Israel and its neighbours, but reset its terms and introduced new areas of dispute.

SHARON 'KING OF ISRAEL': THE OCTOBER WAR OF 1973

The Battle of Abu-Ageila was an operational masterpiece, which made Sharon's reputation, but not quite his career. He was promoted to head Southern Command and was therefore busy during the War of Attrition (1969–70), which involved skirmishing along the Suez Canal. His ambition was to become chief of staff but his awkward personality meant that he had made too many enemies and his route to this post appeared blocked. Eventually, in August 1973, he decided to retire. With Menachem Begin, he founded the Likud, a new right-wing political party. But he was still a reservist. On 6 October, on the holy day of Yom Kippur, Israel was suddenly at war again, this time caught out by Egyptian and Syrian offensives. Egypt got across the Suez Canal, while Syria moved into the Golan Heights.

The surprise attack left Defence Minister Moshe Dayan and Chief of Staff David ('Dado') Elazar with lost authority and a desperate situation. The senior political and military leadership had paid insufficient attention to warnings of a new war, failing to appreciate why Anwar Sadat, Nasser's successor, might want to jolt Israel into negotiations on the future of the occupied Sinai Peninsula. Arab armies were still viewed through the lens of 1967, so inadequate forces had been deployed to defend the east bank of the Suez Canal. Even more alarming at first was the situation on the Golan, as Syrian forces pressed forward, getting closer to Israeli towns and villages. There, everything was thrown into a desperate defence. The air force suffered heavy losses, as it had to support the army before it had a chance to deal with the enemy's air defence missiles. By contrast, it was possible to hold back in the south, as Egyptian forces were still well away from the Israeli heartland. For the moment, until the northern front was sorted out, Elazar's objective for the south was to do no more than defend against new offensives, and unsettle the Egyptians as they tried to consolidate their bridgehead on the Canal's east bank.

General Shmuel ('Shmulik') Gonen was now in charge of Southern Command. As a former subordinate to the two divisional commanders now subordinate to him, Avraham ('Bren') Adan (about to retire from his position as commander of the armoured forces) and Sharon, he was in an awkward position. The third division, deployed to the north of the Sinai, was commanded by General Albert Mandler. He was killed by an artillery shell on 13 October, and replaced by Kalmen Magen. Adan believed Gonen culpable for the slow response to the Egyptian attack and disliked his approach to command. Gonen, he later observed, tended to impose discipline through intimidation, impulsively punishing soldiers he thought had let him down, while staying calm and controlled when talking to superiors – a 'bicycle rider' general, pressing hard downwards while always looking upward.[12]

Sharon was if anything more dismissive. He did not rate Gonen and treated him at best with condescension. On 7 October, he reassured Gonen that he was not out to steal his thunder ('You can win the war'). By the end of the next day, he was convinced Gonen was not up to the job and made no secret of his disrespect. His relations with Elazar were also poor. He saw him as responsible for the terrible situation the country faced, and as one of those who had got in the way of his promotion to the top job.

He respected Dayan, who was still minister of defence. Dayan had supported him during his career and provided a role model. He liked the way Dayan conveyed 'his intentions in an ambiguous way, leaving plenty of room for initiative and interpretation . . . If the result was success, fine. But if it was failure, well then, the responsibility was not his but yours.'[13] He had also noted how well Dayan had cultivated his own dashing reputation, paying close attention to his media image, so that there was a popular clamour for him to join the government in 1967. Sharon was conscious of these matters too and made sure that reporters had been with his HQ in 1967. He did so again now, even while suspecting that the IDF press office was telling reporters to go elsewhere. Those around Sharon at his HQ were loyal and supportive, sharing his confidence that his division would be the one to save Israel, despite the incompetence of the country's leaders. From the start of the war, his staff were aware of his contempt for Gonen and Elazar, as well as 'his promise that at the end of the war he would bring those responsible to account'.[14]

He was after all a politician as well as a general. His peacetime occupation was to oppose the government. At a time of national emergency, party differences might be expected to be pushed to one side, but Sharon suspected from the start that he was being marginalized by the military establishment in order to undermine his future political career, and became particularly irritated when he thought Adan was being favoured as operational responsibilities were handed out. Adan was Labour, and it was as if there were a 'Likud division' and a 'Labour division'. For his part, Adan began the war viewing Sharon as 'an excellent combat commander who had unusual tactical perception and first-rate planning and execution ability'. He was also aware that he lacked loyalty to his superiors.[15] By the end of the war, he was furious with Sharon for his self-promotion, first on the field of battle and then in shaping the public story of the war.

On the evening of 7 October, the commanders met to formulate plans for the next day's counter-attacks against Egypt. Elazar was still unsure about how well the battle would go against Syria. Reflecting the delicacy of the situation, the plan for the southern front developed at the HQ was restrained. He ruled against efforts to uproot the Egyptian bridgeheads or cross the Canal. Some response to the Egyptian advance was needed but this was not yet the time for major risk-taking. The local commanders, less aware of the full extent, pain and tightness of the battle in the north, were in a more offensive frame of mind. Sharon, unsurprisingly, took the view that the Egyptian 2nd and 3rd Armies, which had crossed the Canal, should be hit with maximum force before they could consolidate their positions. An additional factor was Sharon's conviction, developed during the War of Independence, that nobody should be abandoned on the battlefield, including the wounded and dead. He put a high premium on rescuing the men trapped in the forts along the old defensive line by the Canal. Gonen was no more inclined than Sharon to opt for a largely defensive role, and saw possibilities for clearing areas of Egyptian forces and rescuing trapped men.

But there was still uncertainty about what the Egyptians were up to, and the Israeli command structures were inadequate to cope with complex operations that required close coordination. Between GHQ and Southern Command, noted Adan, there was 'no common language', and the situation was even worse between Southern Command and the divisions in the field. Nor was Gonen the man for the moment. He began with an agreed plan, but then kept revising it. He assumed that the IDF would enjoy tactical superiority, without good intelligence on Egyptian capabilities or apparent awareness about the problems that would be caused because of a lack of artillery and air support. On the morning of 8 October, a few early encounters with Egyptian forces were taken as evidence that there was not too much to fear. He did not go to the front to see for himself, but instead tried to control the battle from his HQ based on what he thought was happening. He kept changing his mind, with the result that orders were issued contradicting those that had gone before.

Adan's division suffered particularly badly. He received 'a bewildering series of orders and counter-orders, bordering on the manic', at times to stay a safe distance from the Canal, at times to cross it, and then at a variety of places, while proceeding south to meet an Egyptian tank force.[16] He struggled to cope. His three brigades became separated and uncoordinated. One found itself engaging with an Egyptian division and lost some 50 tanks. When Adan complained to Gonen that his orders showed no knowledge of battlefield realities, Gonen countered that he had not been kept informed, so he assumed all was well. Nor was Adan happy with Sharon for not helping him out when ordered to do so.[17] Sharon explained that he too was unhappy with constantly changing orders. He had been told to move south to follow up the non-existent success of Adan's division, which meant abandoning a position from which he could have blocked an Egyptian advance or launched one of his own. He had protested and urged Gonen to come and see for himself. The response, in what became something of a pattern for Gonen, was to warn Sharon that disobedience would lead to immediate dismissal.

A costly day ended with many dead and nothing achieved. The strategic dilemma was as before. Elazar and Dayan now shared the low opinion of Gonen. He seemed unable to manage a battle on his own, and had little authority left with Adan, let alone Sharon. Instead of taking away his command, however, they installed the former chief of staff Haim Bar-Lev in Gonen's HQ. He was described as Elazar's 'personal representative', though it was clear that he was the man in charge. Bar-Lev was a calmer and more authoritative figure, but he too got little respect from Sharon, whose preferred remedy would have been the much simpler one of putting him back in charge of Southern Command.

There was another day left before Bar-Lev could take over. In the light of this and the previous day's losses, Elazar took a cautious approach, to prevent further 'erosion of our forces', to repair and replace equipment and bring in reserves. His orders for 9 October, therefore, repeated a number of times, were to 'stick to the principle of a defensive battle, without too much manoeuvring'.

Sharon began the day as ordered with his three brigades conducting a holding operation in anticipation of an Egyptian advance. His instinct was still, however, to ignore orders and to push against the Egyptian bridgeheads, looking for their weak spots. Adan had been allowed to approach the Canal the previous day. Sharon decided that it was his turn. He therefore encouraged his commanders to move in that direction, and then use their initiative. Gonen realized that two of Sharon's brigades were moving towards the Canal, and rang to ask what was going on. His calls were ignored. He then flew by helicopter to Sharon's HQ to talk to him face to face. Sharon agreed to stop the advances, but then carried on as before as soon as Gonen left.

Sharon's unauthorized move provided one piece of vital intelligence. When a reconnaissance probe reached the Canal, it found a one-mile gap between the areas occupied by the Egyptian 2nd and 3rd Armies. This meant that the Canal could potentially be reached, without having to fight through the Egyptian bridgehead. Sharon enthusiastically rang Gonen: 'We can touch the water of the lake.' He asked to take bridging equipment and assault rafts to push across, before the Egyptians discovered the gap and closed it. Elazar was now following Sharon closely, and on hearing this request was furious: 'Get him out of there! I say he's not to cross. Not to cross! Not to cross!' Elsewhere, Sharon's initiative had led to another tough fight and damage to 50 tanks, 18 of which had to be left behind.

Gonen rang Elazar and asked that Sharon be relieved of his command. Elazar complained to Dayan about Sharon's plans: 'It borders on madness. I'm being sucked into a reckless adventure, a gamble I can't afford to risk.' Transcripts show Elazar describing Sharon's actions as a 'war crime', as acting against orders. 'And I'm listening to him on the radio, and I see that he's lying to me. And now he's asking for permission to cross to the second bank.'[18] Dayan agreed that Sharon's insubordination was unacceptable, observing, 'He has a personal problem and it's called Ariel Sharon. It won't do for him to be sitting in a bunker like other commanders.'[19] Adan noted ruefully in his memoir that while the unwise attacks into which he had been pushed were sharply scrutinized, those of 9 October got relatively little attention, though they were conducted contrary to the wishes of the higher command.[20]

The next day, still convinced that a great opportunity to turn the war round was being lost, Sharon presented his plan for crossing the Canal to Bar-Lev. He was accompanied by his brigade commanders. Bar-Lev asked them for their views. To Sharon's consternation, they also objected to the plan, on the grounds that they were not ready. It would lead to more casualties, with a low probability of a breakthrough. Although shocked, because he assumed his subordinates shared his view, since they had worked on the plan, Sharon had to take these objections seriously. His whole philosophy assumed that those closest to the action were the best judges of tactical possibilities. It also indicated some wariness among those under his command about Sharon's risk-taking propensities.

His preference for the offensive over the defensive always risked his forward troops becoming exposed. This would be particularly true if some got to the other side of the Canal and could not properly be re-inforced. At a time when there was still hard fighting under way on the Syrian front and there were uncertainties about Egyptian dispositions, Sharon's push was reckless. Crossing the Canal was not a matter for tactical initiative. It was a big strategic decision, and one for the government. It required confidence that any move could be both successful and decisive.

This was a time when confidence was in short supply. The painful consequences of the early Arab successes had left Dayan despondent. He wondered whether the loss of some of the Sinai should be accepted, with forces moved back to a more defensive line. Prime Minister Golda Meir feared the consequences of retreating to lines that would be even harder to defend, in a move that would be viewed by enemies and friends alike as accepting defeat. She wanted the lost territory retaken, and saw the attraction of a Canal crossing, with a marauding force of 200 tanks neutralizing Egyptian air defence missiles and distracting its forces. But she was also fearful of the obvious danger of a substantial force getting trapped on the Egyptian side of the Canal with no means of escape. 'It'll be a catastrophe,' observed the prime minister of Sharon's plan. 'He'll be stuck over there, in their hands.' Elazar reassured her that nothing would be done 'in the present situation. Only if things improve.'[21] For the moment, defence had to be the priority.

Israel dared not wait too long before going on the offensive. The country was straining under the human and material costs of the war. As with its other wars, international pressure would soon build up for a ceasefire. Once it came, wherever the opposing forces happened to be at the time would become the new lines. It was still in deficit on the Egyptian front, so, if Sadat decided to cash in his winnings and agree a ceasefire, this would represent a defeat for Israel. It would raise the prospect of a long war of attrition, with persistent heavy defensive demands, which the country could ill afford. This was the attraction of a Canal crossing, since it would strengthen Israel's position vis-à-vis Egypt, but it carried an enormous risk if the attacking force got trapped. The alternative, upon which the government decided, was to continue pushing forward towards Damascus, now that the initial Syrian assault had been beaten back, in the hope that the pressure on the Syrian capital would provide a bargaining chip. But this was also a hard slog. By the evening of 11 October, progress had been made, but at a high cost, and there was still some distance to travel.

It was, however, sufficient to set in motion a chain of events that changed the dynamic of the war – a good example of how the political consequences of an operation can exceed the purely military. Syria's leader, Hafez al-Assad, was sufficiently alarmed to appeal to Sadat to attack Israeli forces in Sinai to relieve the pressure. Sadat was reluctant. He was aware of the danger of his tanks getting too far ahead of his air defences, and had achieved enough territory already to suit his political needs. Yet pressed by Assad that Thursday night, and over the objections of his war minister, he ordered two tank divisions to cross the Canal and attack Israeli tank formations in the Sinai.

That evening Elazar, who was fearful that the thrust to Damascus was not going to make much more progress, and that Egyptian forces on the east bank of the Canal would be hard to dislodge, began arguing that perhaps a ceasefire should be considered, to give the country a breathing space so it could replenish its losses. As the cabinet was discussing this unwelcome prospect, vital intelligence came in, reporting on Sadat's order, not long after it had been issued, that his tank divisions should launch a new offensive. The mood changed immediately. Now was a chance to deal the Egyptians a blow and clear a way for a Canal crossing. In terms of their strategy, this was just as well.

The next morning Israeli troops moving towards Damascus had come across a large Iraqi force, which had been sent to support Assad. They engaged successfully with the Iraqis, but their advance was now held up. Meanwhile, the Americans were picking up signs that the Soviets were ready to act to protect Assad's regime. When US Secretary of State Henry Kissinger received notice that Israel was prepared to accept a ceasefire, he assumed this was because of weakness, and he advised the Israelis to 'stick to your course'. The Israeli ambassador explained that the American resupply effort had been too slow, leaving Kissinger to assume that the IDF was so depleted that it could not cope. To add to the effect, the ambassador passed on the news that the Egyptians were about to launch a new offensive in the Sinai. This had the desired effect of spurring the Nixon administration into action. As for the ceasefire, the Israeli reasoning was quite different to what Kissinger assumed (he warned colleagues that Israel 'was now in deep trouble in the Sinai'). They accepted it because they knew that Sadat could not accept one while his offensive was under way. Rather than fearing the arrival of Egyptian tanks, they welcomed the opportunity it would bring.[22]

The Israeli plan was to set a trap for the advancing Egyptian forces. A tank battle on Israel's terms would deal the Egyptians a heavy blow, and, as these divisions had come from the east side of the Canal, there would then be fewer forces to be faced when the Israelis were able to get there. On 14 October, the Egyptian offensive, involving some 400 tanks in six separate thrusts, was caught in the trap and badly mauled. By late afternoon, half the tanks had been destroyed and the Egyptian sally was over.

For Israel, it was now the time to move to the offence. That evening, Dayan and Elazar presented a plan for the Canal crossing to the cabinet. Though there were still misgivings about a substantial unit getting trapped, the commanders' assurances were accepted. In the plan put to the cabinet, one division would cross in the first instance. If this was successful, the second division would follow.[23]

Sharon was frustrated that it had taken this long. The previous day he had lobbied Elazar unsuccessfully and then tried to go over his head to Dayan. He left a message with Dayan's daughter, Yael, whom he had got to know during the 1967 War. She was asked to tell her father:

> the whole division here is stamping its feet. The horses are ready for battle. You remember the picture – like the eve of the Six Day War. Explain this to him. He must understand that there's enough spirit here to break the Egyptians. Otherwise we'll enter a cease-fire in our present miserable situation.

When he attended Bar-Lev's briefing on 15 October, he discovered to his horror that the plan was for his paratrooper battalion to execute the crossing, but then, once a foothold had been established, the rest of his division would remain on the east bank to widen the corridor. 'We must expand the bridgehead at least four kilometres to the north,' explained Bar-Lev, 'and this task, Arik, remains yours until the end.' When Sharon queried this, Bar-Lev replied: 'Before you get to the Cairo Hilton you will need to be released from your assignment at the bridgehead.'

For the moment, Sharon's priority was to get his battalion over the Canal. His plan was typically both complex and audacious. To give it time to get through the gap between the Egyptian 2nd and 3rd Armies, there would be diversions and distracting attacks. Bar-Lev left Sharon with the decision on whether to go the evening of 15 October or wait until the next day. It was not in his nature to wait. 'The Egyptians will change their deployment or the Jews will change their mind.' Yet he was not really ready. The pre-assembled bridge could not be got into position in time. Instead, relatively flimsy Gillois rafts were used to ferry men and equipment, including tanks, across the Canal, but they did the job. Far more costly was a diversionary attack that took one of Sharon's brigades inadvertently into the middle of the Egyptian infantry division, which led to intense and ferocious fighting. Sharon recorded the aftermath:

Wreckage littered the desert. Here and there Israeli and Egyptian tanks had destroyed each other at a distance of a few meters, barrel to barrel. It was as if a hand-to-hand battle of armor had taken place. And inside those tanks and next to them lay their dead crews. Coming close, you could see Egyptian and Jewish dead lying side by side, soldiers who had jumped from their burning tanks and had died together.[24]

The strategic purpose was nonetheless achieved. The Canal was crossed with the enemy failing to realize what was going on. The battalion that reached the other side of the Canal was soon at work taking out five surface-to-air missile sites and overrunning some Egyptian positions. But the numbers were not there to expand the bridgehead and getting reinforcements over was not straightforward. Sharon 'got an order from Southern Command', that he described as being 'so outrageous I at first refused to believe it. All crossing activity . . . was to cease immediately. Not a single additional tank or man was to be transferred. According to them, we were cut off, surrounded by Egyptian forces.'[25]

The proposal was consistent with Bar-Lev's original concept. Adan's division was to cross, while Sharon's was to widen the eastern bridgehead and defend it. The reason for the delay was concern about relying on rafts. The bridge still needed to be got into position and this required Adan to create a corridor through Egyptian forces. This was a demanding operation, yet Sharon was impatient. 'Why is he holding things up?' When Adan heard this, he was furious. As far as he was concerned, he had got into position on 17 October, with little help from Sharon. As far as Bar-Lev and Elazar were concerned, Sharon was fighting his own war with little regard to the needs of the rest of the IDF. He not only showed contempt for his orders, but had failed to report properly on the scale of the Egyptian resistance his men had encountered and the state of the roads. The episode could have ended in disaster if the Egyptians had been quicker on the uptake.

To add to Sharon's troubles, his HQ came under attack, with incoming artillery fire. He defended his position with a small force until rescued. By this time, his head had been cut by shrapnel. The bandage to stop it bleeding provided an affecting image, bolstering his reputation as a heroic leader. Bar-Lev, Elazar and Adan were unimpressed when he went to meet them for a desert conference. According to Sharon, when Bar-Lev complained about the great distance 'between what you promised to do and what you have done', he only just stopped himself slapping his commanding officer in the face. Only Dayan, who was also there, showed any appreciation for what Sharon's men had been through and the sacrifices they had made. Sharon noted in his own memoir how they had fought with 'total self-sacrifice'. In one brigade, all the senior commanders had been killed and replaced twice over.[26] He also noted the complete lack of trust. Sharon was convinced that he was a victim of discrimination. Gonen and Bar-Lev saw simple insubordination and self-promotion, with his making sure his achievement in getting across the Canal was well known at home.[27] They were still pressing Elazar to demand Sharon's removal. Dayan told them to stop even trying.

Sharon was ordered to move against Egyptian forces that were shelling the bridge from the stronghold by the side of the Canal known as 'Missouri'. The Egyptians were certainly causing many casualties, but Sharon argued that more would be caused by the assault. It would make more sense to concentrate on the west side of the Canal, he argued. The Israeli move had jolted Sadat, who was now pushing for a ceasefire. Meir judged that there were only a few days left before the Americans and the Soviets would agree to terms. Dayan sympathized with Sharon's complaint, but he did not feel that he could rescind the order. Sharon continued to argue: 'I railed against it. I tried every way I knew to get the order rescinded. It would be a useless gesture, an absolutely needless waste of lives.' Unable to change the order, he obeyed it. On 21 October, Tuvia Raviv's brigade attacked the stronghold with the painful consequences anticipated.

> I stood on the rampart on the western bank and watched Tuvia's tanks and APC's rush the Egyptian positions. I saw them penetrate deep into the defenses, and as they did I saw them hit by a torrent of RPG's, Saggers, and tank fire. One after another Tuvia's vehicles stopped and burst into flame. It was a sight that sickened all of us who were watching.[28]

When he was ordered to bring back his men from the other side of the Canal to help with another push, he replied, 'No way.' Gonen tried once more: 'So I say reinforce!' The same reply: 'No way!' 'You should know,' responded Gonen, 'this is insubordination.' Sharon confirmed the charge: 'Oh come on, leave me alone with that kind of talk.'

Many years later, he would write: 'I cannot free myself from the feeling that one of the reasons they were pressing me to attack the [Egyptian]

Sixteenth and Twenty-first divisions on the east side of the canal was not because they considered the corridor too narrow, but because they wanted to keep my troops on the eastern side.' Past antagonisms had been 'augmented now by political considerations'.[29] Now Dayan interceded. He asked Yisrael Tal, the deputy chief of staff, to review the arguments 'and issue appropriate orders'. Elazar agreed and told Tal that there was 'a limit to how often you can tell a senior commander who's in the field and thinks he can't do it, and thinks he'll have casualties. That morning – I thought, enough is enough!' Tal called Gonen and told him to call off the attack.[30]

Dayan chastised Gonen: 'There is a conditioned reflex in this Command against every suggestion from Sharon.' When Gonen complained, 'Arik is conducting his own private war', Dayan picked upon one of Sharon's themes: 'There are those who say that it's this war room that has been infiltrated by political considerations.' The antipathy to Sharon was clouding judgements about how his units could best be used. 'I have to admit,' Dayan explained to Elazar, 'I prefer Arik's pressures and initiatives tenfold to the hesitations and excuses of other divisional commanders ... Better a noble steed that you have to restrain than a lazy ox you have to beat.' But Dayan had also told Sharon, when first appointing him to a command in the 1950s: 'it was not enough to beat the Arabs; one must also learn to live with the Jews.'[31]

The next day the ceasefire came, although it took another three days before the Israelis felt that they had sufficiently consolidated their position on the west side of the Canal to be ready for the subsequent negotiations. Militarily, it was an Israeli victory. The IDF destroyed or captured 2,250 enemy tanks, while 400 Israeli tanks were destroyed and another 600 disabled but repaired. But politically it was a draw, and the cost had been high. Israel had 2,656 dead and 7,250 wounded. Arab figures for their dead and wounded were 8,528 and 19,540 respectively, although the Israelis believed that the actual numbers were much higher.

Still nursing his grievances, Sharon sought to influence the emerging story of the war. He was already getting credit for the first successful crossing. In addition, as Landau notes, 'With one superficial head wound, Sharon had dealt his rivals a mortal blow in the public-relations race for glory.'[32] He was after credit for himself, but also wanted to deny it to the other senior commanders. Interviews with the foreign press, which avoided local censorship, were against the standing orders of the IDF. Regardless, in November the *New York Times* carried Sharon's account of the Sinai campaign, in which he naturally appeared centre stage. His complaints were reported about the long delays in getting reinforcements across the Canal, and the failure of the senior commanders to 'understand the element of time' or even to visit the front to see for themselves. Only Dayan was exempted from this criticism. The minister of defence was 'right in this case'.[33]

An article written by one of his friends, Professor Amos Perlmutter, published in early 1974 opened by exaggerating Sharon's role, as if only his units were involved in crossing the Canal, and had him being cheered by his troops as 'Arik, King of Israel'. Here more condescension was shown towards Dayan for failing to follow through with his support ('He never imposes his will; his problem is he has no feeling for power'), while Sharon's major grievance was aired in inflammatory terms:

> From the first day of the war, politics was more important than military considerations or military strategy. When at last it was decided that the time had come to cross the canal, everyone was busy discussing who would carry out the crossing – which political party would get the prestige. I told them 'Listen, I am in command of 15,000 soldiers now. But in the end I'll screw you all. First I'll cross the canal and screw the Egyptians and then I'll come back and screw all of you, and you'll all have to wear helmets.'[34]

Prime Minister Meir considered Sharon's behaviour 'scandalous', undermining military discipline, and almost a call to mutiny. Dayan said little. His lenient attitude towards Sharon, protecting him during the war and now observing that words did not cost lives, was not popular. His colleagues noted that he had been treated more positively by Sharon. Soon Sharon's reserve command was revoked and Dayan did nothing to prevent this. He might have made the attempt, but then he heard that, in Sharon's farewell address to his troops, he said victory had been won 'despite the blunders and mistakes, despite the loss of control and authority'.

SHARON'S WAR: LEBANON 1982

Sharon left then in defiant disgrace. In 1977, he became a member of a Likud-led government. Despite his evident desire for the Ministry of

Defence, Prime Minister Menachem Begin had resisted giving it to him because his aggressive and truculent nature unnerved his colleagues. Eventually, in 1981, he got the job he wanted. The security problem was no longer Egypt, which had signed a peace treaty with Israel in 1979. The focus was now on the occupied territories, where Begin had been encouraging a rapid expansion of settlements. The Palestine Liberation Organization (PLO) was mounting attacks on Israel from its bases in southern Lebanon. As tensions rose, Begin needed a credible military figure in charge at Defence.

Sharon moved into position with a clear plan. He retired or moved unsympathetic senior commanders. He knew those around him. Chief of Staff Raful Eitan had served under Sharon when he was first a battalion and then a brigade commander. Amir Drori, at Northern Command, had been his head of operations in Southern Command, and also served under Eitan in the October War and then in Northern Command. Sharon also created his own support separate from the general staff. The National Security Unit in the Ministry of Defence had its own situation room to provide him with advice as needed, much to the chagrin of senior military commanders, who saw this as a source of confusion.[35] He also made sure that he controlled information to the press, public and the cabinet, so that nobody could be sure what he was up to.

Lebanon was his priority. The IDF had moved in and out of Southern Lebanon in the past, and was widely expected to do so again soon. But how far would they need to go? The consensus was far enough to put northern Israel out of the range of PLO rockets – about 40 kilometres. Beyond that, any operation could get tricky, because of the risk of coming up against Syrian forces. Sharon, however, did not shrink from this prospect. Indeed, his ambition was greater: he wanted to get a government in Beirut able to sign a peace treaty with Israel. He was in contact with Bashir Gemayel and his brother Amir, sons of Pierre Gemayel, the elderly leader of the Christian Maronite Phalange party. They were certainly keen on the idea that Israel might help them expel Syrian forces lodged in their country. Beyond that, they were naturally cautious. They did no more than play Sharon along in his hopes for a treaty. Always ready to believe the worst of his enemies, Sharon was prepared to believe the best of his friends. Others in the Israeli intelligence agencies were more sceptical. They doubted that the Phalangists were up to much militarily, let alone interested in a peace treaty, given the uproar that would create at home and in the rest of the Arab world.

On 3 June 1982, an attempted assassination badly wounded the Israeli ambassador to London. By the time the cabinet met to discuss a response, Begin had already decided with Eitan that there would be limited strikes against PLO bases in Lebanon. This was even though it was known that a separate Palestinian group was responsible (the Iraq-based Abu Nidal's) and that the PLO was pre-programmed to respond to any Israeli attacks with rocket fire against Israeli towns and villages in Galilee. In authorizing the strikes, therefore, the cabinet was in effect authorizing further escalation.

Sharon, out of the country on 3 June, was back for the cabinet debate two days later. The PLO had launched a rocket barrage into Israel from southern Lebanon as anticipated. A plan for the IDF to destroy PLO bases was ready for approval. This would require pushing some 40 kilometres into Lebanon. But would this be the end of the matter? One minister, Mordechai Zippori, with long military experience, was suspicious of Sharon's intentions and tried to pin him down. Was there an actual line to which the IDF would advance? Would terrorists in the Syrian sector be attacked? When Begin said there was no intention of attacking the Syrians, Zippori replied that contact was nevertheless likely. Another minister mentioned Beirut. Sharon confirmed that the purpose of the operation was solely defensive – to drive the PLO's rockets and artillery 'out of the range of our settlements'. The 40-kilometre range was 'what the Cabinet has approved'. Zippori pressed on the timetable. Sharon answered that it should all take up to 24 hours. Begin then observed, 'In war, you know how it begins but you never know how it ends', adding, 'nothing will be done without a Cabinet decision.' Some ministers noted the doubtful expressions of the intelligence officers present when it was suggested that fighting with Syria could be avoided. The published cabinet communiqué noted that 'the Syrian army will not be attacked unless it attacks our forces.'[36]

As Israeli armoured columns moved through populated areas, the fighting was more ferocious and the casualties, including civilian, more severe than envisaged. A battle to take a Palestinian stronghold at the old Beaufort Castle proved costly; a manoeuvre to persuade Syrian units to get out of the way did not work. On 8 June, Begin told the Knesset (Israeli parliament) that the only aim was to get to the

40-kilometre line. If this was done, 'all fighting will cease'. He appealed to the Syrian president 'to instruct the Syrian army not to harm Israeli soldiers'. Yet, by this time, Israeli and Syrian units were already fighting each other. The prime minister was evidently out of touch.

Sharon told Northern Command that, as it was unclear how the cabinet would react to an all-out attack on the Syrians, 'we must nibble away at them without creating the impression of a full-scale war'. The next morning one senior general, not present the previous day, challenged Sharon. Did not a direct move against the Syrians 'contradict the objectives set by the cabinet'? Another asked whether the IDF was ready for the action to come. After blaming the Syrians for getting in the way, Sharon added: 'I want you to know that every order, every one, is anchored in Cabinet decisions!'[37] The objective set was the Beirut–Damascus road, well beyond 40 kilometres into Lebanon. Should this be cut, the 7,000-strong Syrian force in Beirut would be separated from its home base and the Palestinians would be trapped. The main obstacle was Syrian surface-to-air missile batteries that could provide their troops cover against Israeli air attacks, as they had done in the early stages of the October War.

Although the field commanders understood the logic of Sharon's moves, these were never spelt out for the cabinet. He knowingly muddled what was defensive and what was offensive. On 8 June, he asked ministers 'to stop walking around with a ruler and measuring the kilometres all day long', adding that 'it is impossible to wage a war with tweezers.'[38] When the cabinet met on 9 June, they saw that the 40-kilometre limit had been abandoned and that, despite reassurances, there were now clashes with the Syrians. Sharon played on the vulnerability of Israeli troops to artillery fire and of Israeli aircraft to air defences. That day, a devastating attack was mounted on the Syrian SAM batteries, leaving all damaged or destroyed, much to the distress of not only the Syrians but also their Soviet suppliers. That day too, the Syrians lost 29 aircraft and Israel none. On the ground, Syrian losses were likewise severe, far more so than those of the Israelis. Yet Israeli losses too were mounting. Meanwhile, the coastal fighting against Palestinian units was leading to damage to infrastructure and civilian casualties, prompting international criticism. And it was still not clear how the war would end.

By 10 June, the IDF reached the outskirts of Beirut. Sharon now explained to the cabinet that the IDF were looking to cut the road to

Damascus but that it would be tricky. Though troops were closing in on the city, their orders were not to advance further. The preference, he explained, was for the Lebanese government and army to deal with the Palestinian fighters inside the city. As for linking up with the Phalange, 'We won't initiate it, but if they approach us, we won't reject them out of hand.'[39] This was misleading. There was already liaison between the IDF and the Phalange. On 11 June, one minister, Yitzhak Berman, commented: 'Arik, perhaps you'll be good enough to tell us what you're going to ask us to approve the day after tomorrow so that you can secure what you're going to ask us to approve tomorrow morning.'[40]

Sharon's objective was to get the Gemayels in control of Lebanon and ready to sign a peace treaty. It was not clear if what had now become a siege could achieve this. On 22 June, he ordered the IDF to intensify the pressure by moving further down the highway. The fighting was heavy. The IDF had already lost some 300 men and now another 28 were killed. The cabinet were getting restive, complaining of the losses and lack of consultation. By not entering Beirut, and with the Phalange taking few risks, all the Israelis could do was to surround the area in which the Palestinians had dug in. The Americans were trying to broker a deal that would see the PLO evacuated. Palestinian leader Yasser Arafat saw the siege, with all the suffering it entailed, as a way of keeping the Palestinian cause in the headlines. Sharon looked at West Beirut and saw a terrorist HQ. Others, including the Reagan administration, saw the heavily populated capital of a sovereign country surrounded by invading forces. The Israeli cabinet was kept in the dark. At one point, when Begin was in Washington, the acting prime minister, Simcha Ehrlich, observed that, when he tried to contact the defence minister, he was never available. Sharon was reported to have commented, while visiting the front lines, 'In the morning I fight the terrorists, and in the evening I go back to Jerusalem to fight in Cabinet.'[41]

By this time, however, dissent was developing within the IDF, as well as in cabinet. When Deputy Chief of Staff Moshe Levi visited a battalion of parachute reservists who had suffered heavy losses, he was berated by a company commander. They were losing confidence in their orders. 'The army carries out the orders of the civilian echelon,' insisted Levi. 'That's democracy.' The junior officer forcefully disagreed. When in mid-July Drori presented a plan for the conquest of West Beirut, brigade commanders warned that they were not ready and that casualties would be heavy. They also queried the purpose and wisdom of the operation. Dissent began to become open. Sharon was no longer so welcome when he visited front-line units. Others held their tongues even when receiving orders that they knew would lead to many casualties.

> First off, if I resign now, it won't prevent the war. They'll appoint another, less experienced commander and there will be even more casualties. My responsibility to my soldiers requires me to stay with them in battle. And second, and I'm not ashamed to say this, after the war, promotions will be based on your location [in the war].[42]

The Americans were becoming irritated and impatient as Israeli shelling caused horrific civilian losses, to which Begin responded with a stubborn self-righteousness. Eventually, he saw the danger of a rift with the US, and that Sharon was acting on his own impulses. On 30 July, he noted, cryptically, at a cabinet meeting that: 'I always know about everything. Some things I know about before, and some things after.'

The weeks went by. Still the siege continued. Vicious air raids on 16 August led Begin to promise Reagan that they would stop. When Begin heard from one of his ministers that reserves were being called up, he challenged Sharon, who confirmed that he had approved the move in case the city needed to be stormed. The need was 'obvious'. 'Obvious?' replied Begin. 'What do you mean obvious? How can you do that without [my] approval? So many people know and the prime minister doesn't know.'[43] Sharon was doing everything possible to thwart an American plan to send in a force to facilitate the evacuation of the PLO fighters, even after the cabinet approved the plan in principle. But he was now increasingly isolated, no longer even supported by Begin. Control over the air force was taken away from him.

Beginning on 21 August, 14,398 Palestinian and Syrian fighters were evacuated. On 23 August, Bashir Gemayel was elected president by the Lebanese parliament, under the country's complex constitution that gave this spot to Christian representatives, while others were reserved for Muslims. He insisted that there had been no collusion with Israel and denied any interest in a peace treaty. To those who had been sceptical about his intentions from the start, this was hardly a surprise. The hopes of Begin and Sharon that they could re-engineer the Middle East by getting a new peace treaty with a friendly Lebanon were falling away. Though the Syrians had not been expelled and international support had been forfeited, if Israel had withdrawn at this point, they would have left with some strategic gains.

Despite so many of the Palestinian fighters having left Beirut, Begin and Sharon remained convinced that militants and weapons stores had been left in West Beirut and these needed cleaning out. Sharon advised, and Begin agreed, that this was a job for the Phalangists, as Israel had already suffered enough casualties. It was not clear whether this would require a limited 'search and destroy' operation or something much more extensive. The head of IDF intelligence, Yehoshua Saguy, who had misgivings about working with the Phalangists from the start, warned of the danger of facilitating acts of revenge against Palestinian civilians now that they no longer had their fighters to protect them. On 14 September, while this was being debated, Gemayel was assassinated. Begin, Sharon and Eitan decided that they must get a grip on the situation. The IDF was ordered into West Beirut.

The Americans were once again furious at a violation of the ceasefire agreement, noting the contradictory explanations – a 'precautionary' move according to Begin, to stop acts of Christian revenge, but necessary according to Sharon, because they knew of at least 2,000 'terrorists' still in the city. In this febrile atmosphere, Eitan raised the possibility with the Phalange that they might occupy the Palestinian refugee camps under IDF 'supervision' to seek out fighters and weapons caches. They agreed. On 18 September, the northern commander, Amir Drori, briefed the Phalange officers due to carry out the operation. According to Sharon, they were told to 'be careful in their identification of the Palestinian terrorists', while civilians were not to be harmed. But the terrorists, if they existed, would be dressed as civilians. In any case, the Phalangists were not in a mood to discriminate.

As the cabinet met that evening, the Phalange had already entered the Sabra and Shatila camps. One minister spoke with foreboding: 'I know what the meaning of revenge is for them, what kind of slaughter.' The most pressing issue for ministers at that time, however, was the entry of the IDF into West Beirut without any cabinet consideration. The communiqué drafted by Begin explained that it had been necessary 'to forestall the danger of violence, bloodshed and chaos, as some 2,000 terrorists, equipped with modern and heavy weapons, have remained in Beirut'.[44] There were undoubtedly some fighters left in the camps, although the number was probably closer to 200 than to 2,000. Caches of weapons were also found. Whatever the rationale for an anti-terrorist operation that was not what the Phalange had in mind. This was an anti-Palestinian operation, designed to revenge Bashir's death and encourage Palestinian flight from Beirut.

The IDF let the Phalangists go into the camps unaccompanied and had little idea what was going on. There were soon hints that unarmed civilians were being murdered by marauding militia men. No action was taken. It was not until well into the next day that it became apparent that all was not well, and even longer before the Phalange operation was shut down. Drori phoned Eitan to warn him that there appeared to have been many random shootings. At 15.30 Eitan got to the Phalange HQ, where he was told that there were no problems. Sabra and Shatila had been taken, though with some casualties. They asked for tractors 'so they would be able to destroy the tunnels and trenches they had discovered'. At 21.00 Eitan called Sharon and told him that there had been civilian deaths: 'They went too far.'[45]

Hundreds had been killed. The exact numbers could not be ascertained. In the face of massive condemnation at home and abroad, the government's claims that this was nothing to do with them were dismissed. An inquiry was set up, this time under Yitzhak Kahan, the president of the Supreme Court. Kahan reported on 8 February 1983. Begin was exonerated because 'he was entitled to rely on the optimistic and calming report of the Defence Minister that the entire operation was proceeding without any hitches and in the most satisfactory manner.' As for Sharon, however, he bore 'personal responsibility' and should therefore resign. He had disregarded the risks and taken no measures to ensure that there were no massacres. Neither he nor Eitan could claim that they had no idea that the Phalangists were going into the camps, because they had sent them.

Sharon had never been candid with his colleagues about what he was trying to achieve in Lebanon. At each stage, he emphasized short-term factors to justify moving to the next stage. There had been no chance for a serious debate about the realism of the political objectives or the costs of getting stuck in Beirut. Yet while there were grumbles and misgivings, his colleagues did not challenge him 'until the nation hovered on the brink of disaster'.[46] Begin and Eitan were also culpable. They set things in motion before Sharon returned from his foreign visit. Begin assumed that Israel only had implacable foes, all acting in the spirit of the Nazis, and with whom there could be no accommodation. He understood the attraction of a deal with the Maronite Christians. Chief of Staff Eitan had no doubt about the need to act tough and was aware of Sharon's ambitions. Though wary about taking on the Syrians, he managed to absent himself from cabinet meetings when the issue was likely to arise. He was always content to let Sharon argue for his own plan and never offered qualifications. Schulze refers to groupthink: 'The belief in Maronite reliability, the inherent morality of the war, and military strength deluded the various decision-makers to Israel's vulnerability.'[47]

In his memoirs, Sharon insisted that:

> The political echelon would maintain firm direction of the battlefield. As a result I made sure that the cabinet was kept informed of every significant development and potential development. I saw to it that every decision was made in cabinet and that orders were issued to the army only after the cabinet had deliberated and made up its mind.[48]

Landau emphasizes the extent to which Sharon kept Begin in the loop and notes that ministers who expressed concern at key cabinet meetings knew what lay in store and assumed that their colleagues could also work this out. In this respect, they were not duped.[49]

But even Begin complained about only being included in the loop late in the day. It was Sharon rather than Begin who exercised control over the military operation. He decided what that cabinet could be told about the operations and what the generals could be told about cabinet decisions. His communications were selective and often tendentious, and deliberations in cabinet at times took place after orders had been issued. He used short-term arguments for escalation, that without it IDF lives would be put in danger, while saying little about his longer-term political objectives. He did not dwell on the likelihood that the initial incursion would come up against the Syrians, or that, when it did, the logical next steps would be getting to the Beirut–Damascus highway and taking out the Syrian SAM network.[50] This is why Begin was let off the hook by the Kahan Commission. It was assumed that Sharon was always the instigator and that he had followed on behind. It made no difference. The prime minister was broken by the experience and soon left office.

After failing to get the cabinet to reject the Kahan report, Sharon resigned. He did not, however, stay away from high office. He remained the voice of the uncompromising, tough-minded right. For the next two decades, he had a variety of government jobs, well away from the IDF, until eventually he became prime minister in 2001, initially cracking down on a Palestinian insurrection before authorizing a complete withdrawal from the Gaza Strip. At the point when he was cut down by a stroke in 2006 (which left him in a vegetative state until 2014), he was recasting himself in more moderate tones.

CONCLUSION: ORDERS AND OBEDIENCE

Throughout his career Sharon saw the chain of command as something to be circumvented and manipulated. When he was directly engaged in operations, as a divisional commander in two major wars, and then as defence minister in a third, he was as convinced of his own natural aptitude for military operations as he was dismissive of others. What made the difference in 1982 was that he now fancied himself as a grand strategist, capable of creating a new political reality in Lebanon, even though those who knew about the country thought his ideas delusional. So long as Sharon was kept under some sort of control, he could be a highly effective commander; when the control was absent, the consequences were disastrous.

Sharon was admired by those serving under him. He not only had a commanding presence, staying cool under fire, and rarely needing to raise his voice to make a point, but was also known for his ability to read a battle – the *coup d'œil* – and take difficult decisions. He worked his subordinates hard, and was ready to dismiss those who did not come up to scratch, but, once they had his trust, he would support them as they fought tough battles. He believed his place to be at the front, and not in some safe but distant command centre well to the rear.

> You read these days that in modern warfare and especially in future warfare commanders will be wearing white gowns and pressing buttons from high-technology command centres far from the battlefield. But in fact, reality is exactly the reverse. Firepower today is so massive that the battlefield situation can change in an instant. At the canal I saw a company of tanks disappear in less than a minute . . . With events like these there was no substitute for being forward. You could not rely on information given

to you through the normal channels – not your intelligence channel, your operations channel, your administrative channel. Nothing.

It was vital 'to be on the spot looking at developments firsthand, as they happened'. In addition, as a divisional commander, giving life-or-death orders, he believed that those he commanded 'were more secure knowing that I was right there, seeing their problems with my own eyes'. If he 'gave them even the hardest orders, involving the gravest danger', they knew he did so 'on the basis of immediate personal knowledge. And consequently they were willing to do whatever was necessary, despite the risks.'[51]

This helps explain why Sharon's problems with the chain of command were not with those below but with those above, even though he lost the trust of junior officers who felt that they had been misled into a costly and cruel war in Lebanon. He was critical of his superiors during the October War for not getting forward. Much later, when prime minister and meeting veterans of his division, he remarked that the commander in the field is better placed to grasp a situation than his superiors. 'I believe that if there is no officer senior to you in the area, you can ignore or change an order.'

A book on command in the October War written by two officers who had served with Sharon claimed that he 'did not explicitly contravene a single order and that at no time did he dare to violate a clear and unequivocal command. Most likely, he did not carry out this or that order exactly in the spirit of the commander', but if so that would have been the fault of the order. It should not 'leave any room for interpretation by an experienced, assertive, creative subordinate'. When a senior commander was opposed to an offensive initiative, for example, the orders needed to be 'scrupulously and unambiguously worded so that they would reach the lower levels exactly as intended'.

An order is one of the most important tools of a commander. A fundamental skill in the art of leading – especially at the generalship level – is the ability to issue a clear and precise order that is incapable of being misunderstood, does not meander, is not overly poetic or semantically ambiguous, and is independent of the spirit of the commander (or the spirit of the order) as a factor that completes it. Every commander – not to mention a general officer – should remember that a subordinate does not always see eye to eye with him.[52]

This was disingenuous. Even when given clear orders, Sharon at times ignored them or tried to get them overturned by appealing to an even more senior figure. Some orders, especially those setting limits on potential action, were stated in sharp and unambiguous terms, yet Sharon's view was that no orders could be truly reliable if issued far away from the battle. In fast-moving and fluid situations, they could not cover every eventuality. This is what Sharon claimed to have learned from Dayan. It had become part of Israeli military culture that local commanders should take the initiative, so long as they accepted responsibility for the outcome and were acting in accordance with their superior's intent.

The Israeli experience showed how this approach could have great advantages when field commanders faced situations that could not be appreciated by headquarters. It would never make sense to frame orders in such a way as to permit no deviation and demand that they be followed exactly. But delegating command authority created its own problems. First, the high command had a wider view, and could know of possibilities, diplomatic as well as military, that should affect priorities and calculations of risk. Second, enormous problems of coordination could result when units were acting independently in the same area. Third, both sets of problems could be managed better with good communications used for candid and informative messages. Fourth, equally important was trust – were sensible orders coming down the chain of command and was any variation warranted by the situation on the ground? This was not just a matter of field commanders taking responsibility for actions. It was about convincing others that they were acting responsibly.

When senior commanders were not on the spot, their advice would depend on what they knew of the situation. That in turn depended on the quality of the reports back to headquarters from the front. If orders were then not followed as intended, then that might be because they were poorly communicated and open to interpretation. Communications were therefore critical to how well command led to control. This was why Sharon became a stickler for minutes, to show that the authority was there for every action he took. Equally, his own reporting made it harder for his superiors to pin him down. Sharon understood how his troubles after the 1956 War had resulted from a lack of evidence proving his authority to act as he did. After that he 'became a champion of documentation, a suppressor of spontaneity, a meticulous note-taker, sometimes with a carbon copy, documenting it all in a note pad'.[53]

Yet the information sent to his superiors was rarely sufficient for an informed opinion of his proposals. Elazar noted the sloppiness of his reports during the October War. He would speak of an 'ambush', an 'obstacle' or a 'position that will not surrender', without being clear that he was facing a major problem that endangered the whole operation. He never used terminology that might lead to him being held back.[54] During the arguments surrounding the crossing of the Canal, Gonen complained of claims about broken equipment or shortages of ammunition that could easily have been falsified, to be used to justify not doing what he had been ordered to do.

In an interview with an Israeli paper, on 25 January 1974, Sharon explained his philosophy, which challenged directly traditional views of the chain of command:

> When I receive an order, I treat it according to three values: the first, and most important, is the good of the state. The state is the supreme thing. The second value is my obligation to my subordinates, and the third value is my obligation to my superiors.[55]

This was an explicit disavowal of the normal principles of command in a democratic society. Only at the highest, governmental level could the interests of the state be properly identified and the full operational environment properly understood. Sharon was saying that his assessments of the interests of the state should take precedence over those of the government, while his duty of care to his subordinates took precedence over his duty of obedience to his superiors. His views were considered sufficiently incendiary to be discussed by senior members of the government and the IDF in April 1974.

They had in front of them Gonen's formal complaint about Sharon's 'long chain of dereliction of duty and discipline', of 'failing to carry out his missions and orders in battle, refusing to follow orders, not adhering to objectives laid out by command, and bypassing the chain of command during battle'. Elazar noted that, in addition to Gonen, the military advocate general and the attorney general had also recommended disciplinary action. Bar-Lev said he had twice recommended dismissal:

> I was told that for certain reasons it had been decided not to do so. I did not sign the appointment of Sharon as a divisional commander and I could not cancel it. I wouldn't have made this recommendation if I

thought he was a first class divisional commander. I was not a great admirer of him as a great divisional commander. On this subject I differ from the defence minister [Dayan]. So I think that in this war only good would have come out of it if he had been removed earlier. But my recommendation was not accepted.[56]

Later, in his evidence to the Agranat Commission, established to look into how the country had been caught by surprise on 6 October, Sharon denied disobeying orders. Either the orders had not been received, or had been communicated imperfectly, or were hard to understand. His only regret was that he had obeyed bad decisions. As a basic rule, he said, orders should be obeyed but special situations could arise:

> You're in the field, and no more senior commander is with you, and you receive an order which you know that, if executed, will result in the deaths of a great many of your men but will also produce the most negligible gain. If you have no one to address your arguments to, then perhaps you need to take a decision yourself. Such situations are very rare indeed. But I was in such a situation at that time, although I did carry out the order. But to this day I believe I should not have done so. It indeed resulted in very heavy casualties and in virtually zero gains. In my view this was the classic case in which a commander needs to say, 'We are not carrying out this order, no way.'[57]

He was once again pointing back to the scarring events of 21 October 1973, when he had no choice but to obey and the results had been as he anticipated. He faulted Gonen for staying in his command post and so not assessing the situation directly. Gonen had few supporters, even among those annoyed with Sharon, and he was the one who took the brunt of the commission's criticisms. It determined that he was 'responsible in large part for the dangerous situation in which our forces were caught'. This gave Sharon's defence more weight, and not only because retrospective assessments on how the chain of command functioned tend to be influenced by results. This was the strongest case for insubordination and was one reason to favour a degree of decentralization in decision-making. Those closest to the action can appreciate the dangers of particular moves directly and see opportunities that might be missed by those in a distant headquarters. But the distant headquarters will still have an overview of the war and be best placed to decide on priorities without having their hand forced by an impetuous local commander.

Sharon was a unique case, partly because of his personality and political philosophy, and partly because of circumstances. He did not want anyone to share in his decisions, and so went out of his way to make it difficult for them to do so. In 1973, he was an opposition politician back in uniform, aware that the government had messed things up. His superior officer was a former subordinate who gave every appearance of being unable to cope with the demands being placed on him. As Sharon knew that those further above him in the chain of command, other than Dayan, wanted him dismissed, he saw no point in making much of an effort to appease them. Relieving him of his command would have been a massive step, of MacArthur-like proportions, especially without evidence of a major command failure. Sharon rationalized his insubordination in 1973 by explaining that he had been sent bad orders. The real explanation was that he was no longer trusted by his senior commanders, so they sent him orders to control him, which he found unfair and unwise, and so tried to evade, adding to the distrust.

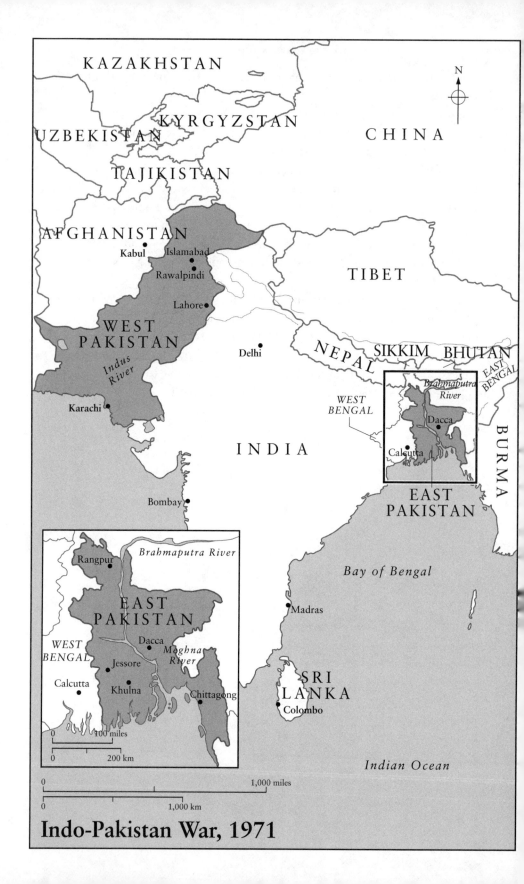

Indo-Pakistan War, 1971

5
Civil War:
The Surrender of East Pakistan

*[T]he involvement of the Pakistan Army in Martial Law duties
and civil administration had a highly corrupting influence, seriously detracting from the professional duties of the Army and
affecting the quality of training which the Officers could impart
to their units and formations, for the obvious reason that they
did not have enough time available for this purpose, and many
of them also lost the inclination to do so.*

Hamoodur Rahman Commission Report, 1974

Sharon always trusted himself to make better command decisions than
anyone else, but when, as was often the case, the actions and the consequences might be contentious, he was keen to demonstrate that he had
not been truly insubordinate. He found orders from his superiors, or,
when minister of defence, decisions of the cabinet, that gave him the
necessary latitude. Not all commanders, however, want latitude, especially when the outcome of an operation may be costly and unpopular.
In such circumstances, they will seek a direct and unequivocal order to
absolve them of any responsibility.

A formal surrender of an army to an enemy officer represents the
ultimate humiliation. It was one the French avoided at Dien Bien Phu by
allowing the base to be overrun. In December 1971, Pakistani forces
defending East Pakistan surrendered to Indian forces. In this chapter, we
see the desperation of the Pakistani general to avoid surrender and,
when it became unavoidable, to get a direct order from his president
and commander-in-chief to do so. In this case, the president and the
commander-in-chief were the same person, and so these events

introduce the question of the impact of military dictatorships on operational performance.

In previous chapters, we have observed tensions in civil–military relations, but only in the case of France did these get close to producing a military coup. Kennedy worried about one; Sharon mused openly; de Gaulle almost came to power through one, although in the end he stayed on the right side of a constitutional transfer of power. Elsewhere, where coups succeeded, they were often the result of a politicized officer corps acting against an ideologically hostile civilian government, as in Turkey in 1960, Brazil in 1964, Argentina in 1966 and Greece in 1967. Countries prone to chronic political instability, including many former colonies, often suffered cycles of alternating civilian and military rule. Military dictators normally came to power not because of external conflicts, but because of disorder and disunity at home, circumstances that allow the personal ambitions of the new supreme leader to assert themselves. In Pakistan, military rule had been the norm since 1958, and, while elections were held in December 1970, they revealed such divisions in the country that the military, led by General Agha Mohammed Yahya Khan, took supreme power. In the end, his policies hastened the break-up of the country. By contrast, India, with a clear division of responsibilities between the government and the armed forces, achieved its objectives.

Military rulers claim legitimacy on the grounds that they can run their countries better than civilians. They take it for granted that they will be more effective in dealing with external threats, because they will be bold and decisive, whereas feeble civilians vacillate. Political direction and military action can come together in one person. Yet, as we shall see in this and later chapters, dictatorships can perform very badly when it comes to fighting wars. In some cases, this can be explained by supreme leaders having promoted themselves to the highest military rank despite having had very little military experience. But that was not the case in Pakistan. The generals who took power in Pakistan were professional soldiers and had seen battle.

PAKISTAN'S DICTATORS

The pattern of military rule was established in Pakistan in 1958, when the then army commander-in-chief, General Ayub Khan, seized power.

In his time, Ayub epitomized the 'man on horseback', the strong man in uniform determined to save his country from chaos and disarray.[1] Ayub looked the part. Tall, with a bearing and accent acquired during his years with the British Indian Army, he set about imposing order, in the belief that this would enable Pakistan to thrive.[2] At first, he was rewarded with significant economic growth, and was hailed as a model of authoritarian modernization, imposing the discipline necessary to hold a fissiparous country together and setting it on a path to development.[3] He reinforced his position by promoting himself to the position of field marshal, ensuring that he outranked any potential rivals in the armed forces, and then with a new constitution. This came into force after martial law ended in 1962. But soon his hold over the country began to weaken. A brief, costly and unsatisfactory war with India over Kashmir in 1965 was followed by an economic recession. Demonstrations began against his rule.

The most dangerous aspect of the unrest lay in how much it exposed the tensions between East and West Pakistan. Holding together a country with two parts separated by 1,000 miles had been a challenge from the start. East Pakistan was the result of splitting the old state of Bengal at the time of partition in 1947, the western part staying with India. The lingering resentments were made worse by the evident inequality between the two. Although the East's population was larger, it was disadvantaged socially and economically. The capital was in the new city of Islamabad in the West, with the military HQ in nearby Rawalpindi. West Pakistanis dominated the senior ranks of the armed forces and the upper echelons of the bureaucracy. For these reasons, the East was demanding greater autonomy.

After a major heart attack in 1968, Ayub knew his days in office were numbered. Handing over to a civilian leader was complicated by the polarization and weak political processes of the past decade. The country's two most popular political figures represented incompatible visions for the country's future. Sheikh Mujibur Rahman (Mujib), of the Awami League, demanded more autonomy for the East. In this he was opposed by former foreign minister Zulfikar Ali Bhutto of the Pakistan's People's Party (PPP), based in the West. As Ayub struggled to find a way forward, waiting in the wings was General Agha Mohammed Yahya Khan, commander-in-chief of the army, and Ayub's protégé. His moment came in March 1969. Invoking his field marshal's rank, Ayub ordered Yahya to impose martial law. He warned that Pakistan was 'going up in flames'. It was the army's duty to get the country back on track.[4] And so Yahya took over as president.

Yahya reached the top with powerful support in the hierarchy. As an officer, he was competent enough, ready to take the lead, though he had hardly shone during the Indo-Pakistani War of 1965. A brisk, confident figure, uninterested in the detail of command, Yahya was unreflective and stubborn, reluctant to change his mind once it was made up. When faced with contrary arguments, his instinct was to procrastinate rather than modify his views. He also had a well-known weakness for drink and female company. The officers he gathered around him were known to share his tastes. They were tellingly referred to as the 'whisky group'. Normal appointment procedures were circumvented to get loyal officers into key positions.

Implementing martial law was the easy part. It had been done before and so now only required 'brushing off a few old orders and documents and imposing them anew'.[5] Governing the country was a different matter. An HQ was established in the President's House in Rawalpindi, separate from the military command and headed by General S. M. G. Peerzada as principal staff officer. He became de facto prime minister, as he took many of the key decisions. A commanders-in-chief committee was given responsibility for decisions on military affairs and for handling communications between the president and the armed services. For policymaking, a council of administration was created, chaired by Yahya, who also took charge of the ministries of Defence and Foreign Affairs. The other departmental briefs were handed out to the other chiefs until a civilian cabinet was established in August 1969. A national security council was also established. But none of these bodies functioned effectively. Yahya preferred to work only with the small group of officers he trusted.

CRACKDOWN IN THE EAST

In principle, the military government was supposed to be temporary. The first aim was to end 'administrative laxity and chaos'; the second to get in place a constitutional government. The model Yahya appeared to have in mind was one in which the military guaranteed order while the civilians administered the country, although he made little secret of his readiness to hold on to total power if necessary. When elections were held in December 1970, the result underscored the country's divisions. Mujib's Awami League dominated the East (winning 160 out of 162 seats) and Bhutto was strongest in the West. It was, however, Mujib who had the parliamentary numbers to form a government, and it was Mujib who most threatened the unity of the country.

Yahya tried to find a political agreement that satisfied Mujib without him actually taking power. But he had no talent for compromise and was encouraged by Bhutto not to make any concessions that could undermine unity and the West's dominance. For his part, Mujib could not back away from his central demand for greater autonomy for the East. This was the demand at the core of the 'six points' on which he had long campaigned.

Yahya interpreted this as defiance. He felt that his authority was not being respected. At a meeting on 20 February 1971, he complained that Mujib was not 'behaving' and needed to be sorted out, as if he were a subordinate officer.[6] The army remained preoccupied with India, a country they had been fighting intermittently for over two decades, and which was assumed to be behind every security threat. This was not a world view that left much scope for political complexity. Instead, the inclination was to see any challenge as being tantamount to treason. Moreover, there was an institutional interest in preventing the East gaining more autonomy: if that happened, the government could be denied the tax revenues necessary to sustain the armed forces in the style to which they had become accustomed.

The only way to stop Mujib was to delay parliament convening. But, unless this somehow jolted the political class into finding an agreed way forward, it was a move that pointed back to martial law. Only this time East Pakistanis would be even more aggrieved than before. Perhaps Yahya thought that the Awami League would moderate their demands when faced with the prospect of force. He was advised that this was not the case. From the East, the governor and senior military officers warned of the uproar should the assembly be postponed. Mujib and the Awami League would resist rather than 'knuckle under'. Yahya's reaction to this advice was to sack the then governor. He was confident that 'firm military action' would deter mass unrest. 'A whiff of the grapeshot would suffice.'[7]

On 20 February 1971, the military began to prepare for a crackdown. Reinforcements were sent to Dacca (which later came to be known as Dhaka), the East's capital. On 1 March, the assembly was postponed. Uproar followed as predicted. There were strikes and roadblocks in Dacca. 'It is the duty of the Pakistan Armed Forces,' Yahya insisted on 6 March, 'to ensure the integrity, solidarity and security of Pakistan, a duty in which they have never failed.'[8] But faced with a situation that he could not yet control, Yahya stepped back. He needed more troops to enforce martial law. While this was being arranged, he revived the political track. Now 25 March was set as the date when the assembly would meet. He agreed to go to Dacca to try to find a way forward. The curfews were lifted and most troops went back to barracks.

Those around Yahya encouraged a tough stance, shutting out officers and officials who knew the East, preventing them from getting their concerns to him. Any individual urging a more conciliatory approach was, by definition, far too sympathetic to the Awami League, and so a virtual traitor to Pakistan. Instead, the information passed on to Yahya came through military and intelligence channels controlled by hardliners who favoured a crackdown and provided caricatured views of Bengali attitudes. They encouraged the developing narrative that the bombastic, defiant posturing of Mujib and his supporters would melt away as soon as they were staring down the barrels of guns.

Although Yahya went to Dacca on 15 March to see if he could get a political settlement, his clumsy manoeuvres had hardened attitudes. In the East's capital, he was warned of the strength of local feeling and that there was no military solution to the crisis. Suppressing the Bengalis would be 'an act of madness'. When Yahya tried to reassure Mujib that his six points were taken seriously, he was held back by Bhutto, warning that such a challenge to the country's unity could lead to agitation in the West. In the end, Yahya could not escape the conviction that unity and Western dominance of the political order could only be enforced through coercion. By acting tough with Mujib, he believed he could extract sufficient compromises to reach a position to satisfy Bhutto, and that, if he failed, he needed to be ready for a crackdown in the East.

Lieutenant General Sahibzada Yaqub Khan, the eastern commander, now added the role of governor to his duties. He too was reluctant to use force to put down the rebellion, and warned that military action would have limited value if not accompanied by complimentary economic and political measures.[9] This confirmed Yahya in his view that he was being let down by local military commanders, who were insufficiently robust. 'A first class army in East Pakistan', he declared, 'is completely demoralized because of two old women.' On 6 March, Yaqub was forced to resign and was replaced by Lieutenant General Tikka Khan, an officer with a reputation for following orders to the letter and a mind 'unclouded by strategic thinking or complicated vocabulary'.[10] Tikka instructed the generals Farman Ali and Khadim Raja to draft operational orders for military action to reinstate public order and central authority in East Pakistan. These were drafted on 18 March, just a few days after Yahya arrived in Dacca. He was there as much to prepare for the crackdown as to seek a settlement. East Pakistani military units and police were to be disarmed. The leaders of the Awami League and rebel student leaders were to be arrested. A political solution was no longer feasible; a military solution must be pursued.

On 23 March, the generals visited brigade commanders to hand over direct orders to prepare operations.[11] Two days later, Yahya met with senior army officers in Dacca and gave the go-ahead. At 18.00, divisional commanders were told that the operation would begin an hour after midnight. This was timed to coincide with Yahya arriving back in Karachi. But news of his departure soon reached the Awami League. Activists went onto the streets, once again putting up roadblocks and barricades. The army brought forward what was now called 'Operation Searchlight' by an hour. Mujib was arrested and his party was banned. Yahya denounced him, as an 'enemy of Pakistan', accusing him of attacking the country's 'solidarity and integrity', a crime which could not 'go unpunished'.

By the end of March, the army controlled Dacca but it took two months to get a degree of control over the rest of the East. The violence was not all one way. Minorities in the East were targeted by Awami League militants. Nonetheless, the army's campaign of suppression led to shocking stories of rape and plunder, of human rights violated and unarmed people murdered. The minority Bengali Hindu population, assumed to be inherently subversive, was singled out for especially harsh treatment. The initial crackdown on Awami League supporters and students prompted an army mutiny in the East, a consequence apparently not anticipated when the plans for mass arrests were drawn up. This left an army of around 45,000, plus some paramilitaries, seeking to control a population of around 75 million, which was becoming progressively more hostile and fearful. A flow of refugees into India eventually became a torrent. At first the numbers were in the thousands, but by late May the refugee population was some 3.5 million and by mid-July it had reached 6.9 million. The 1,000 camps and reception centres close to the border exceeded the ability of local officials to cope and raised serious health problems.

INDIA PREPARES

In India, Prime Minister Indira Gandhi watched these events warily. Politically, she was in good shape as her Congress Party had just won a handsome electoral victory. There was no pressure to rush into action. She assumed and hoped that a settlement would be reached between the two parts of Pakistan. There were risks in continued instability, especially if it began to spill over into West Bengal. Yet she was also aware of three arguments for intervention, which grew in influence as spring moved into summer. The first was that the refugees pouring across the border represented a form of 'demographic aggression', imposing unwanted burdens on India. They also highlighted that this was a crisis with humanitarian as well as political dimensions, and could not be left to sort itself out. Second, hawks in the government argued that, with Pakistan in such disarray, military action represented an opportunity to remove it as a threat to India once and for all. A third consideration was the fear of communist influence in West Bengal. India had been dealing with Naxalite left-wing violence for some time and did not want to see such sentiments take hold in East Pakistan or revive in West Bengal.[12]

On 25 March, as the crackdown was under way in East Pakistan, Gandhi met Defence Minister Jagjivan Ram, who believed that India needed to intervene, and Army Chief General S. H. F. J. 'Sam' Manekshaw, chairman of the Chiefs of Staff Committee (COSC), who was more cautious. In Manekshaw's account, late in April, Gandhi asked him during a cabinet meeting if he was prepared to go to war with Pakistan. He replied that he was not, pointing to a lack of operational readiness, inadequate logistics and adverse weather conditions.[13]

The optimum time for war was late in the year, when the entry points into East Pakistan would not be waterlogged and snow had returned to the Tibetan passes that would impede any possible Chinese intervention in support of Pakistan. Though this was unlikely, troops would need to be kept close to the Chinese border, just in case. Gandhi also had to take account of international opinion. If India started a war against Pakistan to support secession, it would be acting against the UN Charter and would get little support in the Security Council, other than perhaps from the Soviet Union. As part of her intensive diplomatic initiative, Gandhi managed to get the Soviet Union to agree to a treaty of friendship in August 1971.

India could not, however, be neutral in the dispute. It was bound to be drawn into supporting what was now the nascent state of Bangladesh. The Pakistan consular building in Calcutta had been taken over by defecting diplomats and handed over to the government-in-exile of Bangladesh. Indian officials worked with the Awami League leaders to draft its declaration of independence. The Bangladeshi liberation army, the Mukti Bahini, with regular and irregular units, was boosted when more than half of the Bengali/East Pakistani regular troops joined them, led by Colonel M. A. G. Usmani, who had been deputy director of military operations in general headquarters (GHQ) Rawalpindi. It was a credible force. Young men from the burgeoning refugee camps added to its numbers. They would not sit passively on the Indian side of the border.

Although the Indian government recognized that it would be unfortunate if the Awami League appeared to be no more than an instrument of Indian policy, they still trained and armed the Mukti Bahini, because they wished to keep it under some control, not least to ensure that it was led by moderate members of the League. India's own army also moved close to the border with the East, taking over from the Border Security Force at the end of April, because the still-loyal Pakistani army was in control on the other side. As training and equipment improved, irregular units of the Mukti Bahini began a campaign of guerrilla warfare in East Pakistan, including bombing and assassination. This prompted a harsh response from the Pakistani authorities as well as a strong anti-Indian movement in West Pakistan, demanding that India be punished for supporting the insurgents.

By October, this dynamic was making war increasingly likely. India held back from a full mobilization, but reinforced the border areas. The

Mukti Bahini stepped up attacks against Pakistan border posts, sometimes supported by Indian artillery fire, and also started to take salients in East Pakistan in readiness to support a more substantial intervention later. India's pretence that it was not directly supporting the Mukti Bahini was no longer credible. By November 1971, war was being demanded in demonstrations and newspapers in Islamabad and Delhi. It was evident that open hostilities would come as soon as the land was sufficiently dry to allow ground offensives.

India prepared for war with an orthodox chain of command. Political control was exercised by Prime Minister Gandhi. There was no defence committee, but there was the Political Affairs Committee (PAC), the rough equivalent of the US National Security Council, on which key cabinet ministers served and to which the three service chiefs were on occasion invited. The Secretaries Committee supported the PAC with coordination and implementation. Thus, the civilian bureaucracy played an important role in the decision-making process, both as a channel of communication to the prime minister and in its policy recommendations. Manekshaw chaired the chiefs of staff, and was also army chief. The navy and air force chiefs, Admiral S. M. Nanda and Air Marshal P. C. Lal, enjoyed autonomy, had the independent right to meet with the civilian leadership and were not directly under his command.

Manekshaw had his own informal meetings with Gandhi, with whom he had a good working relationship, although the line of authority was supposed to work through Defence Minister Ram. Gandhi used the senior diplomat D. P. Dhar to serve as her liaison with Manekshaw. There was also the Joint Intelligence Committee, consisting of representatives from the Research and Analysis Wing (RAW), the Intelligence Bureau and the three services. During the crisis neither the cabinet nor parliament played much of a role.

The eastern commander was Lieutenant General Jagjit Singh Aurora, although the more dynamic figure in the local command was his chief of staff, Major General 'Jake' Jacob. Jacob, who was Jewish, considered Manekshaw to be anti-Semitic, and later recalled his saying when he appointed Aurora that he had little confidence in his, but 'I like to have him as a doormat.'[14] Yet Manekshaw allowed the local commands considerable autonomy in executing the war plans. For the purposes of the war, the Mukti Bahini forces were organized as three brigades and came to be integrated into the Indian Army, under overall Indian command.

PAKISTAN'S CONFUSED STRATEGY

By contrast, the Pakistani command structure was dysfunctional. The flaws in the system reflected Yahya's own failings and were compounded by them. Rather than clarify roles and responsibilities, martial law created confusion. Yahya was unable to manage the multiple demands on his time – setting domestic and foreign policy, looking after the army and providing operational direction to all three services in the event of war, and this led to uncertainty and delay in coming to decisions and issuing commands. During this crisis, he offered little direction, possibly because at key moments he was drunk. Army officers ran the state, with two brigadiers responsible for much of the civilian bureaucracy. Yet the state institutions that might have coordinated the national effort and provided some direction were left inactive.[15] After his visit in March, he did not return to East Pakistan, or show much interest in how his forces there were supposed to cope. When war came, he asked rhetorically what he could do for East Pakistan, and then answered that he could 'only pray'. It was left to subordinate commanders to prosecute the war as best they could.

His deputy and drinking companion, General Abdul Hamid Khan, became chief of staff of the army, and so, when his boss became president, in effect commander-in-chief. But he was still second-in-command and cautious when it came to taking big decisions. General Gul Hassan Khan, the chief of the general staff, was more active, but described as 'short on strategic vision', in charge of a conventional army caught in an unconventional conflict 'beyond his ken'.[16] He complained that although he was responsible for conveying orders to the field, he was kept totally in the dark by those around Yahya and did not know what was being planned. This meant a lack of direction from headquarters and few opportunities for field commanders to review plans. The confusion this caused was compounded by tensions between the officers responsible for martial law and those responsible for operations.

This confusion was painfully evident in Dacca. After 25 March 1971, the civil administration collapsed and the burden of running East Pakistan fell to army officers, although some civilians were transferred from the West to help. Those from the East who stayed in position were viewed with suspicion. In April, Tikka handed over the Eastern

Command, just one of his many responsibilities, to Lieutenant General Amir Abdullah Khan Niazi. Tikka remained martial law administrator, and so his role and Niazi's overlapped, as they shared command functions, until September, when Niazi also became martial law administrator. Tikka was replaced by a civilian governor, Dr Abdul Motaleb Malik, who was largely a figurehead. Without an effective civil administration, he was unable to assert his authority. He was supported and influenced by his chief secretary, Muzaffar Hussain, and military adviser, General Rao Farman Ali.

As Niazi was the one who eventually surrendered to Indian forces, and was then taken prisoner, he became a scapegoat for wider failings in the Pakistani system. The Hamoodur Rahman Commission, set up after the war to investigate what had gone wrong, certainly went out of its way to put all his actions in the worst possible light.[17] Niazi later wrote his own exculpatory memoir, blaming others for the debacle and describing a dazzling set of conspiracies.[18] The kindest assessment is that he had been promoted above his competence.[19] Then 54, he was appointed in part because few other officers were prepared to take on the task. He had seen extensive service under the British and had been decorated, but his strength lay in tactics and not strategy. One characteristic became very evident during the war: 'his rigid ideas and his false sense of pride of not falling back in the face of the enemy'.[20] An officer attempting to handle public relations in Dacca, Major Siddiq Salik, reported that, when he worried about the lack of troops and resources, Niazi replied: 'In war, it is not the number but generalship that counts.'[21] This tendency to bluster led one of his subordinate commanders to describe him as a 'jackal who masqueraded as a tiger'.[22]

The Hamoodur Rahman Commission referred to Niazi's past 'reputation in sex matters'. According to one account, in responding to reports of sexual misconduct against East Pakistani women, he observed, 'One cannot fight a war here in East Pakistan and go all the way to West Pakistan to have an ejaculation.' One of the witnesses to the Commission testified that: 'The troops used to say that when the Commander was himself a rapist, how could they be stopped?'[23] For whatever reason sexual abuse was rife, leaving its own bitter legacy.[24] The Commission also condemned Yahya for his decadence. There was, it noted, a general problem of senior army officers succumbing to the 'corruption arising out of the performance of Martial Law duties, lust for wine and women and greed for land and houses.' This meant that they lost the will to fight but also 'the professional competence necessary for taking the vital and critical decisions demanded of them for the successful prosecution of the war'.[25]

Niazi led an army of occupation, with poor equipment, that could barely cope with the challenges it faced. He got little help from Yahya or the high command. The limited naval and air forces committed to the East were supposed to work with the army but they were not under his command. He had been given, he wrote in his memoir, 'a rudderless ship with a broken mast to take across the stormy seas, with no lighthouse for me in any direction'.[26]

Initially, he had some success, pushing Mukti Bahini units back and establishing some control over the border. On 17 May, he sent a boastful message to GHQ claiming to have defeated the enemy in the towns and taken out 30,000 rebels, chasing many of them into India.[27] According to his memoir, he felt sufficiently emboldened by June to argue with Hamid that he should push across the border into Indian territory to get at the Mukti Bahini's sanctuaries. He argued that the Indians would not be able to cope, and that the resulting disarray in the border areas would clog up their communications. His plans extended to an air raid on Calcutta to create even more panic and chaos. To do all this he would need serious reinforcements. This would, he recognized, mean war with India, but it would be on Pakistani terms. Hamid explained that the government did not want an open war with India. He was not to enter Indian territory, although any 'hostile elements' entering from India should be evicted.[28]

Pakistan's strategic assumption at this stage, which largely corresponded to thinking in New Delhi, was that India would mount a limited campaign to take an area of East Pakistan large enough to install a provisional government and to destabilize Pakistani forces in the rest of the country. It would counter any Indian offensive in the East by mounting one of its own in the West, where it was stronger, to distract the Indians and hurt India sufficiently to get an agreed settlement. Pakistan would thus have to fight a defensive war in the East and an offensive one in the West. India faced the opposite challenge, although it was better placed to move from a defensive to an offensive war in the West and it had internal lines of communication that would make it easier to move men, material and equipment from one front to another.

Niazi described his orders from the Pakistani GHQ: 'Evict guerrillas. Do not allow any chunk of territory to fall into enemy hands, which they can declare as Bangladesh. Defend East Pakistan against external aggression.'[29] This imposed contradictory demands on his force. Counter-insurgency required dispersal, while a forward defence required strong forces at the border. The inability to win the counter-insurgency campaign complicated the more conventional defensive endeavours, as the Mukti Bahini could interfere with any movements of troops. In addition, his men were exhausted by the guerrilla campaign, fought without proper logistical backup. Then there was the question of what a 'chunk of territory' meant. It implied that the loss of some territory would be tolerable. If not conceding an inch was at one extreme, at the other was concentrating defence on what was known as the Dacca Bowl, that is, the area around the capital surrounded by the Ganges, Brahmaputra and Meghna Rivers.

Even in May, when the military position was at its strongest, Pakistani forces were overstretched, so dispersed that their logistic systems could not support them and they had to find supplies from local sources. All this encouraged a sense of insecurity, so that troops ended up 'chasing ghosts', as they were sent on pointless raids or into ambushes. The size of the territory to be covered, and his relatively small force, with no reserves and only a squadron of old aircraft to provide air cover, rendered all Niazi's plans unrealistic. His strategy to defend Dacca at all costs was formulated on the basis that the population of the East would have been pacified and no longer hostile, and that India would support an invasion by Mukti Bahini rather than embark on one itself. The aim of defending Dacca got lost in a compromise, which meant deploying first along the border but then falling back to supposed fortresses close to selected towns, and after that on to prepared positions around Dacca. But, because Niazi lacked reserves, he had to rely on units getting out of forward positions in time to take up new ones further back. Not only were his command structures unable to support complex moves of this sort, the need for the units to get out was undermined by his injunction that they should fight on until they were unable to continue.[30]

This was always a strategy geared to buying time, at best to be used to launch a campaign from the West against India and at worst for a ceasefire resolution to be adopted by the Security Council.[31] In the Security Council, India had a friend in the Soviet Union, while China backed

Pakistan. The only new complication was that – in a move that Pakistan had helped facilitate – the United States was edging closer to China in a geopolitical game. That July, Henry Kissinger had made his breakthrough visit to Beijing. As the two communist giants became increasingly hostile to each other, the Americans had seen an opportunity to gain some leverage over the Soviets as they sought a negotiated settlement in the Vietnam War.

NIAZI'S DESPERATE DEFENCE

By 20 November, the more aggressive Mukti Bahini campaign, now actively supported by Indian forces, had taken most of the border outposts and had forward bases inside East Pakistan territory. Hassan urged Yahya to open the western front, but he was reluctant to do so. Eventually, on the 23 November, he was asked to visit the operations room at GHQ and was pushed again. Although he did declare a state of emergency in all of Pakistan and told his people to prepare for war, he still procrastinated, hoping to get a boost from China. Senior officers, with Zulfikar Bhutto, were sent to Beijing. There they found their hosts not expecting war, urging a political settlement and making no commitment to come to Pakistan's aid.

There was a strategic rationale behind the decision to take the war to the West, but it was still an extraordinary gamble, when forces in the East were struggling to cope with an insurgency and would soon have to take on a major Indian offensive. At the time, India had 833,800 men supported by 1,450 tanks and 3,000 artillery pieces. It could sustain losses and replace them. Pakistan, by contrast, had a total army of 395,000 men with 850 tanks and 800 guns. India enjoyed air superiority, sufficient to prevent airborne reinforcements from the West to the East. Pakistan's decision to go to war was founded on unwarranted bravado in the higher ranks of the military as well as public opinion, bolstered by a belief in the superiority of Pakistan's forces.

After Yahya took the decision to go to war, on 29 November, few were informed of what was planned.[32] General Hassan, who heard little from Yahya and his coterie, turned to the local media to find out what was going on, but he found the news outlets 'so heavily sedated' that they learned nothing.[33]

The start date was originally 2 December; it then was moved back to the next day. Coincidentally, in late November, Mrs Gandhi had authorized Indian forces to begin a full-scale attack on East Pakistan on 4 December. On the evening of 3 December, just before 18.00, the Pakistan Air Force launched pre-emptive strikes against eleven airfields in north-western India. If the aim was to mimic the Israel attack on the Egyptian Air Force of June 1967, it failed. With only 50 aircraft involved, the Pakistanis caused little damage. India was content to be absolved of any blame for starting the war.

Mrs Gandhi met with Manekshaw, and then her cabinet, that evening. Plans for the Indian offensive the next day were confirmed. Bangladesh was now formally recognized as an independent state. For the moment, the military objective was simply to capture sufficient territory to install the Bangladeshi government; taking Dacca itself was not regarded as essential. The Indian high command assumed that once a significant chunk of the country was lost Pakistani resistance would collapse, with the army left fragmented and unable to recover, while taking Dacca would be operationally demanding. At least one large river would have to be crossed, followed by a dash to the capital, which would be challenging for an army that tended to be methodical and disinclined to improvise, relying as it did on infantry divisions with few mechanized units.[34] Even if a move to Dacca was feasible, there was unlikely to be sufficient time in the face of international pressures for a ceasefire.

Jacob at Eastern Command was never convinced by this strategy and argued against it from when the first plans were being developed in July. He believed Dacca could be captured, so long as that was set as the prime objective and forces were ordered to follow a clear path towards it, isolating and bypassing any Pakistani strongholds they came across en route. When Manekshaw visited Eastern Command HQ in Calcutta in early August, Jacob argued his case. The subordinate commanders agreed. Lieutenant General Sagat Singh, commander of IV Corps, saw a route across the Meghna River and straight on to Dacca. Manekshaw was unconvinced. 'Don't you see if we take Khulna and Chittagong, Dacca will automatically fall?' Yet, even without any formal plan to take Dacca, Jacob had one in mind, and commanders such as Singh intended to exploit an opportunity to get there if one presented itself.

In October, the Indian objective had been 'to assist the Mukti Bahini in liberating a part of Bangladesh, where the refugees could be sent to live under their own Bangladesh government'. Territory would be taken up to the Brahmaputra and Meghna Rivers. Nothing had changed by 3 December. The aim was 'to gain as much ground as possible in the east, to neutralize Pakistani forces there to the extent we could and to establish a base as it were for a possible state of Bangladesh'. Because of likely demands from the Security Council, the cautious view was that those 'commanding the East should work to limited objectives, but go about achieving them as rapidly as possible'.[35]

The Pakistani effort to move the main thrust of the war from the East to the West not so much failed as barely got started.[36] Ground operations were launched in Kashmir and Punjab, with a minor armoured operation in Rajasthan, but their gains were limited, and India soon mounted a counteroffensive. After one major tank battle, thereafter there was little of the drama that marked the eastern front. The Indians took advantage of their air superiority to keep Pakistani forces pinned down, while in two impressively executed operations the Indian Navy used missile patrol boats to inflict large losses on the Pakistan Navy off the coast of Karachi. This hit Karachi's fuel supplies, including a number of oil tankers. The Pakistan plan depended on India moving units from the south to cope with the initial Pakistani offensive in the west. As this made no progress, India did not need to move its forces and so there was no opportunity for a counterpunch. Pakistani units, prepared to participate in this second stage of the offensive, waited in vain for the order to move.

To the East, the Indian offensive proceeded largely according to plan. Jessore was captured on 7 December, as the Pakistani garrison withdrew. But at various points the offensive met resistance, and there were some tough fights. Khulna did not fall under Indian control until 16 December. It did not therefore move as quickly as the Indians would have liked, other than on the eastern side, where Sagat Singh kept on pushing forward. Once it was apparent that India had the upper hand, there were soon questions in Delhi about whether the strategy was sufficiently ambitious. On 9 December, the prime minister's secretariat expressed doubts that 10 million refugees would return quickly to their homeland 'so long as the armies of West Pakistan continue to operate in Bangla Desh', adding that 'a mere cease-fire which does not simultaneously go into the basic causes of the conflict will prove . . . illusory.'[37] The high command now accepted that it would not be enough to take territory. It was necessary to get to Dacca. Yet, because the Pakistanis were losing, it was also clear that they would press for a ceasefire as soon as possible. As Eastern Command had reached this view before the war, in effect Delhi was catching up with its frontline commanders.

Niazi's war had begun with the increasing Mukti Bahini actions in November, which is what led to his original requests for reinforcements. The delays in these reaching the East led him to urge that they be sent 'on emergency basis as done during war'. Even when they arrived this would still not be enough. He wanted two more infantry battalions along with a squadron of tanks and a brigade HQ, urging that these were 'extremely essential' and should be 'despatched immediately'.[38] No response came from GHQ, but he did get a warning that the main enemy objective was Chittagong. He was told to reinforce its defences 'by pulling out troops from less important sectors as necessary'.[39] On 28 November, as the main war drew closer, Niazi acknowledged a 'highly inspiring appreciation at performance of our basic duty EASTERN COMMAND and myself', and sent reassurances of 'high morale and fine shape'. All ranks were 'imbued with true spirit of extreme sacrifice to zealously defend the priceless honour, integrity and solidarity of our beloved PAKISTAN'. His command was 'at the highest STATE of readiness to teach a lasting lesson to HINDUSTAN should they dare cast an evil eye on our sacred soil in any manner'. This, he described, as a 'grand opportunity afforded'.[40]

The tone soon changed. He had been given no advance warning of the planned Pakistani air strike and found out about the start of the war on the radio. On 5 December, with hostilities now under way in the West, Niazi was informed that India would 'shortly launch a full scale offensive against EAST PAKISTAN'. This meant 'total war'. He must therefore deploy his forces 'in accordance with your operational task'.[41] This was followed up by a message explaining that the enemy would 'attempt to capture EAST PAKISTAN as swiftly as possible and then shift maximum forces to face WEST PAKISTAN'. This 'must NOT be allowed to happen'. His priority therefore must not be to hold on to territory. Some losses would be 'insignificant'. Instead, he must keep 'the maximum enemy force involved in EAST PAKISTAN'. He was urged to 'keep up your magnificent work against such heavy odds'. Niazi was given no reason to suppose that anything would be done to redress the 'heavy odds' he faced, unless help came in the form of

'CHINESE activities very soon', although what these might be was not spelt out.[42]

The already shaky foundations of Pakistan's strategy became even shakier with the failure to achieve a breakthrough on the western front.[43] As their orders to Niazi explained, Yahya and Hamid wished the East to hang on for as long as possible, to keep Indian forces tied down and prevent them from moving to the western front. At the same time, because of the potentially fraught situation in the West, they were reluctant to send reinforcements to the East, as it was a lost cause. In any case, with supply lines vulnerable to air and naval attack, it was not clear how they could be sent. After requesting reinforcements in November, Niazi was promised eight infantry battalions and an engineer battalion. In the event, only five battalions were sent. The three that did not arrive Niazi had intended to serve as the strategic reserve in Dacca.

Niazi's situation report of 6 December emphasized just how heavy the odds against him were. The enemy offensive involved

> eight divisions supported by four tank regiments, full complement of support service elements in addition to 39 battalions BORDER SECURITY FORCE and 60-70 thousand trained rebels, backed by the Indian air force sending rockets and napalm against his defensive positions, while rebel forces cut lines of communication by destroying roads/bridges/rail ferries/boats etc.

In addition, he reported, the local population was 'against us'. It was therefore already 'difficult to reinforce or replenish or readjust positions'. Pakistani units had been engaged in active operations since March with no 'rest or relief'. They were 'now committed to very intense battle' without their 'own tank, artillery and air support', and were already suffering losses of men and materiel. Yet, despite the odds, 'own troops inflicted heavy casualties on enemy and caused maximum possible attrition on them', so that they had 'paid heavy cost for each success in terms of ground'.

His plan was to move back to 'pre-planned line of defensives ... resorting to fortress/strong point basis'. The promise was then to 'fight it out last man last round'. However, could the help from China be 'expedited'?[44] The main conclusion that GHQ would have drawn from this message was that there was not much hope of keeping a large Indian force occupied for any length of time. The response was to encourage

Niazi to keep going – 'the outstanding combat performance of all ranks is a matter of great pride' – and to emphasize that he must be prepared to trade space for time. He was to 'hold positions tactically in strength without any territorial considerations including CHITTAGONG with a view to maintaining the entity of your force intact and inflicting maximum possible attrition in men and materiel on the enemy'.[45] Yet while trading space for time argued for nimble moves out of trouble to keep the army in a decent shape for the next challenge, Niazi continued to insist that no unit could pull back until it had suffered at least 75 per cent casualties.[46]

Retreats are hard to conduct under the best of circumstances. The challenge becomes even greater when the withdrawals must take place in what is in effect hostile territory. In this case, there was also a clear contradiction between the strategic imperative to hold out for as long as possible and the tactical need to get out in a timely fashion to reinforce defensive lines to the rear.

SURRENDER COMES TO DACCA

There was a small group running affairs in Dacca – Governor Malik, Chief Secretary Muzaffar Hussain and the military adviser General Rao Farman Ali, along with General Niazi. They now faced a predicament. The military situation could only get worse. The orders were to play for time. According to his memoirs, and the signals he sent at the time, Niazi was going to keep on fighting until his orders changed. Those around the governor were less convinced. They were looking for a way to bring matters to a close in the East as soon as possible. The accounts about what went on differ to a degree, largely on the question of whether Niazi colluded with the political initiatives they took. Farman, in particular, was subsequently keen to refute the idea that the initiatives were his alone.[47] Other than for the impact on their reputations, the dispute is beside the point. The political logic that the governor's group followed was reasonable in the absence of clear direction from Yahya.

On the evening of 6 December, Malik was briefed by Niazi. This led him to believe that matters were under control. By the next morning, the situation had worsened and Niazi was called to the Governor's House. Farman described the general as being 'in a terrible shape, haggard, obviously had no sleep' and soon 'crying loudly'. After the commander had recovered his composure, the three agreed that with the situation so dire a peaceful solution had to be found. According to Farman, as he left, however, Niazi remarked that any message should be sent from the Governor's House, and Farman agreed, as 'I thought it was important for the morale of the troops to keep up the image of the Commander.' Niazi remarked only on the governor's natural concern about the turn of events, and how the letter then sent to Yahya was drafted without his knowledge and overstated the problems his forces faced.

This letter urged that Pakistan propose a political solution at the United Nations. It reported that Niazi's troops were fighting 'heroically but against heavy odds without adequate armour and air support'. And it claimed that food and fuel supplies were running low. The letter also introduced a theme that was emphasized increasingly in explaining the risks of delaying a ceasefire: 'Law and order situation in areas vacated Army pathetic as thousands of pro-Pakistan elements being butchered by rebels. Millions of non-Bengalis and loyal elements are awaiting death.' If there was to be no outside help, then he 'beseeched' Yahya

> to negotiate so that a civilised and peaceful transfer takes place and mil-
> lions of lives are saved and untold misery avoided. Is it worth sacrificing
> so much when the end seems inevitable? If help is coming we will fight on
> whatever consequences there may be. Request be kept informed.[48]

Yahya's response on 8 December urged that the fight be continued. He promised that a high-powered delegation was being 'rushed' to the United Nations and added a reminder that a 'full scale and bitter war' was also going on in the West.

> Please rest assured that I am fully alive to the terrible situation that you
> are facing. Chief of Staff is being directed by me to instruct General Niazi
> regarding the military strategy to be adopted. You on your part and your
> government should adopt strongest measures in the fields of food ration-
> ing and curtailing supply of all essential items as on war footing to be
> able to last for a maximum period of time and preventing a collapse. God
> be with you. We are all praying.[49]

As there was no evidence of any political movement on 9 December, the governor tried again. The enemy was 'likely to be at the outskirts of

Dacca any day, if no outside help forthcoming'. The local population had welcomed the Indian Army and was giving them support. The UN secretary general's representative, who was in Dacca, had suggested that 'Dacca city may be declared as an open city to save lives of civilians especially non-Bengalis.' He was 'favourably inclined to accept the offer' and recommended that it be approved. He did however note that Niazi did not agree, as 'his orders are to fight to the last and [the UN proposal] would amount to giving up Dacca'. Without an 'immediate cease-fire and political settlement', it was unlikely that they could prevent Indian troops soon being able to move from the East wing to the West wing. This would result in a 'meaningless' sacrifice of West Pakistan, now the East was a lost cause.[50]

The reply from Yahya was curious. In view 'of our complete isolation from each other', he was leaving decisions about East Pakistan 'to your good sense and judgement'. Niazi was to take his orders from Malik ('I am instructing General Niazi simultaneously to accept your decision and arrange things accordingly'). Malik could 'go ahead and ensure the safety of our armed forces by all political means that you will adopt with our opponent'.[51] This was an extraordinary abdication of responsibility. Yahya was far better placed than Malik to take action, whether by instructing his delegation at the United Nations in New York or dealing directly with the imprisoned Mujib. A separate peace arranged from Dacca unavoidably implied a separate East Pakistan. The group in Dacca was isolated, beleaguered and in no position to manage any complicated diplomatic negotiations.

Nonetheless, as they had been given the latitude by the president, the governor's group took advantage. A signal was drafted with a proposal to be put to the United Nations. This would invite the elected representatives of East Pakistan to 'arrange for the peaceful formation of a government in Dacca'. It looked forward to an immediate ceasefire, repatriation of armed forces and civilian personnel to West Pakistan, safety of all people settled in East Pakistan since 1947, and a guarantee of no reprisals. It was a proposal for a settlement but not surrender. This would 'not be considered and does not arise'.[52] Chief Secretary Muzzafar, who had drafted the letter, went with Farman to Niazi to get his approval. According to Farman, one of Niazi's officers responded enthusiastically – 'That's it. This is the only course open now.' Niazi asked in what capacity he was asked to approve the proposal. Muzzafar said as a member of the High Powered Committee (the senior group running East Pakistan). Niazi said that he wanted Yahya to confirm that the proposal was acceptable: 'I was extremely unhappy with the contents of the note. It meant the death knell for a united Pakistan and great ignominy for the country, the Pakistan Army.' The men debated how this should be handled, eventually agreeing that Niazi would neither approve nor disapprove but await Yahya's orders. The message concluded: 'General Niazi has been consulted and submits himself to your command.'[53]

The signal to Yahya opened: 'As the responsibility of taking the final and fateful decision has been given to me I am handing over the following note to [UN] Assistant Secretary-General Mr Paul Mark Henri [Paul-Marc Henry] after your approval.' It was therefore reasonable to assume that it would go to Yahya before any approach was made to Henry. When Muzzafar and Farman returned to the Governor's House from Niazi, however, Henry was present. Farman reports he was asked by the governor to hand over a copy of the signal to Henry.[54] Given that Yahya had delegated responsibility to Malik, and told Niazi to follow Malik's instructions, the president should still not have been surprised at this, even though normally it would be expected that such proposals would be communicated to the United Nations from his office. In the event, on discovering that Henry already had the note, Yahya was furious. The governor had 'gone much beyond' his brief. He had assumed that the aim was to get a ceasefire, yet these proposals would mean accepting 'an independent East Pakistan'. All that was required was 'a limited action . . . to end hostilities in East Pakistan', which is what his own draft proposed.[55]

Although Yahya tried to countermand the governor's proposal, and blamed Farman for acting without authorization, there was no way to pull the proposal back. It was soon circulating in New York and in the media. Niazi says he tried to reach the president and the chief of the army staff but failed to do so. These developments were not going to lift the fighting spirit of demoralized troops. It would be pointless to sacrifice their lives when a ceasefire was imminent. Certainly, the Indians saw it as a positive sign but also a reason to push forward. It was evident that the enemy was rattled but also that efforts would now intensify to get a ceasefire. India's response to the proposals contained in the Malik/Farman letter was to demand an unconditional surrender. Manekshaw had no intention of agreeing to conditions, let alone a limited ceasefire.

The enemy was in no position to fight on. The letter also revealed that Yahya could be ignored. He therefore addressed his demand to Farman, who had signed the letter, and urged surrender: 'My forces are now closing in around Dacca and your garrisons there are within the range of my artillery.' Further resistance was 'senseless' while surrender would bring 'complete protection and just treatment under Geneva convention'.[56]

At first, Manekshaw's worries that the pressure for a ceasefire would become irresistible led him to order that all towns bypassed up to this point should now be taken, to get them under Indian control. As this would have taken momentum away from the drive to Dacca, which was now the agreed objective, the field commanders were instructed by Jacob to ignore this order and keep going. To the fore was Sagat Singh's IV Corps. He had seen Dacca as the 'final answer' from the start, and had decided 'to go beyond my assigned task'.[57] This he did with great energy and improvisation, reaching the eastern bank of Meghna River on 9 December. Having found the bridge blown up by retreating Pakistani forces and without craft to get across the river, Singh arranged for an airlift of a sizeable force. By the morning of 11 December, about 650 Indian troops were on the river's west bank. Although Niazi knew that Singh was advancing in his direction, he assigned no additional forces to meet him. Singh was therefore able to outflank the Pakistani defences and cut off any withdrawal towards Dacca.[58] It was only on this day, with the army having in effect set its own war objectives, that the government caught up and the prime minister issued a written directive to the chiefs of staff for the total liberation of Bangladesh.[59]

Niazi, despite his increasingly hopeless position, still insisted that his intention was to fight to the bitter end. He reported on 10 December that his 'formations' were isolated in their ill-prepared fortresses and facing 'liquidation', owing to the enemy's overwhelming strength. The local population were so hostile that they were 'all out to destroy own troops in entire area'. Yet still his orders were 'to hold on last man last round which may NOT be too long due very prolonged operations and fighting troops totally tired'. Ammunition stocks were being used up quickly in fighting, and also destroyed through enemy action. This report was 'submitted for information and advice'.[60]

From GHQ at Rawalpindi came the message that help might be on the way. For this reason, Yahya urged Malik not to be too hasty. 'Very important diplomatic and military moves are taking place by our friends. It is essential that we hold on for another thirty six hours at all costs.'[61] Niazi was told that the US 7th Fleet would soon be in position, and the Chinese had activated a front against India. In the face of strong international pressure, 'INDIA is therefore desperately in a hurry to take maximum possible action against you in EAST PAKISTAN to achieve a fait accompli before events both political and military are against them.' It was 'therefore all the more vital for you to hold out'. This was what the president desired. The signal ended 'good luck to you'.[62] In his memoir, Niazi reports that Gul Hassan telephoned him saying 'yellows coming from the north and whites from the south'.[63]

This was beyond wishful thinking. The Americans were now aware that the Chinese had no interest in a military intervention, so their objectives were focused on saving West Pakistan. East Pakistan was assumed lost. At any rate, Niazi could not hold on. He tried to explain that, unless this support came soon, it would be too late. Enemy units had already been dropped by helicopter near Dacca. If 'friends' were going to get to Dacca, he requested that they arrive 'by air first light 12 Dec'.[64] Without this his situation was 'doubtlessly extremely critical but will turn DACCA into fortress and fight it out till end'.[65] In an effort to convey the urgency of the situation, Niazi sent an unclassified message reporting that a prisoner had been sent back with a message that, if there were no surrender, 'we will HAND over all your prisoners to MUKTI-BHANI for butchery', and urged that this be taken up with 'world red cross authorities'.[66] After expressing his determination to 'fight it out', he now warned that the city was surrounded by rebels and the Indian army was advancing. If the Chinese were coming, they must engage the enemy around Dacca rather than put pressure on India's border. 'Promised assistance must take practical shape by 14 Dec.'[67]

On 14 December, he was told that the Security Council was 'most likely to order a cease-fire'. Niazi was therefore urged by GHQ to 'hold out' to prevent the Indians taking Dacca before it was passed. 'I am saying this with full realization of the most critical situation that you and your command are facing so valiantly.'[68] A resolution proposed by Poland, acting as a proxy for the Soviet Union, was ready for discussion in the Security Council and Yahya wanted to accept it. But Bhutto, once again foreign minister (he had held the post under Ayub Khan), who had been sent to New York, refused to do so. He stormed out of the

Council: 'I will not be a party to the ignominious surrender of part of my country. You can take your Security Council. Here you are. I am going.' The best assumption is that Bhutto, aware that he would be well positioned to take power in the rump Pakistan, wanted to see the army humiliated to get them out of the way.[69]

Now in a hopeless position, Yahya sent a message to both Malik and Niazi:

> You have fought a heroic battle against overwhelming odds. The nation is proud of you and the world full of admiration. I have done all that is humanly possible to find an acceptable solution to the problem. You have now reached a stage when further resistance is no longer humanly possible nor will it serve any useful purpose. It will only lead to further loss of life and destruction. You should now take all necessary measures to stop the fighting and preserve the lives of all armed forces personnel, all those from West Pakistan and all loyal elements.

As this was unclassified, Niazi worried that it might be an Indian trick. His staff called GHQ to validate its authenticity.[70] At about noon on 14 December, Niazi got through to Gul Hassan, who said he did not know anything about Yayha's orders and so Niazi should speak to him directly.

Also, on 14 December, at around 11.00, Indian intelligence discovered that Malik had called a meeting at his house for noon that day to discuss Yahya's message. Within the hour, the Indian Air Force had located the Governor's House and fired rockets into the conference room. Malik hid under a table, while writing a resignation letter to Yahya.[71] Yet having done this, he still felt something should be done about Yahya's instruction. Niazi, in his fortified bunker, said he was seeking clarification from GHQ, but his current intention was to fight on.[72] Farman left the bunker to meet with Malik. They drafted a reply accepting a ceasefire, adding that they would hand over 'peacefully the administration of East Pakistan as arranged by the UN'. This last clause was still further than Yahya wished to go, but it was hard to see how it could be avoided. Malik and Farman approached the US consul general and asked him to transmit their proposal to New Delhi.

Niazi sent a signal the next morning (15 December) reaffirming his intention to fight on. He received a letter from Malik repeating the president's message that 'you should take all necessary measures to stop the fighting and preserve the lives of all armed forces personnel, all those from West Pakistan and all loyal elements.' With continuing hostilities, there would be more 'loss of life and disaster'. 'I request you to do the needful.'

That evening, Hamid contacted him and ordered him to 'act accordingly' and 'stop the war'. According to Niazi, he argued against this order, but Hamid 'repeated it three or four times'. GHQ wanted the war to end quickly before West Pakistan was put in danger.

> I asked to speak to the President. General Hamid told me that he was in the bathroom. Actually he was not in the bathroom; he had passed out, being too drunk. Air Marshal Rahim Khan, who seemed drunk to me, then spoke to me and insisted that I must obey the President's orders.

Niazi still hoped to avoid a formal surrender. His conditions for a ceasefire as sent to Manekshaw avoided surrender by proposing to regroup 'Pakistan Armed Forces in designated areas to be mutually agreed upon between the commanders of the opposing forces'. Manekshaw's reply was received late on 15 December. He offered assurances on safety (observing that he had already done so in two messages to General Farman), but required that Niazi 'issue orders to all forces under your command in Bangladesh to cease fire immediately and surrender to my advancing forces wherever they are located'. Niazi sent the message to GHQ. The response from GHQ came quickly: 'while I leave to you the decision I suggest that you accept the terms laid down by Chief of Staff INDIA as they appear to meet your requirements', adding that this is 'a purely local military decision and has NO repeat NO bearing on the political outcome which has to be decided separately'.[73] They were clinging to the illusion that military defeat did not imply political defeat.

On the morning of 16 December, Niazi sought an extension of the ceasefire until 15.00 and suggested a 'preliminary staff meeting' in Dacca. 'Meantime we are going ahead with ceasefire formalities.' Manekshaw told Jacob to go to Dacca and take the surrender. Indian General Gandharva Nagra, outside of Dacca, sent three officers to Niazi with a message: 'My dear Abdullah, I am here. The game is up. I suggest you give yourself up to me, and I will look after you.' At 09.00 the messengers returned with a major of the Pakistan army to make the arrangements. Nagra and his officers went to Niazi's HQ, whereupon

Niazi broke down, complaining, 'Those bastards at higher headquarters at Pindi have let me down.'[74]

At 13.00 they were joined by Jacob. By now Farman was also present. Jacob read out the surrender document, sent to him by Manekshaw. Both Niazi and Farman refused to surrender. Jacob tried to convince them until, exasperated, he took Niazi aside and said, 'If you refuse to surrender, I will wash my hands off anything that happens. I give you 30 minutes to consider the proposal. If you refuse after 30 minutes, I will order the resumption of hostilities and bombing of Dacca.' Jacob left the room and returned as promised. He then asked Niazi again if he accepted the surrender. When he got no reply, he said: 'I take it as accepted. You will surrender on the Race Course in front of the people of Dacca.' Jacob also demanded an honour guard for General Aurora, who was on his way to sign the document for the Indian forces. At 16.44 on 16 December, Aurora and Niazi signed the Instrument of Surrender. India announced a unilateral ceasefire on the western front. Over 90,000 personnel (79,000 military and 12,000 or so civilian), including Niazi and Farman, were taken prisoner.[75]

CONCLUSION:
A FAILURE OF DICTATORSHIP

The finale had a whiff of inevitability to it. The movement to detach East from West Pakistan was powerful and grew with each misstep by Yahya. Early in 1971, this movement might have been accommodated by political means, most simply by accepting the election results. Once that course had been rejected, Yahya lacked the negotiating skills and the vision to hold the country together. He stuck to a hard line, urged on by Bhutto, who could see how his own political ambitions might be better achieved if the two parts of the country went their separate ways. At each crucial moment, Yahya looked to a military rather than a political solution, yet he showed little grasp of what a military solution might require, especially when it came to war with India. As a politician, he was inept; as a commander, he was absent. The senior generals around him did little to fill the gap. They stayed away from the East and concentrated on the security of West Pakistan, even if this meant sacrificing the East.

The strategy they adopted – an offensive war in the West and a defensive war in the East – was ill thought out and poorly executed. The opening air strikes were not of a size to make a difference, and were never likely to relieve the pressure on the East. By the time they were launched, India was mobilized and ready to advance in the East. If Pakistan was determined to start a war with India, it might have made some sense to push back against the Mukti Bahini bases across the border, as India would have struggled with an invasion in the summer, and there would at least have been a rationale for incursions in terms of 'hot pursuit'. This might have made for a longer and more difficult war, although in the end Pakistan's underlying weaknesses in the East, including the hostility of the local population and its vulnerable supply lines, would still have told. The basic problem was the need to mount a defensive campaign in politically hostile territory with inadequate resources.

Pakistan had a case that active Indian support for the Mukti Bahini constituted an act of aggression, but going on the offensive with air strikes let India off the hook with an overt act of war. By this time there was little international sympathy for its position, because of persistent reports of extensive atrocities in the East.[76] In these circumstances, did Niazi have much of a chance? Gul Hassan later complained that Niazi's professional ceiling was 'no more than that of a company commander'. The Eastern Command could have held out for more than 13 days, but 'with Niazi at the helm, they had no chance.'[77] Yet Hassan could have had him replaced, assuming that there was another commander of greater competence who was prepared to take on such a thankless task. However deficient Niazi was, he got little support during the campaign. He was stuck with a poorly conceived defensive strategy at the national level. His problems were then accentuated by his own delusions and stubbornness.

When war came, the only issue was where and how he would cede territory to buy time, in the hope that a ceasefire would spare him the final ignominy of surrender. A more elaborate defence of Dacca was an option, but India then would have had few problems seizing sufficient territory early on to install the Bangladesh government and put pressure on the supply lines. In addition, in Sagat Singh, the Indians had the more imaginative and daring commander, pushing through to Dacca, bypassing Pakistani positions and avoiding distractions. It is possible to imagine a different outcome but probably only if India had contented itself with more limited objectives and more restrained tactics.

Because of the failings of the Pakistani command system and the lack of clear policy direction coming from Yahya and his aides, the group in charge in Dacca was left alone to sort out what to do. Malik and Farman were realistic in accepting the logic of being cut loose to make their own deal with the advancing Indian forces. While his commanders in the field were fighting their individual battles with little coordination, Niazi presented himself as one who always followed his orders, even to the bitter end, despite the orders he received being expressed in vague or incoherent terms. Being ordered to surrender would absolve him of responsibility for the outcome. As the orders sent from Rawalpindi were largely geared to the security of West Pakistan and not the East, they were never likely to help him. While Yahya delegated authority for ceasefire negotiations, he resisted the implication that this meant delegating responsibility for the political consequences.

Military rule always carries the potential for this sort of dysfunction, although this was an extreme case. The supposition is that by combining the political and military roles in one person they become truly integrated. With an accomplished leader, capable of managing the complex trade-offs this may require, and knowing when and how to take advice, this might work. In practice, few leaders can stay on top of both the political and military decision-making processes, and certainly Yahya was not one of them. The egocentricity that leads an individual to have the confidence to act as a supreme leader encourages sycophancy over challenge. Instead of greater clarity, dictatorship is as likely to lead to confusion, and skewed priorities.

In an investigation of why some authoritarian regimes fight wars poorly, Caitlin Talmadge points to the impact of 'coup-proofing'. Unsuccessful regimes suffer from being organized to prevent coups rather than deal with external threats.[78] In the Pakistani case, the problem was different, although the outcome was similar. This was not a skilful politician seizing power and then making himself the commander-in-chief, without displaying any prior military competence; it was a case of a senior military figure using his position at the top of the armed forces to become a political leader, without having shown any prior aptitude for politics. When power was concentrated at the top, and then wielded crudely and insensitively, the result was fragmentation below. This was because of cronyism and factionalism, as much as a fear of coups. Critical, independent voices were excluded. One should not therefore underestimate the importance of issues of competence and character in these situations. It was always going to be difficult to prevent separation, but, if Yahya had been a gifted commander and an astute politician, he might have been able to justify his supreme power and hold Pakistan together, even though the forces pulling the country apart were formidable. The choices he made meant that the separation, when it came, was accompanied by great suffering and bloodshed, and that it took the form of a full divorce rather than a new modus vivendi.

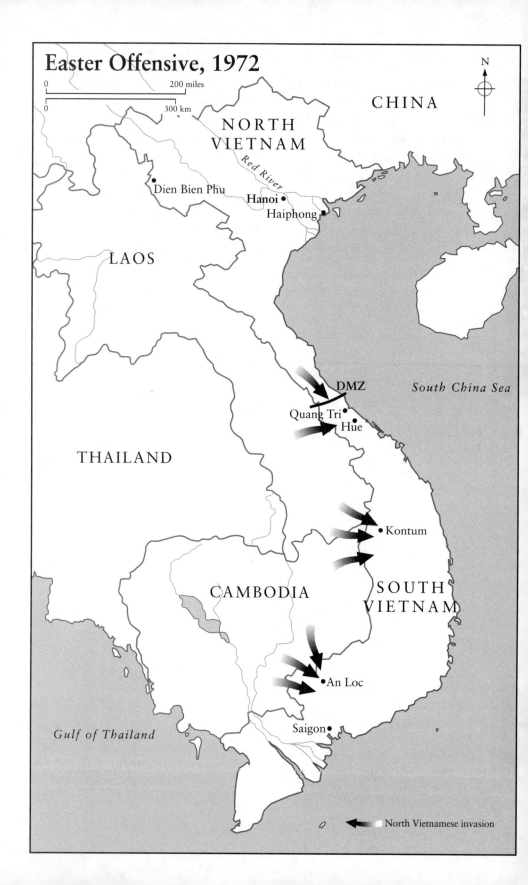

Easter Offensive, 1972

0   200 miles

0   300 km

N

CHINA

NORTH VIETNAM

Red River

Dien Bien Phu

Hanoi

Haiphong

LAOS

DMZ

South China Sea

Quang Tri

Hue

THAILAND

Kontum

CAMBODIA

SOUTH VIETNAM

Gulf of Thailand

An Loc

Saigon

North Vietnamese invasion

1. President Harry S. Truman meets General Douglas MacArthur as he arrives at Wake Island, 15 October 1950.

2. One of the most striking images of the stresses of command. In August 1950, in the early stages of the US intervention in Korea, Marine Capt. Francis 'Ike' Fenton has just lost half his company, run out of ammunition, is no longer in communication with his HQ, and has learnt that this company sergeant has been killed.

3. General René Cogny (*left*), Colonel Christian de Castries (*second left*) and General Henri Navarre (*centre*) confer over maps before the battle of Dien Bien Phu, 1954.

4. President Charles de Gaulle promoted Marcel Bigeard to General during a visit to Algeria, August 1959.

5. As the Cuban Missile Crisis began to wind down, President John F. Kennedy met with Marine Corps Commandant General David Shoup (*left*) and Chief of US Naval Operations, Admiral George Anderson (*centre*) at the White House, 29 October 1962. Both officers had wanted Kennedy to take a more aggressive stance during the crisis.

6. What many believe to be one of the most dangerous moments of the Crisis: Soviet submarine B-59 came to the surface to recharge its batteries after facing pressure from US Naval forces.

7. Israeli troops cross the Suez Canal, 16 October 1973.

8. General Ariel Sharon with Israeli Defence Minister Moshe Dayan on the western bank of the Suez Canal during the Yom Kippur War, October 1973. With his bandaged head, covering a cut caused by shrapnel, Sharon reinforced the image of a heroic general who led from the front.

9. President Yahya Kahn between Army Chief of Staff Lt. General Abdul Hamid Khan (*left*) and Air Force Chief of Staff Air Marshal Abdul Rahim Khan in East Pakistan before the crackdown on the Awami League, March 1971.

10. At 16:44 on 16 December 1971, General Jagit Singh Aurora for India and General Amir Niazi for Pakistan signed the Instrument of Surrender in Dacca.

11. Just before he announces his plans for the Vietnam War, President Richard Nixon confers with Gen. Creighton Abrams, US military commander in Vietnam, at the White House, 12 May 1969.

12. As they push back against the Easter Offensive, South Vietnamese troops watch smoke billowing skywards as B-52 bombs hit a North Vietnamese tank column, 11 April 1972.

13. The carrier HMS *Invincible*, escorted by Royal Navy warships, leaving Portsmouth on 5 April 1982, bound for the Falkland Islands.

14. After sinking the Argentine cruiser, *General Belgrano*, the Nuclear Attack Submarine HMS *Conqueror* returns home flying the Jolly Roger Flag, the traditional marker of a successful 'kill', 1982.

15. Iraqi vehicles caught by American air strikes fleeing Kuwait on the road to Basra, soon known as 'The Highway of Death', 27 February 1991. The carnage led President George H. W. Bush to call for a ceasefire.

16. Despite losing two wars, Saddam Hussein was re-elected in a referendum as President of Iraq in October 1999, gaining 99.96 percent of the votes.

6

Orders from on High: Responses to North Vietnam's 1972 Offensive

I do not pretend to have any knowledge or experience whatever in military matters. But I do know that military men generally are noted for the courage and loyalty of their character and notorious for the plodding mediocrity of their strategy and tactics.

President Richard Nixon, 15 May 1972[1]

While Truman and Kennedy were anxious to control field commanders to ensure that they did not aggravate an already difficult situation, President Richard Nixon sought control with a view to escalation. He pushed his own operational priorities against the preferences of the field commander. The tensions this created reflected not only the distinctive preferences of a commander-in-chief in Washington and the man on the spot, but also the complexity of the decision-making and command arrangements that had developed in the US national security establishment a quarter of a century into the Cold War. Authority to approve missions was widely distributed. Even when there was no intention to frustrate the president's wishes, and at times this was the case, the bureaucracy could be unyielding, illustrating what Andrew Bacevich describes as 'the dirty little secret of American civil-military relations . . . the commander in chief does not command the military establishment; he cajoles it, negotiates with it, and, as necessary, appeases it'.[2]

The American engagement in Vietnam stepped up after the French withdrawal, which followed the 1954 Geneva Conference. This left Vietnam divided into two. The Americans then worked to sustain the South in the face of a persistent communist insurgency. As the security situation worsened in the early 1960s, President Kennedy increased the number of military advisers in the South but resisted a more direct military commitment. He was also anxious for a southern government more deserving of American support. President Ngo Dinh Diem had a narrow political base, and a reputation for corrupt and dictatorial methods.

In the face of popular unrest in the summer of 1963, the idea took hold in Washington that only with a more inclusive and responsible government could the South survive. It tolerated plots against the South Vietnamese leadership. In November 1963, Diem was assassinated, a few weeks before Kennedy was also killed. But instead of better government in the capital Saigon, the result was more instability and a succession of coups. By 1965, the situation had become so bad that President Lyndon Johnson felt he had no choice but to approve a major American escalation. It began with an air campaign, but soon involved ground forces. From the start, Johnson was sceptical about whether this could bring about a military victory, yet felt bound by the political imperative of not 'losing' another state to communism. He was also anxious to keep the war contained, meaning that nothing should be done to bring China or the Soviet Union into the war. The memory of MacArthur's dash to the Yalu in 1950 still ran deep.

On 30 January 1968, when Johnson thought the corner might have been turned, a major offensive was launched by North Vietnam against the South, known as the Tet Offensive. A combined force of 80,000 North Vietnamese troops and Viet Cong guerrilla forces was directed against towns and cities. Although it did not achieve its objective of triggering a rebellion against the government in Saigon, it was nonetheless seen as a political success. The complacency of the American commanders in Vietnam was punctured. Johnson gave up on his presidency, and he ordered a bombing halt to allow peace talks to begin.

These political gains came at a heavy price for the communists. Territory seized was not held and their units were badly mauled in the fighting. The Viet Cong never fully recovered and began to lose its grip on the South's countryside. It took some four years for the Communist Party leadership, with Soviet and Chinese help, to rebuild its military strength. By the end of 1971, it was ready for another major military operation, hoping for even greater political effects than 1968. They intended to throw the bulk of their forces into a multi-pronged invasion of the South.

The immediate effect of the Easter Offensive that began on 30 March 1972 was once again to rattle the Americans and their South Vietnamese allies. This time, however, the North's advances were reversed. Immense pressure was put on both the South Vietnamese, largely responsible for ground operations, and the Americans, who contributed air power. As the South Vietnamese buckled, their inadequate command structures had to be revised. Meanwhile a tension developed on the American side between the local commanders, desperate to support their faltering Vietnamese allies, and the president, whose priority was to coerce the North Vietnamese government in Hanoi to make concessions in the Paris peace talks. The response to the North Vietnamese in the spring of 1972, therefore, illuminates not only the problems of aligning land and air operations when they are the responsibility of different countries, but also the consequences of a president getting directly involved in operational decisions and seeking to set military priorities.

A FRAGMENTED COMMAND

Richard Nixon won the 1968 presidential election in the aftermath of Tet. Nixon was a hawkish, divisive figure, but also well versed in foreign policy issues and pragmatic when necessary. The main plank of his new strategy, announced on 20 April 1969, was 'Vietnamization', strengthening the ability of the South Vietnamese army's front-line combat forces to cope without American support. Over the next three years, this resulted in a reduction of US force levels from 543,000 at the start of the administration to 69,000 by April 1972. The last combat troops were withdrawn on 12 August that year. In 1968, the United States was losing 300 men a week. By 1972, the numbers were closer to 30. This, along with the troop withdrawals and the announced end of conscription for 1973, reduced the impact of the war on the American people and the intensity of the discontent. Yet the war remained deeply unpopular in the United States. Nixon's decision, in April 1970, to extend it into Cambodia to interdict North Vietnamese supply lines caused mass protests, which alarmed the administration. Congress was controlled by the Democrats, who were loath to support any additional measures, including support to the South Vietnamese, and were looking for ways to cut back on all defence spending. This left the administration anxious to avoid measures that could appear inflammatory.

The declared objective was to get to a situation where South Vietnamese President Nguyen Van Thieu could cope without American forces. The Paris peace talks set in motion by Johnson in 1968 had failed to make progress. The United States had rejected North Vietnam's demand that Thieu resign as a precondition for an agreement, while North Vietnam dismissed the American demand that all communist forces leave the South. To add to the pressure on the North's leadership in Hanoi, Nixon played on Sino-Soviet rivalry. The two great communist powers had become more antagonistic towards each other than they were to the traditional capitalist enemy. Nixon wanted them both to accept that the prize of a developing accommodation with the United States must come at the expense of their support for Hanoi. Historic visits were scheduled for Nixon to Beijing in late February and to Moscow in late May 1972.

For a politician, Nixon was unusually socially awkward and wary of direct personal confrontation. Suspicious and resentful, he tended to harbour grudges, confiding only in a small group of courtiers-cum-advisers, trusted to execute his wishes. Dr Henry Kissinger, his national security advisor, was an unlikely member of this group. He was a Harvard professor and, until he was recruited by Nixon, more associated with the liberal wing of the Republican Party. Kissinger had been studying power politics for years. Alongside a talent for high-level diplomacy was one for bureaucratic intrigue, both pursued with great energy. He shared with his boss a penchant for secrecy to ensure the maximum freedom of manoeuvre. As well as working through official channels, he used his own back channels to any entity with whom he was trying to negotiate, including North Vietnam.

Both men had served during the Second World War, Nixon in the navy, where his duties were largely administrative, and Kissinger, as an émigré from Nazi Germany, in army intelligence. Kissinger's academic career, rooted in the study of nineteenth-century statecraft, had most recently focused on issues of nuclear strategy, encouraging a view of military force as a form of political signalling. Neither man had a feel for the inherent chaos of combat, often seeing as excuses the many factors that could frustrate the best planned operations, including bad weather. Both regularly complained about the military's ineptitude and lack of imagination. Kissinger's deputy for military affairs, General Alexander Haig, who had seen combat in Korea and commanded an infantry brigade in Vietnam, was able to counter some of the harsher judgements on his military colleagues. He came to play an influential role in managing relationships between Nixon and Kissinger on the one hand, and the military leadership on the other, and eventually became an independent source of military advice to Nixon.

The shared liking for secrecy, and suspicion that others in government were disloyal (Nixon's concern), incompetent (Kissinger's complaint), or simply following agendas of their own, led to a concentration of power in the National Security Council (NSC) staff. The State Department was largely marginalized. This was not an option for the Pentagon. The Department of Defense was responsible for the execution of policies, however much Nixon and Kissinger wished to limit its role in their formulation. The Secretary of Defense, Melvin Laird, had seen active service in the navy during the war, enjoyed his own independent political base as a former congressman, and was an accomplished bureaucratic infighter. He was also trying to manage a major transformation of the military at a time when the public mood encouraged reductions in their budgets.

Laird had a direct role in approving military operations, and, in this role, he had got off to a bad start with Nixon. In April 1969, North Korea downed a navy EC-121 reconnaissance aircraft over the Sea of Japan. Laird decided to suspend flights rather than risk further incidents, but he did not bother to tell the White House. Haig recalled that when trying to find out what had happened, he faced 'a Pentagon stone wall composed of delays, excuses, and obfuscation'. Nixon wanted to keep the flights going, despite the incident, yet it took three weeks before they resumed, leaving an impression of presidential indecisiveness.[3] 'Thanks to this incident,' Nixon observed in his memoir, 'I learned early in my administration that a President must keep a constant check not just on the way his orders are being followed, but on whether they are being followed at all.'[4]

Yet rather than deal with Laird directly, Nixon directed Kissinger to read him 'the riot act'. Haig doubted that the secretary would be brought to heel by 'mere messengers', and so it proved.[5] On 12 September 1969, Laird sent a memo to his senior officials observing that: 'From time to time requests bearing the ostensible imprimatur of the President will be transmitted from the White House to officials in the Department of Defense. No execution of such orders will be initiated until a check has been made with the Secretary of Defense or the Deputy Secretary of Defense.'[6]

All this left Nixon wary of Laird, whose judgement he rarely sought and often disparaged when it was offered. But, without Laird's active engagement, the White House was unable to get the Pentagon to implement its policies. When the levers of command were pulled, often little seemed to happen. It was as if the president and his closest aides were 'a film of dust on top of the table', with the vast, established bureaucracy underneath.[7] Nixon's frustration was understandable but his response – keeping tight control of decision-making in the White House – was never likely to encourage a creative response from those left in the dark.

This left Admiral Thomas Moorer, chairman of the Joint Chiefs of Staff, as the vital link between the Pentagon and the White House. He had not served in Vietnam, and as a naval aviator had a limited grasp of land warfare, certainly not enough to offer a critical commentary on reports coming up from the field. His position had also been compromised. When he became chairman in 1970, the military hierarchy had already come to the view that the secrecy surrounding the NSC under Kissinger was hampering their work. An enlisted man, Yeoman Charles Radford, was deputed to steal documents from the NSC and send them to the Pentagon. When some of these documents appeared in press columns, in December 1971, the NSC soon worked out that Radford was culpable, but were surprised to discover that his main client was the Chiefs.

Nixon was furious and wanted to prosecute, but was persuaded to use the incident as a lever over Moorer. The chairman was, as one Nixon aide put it, 'preshrunk'.[8] To improve his position, Moorer went out of his way to demonstrate his loyalty to the president. When he explained, on 1 February 1972, that his first duty had to be to Nixon, Laird complained 'no wonder I get scooped all the time, the White House knows more than I do.' Two days after this conversation, Nixon told him that 'this frank exchange between the Commander-in-Chief and the military forces must be in operation at all times', even though 'there were influences in the OSD [Office of the Secretary of Defense] that wanted to go in the other direction'. Nixon emphasized that he was the only one who had been elected.[9] Thereafter, Moorer and the White House maintained their own confidential channel of communications. Moorer found the role he was having to play uncomfortable, observing at one point that, while he understood that the president and Laird had different fish to fry, he did 'not particularly enjoy the fact that they both fry their fish in my pan!'[10]

For this to work, Moorer could not worry about getting a consensus with the other chiefs or indeed make much of an effort to keep them informed. Nor did the individual chiefs push hard. They were 'overworked and engrossed with individual service problems' and so were prone to agree with the 'simplest solution'. The Joint Staff, working for Moorer, was responsible for developing operational concepts. This was described by an officer involved at that time as 'a multiservice, overmanned bureaucracy, rife with service rivalries, and deeply mired in a labyrinth of tedious and time-consuming procedures'. In principle, the staff could challenge operational plans emanating from the field commander; in practice, there was a 'long-standing tradition' of not doing so.[11]

General Creighton Abrams, commander of the US Military Assistance Command, Vietnam (COMUSMACV), was responsible for operations within South Vietnam and just across the Demilitarized Zone (DMZ) into the North. A celebrated armoured commander from the Second World War, Abrams had been in position since 1968, having been deputy commander the previous year. At first his appointment was greeted with enthusiasm, as if he could find a route to victory that had eluded his predecessors. Journalists spoke of his 'flair', bringing 'candor, humor, self-effacement and common-sense skepticism' to the task, foreshadowing 'a significant change' in strategy.[12] But the demands and frustrations of the job had worn him down and blunted his edge. He was repairing a demoralized and often undisciplined American army, while at the same time running it down and building up South Vietnamese forces. To keep Washington off his back, he inclined to the military habit, which had caused so many problems earlier in the war, of sending back over-optimistic reports, assuring his superiors that all was well, so their input was not required.

His dutiful implementation of the Vietnamization project tied him closely to Laird, whose priority was to get the US commitment reduced as quickly as possible for both political and budgetary reasons. His closeness to Laird did not help him with Nixon and Kissinger. Both distrusted his judgement, and derided him as being tired, unimaginative and too fond of alcohol, none of which was wholly untrue. At one point, after the North's offensive had begun, they were sufficiently irritated that Kissinger asked Laird for the names of possible replacements. Laird ignored him. Abrams was due to step down at the end of June and become army chief of staff. Nixon opposed this, but Laird could insist. When appointed, he had obtained control over personnel matters, which he did not intend to relinquish. 'More wars have been lost through reluctance to change commanders than for any other reason,' observed Nixon at one point.[13] This was a debatable proposition; at any rate, unlike previous war presidents, he was unable to act upon it.

Over these critical months, the president therefore depended on a field commander in whom he had little confidence and who regularly argued back against his orders, especially when it came to the most effective use of air power, and an unsympathetic secretary of defense whom he felt unable to remove. Abrams reported to Admiral John McCain, Commander of Pacific Command (PACOM), based in Hawaii. McCain's son, also called John and a naval aviator, who would later before a senator and candidate for the presidency, was then languishing in a North Vietnamese prisoner-of-war camp, after being shot down in 1967.

McCain senior was responsible for any operations into the heartlands of North Vietnam. When President Johnson halted the air raids over the North, he had removed a potential source of friction between McCain and Abrams. They had, at any rate, developed a good working relationship, with their staff in regular touch with each other. Nonetheless, administrative control of air power was confusing, with different structures in place according to the location of the units, whether inside or outside Vietnam. Tactical air power was provided by the 7th Air Force, at the start of the year under the command of General John Lavelle. The United States Air Force (USAF) reporting line went back through the Pacific Air Forces under the command of General Lew Clay to the chief of staff, General John Ryan. As the offensive began there were active discussions between Abrams and McCain about whether there were ways of simplifying these command arrangements. At the start of the year, Abrams had begun to slim down his HQ from 1,844 to 1,058, and was looking for a way to employ the air element more effectively, but no new structure had yet been agreed.[14]

SOUTH VIETNAM'S COUP-PROOFED
CHAIN OF COMMAND

Abrams's ability to influence the course of land operations largely depended on his network of American advisers embedded with South Vietnamese forces. He also worked with the large embassy in Saigon, headed by Ambassador Ellsworth Bunker, who had been in post since 1967. Overall, political direction came from President Thieu. He had a long army career, starting with the French. In 1963, he was part of the coup that overthrew President Diem. Out of the subsequent instability, Thieu had eventually emerged as an elected president in 1967. He consolidated his position in a further, rigged election in 1971, after opposition figures had been arrested. None stood against him in the election. His deputy Air Marshal Nguyen Cao Ky was marginalized. All military promotions were geared to these domestic struggles and rendering the army as coup-proof as possible. Thieu was aware that demotions created grievances and that successful, popular generals might pose a threat. Little attention was paid to the consequences of these actions for military effectiveness. Few officers were promoted for superior battlefield performance; incompetent officers were left in place; little time was found for training programmes. Because of the military's continuing role in governance, a senior officer's time was taken up with administering his district, dealing with bureaucracies and budgets, as well as security.[15]

As an institution, the Army of the Republic of Vietnam (ARVN) was isolated from the population. As a result of Vietnamization, the ARVN was well equipped and numbered well over 1 million men, although less than 20 per cent of these were regular combat troops, and others were in regional and popular forces. There were good reasons to doubt its effectiveness. A RAND report for the American government in 1970 pointed to an officer corps with little understanding of rural life or their peasant soldiers, prone to factionalism and corruption because of meagre wages, and lacking in a professional ethos. With the relationship between military skill and promotion broken, morale was low and junior officers had little confidence in their generals.[16]

The ARVN was organized into four corps, each responsible for a military region (MR). There was also an elite strategic reserve, made up of airborne and marine units that could be deployed anywhere in the country to meet pressing challenges. The Airborne Division also had an occasional role as the president's praetorian guard, although, by virtue of being elite, it was also well placed to mount a coup as well as defend against one, which is why Thieu eventually broke it up.

The command arrangements reflected this fractured system. Thieu, following Diem, had separate chains of command for elite forces, so that if one turned against him, he could call on another as a counter. Officers did not stay in their commands for long, to prevent their acquiring a loyal following among their troops. One American study describes how the conflicted and duplicated chains of command, and the deliberate separation of major agencies from each other, hampered 'coordination, rapid staff action, and decision-making', and so inhibited operations.[17] Thieu did not want his generals to meet too often lest the conversation turn to the kind of plot that had overturned his predecessors.

The consequences of this mismanagement became apparent in late 1970 in an operation designed to demonstrate the progress the ARVN had made. The plan for Lam Son 719 involved three of its best divisions, including those from the strategic reserve, attacking the North's supply lines across the border in Laos, establishing a base that could be used to inflict damage for three months before the troops were withdrawn. The practicalities had not been thought through. This area of Laos was heavily defended. Because Congress had forbidden US troops to enter Cambodia or Laos, the ARVN would be operating on its own, on a larger scale than ever before attempted, and on unfamiliar terrain. The assets targeted were too vital for the North to give up without a serious fight.

The operation, which began in February 1971, was notionally under the command of I Corps commander Lieutenant General Hoang Xuan Lam, who enjoyed his position not because of any evident military talent but because he was close to Thieu. He was known as 'Bloody Hands' because of the consequences of his operational inadequacies and was unable to exercise authority over his divisional commanders: they obeyed orders only when it suited them. The airborne and armoured forces were under Lieutenant General Du Quoc Dong, another close ally of Thieu. Lieutenant General Le Nguyen Khang, commanding the marines, was an ally of Ky. He stayed in Saigon for Lam Son 719. The operation was beginning to develop some momentum when it suddenly halted. This was because Thieu had told Lam to halt once 3,000 casualties had been suffered. Thieu's meddling, which later included replacing one division by another, was apparently animated by his concern to ensure elite units were in shape to defend him if necessary.

As the North Vietnamese, benefiting from good intelligence about what was happening, rushed forces into position, Thieu changed his mind and ordered a rapid move forward. But, when the Americans urged him to back up his vulnerable forward units, he said he would only do that with US forces, which he knew was out of the question. As a result, the operation turned into a rout. Davidson blamed the failure on that 'old bugaboo, lack of unity of command'. Nobody took charge of Lam Son 719, and nobody really commanded it. It 'drifted along, blown about by the winds of Thieu's political needs'.[18] If anything, this understates the problem. One officer later described how Lam was ignored by Dong and Khang, who would only take orders from Saigon. 'They contested Lam's orders and directives at every opportunity.' In the face of this insubordination, Lam asked Thieu to back him up, but he failed to do so, because of their importance to the stability of the regime. Lam had performed poorly. He had taken time off every day for his regular game of tennis. Thieu realized that the best course might be to replace Lam. Unfortunately, the man designated to be his replacement was killed in a helicopter crash on his way to take to charge, so Lam stayed.[19]

AUTHORITY FOR AIR STRIKES

On 2 February 1972, the US National Security Council noted the weakness of the South's army, still at only 60 per cent of authorized strength and with a weak leadership. Laird argued against major reinforcements, not least because he did not want to 'indicate that we do not have much confidence in the Vietnamization program'. Nixon, however, was less confident and sensed the danger should the United States be caught short. In a move that made a significant difference to the later fighting, he ordered Laird to send another aircraft carrier to add to the three already in the vicinity of Vietnam. More B-52s would be deployed and 'all existing sortie restrictions for both B-52 and tactical air missions during the current dry season in South Vietnam' would be removed. He agreed that Abrams should have authority to strike SAM sites in North Vietnam and Laos. There was a crucial proviso. These strikes could only be exercised once the enemy offensive began and 'only after final clearance with the President'.[20]

Nixon would not agree to a conspicuous military initiative, likely to trigger protests at home and denunciations abroad. Commanders could step up action but only surreptitiously. One loophole was found in the terms of the bombing halt ordered by Johnson in October 1968. Unarmed reconnaissance aircraft could still fly over the North to check on whether quantities of men and supplies were being moved into the South. If they were attacked, then the United States could mount 'protective reaction strikes' against North Vietnamese air defences in retaliation. In November 1970, Nixon announced the rules of engagement:

> If our planes are fired upon, I will not only order that they return the fire, but I will order that the missile site be destroyed and that the military complex around that site which supports it also be destroyed by bombing.[21]

In July 1971, these were slightly amended. The American aircraft now had a radar warning receiver to alert the pilots if enemy radars were locking on. This moved the 'reaction' part forward, as they could strike before anti-aircraft guns began to fire or surface-to-air missiles (SAMs) were launched. The new rules allowed any air defence site to be attacked 'which fires at or is activated against US aircraft conducting missions over Laos or North Vietnam'.

As it was rare for the North's defences to ignore aircraft intruding into its airspace, missions could be conducted over choice targets. So long as enemy air defences played their part and locked on as expected to one of the incoming aircraft, an attack on the target was then permitted. Once air defences could be used as an excuse, missions against high-value targets could be prepared in advance. In this way, a rule designed to permit a defensive response to an attack on an unarmed plane was used to justify an aggressive approach to targets of choice by inviting enemy fire. They might still be called 'protective reaction' attacks, but they were not truly reactive and could be deemed pre-planned. One indicator that the North was planning something was air defences being strengthened on the Northern side along routes leading towards the South. Anything that could be done to degrade them prior to an invasion would make it easier to mount attacks on supply lines.

At an early December conference in Honolulu, it was agreed that 'field commanders must be more aggressive and more flexible in apply- ing the existing authorities for attacking NV air defenses.' As the deputy commander of the 7th Air Force put it: 'What they were saying if they [North Vietnamese] give you the slightest provocation, then you go ahead and zap them.' In late January 1972, after pleas from Moorer, the rules were changed again, to permit attacks against the more advanced air defence radars 'when MiGs were airborne and indicated hostile intent'.[22] All that was really left was situations in which MiGs were sta- tionary on the ground, which could not really be deemed to be showing hostile intent.

The extent to which these authorities were being stretched beyond their natural limits did not go unnoticed. In early March, a US senator received a letter from an enlisted man accusing Lavelle, the 7th Air Force commander, of false reporting, so that unprovoked attacks appeared as provoked. In response, the air force chief of staff, General John D. Ryan, sent his inspector general to Vietnam to investigate. Although Lavelle had been encouraged by higher officials to interpret the rule expansively, it was politically awkward to acknowledge it once the issue was out in the open. Lavelle was accused of having interpreted 'these protective reaction rules so liberally as to violate them in both letter and spirit'. He was recalled to Washington and relieved of his command on grounds of health. Commentators assumed that there was some truth in the complaint and that Lavelle had stretched 'his author- ity and [had done so] out of impatience with rules of engagement that he (and most other commanders) resented as hindering their operations and endangering the lives of their men'.[23] As the full story was pieced together, he was vindicated. He was acting as all his superiors had wanted him to act.[24]

Nixon and his senior commanders had been content for 'protective reaction' to mean 'preventive reaction', but they wished to avoid any public indication that the United States was moving to a more provoca- tive stance. The war was supposed to be being wound down, not ratcheted up. At an NSC meeting Nixon urged:

We don't want to do anything that is stupid. We don't want to do any- thing that unnecessarily exacerbates our public in the country, the ugly youth. We must realize that as support for what we're doing – or, shall we put it, as the level of criticism of what we do escalates, it encourages the enemy.[25]

A further consideration was his landmark summit with the Chinese leadership, scheduled for 17 February 1972. Developments in Vietnam must not act as a distraction. Nixon worried that, if Abrams was given 'blanket authority' to attack North Vietnamese SAMs, 'it'll get out'. Abrams was instructed not to 'put out extensive briefings with regard to our military activities from now' til we get back from China. Do it, but don't say it . . . he is not to build it up publicly for the duration. And, if it does get out, to the extent it does, he says it's a protective reaction strike.'[26] Laird sent Moorer a memo on 5 February authorizing air strikes on any target in the northern portion of the Demilitarized Zone (DMZ), separating North from South Vietnam, whenever Abrams 'determines the NV are using the area in preparation for an attack southward'. He added 'no public announcement of any kind will be made with regard to these actions.'[27]

On 8 March, with Nixon back from China, Abrams pressed for explicit authority to disrupt the North's preparations for an invasion, which now seemed imminent. He wanted to attack targets north of the DMZ, including aircraft, radars and SAMs, as well as supply lines. His request was supported by McCain and Moorer before reaching Laird. The secretary of defense remained concerned about the domestic reaction, and recommended something much milder, with attacks confined to border areas. Kissinger, worrying about the Chinese reaction, watered the proposals down further.

When the offensive came, on 30 March, Abrams requested that the past conditional authorizations now be activated urgently. On 1 April, McCain observed to Moorer:

> For the past two and one half months, General Abrams and I have consistently requested the authority to conduct those operations deemed necessary to preclude generation of the critical enemy threat which was predicted and now has developed. Many of the requests either have been denied, or approved with seriously limiting provisions.

Pointing to the worrying situation already apparent as the ARVN tried to cope, McCain argued that it was now 'imperative' to give the tactical commander more freedom of action. To deny this was to 'invite physical and eventual political occupation of a portion of South Vietnam by North Vietnamese force of arms.'[28] Having received this message and discussed it with Laird, Kissinger replied that Abrams had 'the authority to hit north of the 25 miles north of the DMZ', although a more expansive authority still needed Laird's sign-off, which took time to arrive. The next day, as Nixon complained about the military's lame response, Moorer reminded him that the White House had pushed back against Abrams's earlier requests. He noted in his diary that the president had 'apparently forgotten that on Saturday, 18 March, he had personally signed a paper turning down the authorities'.[29]

NORTH VIETNAM LAUNCHES ITS OFFENSIVE

The North Vietnamese leader, Le Duan, who had been first secretary of the North Vietnamese Communist Party since 1960, made it his business to avoid publicity, insisting that he was no more than a member of a collective leadership. He lacked the charisma of Ho Chi Minh and the military expertise of Giáp, and showed no interest in a cult of personality. What he had was an iron grip over the party apparatus, and a resolute determination to see the war through to the end. Vietnam's war strategy was his, executed with the help of his right-hand man, Le Duc Tho, who worked the back channel with Kissinger. Le Duan had come to power after the Geneva Accords as one of the 'Southern-firsters', who were not prepared simply to consolidate the party's position in the North but wanted to complete the country's unification under communist rule.[30]

His last major push, the 1968 Tet Offensive, shook the Americans and led to the policy of Vietnamization. Le Duan saw this as a mixed blessing. It reduced the South's military support, but politically made it harder to present the war as one against foreign intervention. After 1968, the Viet Cong was also too weak to sustain the insurgency in the South or even provide much support to the next offensive. This offensive would therefore need to take the form of a straightforward conventional invasion, intended to expose the fragility of South Vietnamese forces and the weakness of its government and hopefully lead to their collapse. The timing reflected the success of Nixon's strategy of cultivating the two communist giants – China and the Soviet Union – and playing them off against each other, to the detriment of North Vietnam. It would make more sense to wait until the American withdrawal had gone further, but Le Duan hoped that an invasion would remind his erstwhile allies that they should support their Vietnamese comrades. Also, this was an election year, and he assumed that Nixon would not want to take military risks. He was optimistic that by throwing all available forces into the invasion, the South would crumble and provide a 'total victory'.

The offensive began on 30 March with three North Vietnamese Army (NVA) divisions crossing the Demilitarized Zone (DMZ) against South Vietnam's Military Region 1 (MR1), backed by tanks and 130 mm heavy artillery. It was followed by attacks on MR3 on 4 April, and MR2 a week later. Eventually it involved 120,000 men, almost all the NVA then available. This was far removed from the guerrilla warfare of the 1960s. Hanoi called it the Nguyen Hue campaign, in honour of the eighteenth-century Vietnamese emperor who had liberated Vietnam from foreign rule (Chinese). The Americans called it the Easter Offensive, because of its timing.

Nixon claimed to want to avoid the sort of 'micromanagement' of operations for which Johnson had been much criticized. Yet, with news of the NVA's advances, and conscious of the high stakes for both his presidency and his grand strategy, he took on a more active role as commander-in-chief. 'I don't think anybody realizes how far I am prepared to go to save this,' he observed on 4 April. 'We have no option but to win this . . . whatever is necessary to stop this thing has to be done.'[31] He was also aware, in a way that the field commanders could not be, how much the invasion and the Paris talks were linked. Hanoi had abandoned the talks on 23 March. The invasion had begun a week later. Both sides were conscious of how their bargaining positions in any future talks might depend on how the latest stage of fighting played out.

Suspecting that Laird was editing reports from the front to hide how bad things were on the ground, Nixon emphasized to Moorer on 3 April: 'I am the commander in chief, and not the secretary of defense, is that clear?' He demanded, not unreasonably, a daily briefing to be received 'directly' and 'unsanitized'. He then turned his ire upon Abrams, asking whether he saw his job as being 'just do it by the numbers' or to 'try to see that this kind of offensive is stopped'? He wondered whether Abrams had been drinking too much and should be ordered to go 'on the wagon'.

This was followed by strategic advice to be passed to Abrams to concentrate air assets 'in areas that will provide shock treatment'.[32]

Moorer did his best to recast this in a form that could be passed on. That afternoon he sent McCain and Abrams a message:

> The President has clearly stated that he expects imaginative, aggressive and continuous attention to be focused on the current crisis throughout the unified command system. Request you advise me immediately of any additional authorities and resources which you require.[33]

When it came to Nixon's demand to concentrate air assets to shock the North, which in practice meant committing the entire B-52 strength to MR1, Moorer passed this on only as a suggestion. Abrams was still furious. He would resign if Washington was going to dictate his air allocations. He was 'sick and tired of the direction of the tactical effort in South Vietnam by people who did not know anything about it'. Moorer replied that he 'was sick and tired of all these calls and messages from across the river here too but that is the way life is'.[34] Moorer calmed everyone down, in the process irritating Nixon, who now suspected that the chairman was in league with Laird to obstruct his efforts.

Meanwhile, Nixon and Kissinger had taken advantage of the dismissal of General Lavelle as commander of the 7th Air Force (the unfairness of which Nixon clearly understood) by replacing him with General John Vogt, the current director of the Joint Staff, a man they both knew and trusted. He had even attended courses by Kissinger at Harvard. This was not the choice of the air force hierarchy or those in Saigon. Lavelle's deputy, General McNickle, had more relevant experience. Vogt had in fact proposed himself for the role. After telling Kissinger how distressed he was 'with the way the military and particularly the Air Force were handling the Vietnam situation', by not carrying out presidential orders or coming up with ideas of their own, he commented that he would 'give up his 4th star' (which turned out to be unnecessary) to be assigned to Vietnam to straighten everything out. Kissinger thought his assignment a good idea, as did Nixon.

On 6 April, before Vogt left for Saigon, he met Nixon to hear about how upset the president was with the military, and how he must 'bypass Abrams' and 'get things done'. Vogt was told that if the air force 'screws it up, as it has screwed up before ... this is probably the last time the Air Force is going to have a combat role'. At this point Vogt argued for a more expansive role than just air commander.[35] Nixon liked the idea of one man in charge of the entire air war in Southeast Asia, circumventing McCain and Abrams. Vogt saw the attraction of being able to direct operations without constantly responding to demands coming in from different directions. Neither Nixon nor Vogt was aware of prolonged discussions then under way in theatre to change the command structure. The timing for Vogt was therefore poor. When he reached Saigon, nothing had been done to elevate his position. 'So . . . I ran into the same problems that all my predecessors had run into. I had bosses all over the place.'[36] In addition to Ryan, Clay and Abrams, he now had to attend to the needs of the White House, while facing suspicion in Saigon precisely for that reason. Nonetheless, he became a reliable source of information, sending Moorer daily reports through air force channels. Moorer in turn passed Vogt's reports on to Kissinger.

Because US land forces had been severely depleted by March 1972, the big issues concerned what needed to be done to get the ARVN fighting back effectively and the role of US air power. At the start of this campaign, tactical air power was also less than half of what it had been up to Tet – 710 tactical aircraft in 1968 had fallen to just 329 in 1972, and carriers were down from six to just two, with marine air units back in Japan. Over the course of the campaign, the USAF doubled its forces, the marines moved back, and the navy sent four more carriers. This eased the debates over priorities, but during the first weeks of the campaign they were still intense. It was understood that most of the air support must be devoted to directly backing South Vietnamese forces. The issue was how much should be diverted to attacks on targets in the North, and especially around the two Northern cities of Hanoi and Haiphong.

Nixon's view was that this should be a high priority. On this, he was in a minority in his own government. In part, this stemmed from his doubts about the ability of the ARVN to deal with the North's offensive. His preferred alternative was to put heavy pressure on Hanoi to compel them to stop. One consideration was that helping the South cope with the onslaught would not be a game-changer. At best, there would be a return to the previous impasse. Only by convincing Hanoi that it must negotiate seriously could a political outcome be found that would give the South a chance over the longer term, when they could no longer rely on American forces getting them out of a fix. He also thought it important, out of regard for the US's position in the world, that it should still be willing and able to respond vigorously to aggressive acts. In addition to showing the North that 'we aren't screwing around',[37] Nixon wanted to demonstrate to Moscow and Beijing that he would still prosecute the war vigorously, despite his readiness to improve relations with them both. This was not simply a response to the exigencies of the situation. He had been looking for an excuse to coerce the North for some time, and did not intend to waste it now one had been provided.

The most sceptical voice at the senior levels of government was Laird's. He was worried that the sort of escalation Nixon had in mind carried political risks for uncertain military gain. He warned of more international and domestic uproar. Punitive strikes were best held in reserve as a threat rather than used up straight away.[38] He urged that the B-52s be 'used primarily against enemy forces in-country', where the outcome would be determined.[39] On this key point, Abrams and McCain strongly agreed. As for the politics, they had no objection in principle to bombing the North. The point about their current preferences was only that they reflected the state of the war. It might have made a lot of sense to have attacked targets in the North as it prepared the invasion (when they were denied the authority), but now, when the ARVN was struggling, the front line had to be the priority. Unsurprisingly, this was also the view of the South Vietnamese generals. One of them, Ly Tong Ba, remarked: 'If the B-52 strikes only strategic targets they can strike only Hanoi. From the 17th parallel south I say that the best strategic targets for the B-52s is right in front of my positions.'[40]

SOUTH VIETNAM'S ARMY STRUGGLES

Unfortunately, the ARVN's problems were not solely the result of inadequate air support, but had more to do with fundamental issues of command. General Hoang Xuan Lam was still the overall corps commander in MR1, just south of the DMZ. One of his key subordinates was General Vu Van Giai, in charge of the 3rd ARVN Division. From the start, there were concerns that they were not up to the challenge. On 1 April, Abrams reported back to Washington that the situation in

Quang Tri City, a provincial capital in MR1, was 'bad and it's going to get worse'. The next day, Camp Carroll, a key point on the defensive perimeter, fell. The American advisers blamed regimental leaders who were 'defeatist at best, communist agents at worst'. The latter point was not hyperbolic. One erstwhile regimental commander was soon broadcasting an appeal from Hanoi to the ARVN soldiers, urging them to defect.[41]

There were other sources of confusion. When a US EB-66 electronic intelligence aircraft was shot down, the effort to rescue a surviving crew member effectively precluded other air operations while it was ongoing. Even when assets were available, it was not always possible to identify vital targets in a timely manner. In MR1, although not in the other regions, the South Vietnamese were responsible for controlling tactical air. They were not yet used to the systems and failed to make the optimal allocations of aircraft to targets. There were not enough forward air controllers and the information they sent was often neither timely nor accurate.

At every level of command, there was American advice for the South Vietnamese, but it was not always taken. Some of the most intense interactions between the advisers and the ARVN took place at the lower levels. As one adviser noted, in his chain of command as in the ARVN's, the inclination was 'to say nothing and leave all the responsibility to those in contact with the enemy'. At that point, there was no choice. 'Our decisions were made of grave combat necessity.' Marine Lieutenant Colonel Gerald Turley found himself, after only a few days in theatre, appointed as de facto adviser to the 3rd ARVN division tactical operations centre. This was because his superior had left with General Giai to relocate his HQ at a safer place, leaving no orders about how to manage the battle still under way. At the command to move,

> ARVN staff officers and their enlisted men simply stood up, grabbed their personal gear, and left the bunker. Radios were left on and simply abandoned; maps and classified materials lay where last used and unguarded ... Order melted into chaos as frightened men, who had ceased to be soldiers, ran for the nearest vehicle.[42]

When NVA tanks approached a key bridge, Turley asked that it be destroyed, but this was vetoed because it would later be needed for a counter-attack. He then asked the ARVN to reinforce it. A brigade commander agreed after the divisional chief of staff refused. In the end, still acting against orders, he told a US infantry adviser to blow up the bridge. Which he did.[43]

Despite the early pressure, the position in MR1 at first stabilized. When the NVA attacked a marine firebase at Quang Tri City, on 9 April, it had to withdraw following serious resistance. With substantial reinforcements arriving, General Lam judged this to be an opportune moment for a counteroffensive. In what turned out to be a serious strategic error, he judged that he could turn the situation round in short order, even though his subordinates argued that his priority should be improving the defences around Quang Tri.

Lam's knowledge of the front was sketchy. He never visited to assess the situation for himself and worked from reports received by his HQ. As a commander, he was not good at either receiving or passing on unwelcome news. He checked his horoscope to identify the best hour for the offensive to begin. The man responsible for executing his plan, General Giai, in charge of the 3rd ARVN Division, was a more professional soldier, but he was given orders that were unrealistic. In one respect, he looked to be in a good position. More units were assigned to him and so he notionally commanded a powerful force: 23 battalions, organized into nine brigades, plus territorial forces. Unfortunately, he lacked the capacity to control them. The additional units did not arrive with any extra logistical and communications support, or any respect for Giai's authority. One reason he was handed the marine units was because Lam had fallen out with Khang, the Marine Corps commander, at Lam Son 719. It therefore suited Lam that Giai cope with Khang's insubordination. Unlike Lam, Giai was prepared to move among his subordinate commands to get their appreciation of situations. But with so many different units, he was on constant visits, which often meant that he was unavailable when decisions needed to be made.

For all these reasons, from the opening shots on 14 April, Giai struggled to get his offensive moving. From his subordinate commands came many reasons for not advancing when they were ordered to do so, from fatigue to complaints that not enough had been done with air support to clear a path for them. With increasing casualties, they hunkered down rather than attempting to break through the enemy lines. When the marine brigades and ranger groups received orders from 3rd Division, they sent them back to their own headquarters for approval before execution.[44] Adding to the confusion, Lam was issuing his own orders directly to brigade commanders.[45] Unsurprisingly, the offensive achieved little and petered out. Even with the backing of over 400 attack sorties from the air, the net gain was about two kilometres.

Soon the North resumed its offensive. The ARVN fought back with little cohesion or confidence. By 29 April, the defensive line had contracted. Abrams could not even employ naval gunfire in support, because enemy and friendly units were too close to each other. The forward air controllers had a similar problem, with a risk of collisions as the skies became crowded. On 30 April, Giai decided to withdraw from Quang Tri City. The breakdown in his relations with his senior staff meant that he drew up his evacuation plan in secrecy, undermining further whatever trust was left with his subordinates. When Lam was informed of the plan, he raised no objections; but when Thieu found out, he was adamant that there should be no withdrawal. The Paris peace talks were about to resume, and the loss of a provincial capital would not provide a propitious backdrop. Thieu, who had probably not been informed of the gravity of the situation, told Lam, and then Lam told Giai: units must hold their positions 'at all costs'.

The effect was the opposite to that intended, injecting confusion rather than resolve into the defence. It was too late for Giai to reverse course, but he felt obliged to try. Those who received the new orders were in no position to implement them, even if they wished to do so. What might have been an orderly retreat became disorderly, with vital equipment left behind. Eventually Giai escaped with US advisers on a helicopter, fired upon as they left. Fleeing civilians were battered by enemy artillery.[46] This was the first provincial capital to fall, but others now looked vulnerable. At Hue, disconsolate and disorganized troops appeared more as a menace to the local people than their protectors. An Loc, to the north of Saigon, was under siege.

The situation was desperate. A few days earlier Abrams had given Nixon a moderately upbeat account of the fighting, labelling the leadership in MR 1 as 'outstanding: aggressive and competent'.[47] If the ARVN had not 'stood and fought', then 'ten times the air power could not have done the job'. He added, 'they will continue to hold'. A week later, the prognosis was far less encouraging. Vogt called Moorer to tell him Quang Tri was 'about done'. On 1 May, the city was abandoned. Abrams reported that the problem was dissension among ARVN commanders:

I must report that as the pressure has mounted and the battle has become brutal, the senior military leadership has begun to bend and in some cases break. In adversity it is losing its will and cannot be depended upon to take the necessary measures to stand and fight.

Privately he fumed that the ARVN had not lost tanks because of enemy tanks knocking them out. 'The ARVN lost tanks because, *goddam it*, they abandoned them.'[48] The problem, Vogt told Moorer, was not that the 'friendlies' were 'under pressure but . . . because it's too hot'. ARVN soldiers broke and ran when they came under artillery fire. Close air support was difficult when no defensive line was being held. Vogt also reported on how US army officers had been too slow to realize how perilous the situation was.[49] Laird acknowledged the need for better leadership. The generals needed 'backbone', a 'kick up the ass'.[50]

On 2 May, Abrams and Bunker visited Thieu to deliver the kick. They told him that the ARVN had lost the will to fight and that total capitulation might occur at any moment, putting at risk 'all that had been accomplished over the last four years'. 'No amount of air support would be effective unless there is also the will on the part of ground forces.' This required effective field commanders. It says a lot for Kissinger's lack of interest in the land war that when he read Bunker's report of the meeting he was appalled. 'It is a self-serving egg-sucking, panicky lecture by Abrams. Does he think Thieu needs instruction on the gravity of his situation? He cannot make up now for his errors of the past two years.' He told Bunker to reassure Thieu of US support.[51]

In this case, Abrams was right and Thieu got the message. When Bunker returned with the message of fulsome support the next day, as demanded by Kissinger, Thieu acknowledged 'serious defects in leadership, organization and planning' and outlined the changes he had agreed the previous evening with his senior commanders.[52] General Minh, in charge of MR3, was too close to Thieu to be moved, although he was told 'he must act decisively and kill the enemy', advice that one might not normally expect to give to a top commander at this stage in a war. General Dzu of MR2 was to be removed once a replacement was found, although this turned out to be difficult. Khang was removed from his command of the Marine Division. The big change was that Lam was dismissed and replaced by General Ngo Quang Truong, who came from the elite Airborne Division and had been in charge of MR4. The hapless

General Giai, who had done what he could, was not only removed but disgraced by Thieu, ending up in prison, where he remained until the North took Saigon in 1975.

Truong was unique in his effectiveness. He had avoided politics. His division had been engaged in an area close to the North Vietnamese border, where some competence was required, which was well away from the intrigues of Saigon. He had anticipated his move to MR1, preparing a small staff to work with him. They immediately flew to Hue, where his presence, as the man who had secured the city during the 1968 Tet Offensive, was a boost to morale. At Bunker's urging, Thieu made his own visit to demonstrate his commitment to the town's defence. Soon Truong had restructured his corps' command and control.

> A Forward Headquarters for I Corps was established at Hue. It was staffed by senior officers who had solid military backgrounds, both in the field and in staff work, a rare assemblage of talents from all three services and service branches. I had wanted to make sure that they knew how to use sensibly and coordinate effectively all corps combat components and supporting units in a conventional warfare environment.

According to his account, he restored confidence among combat units by reassuring them 'that from now on they would be directed, supported and cared for in a correct manner, while also warning that deserters would be shot'.[53]

By 8 May, he had organized the defence and brought in reinforcements. The Northern forces, optimistic after their recent gains, were advancing towards Hue. But their lines of supply were becoming stretched and this provided opportunities for air strikes, while Truong began to build up confidence among his subordinate commanders by getting them to engage in limited operations. These also served to keep the NVA units off-balance and stall their offensive. It took weeks before they withdrew back across the DMZ, but this was the point where the tide began to turn.

NIXON ORDERS AIR STRIKES AGAINST THE NORTH

The many tense moments from the start of the invasion until the point where the tide of battle began to turn explain the urgency behind the pleas by Abrams and McCain to keep the air effort focused on what was going on inside South Vietnam, while Nixon insisted that some of the air effort should be diverted to punitive attacks against targets in the North.

Nixon first demanded strikes against the North on 6 April. Two days later, on 8 April, Moorer reported to Abrams and McCain that, because nothing had happened, 'the President was extremely out of patience with me this morning'. He told them that they would soon receive a directive to conduct a B-52 bombing attack on North Vietnam. This would have political as well as military objectives. The president wished to send 'a clear message that he intends to use whatever force is necessary in light of this flagrant invasion'. Nixon had observed that his commanders had asked for the authority to strike well to the north of the DMZ, yet when given it they just continued with routine operations.

> I cannot impress upon you too strongly how intensely involved the President is in this operation, how determined he is that the enemy does not succeed in their objectives, and how forthcoming he is when presented with requests for authorities and additional resources – however, he does expect immediate action and forceful response.[54]

Whatever the political rationale, the timing looked poor to Abrams. He was receiving numerous requests for air support from hard-pressed ARVN units. 'The risks remain unchanged and in my view are grave.'[55] Vogt reported Abrams's reluctance to 'even release carriers to any operations north of the DMZ unless they are immediately associated with the battle front'. Every time a corps commander was called, Vogt noted, 'they [the commanders] tell him they are hanging on because of the tacair [tactical air], send more.'[56] Supported by McCain and President Thieu, Abrams urged delay:

> The full weight of the B-52 effort should be applied against the enemy forces and their logistics that are already deployed out of NVN and are in position in SVN and the immediate approaches thereto.[57]

Nixon, irritated that he was being set up for blame if the communists made progress, decided to cancel the strike. But it was late in the day. The attacking force was an hour from Haiphong. Moorer happened to be with Laird when the order came through to cancel. He decided that it had arrived too late, as the B-52s would just end up jettisoning their bombs, and the crews would lose confidence in their commanders.

These 'strategic' B-52 attacks of 10 April therefore went ahead. The main lesson to be drawn was that an enormous effort was required to attack heavily defended targets in the North, potentially for very little gain. The strike force involved two groups, each with 6 B-52s. To protect them there were 8 aircraft to counter MiGs, another 10 to suppress SAM sites and 4 to jam the North's radars. Fifteen minutes before the B-52s arrived over their targets 20 F-4s laid a chaff corridor to confuse the enemy's fire-control radars. From offshore, the navy provided 10 more aircraft – 4 fighters, 4 to suppress SAMs and 2 jammers. All the aircraft returned safely, but the 'disappointing' result was that all this effort, involving 70 aircraft, led merely to the destruction of 50 tons of fuel and some damage to rail lines and cars. These meagre results reinforced those who felt for the moment that all resources should be devoted to the immediate demands of the land battle.[58]

On 14 April, once again the White House ordered McCain to prepare for a heavy attack against Haiphong. Vogt warned Moorer that 'Abrams was preparing a message requesting cancellation of the strikes in NVN', although the actual message, soon received, was to delay rather than cancel. Nixon's reaction, as described, was that he 'practically went into orbit' (Kissinger) or was driven 'up the bulkhead' (Haig). It confirmed Nixon's 'suspicions that Abrams is receiving instructions from Laird contrary to the instructions issued by the President'.

Moorer went back to remind McCain and Abrams that, while the proposed strikes might not help with the land battle, there were other high-level considerations in play. These were about signalling determination and resolve, especially in the light of the active diplomacy then under way with the Soviet Union.[59] On 16 April, 20 B-52s attacked Haiphong's oil storage facilities, this time with more success. Although four Soviet ships were hit in Haiphong harbour, it was noted that Moscow did not withdraw an invitation to Kissinger to discuss the escalation. The Soviet Union would not put pressure on Hanoi, but it would help to get negotiations under way. The Paris talks would start again. Kissinger would meet his interlocutor, Le Duc Tho, on 2 May.

Kissinger sent Haig to explain to Abrams the importance of the northern air campaign as part 'of a progressive and heavy escalation being made for political purposes in an effort to negotiate the war', and to remind him that it was the president that had directed the augmentation of US forces in Indochina amounting to three aircraft carriers, sixteen destroyers, two cruisers, three air force tactical squadrons, and three marine tactical squadrons, without receiving a single request from Abrams. Yet however many forces had been sent, Abrams seemed to need them all for in-country attacks. Haig reported back that Abrams would divert 'whatever is necessary to support the diplomatic hand'.[60]

On 26 April, anxious to convey the impression that his Vietnam policy was on an even course and encouraged by an over-optimistic situation report from Abrams, Nixon informed the American people that there would be a further 20,000-man withdrawal of US forces over the next two months. So long as the US continued to 'provide air and sea support, the enemy will fail'.[61] The timing was unfortunate. The next day the Northern army began its drive to take Quang Tri City. For Abrams, this was no time to divert resources away from the battle at hand. Time was running out for attacks on the Hanoi–Haiphong complex. For Nixon, the focus had to shift.

Nixon ended April as he had begun, pushing for the 'absolute maximum number of sorties' to be flown. 'There are to be no excuses and there is no appeal.'[62] While this was a general exhortation without any particular target set in mind, he remained fixated on striking Hanoi and Haiphong. The earlier strikes in April, however limited, had set the precedents. 'In effect,' he wrote to Kissinger, 'we have crossed the Rubicon and now we must win – not just a temporary respite from this battle, but if possible, tip the balance in favor of the South Vietnamese for battles to come when we no longer will be able to help them with major air strikes.' Kissinger was told to deliver the following warning to Hanoi:

> In a nutshell you should tell them that they have violated all understandings, they [have] stepped up the war, they have refused to negotiate seriously. As a result, the President has had enough and now you have only one message to give them – Settle or else![63]

When Kissinger met Le Duc Tho at the start of May, there was only more intransigence. From Hanoi's perspective, the military situation did not create any imperatives for new concessions. Nixon felt that he dare not relax the pressure. The Moscow summit with President Brezhnev later in the month might be put at risk by more attacks. But if the summit went ahead despite the attacks, that might add to the pressure. Hanoi would see that Soviet support was conditional. In addition, Nixon did not want to wait much longer. Soon the presidential election campaign would limit his options. Nixon told Kissinger he wanted to 'belt the hell out of them' to demonstrate that the United States was not going to accept meekly the loss of the South and to jolt the North into more concessions in Paris. Moorer was now asked by the White House to prepare B-52 strikes against the North for 5 May. Haig explained that Abrams would be told 'that, by God, he's going to have to count on losing those assets'.[64]

Once again Abrams resisted. Once again, he did so by describing a dire situation, with enemy divisions on the move and more provincial capitals to be defended. Vital command changes had been made, but were only just starting to take effect. Thieu had sent him specific and urgent requests for air support. 'We must stay with them at this critical time and apply the air power where the immediate effect is greatest.' If the operation must go ahead ('for reasons not known to us here'), it would best undertaken by the navy from its carriers, 'leaving the B-52 and 7AF effort for in-country use'. Later in the day, McCain wrote to Moorer confirming that he was 'in full agreement'.[65]

Kissinger sent an almost routine response to Bunker. The president was now 'nearing the end of his patience' with Abrams and his inability to appreciate that the United States was 'playing a more complex game with the Soviets involving matters which extend far beyond the battle in Vietnam crucial as it is'. Once again, he was to be reminded that he only had the air assets at all because the president had decided to send all the extra capabilities. The main purpose of the message was to get Bunker to act as the conduit to Abrams for the president's thinking. He should only respond to messages that came through this direct route: 'any contrary signals, no matter what the source, are inaccurate.' Yet, without any more fuss, Abrams should be told that he had got his way. 'In the interim, the President has, in the light of General Abrams' official recommendation, deferred action on the 48-hour Hanoi/ Haiphong strikes.'[66]

There are two significant aspects to this message. First, while Kissinger might have accurately portrayed how Nixon would have reacted to the messages from Abrams and McCain, the president had not actually seen them. Kissinger played them down when he met Nixon ('We've heard from Abrams, incidentally'). He blamed 'Laird, that bastard' for 'crossed signals', suggesting to Abrams that Nixon would actually welcome an excuse not to bomb Hanoi and Haiphong. Nixon accepted this ('Laird is so tricky that he's capable of that'), leading to an odd discussion about Laird's motives, including potential political ambitions.[67] The second aspect is that it is not actually a concession to Abrams to defer the bombing. By the time his message was received, Kissinger and Nixon were already working on a much more ambitious plan.

HITTING HANOI AND HAIPHONG

Nixon's new plan was developed largely in conversation with Kissinger and Moorer, who had to get the work done to prepare the options. When Moorer met with Nixon early evening on 4 May he was greeted by: 'Admiral, what I am going to say to you now is in total confidence of the relationship with the Commander-in-Chief and the Chairman of the Chiefs of Staff. Nothing is to go to the Secretary. Nothing is to go to Vietnam. Is that clear?'[68]

Neither the State Department nor the Pentagon was involved in the process. The planning for what became Operation Linebacker was undertaken by the Joint Chiefs staff, without any reference to McCain and Abrams, and without the Chiefs meeting to discuss the options. Laird was only told as late as possible what was going to happen, though he would be needed to approve the orders. Only once the decision was close to being announced, on 8 May, was the National Security Council convened. Nor was Thieu to be let into the secret until hours before the presidential announcement, scheduled for 8 May.

The aim of such a massive assault was coercive: to put maximum pressure on Hanoi to agree a negotiating position that the United States could accept. Nixon told Kissinger:

> We're going to cream them, now that's what we're gonna do. This isn't in anger or anything – this old thing that I'm petulant and everything, that's bullshit ... warn them that no point in waiting out until after election because he'd still be in power and I really will go wild.

He was not prepared to accept restraints if that diminished the effects. If some Soviet ships were struck in Haiphong harbour that would be unfortunate. If some bombs 'slopped over' and hit civilians, that would be 'too bad'.[69]

The new approach involved a shift of focus, putting pressure on Hanoi by cutting it off from all supplies, including those coming from the sea. In addition to strikes against its land routes, the initial idea was to impose a blockade. The mining of Haiphong and other harbours was then added. Here they could take advantage of an 'off-the-shelf' plan, left over from the Johnson years. As late as 6 May, when Kissinger met Moorer, the plan was to mine all North Vietnamese ports, blockade the entire coast of North Vietnam, and strike military and military-related targets throughout North Vietnam, save for a 25-kilometre restricted barrier south of North Vietnam's border with communist China. An opportunity would be provided for shipping to depart Haiphong and other North Vietnamese ports before the mines would be activated. The blockade element of the plan was then dropped. Kissinger preferred mining because, perhaps with the Cuban experience in mind, it avoided 'the repeated confrontations of a blockade enforced by intercepting ships'.[70]

The objective, as Kissinger explained to Bunker, was to cut off supplies coming by sea but also 'to interdict internal DRV logistics routes and above all, through early and massive application of firepower against rail lines, to preclude or at least severely complicate development of rail from China as a compensating source of supply'.

> To put it in the bluntest terms, we are not interested in half-measures; we want to demonstrate to Hanoi that we really mean business; and we want to strike in a fashion that maximizes their difficulties in sorting out what their priorities should be in responding to these retaliatory actions.
>
> There should be no question in either your or General Abrams' mind that we want to devote the necessary assets to this action. If in your judgment the assets required for operations in the North lead you to conclude that more air is needed to meet tactical exigencies in the South, then that air should be promptly requested and we will get it to you.
>
> [We] 'cannot overemphasize importance of point that steps we plan to take must be accompanied by absolutely maximum GVN effort in days and weeks ahead to turn back NVA offensive. With the dramatic new U.S. measures contemplated we believe this can be accomplished.'[71]

On 8 May 1972, at 21.00, Nixon addressed the nation in a televised speech on the mining of Haiphong harbour and other North

Vietnamese ports. After describing the chosen course of action, he said that it would be stopped when all American prisoners of war were returned and there was 'an internationally supervised cease-fire through-out Indochina'. Once that was achieved all American forces would be withdrawn from Vietnam 'within four months'.[72] As Nixon was escalat-ing his military means there was no corresponding escalation in his political objectives. He required concessions from Hanoi but not capitulation.

As he delivered the address, US Navy A-6 and A-7 aircraft sowed Haiphong harbour with mines. They were set with a 72-hour delay, allowing foreign shipping a chance to leave the port. The operation denied an estimated nearly two-thirds of foreign aid to the North. The original Linebacker directive stated:

> It is essential that strike forces exercise care in weapons selection to minimize civilian casualties and avoid third country shipping, known or suspected PW [Prisoner of War] camps, hospitals, and religious shrines.

There was still to be a Chinese buffer zone, although only 15 miles from the border. At first there were also 10-mile restricted zones around Hanoi and Haiphong but these were later removed. Only targets inside either the restricted or buffer zones required high-level approval.

Although Abrams found out about Linebacker only late in the day, he raised no objections. Unlike Laird, he had never been opposed to the strikes against the North on political grounds. His concerns were purely operational, especially while the situation on the ground was desperate. Yet now he was more confident. He had already got some of the command changes he wanted from Thieu, and he could use this major escalation to get more. When Bunker and Abrams met Thieu to deliver the president's message, they stressed the need to deal with the 'failures of leadership and organization' in the Viet-namese air force:

> the time has come when the most competent officers who can lead and command the loyalty and allegiance of their units must be placed in charge regardless of any considerations, political or other. Half measures or compromises will no longer suffice.[73]

There were also already signs that the North's offensive was running out of steam, owing to a combination of better commanders in the

South and fatigue, with some poor decision-making by the North's commanders.

In addition, there was no longer great competition for air assets. In March 1972, the USAF had 76 fighter and attack aircraft. There were two carriers with 96 aircraft at sea. Another 114 jets were based in Thailand. By the end of May, the numbers of fighter aircraft had more than doubled, and there were now 171 B-52s based in Guam and Thailand, up from 83. Another four carriers had arrived on the scene. The number of sorties flown steadily rose: 4,237 in March, 17,161 in April and 18,444 in May.[74] Abrams had been promised that more assets would be made available should there be 'tactical exigencies' in the South.

Despite much discussion about the advantages of a unified command system for the air war, targeting was still divided between the navy's carriers and 7th Air Force HQ, with limited coordination between the two.[75] In many ways the USAF struggled more with the demands of the campaign. Their procedures tended to be more cumbersome, still requiring some 80 aircraft to mount their raids. They could get frustrated by the weather or diverted by the demands of the continuing land battles in the South, and they were not as well prepared as the navy aircraft for dogfights with the North Vietnamese MiG aircraft. The navy were able to operate with greater flexibility, attacking multiple targets in a single day.

Although there was a dramatic shift in the allocations, with half of the assets being devoted to the North, rather than 13 per cent as before, new types of 'precision-guided munitions' (PGMs), such as the Paveway laser guided bomb and the Walleye optically guided bomb, changed the way the air campaign could be waged.[76] It was possible to think in terms of targets destroyed per mission rather than number of missions needed to destroy one target. This 'smart' ordnance had been available since the late 1960s, but this was the first opportunity for serious operational use, against bridges, rail yards, power plants and industrial targets. For Vogt, PGMs influenced his approach to Linebacker. The 'dumb' bombs used in abundance over both South and North Vietnam risked substantial civilian casualties, which, if they occurred too often, could put certain targets off limits.[77]

Vogt's problem in relying on PGMs was that they were expensive and still scarce. He had only six of the Pave Knife laser guidance pods that ensured that the bombs reached the right targets. So, each strike involved few aircraft and weapons directly, but an enormous support package when they went against defended areas. The air force ended up conducting one mission a day, but they did so with great accuracy. Up to this point, the destruction of specific targets would have been largely a matter of luck. To destroy a single bridge, hundreds of sorties would be required with no guarantee of success. Knowing their importance, the North Vietnamese had made bridges 'flak-traps for aircraft'. Now, a vital target could be taken out with just a few sorties, even in highly populated areas.[78] The new 'smart' laser-guided bomb could be dropped from above conventional anti-aircraft fire, without having to dive through it in the hope of scoring a hit with a dumb bomb.

The point was made quickly on 10 May, when the Doumer Bridge, which was a mile long and a key part of the supply route from China to Vietnam, was badly damaged, and then finished off the next day. For Abrams, the advantage of Vogt's approach was that he did not need the B-52s, which could be used instead to attack the NVA in the South. The navy's concept was different. It involved a deck load of aircraft (about 30) from a carrier putting the maximum ordnance on high-value targets with a minimum of time and risk. With three carriers on station, the navy could mount two or three strikes a day, largely against targets in coastal areas. This meant that the navy contributed more than 60 per cent of total sorties.

The introduction of PGMs was an important innovation, eventually transformational in its effects on warfare, and was remarked upon at the time. Yet it was not discussed at the high-level meetings with Nixon and Kissinger. In general, they showed little interest in operational factors, often seeing them as excuses for inaction. The continual focus on the North's air defences appeared a distraction. A brief conversation between Kissinger and Moorer, after Linebacker was approved, was revealing. Do not 'fritter our stuff away on secondary targets', Kissinger told the chairman. 'No air defense except minimum necessary.' The target should be 'railroad marshalling yard outside Hanoi as quickly as possible' to give Hanoi a jolt. Moorer explained that Vogt and Abrams wanted to go with 'smart weapons' for the 'road highway bridge [Doumer] that goes into Hanoi' and that this could be done faster than immediate use of B-52s. Kissinger did not object, but it appears that this was the first he had heard about Vogt's operational concept.[79]

The value of PGMs was that they allowed specific targets to be taken out with far greater efficiency than before with far less collateral damage. Nixon saw the use of force in more psychological terms. Thus, when the air force resisted sending more B-52s to Vietnam – because they were committed to nuclear deterrence, the models available had smaller bomb loads than later models, and the air force was content with its smart weapons – Nixon was perturbed. With Kissinger, he took the view that the sheer weight of ordnance being dropped on the North was important in itself, and they were irritated with the air force for mounting so few sorties conducted at such high altitudes. Nixon believed that 'the psychological effect of having 100 more B-52s on the line in Vietnam would be enormous'. On 19 May, he described himself

> thoroughly disgusted with the consistent failure to carry out orders that I have given over the past three and a half years, and particularly in the past critical eight weeks, with regard to Vietnam.

He was less interested in the military effects of the bombing than its political effects.

The Pentagon, he complained, had given him the 'run around' and sometimes 'deliberate sabotage'. If there was any further insubordination, he would be looking for the resignation of the man responsible and not 'the one down the line in the woodwork'. The commanders had been playing 'how not to lose' for so long that they could not bring themselves to start playing 'how to win'. He had therefore decided that the air force should have no command role in the strikes against the Hanoi–Haiphong area. 'The orders will be given directly from a Naval commander whom I will select.' He asked that his 'utter disgust' be conveyed to Moorer for him to pass on to the Chiefs, and also to Abrams and Bunker in the field. 'It is time for these people either to shape up or get out.'[80]

Yet the same day he received optimistic reports from Abrams. Ten days earlier the fear was that An Loc would soon fall and that battles for Hue and Kontum would be raging. Instead, the enemy was in difficulty in each area.[81] The accuracy of the air campaign and the mining of Haiphong harbour had added to Hanoi's problems, as their supply chains were disrupted, affecting its ability to support its troops in the South and also supply its own population. Moreover, Hanoi could not but fail to notice the priority given by both Moscow and Beijing to their relations with the United States. If anything, Moscow appeared to resent the way the North had put them on the spot. Soon Hanoi was complaining about the tendencies of its patrons to compromise: 'The revolution is a path strewn with fragrant flowers. Opportunism is a fetid quagmire.'[82]

CONCLUSION:
DEMANDING ESCALATION

When the battle was over, the North Vietnamese acknowledged that their plan had been too ambitious, so that their forces had become overextended. It had been a mistake to fight on three fronts at once rather than concentrate with overwhelming force at one spot. They had not mastered the special demands of conventional warfare in the face of a powerful air force.[83] Eventually, in August, they accepted that a better strategy might be to negotiate to get a complete American withdrawal and then deal with Thieu directly. The Communist Party politburo voted in favour of negotiation, and by September the invasion had petered out. Nixon got concessions from Hanoi and almost a deal by the end of the year. In the event, it took Linebacker 2, another round of heavy bombing of Hanoi in late December 1972 (this time with B-52s) to conclude the agreement, although what was signed after that was not so different from what had been agreed just before, or even what could probably have been agreed in 1969. Hanoi knew that it would be months, even years, before they would be ready to launch another attack. Before that time, it wanted American air power out of the way. This, more than anything else, was the reason why there was a readiness to compromise in the negotiations. Their only bottom line was that they should not be prevented from continuing the struggle in the future, and they were not.

This was a tactical victory for the South. Out of around 50,000 casualties, some 11,000 men were killed. Around 300 Americans were also killed. The NVA casualties were far higher – Hastings suggests double those of the South, along with 250 tanks and most of their heavy artillery. Some 25,000 civilians perished, and the bombing, along with the naval gunfire and artillery, left towns and cities battered and the people exhausted.[84] The fighting had been, as Abrams acknowledged, extraordinarily 'brutal'. It would take time before another communist offensive would be ready, but, when it came three years later, the ARVN lacked American support and was unable to cope.

Talmadge used the ARVN as an example of the problems authoritarian regimes face in battle because of 'coup-proofing'. North Vietnam's regime was even more authoritarian, and there were power struggles within the leadership, but there was no threat of a military coup. And while Communist Party commissars were present in all combat units, and ensured conformity to the party line, they did not interfere in combat decision-making. The North's army was altogether more professional, in its training as well as command structures, than that of the South.[85]

The ARVN operational failings evident during the first weeks of the Easter Offensive were not easy to rectify, and certainly not by empowering a few good generals. Senior commanders were still too far away from the front lines to appreciate the state of the fighting, too ready to give orders that made little sense in the circumstances, and unconvincing when trying to persuade their men to fight hard and take risks. Against American advice, Thieu insisted that no territory should be ceded. The period after early May showed that improved command structures and better commanders could make a difference to the ARVN's performance. But it was also the case that US air support, normally available and so effective, had become a prop on which the ARVN tactical commanders had come to rely, even to the point of not bothering to employ their own supporting weapons.[86] Abrams complained at one point about 'a kind of psychosis' among the ARVN commanders, who had 'an idea that you should use the air to kill *all* of the enemy. When I say *all* I mean the *last goddam one*, and *then* he will advance.' On 4 May, he worried that, unlike their American advisers, the Vietnamese lacked a 'can do' attitude.[87] Without these essential elements, the South would have fallen in 1972 and did fall in 1975.

As a case study in supreme command, Nixon's performance illustrated the difficulties of a political 'commander-in-chief' seeking to impose his will on the course of a battle, with field commanders who do not share his priorities. His most important decision was taken in February, when he directed that more carriers and aircraft should be sent to Southeast Asia. Without those extra capabilities, the position on the ground in April would have been even more desperate and Abrams would have been even more reluctant to spare any air assets to attack targets in the North. Nixon showed great impatience with his field commanders and was rightly wary of a military tendency to send routinely positive reports. But other than his conversation with Vogt before he left for Saigon, Nixon did not speak to them directly, and he interpreted their arguments as excuses to hide their indolence and lack of imagination, or as proxies for what he assumed to be Laird's desire to sabotage his strategy.

Despite being president, Nixon struggled with the internal politics of his own administration, largely because Laird had ensured that he kept control of appointments and insisted on his role in the chain of command. Nixon had failed to convince others of his strategy, not least because he held its development tight and therefore struggled to explain what would be gained politically by diverting desperately needed air assets to attacks on Hanoi. Moorer worked hard keeping the peace between Nixon and Abrams, including by not revealing what the president had been saying in private. Eventually, as the situation in the South stabilized, Nixon was able to follow a punitive strategy and this succeeded in getting Hanoi back to negotiations. Whatever resulted from the negotiations, the anti-war sentiment in the United States, as reflected in Congress, meant that Saigon would be expected to manage without American air power in the future. By the time of the North's next offensive in 1975, Nixon was gone because of the Watergate scandal, and the Americans had lost completely whatever tolerance they had for the Vietnam War.

7

Command in Theatre:
The Falklands Campaign

[C]ommand centres become like islands occupied by close asso-ciates. Within each such centre, the combination of isolation, intensity of work, abundant adrenalin and stress, and the com-radeship such pressures can generate, may create insular states of corporate mind.

Admiral Sir Sandy Woodward[1]

On 2 April 1982, Argentine forces occupied the territory that Argentin-ians know as the Islas Malvinas and the British call the Falkland Islands. The British government in London was caught off guard. This was a dispute of long standing. The historic claims to discovery and owner-ship went back to previous centuries, and the specific Argentine grievance to January 1833, when it was claimed the British had illegally seized their territory. There had been negotiations to resolve the dispute in 1968, but, after parliamentary objections, the British government promised not to transfer sovereignty to Argentina against the wishes of the islanders. Thereafter, there were regular discussions between Argen-tina and the United Kingdom on the topic. An attempt by Margaret Thatcher's government to find a way through the dispute in 1980 ended with more parliamentary fury, leading the Argentinians to lose patience with what they saw as British procrastination. In late 1981, plans to seize the islands were dusted down and updated in Buenos Aires. In mid-March 1982, before these plans could be realized, an apparently trivial crisis blew up over an Argentine presence in the related territory of South Georgia. The Argentine junta concluded that this crisis was being used by Britain to strengthen its military position and thwart the

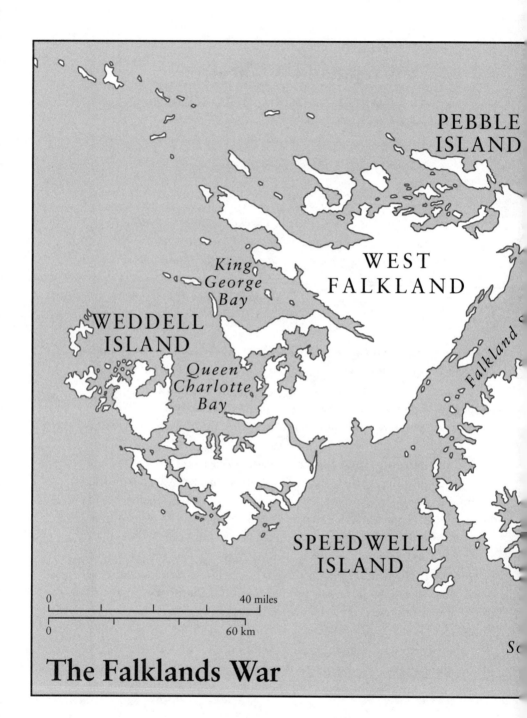

PEBBLE
ISLAND

WEST
FALKLAND

*King
George
Bay*

WEDDELL
ISLAND

*Queen
Charlotte
Bay*

Falkland S

| 0 | | | | 40 miles |
| 0 | | | | 60 km |

SPEEDWELL
ISLAND

So

The Falklands War

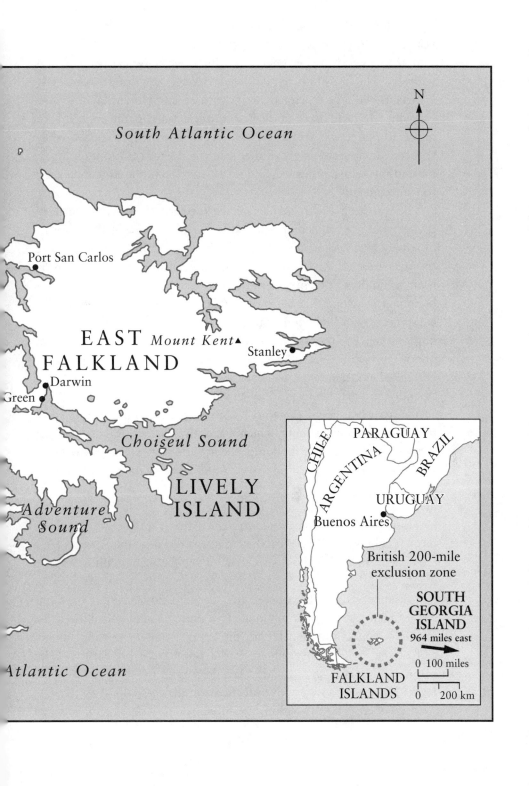

South Atlantic Ocean

N

Port San Carlos

EAST *Mount Kent*▲
FALKLAND   Stanley ●

Darwin ●
Green ●

Choiseul Sound

LIVELY
ISLAND

*Adventure
Sound*

Atlantic Ocean

CHILE   PARAGUAY

ARGENTINA   BRAZIL

URUGUAY
Buenos Aires ●

British 200-mile
exclusion zone

SOUTH
GEORGIA
ISLAND
964 miles east →

0   100 miles

FALKLAND
ISLANDS   0   200 km

occupation of the Falklands they were already planning for later in the year, and so they brought forward their plans.[2] In response to the invasion, the United Kingdom sent a task force led by two aircraft carriers, with Sea Harrier jump jets and helicopters, supported by as many escorts as could be mustered, along with an amphibious landing force carrying a brigade made up of Royal Marines and paratroopers. Later another brigade was sent as reinforcement. The military contest which ensued was extremely tight. Either side could have come out on top. In the end the British prevailed, and on 14 June 1982 the Argentine garrison surrendered.

The war itself was relatively straightforward. Other countries were engaged but not belligerent. The conflict was contained by the problems of supply and reinforcement faced by both sides. In the first instance, this was a naval campaign, as the British needed to land forces on the islands and protect them as they did so. Once this had been achieved, it became a confrontation between regular forces equipped with similar equipment, with limited armour and some air power. Both sides were improvising. The tiny population – some 1,800 inhabitants – were an important factor to be taken into account as British troops approached populated areas, for example when it came to the use of artillery. It was 'friendly' fire that led to the only civilian casualties.[3]

The two command structures were very different. Argentina was then run by a military junta, which meant that the political and military spheres were merged at the top of the government. This war, therefore, provides another opportunity to consider the effectiveness of military dictatorships in wartime. As in the Pakistani case, it shows how the demands of government and suppression of opposition forces can lead to a loss of military professionalism. The major war the junta had previously fought was the 'dirty' one begun in 1975 against an urban guerrilla movement, including those suspected of sympathizing with the movement, which left thousands of victims (known as the 'desaparecidos' or the 'disappeareds') unaccounted for. Coordination between the three Argentinian services was minimal. The United Kingdom followed the standard democratic model, with the military under the political control of the civilian government. It did not have a pre-existing joint command in place, so one had to be constructed for the conflict by the Royal Navy, which was in overall charge of the campaign.

There were tensions within the British chain of command, between the command HQ in London and the various theatre commanders. These tensions were aggravated because of a feature shared with the Arab-Israeli wars and the 1971 Indo-Pakistani War, that is, the problem of synchronizing military operations with diplomatic activity. There was international pressure for a negotiated settlement or at least a ceasefire to end the fighting. The effect of this pressure, especially when coupled with anxiety about the effects of deteriorating weather conditions, was to turn the conflict into something of a race against time. At first, the British hoped that the task force would strengthen its hand in negotiations with Argentina, conducted first under American and then under UN auspices.

THE UK COMMAND STRUCTURE

Prior to the Argentine invasion, the UK intelligence community had sensed danger but assumed that the Argentine junta would not attempt to seize the Falklands without first trying other measures, such as blockading the islands. This idea had in fact already been dismissed by the junta. The government in London realized what was going on barely two days before the islands were invaded. The initial advice was that little could be done militarily. By chance, the first sea lord, Admiral Sir Henry Leach, returned to the Ministry of Defence on the evening of 31 March from a visit to Portsmouth to find an alarming intelligence report warning of an imminent Argentine landing on the Falklands. He set off to find the prime minister, then meeting with ministers and officials, but no officers, in her rooms in parliament.

In his memoir, he described the 'aura of gloom and uncertainty' that greeted him as – uninvited – he entered Prime Minister Margaret Thatcher's rooms in parliament that evening. Contrary to the official advice from civilians in the Ministry of Defence, he insisted that it would be possible to send a substantial task force to the South Atlantic that would in principle be able to retake the islands and restore British administration. His record of the subsequent conversation has Thatcher welcoming this advice, but also displaying her ignorance of the state of the armed forces, for example being unaware that the country's largest aircraft carrier was in the process of being scrapped and that it would take weeks not days for the task force to reach its destination. When she asked if the islands really could be recaptured, he replied, 'Yes, we *could*, and in my judgement (although it is not my business to say so) we *should*.' When pressed, he explained: 'Because if we do not, or if we pussyfoot in our actions and do not achieve complete success, in another two months we shall be living in a different country whose word counts for little.' While the prime minister seized on his advice as a political life-line, other ministers were more sceptical and needed to be persuaded, which took until the next day. When Admiral Sir John Fieldhouse, commander-in-chief fleet (CINCFLEET), who would be in charge of the operation, asked for more time, Leach insisted that there was none. He was not unique among commanders in wanting to act before politicians had a chance to change their minds. 'My greatest anxiety was now to get the Task Force away before political resolve weakened.'[4] This set in motion what was named Operation Corporate. The first elements of the force sailed on 5 April, the next Monday.

The possibility of losing sovereign territory to a military junta presented Thatcher with a dismal prospect. In April 1982, she was not the dominant figure she later became – partly because of her handling of the war. Up to this point, her government had been buffeted by harsh economic conditions and she was disliked and distrusted by members of her own government. Her premiership was at risk if she was unable to find a response to the Argentine action, but also if she attempted to recover the islands and failed. She had to work hard to keep her colleagues with her. At the same time, she did not want to be in a position where she required agreement for each diplomatic and military step from her large and leaky cabinet. A small war cabinet was therefore established 'to keep under review political and military developments relating to the South Atlantic and the Falkland Islands'.[5] The full cabinet was kept informed about the course of the campaign, and asked to confirm, if not quite take, the big decisions.

The composition of the war cabinet was determined by ministerial responsibilities and political balance. The foreign and defence secretaries (Francis Pym and John Nott) had to be present, but the chancellor of the exchequer was excluded, after Thatcher was advised that financial issues could not be allowed to dictate the military strategy. Also present was Deputy Prime Minister Sir William Whitelaw, and a relatively junior member of the cabinet, Cecil Parkinson, chairman of the Conservative Party, a probable hawk and thus able to counteract Whitelaw's supposed dovishness. In the event, Whitelaw stayed loyal to Thatcher. At the time, Pym was assumed by many political commentators to be the natural replacement for Thatcher should she need to resign. He was, however, hesitant in manner, disliked open confrontations and was no match for her in debate. He was also new to the job, having taken over from the more formidable Lord Carrington, who had resigned, with most of the rest of his Foreign Office team, because of the Argentine invasion. Although, by dint of his post and his personal inclinations, Pym pushed the hardest for a diplomatic solution, he never did so from a position of political strength. The attorney general (Sir Michael Havers) also attended regularly because of the many legal matters to be addressed.

Despite this group meeting almost daily through the crisis, Thatcher was in many ways on her own. She could not be sure of her colleagues' commitment to military action. Nott felt uneasy about an operation that undermined the rationale for his defence review of the previous year, which when implemented would have removed the only occasional naval presence in the South Atlantic; his intended cuts would also have left the Royal Navy unable to manage Operation Corporate. Pym (to her mind) was too enthusiastic in his diplomacy, and Whitelaw's and Parkinson's other responsibilities limited their contributions. Her private office had a small staff that could not provide forensic critiques of the advice coming from the Ministry of Defence and the Foreign Office. To cope, she put in the hours herself. Famously able to manage on a few hours' sleep, she worked late into the night to get on top of the detail.

She was also conscious of the fact that she was the only one round the table without military experience. Havers had been in the navy during the Second World War. Both Whitelaw, who served as a tank commander in Normandy, and Pym, who was in the North African and Italian campaigns, had been awarded Military Crosses. Nott had post-war army experience with the Gurkhas. Parkinson had done his national service in the RAF. Although she had the reputation of a hardliner with regard to the Soviet Union, she had also supported Nott in his defence review, which had been bruising and had left its marks on the senior levels of the government and the military. One former minister commented that, if she had been 'a man and if she'd been in the forces during the war', she would not have gone to war because 'she'd have been aware how dreadfully wrong everything was likely to go'.[6]

Even her closest international ally turned out to be unreliable. To her chagrin, President Ronald Reagan was to the fore in pushing for a settlement, assuming common ground could be found between aggressor and aggrieved. On the UN Security Council (other than France, whose President François Mitterrand turned out to be the most sympathetic of her allies), the other European members at the time, Spain and Ireland, both had their own territorial disputes with the United Kingdom.[7] The complexities and pressures of the situation were intense. Much of her time was taken up by the domestic and international ramifications of the conflict, especially the various proposals for a settlement.

The main mechanism for discussing military matters in the war cabinet was through consideration of rules of engagement (ROE). These set the limits on what commanders might do, balancing legal and diplomatic considerations with military imperatives. They set the limits on what commanders could authorize, with the implication that what was not prohibited was encouraged. Agreeing the rules consumed considerable amounts of time on the parts of staff, senior officials, chiefs of staff and ministers, often on the minutiae. Existing maritime ROE documentation was adapted using caveats, exceptions and suffixes, which at times led to inconsistencies.

In her memoir, recalling her initial introduction to ROE, when the issue of whether or not to retake South Georgia arose, she noted this was the 'first time any of us had the awesome responsibility of ensuring that our Armed Forces had the right instructions'.[8] Beyond these discussions, there was limited civilian engagement with the military strategy. Not only was Nott ambivalent about the operation, but he also took the view that he should not take an active role in reviewing orders other than as a member of the war cabinet. Nor did he think that other departments, especially the Foreign Office, should be consulted on operational issues. The cabinet secretary did organize a meeting of the civil service heads of departments to ensure that war cabinet decisions were implemented but this had little bearing on military operations. By herself, Thatcher lacked both the means and the inclination to second guess the military. At one point, she observed: 'You can't fight a battle around a Cabinet table.'[9]

In the circumstances, she was fortunate to have Admiral Sir Terence Lewin as chief of the defence staff (CDS). Another wartime veteran, he had long experience, was popular with those who served under him, and was politically astute and decisive. He worked hard to earn her trust. Thatcher's private secretary observed that Lewin 'exuded calm, confidence, experience and a charm to which she was not immune'.[10] She came to rely on his judgements and Lewin therefore largely got his way – 'If that's what CDS wants, he must have it.' Even when it came to the key political task – setting the war aims – Lewin took the initiative. When Argentina seized the Falklands, he had been in New Zealand. When he rushed back, he realized that nobody had bothered to set down objectives for the task force. He worked out his own formulation: 'to bring about the withdrawal of Argentine forces from the Falkland Islands and dependencies, and the re-establishment of British administration there, as quickly as possible. Military deployments and operations are directed to the support of this aim.'[11] He told Thatcher: 'You need an objective, here it is.' It was adopted by the war cabinet. There was remarkably little civil–military friction. Thatcher shaped the diplomatic strategy but when it came to the military strategy she was largely following the advice of Lewin and Fieldhouse.

Coincidentally, not long before the start of the war Lewin had instigated a change in his formal role by which he became 'the principal military adviser to the Secretary of State and to the Government in his own right, and no longer as chairman of a committee with collective responsibility'. The corollary of this was that the Chiefs of Staff Committee had a diminished role. It was consulted for the benefit of their advice, but there was no need for Lewin to worry about getting a consensus. Because of the defence review, interservice relations were still uneasy. As Leach, known to be furious about the review, had persuaded the prime minister that retaking the Falklands was entirely possible, there was some suspicion that he had done so to demonstrate the Royal Navy's continued worth to the country. The chief of air staff (Air Chief Marshal Sir Michael Beetham) and the chief of the general staff (General Sir Edwin Bramall) accepted that a task force must be sent, but they were wary about where it all might lead. As this was largely a naval operation, they were content in the first instance to take a back seat.

The war cabinet and the chiefs of staff were important parts of the policymaking process in London, but the core chain of command was tight, passing directly from Thatcher to Lewin, and then on to the task force commander. On the military side, other than bringing in air and land advice to the naval HQ at Northwood, established command structures were employed for the campaign, and individuals were maintained in their positions. With so much to be done quickly, changing structures or personalities was considered too disruptive. Fieldhouse, as CINCFLEET, became the overall commander of Corporate. Operational command was vested in flag officer First Flotilla, Rear Admiral John ('Sandy') Woodward, who became combined commander of the task force. In addition, there were four commander task units (CTUs). Woodward also commanded the Carrier Battle Group; Commodore Michael Clapp, commodore amphibious warfare (COMAW), commanded the Amphibious Task Force; Brigadier Julian Thompson, commander 3 Commando Brigade, commanded the landing group; and Captain Brian Young commanded a fourth group, to retake South Georgia. The initial presentation of the command structure suggested that these other groups were under Woodward, but it was not wholly clear, because they all had their own relations with Fieldhouse and there would be practical difficulties for Woodward if he tried to manage the whole campaign while also concentrating on the special demands of the carrier task force.[12]

The potential problems soon became evident. Thompson travelled with Clapp on his command ship, HMS *Fearless*, while Woodward was far away on his flagship, HMS *Hermes*. Communications tended to be through signals. Voice communications depended on the unsatisfactory Defence Secure Speech System (DSSS), which only permitted conversations between two people, who often could not understand what each other was saying. There was no possibility for conference calls, so senior commanders had conversations on the same issue without being aware of what others had been saying. Woodward had the latest communications equipment. Clapp had satellite communications on HMS *Fearless* but he was unsure of their reliability, and they were useless when trying to communicate to many of the ships under his command, such as the royal fleet auxiliaries (RFAs) and merchant ships, which had only basic kit. Thompson recalled a 'small dark box on the bridge of HMS *Fearless*, perhaps in rough weather, where you have to hold on with one hand, holding the telephone with the other while you take notes with the third hand which of course you don't have, and the thing keeps cutting in and out – it was very frustrating'.[13] Even ship-to-shore communications were problematic. This created difficulties between

Clapp and Thompson, once the latter had joined troops on the beachhead, though they had worked closely together on *Fearless*.

As a commander, Woodward was experienced, professional, decisive and correct, but also brusque. He was frustrated by two limitations on his ability to exercise command. He had some control over air operations, but he was not an aviator himself and lacked his own air adviser. The person best placed to advise was Captain Linley ('Lyn') Middleton, the captain of HMS *Hermes*, who was an aviator. But the relationship between the two was frosty, as he did not trust Middleton's judgement. The mistrust was mutual. Middleton later complained that Woodward should have exerted command over *Hermes* as if he were 'in a separate ship', sending him a signal when he wanted something done, but he did not do so. He added that this led to a 'whole lot of things ... that are not down on paper'.[14] The second limitation related to submarines. Woodward had served with distinction in submarines and had views on how they should be operated, yet here control was retained by Northwood, under the flag officer submarines (FOSM), Vice Admiral Peter Herbert, who reported directly to Fieldhouse. Woodward saw the requirement to work through Herbert as a source of delay and inefficiency. The view in Northwood was that any use of nuclear-powered submarines was highly political, and for that reason control could not be delegated.

The most serious tensions emerged between Woodward, on the one hand, and Clapp and Thompson, on the other. Factors of personality played a role, but the origins of the tensions lay in ambiguities of the command structure, made worse by the separate conversations the individual commanders had with Fieldhouse about objectives and priorities. Further aggravation resulted from the circumstances of their first meeting as commanders on 16 April, when the task force had gathered at Ascension Island, the island midway between the United Kingdom and the Falklands which had the twin advantages of being owned by the United Kingdom and having an airport.

Woodward was initially designated 'senior task group commander'. He had two stars. The others had one. But although he outranked them, they were in charge of their own forces, and he had no special competence when it came to amphibious or land operations. Nonetheless, the initial command arrangements had put Woodward in charge of all three task groups heading south. Woodward, however, had been told 'to make haste' to get to the South Atlantic as soon as possible. Although he assumed that the amphibious force would come with him when he left, Fieldhouse had also agreed with Clapp that before his group moved out of Ascension he could reorganize the equipment and stores that had been pushed onto his ships before they left. To get the speediest possible getaway from the United Kingdom, little thought had been given to whether they were in the right order for being taken out to the bridge-head quickly and efficiently after the landing.

More seriously, Fieldhouse had asked Woodward to consider a wide range of possibilities for the task force once it reached the Falklands. An early ceasefire might require him to hold a position at sea for some time; the war cabinet might decide to mount a blockade to prevent Argentine forces being resupplied as an alternative rather than as a precursor to a landing. Even with a landing, practical problems or a ceasefire might confine the British to an enclave which would need to be defensible. Or else a landing could be followed by a move to repossess. Woodward also had to worry about the durability of his battle group. The loss of one of his two carriers – HMS *Hermes* and HMS *Invincible* – to enemy action at any time would mark the end of the campaign, but so could the wear and tear caused by weeks at sea. So, after a landing, whatever the next steps, one of his first priorities would be to establish an airstrip. Fieldhouse had also suggested that consideration should be given to West Falkland for the landing, although most of the population and enemy units were on East Falkland.

These wider considerations were appropriate for a theatre commander. Clapp and Thompson, however, were focused on their biggest challenge: to land safely, sufficiently close to the Falklands capital, Stanley, to be able to repossess it if necessary, but not so close that the landing might be opposed from the main Argentine garrison, which was based there. They were also worried about the threat to the landing force from the Argentine air and naval forces, and so needed reassurance that these threats would be addressed prior to the landing.

While at Ascension, Clapp had invited Woodward to visit him on his command ship, *Fearless*, and Woodward had accepted, but his acceptance had failed to get through. So, he arrived unexpectedly at a time when Clapp was busy. Thompson arranged for him to have what he thought to be a useful briefing about the topography of the Falklands, which an irritated Woodward ended abruptly as a waste of time. The discussion on landing sites went badly. Thompson found the idea of a landing on West Falkland 'grotesque' as it would mean landing closer to mainland air bases and then require another landing to get onto East Falkland and closer to Stanley.

In their memoirs, especially their later editions, these commanders showed more appreciation for each other's positions. Thompson acknowledged that he should have provided a more reasoned response to Woodward's suggestion. He blamed Northwood for the 'ensuing acrimony' by promulgating 'a structure of three co-equal commanders, and then arbitrarily, and without ever telling the other two, treat one of the commanders as if he was the overall boss on some occasions, which they did a number of times'.[15] Woodward also observed that the problems resulted from commanders working with their distinctive and not necessarily complementary sets of orders from the same commander-in-chief.

Woodward also claims to have been unaware of the unfortunate impression left behind after his visit to *Fearless*, such that it had few consequences for him. On board *Fearless*, Thompson's report was that Woodward's style was 'totally at odds with mine, and Clapp's'. Clapp recalled, 'Trust was broken and it would take a long time to repair.'[16] Southby-Tailyour, the marine whose briefing had been cut short by Woodward, found him 'arrogant, argumentative and bullying'. Thereafter, messages from Woodward were 'read against the background knowledge that it was likely to be a dictum and would not be seeking advice or confirmation ... [S]ympathy for, and understanding of our problems was to be in very short supply.'[17] Woodward later noted:

> After I had left to go back to *Hermes*, the whole meeting was debriefed to Mike Clapp as interference, arrogance, total lack of sympathy or even 'wish-to-know' from an admiral who plainly thought he was in charge of everything, including them. Hardly surprising, because at that particular moment and for the next day and a half, I believed I *was* in charge and that as they had presented no major problems standing in the way of obeying my C-in-C's order, there was a range of matters I needed to settle with them, there and then.[18]

The next day, 17 April, Fieldhouse flew to Ascension to meet the three commanders on *Hermes*. Concern about the geographic spread of the forces notionally under Woodward's command and their disparate roles, especially with a new task group formed to retake South Georgia, and Clapp's belief that he needed a direct relationship with the commander-in-chief, led to some clarification. All four task group commanders would report directly to Fieldhouse, although Woodward would still be *primus inter pares*. As the staff work progressed on the location and timing of the landing, the options narrowed and consensus was reached. The wariness from the amphibious force about whether Woodward would look after their interests remained. For the moment, however, they were left behind at Ascension, sorting out their stores, while the battle group steamed on. They were not to come together again until mid-May, in the run-up to the landing.

As the task force set sail, the United Kingdom had declared a 200-mile maritime exclusion zone around the Falklands, as an assertion of sovereignty but also to inhibit Argentine efforts at resupply. Once the carriers were in position, at the end of April, this became a total exclusion zone (TEZ), giving notice that any air traffic between the mainland and the Falklands could also be attacked. Declaring this zone had proved to be a successful tactic, gaining Britain the initiative, demonstrating purpose, inhibiting Argentine resupply efforts and legitimizing British actions. But it had also encouraged the view that it was a combat-inclusive zone, despite the rider that ships 'interfering with the mission of the Task force' outside the zone could still be attacked. Now that the main combat phase of the operation was about to begin, Fieldhouse wanted to change the rules to 'permit all attacks on Argentine naval vessels on the high seas'. If this had been agreed, later controversies would have been avoided. In the first instance, however, the war cabinet would only agree to make a specific change to cover the Argentine carrier, the 25 *de Mayo* (which had originally been built for the Royal Navy in 1943). Clearly, an aircraft carrier could pose a threat from well outside the exclusion zone to British ships within it, simply because of the range of its aircraft. This was agreed on 30 April. The next day, Woodward began the next stage of his campaign. Special forces were inserted on the islands to acquire intelligence on the disposition and capabilities of Argentine units defending them. His main priority was to reduce the threat posed to the future landings by the Argentine navy and air force by encouraging them to come out and fight, through giving them the impression that the main landings were under way.

SINKING THE *BELGRANO*

The Argentine command structure was unwieldy. In their military (as opposed to political) role, the members of the junta as commanders-in-chief of the three services formed the Military Committee, which was in charge of the whole operation. Within the junta, Admiral Jorge Anaya, the head of the navy, had been the one pushing hardest to retrieve the islands. The head of the air force, General Basilio Lami Dozo, was more cautious. The head of the junta was Army General Leopoldo Galtieri, who represented the more hardline faction within the military and had mounted a palace coup against General Roberto Viola, who was looking to open up the country politically. Galtieri's background was as an engineer officer. He had risen to the top through patronage, but had little grasp of the operational issues that needed to be addressed as confrontation loomed with the United Kingdom. The Argentinian system was devised more to manage co-existence among the services – each had precisely a third of the budget – than coordination. There were no unified commands or even substantial inter-force communication. The Ministry of Defence and the joint chiefs were both weak and acted independently from one another.

Argentina had been caught by surprise by the British decision to send a task force. The initial plan involved establishing a garrison of 500 men, but when London announced that it was sending a task force more troops were rushed to the island, putting the numbers up to 2,500. The armed forces had to gear up for a far more demanding operation than the one they had planned. Vice Admiral Juan Lombardo was put in command of the South Atlantic Theatre of Operations (TOAS). This was primarily a naval command, located at Puerto Belgrano naval base. Any attempt to act as a single operational commander was hampered by 'multiple interference and overlapping responsibilities'.[19] A separate Air Force South (FAS) command was supposed to coordinate its activities with TOAS but it was accountable to the junta and not Lombardo. There was no in-theatre commander to coordinate efforts. On the islands, Brigadier General Mario Menéndez was installed, first as military governor and then commander of the Joint Force of the Malvinas Military Garrison. He was given responsibility for the general direction of operations on the islands. Under him, there were separate land, air and sea commands, each of which had their own independent logistical and supply organization, although the army could not supply its forces without air or naval support. This caused major problems for the garrison once the fighting began.

Menéndez was not informed about Lombardo's plans until 23 April, long after they had been completed. The key message from Lombardo was that the navy would be unable to break the blockade of the islands by getting merchant ships to supply the garrison, because of the risk of enemy air and submarine attacks. Yet Galtieri appeared oblivious to these problems. When he visited the islands on 9 April, he ordered yet more reinforcements, without consulting his staff or Menéndez, who was then faced with significant logistical problems. He visited again on 22 April, and was still concerned that there were insufficient troops to provide reserves and to cover the islands. This led to the despatch of an extra brigade, causing further headaches for Menéndez and his staff, who had to incorporate the extra men into their plans and work out how to look after them. The British blockade meant that they could not travel by sea and so had to be airlifted to the Falklands without their heavy equipment. Moreover, Galtieri demanded that the extra forces be deployed in positions that would demonstrate Argentina's complete occupation of the islands, even though this would minimize any military benefit they might offer.[20]

The Argentine Navy had deployed all its seaworthy ships from mid-April. This was Naval Task Force 79, commanded by Rear Admiral Gualter Allara. He was a highly capable officer, who had once commanded the carrier 25 de Mayo. He had also spent some time in London, so was familiar with the Royal Navy. On 30 April, he divided his task force into three groups – the carrier group (TF-29.1) to the north, a group of three corvettes (TF-29.2) to the south, and one led by the venerable cruiser General Belgrano (TF 29.3). On 1 May, all three groups were ordered to move towards the estimated position of the enemy. Four Grumman S-2E Tracker reconnaissance aircraft, operating from the carrier, were sent to find the British task force. Shortly after 15.30 one of these Trackers detected the main battle group in a position north of the Falklands, within range of the carrier's strike aircraft. At dusk, another Tracker located the British ships about 60 miles south-east of the Argentine carrier.

Lombardo had received a report not from Menéndez but from Rear

Admiral Edgardo Otero, the senior naval officer on the islands, that aircraft had been shot down and that there were British troops on the beach. The moment had come. Lombardo signalled Allara that there was an opportunity to attack the British and that he had 'freedom of action' to do so.[21] At 20.07 local time, Allara ordered offensive operations, instructing the carrier group to deploy to a spot from where it could launch air attacks at first light, and then to move back to a safe position. On board the carrier, six A-4Q Skyhawks were prepared for launch early on 2 May, with another aircraft kept in reserve and as a tanker.

The aim was to catch the enemy by surprise. Following the air attacks, the intention was for the three small corvettes of TF-79.2, difficult to pick up because of their low silhouettes, to get in among the UK task force with their Exocets. The third group (TF-79.3), led by the cruiser *Belgrano*, and commanded by Captain Héctor Bonzo, was to close in to deal with any surface units operating to the south of the Falklands. They were cautioned to attack only under favourable conditions. At 22.13, Lombardo urged an early reconnaissance followed by a massive attack on the British fleet before any of its units had a chance to withdraw.[22]

British intelligence picked up Allara's order, and it was part of an intelligence summary sent to Woodward.[23] The admiral had good reason to be concerned by this report. He was aware of the second Argentine S-2E Tracker that had come close to elements of the task force, which meant that his position was likely known to the enemy. He had only a vague indication of the whereabouts of the Argentine carrier group. The *25 de Mayo* was not where it was supposed to be, which was where the SSN (nuclear submarine) HMS *Splendid* had been told to patrol. During the day, Woodward's group had been busy, seeking out Argentine submarines, directing naval gunfire against Argentine positions on the islands and landing special forces on the islands by helicopter. But in the light of the emerging threat, he now needed to get these missions completed and his units back together.

Just after midnight, a Sea Harrier came across radar contacts from a group of four ships some 200 miles away to the north-west. Woodward assumed correctly that this was the *25 de Mayo*'s group, preparing for a dawn strike. As the *Belgrano* group was also on the move, he could see a pincer movement taking shape. While more intelligence was sought to help locate the carrier for the benefit of the two SSNs hunting it, Woodward could not assume that they would find their quarry. Meanwhile another SSN, HMS *Conqueror*, had found the *Belgrano* group and had been tracking it for some time.

Here, then, was Woodward's dilemma. To the north, he had permission to attack the carrier but no contact; to the south, he had contact but no permission to attack. He therefore wanted an immediate change to the rules. This was to get at the *Belgrano* while he had the chance, but also because he wanted the restrictions on his freedom of action eased, as the campaign moved into a more active phase. Even with new ROE, he would still have lacked the authority to send orders to *Conqueror* – these had to derive from Herbert as FOSM. Regardless, to force the issue, he sent the submarine an order to attack the *Belgrano*. As he expected, this was rescinded at once by Herbert, who, as he hoped, immediately informed Lewin and the chiefs of staff, who were about to meet. This was about 09.00 in the morning of 2 May in London (05.00 in the South Atlantic). Lewin and Woodward quickly decided to ask the war cabinet to extend the ROE, to allow for attacks on all Argentine ships, submarines and auxiliaries outside the TEZ, if they constituted a threat to the task force. They then went to a scheduled lunchtime meeting with the war cabinet at the prime minister's country retreat at Chequers.

On arrival at Chequers, Lewin explained the position to Thatcher, who assembled the ministers and officials already arrived for lunch. They were told that, if the opportunity was not taken, *Conqueror* might lose contact with the *Belgrano*. The request did not seem controversial. Parkinson imagined trying to explain in the aftermath of the sinking of a British carrier why the government had failed to allow the threat to be removed.[24] The discussion lasted no more than twenty minutes. Whitelaw later recalled it as 'one of the simplest decisions that I personally found myself involved in.'[25] The brief record noted that it reflected 'the latest intelligence about the movements and intentions of the Argentine fleet, and of the new situation created by the military events of 1 May'. The only caution came from the attorney general, who warned that the decision would be harder to justify if the attack took place 'a long way away from the Total Exclusion Zone'. He was reassured by Fieldhouse that 'the patrol areas of the British units involved made that very unlikely to happen'.[26] The new ROE referred only to Argentine naval vessels, so there was a continuing restriction on auxiliaries, although Nott was authorized to bring them within the scope of the decision 'at his discretion'. As the decision was disseminated, including within the FCO and on to Pym, who was then in the United States, it was presented as much as a response to the general military situation as to a specific encounter then under way.

The decision was taken around noon London time, and, within an hour, Herbert signalled the new ROE to all his submarines. *Conqueror*, the only submarine in a position to act on the new rules, was experiencing communication problems as a result of a broken mast, so it did not actually get the message until over four hours after it was first transmitted. It had, however, managed to report back that the *Belgrano* group was no longer as expected passing through the TEZ sailing towards the task force, but had changed course. Herbert did not think this made a great deal of difference. The change in the ROE would have come at some point. Even if there had been a requirement to rescind the new ROE, it was not clear how this could be done. In war, chances have to be taken when they arise. The next opportunity might fall to the Argentines. There had been serious clashes the day before, including an attempt to sink British ships. One, HMS *Glamorgan*, had been hit.

Conqueror's observations about the *Belgrano*'s movements provided the only indication that Argentine commanders had changed their plans. Woodward had been correct to worry about a pincer movement, but Allara had decided to withdraw. This was for several reasons. First, to the immense frustration of the Skyhawk squadron, ready to launch an attack, there was a surprising lack of wind. Without the wind, the carrier was unable to get to a sufficient speed to launch its aircraft, at least with a full load of fuel and weapons. With no sign of the wind picking up, the load was reduced from four bombs for each aircraft, then down to three and eventually two, which was not considered sufficient to mount a successful attack. According to the squadron's commander, the calculation was that, with a full load, of the six aircraft, only four would get into a position to drop their bombs, and only two of these would get home. If sixteen 500-pound bombs were released probably only four would hit the target. If the numbers were cut by half, the risk was of a raid of limited impact for the potential loss of four A-4s.[27] Second, Allara's ships had been picked up by the Sea Harrier. Tactical surprise was lost, and his position was compromised. Third, as Allara later remarked, and despite the previous day's information, 'it was possible to verify that the British were not disembarking, and therefore their ships remained concentrated.'

He still wanted to persevere, but Lombardo was concerned that his group was vulnerable. There had been 'no further air attacks on the Malvinas' and now he was unsure of the position of the British carriers. 'The free-ranging enemy still constitutes a strong threat to Task Force 79.' The weather showed no signs of picking up. So, at 01.45 local time on the morning of 2 May, Allara agreed there was little point in carrying on. The pincer movement was called off, and the task groups were ordered 'back to their former positions'. Captain Bonzo received this signal at 02.50.[28] It took another three hours before the *Belgrano* began to turn, suggesting little sense of vulnerability or urgency. *Conqueror* was aware of its new course by 06.00, but it was almost another six hours before it was able to inform Herbert. It took even longer before some of these signals, though intercepted, were decrypted by the British and distributed as intelligence briefs. They had no impact on the events of 2 May.[29]

Without firm intelligence on any Argentine change of plan, Woodward could only infer what had happened. There was no sign of an incoming attack, despite further Sea Harrier surveillance. He still kept his group on a high state of readiness. As the light improved, he prepared to resume the day's operational tasks. It took until noon (by which time he knew that the *Belgrano* had turned away), before he concluded that the Argentines had reversed their decision to attack 'and are now retiring'. This still made little difference to his defensive preparations or his decision to wait until the night before inserting more special forces onto the Falklands and ordering naval gunfire against Argentine positions. To the north, two SSNs were still engaged in their fruitless search for the 25 *de Mayo* group, assuming that it was moving closer to the task force.

The *Belgrano* had turned when Woodward sent his order for it to be attacked. What is striking is that, after he had set the chain of events in motion, it took almost 11 hours before the *Belgrano* was sunk. This had nothing to do with Woodward. The matter was out of his hands once Herbert had rescinded his order to *Conqueror* and turned it into a request for a change in ROE. Although the SSNs were quickly informed of the change to the ROE, surface ships were not told until much later.

(When he received the notice, Woodward repeated his request for *Conqueror* to attack the *Belgrano*, not knowing that the submarine already had its orders to do so.)

This stage, from Woodward's order to the change of ROE being sent to *Conqueror*, took three and a half hours. What then took another seven hours? *Conqueror*'s captain, C. Wreford-Brown, had received neither Woodward's order to attack nor Herbert's cancellation. He had expected to follow the *Belgrano* into the TEZ, but then had noted the change of course, without being sure where the cruiser was headed. All that was clear was that it was skirting the TEZ rather than entering. He had the added difficulty of his damaged radar mast, so when he received his new instructions they were garbled. It therefore took some five and a half hours from the first signal being sent to SSNs about the change of ROE to Wreford-Brown being sure of its contents and reporting back his intention to attack. He spent another two hours getting into an attack position. Just before 16.00 local time, he attacked. He reported back: 'successfully attacked *Belgrano*. Two hits with Mark Eights. Evaded to east.'[30]

The Belgrano had adopted no special measures to reduce its vulnerabilities. Bonzo assumed that the two Exocet-armed destroyers acting as his vanguard, geared to deal with an air attack, were the most likely targets for any British strike, assuming the British knew that his cruiser lacked its own Exocets. Bonzo might have used his destroyers on either side as a screen, or increased his speed and adopted a zig-zag pattern, but nothing was done to complicate Wreford-Brown's attack. The *Belgrano* was following a straight line at 10 knots when one torpedo hit it below the bow and the second in the engine room.[31] Without propulsion and electrical power, the ship began to list and, after thirty minutes, it had to be abandoned. On the ship, some 200 men were killed by the initial explosions and by the subsequent fire. Another 850 took to life rafts as the cruiser began to sink. In all, 321 men died.

After the war, elaborate theories were developed about why the *Belgrano* was attacked so long after it had changed course. One prompt for these theories was that the initial parliamentary statement by Nott on 4 May related the attack to the tactical situation, rather than the wider strategic requirements of the campaign. Nott drew attention to the threat posed to the task force by the *Belgrano* group, and reported that it was 'close to the Total Exclusion Zone and was closing on elements of our Task Force, which was only hours away'. This was a hastily put together statement, based on what was understood by his private office; but it was also misleading, and, when this was eventually pointed out, long after the war was over, the government made matters worse by sticking with its original statement, rather than correcting it.

If the new rules had been in place when Woodward first ordered the attack, the technical problems faced by *Conqueror* might still have caused delays, but the attack would not have appeared to come quite so much out of the blue. As Woodward, along with the other admirals, had wanted the rules to cover all warships, and not just the 25 *de Mayo*, he remained unsure whether he had got 'greatly improved ROE' because 'everyone got a fright when I released (against top orders) CONX [Conqueror] to attack', or because his staff had already been working with Herbert to get the restriction removed.[32]

On 4 May, the Argentines got some revenge when an Exocet missile crippled the destroyer HMS *Sheffield*. That same day, Admiral Anaya ordered Allara to regroup his surface ships in shallow waters. The A-4s from the 25 *de Mayo* were disembarked and were later used in the attacks on the landing force. The reason he gave was that the British were getting satellite information that enabled them to locate Argentine ships. This was not true. It seems most likely that the key information had been the result of the *Belgrano* being spotted leaving the southern port of Ushuaia on 26 April. Anaya later reported that, after his defensive measure, he had come under great pressure to deploy the fleet. He would only reconsider his position if there was 'a plan that could destroy two British capital ships. If that could be achieved I would offer the entire Argentine fleet.'[33]

The significance of the attack on the *Belgrano* was not only that it succeeded, but that so many Argentine sailors died. This had political consequences, which could not have been anticipated in advance. On receiving news of the *Belgrano*'s loss, the Argentine junta abandoned conversations it had been having with the Peruvian government about a possible peace plan. There was a later theory that the attack had been devised with this end in mind – to torpedo a peace plan as much as a warship. But the peace plan was only half-baked by the time of the attack (and would have been even more so, if the attack had taken place when Woodward wished), and nobody at Chequers knew much about it. Indeed, because of the international shock at the loss of life, it was the

British government that took the plan seriously and tried to see if something could be made of it.

FROM THE LANDING TO GOOSE GREEN

For the United Kingdom, the most important consequence of the attack on the *Belgrano* was that Argentine warships thereafter kept their distance. This, however, was known only in retrospect. At the time, military leaders could not be sure that it would continue, and there were still aircraft and submarines to worry about. Other than through attacks on Argentine air assets deployed on the Falklands, and reports on the disposition of Argentine forces from the special forces teams landed on the islands, there were only limited opportunities to reduce the risks to the amphibious force as it made its way to the Falklands. The choice of where to land the amphibious force was a compromise between staying clear of the main body of Argentine forces and reducing vulnerability to attack by air and sea. In the event, the problems came from the air.

After the landing at San Carlos on 21 May, for four days, the ships supporting the landing were subjected to intense attack from Argentine aircraft. The Royal Navy lost a destroyer and two frigates, with a number of other ships damaged. It did not help that many of the air defence systems failed to perform as they should. Fortunately, for the main business of getting men and materiel ashore to the bridgehead, Argentine aircraft tended to attack the escorts, and not the auxiliaries and merchant ships as they unloaded. The most effective cover came from the Sea Harriers. The closer the carriers got to the action, the longer their aircraft could stay on patrol, but this added to the risk that they would be struck. Woodward noted on 23 May that he was feeling 'a bit hassled'. Supporting the amphibious force required him 'well forward', long-term maintenance of carriers required him 'well back', while 'provision of in/out convoys requires me somewhere in the middle'. He accepted that the demands of that week required him to be 'upfront', but, 'I must get clear at the first opportunity.'[34] This led to inevitable tensions between the commands. Woodward was frustrated by how long it was taking to get everything ashore, as much had to be done at night. He did not appreciate the problems with the performance of the air defence systems. Clapp and Thompson were desperate for the air cover, and thought Woodward was being too cautious in not moving his carriers closer to San Carlos.

The landing, and the testing few days that followed, changed the political context. Having got this far, and having taken substantial casualties, ministers no longer expected the conflict to end with anything other than a British victory. There was nothing left to negotiate with Buenos Aires other than the surrender of its forces. But the international community, including the United States, wanted to see negotiations. Thatcher and her colleagues anticipated, correctly, a period when they would be resisting calls for a ceasefire.

All this argued for getting the campaign over with as quickly as possible. In this respect, the task force now suffered because of past equivocation about whether the full repossession of the islands should be an objective. The initial order to Fieldhouse at the start of April was 'to sail a task force'. The emphasis was on a conspicuous display of power and intent to coerce Argentina. Eventually, the mission was changed to achieving a landing on the islands, although that possibility was obviously there from the start. Once the objective became one of repossessing the islands, this required reinforcements. General Edwin Bramall, chief of the general staff, needed convincing that it was necessary to do much more than establish an enclave around the bridgehead. Politically, there was concern about announcing the despatch of more forces while efforts were under way to broker a settlement. At the start of May, a decision was made to send 5 Infantry Brigade to supplement 3 Commando Brigade. The reinforcements left on the requisitioned cruise ship the *Queen Elizabeth 2* in early May, but would not arrive until well after the landing had been completed.

Because a second brigade was being sent, Major General Jeremy Moore, who had been serving as the land adviser at Northwood, proposed to Fieldhouse that a divisional HQ was now needed and that he should command it. With five army battalions to the three Royal Marine commandos, some in the army grumbled about a chain of command that went through admirals to a Royal Marine general, but Moore's appointment made sense. He had been working closely with Fieldhouse up to this point and was familiar with thinking both in the war cabinet and at Northwood. Moore was replaced in his position at Northwood by an army lieutenant general, Sir Richard Trant.

Moore flew to Ascension Island once the final arrangements for the landing were in place and went on to join the QE_2 to sail with 5 Infantry Brigade. Unfortunately, there were soon problems with his satellite communications, which had just been fitted to the QE_2. Other means of communication could be easily accessed by outsiders and so were unsuitable for confidential conversations. Northwood, nonetheless, kept on sending signals to Moore, which were copied to Thompson, and to which neither man was able to respond.[35] Moore had considered flying on ahead, so he could drop by parachute from a Hercules transport to join the forces on the bridgehead earlier. He decided against this on the grounds that the media might go over the top with a parachuting story, and that he would be in a slightly odd position with only a single commander (Thompson) underneath him. He also knew Thompson well and had confidence in him. In the event, he believed he made the wrong decision. There was little he could usefully do while aboard the QE_2, while he would have had a valuable role to play on the Falklands.[36]

Thompson had received his last orders from Moore on 12 May. First, he was to secure a bridgehead that could take reinforcements and 'from which operations to repossess the Falkland Islands can be developed'. He was also to push forward 'to gain information, to establish moral and physical domination over the enemy, and to forward the ultimate objective of repossession'. When Moore arrived with 5 Infantry Brigade he would then 'develop operations for the complete repossession of the Falkland Islands'.[37] There was therefore a clear implication that he should probe and push forward, but that the most substantial operations should wait until 5 Brigade arrived with Moore. But Thompson had to think about his next moves on 24 May; Moore would not arrive until 30 May.

Northwood wanted quick movement. In London, there was a developing view that the Argentines would not respond aggressively to the landing, but would wait for the British to come to them to take the capital, Stanley. If this was the case, there was no point in 3 Brigade hanging around. Trant signalled on 24 May that the enemy 'possesses neither will nor means to mount effective offensive ground operations, and that rapid and powerful action will bring about speedy resolution of overall situation'.[38] Yet there was very little at the time to justify any certainty about how well Argentine units would perform as there had been very few engagements. There could be no doubting the bravery of the pilots who had been flying through British air defences. Moore's effort to get into the mindset of General Menéndez, his opposite number, in charge of the Malvinas garrison, had him looking at a picture of a tough paratrooper. Unfortunately, this was the wrong General Menéndez: the one actually in charge had more of a background in staff work than combat. Thompson, for the moment the responsible commander, was worried about enemy air power, overextended supply lines and vulnerable forward units. San Carlos had been chosen for the landing because it was well away from the main body of Argentine troops, based at Stanley. He assumed, prudently, that Argentina would have some serious defensive plan.

There was, however, one possibility for forward movement. When special forces reached Mount Kent, a key point en route to Stanley, they found it surprisingly empty. Plans now were drawn up to move Special Air Service (SAS) units forward by helicopter. Another option was to attack the substantial Argentine garrison not far away from the bridgehead at the settlements of Darwin and Goose Green. The garrison was not blocking the route to Stanley and had only a limited ability to cause trouble. But there was potential value in a raid to destroy the airfield at the settlements and hurt the enemy before returning to the bridgehead. More than that risked tying up a battalion to guard the recaptured settlements. In London, the appeal of such a raid was that it would provide a visible sign of movement, bolster morale and probably undermine Argentine confidence.

Plans for a raid were developed by 2 Para on 24 May, but then put on hold when intelligence suggested that the garrison was stronger than hitherto presumed. Then, abruptly, all plans had to be reconsidered. News came through that the container ship, the *Atlantic Conveyor*, had been hit by two Exocet missiles, leading to the loss of key supplies, including three out of four Chinook helicopters. Instead of moving forward by helicopter, most of the troops would now have to walk. Goose Green did not seem the best allocation of scarce resources. As Thompson was digesting the news, he received a signal from CINCFLEET, supporting the plan for a quick move to the high ground around Stanley, and keeping Goose Green as a secondary contribution:

Now that 3 Cdo Bde [Commando Brigade] is established ashore the earliest opportunity must be taken to invest Port Stanley from positions on high ground west which dominate it. Enemy forces in Port Stanley must be dominated and harassed although I accept that decision to assault Port Stanley can await further developments. Major psychological advantage would be achieved by separate set piece operation to eliminate enemy in Goose Green/Darwin provided that this does not detract from investment of Port Stanley. My prime concern is to make best speed to invest Stanley.[39]

In the circumstances, Thompson considered this quite unrealistic. When he discussed his options with his senior officers the next morning, he decided that, with so few helicopters, the move to back up the SAS position that had seemed bold the previous day was now too dangerous. Thompson reverted to the view that he should wait for 5 Brigade to arrive, and with it more helicopters.

The loss of the *Atlantic Conveyor* had led the war cabinet to the opposite conclusion. They feared that the campaign was stalling, with potentially serious domestic and international political consequences. After the success of the landing, the interminable process of unloading had been accompanied by Argentine aircraft braving British air defences to attack ships, with some success. If their bombs had been fused properly, it could have been much worse. Now nothing appeared to be happening to move the campaign to its next stage.

Lewin had told the war cabinet to expect early movement. The prime minister's press secretary had observed to reporters, 'We're not going to fiddle around.' Yet that seemed to be precisely what was happening.[40] Whitelaw recalled the war cabinet's concern: 'if we didn't get a move on all the proposals for ceasefires would become stronger ... So a break out was very important.'[41] Nonetheless, Thatcher was scrupulous in relying on the military leadership to understand the political issues she faced, and to formulate their plans accordingly.[42] If anything, the frustration was led by Lewin and Fieldhouse. They worried that Woodward was paying insufficient attention to the land campaign (although this was not his command responsibility), and that Thompson was a typical marine in his inability to think beyond the beaches.

Against this backdrop, Northwood saw the optional raid on Goose Green as an opportunity to regain the initiative. A victory there would demonstrate progress, perhaps encourage Argentine commanders that the British were irresistible, and confirm that there was no pause that

might allow a ceasefire to be negotiated. If Mount Kent was now problematic and waiting for 5 Brigade unacceptable, it would have to be
Goose Green.

Fieldhouse contacted Woodward and told him to go ashore and
shout at Thompson until he moved out of the bridgehead. Woodward
refused. This was a matter beyond his competence and his command
responsibilities. So Fieldhouse got in touch directly. Late morning on 26
May, as Thompson was struggling with this perplexing logistical issue,
the brigadier was called to speak directly to Fieldhouse over the satellite
communication system. Thompson later described the conversation:

> The radio-telephone was as clear as if the call had been coming from next
> door. As clear and unequivocal were the orders from Northwood. The
> Goose Green operation was to be re-mounted and more action was required
> all round. Plainly the people at the back-end were getting restless.[43]

Thompson was unimpressed by the failure to understand the difficulties he faced and the pressures on his staff. He did not disagree that
there was a need to move on. He was preparing to get his men to walk
in the direction of Stanley while 2 Para revived their plans for Goose
Green. Thompson reported this back to Northwood. Fieldhouse sent
back an encouraging and positive signal, in the process at last revealing
the political aspect to his thinking. He explained why 'the pressure upon
HMG to agree a ceasefire is likely to be very great'. This was why it was

> imperative that we keep going at very best possible speed. With this in
> mind you should do all you can to bring the Darwin/Goose Green oper-
> ation to a successful conclusion with Union Jack seen to be flying in
> Darwin.

Should this be achieved, it would be possible 'to claim with justification that we now control large areas of East Falklands. To complete the
package you will understand how important it is to cover ground as
quickly as possible to box him in Stanley.'[44] The immediate military
effort, therefore, was geared to strengthening the British hand if the
pressure to accept a ceasefire became irresistible.

The Darwin/Goose Green operation had moved from a secondary
possibility to a high priority. In the process, its objectives moved from
providing a quick shock to the Argentines to liberating the settlements,
from a raid to repossession. Thompson's orders to 2 Para were to 'carry

out a raid on Goose Green isthmus to capture the settlements before withdrawing in reserve for the main thrust in the north'.[45] There was therefore an ambiguity: capturing the settlements required more than a raid. The commander, Colonel 'H.' Jones, 2 Para, was always more focused on the 'capture' aspects of the plan than the raid, but he was allocated no extra resources to ensure the operation's success. Later, Thompson was critical of himself for not taking charge of this operation and mounting a two-battalion attack.

Thompson still found it difficult to think of this operation as other than secondary to his main goal, and therefore secondary also in terms of the allocation of resources. In London, by contrast, the operation was going to be so vital to restoring faith in eventual victory that conversations between ministers and anxious backbenchers soon reached the media. As 2 Para were getting in position on 27 May, discussing how to catch the enemy unawares, they heard the BBC World Service report that the garrison had already fallen. Aware of the fury, from Lewin down, about the leaks and the pressure that had been put on Thompson, the war cabinet observed that, while it was important to make the earliest possible progress, only the military commanders could take specific operational decisions.

The battle itself revealed another complexity of command. Jones relished the chance to lead his men into battle. Even with the BBC broadcast and intelligence suggesting that the Argentine garrison was stronger than originally supposed, he did not want the operation called off or postponed. His second-in-command, Major Chris Keeble, described Jones as a 'guy who ruled by the bullwhip, rather than a conductor of an orchestra'.[46] His orders group, taking place an hour and a half before the battle was due to start, was rushed, with little time for questions or clarifications. It concluded with an optimistic assertion: 'All previous evidence suggests that if the enemy is hit hard, he will crumble.'[47] The plan required a complex series of movements, conducted at night. Progress was slower than hoped and, as dawn broke on 28 May, appeared stalled. Jones moved to a forward position, rejecting advice about flanking manoeuvres because of the urgency of the situation ('Don't tell me how to run my battle').

He ordered men to go forward, but casualties were being taken. Frustrated, he decided to take the initiative, shouting, 'Come on A Company, get your skirts on.' As he moved forward, he was shot in the back and mortally wounded. Keeble took over. The soldiers of 2 Para pushed forward in circumstances that were still confusing and dangerous. Eventually, they managed to persuade the Argentine garrison, which had not crumbled, that they were surrounded by a larger force. To spare lives, including of civilians, it would be best if they surrendered. The personal bravery of Jones was unquestioned, but his action was controversial, going to the heart of the tension between the heroic commander leading from the front, and the more responsible role of managing the battle from a safe space and adapting tactics to a developing situation. It was decided in London to award him the Victoria Cross, the highest honour for bravery.

Though the decision to take Darwin and Goose Green reflected a need to satisfy political objectives in London, once that decision had been taken, it required a more wholehearted commitment from Thompson. In the event, the success of the operation did provide a political boost and helped with the rest of the campaign. There were tactical lessons learned about night fighting and the importance of firepower. It opened up another route to Stanley. Hew Pike, commanding officer of the sister battalion, 3 Para, later described Goose Green as 'the moral turning point', in that before 'we understood that we had to win, whilst after it, we knew that we would'.[48] This was the battle's objective envisaged by those who had been pressing from London for action. The campaign did not all go smoothly over the subsequent couple of weeks, and the battles to take the ground around Stanley were fiercely fought, but, as these positions fell, Argentine forces, demoralized and with their supplies running out, were ready to give up. A ceasefire was announced on 14 June, and Menéndez surrendered to Moore.

CONCLUSION: POLITICAL AND MILITARY ALIGNMENT

During the course of the war, the Argentine junta made some basic strategic errors, from not reinforcing the runway at Stanley, so it could be used as a base for their more capable combat aircraft, to putting more troops on the islands than could be properly supplied, and then waiting for British troops to come to them rather than patrolling aggressively. The errors might have reflected the failure to anticipate that the British would send a task force, but also the loss of military professionalism resulting from too much time running the country and suppressing domestic opponents. The junta's diplomacy was often inept, especially when they failed to take advantage of diplomatic openings that would have left the British hold on the islands permanently weakened, even if they did not lead to their main objective of an immediate transfer of sovereignty.

The British were under intense pressure from the Reagan administration to agree a settlement. Argentine intransigence, therefore, let Thatcher off the hook, since she was never obliged to implement the concessions she did offer on joint administration of the islands while negotiations on the long-term future of the islands were under way. Even after negotiations had broken down and fighting had begun, there was constant pressure to agree a ceasefire. The government did not need to impress this political reality on the admirals. Both Lewin and Fieldhouse were well aware of the diplomatic aspects of the conflict and Washington's push for concessions during earlier rounds of negotiations. They could see the awkward consequences of having to agree a ceasefire when the job was half done. They also shared the frustration and concern about the effects on domestic political support, as ships were lost and battered, without the land force showing signs of moving on.

Yet, while they fully understood how the risks appeared to the war cabinet, they found it harder to share the travails of the amphibious force – as they went through the time-consuming task of unloading stores and equipment at night, and tried to move out of harm's way before the air raids came – or the shattering impact of losing the *Atlantic Conveyor* and its Chinooks. As is often the case, the logistical aspects of operations were underestimated. The fact that Moore was on his way to the South Atlantic and largely incommunicado added to the problems. He would have been able to mediate between Thompson and Northwood if he had been in a position to do so.

Thatcher was never put in the position of having to adjudicate between competing military advice, and never looked for a second opinion beyond Lewin's. While in practice the command arrangements between the war cabinet and Northwood worked well, or at least lacked tension because of the trust Thatcher put in her commanders, those in the task force worked less well. Fieldhouse assumed that the field commanders would make their tactical decisions according to the logic of the developing situation. He could not attempt to coordinate their operations. The distances were too great, too many factors were in play, his information was too sparse, and action often took place when London was asleep. Thompson believed, along with Clapp, that what was missing was a sympathetic interface between them and Northwood, such as a three-star theatre commander, removed from immediate operational issues:

> He could have decided on priorities, seen for himself what was happening and removed the sources of friction. Perhaps most useful of all, he could have taken the responsibility for speaking direct to Northwood off the backs of the busy group commanders.[49]

At Northwood, an extra layer of command was seen as superfluous. The issue largely arose because of the time it took to get Moore to the South Atlantic. While the task force was still at sea, the three-star would still have needed to be closer either to Woodward or to Clapp/Thompson and the primitive secure communications would still have caused difficulties. With good communications, senior political and military figures may be tempted to meddle in decisions best left to local commanders. With poor communications, the temptations were still there, but the meddling was less well informed. This was also before the introduction of a truly joint headquarters, a development encouraged by this experience, which would have improved the coordination between the naval, land and air forces.

It was a close fight. The outcome was not a foregone conclusion. The Falklands campaign illuminates the importance in such circumstances of individual judgements and chance factors, some quite minor. If the junta had realized that they would be facing a substantial UK task force, would they have taken such a hurried decision to invade, when more Super Étendard aircraft and Exocet missiles would soon be delivered from France? If Leach had not spontaneously intervened in Thatcher's deliberations in the way he did, would the task force have sailed? If, on 1 May, Lombardo had not been misinformed about British actions, might he have held back on pushing his fleet out to engage? Alternatively, Woodward's ruse, in encouraging the Argentines to believe that the full landing was under way, might not only have succeeded in drawing the Argentine Navy into battle, but have done so with the 25 de Mayo being tracked as intended by SSNs. As the carrier was not tracked, different weather conditions could have allowed the Skyhawks to fly from the 25 *de Mayo* and strike the UK task force. Then again, *Conqueror*'s mast might have been so broken that it never received its orders to attack the *Belgrano*. And so on. This is a game that can be played with many military encounters, but there is often a greater tolerance on either side of occasional mishaps and failures, because of the underlying balance of power, or because the conflict will in the end be decided by the strength of the political forces at work. It was not the case with the Falklands, where the conflict could have turned on many small events and conditions. This underlined the importance of tactical judgements, and for that reason alone the quality of the contrasting command structures made a clear operational difference.

Even with its underlying clarity, the campaign highlights how much the perspectives of individual commanders are limited, not only by their experience and background but also their most pressing concerns at any moment in the campaign. Thus, in London there was a shared civilian and military appreciation of the need to keep things moving, because of the pressures resulting from both domestic politics and international diplomacy. When, not long after the war, I had a conversation with Margaret Thatcher about the main lesson she had learned from the conflict, she replied, 'Everything takes much longer than you think it should.'

As the amphibious force faced regular attacks at San Carlos, Woodward had little appreciation of the limits of its air defence systems, but he did know that allowing the Sea Harriers to spend more time engaging with the Argentine air raids meant that his carriers would have to spend more time at risk from an Exocet strike. Losing either *Invincible* or *Hermes* would jeopardize the whole campaign. This led to more tetchy exchanges between the front-line commanders – Woodward, Clapp and Thompson. Yet, as each made their meaning clear, they managed to find a form of mutual accommodation and respect each other's areas of competence. When so much is at stake, and decisions are urgent, emollient personalities tend to be rare. Commanders need a stubborn streak. Flashes of bad temper do not always signal dysfunction. Two decades after these events, in my capacity as official historian of the campaign, I met with Clapp, Thompson and Woodward in my office to go over the command arrangements once again and how they had worked. At one point, as Woodward began to complain about the lack of understanding of the risk to his carriers, Thompson gently interjected, 'But Sandy, we won.'

8

Dictator as Supreme Commander: Saddam Hussein

The ideal revolutionary command should effectively direct all planning and implementation. It must not allow the growth of any other rival centres of power.

Saddam Hussein[1]

A usual route to dictatorship is by means of a military coup. By virtue of their control of the armed forces, top generals can turn themselves into presidents. As we saw with Yahya Khan in Pakistan, advancing to political power by this route does not necessarily equip a general to exercise it effectively. By contrast, Saddam Hussein, Iraq's president from 1979 to 2003, had no military qualifications, but was a member of a revolutionary party, and had learned to be ruthless to survive. He became both a student and an accomplished practitioner of dictatorial power.

Saddam acted in paranoid ways, sure that people were out to kill him, and was convinced that threats of extreme punishment were the best way to persuade subordinates to perform. In power, he was either leading a country at war, or on the verge of going to war. He exemplified the 'personalist boss and strongman' most likely to initiate international conflict, least likely to win, and yet able to survive defeat,[2] and provides a natural case study on the effects of the 'coup-proofing' of armed forces on battlefield effectiveness.[3] Although he was often compared to Hitler, with whom he certainly shared a number of traits, his role model was the Soviet leader Joseph Stalin, whose career he studied. Unlike Hitler, Stalin died with his supreme power still intact.

Personalist dictators combine the political and military strands of command. Any other arrangement means sharing power, which they are

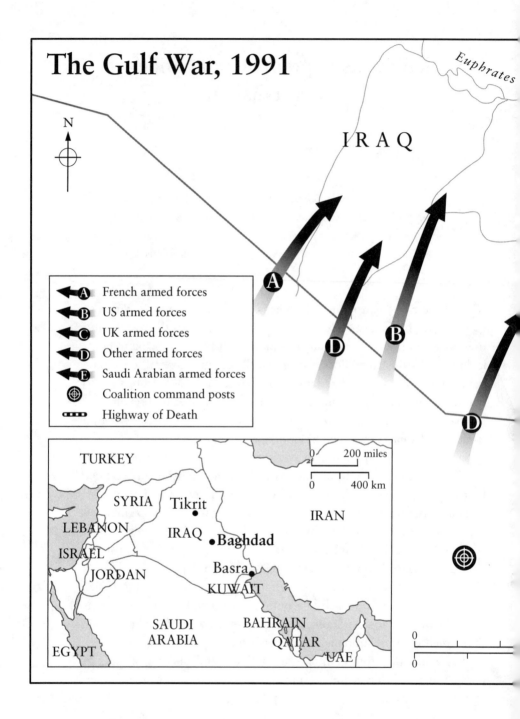

The Gulf War, 1991

Euphrates

IRAQ

N

← Ⓐ	French armed forces
← Ⓑ	US armed forces
← Ⓒ	UK armed forces
← Ⓓ	Other armed forces
← Ⓔ	Saudi Arabian armed forces
⊕	Coalition command posts
▭▭▭	Highway of Death

TURKEY

SYRIA · Tikrit

LEBANON   IRAQ · Baghdad

ISRAEL

JORDAN   Basra ·

KUWAIT

SAUDI
ARABIA   BAHRAIN
QATAR

EGYPT   UAE

IRAN

0   200 miles

0   400 km

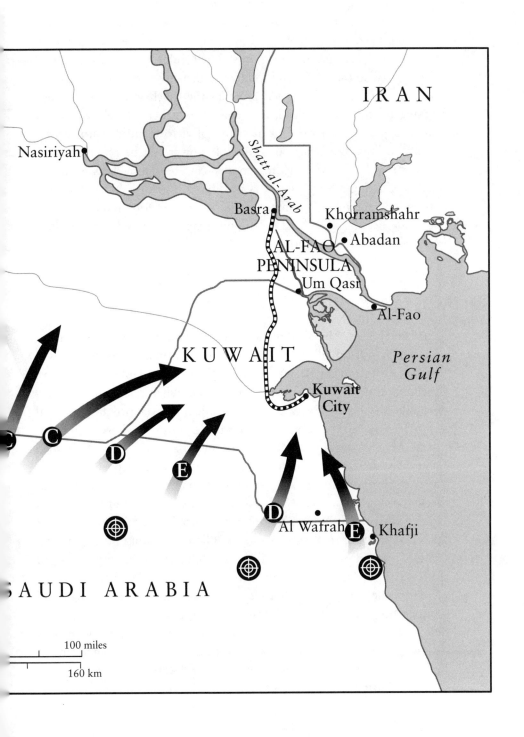

IRAN

Nasiriyah

Shatt al-Arab

Basra

Khorramshahr

Abadan

AL-FAO
PENINSULA

Um Qasr

Al-Fao

KUWAIT

*Persian
Gulf*

Kuwait
City

C C

D

E

D

Al Wafrah

E Khafji

SAUDI ARABIA

100 miles

160 km

loath to do, because it creates rivals for the very top spot. Such leaders are confident in their own judgements and deal ruthlessly with any opponents. They are encouraged by sycophantic advisers and uninhibited by any institutional restraints. Their rule encourages a cult of personality, so that they tend to identify their own interests with those of the state. Personal survival provides the touchstone against which strategic moves are judged, and against which losses elsewhere are secondary. The more obvious measures of victory and defeat need not apply, so long as an aura of invincible power can be retained and a superior will demonstrated. Setbacks can be claimed as victories, because, taking a long view, it is possible to live to fight another day. Assessing Saddam as a commander-in-chief, therefore, requires understanding his ability to hold on to power, against the odds and despite catastrophic miscalculations.

THE DICTATOR

Saddam Hussein Abd al-Majid al-Tikriti was born into a poor family in the northern Iraqi village of Tikrit in 1937. From an early age, he was active in the radical Ba'ath Party, working around plots and coups, spending time in jail and exile. From 1968, when one of these coups brought the Ba'ath Party to power, Saddam developed his personal base. He enjoyed the patronage of his uncle, mentor and eventual president, Ahmed Hassan al-Bakr. By the mid-1970s, he had established himself as de facto leader. In 1979, when he was 42, he pushed al-Bakr to one side and made himself president. Soon his image was being projected around the country. Tall and strong, he looked the part – always a help when establishing a cult of personality. To sustain the image, he avoided wearing reading glasses in public or allowing his slight limp to be captured on film.[4] He paid close attention to the imperatives of survival, in an environment full of threats, fear and distrust.

From the start, he made it clear that his rule would be tough and autocratic. There were no restraints on his power: no press freedom, elections, or any safe means of political expression. No mercy was shown to those who plotted, might be thought to be plotting, or might be inclined to plot in the future against him. 'I know there are scores of people plotting to kill me, and this is not difficult to understand. After all, did we not seize power by plotting against our predecessors?'[5] He was also conscious that his power base was the substantial but still minority Sunni community, and that Kurds, mostly in the north of the country, and Shi'ites, mostly in the south, were opposed to the regime.

Any post of importance Saddam kept for himself – prime minister, commander-in-chief of the armed forces, chairman of the Revolutionary Command Council and secretary general of the Ba'ath Party. Reports were received directly from an extensive network of intelligence agencies. Appointments were controlled, with loyalty the highest priority, and rewarded with lavish gifts, while disloyalty was likely to lead to execution or imprisonment. A special eye was kept on the military, lest any senior figure be tempted to mount a coup.

Although al-Bakr's ties with the officer corps had helped him reach power, once he was there it constituted a threat. One of Saddam's jobs as his deputy was to break it as a political actor, so that it did not continue as an institutional threat to the regime. In 1976, al-Bakr made him a lieutenant general although he had no military background, having failed the entrance exam to the Baghdad Military Academy, so that he was on a par with the chief of staff of the army. As he set about reshaping the senior levels of the army, military professionalism was but a minor consideration in officer recruitment and promotions. One general recalled Saddam describing the army as being like a pet tiger, which made it necessary to pull out 'its eyes, teeth, and claws'.[6] Top commanders were rotated to deny them any opportunity to develop their own power bases.[7] The individuals who gained commands far beyond their experience were expected to show loyalty only to Saddam. They would execute his orders, lacking the confidence to pursue their own initiatives or respond to any suggestions from their subordinates.

Decisions were made in secret. Saddam shared his thoughts with only a few of his closest advisors, who had to judge how far they dared go when asked for their opinions. He wrote his own speeches, to keep control of the narrative surrounding his actions and their consequences. Like many autocratic rulers he encouraged fragmentation and rivalry among his advisers. If he wanted advice, he would ask for it; if he did not, it was unwise to offer it. There was no incentive to criticize or to bring bad news. When subordinates received instructions (which were usually delivered orally), the wise course was to follow them to the letter, however unreasonable or infeasible. This was also the case when orders came from favoured underlings. Criticizing a person chosen by Saddam was tantamount to criticizing him.

In a psychological profile prepared for a US congressional committee in December 1990, Jerrold Post warned against characterizing him as a madman, for he was neither irrational nor unpredictable. He was a 'judicious political calculator', 'shrewdly manipulative' and 'at heart a survivor'.[8] Certainly those who worked with Saddam considered him rational when pondering key decisions, careful and deliberate in his approach, engaging in technical discussions and ready to focus on quite detailed matters. He was sufficiently predictable for his subordinates to be reasonably confident they were following his wishes, even in the absence of formal instructions. According to one, Saddam was 'like a computer: if he received reliable information he would make good decisions, but if the inputs were flawed, the resulting policies would suffer'.[9] A former intelligence chief described him as 'serious'. Although meetings could become tense, 'you don't get intimidated unless he wants to intimidate you'. His problem was a vision 'clouded by a strong propensity for wishful thinking'.[10] A senior general provided a similar assessment. Saddam 'was highly intelligent and, when open-minded, which he was at times, quick to grasp essential points'. This depended on the extent of the difficulties being faced. 'For the most part, however, he tended to confuse reality with what he wished to be true.'[11] His analytical side was therefore combined with another that was deluded and impetuous. He was also described as a 'deep thinker who lay awake at night pondering problems at length before inspiration came to him in dreams'.[12] He was prone to bold and decisive moves, to unsettle his opponents and seize the initiative. At the same time, he was not stubborn. When faced with setbacks or disasters he was prepared to retreat, to fight another day.[13]

TAKING ON IRAN

As the leader of a relatively large Arab state with ample oil reserves, Saddam aspired to establish Iraq as a regional great power and himself as a leader of the Arab people. He made himself president in 1979 because he saw a developing threat to this aspiration. Neighbouring Iran was even more populous – 40 million as against 14 million – and also oil rich with substantial military capabilities. In an earlier spat with Iran, in

1975, Saddam had been obliged as vice president to negotiate an un-favourable deal with the Shah of Iran over the disputed Shatt al-Arab waterway. The year 1979 had begun with the Shah's overthrow and the radical Shi'ite cleric Ayatollah Khomeini becoming supreme leader.

This was always likely to lead to tensions as Iraq, though a majority Shi'ite country, was led by Sunnis. Relations became worse in November 1979, when the Iranian Revolution took a more radical turn and began stirring up trouble among the Shi'ites inside Iraq. By the following spring, Saddam had decided that a response was needed. He was influenced not only by the threat of subversion, but also the opportunities presented by the post-revolutionary chaos in Iran. The revolution had led to purges among the officer class and Iran's armed forces were in disarray. This opened up the possibility of taking back disputed lands and even toppling a hostile regime. After border skirmishes, on 4 September Iran shelled Iraqi cities causing casualties. This was followed by Iraqi attacks on Iranian border posts.

On 16 September 1980, Saddam met with the Revolutionary Command Council to discuss the next steps. He opened by reminding those present of a decision already taken to 'retake our land from Iran'. The question was when to act and with what objectives. Because Iraq had been mobilizing on the Iranian border since the start of the month the situation had become unstable. 'In the beginning,' Saddam explained, 'it was a limited mobilization, but now we have whole divisions mobilizing on the borders.' He supposed that the Iranians were probably asking 'why do they have all these armed forces? What is the need?' This situation could not last long. Maintaining these forces was costly ('[t]he command will not accept draining the resources'), and there was always the possibility that the Iranians would take the initiative. It was therefore necessary to move expeditiously.

The plan was to take back some of the land and then demand the rest, or we will 'grab it back'. The mobilization was intended to make this threat credible. With a metaphor he used twice in the meeting, Saddam insisted: 'We have to stick their noses in the mud so we can impose our political will over them. This cannot take place except militarily.' The aim was to 'put them in a political and military position so they will say yes. Or they would have to pull back their army and assume that the matter is over, and that we can do as we please. We cannot stay on the border forever.'

Should this strategy succeed, as one of those present noted, it would move Iraq 'from one stage to the other', and have a positive effect on the Arab world and internationally. There was however a risk. Would the Iranians act in a 'vast way ... do they have a mind to fight us while they are in this bad military condition?' Saddam was clear that he did not want 'a full-scale war'. He wished to avoid the 'destruction of oil' and 'raids on the cities'. The focus would be on 'military targets', but if Iran escalated there would be a response in kind. If, for example, Iraqi 'oil establishments' were attacked there would be retaliation: 'one situation is met by another.' He concluded:

> What is stopping us from moving forward on all axes and surrounding their armies and imprisoning them? Or doing as we please with some areas [inaudible]? ... No one is saying that there would be no resistance; no one is saying that there would be no losses or dead. The result of our calculations is that we can reach into the heartland of Iran. We want to get to our international borders.[14]

These thoughts on the potential development of the war were not backed by much of a campaign plan. Saddam's core assumption was that turmoil within Iran would lead to its quick collapse and Iraq could get what it wanted. That was the first flaw in his assessment. It led to the second. Iran might fight and so Iraq needed to maximize the advantages of surprise and initiative. Yet, because he wanted to avoid all-out war, his approach was restrained. Insufficient forces were committed to the offensive.

Iraq opened hostilities on 22 September with an attempt to emulate the June 1967 Israeli air strike against the Egyptian Air Force, but without the same success. The next day the army crossed the border. The Iranians struggled with this unexpected offensive, and soon retreated to their cities as they would be easier to defend. But contrary to Saddam's hopes, the regime did not collapse. It opted for escalation rather than concessions. The Iranian navy attacked oil terminals near the port of Al-Fao and its air force attacked Baghdad. Iraq responded with air strikes of its own. Not only was Saddam now experiencing the escalation he had hoped to avoid, but matters were not working out as anticipated on the ground. The terrain was too mountainous for Iraqi troops to make quick progress. In an early battle for the city of

Khorramshahr, they were held up by determined resistance. Eventually, in late October, the city fell, leading Saddam to congratulate himself on a 'victory that generations will talk about a hundred years from now'. He also cautioned that the war was not yet over. It 'could stretch on for a year, maybe less'.[15] It lasted another eight years.

Saddam's next mistake was to lose whatever momentum his forces had gathered by announcing that, since his limited objectives had been achieved, Iraq would now pursue a defensive strategy.[16] The Iranians had used the time gained by resisting at Khorramshahr to reorganize their forces. As they moved to the offensive, they began to gain the upper hand, retaking lost land and preparing to move into Iraq. Saddam, recognizing the shift in the military balance, withdrew from Iranian territory in June 1982 and ordered a robust defensive line to protect Iraqi territory. Although this survived the first onslaught by Iranian forces they kept on coming. Saddam's regular proposals for a ceasefire were ignored.

Away from the struggle for territory, the respective oil industries were under attack, and eventually this extended to all oil traffic in the Gulf. By the time the war ended in 1988, there had been bombardment of cities and use of chemical weapons. The casualties accumulated on both sides, although the oft-quoted figure of a combined total of a million by the time of the ceasefire is probably an exaggeration – the actual total was closer to 250,000 on the Iraqi side and 155,000 on the Iranian.[17] On land, the struggle was shaped by Iraq's desperate efforts to stop Iran seizing even more of its territory. In this respect, Saddam was saved by the ineptitude of the Iranian leadership. Iran's command structure was even more fragmented and dysfunctional than Iraq's, and its tactics were reckless and wasteful.

In February 1986, an Iranian offensive at last succeeded. Following a feint to attack Basra, the main force went to the Al-Fao Peninsula, which it took successfully. Iraqi counter-attacks failed and it was only with difficulty that they stopped Iran moving into Basra. The Iranians exhausted themselves with a series of futile offensives, as the Iraqis reorganized. In mid-April 1988 Al-Fao was retaken and Iraq regained the initiative. In July 1988, Iran accepted a ceasefire. For Saddam, the outcome bore little relation to what had been sought when he started the war, but, after many years on the defensive, a ceasefire with the Iranians off Iraqi territory could be presented as a victory of sorts.

SADDAM AS A MILITARY COMMANDER

Saddam's attitudes towards supreme command developed during the course of this long and vicious war. When it began the Iraqi command structure was not fit for purpose. At the lower levels it was proficient and professional, but its senior levels suffered from both purges and politicization, and political commissars were deployed down to battalion level. For Saddam, membership of the Ba'ath Party was the mark of 'a true natural leader'.[18] On this basis, relatively junior officers, who had not been through staff college nor held intermediate command posts, were propelled into top positions. Once in a post, an officer was apt to be shuffled out relatively quickly, so he did not form too close an attachment to his unit. Conversations across the different branches of the service were actively discouraged. As always with leaders fearful of disloyal generals, Saddam trusted mostly relatives or members of his tribe. Saddam's brother-in-law became minister of defence, moving from colonel to general in a day. As a result, during the invasion of Iran, the senior officers advising Saddam had no experience of commanding large divisions or knowledge of the pitfalls that regularly accompany ambitious attacks on another's territory. Little thought had been given to how the Iranians might fight back.

Even as these pitfalls began to make themselves felt, Saddam held to the view that a deep political commitment and readiness to accept sacrifice for the national cause remained essential qualities. 'The soldier who does not carry on his forehead the emblem of victory or martyrdom, the soldier who does not enjoy defending [his] honourable life and its ... values, such a soldier cannot achieve victory.' Power depended upon 'the bright light of belief and ideological determination'. That could see a country through dark times. The unfortunate logic of this position was that, when things went wrong, it was evident that this light had been dimmed and that the urge to martyrdom had been replaced by cowardice. When 'the non-commissioned officer recognizes that his brigade commander is a coward, how can you expect him to fight with good morale?'[19] Whatever the positive benefits of ideological commitment, it was reinforced by the prospect of execution for backsliding. There was a punishment corps operating in rear areas to maintain adamantine discipline. As Iraqi forces were pushed back in 1981, Saddam ordered that officers, however senior, should not authorize retreats on pain of death. The only exceptions permitted were when odds were greater than 3 to 1. Otherwise, 'we will not accept anything from him [a retreating officer] but a confession that he is a coward or that he failed to [conduct] his battle properly.'[20] In the summer of 1982, when the military position was bleak, some 300 high-ranking officers were executed for poor performance in battle.[21]

Saddam's approach led to a wholly dysfunctional military organization. Commanders were given insufficient information from the top, and were not able to compare notes with fellow commanders. Junior officers were fearful of taking any action without specific authorization from a higher command or at least the local political officer. All incentives were against candid reporting. As reporting failure might lead to execution, it was best to avoid getting into situations that could end in any sort of defeat. Even if such a situation was looming, and reinforcements were needed, mention of setbacks could be a death warrant. This inclination to tell Saddam only what he wanted to hear, or what was safe to tell him, meant that he was poorly informed about the true state of a battle.

Also in 1982 Saddam moved to protect himself against political threats by purging his cabinet. The Revolutionary Command Council, which had become his personal HQ, was streamlined.[22] He created forces outside the military chain of command. The paramilitary Ba'ath army had been formed in 1970 as a counterweight to the regular army. It was 250,000 strong by 1980, and doubled in size during the war with Iran. There was already a Republican Guard, but this was turned into an elite corps. The best commanders were taken from other units to be put in charge of this special, well-equipped, properly-trained armoured force. The overall weakness of the officer class in the early 1980s meant that this took time. After 1986, it was given a further boost as it was expanded to two dozen brigades. Its purpose was to protect Saddam from both his internal and his external enemies.

At the start of the war, Saddam later observed, he told the commanders to 'make the decision and I will take the responsibility for it', without its being presented to him. Soon he wanted to look at the decisions: 'I will say I take the responsibility, you are not responsible until it [is] formed.' Once it was required that all decisions had to be checked with him before action could be taken, the system became drained of initiative. Soon it dawned on him that the climate of fear he had created meant that people were too scared to give him honest appraisals of situations. At a meeting in 1984, he explained that he expected painful truths. 'You know some-times even the brothers at the General Command, they used to keep things away from me . . . The front must report even the painful issues to me, so that I can evaluate the situation and know the factors that caused this pain and make a right decision!' His concern that his subordinates might be too frightened to deliver bad news up the chain of command led him to go to the front and ask his own questions after each battle. 'I do not mean that I do not have confidence in the leaders, no, but I wanted [information] to come out of the soldier's mouth in a way that it can help me conclude something that the corps commander cannot conclude . . . I can evaluate the psychological status in that position.'[23]

The weaknesses in the command structure were exposed by the loss of Al-Fao in 1986. General Maher Abd al-Rashid, whose loyalty was underlined by his daughter's marriage to Saddam's son Qusay, took charge of a small cell to plan a counter-attack. Saddam paid close atten-tion to the planning. Yet when the counter-attack came, it failed with heavy losses. This aggravated tensions between the military and political leadership, with al-Rashid grumbling that Saddam's continual interfer-ence was undermining the military effort. These words got back to Saddam and al-Rashid was recalled to Baghdad. At this point, his fellow officers warned Saddam that if al-Rashid was executed they would mutiny. As this was not so much a coup as a desire to get on with their jobs, and with the war going badly, Saddam gave way. Instead of being executed al-Rashid was decorated (although, once the war was over, he was put under house arrest and Qusay told to divorce his daughter). For now, the generals had more control over decision-making.

The command structure became less centralized and more profes-sional. The field commanders acquired a greater role in the Supreme Command Council.[24] The Republican Guard got a new commander, General Ayad Fayid al-Rawi, who had no connection to Saddam through either his tribe or his birthplace, but instead a record of profes-sionalism and battlefield success. Under his influence, staff work and training were improved. Instead of preparing over-complex operations that required lots of local initiative, tactics were kept simple and geared to each unit's capabilities.

When, in April 1988, the new professionalism paid off and the Iranian position in Al-Fao crumbled, Saddam was happy to take the credit.

Foreign Minister Tariq Aziz reported how, during the eight years of war, 'there was a very deep feeling of self-confidence among the leadership, and among the people, among the Iraqi Armed Forces'. He went on to commend Saddam as 'a wise Commander' with a 'long vision'. Saddam explained: 'Victory is a state within me. I felt it, but I wanted the performance to be a grand one that suits the Iraqis, and the Iraqi Army . . . Not only to achieve our objective and regain Al-Faw, to liberate it, but I wanted our performance to make us reach the grand political, intellectual and psychological euphoric state that we wanted to relay to our enemy.'[25]

He reported how the 'whole world' was talking 'about the new standards of the Iraqi Army'. But the essential quality of 'will' was still to the fore. In a long war, it was 'inevitable that we lose a village here, a city there'. That was not important when the enemy could not defeat 'the will of the Iraqi people'. The outcome of the war bore little relation to the goals set by Saddam when it began. But he had avoided a complete defeat, and had always understood that one advantage of dictatorship was being able to impose a narrative that put the best possible construction on events.

SEIZING KUWAIT

The long war with Iran left Iraq in debt, at a time when revenues were well down because of a collapse in the oil price during the 1980s. The international financial credit Saddam needed to sustain the country was beginning to dry up. In addition, his chemical, biological and nuclear programmes were now attracting the attention of those Western countries that had turned a blind eye when Iraq had been fighting Iran, a country they distrusted even more. The ease with which Soviet bloc autocracies collapsed in 1989 added to Saddam's sense of insecurity. This was all reflected in reports of failed coups, arrests and executions of many officers for their part in conspiracies, real and imagined.[26]

During the first months of 1990, Saddam developed a plan to solve these gathering problems with a single bold move, which would boost both his finances and his power. His forces would occupy and seize Kuwait. The emirate was vulnerable and accessible, as well as lucrative, with great wealth and oil reserves. In 1960 Iraq had opposed Kuwait's independence on the grounds that it was properly part of its inheritance from the Ottoman Empire. Although Kuwait had supported Iraq during the conflict with Iran, Saddam now accused it of engaging in 'economic warfare'. He was especially indignant that Kuwait expected Iraq to repay the loans granted during the war, not least because it was in no position to do so. Another demand was that Kuwait repay Iraq for oil 'stolen' from an oilfield that spread across the two territories. The indictment was set down by Saddam at the end of an Arab summit held in late May 1990. He emphasized the length and cost of the war with Iran and how he had defended the security of all Arabs. There was no response from Kuwait. According to Foreign Minister Tariq Aziz, he asked King Fahd of Saudi Arabia to arrange a summit to discuss the issues. The King promised to try, but nothing happened.[27]

The next month, operational planning began. Lieutenant General al-Rawi, chief of staff of the Republican Guard, was asked by Saddam to 'take a look at the Iraq/Kuwait border', and 'write up a detailed plan to accomplish the task of retrieving Kuwait and massing the troops in the area'.[28] A small planning staff was put together to work in great secrecy, meeting on occasion with Saddam, who gave only oral orders. In one account, by mid-June, two plans had emerged, one for the occupation of the border area and the other for a complete occupation.[29] The General Military Intelligence Directorate (GMID) provided al-Rawi with an analysis of the theatre of operations, details of the Kuwaiti order of battle, and video of the Iraq–Kuwait border on 12 July. On 15 July, Major General al-Razaq's Hammurabi Division received a short-notice movement order to deploy his brigade location near Al-Kut to an area south-west of Basra. He told his subordinates that this was probably just a show of force, and that the threat of using it was a political manoeuvre to put pressure on Kuwait to resolve the increasing political tensions.

As units moved towards the border with Kuwait, on 17 July, Saddam raised the stakes by going public with his indictment, describing Kuwait as being engaged in a 'kind of war against Iraq', fought by economic means as much as 'explosions, killing and coup attempts'. The army deployment was soon picked up, and it had a coercive effect. Talks were arranged for the end of the month between the two sides in Jeddah. The pressure on Kuwait was somewhat compromised, however, as other Arab leaders decided that Saddam was largely bluffing. President Bush accepted this optimistic assessment, despite US intelligence agencies reporting that the forward Iraqi units had the logistical support to advance into Kuwait.

Prior to the talks with Kuwait, Iraq made it clear that definite results were needed rather than more talk of 'fraternity and solidarity'. The Kuwaitis arrived at Jeddah defiant. In their account, they did make a serious financial offer but Izzat Ibrahim, Iraq's vice president, dismissed it and broke off talks, although there was an agreement for the two sides to meet again on 4 August.[30] According to Foreign Minister Tariq Aziz:

> When our delegation, headed by our Vice President, returned from Jeddah, on the 1st of August, telling us that the Kuwaitis were arrogant, and didn't show any sign of reconciliation. So we thought it was futile to wait. We held a meeting of the Revolutionary Command Council, and reached the conclusion that the diplomatic efforts have failed and we gave the green light to the military action.[31]

It is possible that a more generous offer would have led Saddam to change his mind about invasion, but more likely that it would have been hard for the Kuwaitis to come up with anything worth more than the complete acquisition of their country. If a better deal was possible, he could have waited a few more days, although (as with Iran in 1980) he may have been conscious of the costs of keeping forces mobilized for any length of time. There is an issue about whether he felt he had received a 'green light' from US Ambassador April Glaspie a few days earlier, as she denied any interest in the United States getting involved in the dispute. In any event, conversation had been cut short by the news coming through of Saudi mediation.

As for most of the big calls Saddam made, the decision to invade Kuwait was his own – he discussed it only with his son-in-law. There is no record of consultation among the senior echelons of his government and armed forces about the likely risks and costs. Most of the government had no idea what was being planned. The army chief of staff, General Nizar al-Khazraji, recalled 'the invasion was staged by the Republican Guard forces without my knowledge. It came as a surprise to me.' The navy and air force were informed of their tasks only late on in the process. Those military formations involved in the invasion were notified and completed their plans only hours before it began.

General al-Razaq recalls a summons to his HQ on 20 July to be briefed on the general concept for the new war. He swore on the Koran to keep it secret.

I was stunned by the size of the mission. For I thought that at the most we would only reclaim the part of the border which Kuwait had taken from us and which contained quite large oil reserves belonging to the southern oil fields. In astonishment I asked: 'We are going to occupy Kuwait . . . our neighbouring country?'[32]

The plan was still largely conceptual and lacked many of the details necessary for execution. The main challenge was how to achieve surprise, given the distance to be travelled from the staging posts into Kuwait. The Iraqis also lacked some critical intelligence. On 31 July, a detailed list of members of the Kuwaiti government, national council and senior military figures was still being put together. Tactical intelligence was limited, as were the maps, which often had to be those intended for tourists rather than invaders.

That day, before the results of the Jeddah talks were known, al-Razaq was told that the invasion was set for 2 August at 04.00. This tends to support the view that there was little Kuwait could have done to stop it. There was to be no preliminary shelling or protective fire. The objectives were to occupy the city of Kuwait and other cities, and then defend what had been taken. The Tawakalna Division was to take a key air base and the port area south of Kuwait City. A series of commando assaults would seize key territorial and political objectives. Forward units would have to be self-sufficient with their own logistics.

The 16th Republican Guard Special Forces Brigade infiltrated before dawn on 2 August to take vital points. One key task was to seize the ruling family. Once they were in captivity, the idea was to give the emir a choice. If he cooperated, he would be asked to order an end to any resistance, and possibly to continue ruling under Iraq's direction. If he refused to do so, he was to be executed at the palace.[33] But the al-Sabahs were whisked away as soon as it was clear what was happening and escaped to Saudi Arabia. Once safe, the emir was able to rally international support, leading the UN Security Council to demand withdrawal and impose sanctions on Iraq. It also led to an American commitment to deploy troops to Saudi Arabia, in the first instance to defend the kingdom from Iraq, but by October to prepare for a war to liberate Kuwait. The failure to capture the emir irritated Saddam,[34] and was a serious blow to his strategy. As he annexed Kuwait, he had to manufacture a provisional government that lacked credibility from the start.

UNWARRANTED OPTIMISM

Following the occupation of Kuwait on 2 August 1990, the UN Security Council issued an immediate condemnation, demanded that Iraq withdraw and imposed economic sanctions to compel it to comply. When this failed to have an effect, a resolution was passed in November authorizing member states to use 'all necessary means' to eject Iraqi forces from Kuwait and end the illegal occupation. A coalition was formed, led by the United States, with substantial forces from Britain and France, as well as key Arab states, including Egypt, Syria and Saudi Arabia. Saddam further alienated the international community by seizing expatriates and using them as hostages.

A variety of peace plans were canvassed and then discarded, while the build-up of American, British and French forces continued, joined by a number of Arab countries. On 9 January 1991, US Secretary of State James Baker met Tariq Aziz in Geneva for talks, which achieved nothing. The war began with the first American air strikes on 17 January.

A few days earlier, on 13 January, military intelligence chief Wafiq al-Samarrai, alarmed by the prospect of what was to come, provided Saddam with a gloomy assessment.

> I think it comprised seven full pages, handwritten. We showed in it detailed information about the allied build-up and that we thought they had serious intention to launch an air attack and a land attack later on . . . We were quite specific about the targets that would be hit, and that our aircraft would not be able to reach their targets.

Defeat might lead to social disturbances in Iraq or an Iranian invasion. 'These reports really mandated that he should withdraw, but to him that was impossible.' Saddam did not chastise Samarrai for writing the report, but made clear that he did not agree. He was sticking to his view that the Americans could not cope with a long war. 'Perhaps they fight, perhaps they would not.' Saddam insisted:

> Our forces will put up more of a fight than you think. They can dig bunkers and withstand American aerial attacks. They will fight for a long time, and there will be many casualties on both sides. Only we are willing to accept

casualties, the Americans are not. The American people are weak. They would not accept the losses of large numbers of their soldiers.[35]

Saddam was not the first supreme commander to underestimate the enemy, nor the only one to do so by supposing an inferior character and strategic intelligence. 'Every time they calculate what is needed for the next action,' he claimed, 'we will surprise them with something else. This will force them into continual recalculation in light of our surprises and unconventional methods.'[36] He assumed that the popular disillusion exhibited during the Vietnam War would be replicated, as the American people tired of a war being fought for a foreign country and with high casualties dragging on. It was for this reason that, just before the invasion of Kuwait, as he warned the Americans against getting involved, he pointed out to the Ambassador Glaspie that the United States was not a country (unlike Iraq) that could accept '10,000 dead in one battle'. On the day of the invasion he described 'Washington's threats' as 'those of a paper tiger'.[37]

Thereafter, there were regular references to how the war would be a 'new Vietnam'.[38] He contrasted American weakness with Iraq's steely resolve, as demonstrated in the war with Iran. It had 'a unified, experienced political leadership, forged over a span of many years in an environment of struggle and jihad [holy war], which has endowed it with experience in governing and directing combat operations'.[39] His view that the Americans lacked the stomach for a war was reinforced by Baker's readiness to meet Aziz on 9 January 1991, and, even after the start of the air war, the apparent American reluctance to get the land war started.[40] The objective was to play on these fears, denying the enemy a victory until it tired of the struggle. In this respect, Iraq could effectively win by not losing.

> As long as our blood is less, as long as our breath lasts longer, and at the end we can make our enemy feel incompetent. I mean the lower the devastation in our economy, the longer we can last ... the more we can make our enemy hopeless.

He urged his forces to prepare for a long war by not being profligate:

> the most important requirements of the long war are to conserve everything and execute the mission that is given to the men of the armed forces.[41]

But could he entangle the Americans as he hoped in a long and frustrating war involving high casualties? The answer to this question depended on the ability of Iraqi forces to absorb constant air attacks, before drawing the Americans and their allies into a gruelling land battle. 'Whenever someone wants to expel a combatant from some country,' he observed in January 1991, 'he will rely on the "groundpounder".' That was a reference to the foot soldiers who would 'come with a hand grenade and a rifle with a bayonet to fight against the soldier in the trench'.[42] In this contest, size mattered. As the coalition ramped up its numbers, so he ramped up Iraq's. He boasted of the numerous divisions that his country had mobilized, however poorly equipped, trained and motivated.[43] He kept in mind the same simple formula that had influenced him during the war with Iran, that a successful offensive requires a three to one advantage.[44] He relied on a 'pufferfish' defence that would alarm the enemy as capabilities were inflated suddenly.[45]

As his basic understanding of military strategy had been shaped by the war with Iran, Saddam did not appreciate the difference American air power would make. He dismissed warnings as exaggerations. The F117 'stealth' fighters could be 'seen by our shepherds'; cruise missiles could be blinded by firing 'mud and water' at them, so their radars could not function; the claimed ability of Apache helicopters to deal with multiple targets simultaneously over a long distance was 'just a myth';[46] the threat of aerial bombardment could be addressed by dispersing troops and getting them dug in and concealed. In January 1991, he claimed that a visitor to the front would see 'extremely few of the thousands of tanks and million men' and those that could be seen would be 'the ones who are moving along open roads. The others are all dug in and fortified.'[47] His prognosis was that only limited damage could be inflicted prior to the land battle, and, at some point, the enemy would need to accept that it had no choice but to move forward on the ground.[48]

THE BATTLE FOR KHAFJI

As Saddam considered the land war critical, he was frustrated that the Americans seemed content to rely solely on air power. It was of limited solace that he attributed this to the fear they had for the Iraqi army. He therefore pushed his commanders to develop a plan to trigger the land war.

> The plan was to enter into Saudi lands and occupy important locations that are the cornerstone of the mobilization and launching points of allied forces for the purposes of destroying them and engaging them in a land battle at a time and place that suits our troops and not the enemy's.[49]

The target was Khafji, a Saudi Arabian town close to the border with Kuwait. The Saudis had evacuated its population before the start of hostilities because of its vulnerability to Iraqi artillery. As it lacked any obvious strategic significance, it was lightly defended by Saudi and Qatari personnel. For Iraqi purposes, Khafji was perfect: an accessible target close to the border, providing an opportunity to hit the coalition, and demonstrate Iraqi military prowess and determination. The small garrison was assessed as likely to withdraw in the face of a superior Iraqi force.

In 2004, when he was being interrogated by the FBI, Saddam was asked who had planned the Khafji operation. He answered simply, 'Me.'[50] The Republican Guard developed three alternative plans, depending on how deep into Saudi Arabia it was intended to go. Khafji was the closest and therefore most realistic objective, with the other two available in the event that initial success enabled the attacking force to switch to more ambitious objectives. According to the army chief of staff, they were to be told by Saddam only at that moment which plan to execute.[51] From the start, therefore, the military objectives of the operation were unclear.

The operation was conceived of as a raid. Rather than seeking to occupy and hold the town, the aim was to drag the enemy 'into engagements with ground formations in the most expeditious manner or the fastest way possible'. After destroying oil facilities and enemy units, the attacking force would 'return to the main launching area'. A large enough force might allow the town to be held for longer, with a greater chance of drawing the coalition into attritional warfare. The defence minister and the chiefs of staff went so far as to recommend to Saddam 'that our forces could use the city as a safe base from which any further attacks deeper in the Saudi territory, where the invaders forces [sic] were concentrated, could be launched from'.

The plan was ready to go by 02.00 on 27 January 1991. Saddam briefed the relevant commanders personally. This required them to make a hazardous journey through Kuwait back to the command HQ at Basra, from where they were taken to a house being used by Saddam away from the main HQ. He was following his own advice on staying safe from attack and keeping messages secret. Headquarters, he had demanded, must be 'covered, fortified, and kept secret', with alternative buildings available, regular rotation between these sites, and civilian transport used in preference to staff cars. Because Iraqi communications might be intercepted, messages were not to be sent by phone, but delivered in person or by liaison officers by hand. The army commanders who would be undertaking the operation were therefore taken to this secret location to be given their orders. Saddam met them, accompanied by the joint chiefs of staff, some members of the general command and commanders of the relevant divisions and corps. According to Major General Mahmaud, commander of III Corps, after asking the assembled commanders about the condition of their forces and their readiness for the coming battle, Saddam dictated a series of directives for the upcoming attack.

Beginning with a lesson drawn from the war with Iran, Saddam emphasized the importance of challenging the enemy. Once Iraq had 'got involved in a serious way, the image of the enemy, which had long been highly thought of, got tarnished and collapsed'. It would be possible to get quick results by 'hunting' down the enemy so long as this was done 'in a calculated way and with decisiveness'. Fortunately, the Americans lacked 'the same level of determination as the Iranian enemy'. They might collapse, if confronted 'in a determined way'. For this reason, any losses in the coming battles could 'spare the blood of thousands of Iraqi people . . . hence we should take the battle very seriously due to its expected results'.

This was the message that the commanders were to take back even 'to the lowest-ranking fighter in the field' as they prepared for their first confrontation:

> should it fail, it would reflect negatively on our soldiers and result in a positive signal for the enemy . . . Should we succeed, then the war duration will be short, and there will be less bloodshed and the enemy's wailing and mourning will be heard everywhere.

The plan required elements of III Corps to seize and hold Khafji in the main effort, while two divisions from IV Corps would act in support to inflict 'the maximum amount of casualties and to capture prisoners'. It would be the job of the armoured divisions to distract enemy air power away from the town, while the mechanized divisions conducted the raid. After the orders were issued on 27 January, two days were spent getting artillery and armour into position. Consideration was given to how best to conceal movements, including using smoke from oilfields. The challenge was to get to Khafji quickly, and then dig in before they were spotted, to be 'underground before sunlight on 30 January'.

At 20.00 on 29 January, the diversionary force entered Saudi territory, while the 5th Mechanized Division of III Corps went off towards Khafji. The 6th Brigade, one of the units tasked with attracting enemy attention, did this too well and was effectively destroyed, providing a sobering introduction to enemy air capabilities. The brigade was 'spiritually collapsed' and its commander was relieved of his command. Other units wishing to avoid the same fate became inhibited in their movements. Supplies could only be delivered at night. One result of this was that many vehicles assigned to the attack could not be maintained and had to be abandoned. Marines in fast patrol boats were caught by Royal Navy helicopters.

The units rushing to get to Khafji were more successful. The southern outskirts of the town were reached before midnight. By early morning on 30 January, the north and western sides had been secured. Soon personnel and equipment were being put 'underground'. There was only one engagement, with a small Saudi Arabian border patrol.

At this point, the ambiguity about objectives kicked in. If this was just a raid, intended to make a point about the capabilities of the Iraqi army, then it would make sense to return quickly to Kuwait as envisaged. The alternative was to stay in position to engage more with coalition forces. Curiously, instead of taking a view, the General Command told the III Corps commander, Major General Mahmaud, that he could decide whether to stay or withdraw. Perhaps with the prospect of more glory to come and worried that Saddam would take a dim view of apparent cowardice, he decided to stay, and even considered using Khafji as 'a safe base' from which to mount an even more demanding operation to take another port town, Mish'ab. This was also one of the options prepared during the planning process, but was quite unrealistic, as Mish'ab was well to the south and no serious preparations had been made for an operation of this sort. It would only make any sense if there had been a palpable enemy collapse after the surprise Iraqi offensive. This was well understood by the commander of III Corps' 5th Division in Khafji. His division had been chosen because it was designed for rapid operations, which meant that it carried limited supplies and supporting arms. It was not designed for a defensive role, especially in the face of air attacks. He understood his task to be one of starting the attack 'at the last light of the day, and to come back at the first light [of] the following day'. Even after being so advised, Mahmaud replied that nonetheless the division would stay and defend Khafji.

After Iraqi units were surveyed by an American drone at first light, they were subjected to an intense and continuous air and artillery bombardment. Major air raids began in the early hours of 31 January. The divisional commander later recalled his men saying, 'Sir, protect me from the air and I will fight and take care of the land units.' This he could not do. 'Our fighters were heroes, they were disciplined and the commanders were excellent. However, the enemy's technical ability is too great.' As the air attacks created gaps in the Iraqi defences, coalition forces reached the edge of the town. The 5th Division commander requested permission from his III Corps commander to pull back into more defensible positions. Although Mahmaud had delegated authority, and had taken the decision to require 5th Division to stay and fight, he now thought it prudent to ask Baghdad's permission to withdraw. This was soon granted, but he then decided that the movement should not take place before dark. At 18.00 that evening, the order came for 5th Division to pull out of Khafji and return to its original position in Kuwait. While waiting to leave, it endured more air attacks. Eventually, somewhat battered, it got back to Kuwait.

If the aim was to unnerve the coalition, the operation failed. It left coalition commanders largely puzzled. At CENTCOM General Norman Schwarzkopf could not see any military logic. He described the operation as being 'about as significant as a mosquito on an elephant'.[52] To be sure the Iraqis had achieved surprise, but made no tangible gains. The Saudi units that had done most of the fighting had their morale boosted, while the Iraqis should now appreciate their vulnerability to air strikes. Saddam, however, was pleased. His army had shown that it had the will to mount complex operations in adverse conditions against a technically superior enemy. Never one to acknowledge defeat, he pronounced the battle a 'success' because it 'had defamed the enemy'.

CHAOTIC RETREAT

If Khafji was intended to bring forward the start of the land war it failed. Through February, much of Iraq's strategic military infrastructure continued to be devastated by air strikes. Instead of invading Kuwait, the coalition preferred to 'prepare the battlefield' through constant strikes against Iraqi positions. Neither the Iraqi air force nor the Iraqi navy could play much of a role in the face of superior coalition capabilities. One of the curiosities of the war was Saddam's decision to send ships and 137 aircraft for safe keeping in Iran. It is not clear if he was given any assurances, but, once the aircraft and ships arrived, the Iranians showed no inclination to hand them back to their bitter enemy of recent times.

Meanwhile, movement on the ground became increasingly hazardous, supply lines were disrupted and much Iraqi equipment was destroyed. A deserter described the miserable situation faced by soldiers at the front. They only got one meal a day, which was normally rice without meat. Water was scarce. They were exposed to regular bombardment, which they were unable to resist. Equipment was not replaced, and the bodies of the dead were left where they fell. To cap this, the soldiers did not believe in the cause for which they had been put in Kuwait. As a result, they were 'all thinking about surrendering to the Allied forces'.[53]

It may be that the extent of the damage and the declining morale was not fully appreciated in Baghdad and the Command HQ in Basra. Communications were poor, and field commanders were reluctant to convey bleak news. Saddam was inclined to see reports in the Western media about the damage being done as propaganda. Little change, therefore, was made to Iraqi deployments in Kuwait. On paper, there was an enormous commitment of some 43 divisions, although actual numbers of troops were fewer than supposed because of desertions. The plan was still for the front-line forces to absorb and contain the initial thrusts from the enemy, while more mobile armoured and mechanized divisions dealt with any breakthroughs. Behind them, the Republican Guard, along with some heavy formations from the army, would mount counter-attacks as well as prepare to defend southern Iraq, should this become necessary.

On the morning of 24 February, the coalition began its advance into Kuwait. During the first hours, Saddam was confident that 'our units remain excellent'. Soon a degree of urgency began to enter the discussions, largely prompted by Western media reports of Iraqi forces being overrun and surrendering. As nothing untoward had yet been reported back to Baghdad, Saddam's initial reaction was that these were lies and that everything was under control. His forward commanders were as much in the dark about the progress of the coalition offensive as Saddam's HQ. Major General Mahmaud, the commander of III Corps, had no idea just how far enemy forces had penetrated and how many of his brigades had already been destroyed. Even late in the day, he was still describing the situation as 'settled', confident that he had inflicted heavy casualties on the enemy.

A counter-attack was even prepared for early on 25 February. When it was launched, visibility was poor, a consequence of morning fog and the smoke from the burning oil wells, which had been set aflame just before the start of the land war by the Iraqis. Movement was slow. Although the corps commander claimed early success against the lead American units, as the air strikes came in severe casualties were sustained. The attack failed. What was left of III Corps withdrew into Kuwait City, preparing to fight for it. Yet a startling new order now came from Saddam: all remaining units were to withdraw towards Basra 'to cover the border [area] so we can distribute our divisions within the [Iraqi] cities'.[54]

A quick decision had been taken that morning. It was becoming evident that the army would be overwhelmed if it tried to defend Kuwait City. If they were defeated, then the coalition could move into the Iraqi homeland with little to stop them. Somehow the army had to be brought back to defend Iraq. Given the bombast that had gone before, Saddam and his senior commanders recognized that this retreat could be shameful and demoralizing. Saddam called his chief of staff in the forward HQ at Basra, Lieutenant General Husayn Rashid Muhammad, at 20.30 on 25 February from Baghdad.

> Husayn, I do not want our army to panic. Our soldiers do not like humiliation; they like to uphold their pride. Our goal is now to return our soldiers [to Iraq], but we want them to return with their heads up high [and] without humiliation.[55]

The troops must be extricated with their 'fighting spirit' intact. All military equipment that could not be removed was to be destroyed. The returning forces would then form a new 'protective line' to be established along the border towns. A full written order would be delivered to the forward HQ the next morning.

The withdrawal plan was put together in a hurry by members of the army staff, and then approved by the minister of defence and the army chief of staff. It had two aspects. The first was how to get the forces back to southern Iraq; the second was how they should prepare new defences once they got there. The first part of the plan depended on finding ways to keep traffic moving out of Kuwait, given the dire state of the road network. Some protection would be provided by Republican Guard divisions until they too had to get back to protect the southernmost city of Basra. The second part, according to the army chief of staff, involved 'instructions on how to fight in the cities and how we should be close to the cities. It listed instructions on mobilizing the citizens . . . the armed forces were to enter the city and fight [in] an urban warfare style. So we envisioned a huge confrontation [against the coalition] or [at least] a great challenge given our modest capabilities.' The order stipulated that once they had left Kuwait the forces would move to defend the cities of the south in cooperation with militias.[56] Early on the morning of 26 February, Saddam announced in a broadcast that 'on this day, our valiant armed forces will complete their withdrawal from Kuwait'. This would be the end of an 'epic duel' that had begun on 16 January, and that the 'harvest of the Mother of All Battles [has] succeeded'.

The first challenge was to get orders to the field commanders. Attempts were made to contact them about what was coming, but it was impossible to talk to those in Kuwait City. Communications between the forward HQ in Basra and the tactical HQs in Kuwait were barely functioning. As staff officers tried to deliver the messages in person, they were driving on bomb-marked roads, against the traffic and in the face of air attacks, leading to a number being killed. If they reached the tactical HQs, there were often no commanders to be found. A radio announcement that troops were to withdraw 'in an organized way to positions they held prior to 1 August 1990' was all that many of those commanding forces in Kuwait heard. This caused uncertainty and anxiety, not helped by rumours that the messages were false. Those that received the orders were not sure what to do with them. They were under continual bombardment, vehicles were burning and the weather was awful. Separate chains of command for the army and Republican Guard did not help. Communication between the two was poor, so that the retreating army had little information even on the position of the Republican Guard.

A withdrawal on this scale would have been difficult under the best of circumstances, and these were not the best. There could be no orderly retreat, with careful sequencing and a degree of covering fire. Instead, the retreat was disorderly. Dispersed units were unable to rejoin their parent organizations, and all scrambled to get away as quickly as possible. When units came across each other, they feared they were facing the enemy. Soon the roads were blocked, causing even more confusion – the local command structures effectively collapsed. In some cases, the orders to tactical commanders were coming from Ba'ath Party cadres, as nothing was getting through from the top. To add to the confusion, at 07.00 on 26 February, the orders changed. Having previously demanded that equipment be destroyed, now Saddam sent orders to the corps commanders that they must 'evacuate all equipment and wounded'. The army staff in Basra tried to adjust the withdrawal plan with a new sequence, but they lacked the information of the situation on the ground to be able to send realistic instructions.

While this was going on, the US 2nd Armored Cavalry Regiment came across the Tawakalna Republican Guard Division, in Iraq but close to the border with Kuwait. In what came to be called the Battle of 73 Easting, this relatively small force destroyed numerous tanks. In the official Iraqi account, however, the Tawakalna Division 'was able thanks to its good training and high spirits to engage in the battle with the enemy on the 26th of February and to inflict on him huge losses obliging him to interrupt his [attack] on al-Basra'.[57] The account indicates how everything was now viewed through the presumed framework of an allied drive towards Basra, and so anything which supposedly delayed or stopped the developing threat to Iraq became a victory.

On 27 February, Saddam wrote a long missive to the 'Advanced General Headquarters' in Basra. Stripped of the flowery rhetoric, the key message was bleak. The demand was to 'protect the safety, humanity, psychology, and the equipment of our armed forces'. This was required 'to enter the battle and to prove the abilities of Jihad against the infidelity and the treason at this stage'.

This means we have to give up the idea of defending all territories, properties, and roads of Iraq for some time and to pick what we should defend
from cities, territories, and properties. We have to accept the idea of not
being able to make all the roads coming out of this city to another city
open all the way. According to this brief analysis, the defence preparations that we thought to apply before the 27th of February are incorrect,
because you are familiar with our available capabilities.

The immediate goal was to ensure 'the best possible safety for the
fighters and their weapons, to raise their morale, and to raise their fighting spirit'. The defence was 'to line up along the edge of Basra city'.
Preparation should be made to defend Basra (and if necessary other
cities) from the inside of the city as well as the periphery. The aim was to
'protect the fighters and their weapons from the beasts and enables [*sic*]
us to push them back, if they were to imagine that they could enter the
city'. In order to ensure that there was sufficient 'food, supplies, weapons, and ammunition', civilians might need to be evacuated, although
there seemed to be discretion here depending on local morale.

Saddam's letter was followed up with yet another revision to the withdrawal order to 'reset for the defence of our borders and cities', with each
corps and Republican Guard division given an elaborate set of movements for them to take up a specific area of geographic responsibility. To
add to the urgency, they now realized that the coalition's 'left hook' of
armoured divisions could cut off the escape route from Kuwait into Iraq.
That morning, Saddam was told by the commander of the Republican
Guard that two divisions had been attacked and were struggling to cope.
'The enemy is continuing [its] assault and there was a heavy bombardment by helicopters against the troops of the Nebuchadnezzar Division.'
He asked for reinforcements. The need was met by the 10th Division (II
Corps), which was put under Republican Guard command.

SAVED BY A CEASEFIRE

Saddam now faced the overwhelming American superiority about
which he had been warned. As coalition forces moved to cut the road
between Baghdad and Basra, the Republican Guard and regular Iraqi
forces were both about to be isolated and destroyed. A depressed and

exhausted Saddam lashed out, accusing five senior officers of betrayal and ordering their immediate execution. He assigned new tasks to units, while lamenting, 'We do not know what God will bring upon us tomorrow.'

The disarray in which his forces were retreating may have spared him the humiliation of having to plead for a ceasefire. Instead, as he was contemplating defeat, he was offered one. After American aircraft attacked the front of the convoy trying to get from Kuwait to Basra on the bomb-damaged highway, trapped vehicles, unable to move, were struck and troops scattered. Western media was reporting 'turkey shoots' and 'rabbits in a sack'. This provided a troubling set of images and headlines when President George H. Bush met that morning with his top aides. They undermined the positive message of Kuwait's liberation. This was their core objective, and it had almost been achieved. By the next morning, the land campaign would have lasted 100 hours, so stopping the war at that point had a certain symbolic appeal. General Norman Schwarzkopf, commanding coalition forces, was asked for his view. He agreed that for 'all intents and purposes' Iraqi forces had been destroyed. He added: 'I'll check with my commanders, but unless they've hit some snag I don't know about, we can stop.' The position, as he soon reported back, was not so clear-cut. Iraqi forces were at least another day away from being truly trapped and some could still escape. Regardless, the president and his advisers decided that enough had been achieved and 'a battle of annihilation' was best avoided. A ceasefire was ordered. Some of Iraq's most capable forces escaped.[58] Whatever Bush's ultimate intention, if the war had continued for another day, with the prospect of all his forces being cut off, it is possible that Saddam would have fled.

This was not quite the way President Bush had hoped the war would end. He had described Saddam as a monster, comparing him with Adolf Hitler, and wanted his defeat to be unambiguous.[59] The models he had in mind, left over from the Second World War, were either of suicide in a bunker, as with Hitler, or a ceremonial surrender, along the lines of that of the Japanese on the USS *Missouri* in 1945. But having chosen to legitimize military action through the United Nations, working closely with Arab states and the Soviet Union, he was advised by his national security staff not to insist on such a decisive conclusion. He pushed back, but accepted that he must stick with objectives designed to secure the widest possible international coalition.[60] Still, once the war was under way, Bush spoke of Saddam as if he were the target, and opposition forces in Iraq could be forgiven for believing that they had Bush's active support for an insurrection. On 15 February, he urged the Iraqi people to 'take matters into their own hands, to force Saddam Hussein the dictator to step aside'. That day, with Soviet President Gorbachev trying to mediate on the eve of the ground offensive, he wrote in his diary: 'I don't see how it will work with Saddam in power.' Five days later, on 20 February, he expressed the same thought to his diary:

> What is victory – what is complete victory? Our goal is not the elimination of Saddam Hussein, yet in many ways it's the only answer in order to get a new start for Iraq in the family of nations.[61]

But the war aims were confined to liberating Kuwait and there was no plan to go further. Attempting to topple Saddam directly would break faith with a promise to stick to limited, internationally approved objectives, as well as require a challenging military operation. It could end up with the United States occupying a country it would be unable to govern. Some comfort was found in the thought that no leader could survive such a humiliating and costly defeat. The decision, despite contrasting public statements, was to leave his fate to the Iraqis. They would finish the job, either by a coup or an insurrection.

Wafiq al-Samarrai later reported how, up to the moment when Bush announced his ceasefire, the mood in Baghdad was gloomy and anxious. Saddam was tense and tired, close to tears. With the announcement, everything changed. 'Soon he was laughing and kidding and joking and talking about Bush.' Two hours later:

> Saddam came with his escort and media people to our headquarters and started to issue orders by phone. He became a hero and he felt that everything was now subdued and there is no more danger, and well, we have this legend in our history. He was feeling himself as a great, great hero. He started to go like 'We won, we won!'[62]

He claimed in a broadcast that he was the real victor, that Bush had only agreed the ceasefire to 'preserve the forces fleeing the fist of the heroic men of the Republican Guard'. The Iraqis had demolished the 'aura of the United States, the empire of evil, terror and aggression'.[63] Bush noted this with a degree of alarm. 'It hasn't been a clean end – there is no battleship *Missouri* surrender. This is what's missing to make this akin to WWII, to separate Kuwait from Korea and Vietnam.'[64]

Some weeks later, Saddam was already mythologizing these events. On the erroneous assumption that the American plan was to occupy Iraq, he credited the demonstrated superiority of his forces as explaining why Bush held back. '[We] considered the American strikes unsuccessful, regardless of their superiority. The morale and spirit of our people were the most critical issue, and it did not depend on just one situation, such as the number of damaged tanks, etc.'[65] As Saddam told his military staff on 3 March:

> Let's suppose that they militarily won . . . let God and the people be the witness. See how big their shame is. See how worried they were before they began their attack . . . their attack on Baghdad . . . There has been a reunion of the strongest powers existing in the world of the devils and the infidels. The strongest scientific, technological, and military powers [as well as] those with the highest financial and economic potentials [that] exist in the region and the world without any exception; they all got together against us and they did not succeed despite what happened. They did not dare attack Baghdad.[66]

Out of this moment came a self-serving narrative that there was something special about the forces he led in his own special way. 'I am very sure the criminal Bush did not expedite the ceasefire until he realized that our armor was [resisting] . . . He probably said to himself, "It is very apparent that he [Saddam] is going to cause us damage."' Later the narrative was embroidered with claims that the coalition were starting to experience serious losses.[67]

CONCLUSION:
CONTROLLING THE NARRATIVE

Bush's misgivings about concluding the war without a formal act of surrender by Saddam were warranted. Rather than be forced to sign a humiliating instrument of surrender, which had been his ambition for the Emir of Kuwait, Saddam was allowed to spin his own story about his great triumph: how, once again, as with Iran, he had fought a powerful and implacable foe to a standstill. Just as seriously, the terms of the ceasefire were not agreed until after it had been announced by the coalition. General Schwarzkopf viewed the discussions as a military matter about the separation of forces. Most importantly, because of the state of the roads, he allowed the Iraqis to use helicopters to complete the withdrawal of their forces. This turned out to be a crucial concession (Schwarzkopf later claimed he had been 'suckered'). Just as the war with the coalition came to an end, there were mass uprisings in Kurdish and Shi'ite areas. Coalition forces watched as they were put down with Saddam's customary ruthlessness, helped by the availability of his helicopters.[68] Eventually, as the Kurds were being driven into a desperate situation, the coalition intervened to provide them with 'safe havens', effectively providing them with their own autonomous territory.

As is often the case with narratives that look delusional from the outside, it is difficult to be sure whether a line had been adopted to persuade people that things were better than they really were, or whether this is what was actually believed. Saddam's narrative was that he had won. Although the effort to restore the Kuwaiti 'branch' to the Iraqi 'tree' had failed, his regime had survived its most severe trial. He was like an amateur boxer enjoying a moral victory after staying in the ring for ten rounds with the heavyweight champion. Survival was taken to be the result of the 'morale and faith' that allowed Iraq to cope with a stronger opponent.[69] Bush's defeat in the November 1992 presidential election confirmed Saddam's sense of personal triumph.

The narrative had important implications for the future, as Saddam claimed that the Americans would be deterred because of the shock they had received in 1991. 'After [America's] experiences with us, which did not achieve its end regardless of [our] withdrawal from Kuwait, they might wonder how much force they need to deploy this time to achieve what they failed to do last time.'[70] The professional military knew full well what they had been up against, and how they had barely coped with onslaughts from the air and then on the land. All of this had to be played down. Thus, Saddam told those doing a study into air power that they must not give the enemy a 'free advertisement' by illustrating the high enemy hit rate. This would only harm Iraqi fighters 'psychologically'. He added ominously, 'I'm sure that you do not mean this. Correct the study.'[71]

In the autumn of 1994, he appeared sufficiently confident that he prepared to invade Kuwait once again, and moved two divisions into position. He was told by the commander of the Republican Guard that his forces could accomplish the mission. When division commanders expressed doubts, he told them that Iraq would prevail in 'a spiritual battle'. The naysayers were advised 'not to read so much'.[72] In the event, a quick deployment of American troops dissuaded him from taking the plans further.[73]

A year later, at a conference attended by Saddam in December 1995, a senior officer of the Republican Guard spoke on the growing gap between American and Iraqi capabilities. He explained the ease with which the Americans would be able to destroy any targets. They would no longer depend on a heavy mechanized force. Saddam complained that he was a 'mental hostage of American thinking', observing that, if this view was right, all the assembled officers would already be dead. The effect of this censure was that those who made subsequent presentations toned down their comments, to avoid diverging from the claims of past victory and recovered military strength.[74]

Through the 1990s, Saddam worked hard to control the narrative and assert his own strategic genius. Going back even to the Iran–Iraq War, he reminded subordinates of how he then analysed the Iranians, through 'deduction and some of it through invention and connecting the dots, all without some hard evidence'.[75] All this was accompanied by a return to the climate of fear that led officers to dare to pass on only good news, promising that problems had been fixed when they were worse than ever. It was too dangerous for those low down the chain of command to take a decision. Every issue, however minor, was passed back up. Professionals were crowded out and again replaced by loyalists. Senior positions were filled by individuals who lacked not only the motive but also the intelligence to mount a coup. They learned to keep any doubts to themselves and say only what was expected. They looked out for the regime's spies, not to avoid them, but to ensure that they were present to hear that nothing inappropriate was being said in important meetings.

By the time the next great – and terminal – clash came with the United States in 2003, the command structures were wholly dysfunctional. Planning for the war was perfunctory. Saddam was only concerned about the defence of Baghdad. Here, the plan involved a series of concentric circles around the capital from which Republican

Guard divisions would withdraw on orders, until they fought to the death when the inner sanctuary had been reached. When the field commanders wondered how this might possibly work, they were told by Hussein Qusay, Saddam's son (who had been put in charge of the Republican Guard), that there could be no changes to the plan, because Saddam had already signed off on it. When US forces reached Baghdad in April 2003, they had little difficulty pushing the defending units aside.

In the same way as Stalin, Saddam relied on his ruthlessness, purging potential rivals and plotters before they could make a move. Like Stalin, he could also be tactically adept when his regime's survival was at stake. After he was caught by surprise by the German invasion of June 1941, Stalin knew that he needed his generals. Saddam came to the same conclusion in 1986. Then he used his position to frame the narrative to ensure that he gained credit for their achievements and to deflect blame for initiating foolish wars in the first place. He pulled off the same trick in 1991, despite an even worse defeat. A general who had led troops into one disastrous battle after another would be condemned for recklessness and shamed for the consequential losses, and then struggle to salvage his career.

This was an advantage of dictatorship. Saddam the political leader could rescue Saddam the military leader. Because his core objective was his own survival, and because he was still in charge as the dust settled after both the 1980–88 and the 1991 wars, he claimed victory, despite wholly failing to achieve his military or political objectives. Dictatorship offers the ability to control the official narrative of events. Members of the audience may know or suspect a different reality, but they are obliged to keep their doubts private. This is how Saddam turned the fortuitous ceasefire that ended the Gulf War into a vindication of his strategic prowess and a demonstration the great spirit of the Iraqi armed forces. By acting out his narrative, as if it were correct, however, he perpetuated delusion, discouraged candour, punished competence and created the conditions for his eventual downfall.

9

Command in a Fragile State:
Guevara, Kabila and the Congo

[T]here are too many armed men; what we lack are soldiers.
Ernesto ('Che') Guevara, letter to
Fidel Castro, 5 October 1965[1]

Even a committed army can soon descend into a sorry, desperate state when it faces overwhelming odds. Both the Pakistani and the Iraqi armies lost coherence and discipline as defeat loomed. In these circumstances, command becomes impossible, with the fog of war thicker than usual, and communications haphazard and disrupted. Orders are sent from headquarters by people who have no idea what is going on, to front-line officers unable to receive them, possibly because they are dead or captured. Soldiers look for ways to desert or surrender, and to avoid getting killed for a lost cause. In this chapter, we look at uncommitted armies that start in disarray and, even before the opening shots, are unprepared for combat. The chain of command barely functions, so that orders are habitually disregarded; a lack of training means that there is little idea about what to do with those orders that are received; troops and their officers are less interested in preparing for combat than making money, especially if their wages are minimal and often left unpaid.

The armies of this sort described in this chapter were beaten by those that were not. The Congo's armies had chronic problems from the start: feeble institutions, amateurish generals, a corrupt officer corps, and underpaid and ill-disciplined soldiers. As the Cuban revolutionary Che Guevara discovered, these problems were not confined to those who fought for the regime. They also afflicted those who rebelled against it. The first part of this chapter describes how Guevara came to the Congo

Congo/Zaire

CENTRAL AFRICAN REPU

CAMEROON

EQUATORIAL
GUINEA

GABON

REPUBLIC OF THE CONGO

Congo River

Sta
(Ki:

CONGO /Z

Kasai River

Léopoldville
(Kinshasa)

Atlantic
Ocean

N

ANGOLA

0   1,000 miles

0   2,000 km

0

400 mil

0

500 km

in 1965 to help turn a militia into a serious fighting force. He believed he could act as an agent of revolutionary change. He presented himself as an internationalist, confident in the potentially transformational character of bold military action, but soon found that his ideological zeal and desire for military discipline were not shared by his local inter-locutors. He made no headway. The fighters were poorly led, with a limited commitment to their cause, and wary of military actions that promised danger but little reward, menacing the local population as much as the regime did. The second part of this chapter demonstrates the inability of Congolese armies in the 1990s to cope with the profes-sionalism of Rwandan forces. It also underlines the point that military victories by themselves are insufficient when the politics has been poorly judged.

The link between the two parts of the chapter is Laurent-Désiré Kabila. He was Guevara's chosen protégé, because he knew the right things to say to gain the Cuban's attention, presenting himself as another Marxist revolutionary. He had a long career in this guise, though his successes were marked by survival as much as blows against the state. He survived so well that, 30 years after Guevara had given up on him and the Congo, he became the public face of an insurgency against a rotten regime, with an army led by Rwandans. Guevara was always the hero in his own story; Kabila was anything other than heroic, yet he was the one who eventually led a successful rebellion, albeit in singular and temporary circumstances.

The Democratic Republic of the Congo, one of the largest countries in Africa, suffered a series of calamitous wars following independence from Belgium in 1960. Although there were interludes, truces and trea-ties, fighting was never far away. These were wars of militias as well as armies, of commanders with more interest in position and plunder than patriotism and professionalism. The lack of strong loyalties to states or institutions was reflected in the feeble responses of governments when challenged, but also the limp nature of the challenges. Revolution and counter-revolution were often conducted viciously but without much conviction. Although ideology is relevant to this story, tribal and ethnic ties loom larger. However much an uncompromising revolutionary such as Guevara sought to forge unity among the oppressed masses by insist-ing that imperialism was the common enemy, the masses turned out to be divided in many ways.

AN ASPIRING WARLORD

Patrice-Émery Lumumba was the first prime minister of Congo when the country obtained its independence from Belgium in 1960, sharing much with Guevara. Both were charismatic, smart, left-wing firebrands, whose reputations live on as thwarted martyrs. Lumumba's moment in power was brief. Immediately after independence he faced multiple challenges: an army mutiny; the secession of the mineral-rich Katanga Province, led by Moïse Tshombe; and the return of Belgian troops. He asked the United Nations to intervene to help hold the country together. When he also sought assistance from the Soviet Union, he turned the West against him. After being deposed in September 1960 by President Joseph Kasavubu, supported by Commander-in-Chief Joseph Mobutu, he led a short-lived rebellion. Mobutu's forces captured him and handed him over to Tshombe in Katanga, where he was executed in January 1961 by secessionists and Belgian officers.[2]

The country was hit by unrest and lawlessness. The Armée Nationale Congolaise (ANC) had shown little interest in resisting the rebels. It had grown quickly from 10,000 to 30,000 after independence, but it lacked a command structure and experienced regular mutinies: the troops were poorly paid and resorted to lawlessness to supplement their income. The officer corps suffered from incompetence and criminality, with few able to give orders with any confidence that they would be obeyed.

Against this army, disparate rebellions were launched, but they lacked direction and discipline. The most effective involved rebels, describing themselves as Simbas ('lions'), who launched an offensive that led to the city of Kindu being taken on 21 July 1964, then Stanleyville, the country's third-largest city, on 4 August. Soon they were controlling a third of the Congo. It was led by some former members of parliament (the parliament had been closed down in 1963), who formed a government-in-exile known as the Comité National de Libération (CNL). The rebellion was led by Christophe Gbenye, the former minister of the interior, with Gaston Soumialot, his defence minister. They were supported by the more radical African countries such as Egypt and Tanzania, who helped them obtain arms. For Belgium, the former colonial power, the most alarming feature of the Simba rebellion was the explicit threat posed to the large numbers of their nationals stuck in rebel territory. Soumialot warned: 'I do not guarantee the safety of the Europeans of countries who are meddling in our affairs.' Reports from rebel areas, of economic chaos and random murders, were alarming. The Simbas' relations with the local population were at first better than those of the ANC, though they soon deteriorated.

Desperate to stop the rebellion, President Kasavubu recalled the hardline and anti-communist Tshombe from exile and made him prime minister. Using the threat of communist influence, he called for help from the United States, Belgium and South Africa. His troops were bolstered by the arrival of some 400 white mercenaries recruited from Rhodesia and South Africa, commanded by former British officer Colonel Mike Hoare,[3] who called his force '5 Commando'. On the government side were also the first Cubans to participate in the conflict, in this case anti-communist exiles, who flew aircraft against the rebels. Instead of giving recognition to Gbenye's new People's Republic, the recently formed Organization of African Unity urged ceasefires and reconciliation. As the mercenaries pressed forward towards Stanleyville, acting brutally as they went, the rebels placed all Europeans in the city under house arrest. In late November 1964, a combination of Belgian paratroopers, dropped by American transport aircraft, combined with mercenaries to take back Stanleyville. This concluded with 85 white hostages being killed, although another 1,800 were rescued. This pattern continued as the rebels were pushed out of other towns. Many more Africans than Europeans were killed, although this attracted less notice. By November 1964, the rebels had been pushed back to territory in eastern Congo, supplied from Tanzania over Lake Tanganyika.[4]

Kabila was born in north Katanga in 1939. His father was in the colonial administration and, after independence, had been sympathetic to the pro-Western secessionists in Katanga. Breaking with his father, Kabila's early politics were Lumumbaist, and he did not abandon this even after youths associated with the movement murdered his father. Kabila was already aspiring to leadership positions. Although his education did not go beyond primary level (which was more than most Congolese), he was intelligent, a voracious reader, and spoke fluent French along with native languages.[5] His ascent began early, starting with a prominent role among the Lumumbaist youth of his area. By July 1961, he was participating in a World Youth Forum in Moscow, which piqued his interest in Marxism. He then worked as cabinet director for the local minister of information in north Katanga, before quickly becoming a member of the provincial assembly.

In the summer of 1963, he edged towards armed struggle when he joined Gbenye and Sounialot's CNL. He became Soumialot's deputy and travelled to eastern Congo in January 1964 to launch operations. That May with some young Lumumbaist friends he tried to incite a mutiny in north Katanga. This collapsed when the soldiers realized that they were not going to get the better salaries promised. The main result was to prompt repressive measures by the army. Remnants of this group made contact with rebels fighting in the north, who then managed to take Albertville in July.[6]

Kabila was not involved in this fighting, having been travelling to gain support for the rebellion outside of Congo. Yet he had now shown sufficient commitment to count as a rebel leader, and was supposedly local commander in the eastern Congo. His base was Kigoma, on the Tanzanian side of Lake Tanganyika. This was the main supply point for the rebels, especially now that the Simba rebellion had largely lost its earlier gains. The location and the timing added to Kabila's influence. In November 1964, he was appointed the CNL's foreign affairs secretary and ambassador plenipotentiary to Tanzania, Kenya and Uganda. On 24 April 1965, he became the second vice president of the Supreme Council of the Revolution. These activities took precedence over his military role, which had never been prominent, and he spent little time at the front. The Tanzanian capital, Dar es Salaam, where the beleaguered CNL elite was in residence, was more comfortable. More importantly, he realized that, while he could delegate his command responsibilities, he could not expect others to look after his political career.

He was still only 25 and hugely ambitious. He might not have had Lumumba's star quality, but he was credited with an 'unusual type of charm that entailed a mixture of flattery, determination to pursue his goals, and a working-class Congolese humor that enabled him to connect with, and endear himself to, broad sections of society'.[7]

CHE GUEVARA LOOKS FOR
A NEW REVOLUTION

Guevara joined Fidel Castro's revolutionary group fighting the Cuban dictatorship in 1956. Although by origin a doctor from Argentina, he became Castro's second in command, one of a bedraggled group of 22 who gathered in the Sierra Maestra mountains after most of their comrades who had landed with them in Cuba had been killed or captured. They persevered, avoided capture and grew in strength. In January 1959, the dictatorship collapsed and Castro was installed as the country's new leader. Over those few years of revolution, Guevara developed a formidable reputation not only as a guerrilla commander, demonstrating total commitment to the cause, but also as an educator as well as a fighter. This was combined with rigid discipline. He was ready to execute traitors or deserters. Castro admired his comrade's commitment, intelligence and daring, and how he established his authority over his troops, but he also worried about his propensity to take risks and his 'tendency toward foolhardiness'.[8]

Still only 30 at the time of the revolution, Guevara then held a variety of government jobs under Castro. Engaging and intelligent, Guevara was happy to describe himself as an adventurer, as something of a Don Quixote figure. Running a ministry, however, was not his natural vocation. He was soon eager to return to what he saw as his true calling – a professional revolutionary, with an international perspective. He even had his own theory of guerrilla warfare, developed out of the Cuban experience, which he wished to apply in other settings. Unfortunately, his theory was flawed. He simplified the complex history of the Cuban revolution, playing down the importance of the moderate political stance adopted by Castro as he sought to gain popular support, and the part played by the urban working class and its leadership.[9] He exaggerated the importance of demonstrative military action, and the significance of American imperialism as a shared enemy and potentially a unifying factor for rebellious movements across the globe.

Guevara's revolutionary theory reflected the impatience of its author: there was no need to wait for the right conditions as the insurrection could create them. In underdeveloped countries, he argued, the countryside was the basic area of armed struggle, and here popular forces could win against an army.[10] These ideas reinforced the mystique surrounding Guevara, with his trademark beard, beret and cigar, telling of how resolute and committed revolutionaries could inspire others to follow them and take on the ruling classes.[11] Guevara intended to apply his thinking in his native Argentina, but the guerrilla group there was liquidated before he had a chance to join them.

Guevara's expansive view of the possibility of an international uprising against American imperialism, anticipating numerous separate insurgencies coalescing to inflict a decisive blow, meant that he could have chosen any of a number of locations with revolutionary potential, but, when touring Africa early in 1965, he settled on the Congo. He did so despite being unimpressed with the quality of the rebel leadership when he met them in Dar es Salaam. 'They had turned their situation into a veritable profession,' he noted, 'a job that was nearly always comfortable and sometimes lucrative.'[12] They were preoccupied as much with their many internal disputes and rivalries as they were with the enemy. Compared with Soumaliot, whom he found vague, Guevara was impressed with his young lieutenant. Kabila was 'clear, concrete and firm' when talking about the revolution.

Kabila certainly knew the right things to say. He told Guevara that he had just arrived 'from the interior' of the Congo (which turned out to be untrue) and that he 'understood perfectly that the principal enemy was North American imperialism'. Against this enemy he was ready to fight to the end. This declaration plus his 'self-assuredness' left Guevara with 'a very good impression' – so much so that in the name of the Cuban government, he immediately

> offered some 30 instructors and whatever arms we might have and he accepted with pleasure; he recommended speed in the delivery of both things.

At this point, Guevara did not offer himself, because, still a member of the government, he was in no position to do so.

Some other 'freedom fighters' he met were less sympathetic to his message. Their view was parochial. They doubted the concept of an international struggle against American imperialism, and could not see the value of bringing in militants from other struggles in Africa. They observed that 'their people, mistreated and debased by imperialism, would protest if anybody was killed in a war to free another country, rather than by the oppressors in their own country'. There was little interest in receiving Cuban trainers. They were far more attracted by the idea of being trained abroad, as a number had been in China. Guevara chided them that this would be costly and wasteful. 'Guerrilla fighters were forged on the battlefield not in academies.' With the condescension that marks his diaries he observed: 'Africa had a long way to go before it achieved real revolutionary maturity.'[13]

Having returned from his trip to get Castro's blessing and put his affairs in order, Guevara then disappeared from Cuba at the end of March in an elaborate disguise, prompting numerous rumours about why he had left and where he was going. He had arranged for volunteers, all black, to be recruited in Cuba, who were soon also on their way to Tanzania, leaving in dribs and drabs and eventually numbering over a 100. Instead of a training group, Guevara was to command a small force, suitable for combat. The idea was entirely his own. He persuaded Castro of its wisdom, but not friendly African leaders such as presidents Nyerere of Tanzania and Nasser of Egypt. Nasser warned him 'not to become another Tarzan, a white man coming among black men, leading them and protecting them . . . it can't be done'.[14] Certainly neither Soumaliot nor Kabila knew what he had in mind. They had signed up for only 30 military instructors.

Guevara intended to impose himself. His calculation was that once he was in place it would be difficult for his hosts to turn him away. 'I was blackmailing them with my presence.'[15] This created a tension that undermined the operation from the start. The Congolese either had to subject themselves to his command, which they did not wish to do, or Kabila had to insist that Guevara accept his command. This would be a daunting prospect for someone so young and inexperienced, and who was by no means devoting himself to his military duties. Yet without being part of a local force, if Guevara took any separate military initiative, in effect he would be initiating a war between Cuba and the Congo.

THE REVOLUTION FAILS

While Guevara was relinquishing his political positions to concentrate on fighting, Kabila, supposedly already a commander, was acquiring ever more grandiose titles and roles. The consequential neglect of his command was apparent as soon Guevara arrived at Kigoma on the shore of Lake Tanganyika. This was ostensibly the launch pad for operations into the Congo, but, as Guevara later observed, the town was a 'nefarious influence', with brothels, liquor and safety from actual combat.

This was about as far as Kabila got when he claimed to be 'in the interior'. Appalled at the licentiousness, Guevara hurried to get into rebel territory across the lake, arriving on 24 April at the base area of Kibamba. There he found a substantial and well-armed detachment of the Popular Liberation Army. Morale, however, was poor. The troops rarely saw their leaders, and they were disgruntled about being left in the field while their commanders had fun in Kigoma. The idea of integrating Cubans into their ranks and having a Cuban sit in on the meetings of their general staff evoked no enthusiasm. (Guevara, still anonymous, was presenting his second-in-command, Victor Dreke, as the leader of the group.)

The rank and file were ordinary peasants, who had their own distinctive culture and loyalties. This included a belief in magical potions – Dawa – that could keep them, but also the enemy, safe from bullets. Dawa fascinated Guevara. It involved special drinks and signs, yet, according to the belief, whether it worked depended on not only the witch doctor's power but also the fighter's own conviction in its strength and his good behaviour, such as not stealing another's goods or women. Political enlightenment, he noted, after discussing this with an apparently committed leftist officer, was no barrier to embracing Dawa as an article of faith.

After a few days, Guevara revealed his true identity to Kabila's local commander, Godefrei Tchamlesso. Tchamlesso was less than thrilled, fearing an 'international scandal'. He hurried back to Dar es Salaam to tell Kabila of Guevara's presence. Guevara proposed a five-week training programme for companies of 100 men, to be followed by some actual combat. But there was no response from Kabila, so he and his men were left with little to do, and weeks were lost to illness. Kabila, meanwhile, stayed away, busy with his higher political duties, but also unsure what to do with a force that in principle could take on the mercenaries, but that he would have to command under the shadow of one of the most famous guerrilla leaders of the age. He decided that his chief of staff, Laurent Mitoudidi, could act as liaison, with an injunction that Guevara must keep his identity secret.

Eventually, Mitoudidi brought an order from Kabila for an attack using two columns against an enemy bastion at Albertville held by a large contingent of mercenaries and Congolese soldiers. Guevara found the plan absurd. He had few troops (many were now sick), intelligence was poor and no proper preparations had been made. He sent Kabila an extensive report explaining why the most important task was to train and prepare for an anti-imperialist offensive. Targets had to be chosen carefully. He proposed that the rebels fight in mixed units, commanded in the first instance by Cubans (playing a similar role to Hoare's mercenaries in respect of those of the government). Kabila was effectively asked to cede strategy and command. 'We would guarantee direction of the fighting,' Guevara promised, 'in line with our concept of guerrilla warfare.'[16]

He got no reply, and saw little prospect in turning the Congolese troops into a fighting force. It dawned on him that his band of dedicated revolutionaries had entered a make-believe world. Exaggerations were routine: handfuls of men were claimed as large battalions, on their way to 'fronts' where there was no fighting. The soldiers sought to keep their distance from the enemy; the local commanders got drunk, while the senior commanders were largely absent, boasting about battles that had never occurred.[17] The only people with reason to fear this army were the local peasants, who frequently suffered 'outrages and mistreatment' at their hands. 'The characteristic of the Popular Liberation Army', Guevara lamented, 'was that of a parasitic army.'[18] He did have some hope for Mitoudidi, who tried to get his men to take the fight seriously, for example by punishing excessive drinking, but then he drowned in an accident crossing Lake Tanganyika.

After some time, he was replaced by Mudandi, a Chinese-trained Rwandan Tutsi, who came from Dar es Salaam with new battle orders. As we shall discuss shortly, the Tutsis had their own grievances, and were active rebels, but still had an uneasy relationship with the Congolese. The target was to be the Front de Force, the strongest garrison in the southern region, close to a hydroelectric plant. It had some 400 defenders. Kabila wanted conspicuous assaults on prominent enemy positions, in contrast to Guevara's guerrilla philosophy, which depended on ambushes and sabotage to undermine the enemy's confidence and was bound to be a 'slow and tenacious process'. Regardless, Guevara felt he had to accept the mission, as he was supposed to be serving the rebels. There was yet more frustration when he was told that Kabila would not allow him to take part, as he would be too much of a high-profile casualty. 'I can assure you as a man of action, I am impatient,' Guevara wrote to Kabila, adding that he was not implying any criticism. Kabila did not change his mind.[19]

The outcome was as Guevara feared. On 20 June 1965, a force of 160 local rebels plus 44 Cubans, divided into four and then mounted an attack with mortars and machine guns. Of the local men, 60 deserted before the fighting began and many others did not fire a shot. 'Every one of our fighters had the sad experience of seeing troops going into battle break up the moment the fighting began, dumping their priceless weapons anywhere to escape faster.' The Congolese withdrew as they took casualties, later blaming bad Dawa. The Cubans, having lost four dead, saw no point in continuing. Sixteen Rwandans were also killed. When Hoare's men found a Cuban passport and itinerary in the knapsack of one of the dead, their cover was now lost. The enemy now knew of the Cuban presence.

The situation in Kibamba was not helped by tensions between the Rwandans and Congolese. Mudandi shared Guevara's irritation with Congolese who would not fight for their own country. Kabila was accused of neglecting his men at the front, and a mutinous mood was developing. Guevara's own frustration at Kabila's continuing excuses for his non-appearance was not helped by little notes urging him 'to have courage and patience' and to remember that he was 'a revolutionary and had to withstand such difficulties'. Guevara realized that Kabila did not get 'the least pleasure' from his guest, whether because of 'fear, jealousy, or wounded feelings over the method I employed in coming'.[20]

On 7 July, Kabila at last arrived at the camp with a new commander, Ildefonse Masengo. But he only stayed five days before he had to go back to his politicking in Dar es Salaam, where there was a complex power struggle under way. Guevara noted that while their true commander was there the Congolese got busy, but then slackened again as soon as he left. When he said that he would take personal command of training and fighting, Kabila replied that a world-renowned revolutionary should not be risking his life on the front. Guevara promised that he knew how to take care of himself and was not seeking glory. He came up with plans for improved training and a new unified command structure, but got nothing but evasions from Kabila. Later Masengo did permit him to establish small teams of Cuban, Congolese and Rwandan fighters, to mount properly prepared but small-scale ambushes. The results remained frustrating. Five enemy soldiers were killed in a truck. The Rwandans fled from the shooting, but returned to take control of cases of liquor found in the truck. Guevara could not see how a war fought this way could end quickly 'unless something changed in how the war was directed – an ever more distant possibility'.[21]

Eventually, in mid-August, Guevara's patience ran out, and he decided to take command in the field without Kabila's consent. He returned to the target at Front de Force, intending to take stock of the troops and terrain, and to assess the prospects for action. 'I couldn't get Kabila to come,' he told his men. 'If he wants me to return to the base, he will have to come.'[22] On 11 September, under his command, 40 Congolese, 10 Rwandans and 30 Cubans ambushed an enemy convoy. It was the same problem as before in that the Congolese withdrew quickly, although this time the Rwandans held their ground. He suffered no casualties, and captured some weapons, ammunition and documents.

Meanwhile, the wider rebellion was suffering from rivalry and factionalism. There was some fighting between pro-Gbenye and pro-Soumaliot groups. When Guevara met other local commanders, they showed neither interest in sending him men to train nor evidence that they actually had forces available to be trained. The gap between his aspirations and the harsh reality of the situation was clear. He wanted to create a 'perfectly armed, well-equipped, independent column that can be both a shock force and a model'. Such a force would change 'the panorama' considerably, but until that was done, 'it will be impossible to organize a revolutionary army; for the low quality of the chiefs prevents it.'[23]

Meanwhile, back in Cuba, Castro had been sufficiently enthused by specious reports of military progress, after a meeting with Soumaliot, to want to send more Cubans. They 'have sold you a huge streetcar', Guevara wrote to Castro. 'It would be tiresome to list the large number of lies they have told.' Sending any more men to the Congo would be harmful 'unless we decide, once and for all, to fight on our own. In that case, I will need a division, and we will have to see how many the enemy will throw against us.' For the moment: 'I don't need good men; here, I need supermen.'[24]

If anything, the presence of the Cubans helped the government more than the rebels. Tshombe used the spectre of communist Cubans infiltrating the Congo to get American and Belgian backing. Hoare's mercenaries began an offensive that soon had the rebels on the back foot. On 13 October, the political context changed again when President Kasavubu dismissed Tshombe, realizing that he would never get support from the other Africa governments while the hardline anti-communist was prime minister. This led to an attempt at political reconciliation, which the more radical African governments encouraged. The combination of the successful offensive against the rebels, the loss of the support of radical African states and the possibility of a political settlement all put the Cuban position in doubt.

In late October, having been pushed back, Guevara prepared for a last stand against an advancing enemy. But, after the Congolese fled the Kibamba base, and against all his instincts, he decided to retreat, as he was close to being surrounded. His men saw little point in a defiant act of resistance on behalf of an evaporated liberation movement. On 1 November, an urgent message came from Dar es Salaam that the Tanzanian government had decided to wind up the Cuban expeditionary force. This was 'the coup de grâce for a moribund revolution'. Yet still Guevara did not want to leave, resisting entreaties from Castro. With a small band of dedicated men, he was prepared to connect with other rebel groups. In the end, it was too much to ask of others. On 20 November, he crossed Lake Tanganyika back into Tanzania. 'All the Congolese leaders', he wrote, 'were in full retreat, the peasants had become increasingly hostile.' The next day he reached the Cuban embassy in Dar es Salaam and began to write his own account: 'This is a history of a failure.'[25]

'If I had been a better soldier,' he wrote, 'I would have been able to have a greater influence.' That was not actually the problem. He was a foreigner inserting himself into a conflict that he did not understand, seeking to turn it into a struggle against the Americans rather than the local despot, promoting a concept of a revolutionary army far removed from the harsh realities of the Congo. By getting his hardened veterans to work with the Congolese fighters, he sought to 'promote what we called the "Cubanization" of the Congolese'. As he came to recognize, the influence was if anything in the other direction.[26] He wanted his force to be a determined and clear-sighted vanguard, but it became something more chaotic. He was seeking to clone himself as a model of revolutionary command, without questioning whether this made sense in the circumstances of the Congo in 1965.

Early on, in seeking to explain the importance of training to his hosts, he noted that of 'every 100 men two or three might become command cadres'. Later, he complained to Kabila about a 'lack of a single central command with real power over all the fronts, to bring what in military terms is called the unity of doctrine', and of insufficient 'cadres' that had a 'high enough cultural level and absolute fidelity to the revolutionary cause. The consequence of this is the proliferation of local chiefs with authority of their own and tactical and strategic freedom of action.'[27] He despaired of the Congolese soldiers who held back from a struggle for which they had sworn to die, asking if they understood the meaning of the phrase 'If necessary, unto death.'[28] Guevara was always prepared to die for his ideals and in the end that is what he did – in October 1967, in Bolivia, where he was captured and executed at the end of another failed insurgency. In the Congo, as elsewhere, individual fighters and their local officers did not share his readiness for sacrifice in the name of the revolution, whatever the ideological claims and boasts of military prowess made by their leaders.

KABILA'S WILDERNESS YEARS

Much later, when Kabila was in power, Guevara's posthumously published diary carried an unflattering portrait. Kabila was judged to have the 'genuine qualities of a mass leader', but lacked 'revolutionary seriousness, an ideology that can guide action, a spirit of sacrifice that accompanies one's action' (qualities that Guevara certainly saw in himself). 'I have grave doubts', the report card concluded, 'about his ability to overcome his defects in the environment in which he operates.' Another Cuban observed of Kabila that, with such leaders, 'Africa can expect to have long centuries of slavery and colonialism'.[29] Godefrei Tchamlesso, who was close to Kabila at this time and later emigrated to Cuba, had a similar assessment. He never questioned Kabila's revolutionary credentials or his 'capacity as a leader'. He was, however, 'looking for a soft billet, and he didn't have enough – any, in fact – military experience'. He was an 'agitator' who

> lacked the seriousness, the self-assurance, the knowledge and the innate talent you can see in a Fidel and that you can see in other leaders, who

headed the guerrilla force ... He was more of a politician who knew about urban insurrections and how to conspire in the streets.[30]

From the perspective of 1965, Kabila's later rise to power would have come as a surprise. The retreat from Kibamba, leaving large amounts of materiel and documents behind, harmed his reputation. He took the opportunity to reinvent himself. In March 1966, he arrived in Nanjing in China for six months of military training. While he was there, the Cultural Revolution was launched by Mao Zedong, celebrating extreme radicalism and intense self-criticism. Out of this came Kabila's most significant political text – *The Seven Errors*. The first mistake on his list had been a lack of 'precise political education'. The self-criticism continued. Pointedly, he noted that there had been too much reliance 'on external support and advice'. There were observations about waging war 'without goal or sense', a rush to 'seize large towns' while forgetting 'to first take small villages and to work with peasants and workers'. There had been a lack of 'discipline and collaboration', fights over 'ranks and fame', so that 'everybody wanted to be in charge and to get positions for himself and his relatives'.[31]

In late 1967, back from China, he set up the Parti de la Révolution Populaire (PRP) in South Kivu, where he found some remnants of the 1965 rebellion among the Bembe people, who were prepared to work with him. His statelet was organized on Maoist lines, Kabila himself now at the centre of the cult of personality, insisting on strict military discipline and ideological training. Conditions were harsh. Little threat was posed to the regime, but, with some 1,500 potential combatants, Kabila had sufficient force for his own security.

The notional target of this new rebellion was Joseph-Désiré Mobutu. He had formed his military dictatorship following a November 1965 coup, just after the defeat of the rebellion. His highest military rank before independence had been sergeant, which was as far as Congolese were allowed to advance under the Belgians. He had then worked as a typist and journalist, before his arbitrary appointment as chief of staff by Lumumba. After his coup, he continued this unqualified elevation by appointing himself field marshal. His Popular Movement of the Revolution (PMR) became the sole legal party in 1967. The name of the country was changed to Zaire in 1971, and his own to Mobutu Sese Seko in 1972.[32] Backed by the West, and later by China, because he was anti-Soviet, Mobutu's instincts were totalitarian and kleptocratic. The corruption and incompetence of his regime undermined his attempts to suppress the fragments of the rebellion. Kabila's PRP activists in South Kivu, for example, had a more transactional than combative relationship with the Zairean Army. Their presence allowed the army to claim resources for anti-guerrilla operations. In practice, they exchanged uniforms, ammunition and some goods for gold. Despite presenting itself as a secessionist Marxist state, this enclave more resembled 'a network of loosely affiliated businessmen smuggling gold and diamonds for a cut of the extortion and robbery profits'.[33]

One reason for the more transactional approach to armed struggle was the American-Chinese rapprochement of 1972, which was not only ideologically confusing but also led to the limited financial support from China drying up. Kabila got into trouble when, in May 1975, the search for funds led to some of his men kidnapping three Americans and one Dutch student from a research project in Tanzania. The ransom may have helped financially, but the incident drew attention to Kabila's movement acting without restraint. Humiliated, Mobutu launched attacks against the enclave. In 1977, in the face of these attacks, Kabila left with his family to Dar es Salaam. The PRP enclave continued until the early 1980s, when an initiative by the local governor led to many fighters giving up. They now doubted that they could have a role in toppling Mobutu and suspected that they were being used by Kabila for his personal benefit.

Almost a decade presiding over his own territory led Kabila into bad habits. He was authoritarian and quick to stamp out perceived rivals. He was a womanizer (including sleeping with the wives of his commanders, possibly as a way of demonstrating his power over them), who ended up fathering at least 24 children with six women. Yet he had also been able to use his base to establish himself as a leading opponent of Mobutu, and in this guise keep up his international contacts. Later in the 1970s, Kabila was encouraged to work with a Katangese group known as the 'Tigers' based in Angola by the local leftist leader Agostinho Neto. But the PRP no longer had any military clout, and the Tigers did not see Kabila as a leader. When they launched attacks, they did so without any contribution from the PRP.

Kabila then switched his focus to Katanga, where for a while he teamed up with Alphonse Kalabe, who was preparing to start operations against Mobutu. Their men briefly occupied the town of Moba in November 1984, before it was retaken and Kalabe arrested. Kabila entertained the idea of mounting his own operation to take Moba back in June 1985, but by then he only had a dwindling band of exhausted fighters, dubious about a leader who was never with them but instead issued orders from abroad. After this Kabila concentrated on his business, mainly the gold trade, while maintaining his position as a principled opponent of Mobutu, avoiding the bush, but instead 'preferring to hopscotch through the socialist world in search of support for his rebellion', while writing revolutionary pamphlets 'using ornate prose and Marxist jargon'.[34]

RWANDA'S PUPPET

This marginal existence suddenly changed in the summer of 1996, when Kabila was visited at his house in Dar es Salaam by the Rwandan intelligence chief, Patrick Karegeya. The Mobutu regime was ripe for overthrow. The Rwandan and Ugandan governments were ready to make it happen, but they needed an authentic Congolese leadership if the new regime was to have any legitimacy. When they looked for candidates to play this role, they were not exactly spoilt for choice. Soon Kabila was part of a hastily concocted coalition known as the Alliance of Democratic Forces for the Liberation of Congo-Zaire (AFDL).

Mobutu was vulnerable for a number of interrelated reasons. With the end of the Cold War, the West no longer needed him as a bulwark against Soviet influence, and his corruption and brutality had become embarrassing. Up to this point, the rottenness at the core of the regime had been obscured by external support. It was exposed to the full when support was withdrawn after 1990. For a moment Mobutu toyed with the idea of a political transition to a multi-party democracy, but the experiment was never very serious and soon he returned to his repressive ways, only this time against a background of economic failure and indebtedness. The effect on his military capability was catastrophic. There was no money to pay the armed forces. Officers and men sustained themselves by selling to the black market whatever they could lay their hands on, including fuel and equipment. Some turned to outright criminality.

This was also a violent time in the wider 'Great Lakes' region. Behind it was the long-standing conflict between Hutus and Tutsis in Rwanda, which went back to the nineteenth century. The Belgians installed a Tutsi King, despite the majority of the population being Hutu. After the Tutsi monarchy was abolished in 1959, many Tutsis fled into the Congo and Uganda to escape vengeful Hutus. The Tutsi fightback began in 1986, when Yoweri Kaguta Museveni became president of Uganda, after his National Resistance Army (NRA), many of whose members were Tutsi, toppled the government. In October 1990, a Tutsi army in exile, known as the Rwandan Patriotic Army (RPA), invaded northern Rwanda from Uganda. This challenged the regime of Juvénal Habyari-mana, a Hutu, who had taken power in a 1973 military coup. The invasion was blocked by the Rwandan army (known as FAR), sup-ported by Zairian and French troops, and its leader was killed.

After this setback, the RPA regrouped under Colonel Paul Kagame, formerly chief of military intelligence under Museveni, who had attended the US Army's Command and General Staff College at Fort Leavenworth as a Ugandan officer. There then followed a period of inconclusive fighting, with occasional peace negotiations, until April 1994, when Habyarimana was assassinated (along with the president of neighbouring Burundi), when his jet was shot down while landing at Kigali airport, returning from negotiations in Tanzania. The culprits may have been extremist Hutus who were concerned that he was making too many concessions to the Tutsis, or they may have been Rwandans.[35] What followed was a horrific genocide, as the Interahamwe (One Together) and other Hutu paramilitaries massacred opposition politicians, moderate Hutus and, mostly, ordinary Tutsis, in a horrific frenzy of killing. The estimate of those murdered is normally put at some 800,000.

The slaughter did not affect the RPA, who stayed safe in Uganda. They took advantage of the chaotic aftermath of the genocide to launch a new offensive and take the country over. As a gesture of unity, Kagame appointed a Hutu to be the new president of Rwanda, but there was no doubt that he was in charge. Some 1.2 million Hutus now fled to Zaire, including many members of the militias who had been responsible for the genocide. The latter took control of the refugee camps and prepared, with Mobutu's compliance, a counteroffensive into Rwanda. Kagame saw them as a threat not only to the new regime in Rwanda but also to the many Tutsis living in Zaire. The international community was dithering, so he decided that this intolerable situation could be addressed only by entering Zaire to take down the Hutu bases and if possible overthrow Mobutu. Kagame had impressive support from neighbouring African countries, and, having overcome a numerically superior force when invading Rwanda, he was confident of the competence and discipline of his forces.

What he needed was national leaders to provide cover for an external intervention. This is why Karegeya visited Kabila in the summer of 1996. Nyerere, now out of office but still an influential figure, was well aware of Kabila's flaws but nonetheless recommended him. He was an authentic Congolese leader, not a Tutsi, and also had close ties to Tanzania's intelligence services. Kabila was soon in the Rwandan capital, Kigali, with three other figures. André Kisase Ngandu was another rebel leader of a similar vintage to Kabila, who was still leading a few hundred fighters on the Uganda–Zaire border. In addition, there was an architect from North Kivu, and Anselme Masasu Nindaga, a young man from Bukavu who had become a soldier in the Rwandan army, and could appeal to the country's youth.

From the start, Kabila was underestimated. Karegeya thought him an old man who seemed like a 'relic of the past', with his reminiscences about anti-imperialist struggles, and lapses into Marxist theorizing. Searches for Kabila's men who were supposedly still fighting against Mobutu showed that he had no mass following. The few former comrades who eventually joined Kabila in Kigali looked like 'janitors who had lost their brooms'.[36] Kabila was out of touch with the modern world, surprised by new technologies such as laptop computers and satellite phones. It is not hard to see why the Rwandans would have thought him an easy man to control and so a suitable figurehead. But, at 55, he was not that old and, while he may have been an absent and inept military commander, he remained politically shrewd. He soon put himself to the fore of the AFDL, largely wrote its founding document, and had himself named as the spokesman. As the visible face of the movement, and in touch with other exiles from Mobutu's rule, he became de facto leader. Colonel James Kabarebe, who had served as Kagame's aide-de-camp during the 1990–94 Rwandan civil war and was now commander of the Rwandan Presidential Guard, did all the planning and commanded the forces in the field. He was a far more capable military strategist than Kabila, but neither he nor

Kagame had thought through how the politics of the operation was likely to play out.

MOBUTU OVERTHROWN

On paper, the balance of forces at the start of the war clearly favoured Mobutu, with some 60,000 men in his armed forces, compared initially to around 2,500 behind the rebels. Zaire's army had enjoyed supportive links in the past with some of the most capable forces in the world, and many of its officers had trained at the top military academies.

Yet there were pathologies at work that had been present since colonial times. As with the Belgians, military and policing functions were intertwined. When there had been serious trouble they had to look for outside support – in the early years this had come from UN peacekeepers, mercenaries and Belgian paratroopers. As someone who had come to power by means of a coup, Mobutu did not wish to become a victim to one himself. He became a prime example of a dictator 'coup-proofing' his army, whatever the cost in terms of professional competence. He trusted his own paramilitaries more than the regular army, created a variety of units that were pitted against each other, and removed officers, however capable, who might plot against him. Eventually, he concluded that family and ethnicity were the only guarantors of loyalty. By the 1990s, half of the 62 generals in the armed forces came from his home province of Équateur, and a third from his Ngbandi ethnic group.[37]

Compounding all these problems was the country's indebtedness. Soldiers were not paid and could barely feed their families. To be appointed to a command was to acquire a business opportunity, based on extortion or smuggling. The rot went right to the top. The army's chief of staff siphoned fuel from military stocks to run a fleet of taxis; the commander of the Presidential Guard used army trucks for copper smuggling.[38]

The rebel forces were more committed. At the core were many combat veterans, mainly Banyamulenge, ethnic Tutsis who lived in Kivu by the Rwandan border. Rwanda provided the command structure.[39] The fighting between the two forces was occasional and limited, because, for much of the time, the AFDL forces were advancing and the Congolese retreating, often in disarray. There was horrific violence as a result of the Hutu–Tutsi tension at the heart of the conflict. Both communities had reason to be frightened. The Congolese Tutsi saw local hotheads agitate against them. The Hutus in the border camps feared vengeful Tutsis, just as the Rwandans saw the camps as a base from which new offensives might be mounted against them. This was a recipe for a series of massacres in both directions. The humanitarian consequences were appalling. The numbers might not have reached those of the 1994 genocide, but they were still in the hundreds of thousands.

The original Rwandan strategy was to encircle the refugee camps at the border, but to leave an eastern corridor, so that those who wanted to return to Rwanda could do so. At one level, it was extraordinarily successful. Some 800,000 Hutus trekked back to Rwanda, relieved not to be attacked as they did so. The other 400,000, who pushed through to escape to the west, were assumed by the RPA to be the Interahamwe and hardline Hutus who threatened them the most. Rwandan leaders later admitted to 'excesses', put down to the raw memories of the genocide and the fear that its perpetrators were about to return. They noted the failure of the international community to intervene, despite their appeals. From Kagame's perspective, the international relief effort to support the refugee camps allowed his enemies opportunities to hide and plot. In an early battle over Bukavu, the hardline Zairian General Gratien Kabiligi fought his defensive battle in a way that ensured that refugees were in the path of artillery fire, which he seemed to see as a punishment for those Hutus who had refused to flee with his hardliners.[40]

The fall of Bukavu, in October 1996, foreshadowed the future pattern of the conflict. Jason Stearns describes the experiences of Lieutenant Colonel Prosper Nabyolwa, a Zairian officer trained in Belgium and the United States. Because he came from the region, his career had been restricted and his orders came from men without his military education. The other officers were more concerned with their businesses. 'They would come to staff headquarters wearing gold rings and chains, sometimes even sunglasses, smelling of cologne.' In the town, there were 800 presidential guards, 1,000 civil guards and 200 paratroopers, all answering to different chains of command. The paratroopers were working for private security companies. The presidential guards insisted that their role was to protect refugees for the United Nations and refused to go to the front lines. There was little actionable intelligence. Nabyolwa had no idea whether they were facing 300 or 3,000 enemy troops. When he radioed to say he urgently needed one battalion of special forces, the commander of the Presidential Guard answered: 'We have problems in Kinshasa, too, you know. We need the soldiers here.'

As refugees rushed into the town to escape the Rwandans, and ethnic violence began to escalate, Nabyolwa went to the most forward position to rally his troops, just in time to find them getting into a truck: 'Colonel. You are on your own.' Back in the town, he asked his commanding officer to get reinforcements. He said he would travel personally to Kinshasa to do so. Three times he asked Kinshasa for more troops. Nothing came. The only issue was how to retreat. There were ideas about regrouping out of town to prepare a counter-attack, but there was no longer much of an army. When Nabyolwa ordered some troops to rescue a general who was caught in a vulnerable position, he was accused of being a traitor. 'Every time you send us into battle, we get attacked.'[41]

The Rwandans used the chaos and disloyalty on the Zairian side to their advantage, speaking with commanders in Kinshasa and on the front line. 'We had extensive infiltration, we used money, we used friends. It wasn't hard.'[42] Zairian forces barely tried to fight and were content to surrender even to units much smaller than their own. A key part of the rebel strategy was to leave Mobutu's force an escape route, confident that it would be taken. The AFDL units grew as they were joined by the Katagan Tigers and Ugandan units. Unable to rely on his own forces, Mobutu recruited about 280 mercenaries (mainly French and Serbs) under Belgian command, but they were too disorganized to make much impact.

Unlike his Zairian counterparts, Colonel Kabarebe, who masterminded the campaign, led by example, eating with his officers and going to the front line for offensives. When considering tactics, he would listen to what others had to say before deciding. His chain of command led to Kagame and Museveni. Below him, Rwandan officers provided the command structure, although the Rwandan proportion of the rebel forces declined as more Congolese joined.[43]

Ostensibly, these were the forces of the AFDL and Kabila was now recognized as its leader, but he had little to offer on the military side. He was happy to take the credit for the AFDL's advances and made a point of speaking at each town after 'liberation', Kabarebe later recalled:

> Laurent Kabila had strange notions of military tactics. In Kisangani, when we were blocked by the mercenaries, he came to me, urging me to put soldiers up in the trees and, on command, to start shooting in all different directions at once. He said it would confuse the hell out of the enemy![44]

Nor did he attempt to give much political direction. He understood that victory depended on the Rwandans, and therefore that in these situations you had to pay attention to those providing you with a bodyguard. Ngandu, who was far more concerned to demonstrate his autonomy from the Rwandans, lost his bodyguard at one point and was killed. Kabila, by contrast said little and was apparently subservient, earning him the nickname of Ndiyo Bwana ('Yes Sir' in Swahili).

Yet he knew what he was doing, asserting himself more as AFDL forces rolled forward to Kinshasa. When Mbuji-Mayi, the country's diamond hub fell, he rushed forward to get cash. His old home town, Lubumbashi, a copper capital, allowed him to meet with heads of international mining corporations. As the army advanced, he came in behind giving rousing speeches and encouraging youths to join the rebellion. He declared himself the new president, without warning or consultation, before Mobutu had left the capital. Because he had emerged as leader, there was no one to contradict him. Soon he was being approached to meet Mobutu to arrange a transfer of power. This was done with Nelson Mandela presiding on a South African boat on 4 May 1997. But Mobutu refused his demand to step down and returned to Kinshasa.

The old dictator was now dying of pancreatic cancer. The chief of staff he had appointed in December, General Donat Mahele, realized that all was lost and shared concerns that any attempt at resistance would produce a bloodbath in the city. Through the Americans, he worked out with Kabila a plan for him to read a speech telling his troops to stand down when the rebels walked into the town. He would fly to the Zambian capital, Lusaka, where Kabila could be recognized as leader. Although others believed a stand could be made, Mahele persuaded Mobutu to give up. Before he could proceed to the next stage of his plan, however, he was murdered by a gang of former presidential guards.

TO THE NEXT WAR

Kabila had become president because he had pushed himself forward to lead a cobbled together and unnatural coalition, after he had been picked out by the Rwandans from a small pool of politicians with a consistent record of opposing Mobutu. He had provided the public face, and occasional voice, for an uprising to overthrow the regime, but the military campaign had been under Rwandan command. The Rwandans were smarter in the military sphere than in the political.

Any political leader they helped install would face legitimacy questions, but Kabila had particular handicaps. He was a throwback to an earlier period of anti-colonial struggle, with his quaint rhetoric and Maoist theories, 'a political Rip van Winkle whose conspiratorial political style had been frozen at some point in the 1960s'.[45] His ideology demanded national self-reliance and state control of the economy, but the administrative capacity for such an undertaking was completely absent. Zaire now became the Democratic Republic of the Congo (DRC), but a new name could not erase the legacy of a country plundered and degraded by the previous president. The DRC was one of the largest, and potentially richest, African countries, but Kabila was in no position to govern it. A state that lacked robust institutions, the manner of his coming to power and his own political personality combined to provide a weak foundation for stable government. After the Mobutu years, there was a lot of international goodwill towards the DRC, but it was squandered, with companies prepared to invest in the country unable to find a way of doing so. Kabila was erratic and impulsive, with numerous special advisers and no clear lines of responsibility. His comrades and ideas associated with his old party, the PRP, were influential. He sought to consolidate his hold on power, but in doing so he became subject to the same pathologies that had afflicted Mobutu. The DRC became a one-party state, but the party was no longer the AFDL, which had always been an artificial construct and whose other leaders had either been killed or imprisoned.

The situation aggravated Kabila's authoritarian tendencies and encouraged paranoia. Other politicians in the Congo who had also opposed Mobutu enjoyed a larger popular following. He did not enjoy any natural legitimacy and so trusted only members of his family and ethnic group, while putting down opponents, more ruthlessly even than Mobutu, and bribing others. He even followed Mobutu in promoting himself to field marshal. He wanted to run the country along the half-baked Maoist lines he had begun to formulate in the late 1960s, which allowed points of ideology to become matters of dispute.

Most of all, although not a Tutsi, he was perceived to be a puppet of Rwanda. Without them, he would not have achieved power. Rwandan commanders had charted a path to victory. Nindaga described himself as a general and the 'army boss', but only lasted until November before he was thrown in jail. When Kabila was asked that month about the army command structure apart from himself he replied cryptically: 'We are not going to expose ourselves and risk being destroyed by showing ourselves openly . . . We are careful so that the true masters of the army are not known. It is strategic. Please, let us drop the matter.'[46] This was taken correctly as confirmation of Rwandan control.

Real military power rested with James Kabarebe. He was chief of staff of the Forces Armées Congolaises (FAC), but still retained his Rwandan citizenship and commanded a battalion of crack RPA troops in the capital Kinshasa, to look after Kagame's interests as much as Kabila's. Kabarebe stayed close to Joseph, Laurent Kabila's son, who became his deputy; perhaps Kabarebe thought that would cement ties with the father. Joseph saw the Rwandan as his mentor and friend, but Kabarebe's relationship with Laurent Kabila deteriorated. Laurent Kabila began to fear that the Rwandans could replace him as easily as they had put him in position. He also knew that they were unpopular in the country. On 14 July 1998, he abruptly dismissed Kabarebe as chief of staff, but for the moment kept him on as adviser to his successor, Célestin Kifwa. Then, unexpectedly, he visited Cuba for a working meeting with Castro, apparently catching his host by surprise.[47] Whether or not his visit to his former supporter made any difference, on his return, he thanked the Rwandan military for their assistance and asked them to leave.

The consequences were disastrous. Kabarebe left Kinshasa 'quite flustered and eager to strike back'. He took his dismissal by Kabila as a personal, as much as a political, betrayal. When Kagame asked what was going on, he replied, 'You are our chief; if you want to go on being our chief just let me handle this.' Kagame was worried about the lack of planning for such a contingency, such that any operation would be improvised. Kabarebe was convinced that he could rely as before on Congolese troops not putting up a fight. Patrick Karegeya, who had made the initial contact with Kabila, urged caution. He believed the situation could be managed with a combination of flattery and threats, and some external pressure. He thought an invasion of Congo unnecessary: 'it would result in the loss of innocent lives and resources of which we could not afford at the point in time.' Another senior general warned how occupying forces soon get to be resented. In addition, their forces had been fighting for too long and needed a rest. Kagame did not rush, but eventually decided to back Kabarebe.[48]

Meanwhile, Kabila's response to the threat from Rwanda made the situation even worse. His new commander-in-chief, General Célestin Kifwa, was old and incompetent, with a belief in magic potions as an aid to decision-making.[49] The only alternative to the Rwandans and Tutsis as a serious armed force were their most hated enemies, including the Hutu *génocidaires*. He whipped up anti-Tutsi sentiment, losing any Tutsi in the military who might have stayed loyal. Without leadership, the army began to fall apart, and people began to take matters into their own hands. In a chaotic Kinshasa, he told his minister of information, recently recruited from the United States, that he would 'not let our great country be dominated by its tiny neighbour', adding: 'Can a toad swallow an elephant? No!' Without an army, it would still be possible to 'survive with the force of the people – you have to rally them behind us'. This was to be the job of the minister of information. 'In the meantime, I will go and look for allies.'[50]

Militarily, the position soon looked hopeless. One of the best equipped brigades of the Congolese army mutinied. Uganda came in with the Rwandans. Soon the Rwandan units and their proxies had control of much of eastern Congo. Impatient, instead of working his way forward, Kabarebe planned a bold move to take Kinshasa. Using civilian airliners that were effectively hijacked for the purpose, 1,200 troops were airlifted some 1,000 miles to a base close to Kinshasa, with the connivance of the local commander. From the airport, they marched to the Inga Dam and shut down the turbines, depriving Kinshasa of power. But the Rwandans had pushed their luck and not thought through the politics of the operation.

The rebellion was belatedly branded as the work of the Rassemblement Congolais pour la Démocratie (RCD). It was a group without any unifying theme, a mixture of former Mobutuists, leftists and friends of Rwanda. It appeared as what it was: yet another cover for a Rwandan invasion. Kabila fled to Katanga, and called on Angola and Zimbabwe to help him. Against Mobutu, the countries of the region had been either indifferent or pleased to see him go. In this case, they saw Rwanda posing a direct challenge to the DRC's sovereignty and potentially their own. Thus, what started as the break-up of a winning coalition drew in armies from neighbouring countries, and turned the country into a battlefield. The most immediate effect was that Kabarebe and his men risked being trapped. They found a small Angolan airport, and flew in equipment to extend the runway until it was long enough for aircraft that had sufficient room to evacuate the troops.

The war continued through its miserable course, with ceasefires coming and going. The coalition that had overthrown Mobutu soon split again, as Rwanda and Uganda came to blows over what Uganda leader Museveni saw as Rwanda's preoccupation with the security of the Tutsi. The position on the ground was becoming increasingly confusing. On 16 January 2001, Kabila was shot and killed by a bodyguard, with rumours that the assassination was masterminded by Rwanda. His son Joseph became president.

CONCLUSION: POLITICAL POWER AND MILITARY DISCIPLINE

In a perceptive, brief biography of Kabila, Erik Kennes notes how in power Kabila became like Mobutu, with his own personality cult, access to his subordinates' women, and readiness to punish disobedience with death. Mobutu had managed to create a political persona that 'integrated all previous leadership figures in the Congo – from King Leopold II, the colonial Governor General, the customary chief, and the leader who acted as a "good father" during the day and a dangerous sorcerer at night, to the leftist and economically liberal head of state'.[51] In countries with weak state institutions and legal systems, individuals create bespoke power structures around themselves in order to legitimize and secure their rule. The armed forces provide symbols of power and vital sources of protection, but when so much depends on loyalty and trust, competence and integrity come to be valued less than close family or tribal ties. Indeed, few people are more dangerous than those who are both competent and untrustworthy.

Kabila understood from an early age the importance of nurturing a personalized power base and tending to it even at the expense of the revolutionary cause he espoused. That is why he spent time in Dar es Salaam, when Guevara felt he should have been with his troops at the front, and why stories of battle were told to create a useful mythology, even though they bore little relation to a more dispiriting reality. Kabila's success lay in tempering his ambition. Unlike many would-be rebels, he learned to avoid rushing headlong at a stronger enemy, and instead was prepared to find a sanctuary that could be defended, or make a deal that could get him out of trouble, or lie low when this was not possible. None of this required any aptitude for military command, which was just as well, since he showed none. Nor did he show much interest in whatever Guevara and his Cuban colleagues could provide militarily, because they had come without an invitation and their prominence only invited unwanted attention.

By contrast Kagame used his army skilfully and remorselessly to achieve power and then to try to reshape his neighbourhood to remove threats to his regime. His objectives in the Congo (then Zaire) were to eliminate the danger from vengeful Hutus, so he had little interest in what replaced Mobutu. Kabila was available in 1996, with demonstrable durability. As a long-term opponent of Mobutu, he had managed to avoid death or imprisonment. That was all the Rwandans were looking for. Kabila could see at once that they offered sufficient military competence and capability to overthrow Mobutu. He managed to project himself as notional leader of the AFDL, while appearing passive and quiescent to the Rwandans. Victory put him in power, but this was compromised from the start by the fact that his army was commanded by a Rwandan and he appeared dependent upon their strength. With more sensitivity on both sides, the rupture might have been avoided.

The context of chronic insecurity, scarcity and degradation magnified the impact of personal quarrels and social cleavages. The forces fighting were often amateurish, ill-disciplined, and not at all heroic. Command structures were haphazard. Rwandan forces made an impact because they were the most professionally commanded, but this was not always combined with a political sensibility. They did not think through the consequences of yet another attempt to topple a government in a neighbouring state. Kabila immediately looked to Angola and Zimbabwe for his salvation, a possibility that, in their hurry, Kabarebe and Kagame had failed to consider. The result was that, instead of coming to a quick and decisive end, the new war, sustained by opportunities for plunder and trafficking, drew in neighbouring countries and their armies, and the misery of the Congolese people and the destruction of the Congo's infrastructure continued unabated.

10

Command in a Faltering State: The Russian Invasion of Chechnya

Give me a unit of paratroopers and we will sort out the Chechens in a couple of hours.

Pavel Grachev, December 1994

The state identifies its enemies and looks to the armed forces to provide protection against them. The armed forces in turn expect sufficient resources and political support from the state. In normal times, when power structures are stable and business is routine, provisions can be made to deal with potential threats to national security. But there are times when this can all go awry. The state may be weak and its enemies internal as much as external. These are circumstances in which the armed forces are more important than ever, as they control the means of organized violence that underpins the stability of the state. But the armed forces will also be affected by transformational social and political changes and develop their own tensions and divisions. In these circumstances, the military leadership may be unsure about where their loyalties should lie, and anxious about deteriorating capabilities and challenges they are unable to meet. Chains of command are apt to become strained and may even break. When combined with fractures in the political leadership, there could even be a risk of civil war.

These disintegrative pressures were at work in the Russian Federation in the aftermath of the fragmentation of the Soviet Union at the end of 1991. During these tumultuous times, senior military officers confronted fundamental issues of principle, about intervening on behalf of a beleaguered head of state or using armed force to deal with secessionists. Their forces were in disarray, with under-trained and under-fed

Chechnya

0   150 miles

0   200 km

N

R   U   S   S

Sochi

Black Sea

C   A   U   C

0   600 miles

0   1,000 km

Moscow

R U S S I A

GEORGIA

TURKEY

TURKEY   A

I A

Mozdok

CHECHNYA

Grozny

Caspian Sea

Makhachkala

A

S

U

S

DAGESTAN

Tbilisi

ENIA

AZERBAIJAN

troops, and officers suffering from a loss of status and often not paid. None of this encouraged operational effectiveness, which became painfully apparent when they were tasked to suppress the secessionist republic of Chechnya. The campaign was misconceived; planning and preparation were inadequate; execution was poor; generals were insubordinate, leading to resignations and dismissals. There were bitter complaints about both the political and military leadership.

The pressures on the system were enormous, yet it did not fall apart. Instead, it took a more authoritarian turn, as senior figures in the security agencies as well as the military were drawn closer to the centres of power. When the First Chechen War was followed by a Second, this was an opportunity for Yeltsin's successor, Vladimir Putin, to take a tougher stance to impose a degree of order on society.

YELTSIN AND GRACHEV

The leaders of the Russian military during the 1990s had developed their views of their political role during the Soviet years. The Communist Party of the Soviet Union was always aware of the importance of keeping the army firmly in its place. Even when fighting for its survival during the early years of civil war and then in the epic struggle against Nazi Germany, the party inserted commissars in to military units to ensure that they followed the correct political direction. There must be no 'Bonapartism' – a celebrated general seeking to use those under his command to seize power. If military leaders opposed policy, as they did when Nikita Khrushchev sought to cut conventional forces in 1961, they could be dismissed. A few years later, Khrushchev was removed from power by his party colleagues. The generals no doubt privately supported the move, but they stayed silent to show their separation from politics. In return, they were largely able to keep civilians away from their business, and with Khrushchev gone and the party leadership committed to building up the country's military strength, they controlled the Ministry of Defence and spent what they thought was necessary to keep the country safe.

Unfortunately, as a result, the defence establishment became bloated and unaffordable. As this became unsustainable, tensions developed. Chief of Staff Marshal Nikolai Ogarkov was fired in 1984 for complaining about defence spending being held down, reflecting military dismay at the speed with which the United States was successfully incorporating the new digital technologies into its military posture. It got no easier for the military once Mikhail Gorbachev became president in 1985. Finding ways to cut military expenditure became one of his major preoccupations. He sought arms control agreements with the United States, ordered the withdrawal of Soviet forces from Afghanistan, and prepared to reduce conventional forces based in central and eastern Europe.

Hardliners soon had enough of Gorbachev's reforms, especially when they appeared to threaten the unity of the Soviet system. In August 1991, they decided to mount a coup. The planning was led by the head of the KGB, Vladimir Kryuchkov. But it was supported by some senior military figures. Others were opposed, and these divisions ensured that it failed, along with the ineptitude of the plotters and the anti-coup leadership of Boris Yeltsin, president of the Russian Federation. This failure accelerated the very event that the plotters wanted to prevent – the break-up of the Soviet Union. It fragmented into 15 independent states at the end of 1991.

Yeltsin had a keen grasp of the sources of power. With Russia now an independent state, he was initially popular as a reformer, and for his bravery in standing up to hardliners. But the economic changes hurriedly set in motion to enable his country to make a swift transition from state socialism to capitalism resulted in much hardship and inequality. Living standards deteriorated, while corruption was rife and a few made huge fortunes. The Communist Party did not go away, but lost its dominant role, now challenged by new political parties ranging from Western-type liberals to xenophobic reactionaries.

Although Yeltsin lacked military experience – born in 1931 he was too young to have fought in the Great Patriotic War – he understood the importance of controlling the armed forces. The generals were having a difficult time. Although they were the inheritors of the military might of the Soviet Union, their numbers were contracting and their budgets dwindling, while they faced questions of loyalty and accountability. A key figure in the transition was Major General Pavel Grachev. He rose to senior command during the Afghan War of the 1980s, ending up in charge of an airborne regiment and recognized as a 'Hero of the Soviet Union'. The latter was for 'executing of combat missions with minimal casualties'. In 1991, now in charge of the paratroopers, he was drawn into the planning of the coup against Gorbachev. He attended two meetings with the plotters on 5 and 16 August. He later testified that he thought the coup a 'dubious idea', but he did not inform on the plotters. 'I kept my opinion to myself.' On 20 August, with the coup under way and Gorbachev under house arrest, he went with the minister of defence, Air Force General Yevgeny Shaposhnikov, to Yeltsin and promised to defy orders to attack the parliament building known as the White House.[1]

In October 1993, the White House was at the centre of another political crisis, although this time Yeltsin wanted it stormed rather than spared. The origins of the crisis lay in Yeltsin's choice of Alexander Rutskoy, an air force general, to run as his vice president in the 1991 elections. Rutskoy was not a reformer and resisted Yeltsin's policies, with the support of many in the legislature. When the conflict between the two first came to a head in December 1992, Grachev, now minister of defence, was mainly preoccupied with the state of his armed forces and defining their role.[2] He showed no inclination to get involved in the political struggle, sticking to the constitution and insisting on his neutrality. Virtually all of Yeltsin's cabinet took the same position, even when Yeltsin came close to being impeached by the legislature in March 1993.

The crisis erupted again in September 1993. The president met with Grachev, along with Interior Minister Viktor Yerin, Acting Security Minister Nikolai Golushko and Foreign Minister Andrey Kozyrev to inform them that he intended to shut down the Supreme Soviet. According to Yeltsin, he got their support, with Grachev insisting that such tough action should have been taken long before. Nonetheless, when Rutskoy and his supporters made the White House a redoubt, Grachev held back from pushing them out. There was no support for action in the Defence Collegium. This was the body, chaired by the minister of defence, that managed the Ministry of Defence and included the deputy ministers as well as the heads of the general staff directorates and the armed services. Here, there was some sympathy for Rutskoy. Grachev only came down on Yeltsin's side when supporters of Rutskoy used deadly violence, breaking the police cordon around the parliament, and attacking the mayor's office and the TV tower. Even then, he did not rush to act. After declaring martial law, Yeltsin drove to the Ministry of

Defence, where he was given excuses for passivity (soldiers were helping with the harvest). Recognizing that the police could not manage the disturbances, Grachev accepted that the military must act, though he regretted being 'forced to help solve the problems created by political confrontation'. To show he was following constitutional proprieties, he asked for written orders. Yeltsin was irritated but complied. Tanks opened fire on the White House and commandos seized the building.[3]

Bitterness was soon expressed in army circles about rescuing a government that had defamed the army, by suffocating it financially and purging it of unorthodox voices.[4] Grachev published a new military doctrine just a month after the storming of the White House. But with the economy in free fall he was unable to fund the changes. Cutbacks and shortages undermined morale. Moreover, this was a time of enormous uncertainty about what tasks the military might be asked to perform. There were also concerns about corruption in the military, which cast a shadow over Grachev. Huge amounts of money were involved in weapons procurement. In October 1994, a journalist, Dmitri Kholodov, published details of how senior officers had enriched themselves by selling army supplies. Grachev was accused of taking a Mercedes that had been bought in Germany using funds intended for housing repatriated soldiers. For this he earned the nickname 'Pasha-Mercedes'. A parliamentary inquiry was set in motion, but then suspended when Kholodov was killed by an exploding briefcase. Grachev denied being involved, but he could not fully dispel rumours that he was behind the murder.[5]

REBELLION IN CHECHNYA

Chechnya is a constituent republic of the Russian Federation, situated in the North Caucasus. Its largely Muslim population never had an easy relationship with Moscow. They were accused of supporting the Nazis during the war, and many were forcibly removed to Central Asia in the aftermath, only returning after Stalin's death. In November 1991, as the Soviet Union came apart, Dzhokhar Dudayev, a former Soviet air force general, declared Chechnya independent.[6] He then made life extremely difficult for Russians living in the territory, so that many fled. None were allowed any senior roles in the military or security agencies. At the same time, the society and its economy were becoming marked by criminality. It became a haven for gangsters, and this by itself posed a threat to the society and economy (although gangsters were hardly absent from the rest of Russia). There was also a potential threat of interference with oil shipments coming from the Caspian Sea.

Somewhat embarrassingly, this breakaway statelet was also well armed. Shaposhnikov, the Soviet Union's last defence minister and Yeltsin's own military adviser, alleged that Grachev, not long after becoming defence minister in May 1992, had issued an order allowing Chechnya to keep half of all the arms left on its territory by the Soviet Army. Shaposhnikov further alleged that, when this first had been put to him (Shaposhnikov), he had refused. In the event, some 75 per cent of the arms stockpiled by the 12th Motorized Infantry Division were left behind, including 45 tanks, 40,000 automatic weapons, 153 heavy mortars and cannons, 130,000 grenades, 55 armoured troop carriers and 18 Grad rocket launchers. Grachev claimed he had little choice: there were simply not enough forces available to look after such a large arsenal.[7]

Yeltsin wanted to be rid of Dudayev, but he could not find a way. In August 1994, he described the use of force to solve the problem as 'impermissible', but soon changed his mind. He could see few prospects for success in alternative proposals such as blockading areas where Dudayev had influence, including the capital, Grozny, while financing oppositional areas. Nor had he any interest in direct talks with Dudayev to see if there were possibilities for compromise. The Chechen leader appeared wayward, hysterical and generally out of control. Instead, Deputy Prime Minister Sergei Shakhrai persuaded him that the local opposition could do the job for them if they were given some equipment and support.

The opposition, known as the Provisional Chechen Council, were little more than agents of Russian security agencies, with few local roots. Many of their fighters were mercenaries. In late August and mid-October 1994, they were encouraged twice to try to take Grozny. Both operations failed. Felgenhauer notes: 'The rag-tag Chechen opposition gladly took the money and the arms, but never had any serious intention of risking their lives for the sake of Moscow's interests.'[8]

Over time it might have been possible to provide non-military assistance to the opposition to enable it to build up its strength. But Moscow wanted a quick military fix. Yeltsin was anxious about the growing strength of nationalist sentiment in Russia. A far-right extremist, Vladimir Zhirinovsky, had put in a good showing in the Duma elections the previous December. A quick win in Chechnya would enable Yeltsin to appear as a tougher figure. The portfolio was now taken away from Shakhrai and handed to Nationalities Minister Nikolai Yegorov. Dudayev's level of support was still underestimated. The opposition was provided with tanks and active-duty Russian officers for a new operation to take Grozny, launched on 26 November. It was conducted with extraordinary laxity. The government wanted a semblance of deniability, but their help was hardly covert. Journalists knew of the impending attack. Helicopters with Russian markings were engaged in the early attacks on the Chechen units. The presence of Yegorov and his deputy, commanding the operation, was noted. The attack was even announced on Russian television before it began.

The troops were told that they would be backed by special forces, that there would be little opposition and that the people would welcome them.[9] Instead they faced serious resistance, and opposition fighters fled as before, leaving the Russian tanks and crews stranded without any infantry cover. They had no choice but to surrender. Major General Boris Polyakov, commander of the Kantemirov Guards Tank Division, resigned because of the use of his subordinates 'without the knowledge of the command'.[10] Dudayev threatened not only to put these soldiers on trial but also at one point to execute them. It was now impossible for the Kremlin to deny Russia's involvement.

This added to the urgency of the situation. Those ministers with troops at their disposal were known as the 'power ministers'. In addition to Grachev and Yegorov, these were Interior Minister Viktor Yerin, Counter-Intelligence Minister Sergei Stepashin and Aleksandr Korzhakov, the head of the Presidential Guard, who had thousands of troops at his command. This was also a group with which Yeltsin liked to drink. Together they decided on an invasion of Chechnya. Although by this time he was not in the best of shape, a result of the stress and alcohol, there is no reason to suppose that Yeltsin was talked into an invasion against his will. Letting the Chechen leader off the hook would appear as another example of weakness, while a quick war, which is what he was promised by Grachev, would be a show of strength and see off his many critics. Grachev was reported to have told members of the Russian Security Council that the operation 'was going to be a bloodless blitzkrieg' that would not last any longer than 20 December, although this may have been hyperbole more than an actual promise.[11]

The formal decision was taken on 29 November at a meeting of the Security Council. Yeltsin wanted a 'final decision'. Grachev, Yerin and Stepashin recommended a full-scale military operation. Foreign Minister Andrey Kozyrev expressed reservations, as did the head of the Foreign Intelligence Service (SVR), Yevgeni Primakov. They were overruled by the power ministers who saw how their own roles in the still evolving Russian political system might be enhanced. For some, new opportunities for corruption may have played a part, as funds would soon be flowing to support the operation.[12] The decision was not shared widely. The Collegium of the Ministry of Defence and senior generals were excluded. Grachev did not even consult his deputy, General Boris Gromov. Gromov was well regarded, but also Grachev's former commander in Afghanistan, with whom he was reported to have an awkward relationship.[13] Parliament and the public, and indeed many of Yeltsin's advisers, were kept in the dark about what was being planned and left unprepared for what was to come.

Acting as if he could 'order up a huge military operation as easily as ordering up a limousine',[14] on 30 November 1994 Yeltsin signed a secret directive ordering the initiation of activities aimed at the 'restoration of the constitutional order and legality on the territory of the Chechen Republic'. This directive ordered the creation of a special group under the command of Grachev that was primarily tasked with the 'disarmament and liquidation' of 'armed formations' in Chechnya. Later, when he explained the decision to the Russian people, Yeltsin stressed that it was the country's unity: 'Russian soldiers are defending Russia's unity. This is an essential condition for the existence of the Russian state . . . Not one territory has the right to leave Russia.'

Chechnya was viewed, including by the intelligence agencies, as an artificial, gangster-infested state for which few inhabitants could be expected to sacrifice their lives, especially when confronted with the full blast of Russian military power. Yet there were reasons for caution. The formations to be disarmed were 45,000 strong. In addition to the recent failures of opposition forces, studies by the Ministry of Defence noted the possibility of serious resistance. Dudayev and many of those around him were also Soviet veterans, with a good grasp of Russian military thinking. They had been preparing for a Russian offensive for three years and had acquired not only arms but also some mercenaries. They were ready for a guerrilla campaign to tie down Russian forces.

In his memoirs, Yeltsin described the war as a moment when Russia 'parted with one more exceptionally dubious but fond illusion – about the might of our army . . . about its indomitability'. In 1996 he described the Chechen War as the 'most botched war in the history of Russia', a title for which there was some competition.[15] If he had consulted more widely and been less impetuous, the outcome might have been less botched.

The military were in a poor state. The army was described at the time as 'hollow'.[16] It was supposed to have a peacetime establishment of some 1.7 million men, but there was a massive shortfall of conscripts, the result of exemptions, evasion and a lack of fitness among those who turned up. Many of those on contracts suffered from illiteracy, poor health and alcohol or drug abuse, and had histories of criminality. As the Chechen operation was being prepared, in late 1994, the commander of the ground forces admitted that 'we had to take everybody who applied . . . with no choice in professional ability or quality.' Many were 'morally unsavoury characters' or unhealthy. Once in service their treatment tended to make matters worse. They lived in unhygienic, overcrowded conditions. Their diets and health care were inadequate. Bullying, accidents and suicides were regular. The chief military prosecutor reported that, in 1994, more than 2,000 people died because of accidents and crimes. During first six months of 1995, a total of 11,444 crimes occurred in the Russian armed forces, of which draft evasion accounted for half. Though crimes were then rising more generally in Russia, those in the armed forces rose much faster.[17]

In 1992, the plan was to cut the officer corps by 70,000. Instead twice that many left, attracted by higher pay and better conditions elsewhere in the economy. To make up the shortfall, reservists had to be called up. With insufficient numbers of NCOs and officers, there was little training. Soldiers were routinely sent to help bring in the harvest. Instead of adjusting to the lower numbers by reducing the number of units, no changes were made, so that each unit was well under strength and could not deploy on its own. As a result, when Chechnya was invaded, 'every regiment and even battalion was a composite organisation, cobbled together for the occasion'.[18]

Grachev himself characterized the forces at the time as 'hungry, barefoot, and underfinanced'.[19] The Russian military had conducted no large-scale exercises since the demise of the Soviet Union. A letter from eleven top generals was sent to the Duma on 10 December complaining about the army's poor state and lack of combat readiness. General Staff Inspector Colonel S. Baratyanov expressed the bitterness widely felt: 'Reform is increasingly covered with the dirt of immorality ... No matııter what sphere you poke with your finger, you see lies, hypocrisy, deception, and the powerlessness of our higher military leadership everywhere, which is attempting to put up a bold front.'[20]

Planning for Chechnya began in early November, although it is unlikely that it gathered pace until the covert operation collapsed late in the month. General Aleksei Mityukhin, commander of the North Caucasian Military District (NCMD), was responsible for the plan. It was completed without any consultation with senior army commanders, approved on 5 December, and six days later it was implemented. By then, on 11 December, a substantial force of 23,700 men, with tanks and artillery, had been assembled, but in haste. None of the units were at full strength and any gaps had been filled arbitrarily. More than 50 per cent of this force was made up of conscripts. In addition, it was the time of the year when trained soldiers were leaving and young soldiers were being called up. The new soldiers had not trained together and morale was terrible. This was also a time when the weather would be bad and visibility low, which would limit the ability of the air force to act in support.

Troops moved into Chechnya on 11 December from three directions, with the aim of blockading Grozny. The disingenuous claim was that they were going to separate and disarm the warring sides in a civil war. Once this had been achieved, the plan was to transfer authority to the Ministry of Internal Affairs and establish a temporary government. The 'illegal formations' were to be given until 15 December to disarm. The press was told that 'Grozny will not be stormed', and that the local population would not be targeted.[21]

Things did not go well. The advance was slowed down by crowds of unarmed villagers who blocked the roads. In some reports, Russian soldiers were encouraging civilians to disable their vehicles; in others, soldiers got drunk and treated civilians brutally. The troops were unprepared for the fight and so often refused to attack enemy positions. The caution extended to their commanders, who advanced only warily if at all. Grachev blamed the slow start on unreasonable behaviour by local people: 'We never thought that on our own territory, anyone, hiding behind women and children, would shoot their own citizens in army uniform in the back ... local inhabitants, taking advantage of the fact servicemen could not use violence against the peaceful population, have been dragging troops out of their vehicles.'[22] He soon became furious with those in charge of the operation, including Mityukhin, who retired to Moscow, ostensibly with back problems, along with his deputy and other NCMD officers.

His designated replacement was Colonel General Eduard Vorobyov, first deputy commander of the Russian Ground Forces, with a long history of senior command. He arrived at the operational HQ at Mozdok, 55 kilometres from Grozny, on 17 December, having been asked to 'render assistance to the planners there'. He took over command 'on a temporary basis'. He soon reached the conclusion that 'without a decision of Parliament, without a presidential decree, without proper military preparation, this was an adventure.' He was prepared to execute a viable plan, but there was none. The Chechens had been underestimated. Local support was flimsy. The improvised Russian forces were not 'battle worthy'. There had been little preparation, so there were not even proper maps for the tanks' crews. He later explained his predicament:

> The political leadership wanted us to step things up, and to do this we had two options. We could start a huge artillery barrage, which would have been very difficult because of the weather – it was terribly foggy, and visibility was zero. We would be shooting into the fog, essentially, destroying civilians. This is a terrible crime. Artillery also requires reconnaissance operation, but the weather made that impossible as well. The second way was a rapid ground invasion. But the troops we had were just not prepared for this. They were badly trained, they barely knew one another. The truth is they would have needed a month, even three months, to prepare. To throw them into battle – which is what was done, finally – was a crime.

On the morning of 21 December, he reported to the chief of general staff, General Mikhail Kolesnikov, that 'the operation was badly thought out, a sheer adventure.' He argued that the operation should be postponed, until conditions were more propitious and the deficiencies had been addressed. He asked that his views be passed on to Grachev. That evening a furious Grachev flew to Mozdok, after which he said he would take charge personally and appointed Lieutenant General Anatoly Kvashin from the general staff, with Lieutenant General Leonty Shevtsov as his deputy, to run the operation. As requested by Grachev, on the morning of 22 December, Vorobyov submitted his resignation:

> By refusing the job of commander in Chechnya, I have disobeyed an order for the first time in my thirty-eight years as a soldier. Because of this, I cannot remain in office or command my troops. I ask to be dismissed from the Armed Services of the Russian Federation.[23]

One of the articles of the Russian military oath (signed by President Yeltsin in January 1992) had each new recruit swear not 'to use weapons against my own people'. Other senior officers refused to participate on this basis.[24]

CHAOS, INCOMPETENCE AND DEMORALIZATION

The attack on Grozny began on 31 December 1994. On 1 January (his birthday), Grachev estimated that it would take about six days for the town to be cleansed of 'bandit formations'. The attack required the coordination of troops from different units, services and ministries. They came from tank and motor rifle regiments, airborne and naval infantry units, as well as Internal Troops, whose training was largely for riot control. They had no experience of operating together, and arrived with varying levels of combat readiness and equipment. 'In the absence of a supreme commander with the power to direct the efforts of all institutions, the result was chaos. There was no clear allocation of duties between the staffs of the various forces and so there were regular inter-departmental quarrels. Each organisation directed its own forces in ignorance of the actions of others.'[25] Nothing had been rehearsed. The intelligence was poor. The generals were arguing among themselves.

The initial attack was led by mixture of forces from 2nd Motor Rifle Division and Interior Ministry troops, neither of which were prepared for urban warfare. Some units refused to advance. A major commanding a naval infantry assault battalion from the Pacific Fleet considered his men only half trained, and would not send them to Grozny; neither would a Spetsnaz commander, for the same reason. Major General Ivan Babichev, commanding an armoured division, refused to 'wrap bodies round the tracks of his tanks', while Major Viktor Zaytsev of Internal Troops considered this to be 'a strange war with strange objectives ... one was 'to die over yet another instance of the president's and the government's bungling'.[26] Some air force units refused to bomb Grozny.[27]

The plan involved four columns, with tanks followed by infantry, moving in a coordinated attack on the capital, coming together at the Presidential Palace in the town centre. It was if they were on parade, expecting to awe the Chechens into submission without having to undertake any serious fighting. Instead they faced a substantial and determined force, with their own armed vehicles and artillery pieces.[28] One of the Chechen commanders later recalled:

> What struck me at first was that Russian tanks and APCs [Armoured Personnel Carriers] were not even advancing in battle order. They were marching as if on parade ground with only a distance of 5 to 6 meters between each APC. They were unable to manoeuvre or turn around when necessary. This was a suicidal manoeuvre for APCs. What is more, infantry was also advancing in complete disorder among the APCs ...
>
> Our tactics were simple but effective: we let the Russian columns entered [sic] the city, driving along streets where the APCs and tanks could not manoeuvre. When a column was engaged in a narrow avenue, we simply shot the leading APC and the last one of the column. The Russians were sitting ducks.[29]

Russian tanks and APCs could not elevate their guns high enough to shoot back at Chechen ambushers concealed in the upper storeyes of buildings. Substantial numbers were lost.

General Anatoly Kvashnin commanded the main assault force. The advance was on three axes, one led by Lieutenant General Lev Rokhlin from the north, a second by Major General V. Petruk of 19th Motorized Rifle Division from the west, and the third by Major General Nikolai Staskov, deputy commander-in-chief of Airborne Forces, from the east. Chechen fighters concentrated on Rokhlin's force, because Petruk and Staskov had given false reports to Kvashnin about their whereabouts. They later explained that they had held their forces back because of a lack of administrative and air support. Rokhlin's group of some 5,000 men reached the centre and, despite being isolated, held its position, thus sparing Yeltsin and Grachev the ignominy of an unequivocal defeat by Chechen forces. He later refused to accept the Hero of Russia military decoration, on the grounds that a military officer should not be decorated for taking part in a civil conflict.[30]

While the initial operation had been a shambles, the Russians now sought to show the difference that could be made by superior, ruthless forces.[31] The forces were reorganized into three 'Joint Groupings of Federal Forces' with new commanders. High quality units were found for Chechnya, including naval infantry regiments, a paratrooper battalion and Spetsnaz forces. Tactics changed, as troops moved more carefully through Grozny, protecting flanks and taking every building. They were covered by heavy artillery and aerial bombardment, which had the effect of killing numerous civilians but relatively few Chechen fighters. It still took three weeks of hard fighting before Grozny was occupied. The city was now battered and depopulated. Dudayev's forces largely retreated, although there was a final defence of the Chechen Presidential Palace, before it was abandoned under cover of darkness on 18 January 1995.[32] On 26 January, Grozny was turned over to Ministry of Internal Affairs troops. They took another month to clear the city.

On the first day of the attack, the Russian army lost over 100 armoured vehicles, including tanks. Casualties at the height of the battle ran at 100 a day. In less than a month, Russian casualties reached 1,520 soldiers.[33] In the end, the First Chechen War cost the lives of 2,941 army officers and soldiers, 991 servicemen of Internal Troops, 289 police, and as many as 4,000 Chechen fighters.[34] 'One third of Russian servicemen killed in the conflict had served in the armed forces for less than six months, and most were conscripts.'[35]

According to the Ministry of Defence, 557 officers refused to serve in Chechnya and were dismissed. Grachev reported in late January that this included up to seven high-ranking generals, who had refused to carry out orders for combat action and would leave the armed forces as a result. One of those was General Georgiy Kondratev, who had criticized the 'thoughtlessness, poor planning, preparation, and leadership of the troops' actions in this operation'.[36] Major General Ivan Babichev complained: 'Our commanders in Moscow have let us down. They sent us in and then left us on our own.'[37] Some two-thirds of the military were said to disapprove of their use against separatist uprisings in the Russian Federation.[38] In the early days of the battle, 'the Russian army was on the verge of refusing to obey the ridiculous orders of its commanders and government'.[39]

The Security Council congratulated Grachev on the conclusion of military operations in Grozny. When the head of the Duma Defence Committee, Sergey Yushenko, queried the competency of the operation, he was dubbed 'a little toad' and accused of vilifying the deaths of 18-year-olds who died for Russia 'with a smile on their faces'.[40] Grachev later blamed lower-ranking officers:

> The operation to take the town was planned and was carried out with the least losses ... And losses occurred, here I tell you in all honesty, through the absent-mindedness of commanders of the lower units, who sensed an easy victory and quite simply relaxed.

Unsurprisingly, the view from the generals in Chechnya was different.

One observer noted: 'The Russian command is no "command of brothers" but a squabbling group of careerists. There appears to be no concept of professional solidarity within its ranks.'[41] Lieven reports soldiers and officers observing that a 'fish rots from the head', noting that the head referred not only to Yeltsin and Grachev, but 'to an extent the entire military hierarchy, riddled as it is with outrageous corruption and outright theft'.[42] A letter from an anonymous officer provided a litany of complaints against Grachev ('weak, incompetent minister with the mentality of a commander of a troop division'). But he had protected Yeltsin from a putsch, with which the author clearly had sympathy. He warned of the disillusion of the officer corps: 'Trained to fight, many feel only aversion for the slaughter of fellow countrymen, which their government has forced upon them in Chechnya.' While this was going on, the United States and its NATO allies had not let their forces go to pieces: 'We seek to be equal to the strongest. Yeltsin has denied us our most precious professional feeling: a sense of pride in our own might. The military will never forgive him for that.'[43] Grachev's popularity in 1994 was at 20 per cent, while his disapproval rate stood at 50 per cent.[44] The military were also distressed at the lack of popular support, which had been undermined by stories of the privations of the troops and of atrocities perpetrated against Chechens. 'The lack of support among the Russian people left the military feeling betrayed and ostracised.'[45]

CONCLUSION: WEAKNESS AND WAR

The war was still under way in 1996. Rebels raided Grozny to seize weapons in March, and ambushed a Russian convoy on 16 April. Although later that month Dudayev gave away his position in a telephone call and was promptly killed by missiles launched from Russian aircraft, another Chechen commander, Shamil Basayev, managed to find a way into Grozny, causing many Russian casualties. Russia began an artillery bombardment to coerce the Chechens into withdrawing, but the appalled reaction to the impact led to a ceasefire. With no popular backing for the war, Yeltsin now looked for a negotiated settlement. One reached at the end of August left the final status of Chechnya unclear, and included some disarmament measures, but in practice Chechnya had a de facto independence. The costs were heavy: some 8,000 Russian soldiers killed or missing in action, with 52,000 wounded, an unknown number of Chechen civilians and fighters killed (on some counts as many as 100,000), along with up to 35,000 ethnically Russian civilians.[46]

The Chechen War weakened Yeltsin. To compensate for the embarrassment, he needed to mend fences with hardliners in the politico-military establishment. One such figure was General Alexander Lebed, who campaigned in the 1996 presidential election with a promise to make Russia great again. After he came third in the first round, Yeltsin offered a deal if Lebed endorsed him for the next round. Part of the deal was that he was given the post of Security Council secretary; the other part was Grachev's removal. Over the subsequent years, Yeltsin depended even more on the national security establishment, finding it prudent to keep them close. This worked sufficiently for Yeltsin to remain in power until the end of the decade.

The man he anointed as his successor, Vladimir Putin, had been a KGB man in Dresden from 1985 to 1990. After he left Germany and the KGB, he began his political life as a low-profile but highly efficient operator, associated with a prominent reformer in ways that turned out to be lucrative for all in his circle. He worked assiduously for Petersburg mayor Anatoly Sobchak, demonstrating his skills as an administrator and a political fixer. When Sobchak lost his campaign for re-election in 1996, Putin might have been expected to go down with him. Instead, he moved to work for Yeltsin and, once in the Kremlin, was rapidly given one promotion after another. By 1998 he was running the Federal Security Bureau (FSB), the successor to the KGB. The next year he became acting prime minister, and a year later, with Yeltsin's blessing, president. His rapid rise took many observers by surprise. Little was known about him, other than that he was good at bureaucracy, believed in a strong Russian state and wanted Russia to be a great power.

Putin's extraordinary progress was the result of a confluence of a security crisis (over Kosovo, discussed in the next chapter) and the 1998 financial crisis, as well as his shrewd grasp of how to wield power and his capacity for manoeuvre. With Yeltsin's health now failing, members of the security agencies became increasingly influential in governing the country. At first it seemed that the most likely candidate to succeed Putin was another former KGB man, Prime Minister Yevgeny Primakov, who relied on colleagues from the Soviet era to get a grip on the functions of the state, using financial scandals to push reformers aside. Yeltsin became vulnerable as a result of the combined impact of Chechnya, economic crisis and a belief that he was unable to stand up to the West. In May 1999, he rallied sufficiently to sack Primakov, replacing him with Sergei Stepashin, the interior minister and a close ally. But the situation in Chechnya was worsening and Stepashin was associated with the original debacle. Then, unexpectedly, at the end of August, Yeltsin dismissed Stepashin and replaced him as prime minister with Putin. The latter's advantages lay in his loyalty and competence, but he had no public profile. Even later, when Yeltsin announced that he was stepping down and named Putin as his preferred successor, the informed view was that, with a discredited Yeltsin as his patron, and a grey, bureaucratic persona, he stood little chance in an election.[47]

What made the difference was Chechnya. Aslan Maskhadov, who was elected president of Chechnya in January 1997, faced challenges from disparate warlords. Islamist groups became more influential and used Chechnya as a base from which to launch terrorist attacks in Russia, and in particular into neighbouring Dagestan. Russian Internal Affairs troops responded sufficiently to stop these incursions, but then the terrorism became even more outrageous. A series of mysterious and deadly terrorist incidents against civilian types in Moscow and elsewhere (for which many suspected the FSB) was cited by Putin as a reason to take decisive action. In late September 1999, Russian troops were ordered to gain control of Chechnya using 'all available means'.

Putin made sure that this time the generals had a plan. The Russians enjoyed better equipment and more unity of command. The reforms of the 1990s had borne fruit. The Chechens suffered from in-fighting and defections. When the time came to move into Grozny, Russian forces acted cautiously until its occupation on 6 February 2000.[48] By the middle of the year, they were in control of the major towns. From the start, Putin had used the war to show bold leadership, visiting the front and denouncing the enemy. During the final stages of the election campaign in March 2000, the fighting was still under way, and there were calls by some of his rivals for another negotiation. By contrast, Putin promised to 'wipe out the terrorists and bandits'. He was rewarded with a decisive victory.[49] As he was campaigning, Putin was asked by journalists which political leaders he found 'most interesting'. After Napoleon (which was taken as a joke) he offered Charles de Gaulle, a natural choice perhaps for someone who wanted to restore the effectiveness of the state with a strong centralized authority.[50]

While Pakistan fell apart and the Congo suffered endless civil strife, the Russian state held together after it emerged out of the former Soviet Union. This was despite the withdrawal of the Communist Party as a binding political institution, economic upheavals and the disastrous war in Chechnya. Continuity in leadership helped. So did the opportunities for critics and opponents to express them openly without resorting to insurrectionary methods, at least after the clash between Rutskoy and Yeltsin in 1993. There was a semblance of the rule of law, and the state generally continued to function. When the military intervened on Yeltsin's side, it did so grudgingly. Grachev wanted his orders in writing as he tried to preserve a degree of political neutrality. The First Chechen War aggravated all the dissatisfaction already felt within the military about how badly they had been treated since the implosion of the Soviet Union, but dissent led to disgruntled officers resigning or being sacked, not summarily executed. For although there were many problems with the military, they did not act extra-constitutionally, as some had done in 1991. Instead of a military coup, Russia had a spy coup. Yeltsin turned to the security agencies to help him get a grip, which culminated in Putin becoming president. With a mindset nurtured in the secret world of the KGB and its progeny, security became the priority, together with a determination to demonstrate how the state could be tough and decisive.

The Kosovo War

I I

Too Many Cooks: Kosovo in 1999

Sir, I'm not starting World War III for you ...
Mike Jackson, to Wes Clark, June 1999

NATO's war against the Federal Republic of Yugoslavia (which by this time essentially meant Serbia) to stop the persecution of Kosovar Albanians began in March 1999 and concluded that June. It was both successful and deeply unsatisfactory – captured in the title of one of the books about it, *Winning Ugly*.[1] As in the case of the Russians in Chechnya, NATO underestimated the resilience of their adversary, although, unlike the Russians, they made a point of not putting ground forces in harm's way. Instead they largely relied on air power to coerce their adversary, with a suggestion at the end of a land war to come. This meant that, although, as with Chechnya, it was an unpopular war the domestic impact was limited. Unlike Chechnya, it was fought by an alliance. Among individual members there was an uneven commitment to the cause, yet all had opportunities to engage on key decisions, especially when it came to choosing targets for air strikes. Despite the clumsiness and ugliness, NATO sustained enough strength and coherence to see it through. A complex alliance command structure, aggravated by tensions within the US structure, caused problems all the way through the campaign, and then again at the end, when the campaign was over, Serbian leader Slobodan Milosevic had capitulated and a peacekeeping force was to be introduced into Kosovo. Russia expected to be a part of this force, but on its own terms. This created a decision-making tangle, involving NATO, the United States, the United Kingdom and Russia.

General Wesley Clark was US supreme commander in Europe (SACEUR), the position first established by Eisenhower almost half a century earlier. In 1951, Eisenhower's personal standing was immense, while the alliance was smaller and the threat to be addressed sharper and more substantial. The role of SACEUR remained a high profile one through the Cold War, but was less so following the end of the Cold War, when the question of what NATO was for had become moot. Should it be a vehicle for the coordination of Western military power away from Europe as well as within? Under what circumstances should it intervene in the internal affairs of sovereign states? What did it mean for the use of force in what Rupert Smith, Clark's deputy in 1999, described as 'wars among the people'?[2] Belatedly, it had got drawn into the turmoil associated with the break-up of Yugoslavia, first by supporting the government of Bosnia–Hercegovina with air strikes against Serb militias, and then into Kosovo.

Lacking the prestige of an Eisenhower, Clark's position was politically exposed from the start. He was answerable to both the American president and the NATO secretary general. He received backing from the civilians in Washington outside the Pentagon, but within the Pentagon itself he lacked supporters. In theatre, he had profound disagreements with Air Force General Mike Short, head of the US Air Force in Europe, over the focus and intensity of the air campaign, and then, even after the war was finished, with General Mike Jackson, the British commander of the small force that entered Kosovo to keep the peace after Serb forces withdrew.

As we have repeatedly seen, personalities make an enormous difference to command relationships. These were relevant to controversies surrounding Clark's handling of the Kosovo campaign, but behind their disagreements were real and difficult issues, compounded by the limits set by member states on how the war should be prosecuted. Clark's position required him to be intensely political, because he needed to manage a range of conflicting pressures. For many in the Pentagon, this highly visible political role was driven by his ego. The war also illuminated tensions on the Russian side, not least because of Chechnya. Because the Russian leadership was struggling to keep their own small Muslim breakaway statelet in the Federation, with its own demands for self-determination, they easily identified with the Serbs. Much to the frustration of Russian hardliners, including those who recalled NATO as an implacable enemy, Yeltsin did not want to do lasting damage to relations with the West. As a sort of compromise, designed to help the

Serbs, as the peacekeeping force was assembling, the Russian military attempted a poorly thought-out manoeuvre to get a force to Kosovo's Pristina aircraft before NATO's force arrived, as we shall see.

DAMON VERSUS MASSENGALE

Once an Eagle, a novel published in 1968 by Anton Myrer, a Second World War veteran, acquired a cult following in the US Army and Marine Corps. The plot revolves around the contrasting army careers of two men, beginning in the First World War and concluding in Vietnam. Sam Damon, the hero, is an enlisted man who eventually becomes a general. Such a man is a 'mustang', like a wild horse that can be tamed and saddled yet retains its feral instincts. Damon's approach to command is shaped through harsh combat experience. He is determined to look after his men while holding on to his moral compass. A succinct statement of his ethos is made when he responds to a racist colleague who insists that he would never 'take orders from a colored officer'. Sam tells him not only that he should but also that he would. 'Because we all do things we don't like, for the good of the service. All the time. Because we're trained to respect principle over person, rank over failings.'[3] The commitment is to the service and to the chain of command.

The contrast is with Courtney Schuyler Massengale, whose army career began at West Point, and progressed through self-promotion, staff work and a shrewd mastery of military politics. Massengale is a show-off, demonstrating his wide knowledge of military history, yet lacking sufficient insight into the demands of battle to appreciate why his intricate plans are apt to fail. He is the sort who is bothered about the slovenly appearance of troops instead of asking about their gruelling fight. To fit the stereotype, he is also fascistic and uncompromising, just as Damon is humane and pragmatic.

During the Pacific War, and after his operational advice is ignored, Damon prevails in a battle that had been made tougher by Massengale's over-elaborate plan, at a heavy cost to the division he is commanding. Yet it is Massengale who uses this sacrifice to advance his career. The climax of the book comes as the two meet up again in the early 1960s. Massengale, now the four-star general of the US advisory mission to Khotiane, a barely disguised Vietnam, treats the local people with contempt, while advocating taking the war to communist China. The hare-brained scheme Massengale has in mind for Khotiane is an echo of MacArthur's for Korea – seeking to work with the forces of the Nationalist Chinese leader Chiang Kai-shek against the communists, exaggerating the Nationalist contribution, referring to the 'cast-iron guarantees' from the generalissimo, while playing down the risks of all-out war. Damon, asked to offer advice, warns that this is foolishness. While still trying to block the action, he is caught in an ambush. His dying words: 'if it comes to a choice between being a good soldier and a good human being – try to be a good human being.' The model for Massengale was clearly MacArthur, who also makes his own appearance in *Once an Eagle*, and is imagined at one point sitting alone in his study, 'gazing at maps and charts, reflecting darkly on the incompetent and vindictive souls in Washington and – very probably – on the deplorable lack of loyalty on the part of subordinate commanders'.[4]

In 1997, not long after Myrer died, his widow bequeathed the publishing rights to the US Army War College.[5] The College republished it, this time with fulsome endorsements from senior commanders. It was in some respects a surprising book to put on military reading lists. It is a daunting 938 pages, and its battle scenes, though compelling and vivid, are interspersed with stories of stressed marriages and steamy affairs. The MacArthur character gives the book its anti-war tinge, as a warning about generals who want to mount dangerous operations to suit their own ideological agendas as well as their careers.

The book was popular among senior officers for another reason: its value was seen in its depiction of two contrasting approaches to command. Damon and Massengale were recognizable types: one looking out for the troops and the other for personal gain. One has grasped the demands and uncertainties of battle, and the other has mastered staff work and Washington politics. General Charles C. Krulak, commandant of the US Marine Corps, wrote that the book was a 'primer that lays out, through the lives of its two main characters, lessons on how and how not to lead'.[6] The distinction appeared as one between the intellectuals, who liked abstract ideas and became indistinguishable from civilian politicians, and the warriors, who learned through experience and took care of those under their command, between those whose first thought was to please their superiors, and those who paid close attention to their subordinates.

A particular fan of *Once an Eagle* was General Hugh Shelton, chairman of the Joint Chiefs of Staff from 1997 to 2001. When he wanted to exclude a candidate from promotion, he would tell the board of review: 'This is another Courtney Massengale.'[7] It is not hard to see why he might have identified with Sam Damon. He had not been to West Point. With a background in special operations, he had spent much of his career acting as part of a small team in tricky parts of the world, rather than engaging in the cut and thrust of Washington politics. He castigated those who recoiled from battle as 'sissies', while admiring officers who were team players and 'stayed in their lane'. 'I did my best to isolate myself from the political arena and walk squarely down the middle.'[8] Secretary of Defense Bill Cohen described him as 'tall, straight to the point, not a lot of words'.[9] His view of his job as chairman was limited, but traditional. He would advise the president, implement his orders and then support him.

If there was a contemporary Massengale, in counterpoint to Shelton as Damon, it was General Wes Clark. He was the one who had been to West Point, was a Rhodes Scholar, graduated top of his class at the Command and General Staff College, served as a White House fellow and in the Pentagon as director of strategic plans. Although few doubted his intelligence or dedication, Clark attracted an unusual degree of animus. He was regularly described as a self-promoter, always polishing his credentials, and making sure he knew the right people. He was called the 'perfumed prince' and a 'water walker' by those under his command. 'You know who Courtney Massengale is?' journalist Mark Perry was asked. 'Well, Clark is Massengale.'[10]

Yet Clark had proved himself as a warrior, having been wounded in Vietnam. He showed the same competitive drive in the field as he did elsewhere.[11] He himself put the problem down to jealousy. Even his admirers, however, admitted that he could come over as too cold and analytical, and lacked the sort of personality that put others at ease in the army. It did not come naturally to him to 'spit and chew and dip, and wear your cowboy boots, and clip your "ing's"'.[12]

One of Clark's admirers became his patron. Just as Marshall ensured Eisenhower's rise to the top, Shelton's predecessor, John Shalikashvili, promoted Clark against resistance from other senior figures, including the army chief of staff. Shalikashvili, of Georgian parents, born in Ukraine when it was part of the Soviet Union, believed that the United States should play a major role in stabilizing Europe after the turbulence caused by the collapse of the Soviet state. He saw Clark as someone who shared his values, and had been impressed by his role as one of the team that negotiated the 1995 Dayton Agreement, which brought a degree of peace to the former Yugoslav republic of Bosnia–Herzegovina. On this basis, he ensured Clark's appointment as supreme allied commander Europe (SACEUR), a command first held by Eisenhower when NATO's integrated military command was established in 1951.

But when Shalikashvili stepped down in 1997 and was replaced by Shelton, Clark was left with no natural allies at the highest levels of the Pentagon. The new chairman was wary not only of Clark but also of 'humanitarian interventions', operations designed to manage quarrels in distant countries, and unhappy that the United States had ended up with a garrison in Bosnia as part of the Dayton settlement. Secretary of Defense William Cohen was equally unenthusiastic. As a centrist Republican in a Democrat administration, a former senator now in the executive branch, and a critic of past engagements in the former Yugoslavia, he was also uncomfortable with his position in the chain of command. Under the post-Vietnam reforms, as a regional commander, Clark reported directly to him. In practice, Cohen was inclined to delegate managing subordinate commanders to the Joint Chiefs.

AIR WAR IN KOSOVO

President Bill Clinton was also a reluctant intervener – although he was scarred from failing to act during the 1994 Rwanda genocide and then by being caught out by the 1995 massacre of Bosnian Muslims in Srebrenica. He was also under a cloud in 1998, owing to revelations about an affair with Monica Lewinsky, a young White House intern. Clinton was an accomplished politician, with a quick wit, charm and eloquence, which allowed him to win elections, and so cast off his personal failings (mostly), but he had little natural rapport with the military. No president, observed Richard Kohn, 'was ever as reviled by the professional military – treated with such disrespect, or viewed with such contempt'. Nor had any administration 'ever treated the military with more fear and deference on the one hand, and indifference and neglect on the other'.[13] Like so many of his generation, he had avoided the draft to Vietnam, and he spoke to trends in American culture that many in the military disliked. There were toxic disagreements over gender issues and gays. Polling showed members of the military trending strongly Republican. All of this undermined the administration's ability to exercise civilian control. Clinton was distrusted for being 'too nimble, too supple with words, too facile', for being ready to 'go to different meetings and seem to please opposing constituencies'.[14] For all this, Shelton's relations with the president appear to have been professional and amicable, but that was largely because Clinton was wary about imposing his will.

In 1998, there were growing demands for yet another intervention in the former Yugoslavia, as the Serbian President Slobodan Milosevic stepped up his intimidation of the ethnically Albanian, Muslim majority in the province of Kosovo, where Serbs formed only 10 per cent of the population. The aim was to get them to flee into neighbouring countries. After the effort put into bringing the Bosnian War to a conclusion Clinton accepted it would be a big step backwards if there was yet more mayhem and bloodshed, and that this required putting pressure on Milosevic to hold back. Clark was a strong advocate of this approach, in which he had more affinity with Secretary of State Madeleine Albright than with the top level of the Pentagon.

Although in late 1998 Milosevic seemed to have backed off, by early 1999 the conflict resumed, after a final attempt to solve the problem peacefully. NATO threatened bombing unless the persecution of the Kosovar Albanians stopped, and, when this did not happen, the bombing duly started on 24 March. Any hopes that a few days of air strikes would cause him to desist were soon disappointed. The air campaign was extended and the target set expanded. By the time Milosevic eventually capitulated at the start of June, consideration was being given to the use of ground forces to force the issue.

As SACEUR, Clark was responsible for the conduct of the campaign. In this role, he was accountable to NATO Secretary General Javier Solana and the ambassadors to NATO from its 19 members. He was advised by the high-level Military Committee, chaired by German General Klaus Naumann. Clark was also commander of US forces in Europe, accountable to his national chain of command. This potentially subjected him to incompatible pressures from the two chains of command, as he needed to get agreement on both the political objectives and the means to meet them.

The original means – limited air strikes – were chosen less in reference to what was necessary to ensure Milosevic's compliance than to what was politically acceptable domestically. Getting an army into Kosovo would involve considerable logistical challenges and problems of terrain, and risk substantial casualties, to the point where public support for the operation, already uncertain, could evaporate altogether. Clinton simply ruled it out. As the bombing began, he stated publicly, and to the distress of his advisers: 'I do not intend to put our troops in Kosovo to fight a war.'[15] This shaped both NATO and Serb strategy. After it was all over, Clark defended his strategy as 'natural for NATO', on the grounds that it was based on a formula that had worked in Bosnia in 1995, despite the fact that the two episodes were not really comparable. The strategy included the role of air power as a 'low-cost, low-risk statement of political intent', although it is not clear why something low-cost signals anything other than low political intent. It also left open 'other, more difficult, and costly options', although Clinton ruled out the most substantial and difficult option.[16]

The air war was complicated by constant wrangling over targets. All options were individually assessed by reference to their location, military impact, possible casualties and collateral damage, according to the weapons being used. Committees of lawyers at the NATO HQ in Belgium checked for violations of international law and a Joint Target Coordination Board assessed the strategic rationale.[17] Every strike became a quasi-political event, needing decisions from up and down the chain of command, including Admiral James Ellis, the commander-in-chief of Allied Forces Southern Europe, and Air Force General John Jumper, commander USAF in Europe, as well as Clark and Air Force General Mike Short. The process was described as being similar to a head chef ready to cook the greatest meal of his life 'only to find some twenty other self-appointed chefs, arguing about ingredients and cooking times; instead of making the meal better, each managed to subtract some bit of seasoning, diluting the final product'.[18]

It became the sort of campaign the USAF had been desperate to avoid since Vietnam, building up slowly and incrementally, allowing the enemy to adjust, and so losing the potential advantages of shock and surprise. Instead of the 'Instant Thunder' campaign of the 1991 war against Saddam Hussein, the operation was derided as 'Constant Drizzle'.[19] Unsurprisingly, Milosevic's strategy required holding out against this limited pressure, in the hope that the stresses and strains within the alliance would cause it to abandon its campaign.

Clark viewed the war as a land commander. He could not deploy his own army, although he eventually lobbied to do so, and so saw the air campaign initially as a means of reducing the efforts of Serb forces to push Kosovars out of their homes and then out of the country, even if this could not be stopped. Unfortunately, the Serbs proved to be adept at keeping their armour concealed and dispersed, and avoiding stepping out into the open during the day. Without forces on the ground to spot targets and call in strikes, the initial NATO campaign involved many sorties for meagre results. The alternative to looking for 'tactical' targets within Kosovo, which were going to be few and far between, was to adopt a more 'strategic set', taking the war to Belgrade, attacking targets that mattered to the Serb leadership. This was what Short wanted to do from the start. He saw no point in going after field forces, which he later described as a 'high level-of-effort, high-risk, low-payoff option'. Clark warned him that there was no support for his alternative. To add to Short's frustration, he could only at first bomb for two or three nights. 'That's all Washington can stand, that's all some members of the alliance can stand.'[20]

Only as that failed to do the trick and the war dragged on was the target set was expanded. At the start of the war, 219 targets had been selected and approved, largely related to air defences and communications. Half of those had been struck by the end of the third day. Later the concern was that, if Milosevic continued to resist, there would be a risk of running out of targets. At one point, Clark set a goal of finding 2,000. By the end of the war, they had come up with just over 1,000 fixed targets, including civilian infrastructure targets in Belgrade.[21]

Despite wanting to do more, Short spent his time fending off demands to do less. His mood was not helped by Clark's micromanagement. As SACEUR, Clark might have been better placed managing the big strategic questions and keeping alliance members happy, while leaving responsibility for the war's conduct to Ellis. Instead, he wanted to get deep into target choices. In doing so, he gave little respect to Short's views. He judged Short's superior in the American chain of command, General Jumper, to be a more appropriate source of advice, even though he was not formally in the NATO chain of command. Clark described Jumper as 'the senior American airman' and his 'adviser'. He 'had all the technology and communications to keep a real-time read on the operations. As Mike Short's commander in the American chain of command, he also had a certain amount of influence in an advisory capacity.'[22]

The tensions between Clark and Short were evident at the video teleconferences (VTCs). Short disliked these precisely because they allowed senior leadership to get involved in decisions that they should leave to the responsible commanders. During the early days of the war, Clark would ask, 'Are we bombing those ground forces yet, Mike?' The response would be non-committal. Later, when looking at infrastructure targets, Clark would ask about the details of individual targets. The participants would have binders full of targets, and Clark would say 'Let's turn to target number 311', and start to 'raise questions about a target's relevance, expostulate on allied sensitivities, or abort attacks already in progress', or even challenge the intelligence on specific targets ('Isn't that an apartment building?'). Short would be seen 'slumping back in his chair, folding his arms in disgust, and mentally checking out'. Jumper would then step in with a compromise.

In one exchange, Short responded to Clark's requirement to persist with attacks on field forces by saying that these attacks were a waste of assets and should be replaced by missions against downtown Belgrade. He noted that the Serbian special police headquarters in Belgrade was about to be struck.

> Short: 'This is the jewel in the crown.'
> Clark: 'To me, the jewel in the crown is when those B-52s rumble across Kosovo.'
> Short: 'You and I have known for weeks that we have different jewelers.'
> Clark: 'My jeweler outranks yours.'

To those present it was unclear whether Clark was reflecting the political pressures he faced or 'was engaged in a divide-and-rule game by playing on putative "constraints" to his advantage and gathering diverse inputs and opinions until he heard the one he wanted to hear'.[23]

PUSHING FOR A LAND WAR

The mismatch between the military effort and the political objective put Clark in the position of continuing to push for a more substantial commitment. Clark's advocacy role did not go down well in the Pentagon where there was little enthusiasm for the operation. They blamed him for promising an early result from first the threat and then the implementation of a modest air campaign on the grounds that he had seen Milosevic bend to pressure in Bosnia. He had then pushed for escalation when his optimism turned out to be unwarranted. Their irritation grew as Clark pushed for more consideration of the land option. While they could not sack him in the middle of an operation, as that would confirm concerns that NATO was floundering, they at least wanted him to hold back on his advocacy. In his memoir, Clark described a 'divide between those in Washington who thought they understood war' and 'those in Europe who understood Milosevic, the mainsprings of his power, and the way to fight on this continent'.[24]

Clark was focused on a summit in Washington that was to begin on 23 April 1999, marking the alliance's 50th anniversary. A few days before it began, British Prime Minister Tony Blair, who had taken an aggressive stance on the war from the start, went to Brussels to confer directly with Clark – having checked with him and Solana that they would welcome his help 'with open arms'. He returned fortified in his belief that ground forces needed to be considered. This did not go down well at the senior levels of the Pentagon. Clark's advocacy was of increasing concern. They did not want him even to attend the summit. He was only able to get there as SACEUR, with Solana, and not as the senior US commander. Once he arrived at the first reception, he was snubbed by the Pentagon delegation.

Cohen disliked 'the constant drumbeat we were hearing that Wes wanted a large ground plan to move into Serbia'. On returning to Brussels, Clark gave a press briefing in which he commented on the difficulty of getting reliable information on targeting 'without being on the ground'. He got a furious response from Shelton:

> Wes, at the White House meeting today there was a lot of discussion about your press conference. The Secretary of Defense asked me to give you some verbatim guidance, so here it is: "Get your f——g face off the TV. No more briefings. Period. That's it." I just wanted to give it to you like he said it. Do you have any questions?[25]

The air campaign was expanded and still Milosevic would not budge. Targets in Belgrade were struck, at times causing civilian casualties and at other times embarrassment. Hitting the Chinese embassy on 7 May was a mistake, for example, that had a long-term effect on Chinese attitudes towards the West. Meanwhile Blair continued to push for a land campaign. In late May, he asked Clinton whether the bottom line was 'NATO must not lose' or 'NATO must not use ground troops'. Clinton was less than pleased, as the issue was adding to his own political difficulties. As Blair noted, 'Republicans were lining up to cane him either way: weak, or foolhardy.'[26] But Blair's question was to the point. NATO's credibility was now at stake. A combination of the most powerful nations of the world, even though using only a limited portion of their capability, might yet lose to a small and beleaguered country. By late May, Cohen was exploring with his British, French, German and Italian counterparts what might need to be done. The British were already planning their own ground operation. Nonetheless, by early June, the line from the us Joint Chiefs remained that there was 'insufficient domestic and international support for sending ground troops into Kosovo'.[27]

By this time Milosevic realized that his own strategy had failed – NATO was not going to be deflected from its campaign. By continuing to intimidate the Kosovars, forcing people to abandon their homes and seek refuge, he had provided compelling reminders of the humanitarian justification for the NATO operation. There were members of the alliance unhappy about the operation, ready to pick up on any conciliatory gesture from Serbia, but instead the push against the Kosovar people intensified once the bombing began. Some 750,000 people – about a third of the entire population – fled Kosovo. Their evident distress reinforced public support in NATO countries. In the refugee camps, the Kosovo Liberation Army (KLA) regrouped and were able to mount attacks back in their own territory, obliging Serb forces to come out in the open to deal with KLA attacks, which rendered them vulnerable to NATO air strikes. Serbian elites were fearful of the bombing, and also of their country's diplomatic isolation, especially as they appreciated the limits of Russian support. Milosevic's sense of vulnerability was not helped by the news that he was being indicted by the International Criminal Tribunal for the Former Yugoslavia for war crimes.

PEACEKEEPERS

The Russians had watched all of this with mounting frustration. They were opposed to NATO's use of force, which they considered aggressive and in violation of the UN Charter. Their sympathies were with the

Serbs, not least because of the similarities between the Kosovars and Chechens – Islamic groups demanding self-determination. The situation also confirmed all their fears about the growing strength and reach of NATO, as the West expanded its sphere of influence. Yet at the same time Yeltsin was conscious that Russia lacked the economic and military strength to break with the West. To the disgust of the Serbs and his own hardliners, Russian protests did not extend much beyond preventing a vote supporting the NATO action in the UN Security Council (although their own resolution condemning the action was heavily defeated) and cutting back on various forms of cooperation. More drastic steps, such as breaking diplomatic relations, were avoided. Yeltsin decided that the most he could do was help mediate a political settlement and to this end he appointed former prime minister and close ally Viktor Chernomyrdin as his representative.

Chernomyrdin was not able to make much difference to NATO's stance. The Serbs were furious because Chernomyrdin could not offer them a way out, while he was regarded as a virtual traitor by the nationalists in the Duma. There were complaints from hardliners in the government. This included military members of his own delegation, notably Colonel General Leonid Ivashov, chief of the Main Directorate for International Military Cooperation, who had been an early critic of the First Chechen War for its failure to garner public support and 'constant lies which only put a considerable proportion of Russia's population in a negative mood and demoralized the troops'.[28] He worked closely with the like-minded General Anatoly Kvashnin, chief of the general staff.

Strobe Talbott, a friend of Clinton's and the leading State Department negotiator with Russia, recalls in his memoir of this period many instances of Ivashov clashing with Chernomyrdin. On one occasion, when discussing what were in effect Milosevic's surrender terms, Chernomyrdin told Ivashov, 'If you are going to keep interrupting me, you can go outside and smoke a cigarette.' When the terms were agreed, Ivashov insisted that they could not be endorsed until he checked with Defence Minister Marshal Igor Sergeyev. As the two flew to Belgrade to present the terms to Milosevic, Ivashov was heard to mutter about Chernomyrdin, 'I'd like to kill that son of a bitch.'[29] Talbott presumed he was being treated to a display of insubordination and a challenge to civilian rule in Russia. The behaviour of Foreign Minister Igor Ivanov and Defence Minister Sergeyev, as well as Chernomyrdin, suggested real irritation with the role being played by the hardliners; at one point, however, when they consulted Yeltsin, it was clear that, while not being prepared to disavow Chernomyrdin, the Russian president was anxious about acquiring a reputation as a NATO puppet. Ivashov and Kvashnin, who did not trust Sergeyev, had their own direct line to Yeltsin.

On 10 June 1999, Talbott went to Russia to talk to Prime Minister Stepashin and Chernomyrdin about the implementation of the UN resolution which set up the peacekeeping force and the Russian role. The Russian military were adamant that they would not, in Ivashov's words, 'take orders' or 'beg for scraps from NATO's table'.[30] A senior officer on Talbott's team noted that, as Chernomyrdin's influence diminished, Ivashov acquired 'a whole new lease on life'. Instead of being 'permanently pissed off' he was now 'kind of cocky. I don't like the smell of it.' Talbott's dealings with the Foreign Ministry also suggested a change in attitude. Russia's position was that it should have its own 10,000-man force in the northern and eastern parts of Kosovo. When Talbott saw Prime Minister Stepashin, he asked for a reassurance that Russian troops were not preparing to advance into Kosovo in advance of the Kosovo Force (KFOR). He did not quite get it.

By this time, NATO was picking up signs that something was up on the Russian side. The KFOR that was to enter Kosovo for peacekeeping purposes was commanded by Major General Mike Jackson from the United Kingdom, a paratrooper with extensive experience in Northern Ireland and more recently Bosnia. In 1997, he was made commander of NATO's Alliance Rapid Reaction Corps, and it was in that capacity he deployed his headquarters to Macedonia during the early stages of the war. Because of the flow of refugees pouring out of Kosovo, as many as 5,000 on some days, the UN agency for refugees was overwhelmed, so KFOR helped construct and support the camps, although strictly speaking this was not within their remit. With the end of hostilities, Jackson was responsible for negotiating an agreement with the Serb military to enable KFOR to enter Kosovo to oversee the return of refugees and prevent outbreaks of inter-communal violence.

Jackson, as the lone field commander, was directly responsible to Admiral Ellis, who in turn reported to Clark. Jackson's forces came from the contributing nations. The largest contingent came from the UK 3rd Division under the command of Major General Richard Dannatt. As was normal in multinational operations, if a particular country objected to orders from a senior commander they could hold up a 'red card' and opt out. Dannatt held Britain's red card. Both Jackson and Dannatt were accountable to the UK chief of the defence staff, General Sir Charles Guthrie. Guthrie, in turn, had close ties to his US opposite number, Hugh Shelton.

The issue with Russia began to come to a head on the evening of 10 June. The NATO plan divided Kosovo into five sectors, each of which would have a NATO force. KFOR would be under the command of Jackson. Ivashov was vehemently opposed to this arrangement, and continued to insist that Russians must have their own sectors and take orders only from their own commanders. Talbott's delegation began to suspect something was up. The impression was confirmed by a Russian general's observation that Russia had decided to take 'her own train'. The US team was handed a document that showed an interest in the airport at the Kosovar capital, Pristina (which they called Slatina). All this pointed to a move to ensure Russian access to the airport, and to seek to do so by getting to Pristina first, before the NATO contingent.

Early on 11 June, Talbott met, for the first time, Putin, who was now head of the Russian Security Council. Putin impressed with his 'self-control and confidence'. When news came through, as they were talking, of a threat by Ivashov that Russia would make its own move into Kosovo, Putin dismissed it as an 'emotional outburst' with no policy relevance. The orders had in fact already gone out to Russian units in Bosnia, where they were part of a peacekeeping force, to move into Kosovo. Two hundred personnel crossed the Drina River.

With KFOR about to enter Kosovo, NATO received reports that Russian troops had left Bosnia, and were soon expected to arrive in Kosovo. The most benign interpretation was that Russia wanted to be part of KFOR, demonstrating that it was not simply a NATO occupation force and that Serb concerns were being addressed. More worrying was the possibility that they were intending effectively to partition the country, so that the Serbs had their own territory. If they could take the airport at Pristina they could then fly in reinforcements directly from Russia. This was Clark's view. He told Jackson that he did not 'want to be welcomed by a Russian battalion that claims to dominate the airport and then have to negotiate with the Russians for the use of the airport'.[31] He gave Jackson a warning order, preliminary to an actual order, 'to get ready to move by air to occupy Pristina airport'. Jackson 'didn't like this idea one bit'.[32] He saw no need to antagonize the Serbs, who had just agreed to the peaceful entry of KFOR into Serbia, or even the Russians, who had been instrumental in getting Milosevic to concede. If helicopter-borne NATO troops were sent into Serb-held territory, they could get stranded. Nonetheless, Jackson prepared to move two UK companies of 250 troops each and a French battalion of 350 men, although preferably on land rather than by helicopter.

Clark was in touch with Washington through General Joseph Ralston, vice chairman of the Joint Chiefs. Having got initial support for his warning order, just before noon word came back that there was no desire for a confrontation, so only a small force should be sent to Pristina. Secretary of State Albright, who was now in Macedonia to help negotiate the post-war arrangements for Kosovo, got involved and was inclined to follow Clark into taking a hard line. The guidance changed again. A NATO presence was needed on the ground at the airport as a matter of urgency. This led to Jackson receiving a written order from Clark at 13.15 'to move and occupy Pristina airfield'. Yet there was still evidence of a debate under way at the senior levels of the US government, so Jackson, to his relief, was told by Clark to wait, while he gained approval for the operational plan. He took the opportunity to relay his concerns to Clark's British deputy, General Rupert Smith, and to Guthrie.

Meanwhile, the French concluded that this was an operation outside of the UN Security Council Resolution that authorized KFOR, and so they played their red card and withdrew their contingent. The United States at this stage was offering helicopters but no troops. Rupert Smith warned Clark that, without the French, London's interest in the proposed move was waning. Shelton also reported to Clarke that the British wanted to hold, which led him to suggest that they were 'getting soft'.

For 40 minutes from 14.30, Clark had a flurry of phone calls. First, Guthrie called in noting that, while he did not trust the Russians, 'we would need very strong political backing to undertake an operation like this'. Next, at 14.38 there was discussion with Shelton about replacing the French with two US airborne companies using Apache helicopters. At 14.52 Ellis reported on the conversation one of Jackson's team had with the Serbs, in which they had confirmed that they would not consent to any move outside the agreement they had just reached with KFOR. After another conversation with Ralston at 14.54, Clark spoke to Shelton at 15.05 who repeated that UK support was weak and that Cohen was also reluctant to go forward.

Clark backed off. 'We will now wait to see if [Russian President] Yeltsin has lied to the President.' He was still convinced about the need for the operation, but political support was limited while his commanders 'were full of doubts and reservations'.[33] Rather than rush, the plan returned to the original intent for KFOR to enter Kosovo at first light the next morning.

Meanwhile, although Talbott left Moscow for Brussels after meeting Putin, news of the Russian troop movements meant that, soon after take-off, he was called on his aircraft and told to return and 'raise hell' about being misled. When he eventually reached the office of the foreign minister, after watching TV images of a Russian armoured column making its way through cheering Serbian crowds, Ivanov was speaking to his US opposite number, Madeleine Albright, and apparently denying the move which Russian TV had just broadcast. Ivanov claimed to be trying to find a way of arranging matters so that Russian and NATO troops went in together.

Accompanied by Ivanov, Talbott went to visit Sergeyev, who was mainly interested in forms of words that respected Russia's position. The US military team then set out a scheme whereby the Russians would join an initial limited deployment under an American commander wearing a US 'hat' rather than a NATO one. Kvashnin and Ivashov were there with objections. As the meeting progressed, Albright and the Joint Chiefs were kept informed. Sergeyev and his generals, who had been heard arguing, went off to see Yeltsin. They reported back, confirming that Yeltsin wanted a Russian sector outside the NATO chain of command. Eventually Ivanov passed on a message for President Clinton. This promised 'that we aren't going to introduce any forces into Kosovo first or create additional problems, but if NATO goes in, ours will go in right behind them'. Sergeyev promised that the movements would be synchronized.

This was sufficient for Albright to agree that there was still a possibility of working with the Russians. She informed Clark of this at 23.00 on 11 June (01.00 on 12 June Moscow time). Shelton followed up saying that the White House had decided to delay the NATO entry into Kosovo scheduled for the next morning, on the assumption that the Russians would also delay. This was passed on to Jackson, who was now upset that at a late hour he was going to have to delay a move for which orders had been issued and preparations made.

Two hours later, CNN reported that Russian troops had reached Belgrade and were heading south. Talbott asked Sergeyev what this meant, and he was told that the troops would stop at the border with Kosovo, so long as KFOR had not already entered. An hour later, Ivanov complained to Talbott that NATO was deploying. The Americans replied that this was not the case and got confirmation that KFOR was still on the Macedonian side of the border. After another hour, CNN reported that Russian troops had arrived at Pristina airport. Sergeyev at first denied this, but then went off to check. The Americans wondered if there was a riot under way down the hall. Talbott 'heard the thump and crash of articles being hurled against the wall'.[34] Now Ivanov came to speak to Talbott privately, regretting that a column of Russian soldiers had indeed 'accidentally' crossed the border and orders had been issued for them to be out in two hours. He agreed to issue a statement that orders had been issued for it to leave.

Clark's attempt to get some sleep was thwarted at 02.00 on 12 June, when he was handed the unwelcome news that Russian troops had indeed arrived at Pristina, where they had been greeted as heroes. They had yet to go to the airport. The political mood now changed. Clark spoke with Solana and Shelton. Instead of holding back, they now wanted to get KFOR in as soon as possible. Jackson returned to his original plan and soon KFOR was on the move. At 09.00, Jackson was confident that he would get to the airport in a few hours and that, as a Russian speaker, he could handle the Russians. His aim was to manage the situation by controlling Russian access to their supply lines rather than a direct confrontation. At this point, the Russian Ministry of Defence told him as KFOR commander that the 'leading element' of the Russian contingent 'now controlled the airfield at Pristina'.

Talbott again went to see Putin, who 'set about explaining – slowly, calmly, in a voice that was sometimes barely audible – why what he'd promised wouldn't happen had now happened'. He noted that there was a pre-election year struggle in Russia between hawks and doves. Hawks had been responsible for the move, but no one had been killed, and, whatever damage done, nothing compared to that which the United States had inflicted on Yeltsin's prestige by pressing on with strikes. He managed to present himself as both hawk and dove and blame the United

States. Russia was prepared to look for compromises, but in the end, 'no one in Russia should be able to call President Yeltsin a puppet of NATO.'[35]

Talbott's interpretation was that Kvashnin and Ivashov had assumed NATO was trying to get into Kosovo without Russia and that they had moved to pre-empt this. To do so they had rolled over the ministers of defence and foreign affairs. Ivanov now claimed to be upset that he had been taken in by deception. He could see that civilians needed to exercise more control over the military. There was an alternative, however, that they were part of the deception: it would suit the Kremlin for the Americans to believe that the move to Pristina was the responsibility of insubordinate officers.

Clark's fears were now realized. The Russians were trying to create new facts. He wanted KFOR to be able to stop the Russians using the runway to bring in reinforcements. To add to his frustration, the advance of the British contingent to the airport was being slowed by obstacles on the ground, including mines. Nonetheless, by 18.30 on 12 June, KFOR had secured the route into Kosovo and were approaching Pristina. Jackson flew to the airport to contact those Russians who were there. He now felt, as the field commander, he could deal with the situation.

Clark was unconvinced. In his account, following a suggestion from Ralston, he told Ellis to use Apache helicopters to block the Pristina runway during the hours of darkness to prevent Russian IL-76 transports flying in. Ellis passed this onto Jackson, who thought it a very bad idea. Jackson insisted his mission was strictly humanitarian and peace-keeping; he lacked the legal authority to act in a way that could lead to a fight with the Russians. He had insufficient forces for such a contingency. As the weather was terrible, the Apaches could not get in. The problem was not even urgent, because Clark had already managed to prevent a Russian airlift by getting NATO countries surrounding Kosovo to deny Russia the use of their airspace. This was, in fact, the critical factor – Russia's erstwhile allies were now on the other side. Hungary, Bulgaria and Romania denied Russian military overflight rights, so they could not complete their plan. Until they appreciated the extent of this difficulty, which led to a major argument between the Defence and Foreign Ministries, the Russians continued to procrastinate.

At 22.00, Ellis reported Jackson's misgivings back to Clark. Dannatt had been trying to follow the conversation between Jackson and Clark, but he had been hampered by his loss of a video link as Jackson was explaining his plans. By the time it was restored, the moment for sending troops by helicopter had been lost. Dannatt had already been told by London that he should be prepared to use the red card to veto any 'pre-emptive operation'.[36]

Clark decided that he had to go to Macedonia to have it out with Jackson. At 08.40 on 13 June, Clark arrived at Jackson's HQ in Skopje, the Macedonian capital. To Jackson he 'still seemed obsessed by the Russians, and would not focus on anything else'. KFOR's own intelligence assessment was that the Russians had neither the capability nor the political will to confront the international community by flying troops into the airport. 'Again and again I stressed that confrontation was not the answer.'[37] Rather than argue in public, they went into Jackson's office. Clark described Jackson as 'angry and upset'. Jackson recalled: 'I don't mind admitting I was furious.'

> 'Sir, I'm not taking any more orders from Washington.'
> 'Mike, these aren't Washington's orders. They're coming from me.'
> 'By whose authority?'
> 'By my authority, as SACEUR.'
> 'You don't have that authority.'
> 'I do have that authority. I have the Secretary General behind me on this.'
> 'Sir, I'm not starting World War III for you . . .'
> 'I'm not asking you to start World War III. I'm asking you to block runways. It doesn't have to be a confrontation.'
> 'Sir, I'm a three-star general; you can't give me orders like this. I have my judgement.'
> 'Mike, I'm a four-star general and I can tell you these things.'

At this point Clark decided to bring Guthrie into the discussion. Jackson told Guthrie that he was going to have to resign. Guthrie said: 'For God's sake, Mike, don't do that. It would be a disaster.' After they had spoken, Jackson handed the phone to Clark. Guthrie told him that he agreed with Jackson, adding 'and so does Hugh Shelton'. This took the wind out of Clark's sails. He had assumed he was acting as instructed by the Chiefs. Although it was only 03.00 in Washington, he rang Shelton and asked whether his orders were supported. The response was equivocal. Yes, he was supported, but not to the point of confrontation. As Jackson notes this was a contradiction in terms.

As he still had Solana's support, Clark persisted. He gave Jackson a direct order as SACEUR, warning that, if he rejected it, he would have to resign. Jackson dealt with it not by refusing to obey but by suggesting that the best way to block a runway would be with armoured vehicles. Clark agreed and sent out an order for UK 4 Armoured Brigade to place a combat team on short notice to move to the airfield. As Jackson expected, this was referred to London and then on to Dannatt for approval, which was denied. Jackson had been careful to avoid any impression of collusion by not talking directly with Dannatt, but of course Dannatt and Guthrie knew full well what was going on. Shelton spoke to Guthrie, and Cohen spoke to George Robertson, the British defence secretary, and nothing changed. In practice, instead of blocking the runways, British troops moved to block the roads leading from the airfield. With NATO controlling the airspace and nothing able to reach them on land, the Russian contingent had little choice but to cooperate with KFOR.

Clark's problem was that he did not enjoy the confidence of his immediate superiors, whether military or civilian, in the Pentagon. As we have seen, he had more support in the State Department and the White House. Just as Clark's relations with his superiors were poor, Jackson's were good. When forced into a corner, he was sure that the national red card would be raised, so that he would not have to resign his position. Prime Minister Tony Blair was one of those who were engaged on his behalf. Blair recalled that, with 'increasingly frantic calls ricocheting around the system', he spoke to Guthrie, who explained the issue and the need for caution. 'Contrary to all propriety in chains of command,' Blair called Jackson. 'Mike clearly thought fighting the Russians was completely crackers. I told him to play along, ignore the order and stay cool. He sounded relieved.'[38] Jackson makes no mention in his memoirs of this call, noting only that Guthrie was in a meeting with Blair when Shelton tried to contact him at Clark's behest to get the red card reversed. Whatever the quality of Blair's recollection, the anecdote is a reminder of the potential political storm that might have followed if a British general had been obliged to resign in those circumstances.

Meanwhile, Clinton was working on Yeltsin to push him into getting the matter sorted out. On 12 June, Vice President Gore had contacted

Prime Minister Stepashin and complained that Russian forces had 'deployed in Kosovo unilaterally and without warning', reportedly with Yeltsin's approval, and that contrary to the assurances received from Ivanov they had not been withdrawn. These 'mixed signals', he warned, 'will deeply damage Russia's international credibility'. He urged that they build on Talbott's conversations to integrate this force into KFOR to avoid 'a very serious blow to our relationship'. Stepashin denied Yeltsin's role in the decision and made conciliatory noises, while yielding little.[39]

The next morning, 13 June, Clinton spoke with Yeltsin, urging that the issue be resolved as soon as possible, and that his General Zavarzin (a name with which Yeltsin was clearly unfamiliar) work out how to do this with General Jackson. A few days earlier, Clinton had praised the work Russia had done to get Milosevic to withdraw as a 'triumph' for Russian diplomacy. Now he was warning bluntly that he would not be able to meet the Russian president at the imminent meeting in Cologne of the 'Group of Eight' if there was still a stand-off.[40] The following morning, 14 June, Gore was complaining to Stepashin that, though the generals had met, Zavarzin said he was there to listen but still insisted on Russian control of the airport.[41] Later Clinton spoke again with Yeltsin. As he was beginning to say how disappointed he was, Yeltsin came in and conceded on the main points – using the Bosnian model in the first instance to allow Russian forces to work with the NATO command structure. The current detachment would be allowed to stay, but there would be no more deployments until a long-term agreement on Russian participation had been reached.[42]

On 15 June, Sandy Berger, Clinton's national security advisor, spoke, for the first time, to Putin, establishing a 'channel of communication'. He had positive reports of the latest Jackson–Zavarzin meeting. Putin agreed that the two presidents had been able to sort the problem out, adding that he did 'not think that the airport and everything connected to it will be a big issue'.[43]

CONCLUSION: COMPLEX COMMAND

Both Clark and Jackson later acknowledged that fatigue, frustration and stress meant that their conversation was more bad-tempered and emotional than it need have been. This aggravated the tensions that were present anyway. The sensitivity of the matter in contention added to the challenge each posed to the other's position as commander. Jackson resented that his judgement as the commander on the spot was being questioned. Clark wished to assert his authority as supreme commander. Reflecting on the argument, Clark put it down in part to distinctive command philosophies. He noted that in the British system a field commander was always supported. 'They were given their mission and trusted to achieve it without detailed and continuing guidance.' In the American system, by contrast, 'I had seen frequent oversight by higher headquarters, repeated questioning of seemingly insignificant details, and surprisingly little autonomy for field commanders.'[44] Jackson certainly complained about Clark's 'long screwdriver'. Not only did he often bypass Ellis, Jackson's immediate superior, but he had worried from early in the campaign about contingencies not only that were unlikely to happen (such as a Serb invasion), but for which Jackson felt his own team was perfectly capable of planning. Clark was 'something of a loner', Jackson recalled, 'a driven, intensely ambitious man with a piercing stare'. Not all those closest to him were comfortable with his decisions.[45]

This inward-directed 'low' politics of command interacted with the outward-directed 'high' politics. At the heart of the disagreement between the two men was the issue about how best to deal with the Russians. One reason for the distrust of Clark in the Pentagon was that he was the one pushing for escalation. Jackson considered him 'dangerously stuck in a Cold War mentality of confrontation'.[46] There was no desire for a direct confrontation with Russia in the US government, nor in the United Kingdom and France. Clark's assessment of Russia's intentions was however correct.

One mundane factor was the time difference. The United States was five hours behind Europe, where the action was taking place. In addition, Albright, Clark's key ally, was not in Washington but travelling to Macedonia. The issue was handled in a haphazard fashion across the US administration and between allies, as it had been from the start, reflecting the range of views about the salience of the Kosovo campaign and how to prosecute it. The equivocation around him meant that from the start Clark was to the fore framing the strategic debate. He offered advice on whether strategies would work to the political echelon, as he was also responsible for implementing whatever decisions were taken. 'Thus I was deeply involved in the process that gave me the orders to execute.'[47] This was neither inappropriate nor unusual. But it left him running solo without firm guidance from Washington. The early days had not done much for his reputation, because of his claims that it would not take much to get Milosevic to bend to NATO's will. Nor had the final spat with Jackson helped. The British general's judgement that the situation could be addressed calmly was vindicated, although his warning that confrontation could lead to World War III was hyperbolic. The real game-changer was preventing the Russian air transports reaching the airport by denying them overflight rights. If they had reached Pristina when they had originally intended, Jackson's position would have been more difficult.

Two issues emerge from this case. The first concerns the complexity of command arrangements as countries seek to work together, despite having different perspectives and interests. The Russians entered a peacekeeping role, even though they were unhappy at the train of events that led them to this point, and were resistant to do so under NATO's command. Because they could not be sure of getting what they wanted through the normal channels of cooperation, they tried to take unilateral action and present NATO with a fait accompli, by taking Pristina airport and then bringing in the rest of their force by air. Unfortunately, for those who planned this ruse, they had not thought through all the issues, and in particular the need to secure overflying rights to reach Kosovo. Their failure to do so left their small, advanced detachment stranded and eventually dependent upon KFOR for support. They got some concessions in the negotiations on command arrangements that followed, but nothing that made much difference to future political developments. The main impact of the Russian move was to cause consternation on the NATO side and sharp disagreements over how best to respond. The established alliance command structures, which had already been put under stress during the air campaign, could not cope, as member states – first France and then Britain – employed their red cards, and in doing so undermined the authority of the supreme allied commander. Smith as Clark's deputy, wrote at the time that he tried to explain to the allies, that the 'pivotal position of US forces' meant that position of US commanders was assured. 'We must support the US Commanders in their positions, only the US can unseat them; carping in the corridors will weaken the command like a cancer.'[48]

The Kosovo War took longer than initially expected. If Serbia had hung on, then it would have had reason to hope that, because of frustrations among NATO members, the campaign against them would have petered out and led to some sort of negotiated settlement. This did not happen, because NATO appreciated the danger of the alliance appearing to lose, and because the Serbs continued to provide reminders of the original rationale for the war by pushing Kosovars out of their homes. Despite all the tensions on targeting and the role of land forces, Clark managed to sustain the campaign until Milosevic gave up. The Kosovo War was certainly ugly and messy, but, other than two helicopter pilots who died in a crash, there were no American combat casualties; and the core goals of getting Serb forces out of Kosovo and enabling the refugees to return home were met. The war was largely fought from the air, using some 1,000 aircraft operating from bases in Italy and Germany and one aircraft carrier. Clark understood what was at stake, including in the Russian attempt to take Pristina airport.

Clark had managed to sustain a difficult campaign through to a satisfactory conclusion, but this did not save him. A few weeks after it was all over he was told he would not have a second term as SACEUR. The ostensible reason was that they needed a four-star berth for Joe Ralston, who had been passed over for chairman when Shelton got the job. When he was asked to approve the appointment, Clinton appears to have been advised that this was a routine rotation (and was reportedly furious when later told what had happened). Clark was not the first senior general to fall out with his superiors. But he was not summarily dismissed, and his departure did not cause much of a ripple outside of the armed forces. In 2003, he began his own, soon abandoned, campaign for the presidency. Shelton pointedly observed: 'I will tell you the reason he came out of Europe early had to do with integrity and character issues, things that are very near and dear to my heart.' He did not elaborate, but added somewhat unnecessarily, 'Wes won't get my vote.'[49]

Clark's relations with the Chiefs and the civilian leadership in the Pentagon were uneasy from the start. Like MacArthur he was criticized for being highly political, with a similar capacity for self-promotion. The two were also political in a more partisan sense. MacArthur made no secret of his Republican Party sympathies, while after retirement Clark tried to mount a serious presidential campaign, although in his case as a Democrat. These were not the political qualities that led them to fall out of favour. In both cases, it was their readiness to push for escalation, although MacArthur was content to risk a full war with China, while Clark was focused on adding a land component to his options. As supreme commander, Clark could legitimately claim that the choice of political goals and military means were intertwined. He was caught in the gap between the alliance's professed goals in Kosovo and the modest means permitted to achieve them.

Clark's command structure was far more complex than MacArthur's. Unlike MacArthur, he could not shut himself away from the distractions of people demanding conversations. His world was one of constant communications, making it hard to resist any demands for information or consultation from his own and other national capitals, as well as several disparate command centres. The complaints against him as a commander were that he was too controlling, not sufficiently willing to let the responsible commanders make key decisions. Unlike MacArthur, Clark did not lose the confidence of either the president or the secretary of state, but he was out of tune with both the civilian and military leadership in the Pentagon. In the end, the issue was not one of civil–military relations, but more of personality and policy clashes among senior officers. He was presented as a Courtney Massengale figure, to be contrasted with the nobler, less pushy, more empathetic Sam Damon.

Yet the contrast between the two was a false one. Long after welcoming the original bequest for *Once an Eagle* when he was commandant of the staff college, General Robert Scales had second thoughts. The novel conflates 'two views of careerism between the good warrior versus the bad staff officer'. It encouraged officers to be 'contemptuous about serving in the purgatory of the Washington bureaucracy and treat staff time as an unwelcome interlude between assignments in the field'. This affected the quality of the advice provided by soldiers to their civilian masters. Scales offered his heretical thought: 'We need more officers with Courtney's skill as strategists, officers with the ability to think in time, who are able to express themselves with elegance, clarity, conviction, and intellect, and yes, navigate through the swamp of political-military policymaking.'[50] The issue was not so much whether commanders were political. That was unavoidable. The issue was how good they were at politics.

12

From Hybrid Conflict to All-Out War: Russia Fights Ukraine

A dog senses when somebody is afraid of it, and bites.

Vladimir Putin[1]

On 24 February 2022, Vladimir Putin launched a vicious war against Ukraine, causing immense death and destruction, without yielding the anticipated political gains for Russia. The origins of this war go back to the break-up of the Soviet Union in 1991. For many Russians, it was hard to imagine Ukraine as an independent state with its own national identity. Vladimir Putin saw the separation of the two states as unnatural, a source of artificial discord that made no sense in the light of their shared history. He also feared that the closer Ukraine got to the West the more threatening it would become to Russia. This would especially be the case if it joined Western institutions, such as the EU and NATO, but also if it was treated a showcase for a popular democracy with a low tolerance of autocrats.

This chapter includes an unavoidably incomplete analysis of the 2022 war, which had yet to conclude as this book went to press. It is largely concerned with the origins of the conflict in 2014, as Russia annexed Crimea and stirred up trouble in Eastern Ukraine. The links between these events and the later war are self-evident, yet what is striking is how much Putin's own risk calculus changed, from being audacious yet careful in 2014 to becoming reckless in 2022. In 2014, he allowed loosely controlled adventurers to make the running in Eastern Ukraine. In 2022, these adventurers, now in charge of their small statelets, provided the pretexts for Putin's much more ambitious war.

In 2014, Putin dominated Russian politics. He had taken advantage

BELARUS

POLAND

Lviv

U K R

Kyiv

Dnieper R.

ROMANIA

MOLDOVA

N

ODESSA

Russian invasion, 24 February 2022

Zone controlled by separatists
after 2015, plus Crimea

0   200 miles

0   300 km

Ukraine

Blac
Sea

RUSSIA

Sumy

Kharkiv

LUHANSK

DONBAS

Slovyansk

Luhansk

Krasnodon

Donetsk

Snizhne

Marinovka

DONETSK

Pervomayskoye

Mariupol

rson

Sea of
Azov

CRIMEA

Simferopol

evastopol ● Belbeck military
air base

of both Kosovo and the Second Chechen War in his rise to power, and then used them to claim that Russia had regained its strategic aptitude. His position, along with the Russian economy, benefited from high commodity prices. Yet at the same time relations with the West were tense. The Kosovo conflict had confirmed his view that the United States followed double standards when it came to international law. He suspected the United States and its allies of wanting to undermine his regime, by encouraging popular discontent in neighbouring countries as a prelude to drawing them into NATO.

Ukraine was of special concern. In 2013, Viktor Yanukovych, Ukraine's largely pro-Russian president, tried to pursue a generally popular association agreement with the European Union, while at the same time engaging with Putin's alternative proposal for a Russian-led customs union – the Eurasian Union. Putin, however, insisted that a choice be made, and put Yanukovych under intense economic pressure to abandon the association agreement. When the pressure succeeded in November, a popular revolt broke out, known as the EuroMaidan movement after the large square in Kyiv where many of the demonstrations took place. On 22 February, Yanukovych fled the country. A new government was formed from the opposition parties in parliament.

Faced with this setback, Putin decided to respond by annexing Crimea and stirring up discontent in Eastern Ukraine.[2] This had the effect of escalating the crisis. European and North American countries demanded that Russia withdraw from Ukrainian territory and imposed economic sanctions until it did so. The situation stabilized with Crimea left in Russian hands, enclaves in Donetsk and Luhansk (together known as the Donbas) under separatist control, sustained by Russian subsidies but formally still part of Ukraine, and sanctions still in place. It was hard to see how this could be counted as a strategic success, as Ukraine moved closer to the West and away from Russia. At most, Putin had made the best of a bad job, taking away a consolation prize in the form of Crimea, avoiding an obvious defeat, keeping the conflict contained, disrupting Ukraine and deterring the West from getting too involved.

Russian strategy towards Ukraine was aggressive, yet carried out in a form that allowed it to be denied, albeit not very convincingly. In this, it was not dissimilar from what had been attempted in Chechnya, prior to the direct military intervention of December 1994. The Kremlin was said by Western observers to be practising 'hybrid warfare'. The theoretical foundation for this approach was discerned in a 2013 speech by Valery Gerasimov, chief of Russia's general staff. Gerasimov was considering how warfare would evolve now that 'frontal clashes of major military formations' were 'gradually receding into the past', and he pointed to the importance of 'political, economic, informational, humanitarian and other non-military measures', as well as forms of irregular warfare that required firing up local populations and using 'concealed' armed forces.[3] Notably, Gerasimov also had control of the military's main intelligence agency, the GRU, and had established a Special Operations Forces Command.[4]

Later analysis suggested that more had been read into Gerasimov's words than intended. The strategy followed by Russia in 2014 was more an expedient and improvised response to events than something deliberate and properly planned.[5] Nor did hybrid warfare describe a clever innovation, something never tried before. Most wars are hybrid, in that belligerents engage in a variety of activities to hurt and disorient their adversaries. Often these activities follow their own paths and so they may not be well coordinated. The talk of hybrid war suggested that apparently disparate activities were properly integrated to achieve a degree of synergy. As we shall see, this was often far from the case in Ukraine. Russia certainly sought to wrong-foot its adversaries, by bringing together regular and irregular forces, overt and covert activities, combining established forms of military action with cyberattacks and information warfare, but the disparate actions were rarely synchronized to maximize their strategic effect. There were limits on what could be directed and coordinated from the centre.

Although many of the rebels in eastern Ukraine were Russian, and either members of or linked to Russian special forces and security agencies, Moscow never appeared to be wholly in control of their activities, and they squabbled among themselves. There was not a single chain of command but multiple chains, some more tight than others. In Russia, strings were pulled by businessmen and political associates of Putin, as well as the FSB and the GRU. At the other end of the strings were militia leaders in Ukraine. They had their own political agendas, which did not necessarily fit with Putin's or each other's. They took their own decisions on how to fight forces loyal to the Ukrainian government. The core problem was that the rebels wanted Eastern Ukraine to follow

Crimea and be absorbed into Russia, which would require Moscow to mount a major military operation, while Putin wanted the enclaves to be thorns in the side of Ukraine, and any Russian military engagement to be minimal. In the summer of 2014, Russia did have to accept a more overt role to prevent the separatists being defeated. This left the enclaves without any formal status, dependent on Russia for financial and military support, yet still notionally part of Ukraine. Eventually, Putin found the ambiguity in this situation untenable and decided to resolve it through a full-scale war. When he ordered the invasion of Ukraine on 24 February 2022, he cited the vulnerable position of the separatists as the pretext, although his underlying objective was to bring all of Ukraine back into Russia's sphere of influence.

GIRKIN/STRELKOV

One key figure on the rebel side in Ukraine was Igor Vsevolodovich Girkin, better known by his *nom de guerre* Igor Strelkov (the 'Shooter'). Girkin was born in Moscow on 17 December 1970. He turned 21 as the Soviet Union came apart. On his own admission, after graduating from the Moscow Historical and Archival Institute, he did not work in his chosen field but instead followed a family tradition and entered the 'military sphere'.[6] His politics had already moved to a romantic extreme, embracing ultranationalism and advocating, at a time of chaotic transition in Moscow, a return to monarchism. One who knew him then described him as 'living in the beginning of the 20th century'.[7] This belief in the restoration of the Tsarist Empire found an outlet in military re-enactment societies, which allowed him to dress up in old uniforms and carry vintage weapons to relive the battles of past wars. His favourite role appears to have been as an officer of the anti-Bolshevik White Russians during the civil war that began in 1918 and continued until the early 1920s. White Russian General Mikhail Drozdovsky, who was killed in battle in 1919, was his hero. Girkin's distinctive look, with closely cropped hair and thin moustache, was said to be influenced by this period, along with his military tactics. As a commander, he could act decisively, and was sufficiently brave, confident and ruthless to get others to follow him. As a politician, he was trapped in his romantic world view, which left him pursuing unrealistic goals.

He gained his experience by moving around the conflicts that followed the collapse of European communism – in Transnistria, the Russian-backed breakaway in Moldova (1992); on behalf of the Serbian faction in the former Yugoslavian republic of Bosnia (1992–3); and in Chechnya. He had been one of the defenders of the Russian White House in 1993 when it was shelled by Grachev's men. From 1996 to March 2013, he served in the FSB, being trained in front-line intelligence and counter-intelligence, before working in its Department of Protection of Constitutional Order.[8] By his own account, during six years of service in Chechnya, he was wounded twice and suffered from PTSD. He reported to a friend one incident during the Second Chechen War when he rounded up local Chechen activists. When encouraged to publish the story, he said darkly that this would be impossible, because 'the people we captured, as a rule, disappeared without a trace after interrogation'.[9]

Although he was often described in 2014 as a colonel in the FSB, he was by then a reservist. He had left in March 2013 to work as the head of security services at Marshall Capital, founded in 2005 by the businessman Konstantin Malofeev. Malofeev, born in 1974, had earned his money by working closely with Western companies in private equity. Politically, he moved in what he described as 'patriotic and orthodox circles', promoting ultranationalist, monarchist ideologies and fundamentalist Christian values.[10] The characters around Malofeev included a number who played a role supporting the Ukrainian separatists in 2014, including Father Tikhon, Putin's personal confessor, the right-wing ideologist Aleksandr Dugin, and Prince Zurab Chavchavadze, from a Georgian aristocratic family linked to White Russians, who directed Malofeev's St Basil the Great Charitable Foundation.[11]

Malofeev also employed Girkin's old friend Alexander Borodai as a political adviser. The two men met in Moscow after they had both fought in Transnistria.[12] Borodai's background was in journalism.[13] He worked as a military correspondent during the First Chechen War, and then for the ultraconservative *Zavtra* ('Tomorrow') newspaper, for which Girkin also occasionally wrote. In an interview, Prince Chavchavadze described how Borodai, whom he had known since he was a boy, introduced him to Girkin/Strelkov when he was visiting Chechnya around 1996 with Father Tikhon, to bring humanitarian aid to Russian soldiers. There he was told about 'the valiant officer Strelkov, who, in addition to fighting as a knight, is also an amazing strategist, and they really appreciate his advice'.[14]

Ukraine provided a cause for Malofeev's circle. This was in part because Ukraine's separation from Russia was seen as an affront. They found it hard to think of the country as anything other than artificial, and assumed it was ready to break up. This opened the possibility of Russia recovering the eastern parts, known as Novorossiya, which had first been attached to Russia at the time of Catherine the Great. Crimea was an obvious, credible first step in this project. It had been detached from Russia and handed to Ukraine as recently as 1954, when they were both republics of the Soviet Union. To bring forward their territorial project, this group worked with like-minded groups in Ukraine, particularly those attached to the Orthodox Church, who shared their disgust at Western decadence, gay rights being something of an obsession.

Within the Russian government, the person responsible for Ukraine closest to Putin was Vladislav Surkov, the former deputy prime minister and at the time presidential adviser, sometimes described as the Kremlin's 'grey cardinal'. Also engaged, but subordinate to Surkov, was Sergey Glazyev. An economist and former politician, who was half-Ukrainian, he dealt with all matters related to the proposed Eurasian Customs Union. Surkov does not appear to have been close to Malofeev's group, and when things went wrong in Ukraine in 2014, the ultranationalist ideologues held him responsible for failing to take the opportunity to seize Novorossiya. But at first there was a coincidence of interest. Glazyev, who was much more ideologically nationalist, and Malofeev met together in September 2013 to discuss 'saving Ukraine from the homo-Euro integration'.[15] Glazyev had influence. Malofeev had resources.

ANNEXING CRIMEA

The gathering anti-Russian movement in Kyiv prompted opposing pro-Russian sentiment in Crimea. This created secessionist possibilities that were straightforward for Russia to exploit, not least because it had a naval base at Sevastopol, attached to Crimea. During the first weeks of 2014, interested parties from Moscow visited Crimea. On 30 January, Malofeev accompanied a religious delegation to Simferopol, the

Crimean capital. Girkin provided security. He took the opportunity to do some reconnaissance and meet with Sergey Aksyonov, head of the small Russia Unity Party and previously a businessman, with alleged links to organized crime.[16]

Back from his visit, Malofeev sent a memo to Putin's office detailing the vulnerability of Yanukovych and the likelihood that Ukraine would soon disintegrate.[17] The memo urged Putin to use the West's own language on self-determination to take Crimea and a large part of Eastern Ukraine.

> In these circumstances, it seems appropriate to play along the centrifugal aspirations of the various regions of the country, with a view to initiate the accession of its eastern regions to Russia, in one form or another. Crimea and Kharkiv region should become the dominant regions for making such efforts, as there already exist reasonably large groups there that support the idea of maximum integration with Russia.[18]

Malofeev was prepared to put his own resources into the effort. Whether or not this was a quid pro quo, it is notable that on 27 February he settled with VTB, Russia's state bank, which had accused him of misusing a $225 million loan.[19]

Plans to take Crimea gestated during January and February. Surkov also visited the territory in early February, and, by 23 February, when Putin decided to act, the plans were in place. This was the day after Yanukovych fled Kyiv. The president told senior aides that events had 'unfolded in such a manner that we had to start planning how to return Crimea to Russia. We could not leave the region and its people to the whim of fate and the nationalist steamroller.'[20]

Putin kept an eye on the larger picture as events unfolded, prepared to hold back should Ukraine manage to muster a serious response and gain significant support from the international community. But Ukraine was in disarray. There was no minister of defence and no decision-making authority in a position to respond.

Putin's strategy was to present his move as a response to popular pressure rather than opportunistic aggression. This was not, however, a spontaneous uprising. Russia already had substantial forces on the peninsula, including two naval infantry brigades, which had been at half strength and were brought up to full strength. They were used to secure airfields and arms depots.[21] The Russians had also turned the deputy commander of Ukraine's Black Sea Fleet. Special forces were moved by sea and air into Sevastopol. There, on 23 February, a Russian-born engineer, Alexei Chaly, used a mass demonstration against EuroMaidan to depose the mayor and get himself installed instead.[22] Elsewhere, the operation was more coercive. Putin later admitted the role of 'our soldiers' standing behind 'the self-defence forces of Crimea', to make possible 'an open, honest and dignified referendum and help people to express their opinion'.[23] The Ministry of Defence, under his orders, had deployed 'a special division' of the GRU 'together with naval infantry forces and paratroopers'. This was 'under the guise of protection of our military facilities in Crimea'.[24] The Russian troops, with standard uniforms and equipment but no markings, came to be known as the 'little green men', their presence at first vehemently denied and then admitted by Putin.

On the morning of 27 February, government institutions in Crimea, including the parliament in Simferopol, were taken over by notably well-armed men, who claimed to be members of Crimea's 'self-defence force'. They came in fact from the KSO, the new Special Operations Command, supported by other Spetsnaz commandos and naval infantry.[25] They were joined by some local volunteers, including defectors from Ukraine's Berkut riot police. In the parliament, Aksyonov, who had only 4 per cent of the seats but control of the gunmen, got a quorum of the chamber's lawmakers to agree that he was now head of the government, and that there should be a referendum on unity with Russia. More of the 'green men' surrounded Ukraine's Belbeck military air base. On 28 February, Simferopol's civilian airport was seized by Russian forces. Civilian flights were cancelled as Russian transports moved in. Ukrainian bases and military facilities were seized.

Girkin's main role was with the 'self-defence force', which 'forcibly' drove deputies to vote. This contribution Girkin later cited as evidence of his importance, although only as 'part of a large machine'. 'Aksyonov, for example, wouldn't have so easily become the head of Crimea if he hadn't met me.' Without Malofeev there would have been no early backing for the coup in Simferopol. Without all this activity in Crimea, Putin's claim that he was responding to a local initiative would then have been even less credible. It was Malofeev who was able to act 'very fast' and finance the 'self-defence force' led by Girkin.[26] Borodai also worked closely with Aksyonov, describing himself at one point, half-seriously, as 'the minister of propaganda'. Aksyonov still needed an influx of some 1,700 personnel from the GRU to manage Crimea's civilian and military infrastructure.

As Girkin acknowledged, in these closing days of February, he 'wasn't aware of the whole plot'. From the start of the year, when he had begun to pay attention to developments in Ukraine, he appeared to have in mind the formation of a new pro-Russian entity, comparable to Abkhazia in Georgia or Transnistria in Moldova, that would be separate from Ukraine but not part of Russia. It was only as it happened that he realized that annexing territory was a bolder and more provocative step to take, with a much more satisfactory conclusion. As part of Russia, Crimea would avoid the fate of becoming another territory of uncertain sovereignty, of which there were now a number scattered around the former Soviet Union, forever left in a political limbo.

On 4 March, when asked publicly about whether he saw Crimea joining Russia, Putin replied in the negative, but added that this was a matter for the people of Crimea, who had the right of self-determination. Russia would 'in no way provoke any such decision and will not breed such sentiments'.[27] When a referendum was held on 16 March, and provided the expected overwhelming support for the reintegration of Crimea into the Russian Federation, he was happily able to argue that those sentiments existed. When he welcomed Crimea into the Russian Federation, he celebrated the determination of its people to escape from an illegitimate and retrograde government in Kyiv.[28]

Organizing Aksyonov's takeover in Simferopol was not Girkin's only task in Crimea. He led troops to take the airport, and negotiated the withdrawal of Ukrainian naval personnel,[29] by playing on their sense of honour rather than the crude threats favoured by the Russian naval officers present at the talks.[30] The first questions about his role came on 18 March, when two people were killed, as his self-defence forces stormed a facility at Simferopol still held by naval personnel loyal to Ukraine. After this, 'the company was disbanded and its members parted'.[31] Those that stayed were largely anti-Maidan activists from Ukraine who had nowhere else to go. He wrote to Malofeev that he could not do much, as 'my local colleagues and police suspect the devils of what and see me as a dangerous madman'. He was in position only because of his personal ties with Aksyonov, and lacked any official status. This limited his ability to carry out the tasks assigned to him. He soon found a new mission.

ADVANCING TO SLOVYANSK

March and April 2014 provided a test of the Russian thesis of the essential artificiality and fragility of Ukraine. Putin's actual expectations are hard to discern. There were enthusiasts who were waiting for the orders to mount an insurrection, but Putin was cautious. In Crimea he was confident of success, but the situation in Eastern Ukraine was less certain. One group of advisers saw an opportunity to protect Russian speakers, who they believed were at risk from the 'fascist junta' in Kyiv, and to incorporate Novorossiya back into Russia; others worried that it would lead to more trouble with the West for few tangible gains.

Glazyev was one of the hawks. He 'believed that Russia could count on local mobilization to help oust Ukrainian forces and then annex as many as six eastern Ukrainian regions'. Putin was tempted. He was ready to take advantage of any major upheavals in the areas close to the border with Russia, with laws prepared and troops ready to enable him to order an intervention if the conditions were right. But, if the conditions were not right, he could leave Ukraine under its new regime, composed of opponents of Russia, uncertain and unstable as it coped with popular discontent in the east. Putin's public position remained ambiguous. He spoke in terms that envisaged the break-up of Ukraine without making any promises about expanding Russia's borders. It was enough to convince many militants that he would support the separatist cause.[32]

To achieve their objectives, the militants looked to replicate the Crimean formula. This depended on not only the pretence that there was a demand to join Russia but also some tangible evidence. On 1 March, pro-Russian militants took government buildings in the eastern Ukrainian cities of Kharkiv and Donetsk. But there was something performative about the early encounters, often with minor local figures making grand proclamations that few took seriously. Those who hoped for something more dynamic were disappointed. Glazyev spoke to activists in Kharkiv saying that he had 'direct orders – to raise the people in Ukraine where we can'. His message to the activists was to fill the streets, take over local government buildings and then demand Russian help. 'We cannot do everything with force, we use the power to support people, not more. And if there are no people, what support might there be?' In another conversation, he explained: 'It is very important that people appeal to Putin. Mass appeals directly to him with a request to protect, an appeal to Russia, etc.'[33] The protests that came, however, though hailed by Russia, were just not enough. They failed to attract mass support and fizzled out.

Watching from Crimea, Girkin found this frustrating. Given the resources pumped into the Kharkiv protests, they should have developed into something substantial. From his perspective, recovering Novorossiya should be the highest priority – and was vital to the success of the project begun in Crimea. These territories were the 'jewels in the crown of the Russian Empire', but if separated they left Crimea vulnerable. He therefore set in motion what he later described as the 'flywheel of war' and 'reshuffled the cards'.[34] It began when individuals from elsewhere in Ukraine came to Crimea to get directions on how to achieve their own uprisings. Aksyonov, who already had his hands full, asked Girkin to work with them.

He does not seem to have had any specific orders from Moscow, although there were consultations. Having observed what had happened in Crimea, and seen his own expectations exceeded, Girkin assumed that, if he could stir things up sufficiently in eastern Ukraine, Russia would lend a hand. His other assumption was that the only way to provide some momentum to the pro-Russia movement was to provide a powerful military demonstration. Beyond that, he did not have much of a plan.

Part of the reason was that he lacked the manpower and weapons to be too ambitious. Also, in choosing where best to make an impact he was hampered by his lack of knowledge of Ukraine. He later admitted that he 'barely knew the local terrain and had no information sources of my own'.[35] His small force would be lost in cities such as Kharkiv, and Odessa would be insufficiently accessible when the time came for Russian intervention. (Later, on 2 May, after clashes in the city, 42 pro-Russian activists died in a fire at the Trade Union House in Odessa.)

Eventually Girkin settled on Slovyansk in the Donetsk region, a town that was a little out of the way, but large enough to be notable and small enough for his group to be able to make a difference. It was also, as he eventually discovered, easy to surround and hard to defend. He crossed into Ukraine from Crimea with 52 volunteers. They brought with them 250 military uniforms to hand over to the local volunteers he hoped to find on arrival. The aim was to create the impression of an organized force. On 12 April 2014, wearing army fatigues, bulletproof vests and masks, and armed with Kalashnikov rifles, his group captured a number of state buildings.[36] By storming the police department they got hold of assault rifles and pistols. They soon had around 200 volunteers. Faced with direct military action, the new government in Ukraine felt it had to respond and launched an 'anti-terrorist operation', which led to early skirmishes and the first casualties. Girkin attracted notice (as Strelkov) when he first appeared at a 26 April press conference, talking about eight observers from the Organization for Security and Cooperation in Europe (OSCE) who had been taken hostage, accusing them of acting as spies for the Ukrainians.[37]

Elsewhere in the region, other militant groups sprang into action, seizing not only administrative buildings but also those of security forces, which provided them with many of their weapons. Many local police and soldiers defected to the rebels, while those that remained loyal lacked leadership, and their resistance was ineffectual. There were soon struggles going on to gain control of several towns and villages. These were successful in the two provinces of Donetsk and Luhansk. By late April, the separatists could claim a degree of control over a substantial portion of the territory.

Girkin could now feel that with his comrades he had changed the course of Russian and Ukrainian history, building on the annexation of Crimea. The counterfactual history is uncertain. Without Girkin's intervention, there would probably have been continued unrest, but not necessarily the localized and deadly insurgency that followed, and the degree of commitment from Moscow to the resulting enclaves. He later claimed to have 'pressed the launching trigger of war', adding:

> If our squad did not cross the border, at the end all would have been finished as in Kharkiv or Odessa. Practically, the flywheel of war which lasts until now was launched by our squad. And I bear a personal responsibility for what is happening there.[38]

Some confirmation of this claim came from Pavel Gubarev, who was part of the early protests in Donetsk in March before being arrested by the Ukrainians. He recalled that it 'was Girkin who was able to "drag the uprising out of a usual, unarmed and toothless street protest"'.[39] But he could only take matters so far. Russia now needed to play its part.

The separatists believed that they had set the necessary conditions for Moscow to finish off what they had started. They therefore prepared to move to the next step – on the Crimean model – by organizing referendums on 11 May to demonstrate that joining Russia would have popular support.

Putin made play with the Novorossiya concept in a speech on 17 April, suggesting that at this point he had not ruled out drastic action. However, faced with a strong international response to the annexation of Crimea, and signs that the disarray in Ukraine was not as great as at first supposed and that there was no mass clamour in the east to join Russia, he held back. The Kremlin judged that the referendums were premature and asked that they be postponed. This did not dissuade the militants. A report of a key meeting has one saying that Putin's hesitation was in fact a green light:

> This was an act of colossal support for us ... It was a proclamation to the whole world that we are holding a referendum. Thanks to Vladimir Vladimirovich's statements, people from across the world will know that the Donetsk People's Republic will express its will. It was a positioning of the Donetsk Republic as a people's republic.[40]

The meeting decided to press ahead with the ballot. On 11 May, the referendums in Donetsk and Luhansk proclaimed themselves people's republics and declared their independence from Ukraine. Russia said it 'respected' the results, but the request from Donetsk to be 'absorbed' into Russia was ignored.[41] Glazyev might have wanted to go further, but Surkov understood that his boss wanted leverage over Ukraine and not new statelets.[42]

There was an evident tension between, on the one hand, carving out a chunk of Ukraine that would be effectively controlled by Russia and, on the other, gaining influence over Ukrainian decisions to prevent moves inimical to Russian interests. Now it dawned on Girkin that Russia was not going to follow the script. Putin did not regard Donetsk and Luhansk as low-hanging fruit ripe for the picking after all. Having underestimated Russia's ambition in Crimea, Girkin had now overestimated it in the Donbas. 'Initially I assumed that the Crimea scenario would be repeated: Russia would enter.' He later commented. 'That was the best scenario. And the population wanted that. Nobody intended to fight for the Luhansk and Donetsk republics. Initially everybody was for Russia.' Instead, they heard Russian calls for 'dialogue' with Kyiv. Because of the optimistic assumptions about Russian intentions, no preparations had been made to create functional states.[43] 'I didn't think about any kind of state building,' recalled Girkin. 'And then, when I realized that Russia will not take us in, this decision was a shock for us.'[44]

Surkov made sure that the new entities had some governance. Malofeev was in touch with him with names for posts in the Donetsk People's Republic (DNR), including Girkin's, but also that of another one of his former employees with links to the GRU, Denis Pushilin. Pushilin was a former security guard and candy salesman who had previously sold a Ponzi pyramid scheme.[45] Borodai anointed himself prime minister and Girkin as minister of defence of the Donetsk People's Republic (a separate entity was formed in Luhansk). On 12 May, Girkin introduced himself as 'the Supreme Commander of the DNR' and all its 'military units, security, police, customs, border guards, prosecutors, and other paramilitary structures'. From now on, he decreed, 'commanders will carry out only my orders and instructions'. He warned members of Ukrainian militias ('neo-Nazi groups') that they would be detained and killed in the event of resistance, that named members of the 'Kyiv junta' would be prosecuted, and that all military and paramilitary units in Donetsk must either swear their allegiance to the DNR or leave. He concluded by appealing to the Russian Federation for military assistance.[46]

Despite his nominal role as minister of defence, in practice Girkin's main challenge was to run Slovyansk. He had preferred in the past to operate in the shadows, yet now he had to step up to a public role. In this, his background in historical re-enactments may have contributed to the theatrical quality of his public appearances and utterances. At the same time, a stress on his secret service connections, reinforced by erroneous suggestions that he was still an FSB colonel, boosted his image and his assumed influence as a trusted instrument of Russian policy. Borodai expressed his appreciation of how Girkin – as Strelkov – controlled his image, so that he was 'perceived both as a Russian volunteer and on a mission from Moscow'.

But he played his part, and became a symbol. Here he appears at a press conference – so handsome, mysterious, in camouflage, reading yet another [military news] brief. It looked arty; the patriotic media did what they could to portray him a Russian folk hero.[47]

To assert his authority and demonstrate his seriousness of purpose, Girkin ordered that looters would be executed. Later he claimed to have installed a military court and introduced 1941 military laws. 'Under this legislation we tried people and executed the convicted.' Three of these were for looting and another for killing one of his troops.[48] Less severe punishments were announced for drunkenness, drug-dealing and swearing when on radio calls.[49] The brutish side of the occupation was revealed in other calls intercepted by Ukrainian intelligence. Girkin's then subordinate, Igor ('Bes') Bezler, ordered a local Ukrainian politician to be 'neutralized'. Later Girkin issued instructions to dispose of the body, which is 'lying here [in the basement of the separatist headquarters in Slovyansk] and beginning to smell'.[50]

Girkin struggled with the duties of a military commander. As he acknowledged, far from being a specialist in hybrid warfare, he had 'never had to supervise large-scale military operations involving different types of armed forces'. He had been taught military theory but lacked relevant experience. The fighting in Ukraine was at a different level to the sort of operations in which he had previously been engaged in Chechnya, where at most he had commanded a unit of 150 men. Most importantly, he was in a weak position, without reserves and unable to call in artillery or aviation in support. The troops available to him were a mixed bag. Many had combat experience, more so than the Ukrainians he was facing, but the numbers were relatively small: his brigade at its height had just under 2,000 fighters in Slovyansk and neighbouring towns. In small units, they were often effective fighters, able to improvise and take the initiative taking advantage of their local knowledge, but they lacked weapons and struggled with resupply, and the command structures were poor. What they had by way of armoured vehicles and artillery pieces had been seized from the Ukrainians. There was little point in recruiting locals to join the fight when they could not be armed. To make his forces appear more powerful than was the case, Girkin relied on

> disinformation and intimidation, so that the opponent thought that there were more of us and that we were better armed, and that Russia was behind us. We bluffed, pretended that Russian spetznaz were fighting

with us and that rebels only made up the first line of defence. The Ukrainian side feared that we would begin an offensive, and this deprived them of willpower.[51]

At first, Girkin's men and the forces loyal to Ukraine were wary of each other, and avoided any intensive fighting. There was not much above skirmishing until the end of May, when Ukrainian forces started to shell positions in the town. They were now more confident. Girkin believed that this was the result of a growing belief that they would not have to face the Russian army. It was also the result of the election of Petro Poroshenko as Ukraine's president. Although the Ukrainian government had declared an anti-terrorist operation as soon as Girkin seized Slovyansk, Poroshenko was able to inject more drive and urgency into the fight. Girkin was also frustrated by the Ukrainian strategy. Instead of a frontal assault, they decided to lay siege, trapping the rebels inside the town while they shelled their positions.

In early June, the Ukrainians began to employ armoured units. The separatists were now under pressure across the front against an enemy with superior forces. By late June, Girkin had concluded that his position in Slovyansk was hopeless. Some volunteers reached his beleaguered group, but far more were reaching the enemy. Other units had their own battles to fight, and none were going to be able to break through to rescue him. The image might have required a valiant fight to the end, but he concluded that his men would be of more value defending Donetsk, so he decided to withdraw.

The decision about whether to leave Slovyansk was discussed with Moscow. Glazyev talked up the resistance in Slovyansk, comparing it to the defence of Brest, the first major battle against the Nazi invaders in June 1941, claiming that 'they die not only for Donbas, they die for all the people of the Russian world and of all mankind, saving us from a new world war'.[52] Yet martyrdom and a symbolic defeat had limited appeal. Girkin's deputy, former Russian GRU officer Sergey Dubinsky, another of his contacts from Chechnya, discussed the situation with his commanders on the phone on 4 July. One told him: 'You have to convince Pervy [an intriguing nickname for Girkin] that the people have to leave there. Otherwise, we will lose everything.' Dubinsky answered: 'The point is that he has just contacted Moscow, and they won't allow us to leave Slovyansk.' Late that night, the decision was made: 'It's today, today, tonight, all night long.'[53] On 5 July, Girkin organized his men into six columns to leave in stages. Although he lost his armoured unit in an ambush, most got out safely. He left in the second column, which he later accepted was a mistake. As the commander, he should have been the last man out. As Girkin's presence had made Slovyansk the military command centre, this was considered an important victory for Kyiv.[54]

RETREAT TO DONETSK

Returning to the city of Donetsk from his front-line experiences on 5 July, Girkin was unimpressed by how unprepared it was for the next stage of the war. Unlike Slovyansk, however, here he was not in charge. Borodai was running the government, and, while Girkin might have considered himself to be supreme military commander, this was not the view of the other independent militias, with their own leaderships and political agendas, which had sprung up in the Donbas.

Oplot (Stronghold), for example, developed out of an anti-Maidan group that had first come together in Kharkiv in January 2014. Alexander Zakharchenko set up his own branch in Donetsk, and was active in seizing administrative buildings in the city in April 2014. He then became the military commandant of Donetsk, commander of the Oplot brigade and deputy internal affairs minister of the DNR. The Vostok (East) battalion was headed by Alexander Khodakovsky, a former commander of Ukraine's Alpha force in the Donetsk region. Its core was made up of former members of Ukraine's special branch. It first made its appearance as a force of 500 men at a Second World War victory parade on 9 May. It was badly mauled in a fight for Donetsk airport in May (which led to 32 bodies being returned to Russia).[55] Another group, known as the Russian Orthodox Army, was a mixture of Russians and Ukrainians; Kalmius was largely made up of coal miners.[56]

Girkin wanted to turn this complex network of militias into a single army with a unified command.[57] He established a Military Council, but could not overcome the rivalries between the different groups and their lack of interest in working with him. He later regretted the lack of a chief of staff, who might have been able to explain to the disparate leaders what was required of them.[58] Dubinsky, his most important deputy, put together

an agency that came to be known as the 'GRU DNR' and was a combination of intelligence and Spetsnaz units. Dubinsky played a role getting
weapons from Russia into the beleaguered town. After the retreat back to
Donetsk, his agency grew in strength and influence, in part because of
Dubinsky's links with weapons suppliers and intelligence services; he was
able to get hold of equipment and knew what people were up to.

Girkin's arguments with Khodakovsky led to Vostok splitting, with
one part joining him. There were other units, Girkin later noted, 'that
categorically did not want to obey and had their own financial and supply channels'.[59] The other commanders had their own areas to defend,
which they could also exploit to keep themselves in funds. There was
little interest in sharing weapons or stocks, let alone joint operations.
Zakharchenko came to the Military Council only twice. Khodakovsky
got into regular clashes with other militias, but saw Girkin as his main
rival. 'While Strelkov was in Donetsk, there was no communication
between us. I didn't trust him, and he didn't trust me.'[60] He was contemptuous of the retreat from Slovyansk. A well-known figure on the
Russian far-right, Sergey Kurginyan, was invited to Donetsk on 7 July,
to denounce Girkin for betrayal and cowardice, and for leaving caches
of weapons as he rushed to get away. As he spoke, some of Girkin's men
accused him of being a 'professional provocateur'.[61]

Girkin's desire to impose some order on the situation predictably led
to a clash with Borodai. Although he was prime minister, he had not
tried to get a grip on the local administration, much of which was still
run from Kyiv. This included the local mayor. As he lacked the capacity
to take it over, Borodai decided to stick with the current arrangement,
which had the additional advantage that Kyiv paid public sector salaries.
Girkin found this intolerable. When Borodai was visiting Moscow, he
called in the mayor and demanded that he take an oath of allegiance.[62]
The mayor left for Kyiv, leaving the DNR struggling to cope with its bills
and without administrative capacity. The problem was compounded by
the fact that two of the posts in the government, for economics and
taxation, were held by subordinates of Khodakovsky. As they were also
field commanders, they did not spend time on their portfolios. Borodai
decided that the only way to cope was not to raise taxes at all. The
result was that the centre lacked funds, while the local militia bosses
found their own ways to raise taxes, further encouraging gangsterism
and lawlessness.

This was clearly not an entity that could survive on its own. By the start of July, Putin had concluded that having backed the separatists, even half-heartedly, it would be humiliating if they collapsed. These were Russian clients at risk.[63] Surkov oversaw the budgets, with allocations for law enforcement structures, youth support and pensions, as well as for the DNR Ministry of Information, a press centre and a newspaper.[64] At the same time, Borodai was still looking to Malofeev to support his operation. On 12 July, Borodai told Malofeev that the money already sent had run out and that more was needed. Malofeev replied positively.

Surkov also worked to sort out the governance in Donetsk. He was in regular consultations with Borodai, as well as Aksyonov in Crimea, using 'Special Communication Telephones' that 'are gotten through Moscow. Through FSB.' These were available to Girkin, Borodai and Aksyonov, and enabled them to communicate with Moscow. Surkov was described as the 'one who assigns missions'. Lest there be doubts about his loyalty, on 3 July Borodai made it clear that he was 'carrying out orders and protecting the interests of one and only state, the Russian Federation. That's the bottom line.'[65] That day Surkov told Borodai that someone called Antyufeyev 'will be setting off for your place'. They were 'already departing for the south to be combat-ready'.[66] Vladimir Antyufeyev, a former security chief in Transnistria, had been tipped to displace Khodakovsky, who needed to move out of that role, given his poor relations with Girkin.

On 10 July, Antyufeyev held a press conference, with Borodai and Girkin, to explain his new role in charge of State Security, Home Affairs and Justice of the DNR. On 8 June, Girkin had asked the Crimean leader Aksyonov, who was still part of the network supporting militants in the Donbas, to help get military support from Russia. Eventually, this support came, through a chain of command that led to Russian Minister of Defence Sergei Shoigu and General Andrey Serdyukov, a commander of the Southern Military District of the Russian Federation.

The key figure organizing the supply of equipment to the front was Colonel General Andrey Ivanovich Burlaka, one of the top officials in the FSB with responsibility for Ukraine. He was referred to in communications as 'Vladimir Ivanovich'.[67] Burlaka was chief of the operational staff of the FSB's Border Service, and first deputy to its head, who in turn was first deputy to the overall head of the FSB. Burlaka was constantly on the move between Moscow and the three Russian command centres for operations against Ukraine – Rostov, Crimea and Krasnodar.

Burlaka had been given by Shoigu responsibility for organizing the supplies of equipment. On 17 July, he was phoned by a militant with a list of 'things we need'. The list included arms, ammunition, night-vision equipment and armoured vehicles. Burlaka only authorized part of the list, leading to a demand to contact Surkov with any questions, as 'he is the one giving us the tasks'. Burlaka made it clear that he got his instructions from his own boss. On 31 July, one of his staff told Girkin that he would get some equipment, but only after giving two vehicles to another commander. Girkin said he needed it all. 'I need equipment and people, people and equipment, weapons and munitions. None of my people will fulfil orders other than mine.' When Burlaka's man queried this, Girkin observed, 'Vladimir Ivanovich [Burlaka] himself has to give orders to me. But not to command my people over my head. My people will fulfil my orders.'[68]

On 1 July, Burlaka spoke with Borodai and Malofeev about a turf war between Girkin's people (still in Slovyansk) and Bezler's. Some 100 of Girkin's troops were reported ready to defect to Bezler's group. Dubinsky tried to mediate. Bezler refused to be intimidated by 'that faggot in epaulettes'. Girkin threatened to publish compromising material about Bezler, who was then prepared to retaliate by publishing his own information 'on stealing cars, robberies and all kinds of other shit'.[69] Burlaka was unimpressed and told Borodai he wanted to 'eliminate Bezler's groups'. Borodai reported that he had informed and received authorization from 'The Office' (the FSB) to do this, but not yet from Surkov. Not much seems to have come from this, possibly because of Bezler's GRU connections.

Bezler had also been taking initiatives. He had been to Moscow and encouraged the army to get a grip on the increasingly chaotic situation in the Donbas. As a result, in mid-July a headquarters was established in Krasnodon, where there were several retired generals and colonels, some with general staff experience, who were tasked with uniting the command of the republics. One senior Russian commander (using the code name 'Delfin', but believed to be Colonel General Nikolai Fedorovich Tkachev) was present. To Girkin they appeared to be operating independently of Surkov. Tkachev's main task was to organize and consolidate the sundry units operating in Luhansk, where the situation was even more chaotic, but they also expected to have some role in Donetsk. Girkin, who met him not long after he arrived, described him as 'a good military specialist', but with experience only in 'commanding regular troops, where there's discipline, unconditional submission'. Here he had to cope with 'partisan warfare, scattered units'. He struggled to coordinate, let alone command, the more than twenty separate units. Their commanders had no desire to submit to anyone. Yet Girkin does appear to have seen this as the equivalent of a Russian command post that he should respect. In an interview, he spoke of having constant contact with them and of sending them 'operative reports each morning and evening for the sectors in which units under me were fighting'. He did not, however, 'receive any orders from them'.[70]

SHOOTING DOWN MH17

On 16 July 2014, rebel forces were in trouble in Marinovka, a village close to the Russian border. At noon, a commander in the village, Leonid Kharchenko, told Dubinsky that his men were being shot 'down like dogs' by Ukrainian snipers. Unable to even dig trenches for cover, he complained about being 'cannon fodder'. Their positions were being struck by artillery and combat aircraft. 'They are bombarding us, we are constantly under fire.' Losses had been high. Dubinsky promised the senior commander present, Oleg Pulatov, that he would send a few tanks. Pulatov replied that that would be pointless. 'They'll only get burnt to the ground here.' What he really needed was 'long-distance artillery and good anti-aircraft material because the aircraft has operated from great heights, so practically none of our systems could reach it'. Thus apprised of the situation, he rang his opposite number in the 'Vostok' battalion. Because of Ukrainian aircraft, the situation was desperate, unless he could get hold of a Russian Buk anti-aircraft missile. 'If I can get the Buk system early enough in the morning, I can take it there. Then it's okay. If not, I'm in the shit.' Soon he heard back that a Buk would be delivered, and immediately promised Pulatov that, as soon as it arrived, it 'will come your way straight away'.[71]

By this time, Russia was apparently taking the situation seriously enough to have sent one of its combat aircraft into the fray, which shot down a Ukrainian SU23 aircraft. It also agreed, as a matter of urgency, to dispatch a Buk. Dubinsky believed that that would make all the difference, sufficient for him not take up an offer from the Vostok battalion to send troops and tanks to Marinovka. 'Well, the Buk is expected tonight. After that, all our problems should be solved.'[72]

On 17 July, Buk surface-to-air missiles from Russia's 53rd Anti-Aircraft Missile Brigade were sent from Russia across the border, close to the command post at Krasnodon. The Vostok battalion got the missile launcher through the separatist held territory. Dubinsky's men guarded the launcher once it reached the launch site south of Snizhne around 12.45. At 09.30, Dubinsky told Pulatov that he would get the Buk 'any minute now', and told him where to set it up (near Pervomayskoye). The Vostok battalion would also send three tanks. Pulatov's job was to guard the Buk when it had reached its destination.

Once it was in position, Bezler's group spotted a potential target.[73] The Buk crew, who had come with their weapon from Russia, received the information and an order to fire. At 16.19, a missile was launched. Soon Girkin was bragging on social media about another successful interception of what was assumed to be a Ukrainian An-26 military transport. Tragically, it was soon evident that the plane shot down was Malaysia Airlines Flight 17 (MH17), a Boeing 777 on a scheduled passenger flight from Amsterdam to Kuala Lumpur. This led to the loss of 283 passengers and 15 crew.[74]

About 30 minutes later, Dubinsky received a report that a Ukrainian combat aircraft had been downed, and expressed his delight. Half an hour later, when he had a report of Ukrainian artillery bombardments of his soldiers' positions in Marinovka, his first concern was to check that the Buk was out of range and properly guarded. He was now hoping for more support from Russian units to deal with the Ukrainian threat, still ignorant of what had happened. Two hours after the attack, he was told that journalists were asking questions about a missing Malaysian airliner. He still did not link that to the Ukrainian aircraft he was convinced had been brought down by the Buk.

He then went to Girkin's office. Soon he was worried that the two crashes were one and the same. At 20.00, he called Pulatov to ask what happened. He was told that the Buk 'brought down a Sushka [a Sukhoi jet] ... But before that, the Sushka downed the Boeing. They tried to blame us for that.' Dubinsky asked if that was based on observation.

Pulatov insisted it was. 'The "Sushka" hit the Boeing. They saw that from Snezhnoye. After that, the "Sushka" carried on, and the Buk blew it to shreds.' Dubinsky passed this story on at once to Girkin.

> So, here's what happened. A 'Sushka' hit a fucking Boeing. After that, the 'Sushka', as it was on its second round, was brought down by our BUK. And lots and lots of our people saw that. Gyurza just reported that.

Girkin took some time processing the news. Dubinsky observed, 'That's good news, isn't it?' Girkin replied: 'Well, I'm not sure. I don't think so, really.' Dubinsky: 'Well, they are going to blame us anyway, for blowing that thing to pieces.' Later, when he spoke to his men at the crash scene, he interrogated them again on their description of the sequence of events, and they stuck to their version. 'Yes, first there was a bang up there, and then there was our bang.'[75] The Russian Ministry of Defence first adopted this story. When it was clear that only one plane – and not two – had been shot down, they moved to another version, suggesting that it was a Ukrainian Buk that shot down MH17.

In June 2019, the Dutch Public Prosecution Service charged four people with murder and issued international arrest warrants.[76] Those charged were the Ukrainian Leonid Kharchenko, and the three Russians Sergey Dubinsky, Oleg Pulatov and Igor Girkin. Years later, Girkin accepted a 'moral responsibility' for the incident, while still denying that separatist forces shot down the aircraft (allowing for the possibility that the missile was launched by a Russian unit).[77] It is important to keep in mind that the essence of the story was known straight away, not least because of Girkin's post on a Russian social media site – 'We warned you not to fly in our skies.'[78]

The human tragedy of the shooting down of the Malaysian airliner was also a political blow for the separatists and a major distraction. The efforts to soften the impact by pretending that somehow it was Ukraine's fault had the result of prolonging the controversy. The military position did not improve, and by the end of July Girkin was thinking that it might be necessary to evacuate Donetsk. By his account, he changed his mind: 'I realized that it's better to take the fight in Donetsk than all these breakthroughs. In the evening I returned to Donetsk and already, despite the severity of the situation, I did not plan to transfer the headquarters, nothing.' Other accounts suggest that he did order a withdrawal from Donetsk, but the other militia leaders refused to follow.[79]

By this time, in Moscow, there was alarm and frustration with the situation. According to an account from one of the separatists:

> In early August 2014, the Kremlin hosted a closed meeting between President Vladimir Putin and journalists – it was about 50 people, including those who worked in the Donbas. Putin listened to them carefully. All of them literally asked Putin in chorus to send troops to the Donbas and support the small militia that opposed the entire Ukrainian army.[80]

Allowing the separatists to be overrun would be too great a humiliation and might even provoke a nationalist backlash in Russia itself. Putin accepted that regular Russian forces would be needed to push back the Ukrainian offensive. First, he wanted a change in leadership, which was to be orchestrated by Surkov. Surkov had already been controlling events as best he could from Moscow. 'Any call from Moscow was viewed as a call from the office of Lord God himself and ... was implemented immediately.'[81] Borodai resigned as prime minister, although he stayed on for a while as deputy to the Ukrainian Zakharchenko, who took over his role. As Borodai later observed, one reason was that it was hard for Moscow to claim that this was a Ukrainian civil war when so many Russians were in charge. 'At that time, the leadership of the Donetsk People's Republic was a strange spectacle,' he later explained: 'I am from Moscow. My first deputy was from Moscow. The power ministries were controlled by Muscovites, and defense minister Igor Strelkov was also from Moscow. It was a little too blatant from a propaganda perspective.'[82]

On 14 August, Girkin resigned and returned to Russia. Part of the deal may have been that Russia made stepped-up support conditional on his departure. In an interview in 2017, Girkin explained: 'I was ordered to transfer command to Zakharchenko.' When asked why Zakharchenko was chosen, he said he did not know. 'He and Borodai went to meet with Surkov. And apparently he was chosen, that is for the formal head of command. And why and how this happened ... Surkov's choices are always shit.'[83]

By this time, Moscow viewed Girkin as a loose cannon. The leadership was irritated when he criticized Surkov for his 'betrayal' in not supporting a more ambitious policy in April. One former Kremlin official observed that Moscow was frustrated with his strident calls for more Russian intervention. 'He went over there and started this mess ...

and now we are cleaning it up.' [84] Because the Russian media had built him up as a modern-day hero fighting against the odds for the nation, they were now encouraged to bring him down before he became a rallying point for ultranationalists, who thought Putin too soft. A campaign was begun against Girkin, criticizing his unheroic retreat from Slovyansk.[85] In the transcript of an intercepted conversation, Malofeev tried to get Girkin to make it clear that he was not against Putin. He wanted him to give an interview in which he would say: 'I'm an officer, I have a supreme commander. Of course, I don't follow his direct orders, because I am in another country, but I respect him most, I consider him the brightest leader of our time, thanks to whom Russia has risen from its knees, and we all look at it with hope.' When he returned to Russia, Girkin insisted on his support for Putin, while adding that the Russian leader was surrounded by traitors whom Girkin intended to fight.[86]

Thereafter the Kremlin prevented him from going back to the Donbas, and Malofeev was discouraged from sponsoring his activities. He tried to use the prestige he had acquired to enter Russian politics, forming the Novorossiya movement, and allowing a nationalist cult of personality to develop, with a website, superstrelkov.ru. But he failed to find a niche, and his efforts fizzled out.[87]

The Russian regulars who moved to push back the Ukrainians were, imaginatively, described as 'vacationers', military men who volunteered to spend their summer holidays fighting across the border. It did not take long before their superior strength, equipment and tactics prevailed. The change of leadership, however, did not lead to a lasting stability. Now backing away from any thoughts of Novorossiya, Putin moved to a deal with the Ukrainian government that would have Donetsk and Luhansk return to Ukraine but with much more autonomy and veto power. This was the deal at the heart of the Minsk agreements of September 2014 and February 2015. However, it was still unacceptable to the separatists. They never really deviated from their aim of creating the conditions under which their territories could be absorbed back into Russia and had no interest in the alternative plan, which saw their being absorbed back into Ukraine, a development that would remove them from power.

Although both the battle lines and the structure of a possible settlement were now largely set, the conflict continued to rumble on, with regular loss of life and economic damage to all parties. Within both

Donetsk and Luhansk there were regular upheavals, often marked by assassinations. A 2017 report referred to the militias as disorganized, factionalized, rarely working 'effectively with each other on the battle-field', often engaged in 'rampant criminality, particularly theft, smuggling, extortion, and violent assault', and suffering from 'pervasive substance abuse'. The Kremlin's frustration with the local leadership led to regular purges, but also then to commanders with little local following.[88] Girkin was left isolated in Moscow. In 2019, he was reported to be selling a gold medal, presented to him by Malofeev's Charitable Foundation of St Basil the Great, inscribed 'In memory of the reunification of the Crimea with Russia in 2014', with a depiction of Putin wearing a laurel wreath.[89]

FROM HYBRID WAR TO TOTAL WAR

Despite the talk of 'hybrid warfare', which implied a single mastermind pulling together mutually reinforcing strands of activity, the confused lines of command undermined operational effectiveness and blurred the political message. In the first stage of its war with Ukraine, Russia secured Crimea, but then it equivocated about what else it wanted to do. The pretence was maintained that a rebellion was under way as an authentic local reaction to a coup in Kyiv, denying the role of Russian money and guidance, as well as the roles played by its Spetsnaz and eventually regular forces. The militants in view were a mixture of romantics, adventurers, crooks and mercenaries. Inevitably, they often worked at cross purposes, and Moscow struggled to get a grip on their activities. They lacked the capacity to create the insurrectionary conditions that might have persuaded Putin to annex even more territory. Yet they left Russia committed to their defence, with a stake in the viability and security of a chunk of territory in a neighbouring country.

In line with the assumptions of hybrid warfare, Moscow backed up the efforts within Ukraine with both cyber operations and an intensive propaganda campaign. A GRU group mounted multiple attacks on Ukraine's infrastructure, including the electricity grid. Government departments were disabled. Major companies were attacked. The attacks were brazen and caused real damage. Yet they were not synchronized with military developments on the ground or diplomatic initiatives, as the theory might lead one to expect. Nor did they destabilize Ukraine or coerce it into major concessions on the Donbas.[90] Equally, the propaganda machine may have convinced Russians that the Ukrainian leadership was composed of fascists, but it had less effect in Ukraine. It went into overdrive after MH17, but only with the effect of ensuring that the controversy dragged on, including in a Dutch court.

Far from identifying a clever way to bring together a variety of military and other coercive instruments, so that the overall effect was greater than the sum of the individual parts, the Russians had set in motion events that they could not control, led by individuals they struggled to command, for objectives they did not wholly share. Militia groups, however formed, lack the stability and discipline of regular forces. They aspire to be proper armies with ranks and chains of command, but, without strong leadership and military success, they can easily fragment. Even if their leaders are strongly committed to a cause, this may be less of a factor among volunteers, who might be looking for adventure or criminal opportunities.

For their part, the separatist leaders were left frustrated. They looked up to Putin as their commander-in-chief, even if he did not communicate with them directly. They were always dealing with intermediaries and unsure how much the Russian president was taking an interest. As it became clear that he would not pursue their goals, they blamed his advisers, but still hoped that he would once more become the bold leader that had defied the world and annexed Crimea, and revive his offensive against Ukraine. Their position of not being part of either country left the enclaves in a mess. Instead of being able to walk away from the crisis of 2014 with the sole but clear prize of Crimea, Putin was left with a simmering conflict that could only be resolved by admitting political failure, or, alternatively, by taking more overt military action, with a high risk of its escalating into a more demanding and dangerous fight. Sympathy for Ukraine led NATO countries to step up material support. Instead of drawing Ukraine away from the West, Russia pushed it closer. Girkin, who had set all this in motion, was unimpressed. In 2020, he declared the enclaves to be a 'dump', with conditions worse than either Russia or the rest of Ukraine, and where Russia was hated. Nonetheless he remained convinced that Russia and Ukraine should be once more brought together.[91]

By this time, Putin had also become increasingly frustrated by the situation. His plan to use the enclaves to influence Ukrainian politics was getting nowhere. Ukraine no longer accepted any responsibility for their upkeep and so they required substantial Russian subsidies. A former comedian, Volodymyr Zelensky, became Ukraine's president in 2019, and declared himself interested in implementing the Minsk agreements to end the conflict, but to Putin he appeared weak and held back by Ukrainian hardliners. This left Russia with a de facto annexation of Donetsk and Luhansk, which meant that they could no longer be used to influence Ukrainian politics, while Ukraine was almost a de facto part of NATO, from which it was gaining weapons and other forms of military assistance.

Yet while Putin was gloomy about Ukraine in other respects, he was positive about Russia's situation. A substantial effort had been put into modernizing Russia's armed forces. He notified the West about new systems that at least sounded impressive, such as 'hypersonic weapons'. He had used military power effectively to help defeat rebels in Syria, and was using cyberattacks and information campaigns to harass Western states, with few apparent consequences. At home, he had consolidated his position, as his opponents were either murdered or imprisoned, and his hold over the media was strengthened. Prudent macroeconomic management meant that the sanctions imposed by the West after Crimea had been managed, while higher commodity prices meant that financial reserves were healthy. The West appeared unsettled after Donald Trump's presidency, and, as we shall discuss in chapter 15, this impression was confirmed by the botched US withdrawal from Afghanistan in the summer of 2021. He had also helped Alexander Lukashenko, president of Belarus since 1994, to suppress a popular movement, following the familiar pattern of protests over a rigged election in August 2020. Because of this, Belarus was now in effect a client state. One of the consequences of this new alliance, not appreciated as it was forged, was that it gave Russia more options for mounting an offensive against Ukraine. This produced a toxic combination – optimism about Russia's international position, along with pessimism about the political direction being taken by Ukraine.

In the summer of 2021, with his country still suffering from the Covid pandemic, which added to his personal isolation, Putin ruminated on his old themes. In July 2021, he published a 7,000-word essay that went far back into the history of the two countries, leading to the conclusion that Ukraine should never have been allowed to separate from Russia, and that it was now a non-country without a true national identity. He castigated the current leadership, presenting it as an instrument of an anti-Russian Western project that had lost interest in any attempt to resolve the position in the Donbas.[92]

After the publication of Putin's article, what had been a tentative movement of military units to the borders of Ukraine began to pick up pace. In early 2022, an intense debate developed among Western analysts about whether a Russian attack on Ukraine was imminent. Crucial to this debate were detailed assessments of the Russian forces close to border areas, including such details as to whether blood supplies had been delivered to field hospitals.[93] Even while there was little dispute about the core facts of the build-up, which was assessed at its conclusion to involve as many as 190,000 troops, there was far less agreement on what they revealed about Vladimir Putin's intentions. The preparations appeared too complete to be bluff, yet the quality of satellite imagery and other intelligence sources available to the West meant that a credible bluff would always have to look like the real thing.

In early February 2022, British and American intelligence publicly confirmed these assessments.[94] The Russian leadership continued to deny that an invasion was planned, dismissing it as a figment of a fevered Western imagination, while also presenting demands to the West that would require a revision of the European security order so that NATO could pose no threat to Russia, including ruling out Ukraine's membership of the organization. 'We are fed up with loose talk, half-promises, misinterpretations of what happened at different forms of negotiations behind closed doors,' stated Russian Deputy Foreign Minister Sergei Ryabkov. 'We need iron-clad, waterproof, bulletproof, legally binding guarantees. Not assurances, not safeguards, but guarantees.'[95] There were a lot of conversations but no progress.

The main reason why there were doubts about the Russian intentions was that it seemed self-evidently foolish for Russia to attempt to conquer a country the size of France with a population of 44 million. Even the Ukrainian government played down the talk of imminent war, concerned that it would undermine the country's economy.[96] Girkin was also sceptical. Instead of looking forward to the fulfilment of his dreams from 2014, he noted that Ukraine was better prepared militarily than before. A ground invasion would be extremely demanding. 'There aren't nearly enough troops mobilised, or being mobilised,' he was quoted as saying. 'The maximum Putin is doing is a military distraction, possibly to draw troops away from an operation in the Donbas.'[97]

Captured Russian documents, stamped 18 January 2022, show preparations then being made for operations for 15 days between 20 February and 6 March.[98] This does not mean that a final decision had been taken at this point. Whenever Putin decided on war, disregarding those risks that appeared obvious to external observers, he concluded that he had a historic opportunity that should be taken before the moment passed and the troops needed to be withdrawn from the front line.[99] The voices he heard were from his closest advisers, old comrades from the Russian security apparatus and his days in St Petersburg. They shared conspiratorial and reactionary views. These included Nikolai Patrushev, the hawkish chairman of his Security Council and former head of the FSB; security service chief Alexander Bortnikov; and foreign intelligence head Sergei Naryshkin.[100] The logic was that the enclaves in the Donbas were under threat of Ukrainian military action, and must be protected, but that protection required a different government in Kyiv that would have neither the inclination nor the means to contemplate such action in the future.

According to the agreed script, Denis Pushilin, the former GRU man who had been running the DNR since 2018, following the assassination of his predecessor Alexander Zakharchenko by a car bomb, would provide the pretext. The aim was to demonstrate that a Ukrainian offensive was under way, however unlikely that might be for a country surrounded by so many Russian troops poised for an invasion. Ukrainian territory was shelled from the two enclaves, presumably with the intention of goading the Ukrainians into retaliation. Warning that Zelensky 'will soon order the military to go on the offensive, implement a plan to invade the territory of the Donetsk and Luhansk people's republics', Pushilin ordered a 'mass evacuation' of women, children and the elderly into Russia. Putin then backed this with a promise to pay 10,000 rubles to every 'refugee', and ordered officials to go to the Rostov region to support them.[101]

On 21 February, Putin held an extraordinary meeting of his Security Council, later broadcast on Russian TV, ostensibly to discuss whether to recognise the DNR and LNR as independent entities. Presumably because of his fears of Covid, he sat some distance from the members of the Council who were asked for their views on the narrow question of whether these two enclaves should be recognized by Russia. Here

Patrushev pushed his view that the US's 'concrete goal' was the break-up of Russia. Naryshkin did not fare so well, being admonished by Putin for answering the wrong question.[102] That evening, after it had already been announced that the enclaves would be recognized, Putin explained his decision in a tirade in which he expressed all his accumulated grievances, about the West and the government in Kyiv, ending with accounts of the daily provocations by Ukrainian forces in Donetsk and Luhansk. He concluded: 'We want those who seized and continue to hold power in Kyiv to immediately stop hostilities. Otherwise, the responsibility for the possible continuation of the bloodshed will lie entirely on the conscience of Ukraine's ruling regime.'[103]

The next day, the separatist and Russian media reported that an IED (improvised explosive device) had detonated, impacting two vehicles and causing three deaths. This was soon shown to have involved the staged use of cadavers and faked damage.[104] On 24 February, with treaties of 'friendship and mutual assistance' now in place with the DNR and LNR, Putin announced his 'special military operation'. The aim, he insisted, was not to occupy Ukraine but 'to protect people who, for eight years now, have been facing humiliation and genocide perpetrated by the Kyiv regime.' The objectives, however, clearly went beyond the Donbas:

> To this end, we will seek to demilitarise and denazify Ukraine, as well as bring to trial those who perpetrated numerous bloody crimes against civilians, including against citizens of the Russian Federation.[105]

He also called on Ukrainian soldiers to lay down their arms. If they did so they would be able to 'leave the battle zone' and return to their families. The next day, when they had palpably failed to do so, he instead warned that they were allowing a neo-Nazi regime to 'use your children, wives and elders as human shields' and urged them to: 'Take power into your own hands, it will be easier for us to reach agreement.' This appeal was no more effective than the first.[106]

CONCLUSION: AN INEPT INVASION

On 24 February, the surprise was not so much that Ukraine was being invaded, but that it was being done so incompetently. The offensive was mounted from Russia, Crimea and Belarus. The first objective appeared to be to get forces into Kyiv, with groups already inserted into the Ukrainian capital tasked with capturing or assassinating President Zelensky. The second city Kharkiv, close to the Russian border, was another major target, as were areas contiguous to the enclaves in the east. It was not long before it was apparent that the campaign was in serious trouble.[107] None of the most important targets had been taken and Russian forces were suffering high casualties as they were ambushed by Ukrainian forces. Zelensky was not only safe in Kyiv but was turning himself into an inspiring and effective war leader, mobilizing international support for Ukraine's war effort. Although the apparent objectives of subjugating Ukraine and installing a puppet government were always unrealistic, because the Russians never had enough troops to conquer and occupy such a large country, they now looked unlikely to pass the first hurdle of taking major cities. Putin faced the prospect of losing to a country he treated with contempt.

The symptoms of a campaign going badly included failure to achieve command of the air, despite the supposed superiority of the Russian Air Force, and too many axes of advance, none of which could be properly supported. Columns of tanks and their logistic support seemed largely confined to the Ukrainian road network, which meant that they were vulnerable to ambushes and could be diverted by blowing up bridges. The most visible example of these problems was a column of some 60 kilometres in length, which in fact was several columns bunched together, spotted approaching Kyiv. This appeared alarming until it became a symbol of Russia's chronic problems of logistics, with broken down and abandoned vehicles. According to one account, the column was initially stopped by a group of some 30 Ukrainian soldiers who approached it at night by riding through the forest on quad bikes 'equipped with night vision goggles, sniper rifles, remotely detonated mines, drones equipped with thermal imaging cameras and others capable of dropping small 1.5kg bombs'. Once they had destroyed a few vehicles at the head of the column, those behind were stuck, and could also be attacked.[108] Eventually it dispersed. With the smaller columns, there was little understanding of the principles of combined arms. They entered towns and villages without dismounted infantry checking ahead and were caught by Ukrainian fire. Compared with the ineptitude of the Russian offensive, the Ukrainian defence was conceptually coherent and well executed, making effective use of anti-tank, air defence systems and artillery. A month into the campaign, they began to mount counteroffensives.

In response to the setbacks, the Russians began to direct their fire against the civilian population. The readiness to destroy infrastructure and kill people was more than an expression of frustration. It was bound up with a world view that Putin both reflected and encouraged. According to this view anyone who accepted the idea of an independent Ukraine was by definition a Nazi, which served as a catch-all term to describe any enemy of Russia. At the start of the war Russians were encouraged to believe that only a few illegitimate leaders were the Nazis. Once the Ukrainians were resisting en masse it appeared that the bulk of the population now came into this category, and so must be exterminated.[109]

Although the costs to Ukraine were heavy, no military objectives were achieved by the missile, artillery and air attacks on cities. They did not 'soften up' urban areas to make them easier to enter, or coerce Ukrainians into surrender. The symbol of Russian brutality and Ukrainian resistance was the city of Mariupol on the southern coast, which was rendered uninhabitable, with thousands of civilians trapped and then killed. Yet the defenders still forced the Russians to fight for eleven weeks through the rubble. The effect of the pummelling of Ukrainian infrastructure, property and people, as might have been anticipated, was to make Ukrainian forces more determined, especially as they became further encouraged by the military situation on the ground.[110] It was also a factor in encouraging Western countries to increase their economic and material support to Ukraine, including shiifting from purely 'defensive' to more 'offensive' weapons, such as long-range artillery. Civilians, fearful of being caught by Russian advances, fled either to the safer western parts of the country or became refugees. Up to 6.5 million left the country although as the fighting became concentrated in the east, some 2 million returned.[111]

To ensure that NATO countries did not get directly involved in the fight, early in the war Putin invoked the nuclear deterrent.[112] Although these were unusually fraught circumstances, naturally leading to speculation about what would happen if the Russian situation became even more desperate,[113] nuclear weapons may have helped to contain the conflict – deterring direct Western intervention, but also deterring Russia from mounting attacks against the neighbouring NATO countries supporting Ukraine.

Through the first month of the war, the Russian leadership continued to insist that everything was going to plan and was on schedule, although this was obviously not the case. Girkin, who felt under no obligation to help the regime, observed caustically that a 'catastrophically incorrect assessment' of Ukraine's forces had been made. Not only had there been no operational success, Russia was now likely to be 'drawn into a bloody push and pull, a long debilitating and extremely dangerous [war] for the Russian Federation'.[114] His advice on how to improve matters was to be totally uncompromising, establishing new authorities in the 'liberated territories, corresponding to the traditional fiefdoms of Novorossiya', and incorporating them into a new unified state. The war, he insisted, could only be won completely or lost completely.[115]

Rather than accept the risks of total war, the Ministry of Defence opted for a more focused approach. On 25 March, it announced what was widely interpreted as a partial retreat, although it was presented as part of the original plan. The line taken was that after considering two options for its 'special military operation', one of which would have covered the whole of Ukraine while the other would have concentrated on the Donbas, the choice had been made to concentrate its main effort on the 'complete liberation' of the Donbas region. This was because the vast majority of Ukraine's air force and navy had been destroyed, and 93 per cent of Luhansk Oblast and 54 per cent of Donetsk Oblast were already under Russian control.[116] By the end of the first week in April their departure from the Kyiv, Sumy and Chernihiv regions was confirmed. As they withdrew they left behind grisly evidence of murders, rapes, torture and looting. This cast a cloud over what was still a remarkable Ukrainian victory in the first round of the war, achieved against the odds. Putin's original war aims were now out of reach and the horror of these revelations ended any early prospects for peace negotiations.

The Russians began the next round, the battle for the Donbas, with depleted forces but potentially more manageable logistics and opportunities to use their air power. Ukraine, fully mobilized, did not lack for troops but depended on NATO countries for supplies that would keep them in the fight and able to launch counteroffensives. So long as Russian forces were still in occupation of any part of Ukraine, the situation would be unstable and the sanctions imposed by the West, which were squeezing the Russian economy, would remain in place.

Both sides provided estimates of enemy casualties while staying largely silent on their own. Independent analysts were able to keep some sort of tally of equipment losses, using the numerous posts of battle scenes on social media. The most authoritative identified by 24 June almost 4,375 Russian losses (destroyed, damaged, abandoned and captured), including 789 tanks, with the comparable figures for Ukraine of 1,184 items, including 198 tanks.[117] Accurate numbers of casualties were hard to come by. Ukrainian losses over the first four months of the war were over 10,000 service personnel and at least twice as many civilians, while Russian military losses were at least 15,000 and possibly higher.[118]

The UK Ministry of Defence assessed on 8 May that Russia had lost a third of the combat capability that had been assembled at the start of the war.[119] This would explain the evident difficulties faced by the Russians in the fight for the Donbas as they cast around for reserves to replenish front line forces and had to draw on stored equipment that was often obsolete or had been poorly maintained. There was speculation that Putin saw 9 May, the date marking victory in the Great Patriotic War, as a deadline for the army to deliver some victories in this war. As it became apparent that none would be forthcoming, the speculation shifted to the prospect of Putin announcing full mobilization to address the chronic shortages in military manpower. But no such announcement came.[120] Any measures would take too long to bring battlefield benefits and would be deeply unpopular. Girkin lamented that because of these shortages 'our forces are unable to deliver even a limited defeat to the enemy in ground combat.'[121] The Russians adapted their tactics, relying more on artillery to batter Ukrainian defences, as well as the towns and cities they were defending. They concentrated on completing the occupation of Luhansk, which they had achieved by late June at a high cost to their own forces as well as to the Ukrainians. While these battles raged Kyiv waited for the arrival of Western equipment, to enable them to mount counter-offensives. The question became one of whether the Russians would be able make up their shortages in troop numbers, with evidence of poor morale, and then defend territory as tenaciously as Ukrainians. They also had to cope with a developing insurgency in the occupied territories.

What does this tell us about command? We come back to the familiar theme of autocratic decision-making, of leaders supremely confident in their wisdom and insight, egged on by sympathetic courtiers who share the same baleful world view, while disregarding any naysayers who warn of the pitfalls. Those in Moscow in and around the elite were largely in the dark about Putin's plans, and assumed, along with many outside observers, that this was a coercive bluff. When the invasion was launched, many were shocked, aware how badly this could go, with massive Western sanctions and a mission defined in a way that it was impossible to achieve. 'I was shocked because for a long time, I thought that a military operation was not feasible. It was not plausible,' reported Andrey Kortunov, a member of a Kremlin panel of foreign policy advisers.[122] By ignoring experts on Ukraine, Putin made his decision much easier but also much worse.

With his own background in the FSB, he was comforted by reports of agents in place, ready to subvert the Ukrainian state as the invasion started and help install a new administration, though as the days passed there was no obvious return on this investment. A greater puzzle is why there was no military advice on the likely consequences of the invasion. In part, as with some of the other advice he may have received, this was because of the natural tendency in autocracies to tell the leader what it is thought he wants to hear, with assurances that all preparations have been made, eased by a sense that the whole exercise was largely performative and would not lead to anything. It might also have been down to arrogance, similar to that which led to the tactical errors and early failures in Chechnya in 1994–5. Just as Putin imagined an artificial state, feebly led and with little social cohesion, the Russian high command may have assumed an equally feeble Ukrainian force. On the numbers, the Ukrainians were outgunned in all departments, including air power. The last time there had been a direct clash between the two armies, in 2014, the Ukrainian army had been beaten easily and suffered badly.

The flawed underlying political assumptions led to flawed military assumptions. The field commanders were barely given any notice that the 'special military operation' was to begin, and so their plans were rushed. Moscow expected a short campaign, focused with decisive moves on the first day. This meant that elite combat units were given priority over logistics units, which limited their ability to sustain the offensive once the offensive stalled and all the essentials of modern warfare, including food, fuel and ammunition, began to be consumed at a rapid rate. In effect, there were a number of separate wars being fought at once, all facing their own challenges, without an appropriate mechanism to allocate scarce resources between them. When the more focused battle for the Donbas began one individual – General Alexander Dvornikov, the

Southern Military District Commander – was put in charge of the Russian military effort, although in June he was replaced.

Putin's own background was in intelligence operations. So were those closest to him in the decision-making process. Their cast of mind was conspiratorial, convinced that their enemies were constantly manipulating the perceptions of ordinary people as part of plots to destabilize Russia, and so they must do the same. They dealt in covert operations and narratives to which the facts must always be made to fit. This routine manipulation of the truth meant that Putin became trapped by a false narrative he had helped to form. As he realized that the floundering operation in Ukraine was undermining his position and aura, he lashed out first at the FSB, the agency so important in his own rise to power, which became subject to extensive purges. Failed generals were dismissed, along with the Admiral considered culpable for the loss of the *Moskva*, the flagship of the Black Sea Fleet, to an audacious Ukrainian attack. Moscow's frustration was reflected in reports of General Gerasimov visiting the Donbas to give some detailed direction, where he only just avoided being caught by a Ukrainian strike against a command post,[123] and that he was joined by Putin in getting into inappropriate levels of detail in ordering force deployments.[124] It was also possible that such reports reflected attempts by senior officers to deflect blame to where they thought it was due.

As we noted in chapter 10, the Russian military had inherited the Soviet tradition of subordination to the political leadership. By 2022, the military leadership had been in position for many years, and had become embedded in the decision-making process, dependent upon Putin for their positions, but also able to enjoy the rewards the Russian system offered those at the top. They would not have been inclined to offer unwelcome advice, even if it had been sought. The incentives to offer only welcome advice permeated the command structure. This meant that few would have been inclined to point out that the Ukraine operation depended on equipment with parts lost to corrupt practices, or just shoddily maintained, or that the Russian army had not developed tactical concepts to cope with the defensive measures that the enemy was likely to adopt, or that insufficient intelligence had been gathered even to work out what these measures might be. If the operation had been the walkover expected, then none of this might have mattered. But it wasn't, and it did.

13

The War on Terror: The Battle
of Tora Bora

This adversary is one of the world's last bastions of central planning. It governs by dictating five-year plans. From a single capital, it attempts to impose its demands across time zones, continents, oceans, and beyond ... You may think I'm describing one of the last decrepit dictators of the world [but] the adversary's closer to home. It's the Pentagon Bureaucracy.
Secretary of Defense Donald Rumsfeld, 10 September 2001[1]

On 11 September 2001, four civilian aircraft were hijacked by Islamist terrorists and flown at the centres of American political, military and economic power. Two hit the twin towers of the World Trade Center in New York. One hit the Pentagon in Washington. Another was directed at the US Capitol building, but the attack was thwarted by passengers, who overwhelmed the hijackers, although the aircraft still crashed. The death toll of the attacks, soon referred to as simply '9/11', was just below 3,000, although, at well over 10,000, initial casualty estimates were far higher, and this helped shape the immediate reaction to the outrage.

President George W. Bush was determined to respond. From the start, there was compelling evidence identifying the al Qaeda group, led by the Saudi Osama bin Laden, as the responsible party. It was known to be based in Afghanistan, which was then largely under the control of the Taliban, a group with a similar Islamist ideology. The American military had never previously given any thought to the possibility of going to war in Afghanistan. Now they had to plan one as a matter of urgency.

Tora Bora

N

TURKMENISTAN

Maz

IRAN

AFGHANI

Nangarhar Province

RUMSFELD TAKES CONTROL

On 21 September 2001, ten days after the attacks, Bush, along with Vice President Dick Cheney, received Secretary of Defense Donald Rumsfeld and four generals into his private residence at the White House, to be briefed on the state of military planning. The generals included Army General Hugh Shelton, whom we met in chapter 11, and who would be leaving his post as Chairman of the Joint Chiefs of Staff at the end of the month. The others were his successor, Air Force General Richard B. Myers; General Tommy Franks, head of Central Command (CENT-COM), responsible for all operations in the Middle East and Central Asia; and Major General Dell Dailey, head of the US Joint Special Operations Command (JSOC).

The man greeting them had little military experience. Bush joined the Texas Air National Guard in 1968, aged 22, and served until 1974. This was a common way of avoiding Vietnam. It meant two years on active duty learning to fly, but no combat. Now, as president and commander-in-chief, he was for the first time engaged with war planning. The 'officers' dress uniforms with the rows of ribbons highlighted their military expertise', he noted of his guests, adding that this 'was a whole lot more extensive than mine'.[2] Bush had already set the task by demanding, immediately after 9/11, that bin Laden be found 'dead or alive'. Now, with the Taliban apparently still determined to give sanctuary to al Qaeda, Bush concluded that both had to be eliminated. He was content to leave it to the military leadership to determine how this was to be done, and did not intend to interfere with logistics and tactical decisions. He saw his job as ensuring that their plans were consistent with his strategic vision. Like many of his generation, he had been brought up on stories of political 'micromanagement' during the Vietnam War and saw this as something he must avoid. Nonetheless, his impatience set the tone for the planning. It created pressure for an early start to the campaign.

Rumsfeld shared the president's sense of urgency and was much more experienced. He had been a naval aviator in the mid-1950s, and stayed a reservist until 1989, by which time he had acquired the rank of captain. He was now in his second stint as secretary of defense, having first served in Gerald Ford's administration a quarter of a century earlier. He had also been an ambassador to NATO. Unlike Bush, he was not at all humbled by the military expertise around him. He had been dealing with military issues when the current commanders were junior officers. He was keen to start testing his ideas for a 'new way of war', and was not going to be reticent when it came to driving forward the administration's strategy.

Rumsfeld also had strong views about his role in the conduct of the coming war. He ensured that, other than the president, he was the sole civilian in the chain of command, and discouraged collegial decision-making. His main ally was Vice President Richard Cheney, an old colleague of his. Cheney had taken over from Rumsfeld as Ford's chief of staff in 1975, and had been secretary of defense from 1989 to 1993, when Bush's father had been president. These two ruthless and skilled bureaucratic operators marginalized alternative sources of advice, especially Secretary of State Colin Powell, a former chairman of the Joint Chiefs who knew about war planning and was altogether more cautious. The president's national security advisor, Condoleezza Rice, largely saw her role as managing the process and was not inclined to expend capital to change policy.

By September 2001, Rumsfeld's self-confidence, arrogance and disregard for their views had already made him unpopular with the senior echelons of the military. He made no secret of his view that they were slow to act and unimaginative.[3] In return, they objected to his readiness to disparage their advice, but also his curious management style. Underlings would be sent 'snowflakes' – terse one-page and even one-line memos, sometimes giving instructions and sometimes asking questions, sometimes addressing fundamental issues and sometimes raising trivia. Like snowflakes, they made some impact on landing but soon melted away, largely because they were rarely followed up and came too often (at times as a 'blizzard') for subordinates to do much with them. Staff spent days on obscure questions, only to discover that Rumsfeld no longer had any interest in the answer.

The quotation at the head of this chapter, from the day before 9/11, shows how much he believed himself to be fighting Pentagon bureaucracy. Given this attitude, he was unlikely to take a back seat when it came to operations. It was the norm for civilians to defer to professional military judgements in operational matters, as he acknowledged, but in this case an exception had to be made. This was a unique situation.

There was no 'off-the-shelf' doctrine that had been war gamed and practised.[4] Not only did he believe that he was entitled as secretary of defense to get into every issue he thought important, he also could not see any other way to shake the military hierarchy out of its lethargy. The initial military response to the emergency, with familiar options, had confirmed Rumsfeld's prejudices. Unlike the CIA, which had been dabbling in Afghan affairs for three decades and had some agents in place, the military had little knowledge of the country and nothing to build on when devising plans.

At the time, the Chiefs were not best placed to assert themselves. Shelton, as chairman, had been extremely critical of Rumsfeld, which is why his term was not extended when it expired on 30 September. Although the Goldwater–Nichols Act of 1986 designated the chairman as the chief military adviser to the president and National Security Council, Rumsfeld actively, although unsuccessfully, discouraged him from performing this role. Shelton had continued to give his advice directly, later observing that Rumsfeld was 'marking his territory like a little bulldog'.[5] To replace Shelton, Rumsfeld had sought a figure more versed in the emerging military technologies that interested him, but also less likely to contradict him. The hard-working, competent and amiable Myers was judged to be more pliable, and was pushed to concentrate on reforming what was below him, instead of influencing what was above. On 10 October, a few days after a lacklustre start to the Afghanistan campaign, with air strikes making a limited impact, Rumsfeld wrote to Myers complaining that nothing coming out of the bureaucracy was 'thoughtful, creative or actionable'. He suggested that 'down the line' in all parts of the Pentagon there were 'middle-level people making terribly wrong judgments with respect to political risk and military risk, decisions they are not qualified to make and ought not be making'.[6]

The aim of the Goldwater–Nichols Act had been to eliminate the paralysis caused by interservice rivalries as they struggled to find common ground. That is why the chairman had become the sole direct source of military advice. For the same reason, the chiefs of the individual services (known as the 'service chiefs') had been bypassed altogether when it came to operations, with the regional commands (Rumsfeld renamed them 'combatant commands') becoming responsible for their conduct and answerable to the president through the secretary of defense. This did not mean that the service chiefs lacked influence. Under 'Title X', the mandate under which the military functioned, they were required to train, equip and assign forces to the regional commanders, in this case CENTCOM, and so they could offer advice on how operations might best be accomplished.

Franks, for his part, while having little choice but to respond to Rumsfeld, was determined to protect his position in the chain of command and resisted any interference from elsewhere in the Pentagon. He was thus annoyed to be summoned by Shelton to meet the service chiefs at the Pentagon to brief them first on what was still a 'rough concept' on 20 September, the day before he was to present his plan to the president. At the meeting, the four chiefs were present, along with Shelton and Myers, as well as Rumsfeld and his deputy Paul Wolfowitz. The concept behind the plan reflected a developing consensus among the senior figures in the administration. Air strikes against possible al Qaeda targets would not be enough. Getting a major land force into Afghanistan would take too long and provoke local resistance. The best option was to work with local forces opposed to the Taliban regime. Fortunately, such a force existed, known as the Northern Alliance, reasonably well organized and already in control of some 20 per cent of the country. The CIA had come to this conclusion quickly, on 13 September, and had soon convinced Bush of the logic.[7] The core idea therefore was to combine American air power with the Afghan rebels, with the campaign held together on the ground by CIA agents and US special forces.

After the plan had been presented, the questioning began. General Eric Shinseki of the army expressed his scepticism: 'No one's ever fought a war using an indigenous rebel force. What you are proposing is completely unprecedented.' Franks dismissed his concerns: 'I'm fighting this war. You're not.' Shinseki, equally blunt, responded: 'We don't think it'll work.' Franks then stood up and said 'bullshit'. It was his plan and he was 'responsible for its execution'. He then walked out of the room.[8] The next day Franks described Shinseki and the Air Force Chief of Staff General John Jumper as 'Title X motherfuckers'. Franks's behaviour confirmed what the Chiefs had feared. Shelton observed that 'as soon as Tommy was promoted to four-star, he had developed a hell of an ego. It was not evident until he became the CENTCOM commander, then it started coming out in spades.'[9]

Shelton told him that he was missing an opportunity to improve his plan by taking seasoned advice. Franks's view was that the Chiefs were just making pitches for their individual services.[10] He complained to Rumsfeld about 'narrow-minded four-stars' seeking to 'advance their share of the budget at the expense of the mission', insisting that 'unity of command' must prevail. 'I will follow every lawful order that you and the President give me. But I must have command authority to execute those orders.' Rumsfeld concurred.[11] 'Don't pay attention to those assholes. You're my general.'[12]

This all suited Rumsfeld. Both he and Franks disliked having anybody cramp their style. Rumsfeld's aide Doug Feith described how Rumsfeld 'didn't want multiple sources firing CENTCOM ideas that looked like directives or orders. Those came only from himself.'[13] Franks was content with only one source of direction. The result was that neither of these two key figures in the chain of command sought to benefit from the advice of their peers. It also meant that they were dependent upon each other, and while Rumsfeld was pleased that Franks had disengaged from the Chiefs, it did not mean that he was satisfied with either the man or his plan.

Franks was a 'mustang', who had worked his way up after enlisting as a private in 1965. By the time he reached CENTCOM in 2000, his reputation was as a tough battlefield leader, inclined to make his points with profanities. He lacked, as Rumsfeld put it, 'the polish of some of his fellow generals, who had graduated from West Point and spent many years learning the ways of Washington DC'. He was a Sam Damon rather than a Courtney Massengale, though, in this case, the lack of a political sensibility was a major handicap.

Franks conceived his role in narrow terms, and so made little contribution to the intense strategic debates swirling around the administration in the days after 9/11. At first, faced with the challenge of a major operation over unfamiliar terrain in an inaccessible country, he told Rumsfeld that he would need two months to develop a war plan. The response was that that was not good enough and that the 'first cut' should be ready within days. It was this first cut that had been presented to the Chiefs on 20 September and was taken to the president the next day. Rumsfeld felt it necessary to alert Bush prior to the briefing: 'even before you hear the plan, I want to state: You will find it disappointing. I did.'[14] After hearing the plan, Bush decided to wait until something more developed was ready, eventually demanding a proper presentation on

28 September. By this time, two Marine Expeditionary Units (2,000 men each) had been added to the 500 CIA and special forces that would enter Afghanistan.

He might have been Rumsfeld's general, but Franks was given no reason to suppose that he enjoyed the secretary's confidence. Rumsfeld later acknowledged that he provided an 'overabundance of advice', which usually took the form of constant nagging for better plans or a faster operational pace. Here Rumsfeld reflected Bush's impatience. Bush was a man in a hurry. Politically, he needed to respond to this attack on the American people. In his early meetings with the military, he had been regularly alarmed about how long everything was going to take. This was one reason why a major commitment of land forces was ruled out. Air strikes, therefore, began on 7 October, even though not all elements of the plan were in place, few American personnel were in the country and few targets had been identified that were worth bombing. This led to what Franks called 'ten days of hell', marked by apparently futile bombing and little progress on the ground, during which doubts were fulsomely expressed in the media and tempers started to fray in government.

Rumsfeld made it particularly hellish for Franks. The secretary wanted to know what was going on with the air strikes, when there was actually little of value to strike, and why had more not been done to contact Afghan forces. Whereas the first ten-man CIA team had arrived in country on 26 September, the first special forces did not arrive until 19 October. There were a variety of answers to explain the delays, including bad weather, faulty helicopters and locating Afghan commanders. The military's reluctance to put forces at risk until they had dedicated search and rescue teams in position meant that they had to find a forward base. One in Uzbekistan was made available but it still presented a logistical challenge. Franks later recalled Rumsfeld's 'chronic impatience'. Blunt messages came regularly: 'When is something going to happen, General?'; 'I do not see any movement, General Franks'; 'Can you predict when something is going to happen'; 'General Franks, this isn't working. I want you to build options that will work.' Eventually, this got too much for Franks and he offered his resignation, suggesting the secretary find another commander more suited to his tastes.[15] This led Rumsfeld to back off.

The two men were locked together, but it took time before they learned to work with each other. It still fell well short of a partnership. In one meeting, after Rumsfeld had spoken, Bush asked Franks what he thought: 'Sir, I think exactly what my secretary thinks, what he's ever thought, what he will ever think, or whatever he thought he might think.'[16] That December, Rumsfeld described the division of labour in terms which suggested, with some condescension, that Franks was the tactician while he was the strategist. 'He tends to be focused on what he has to do, and what his people have to do. I'm frequently thinking of things that are around the corner, up ahead.'[17]

A further, critical complication came with the leading role taken by the CIA. In contrast to the military, who were slow off the mark, initially coming up with options that seemed torn between the operationally uninspiring and the logistically demanding, the CIA were full of ideas, and had quickly proposed working with the indigenous opposition to the Taliban. Rumsfeld did not like the thought that the CIA would play a prominent and autonomous role in the campaign. He therefore requested at the 21 September meeting with the president that all its operations in Afghanistan be placed under Franks's command.

Even though this was agreed in principle, in practice little control could be exercised from CENTCOM's HQ at Tampa, Florida, over events so far away. Many of the key decisions – in terms of which Afghan groups could take on the fighting, and what could be expected from them and with what equipment – were being made by CIA agents on the ground. Indeed, the only serious effort to find a peaceful solution to the crisis, by persuading the Taliban to abandon bin Laden and hand him over to the Americans (which if pushed harder might have prevented a lot of later grief), was conducted by Robert Grenier, the CIA man in Islamabad, while the State Department remained passive.[18]

Franks and his staff had only a limited understanding of how the CIA went about their business. There was an inherent disconnect between the senior command and the local. CIA Director George Tenet took the view that the teams on the ground should have 'tactical autonomy'. 'Our job in Washington was to provide support and guidance, but basically to get the hell out of the way.' Franks remained bothered by the chain of command. He told Tenet early in October: 'I want you to subordinate your officers in Afghanistan to me.' Tenet responded: 'It ain't gonna happen, Tommy.' He was concerned that the Pentagon bureaucracy would 'stifle our initiative and prevent us from doing the job we were best equipped to do'. He compromised on a memorandum of understanding between CENTCOM and the CIA. The memorandum was drafted, coordinated with CENTCOM and then 'put on the shelf'.[19]

From the start, the Agency had focused on al Qaeda. Their briefings were branded 'No Bin Laden'. Bush's 'dead or alive' demand chimed with this. Rumsfeld later claimed that he was never comfortable with this focus, in part because he was not confident of getting bin Laden, and in part because he wanted to give the 'war on terror' a wider scope, with less of a focus on Afghanistan.[20] The Taliban were understandably the first priority, because, absent their handing him over, it was impossible to get to bin Laden and his associates without first toppling the regime. This would also be a more straightforward task, as the Taliban's defence depended on holding positions from which they could be expelled by superior forces. Al Qaeda had no need to hold territory. It could disperse and regroup, and bin Laden could inspire sympathetic groups and individuals around the world simply by surviving and sending out messages. There was therefore always a possibility that the campaign might end up toppling the Taliban from power, leaving al Qaeda battered and its bases evacuated, but possibly not eliminated or even decapitated. This led to care when making public statements about what victory in Afghanistan might entail. Myers later observed, 'the definition of winning eluded us in the early parts of our campaign against the Terrorists'.[21]

OSAMA BIN LADEN ESCAPES

After a slow start, the campaign plan worked well, as the Northern Alliance, supported by American air strikes against enemy positions, pushed forward and the Taliban fell back in disarray. The capital Kabul fell on 13 November. The Taliban leadership fled back towards Pakistan or southern Afghanistan. Bin Laden was in Jalalabad to the east of the country, and then, with his close partner, Ayman al-Zawahiri, he left for the mountain caves of Tora Bora ('black dust'), in the Spin Ghar ('white mountain') region of Nangarhar Province, 15 kilometres from the Pakistani border. This covered an area almost 10-kilometre square, with valleys as well 12,000 foot peaks. He knew it well. From the early 1980s, it had served as a base for mujahedin fighting the Soviet Union, and he had returned a number of times since. It had fortifications, caves and tunnels, stockpiles of weapons, ammunition and food. It was a natural place for his last stand, with the option of an escape to Pakistan, should he choose to retreat.

Yet at this point, with bin Laden on the run, Rumsfeld and Franks became distracted. The idea that, at some point, Saddam Hussein's regime in Iraq could be targeted under the war on terror had been raised in the immediate aftermath of 9/11. The need to remove Saddam from power had been high on the agenda of many in the administration before 9/11. Even though there were no corroborated links between Saddam Hussein and al Qaeda, Rumsfeld and Cheney now made the case – not difficult to an administration still shaken after being caught out by al Qaeda – that all potential threats must be addressed before they became critical. The administration appeared reluctant at this time to tolerate any conceivable risk of threat.

Meeting with the National Security Council the day after Kabul fell, Bush stressed his reluctance to hang around in Afghanistan, at least in any numbers, expecting that a new government would be in place soon. 'US forces will not stay . . . We've got a job to do with al Qaeda.' Franks had proposed closing the border with Pakistan to stop bin Laden and al Qaeda escaping. Bush, however, wanted to move on. If bin Laden moved elsewhere, he observed, 'we're just going to get him there'.[22] Whether or not this was a formal shift in priorities, it certainly reflected Bush's continuing desire to press forward with his 'global war on terror', as announced just after 9/11, and Rumsfeld's conviction that it was now time to topple Saddam Hussein.

Soon a war against Iraq was moving from speculative discussion to demands for plans to invade and occupy the country. On 27 November, as Franks was working on air support for Afghan units preparing for bin Laden's last stand, he was asked to begin work to review the existing plans for Iraq and report back in a week. His response was 'Son of a bitch . . . no rest for the weary.' He did not suggest that work on the next war might wait until he had finished with the one he was already fighting. Instead, he accepted the distraction. At this point, his memoir abruptly moves away from Afghanistan and starts on planning for the Iraq war.[23] At this critical moment, with both focused on a plan for the next war, neither the secretary of defense nor the operational commander-in-chief could give the hunt for bin Laden their full attention.

Because of the success of the campaign up to this point, the two may have felt that there was no need to change an approach that had served them so well. It could now be applied with little amendment to the next stage. The formula of a light American footprint, with Afghans doing the actual fighting, played well back home, because it reduced the risk of American casualties. It also played well in Afghanistan, because it meant fewer foreign troops and a chance for Afghans to form their own government afterwards. The argument that the alternative of a heavy footprint was likely to turn the population against the Americans, as had happened with the Soviet Union, was persuasive.

The combination of Afghan infantry and American air power had in fact worked so well, much faster than expected, that, by the time Kabul fell on 13 November, little thought had been given to the important change this represented in the operational environment. The enemy was now seeking to hide and escape, rather than stand and fight. The Americans would no longer be fighting with the Northern Alliance, which did not wish to head south or east of Kabul, but would have to find new and as yet untested allies. The local population was more sympathetic to the Taliban and al Qaeda. Elements in the Pakistani government shared this sympathy. The original formula therefore no longer applied. But no thought had been given to a new one, and the rush of events meant that there had been no time to do so. CENTCOM thus did not have a sufficient grasp of the situation on the ground to respond with energy and speed to the situation at Tora Bora.

The previous strategy depended on US air strikes, and these were bound to continue. The key question was whether US ground forces would be involved, and, if so, how and where. Franks decided against putting US troops into this battle. He explained in 2002 that this was because it would take too long before they could be got into position. Our 'Special Forces troopers', he observed, 'were not yet in large numbers, even with those forces that we were providing support to'. He posed as the alternative something similar to the Soviet intervention that had begun in December 1979, initially to bolster a Soviet-backed regime struggling to cope with an insurgency. 'Given the timeframe that would be necessary to introduce conventional forces, and given the fact that, even with more than 600,000 people on the ground inside Afghanistan, the Soviets were never able to get . . . it done.'[24]

This was a poor analogy. Between a few special forces and a large army there were a wide range of possibilities. Most relevant was Task Force 58, a marine force under Brigadier General James Mattis, which was in a forward operating base by late November. Mattis was frustrated that he had been given nothing to do, as well as being limited by Franks to 1,000 men, with another 3,500 left on ships. He was under the control of United States Army Central (ARCENT), then based in Kuwait, which was running the army component of the war for Franks. He concluded that an army general could not figure out what to do with 1,000 marines.[25] For Mattis, it was obvious that he should get his men to Tora Bora as the 'only American unit within reach that had the firepower, leadership, mobility, and shock troops to do the job and finish the fight'. His staff took the view that there were only a few dozen passable routes of retreat:

> I was prepared to deploy Special Ops teams and Marine rifle platoons, all with forward observers who could direct air and artillery fire. At every pass, helicopters would insert overwatch teams equipped with cold-weather gear, forward air controllers, snipers, machine guns, and mortars. Attack aircraft would be on call. Our air could smash the entrances, leaving the terrorists to die inside the caves. If they tried to escape, TF 58 would be waiting at the exits.

Although he sent his proposed scheme to ARCENT in Kuwait, he got no response. In his memoir, he recalls some blunt exchanges ('some described my presentation as highly obscene') in early December. Even though, by 14 December, he had helicopters ready to leave on the Kandahar runway, with troops ready to go, the call never came. In his memoir, he cites a 2005 *New York Times* account claiming that 'the Bush administration later concluded that the refusal of CENTCOM to despatch the Marines ... was the gravest error of the war.'[26] Mattis characterized the error as one of Franks being unable to distinguish between, on the one hand, a heavy armoured land force invading on the scale and in the manner of the Soviets in December 1979 and, on the other, the heliborne, fast-moving light infantry that he could deploy.[27]

While Franks refused to use a substantial force of marines, the CIA went ahead with a few of its agents. Gary Berntsen, a CIA official who had been in Afghanistan in 2000, in charge of a team seeking to capture a senior al Qaeda figure, was now commanding the agency's operation in eastern Afghanistan.[28] In this role he got a number of Afghan

17. Che Guevara in the Congo, 1965.

18. A truck full of soldiers passes by a poster of Laurent-Désiré Kabila, President of the Democratic Republic of the Congo, which reads 'He's our man', in Kinshasa, 11 August 1998.

19. Russian President Boris Yeltsin and Defence Minister Pavel Grachev greet each other, 1993.

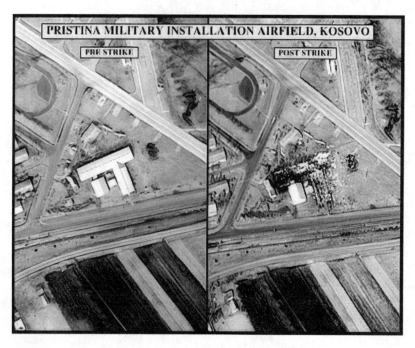

PRISTINA MILITARY INSTALLATION AIRFIELD, KOSOVO

PRE STRIKE

POST STRIKE

20. Pre-strike and post-strike photograph of the Pristina military installation airfield, Kosovo, Serbia, used in a Pentagon briefing on 16 April 1999.

21. British KFOR commander Lieutenant General Mike Jackson looks warily at NATO supreme commander General Wesley Clark as they discuss post-war security arrangements at Pristina airfield, 13 September 1999.

22. Self-proclaimed Prime Minister of the pro-Russian separatist 'Donetsk People's Republic', Alexander Borodai (*centre*), and self-proclaimed Defence Minister, Igor Girkin (Strelkov) (*left*), deliver a press conference in Donetsk, 10 July 2014.

23. Sloviansk city council under control of separatist forces, April 2014.

24. A Russian armoured vehicle burns after street fighting in Kharkiv, Ukraine's second largest city, three days after the Russian invasion, 27 February 2022.

25. Secretary of Defense Donald Rumsfeld looks on as General Tommy Franks, Commander of the US Central Command, gestures during a news conference at the Pentagon after the invasion of Iraq, 9 May 2003.

26. Anti-Taliban Afghan fighters walk past a huge bomb crater in the ruins of an al Qaeda camp in Tora Bora, Afghanistan, 18 December 2001.

27. British soldiers under attack by Iraqi protesters in Basra, September 2005.

28. Prime Minister Tony Blair addresses troops as he arrives in Basra, southern Iraq, for a surprise visit to British soldiers, 4 January 2004.

29. President Barack Obama meets with General Stanley McChrystal, Commander of US Forces in Afghanistan, on Air Force One, 2 October 2009.

30. Russian aircraft deliberately destroyed Nabad al Hayat Surgical Hospital in southern Idlib Province, Syria which served around 200,000 people, 5 May 2019.

31. The Joint Operations Center (JOC) in the United States Central Command, from where all current conflicts are commanded. Live feeds of TV channels – such as *CNN* and *Al Jazeera*, press conferences, ground operations and maps are projected on the giant screens.

32. President Xi Jinping, also chairman of the Central Military Commission, inspects the Chinese People's Liberation Army (PLA) Garrison in Macao Special Administrative Region, 20 December 2019.

warlords to provide the ground forces necessary for any assault, took a decision to call in air strikes at the first possible opportunity, and then called for US forces to support the operation, including blocking the escape routes for al Qaeda from Tora Bora to the Pakistani border. Berntsen was confident that he was reflecting the view of his immediate superiors in his pursuit of bin Laden, although less so of those at the highest levels of government.

Cofer Black, head of counter-terrorism in the CIA, had told those first going into Afghanistan on 19 September that their task was to kill bin Laden and his leadership.[29] Berntsen later explained that the guidance on the Taliban was that it might be possible to get them to negotiate or defect as alternatives to killing them. When it came to al Qaeda, however, the orders were 'kill bin Laden and eliminate every one of them'.[30] He noted later the large 'disconnect' with the Department of Defense. 'I understood my mission was to kill Bin Laden. I'm not sure that everybody in DoD understood that.'[31]

In terms of command, Berntsen worked with the system designed by his immediate superior in the CIA, Hank Crumpton. Whereas 'the military can't go off base without writing up an op [operations] order and having it approved up nine levels', he would just make a decision to proceed. This was a 'very flat chain of command'. Decisions would be made, even on major actions, 'on the spot based on the intelligence we had at hand', without asking permission. It was too complicated and time consuming to explain what was going on back to a distant high command.[32] He had become used to operating on his own when deciding on allies, what could be expected from them and with what equipment. With the Northern Alliance, he had conducted 'eighty percent of the meetings' by himself.[33]

At this stage, Berntsen was not looking for an army contribution. He assumed that, if one came, it would be a full brigade with artillery support, for which there would need to be careful planning, and he did not want to wait. Instead, he put together an 'Eastern Alliance', which he hoped would be equivalent to the 'Northern'. Unfortunately, there was no equivalence. The available Afghan militias were diverse and at odds with each other. Reflecting the urgency of the situation, Berntsen lacked the time to vet them fully. Nor did he feel able to pick some in preference to others. He needed the numbers. So he had to hope that the assembled force of about 1,000 men could work together.

The two key commanders, self-styled 'generals', were Hazarat Ali, who had been suggested by the Northern Alliance, and Haji Zaman, who had been suggested by Pakistan. Both were veterans of the war against the Soviets, but, while Hazarat Ali was poorly educated, Zaman was well-travelled and sophisticated, with a past conviction for drug smuggling. A third warlord, Haji Zahir Qadir, was the son of a former governor of Nangarhar Province and an old foe of Zaman. Each of these men had their own political agendas and a largely transactional approach, literally, to working with the Americans: dollar bills provided essential incentives at key operational moments.

In the absence of Mattis's marines, there were no forces to the south to block off the enemy's escape routes to Pakistan. The administration had hoped that the Pakistanis would help here. A big effort had been put in to get Pakistan on side since 9/11, despite its evident past links with the Taliban and even al Qaeda. The working assumption in Washington, which was at best naive, was that Pakistan would watch its own border and detain any terrorists trying to enter. A 4,000-strong frontier force was promised, but there were both practical and political grounds to be unsure of its effectiveness. The border was long, and there were many routes through it.

On 18 November, Berntsen sent a team to pursue bin Laden from Jalalabad to Tora Bora. On 3 December, four CIA observers accompanied by ten Afghans got close to an al Qaeda camp, with 'trucks, houses, command posts, checkpoints, machine-gun nests, an obstacle course and hundreds of bin Laden's men'.[34] With such a significant and unsuspecting target, Berntsen called in air strikes while he had the chance. For three days, US aircraft hammered away at al Qaeda positions. As a result, those al Qaeda members not caught by the bombardment retreated further south into the mountains to seek refuge in caves. The Afghan forces were spread out to move forward in the hope of trapping the enemy in the mountains. The evident risk was that, instead of being trapped, the enemy might get through to the southern side of the mountains and then take the relatively short journey to the Pakistani border.

Nobody else was consulted about this move, though Berntsen got retrospective authority. The argument for quick action was to take the opportunity to kill key al Qaeda figures while they were there. His concern was not only that it would take time to get the necessary permission, but that it would not be forthcoming:

I did not inform CIA headquarters that I was doing this. I did everything possible to initiate a battle without asking for their permission because I was very concerned that they wouldn't authorize any of it. They would want to know how many people I had. There would have been a slew of questions. I didn't want any questions. I didn't want to hear anything from anybody.

And quite frankly I didn't trust the seventh floor of the CIA [where the senior leadership was located] to do the right thing, because they had not done the right thing for a number of years before that. And I didn't care if I was fired or relieved either. I was just going to do it.[35]

So, after all the manoeuvres in Washington by Rumsfeld, Franks, Tenet and others to secure positions in the chain of command, in the end one man devised his own, opportunistic strategy to achieve what had been the administration's prime strategic objective of taking bin Laden 'dead or alive', and made a point of not checking with any superiors lest they seek to delay or amend his plan. As we have seen, it is not unusual for impatient field commanders (for example, Ariel Sharon, and 'H' Jones in the Falklands) to rush into operations because they fear cancellation if they wait. In this case the argument for early strikes was not tested against the alternative of watching the al Qaeda positions and identifying their weak points, while building up capabilities.

But Berntsen could not take bin Laden without support. As he called in the initial air strikes, he also tried to call in a force of 800 US marines or army rangers. They would be able to move into the caves of Tora Bora to take out al Qaeda and prevent their escape. Crumpton of the CIA describes how Berntsen's deputy rang him on a satellite phone from the base at Tora Bora, speaking in an 'unusually strident tone', asking for reinforcements. 'We can get this bastard, but we need more men. We need them now. Send us some rangers.' Crumpton briefed Tenet and Black. The next morning, he called Franks at Tampa but got nowhere. There were two arguments against sending so many troops. The first was the naive one – that they were not needed, because the Pakistanis would guard the border.[36] The second was that Franks did not intend to change his original formula. The message went back to Berntsen: 'General Franks wants to stick with what has worked, our small teams with our Afghan allies. He also says it will take time to plan. Time to deploy rangers. Too much time.'[37]

A more promising prospect was the special forces who had already been working with Afghan militias. Under the agreed division of labour, it was up to the CIA to make contact with potential Afghan allies, and, once this had been achieved successfully, the special forces would come in to conduct the operation. Berntsen approached Colonel John Mulholland, commander of the special operations force group known as Task Force Dagger. Mulholland was sceptical about the qualities of the Eastern Alliance, and faced his own resource constraints. His teams 'had been burned by warlords who had personnel [*sic*] vendettas and agendas that were counter to the United States objectives'. Hazarat Ali was a relative unknown who had not been vetted to Mulholland's satisfaction. His concern was that his men would get caught in a 'slugfest' trying to get to high ground occupied by the enemy, and be poorly supported by the Afghans and unable to get casualties evacuated by air.[38] Mulholland told Berntsen to get his team in. 'If in a week they're still alive and operating I'll send a team to work with them'.[39] This was one reason why Berntsen wanted to get the battle started. It put pressure on Mulholland.

Still with misgivings, Mulholland did send a small unit of 13 men known as COBRA 25, under Thomas Greer, to work with the Afghans. Greer later wrote of his exploits under the pen name Dalton Fury.[40] Their orders were still tentative. There was to be: 'No maneuver, TGO [terminal guidance operation] ONLY.' They were expected to wear US military uniforms, ostensibly to prevent friendly fire, although this stipulation was soon ignored. More serious were the strict orders to provide the Afghans with 'advice and assistance with air support' but 'not to lead them into battle or venture toward the forward lines'. This raised an immediate and obvious tension with the Afghans. The United States wanted to get bin Laden, yet they did not want to put their people at risk when doing so. The Afghans who were not that bothered about bin Laden appeared to be cannon fodder.

So, when Hazarat Ali met with the American team on their arrival on 6 December, he demanded that they participate directly in combat missions. This led Mulholland to order his men back to Jalalabad, until Ali agreed that they could have only a restricted role. Eventually there was a compromise. The Americans would engage in combat but only alongside Afghan troops. After this unpromising start, relations between the Americans and the Afghans remained uneasy. One big issue became the holy month of Ramadan. The need for Muslims to eat after the day's fasting required by Ramadan meant that positions taken from al Qaeda during the day were abandoned at sunset. Staying up in the mountains overnight was also an unattractive prospect, because of the extreme cold and thin air.

The Americans were unimpressed. There was a notable lack of Afghan commitment. Nothing much could be achieved without regular financial inducements. 'For the most important mission to date in the global war on terror,' observed Greer, 'our nation was relying on a fractious bunch of AK-47-toting lawless bandits and tribal thugs who were not bound by any recognized rules of warfare.' For their part, the Afghans were unimpressed by a collection of fighters who wanted other people to do the fighting for them. If the Americans were so keen to get bin Laden, why had they sent so few men to do the job? As Bergen notes, there were more journalists (around 100) in and around Tora Bora than there were Western soldiers. This also provided an additional complicating factor when supposedly stealthy operations were under way.[41]

On 8 December, command shifted from the CIA to the Special Operations Task Force (SOTF) 11, which now consisted of 50 elite troops as well as a contingent of British special forces.[42] With his team in place, Greer assessed the situation, established observation posts and decided on the next round of air strikes. This was to use a 15,000 pound BLU-82 'Daisy Cutter' that would likely kill anybody close to the explosion. But the bomb did not detonate fully, and landed away from the target area where they assumed bin Laden and Zawahiri might be hiding. Nonetheless, the force of the bomb made the ground shake and seemed to have an effect. On 10 December, American intelligence operators intercepted a message: 'Father [bin Laden] is trying to break through the siege line.' Another intercepted signal offered an even more precise location for bin Laden.

That afternoon, Hazarat Ali asked for some Americans to join him at the front line much higher in the mountains, to call in air strikes in support of a direct attack he proposed to launch against a potentially important al Qaeda position that his men had identified. The urgency of the request gave Greer little time to decide what to do. He chose to send two of his men with an interpreter, if only to demonstrate that Americans were prepared to take risks. Afghan observers now claimed to have spotted bin Laden and requested yet more American support. Greer decided to take his task force up the mountain to join in the fight. First, they had to convince some Afghan guides to go with them. Using Toyota pickups, they began an arduous 10-kilometre drive, only to meet an Afghan convoy passing in the opposite direction, returning home to break their Ramadan fast. Ali promised that they would come right back, but it was hard for Greer to have any confidence that this would be the case. Meanwhile, those still in position came under fire from enemy positions. This led the rest of the Afghan soldiers to withdraw, leaving the two special operators and their translator stranded in a parlous position. With their Afghan guides refusing to go any further and no likelihood of Ali returning, the Special Operations Task Force concentrated on retrieving their men. This was not going to be the night to find bin Laden.[43] Still, enough was now known about al Qaeda positions to call in more air strikes, which began that night and continued nonstop for 17 hours. As al Qaeda retreated further back, the Afghans occupied more forward positions. Greer decided to keep his men more forward, in case there were more sightings of bin Laden.

Now Zaman took an initiative of his own. Relations between his men and Ali's had always been tense. Not only was there little coordination between the two, but at one point they even fought each other. Zaman now claimed to see an opportunity to get bin Laden to surrender. He was not optimistic about the outcome of a direct assault on al Qaeda forces as they were well armed and determined, but some deal might be possible. The coming feast of Eid al-Fitr, ending Ramadan, seemed to be the right moment.[44]

The Afghans and Americans had different concepts of surrender. Many of the Eastern Alliance fighters had little appreciation of the events of 9/11. As al Qaeda was made up of fellow Muslims, they had no problem with the battle being decided by letting them lay down their arms and walk away. For the Americans, such an outcome would be unacceptable, at least when it came to the senior al Qaeda figures who they wanted to capture. On 12 December, the Afghans told the Americans to stop the bombing. At first the Americans complied, but they saw no basis for a negotiation. Berntsen, now back in Kabul, was furious. 'Essentially I used the f-word . . . I was SCREAMING at them on the phone. And telling them, "No cease-fire. No negotiation. We continue airstrikes."'[45]

The bombing resumed. On 14 December, another message from bin Laden was intercepted: 'Our prayers have not been answered. Times are dire ... I'm sorry for getting you involved in this battle, if you can no longer resist, you may surrender with my blessing.' Once again Zaman demanded a ceasefire. But when the next day's intercepts began with what sounded like a pre-recorded sermon, the suspicion developed immediately that the talk of surrender had been a cover to enable bin Laden to escape. He had divided his troops into two columns to move down the mountain towards Pakistan in separate paths as they made their escape, while a few fighters were left to provide cover. One of his guards was left with his satellite phone, letting the Americans pick up what became increasingly misleading signals. In the afternoon of 15 December, Hazarat Ali's people again thought they caught sight of bin Laden. By the afternoon of 16 December, the battle was essentially over. Of the al Qaeda fighters, some 220 were dead and another 52 were captured. Ten days later, a videotape surfaced of bin Laden. He appeared to be visibly aged and contemplating his own death. 'I am just a poor slave of God,' he said. 'If I live or die, the war will continue.' During the 34-minute video, he did not move his entire left side.

The Pakistani troops who were supposed to have prevented al Qaeda fighters entering their country had largely left. On 13 December, five armed Pakistani nationals from the Jaish-e-Mohammed group, which had strong links with both al Qaeda and Pakistani intelligence, had mounted an attack on the Indian parliament. Although the attack failed, a major crisis developed between the two countries. Pakistani forces guarding the border with Afghanistan were moved to deal with a possible conflict with India. Whether or not the timing was deliberate, to provide a distraction to allow the top leadership of al Qaeda to escape, that was the effect.

CONCLUSION: A MISSED OPPORTUNITY

Tora Bora and its aftermath revealed the potential, but also the limitations, of an approach to armed intervention that later became the norm. To avoid inserting a large army into Afghanistan, the Americans worked with local forces that shared their anti-Taliban objectives, supporting them with special forces and air power. This combination was successful largely because the enemy had no counter to the air power. When it came to moving against al Qaeda, the combination worked less well. The Afghan partners were not truly aligned with the Americans on either objectives or tactics. The failure to get bin Laden also exposed a fault line in the American command structure. The Americans on the ground, working with Afghanis, were largely from the CIA, backed up by special forces, and allowed considerable latitude when it came to taking initiatives, often acting before they received formal authorization to do so. By contrast, the military command was hierarchical, with those at the top unresponsive.

Franks was aware that the fact that the man Bush wanted 'dead or alive' at the start of the campaign was able to escape was a black mark against a campaign that was otherwise successful. He was soon rejecting any suggestion that more could and should have been done, first on the grounds that bin Laden might not have been present, and second on the grounds that the United States did not have the troops available to help trap him at Tora Bora. Both lines of defence were dubious, but the first – the claim that the al Qaeda leader might not even have been in Tora Bora at the time – was the weakest. As early as the summer of 2002, Franks dismissed suggestions that bin Laden was even present as 'speculation after the fact', accepting only that 'we had a sense that there were enemy formations in the Tora Bora complex. He was not saying bin Laden and other leaders were not present, only that he had seen no proof that they were.[46] When, in 2004, John Kerry, the Democratic Party's presidential nominee, charged the Bush administration with a major strategic error in allowing bin Laden to escape, Franks repeated this claim.[47] Later, Kerry used his Senate position to investigate and to provide convincing evidence that bin Laden was at Tora Bora.[48] Franks's deputy, General Michael DeLong, wrote in his own memoir that bin Laden was hiding in Tora Bora at the time of the battle. He spoke less definitely in 2004, in support of his former boss, but still had to acknowledge that the prevailing assumption at the time was that the al Qaeda leader was present.[49] Moreover, DeLong also reported that Rumsfeld was anxious for news that there had been progress in the manhunt.

> We were hot on Osama bin Laden's trail. He was definitely there when we hit the caves. Every day during the bombing, Rumsfeld asked me, 'Did we get him? Did we get him?' I would have to answer that we didn't know.[50]

As further evidence, we can note an interview Rumsfeld gave at the time in which he described the current stage of the operation as being about getting bin Laden. 'To finish the job . . . we've got to get the senior al Qaeda people, and we've got to see that the lower level al Qaeda people don't get out there and run loose and destabilize another country or start killing people somewhere else.'[51]

This casts doubt on Bush's own insistence, in his memoir, that the United States was never close to bin Laden, with Tora Bora only mentioned as one of the possibilities.

> I asked our commanders and CIA officials about bin Laden frequently. They were working around the clock to locate him, and they assured me they had the troop levels and resources they needed. If we had ever known for sure where he was, we would have moved heaven and earth to bring him to justice.[52]

It is unclear to what degree the request for more support was raised with Bush, but quite clear that in Washington no great exertions were made to ensure that whatever opportunity was there was taken. Mattis, who certainly assumed that bin Laden was at Tora Bora, and expressed his anger in his memoir that he was not allowed to go after him, blamed himself for failing to invest the time 'to build understanding up the chain of command'. If he wanted his senior commanders to be his advocate, he needed to get on their wavelength, so that his points could be made more effectively.

> When you're the senior commander in a deployed force, time spent sharing your appreciation of the situation on the ground with your seniors is like time spent on reconnaissance: it's seldom wasted.[53]

In practice, however, the time available for such sharing during a frantic, and in many respects improvised, campaign was limited, and the key decision makers were far away in Tampa and Washington.

Franks left a large gap in his memoir where there might have been a discussion of Tora Bora. As he had put such an effort into having total operational control, other decision makers had no trouble noting that whether and how to go after bin Laden was a matter for Franks. The CIA's Crumpton recalled providing 'our best intelligence, including confirmation of UBL's [Osama bin Laden's] presence, and offered our best recommendation but this was ultimately a military decision'.[54]

THE WAR ON TERROR: THE BATTLE OF TORA BORA

From the civilian side, Condoleezza Rice reported that Bush never received any recommendation on the matter. Rumsfeld's section in his memoirs was carefully worded. He made it clear that, whereas he 'was prepared to authorize the deployment of more American troops into the region if the commanders requested them', he never received a request from either Franks or Tenet.

> If someone thought bin Laden was cornered, as later claimed, I found it surprising that Tenet had never called me to urge Franks to support their operation. I can only presume that either their chain of command was not engaged or that they failed to convince Tenet of the quality of their information.

But Rumsfeld had created a hostile command climate. His determination to control everything had led the CIA to give him few chances to control them, and he was kept well away from their command loops. Although Rumsfeld had been given daily briefings on the course and accomplishments of the US military action in Afghanistan, just before the battle a newspaper reported, 'Absent from those briefings are any details or sense of the CIA's covert role in the battles, a secret war that has now remained largely under wraps.'[55] This disconnect between the CIA and CENTCOM meant that those most aware of the situation on the ground were unable to get to Franks when they had vital intelligence on bin Laden. Franks did not want to change a winning formula. There is no evidence that he consulted at all when rejecting the request for ground troops. Instead of an agreed plan to take out the main target in Tora Bora, the CIA agent on the ground was left taking the initiative by calling in air strikes, without any figures higher up the command chain discussing what other preparations might be made before revealing to bin Laden that he had been found.

In his memoir, Rumsfeld related CENTCOM's reasoning against a conventional ground offensive without fully endorsing it and then added,

> I believed a decision of this nature, which hinged on numerous operational details, was best made by the military commander in charge. Franks had to determine whether attempting to apprehend one man on the run, whose whereabouts were not known with certainty, was worth the risks inherent in such a venture. It was not an easy call.[56]

This suggests unusual reticence on his part. We know from DeLong that Rumsfeld was intensely interested in what was going on in Tora Bora. It was Franks's responsibility with an issue of this importance to ensure that the secretary was briefed, and his view sought, even if in the end the operational issues were for the commander. He could also have asked the secretary's view. Franks was doggedly following the line that there was no option other than to back Afghan forces as they pursued an American agenda.

This was exactly the sort of call where the views of the civilian leadership were needed, especially given the status of the 'man on the run'. Yet all the key members of the National Security Council, other than Tenet, denied that they even knew that there was an issue. When Rumsfeld did realize what was going on, when he visited Afghanistan on 20 December, and saw the problems with the Eastern Alliance, he sent a memo to Tenet saying that 'we might be missing an opportunity in Tora Bora and perhaps we should reconsider the earlier decision against bringing in more US Forces'. The message to Franks changed. 'I wanted to know "whether or not we should have had more people on the ground to avoid having so many people get away".'[57] By then, of course, it was too late. The bird had flown.

Peter Bergen argues that letting bin Laden escape when he was in reach was 'one of the greatest military blunders in recent US history'.[58] The most thorough student of the episode, Yaniv Barzilai, describes this battle as 'the largest failure of the campaign'.[59] A more generous assessment saw it as the 'flaw' in what would otherwise be a 'masterpiece'.[60] One issue with the indictment is that there might not have been much more that the Americans could have done to catch him. There is evidence, including the apparent injuries on his left side, that bin Laden was almost caught by the bombing, and, if he had been, the operation would have been considered a great success. Equally, if the marines had moved in, the al Qaeda leadership still might have escaped.

Such battles can be decided by slight margins rather than poor command decisions. The difficulty of manhunts in inhospitable and unfamiliar terrain, when the local population may be sympathetic to those being hunted, should not be underestimated.[61] The battle was fought by a few Americans working with reluctant local allies. The Afghans knew of the Taliban and al Qaeda's local popularity, and how much distrust there was of the Americans. In the end, some were as ready to help bin Laden escape as others were to find him. Tenet later observed that the Pakistanis always knew more than they were telling us – and were 'singularly uncooperative in helping us run these guys down'.[62]

There was nevertheless a problem with a chain of command that was too narrow and resistant to contrary thinking. Rumsfeld, the only one capable of giving Franks a nudge, was not only distracted himself by Iraq, but had also distracted Franks. The two had ensured that they were in controlling positions, but at this critical moment their minds were elsewhere. Ricks, a ferocious critic of Franks, provides an unflattering portrayal: 'dull and arrogant', never offering 'an example of fresh or even mildly offbeat thinking'. In this case, he was 'bumbling ... inattentive, almost as if the battles were someone else's problems'.[63] The charge against Franks, therefore, is that the matter was given no urgent consideration, and that an available option of a marine brigade was not taken seriously. Having got the idea fixed in his head that ground troops meant an American force comparable to that employed – unsuccessfully – by the Soviet Union in the 1980s, he could not imagine alternative ways to use ground forces. Whether the marines could have caught bin Laden as Mattis asserted, it was certainly a proposition worth testing. Senior policymakers, including Bush, claimed that they would have approved whatever was thought necessary to get bin Laden. They were not offered the possibility. The Bush administration and CENTCOM were looking forward to another war in Iraq, leaving Afghanistan as a job largely completed, rather than a work in progress, with a new, inexperienced and under-resourced leadership. Soon the Taliban would be on their way back.

14

A Tale of Two Surges: Iraq 2006–7

I had a feeling that, had we believed in our mission more and not despaired so easily – as indeed our soldiers on the ground showed – we would have played a far greater part in the final battle [for Basra].

Tony Blair[1]

In Afghanistan, President Bush set in motion regime change as a means to an end. He could not get at al Qaeda without first getting rid of the Taliban. In Iraq, in 2003, regime change was the objective from the start, yet there was no more of an idea about how to replace Saddam than there had been about replacing the Taliban's Mullah Omar. Getting rid of Saddam turned out to be a relatively straightforward operation. Coping with the subsequent insurgency was anything but straightforward.

It was not only the Americans who had to find a way to manage a dire security situation. So did other members of the coalition, including the United Kingdom, the most prominent ally of the United States. Until 2007, the two countries appeared to be following similar approaches, but then, with matters apparently spinning out of control, the Americans embarked on a bold move to recover lost ground and defeat the insurgency. The British effectively moved in the other direction, despite the fact that the original rationale for joining the Americans in invading Iraq had been to demonstrate that they were, in Tony Blair's words, 'shoulder-to-shoulder'.

We have seen with Kosovo that partnership, even between these two close allies, can produce frictions. In the case of how to deal with the Russian dash to Pristina airport, a UK commander was in charge on the

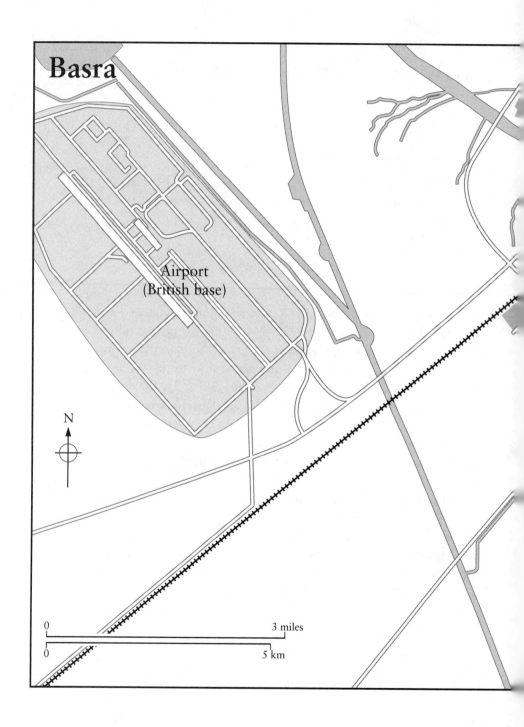

Basra

Airport
(British base)

N

0
3 miles
0
5 km

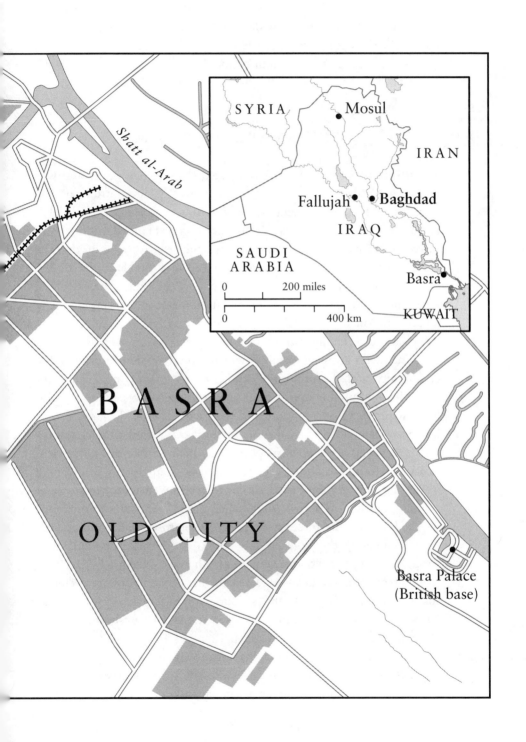

Shatt al-Arab

BASRA

OLD CITY

Basra Palace
(British base)

SYRIA

Mosul

IRAN

Fallujah   Baghdad

IRAQ

SAUDI
ARABIA

0   200 miles

0   400 km

Basra

KUWAIT

ground. His argument with his American superior, though heated and with potentially significant wider implications, was essentially about tactics. In the case of Iraq, the two countries diverged over strategy, which left the United Kingdom exposed as the junior partner in the coalition.

THE AMERICAN SURGE

When Iraq was invaded in March 2003, the only clear war aim was to topple Saddam Hussein's regime. This was achieved after about a month's fighting, and the country was occupied. Not only was the elite removed from power, but the Iraqi state was dismantled and its army disbanded. This led to an administrative and security vacuum that the US-led coalition was unprepared to fill and was unable to do so. The coalition spent the first year of occupation providing the country's government, while the security situation deteriorated rapidly. The administration did not acknowledge until too late the danger of an insurgency directed against the occupation picking up strength; it soon combined with growing sectarian violence between the majority Shi'ite community and the minority Sunni. From the start, any route out depended on building up the Iraqi security forces to cope with the violence without outside support, but that was easier said than done, as had been seen over 30 years earlier in Southeast Asia with 'Vietnamization'. After well over two years of conflict, in November 2005, Bush still explained the basic strategy in these terms. Iraqi forces would take increasing responsibility as coalition forces looked to concentrate on training and hunting down 'high-value targets'. This was the mantra: 'As the Iraqi security forces stand up, coalition forces can stand down.'[2]

Unfortunately, the violence only got worse. American commanders struggled to get a grip on the situation, with inadequate forces that were taking regular casualties – one reason for the operation's declining support at home. General John Abizaid, who took over from Franks at CENTCOM in 2003, recalled his instructions from Bush, Secretary of Defense Donald Rumsfeld and the chairman of the Joint Chiefs to 'minimize casualties'. The president kept on asking, he later recalled, 'Why aren't the Iraqis doing enough to defend their own country?'[3]

An effective counter-insurgency campaign required concentrating on protecting the population. Making force protection the priority got the strategy the wrong way round. Instead of working to detach the militants from the population, the emphasis was put on killing militants, although, as in Vietnam, it was not always possible to distinguish them from ordinary civilians. As the troops went after an enemy that was causing them regular hurt through roadside bombs and ambushes, they became careless about the damage being done to civilian life and property. As a result, the insurgency was boosted. General William Casey, who took over as commander of the Multi-National Force (MNF) in the summer of 2004, gathered his forces into a few large forward-operating bases to keep them safer, taking them further away from the people supposedly being defended.

With minimizing casualties so important, the incentive for junior officers was to stay out of trouble until their tour was over. There was not enough time to make a positive difference, but enough for a negative impact should their units get caught out. The inclination was not to win but to 'CYA (cover your ass)'.[4] Morale declined as units returning for their second and third tours found no improvement, and towns they had previously cleared now back under insurgent control. In these circumstances, excessive risk-taking appeared pointless.

In February 2006, the Golden Dome Mosque at Samarra, 65 miles north of Baghdad and one of the holiest Shi'ite sites, was blown up by an affiliate of al Qaeda in Iraq to provoke a civil war. For a while this appeared to be succeeding, with intense sectarian fighting resulting in hundreds of deaths. In May, months after an election that had been boycotted by many Sunnis, Nouri al-Maliki, a Shi'ite politician with sectarian inclinations, became prime minister. Maliki was soon diverting the American effort away from Jaysh al-Mahdi (JAM), the main Shi'ite militia, linked to the radical Shi'ite cleric and politician Muqtada al-Sadr. Ricks describes an incident in October 2006 when an American soldier was captured by JAM. As checkpoints were being set up close to where he was being held, Maliki told Casey to lift them. 'If that's your order,' said Casey, 'we'll do it, but people will say you don't care about American soldiers, and that you kowtowed to Sadr. Third the Sunnis will read this as a pro-JAM action. Can you accept that?' Maliki said he could.[5]

By the spring of 2006, there was therefore a strong case to be made for a strategic reappraisal, whether it led to an early withdrawal or a larger commitment. The current course pointed only to failure. This was accepted by national security advisor Stephen Hadley, and his predecessor, Condoleezza Rice, now secretary of state. Rumsfeld, however, saw no need for a reappraisal and refused to allow the Pentagon to engage in one. He described Samarra as 'an affirmation of the nature of the struggle you're in rather than a sign that you're losing'.[6] NSC staff were forbidden to interfere in matters that were the prerogative of the chain of command. 'Since you cannot seem to accept the fact,' he told Hadley, 'my only choices are to go to the President and ask him to tell you to stop or to tell anyone in DoD not to respond to the NSC staff. I have decided to take the latter course.'[7]

But Rumsfeld was now running out of political capital. He had disregarded the views of colleagues in government and even regularly ignored the president's requests for action. Behaviour that might have been tolerated if it brought results was now consolidating failure. He was described as following a 'commissar school of management', telling 'folks to advance, not offering his own vision of where to go, instead waiting to watch their choices and then questioning or potentially penalizing them'. As he prodded others, his own preferences were often obscure.[8] The military were fed up with his constant meddling in areas where they were competent, while he failed in his main task of ensuring that their plans matched the president's political objectives.[9]

Over the spring, in what came to be described as a 'revolt of generals', retired senior officers put their complaints against Rumsfeld into print. One called him 'incompetent strategically, operationally and tactically'.[10] The effect, however, was the opposite to that intended. Instead of wondering why figures recently in key positions felt this way, Bush pushed back. 'It pissed me off. I'm not going to have the generals force my hand. I thought it was a PR stunt, and it made me very sympathetic to Don Rumsfeld.'[11] In this way, as Kori Schake notes, the White House 'allowed the political cost of veterans' opposition to be treated as though it were indistinguishable from insubordination by active-duty military'.[12]

Bush had become curiously disengaged from the war's conduct. He gave every impression of relishing the power of the presidency, including its lack of everyday accountability. He observed to the journalist Bob Woodward,

I'm the commander – see, I don't need to explain ... why I say things. That's the interesting thing about being the President. Maybe somebody needs to explain why they say something, but I don't feel like I owe anybody an explanation.[13]

Yet, unlike Rumsfeld, he was instinctively deferential to military views and reluctant to challenge them. He had taken the lesson from Vietnam that presidents should be cautious about second-guessing professional military judgements. General Peter Pace, now chairman of the Joint Chiefs, found him 'always solicitous of the military, less questioning of what he was getting from them. It put him in a position where he wasn't very demanding.'[14] Bush told the *Washington Post*, 'It's important to trust the judgment of the military when they're making military plans ... I'm a strict adherer to the command structure.'[15] The decision-making processes in place, as his chief of staff noted, encouraged, rather than discouraged 'his instinct to defer to the people in uniform'.[16]

In July 2006, Casey mounted two 'Together Forward' operations, which involved US and Iraqi forces working closely together to remove insurgents from their sanctuaries in Baghdad. They made no noticeable difference to the level of violence. This revived the spectre of failure. Bush read the reports of carnage among Iraqis and the constant American casualties and realized that he might lose this war. When Rumsfeld explained, in his favourite analogy, 'You know, we're teaching the Iraqis to ride a bicycle. And at some point, you have to take your hands off the bicycle seat', Bush came back, 'yeah, but Don, we can't afford to have the bicycle turn over. We can't start again.'[17] Bush might be loyal to his subordinates, but there was a larger consideration. 'I couldn't stand the thought of making decisions that enabled defeat.'[18]

Rumsfeld's stubbornness pushed activity elsewhere, with active reviews under way in the National Security Council and the State Department. General Jack Keane, a former vice chairman of the Joint Chiefs, knew many of the senior figures in the army. His former colleagues appeared exhausted, concentrating on coping, having lost confidence in winning. With Frederick and Kimberly Kagan at the American Enterprise Institute, he pushed for a change in approach, channelling the frustration of officers who had no other outlets for their critiques and recommendations about how to salvage the situation.[19] A particular focus was on the Iraq Study Group, a high-level bipartisan effort, which had been holding hearings and visiting the country since late 2005. When it reported at the end of 2006, it concluded that there was no path to guarantee a victory and that the best course was to accelerate withdrawal, getting combat brigades out by the start of 2008. It did, however, contain a one-sentence get-out, saying that a surge could be supported 'if the U.S. commander in Iraq determines that such steps would be effective'.[20]

Once the president concluded that the United States must not be defeated, Hadley, as national security advisor, saw his job as ensuring that Bush had options for avoiding defeat though they had little bureaucratic or popular support. Rice was conflicted over strategy, anxious to support the president, but eventually in favour of stepping back, hoping that the sectarian violence would burn itself out. Hadley believed that, in the short term at least, more troops and bolder tactics were needed, but he did not want to suggest lost confidence in the existing strategy without something to replace it. The policy reviews now undertaken were therefore conducted in secrecy and the conclusions guarded tightly. At issue was whether it really was the case that foreign troops fuelled the insurgency. Abizaid at CENTCOM had an 'antibody theory' of insurgency, according to which 'foreign forces are always rejected'.[21] The alternative view, taken by advocates of the surge, was that the conflict was now about sectarian violence and the Iraqi people would back those who could bring it to an end.

During November and December, the pieces fell into place. The day after the congressional elections, Bush announced that Rumsfeld would be replaced by Robert Gates, who had spent his career in government, and was quiet and professional where Rumsfeld was loud and contrarian. The various studies were completed and presented. On 13 December, Bush and Cheney visited the Pentagon to meet the Joint Chiefs, with both Rumsfeld and Gates present. The Chiefs warned that the key problems in Iraq were political and not military. When Army Chief of Staff General Peter Schoomaker told the president he did not 'have the time to surge and generate enough forces for this thing to go', Bush replied, 'I am the President. And I've got the time.'[22] He also made it clear that the question of assessing public support was his responsibility and not the Chiefs'. When told of concerns that finding the extra units would put an unacceptable strain on ground forces, he asked whether even more damage might be done by another humiliating defeat along Vietnam lines.[23]

On 14 December, a seminar was held for Bush at the White House, where he found academic and professional support for a surge. Keane and Kagan reported on their study. Professor Eliot Cohen of Johns Hopkins University, soon to join the State Department, had written the seminal book on supreme command, which Bush had reportedly read prior to the invasion of Iraq. In it, Cohen stressed that the political leader must ensure that the commanders were up to the job. 'Not a single general has been removed for ineffectiveness during the course of this war,' he noted. 'The current promotion system does not take into account actual effectiveness in counter-insurgency. We need not great guys but effective guys.'[24] On 15 December, Bush met with the National Security Council. He described the options: 'We can hold steady. None of you say it's working. We can redeploy for failure – that's your option, Condi. Or we can surge for success.'[25]

The new strategy took shape as a result of bypassing not only the secretary of defense, but also the Joint Chiefs and Central Command. Even the task of finding the extra units to support the surge was undertaken by a former Pentagon planner working for Hadley. Nonetheless, Bush still needed military support and wished to avoid any visible split with his senior military commanders. Increasing troop numbers was not going to be popular and might not be backed by Congress. To get the high command's support he had to address three objections: given the existing strain on the army and Marine Corps, the extra battalions were unavailable; it was not clear what could be done with 160,000 troops that could not be done with 140,000; the real problems in Iraq lay not with the American military response, but in Iraq's political divisions. Even if more troops improved matters in the short term, the effects would not last. 'Wherever you put American troops it would stabilize the situation – but when they left, it would destabilize the situation.'[26]

Bush dealt with concerns about the morale and readiness of the army and Marine Corps by offering to increase their strength to help them cope, although this would not have much effect in the short term. In the end the Chiefs accepted that, if the president wanted to avoid losing a war, that had to be the priority, however stressful. The chairman, General Pace, understood which way the political wind was blowing and worked to bring his colleagues round in support of the president. The senior commanders had argued against the new strategy, so they were replaced: at CENTCOM Admiral William Fallon took over from

Abizaid, and Casey was promoted out of commanding the Multi-National Force to become chief of staff of the army.

Casey's replacement, General David Petraeus, was ready and waiting. Known for both his physical and intellectual competitiveness, he had taken the counter-insurgency task seriously as a divisional commander in Iraq and then used a posting at Fort Leavenworth, overseeing training and education, to commission a new counter-insurgency manual. He had gathered around him a series of like-minded officers, leading what was in effect his own insurgency within an army dominated by preparations for big wars against peer competitors.[27] He had a ready-made set of concepts and tactics for this situation and was keen to see them applied. Instead of concentrating on hunting down and shooting insurgents, his aim was to hold areas and provide security to the local population.[28]

The most important person to be squared was Iraqi Prime Minister Maliki. His sectarian bias was particularly relevant to one part of the surge project, which was to support tribes in Anbar Province in the Sunni heartland of western Iraq. They had rebelled against al Qaeda in September, and the Americans saw an opportunity to reinforce them with troops and weapons. This was not something favoured by hard-line Shi'ite elements.[29] Bush engaged with Maliki by talking him up rather than down – 'You are my man' – which was a risk when it was unclear that the Iraqi leader deserved a presidential embrace or would give much in return.[30] Maliki still needed the Americans, and so, after a lot of pressure, including direct meetings with Bush, he agreed to commit additional Iraqi brigades. He also needed to neutralize Muqtada al-Sadr as JAM was the main source of Shi'ite violence. Four days before Bush made his announcement on the surge, Maliki made a speech in which he promised no safe havens for the militias.[31]

On 10 January 2007, in a nationally televised address, President George W. Bush announced a new strategy for the painful war that had been under way in Iraq since March 2003, which showed no signs of reaching a satisfactory conclusion. Popular dissatisfaction had led to the defeat of his Republican Party in the mid-term elections. In the face of this discontent, a natural response, and one that was widely expected, would have been to announce a reduced American commitment. Instead, Bush went in the opposite direction. An extra 20,000 soldiers were to be sent to Iraq, the majority to Baghdad. In addition, units already serving elsewhere would have their tours extended. The aim was still to establish a 'unified, democratic federal Iraq that can govern itself, defend itself, and sustain itself'. To this end, the US military would 'help Iraqis clear and secure neighborhoods, to help them protect the local population, and to help ensure that the Iraqi forces left behind are capable of providing the security'.[32] Although this was known as the 'surge', it was about not only extra troops but also a change in strategy.

Bush's decision, taken after much study and deliberation, and widespread consultation, provided a striking contrast to his decision to occupy Iraq in the first place, which was taken almost by default, disregarding the many warnings about the consequences. In both cases, the outcomes reflected Bush's decisiveness. Now his determination to avoid defeat was not matched by any optimism among his senior advisers. Only Hadley, his national security advisor, was fully behind the decision. The secretary of state was unconvinced; the chairman of the Joint Chiefs was giving grudging support; while the new secretary of defense took a neutral position on the chances of success. Yet, nine months later, when Petraeus was able to give a buoyant progress report to Congress, showing a much-improved security situation, the new strategy was claimed as a triumph. At CENTCOM, Fallon questioned Petraeus's push for higher numbers, but it was Petraeus who had the better line to the White House, and not his notional boss. By the following May, Fallon was out, replaced by Petraeus.[33]

The extra troops and an energetic commander with a ready strategy made a difference, but the political conditions were also in place. The opportunity to turn the position around in Anbar Province, for example, was the result of a local reaction against al Qaeda's brutal methods, but it was still combined with wariness about the intentions of the Shi'ite-dominated government in Baghdad. So long as Maliki was prepared to take on the Shi'ite militias, then the extremists on both sides were being challenged and the country could step away from the brink of civil war. But there was always a question about whether short-term gains could endure. The security situation continued to improve, while Bush was in office. After he left at the start of 2009, and once President Obama acted on his promise to withdraw, Maliki's sectarian interests and his dislike of having foreign troops in Iraq reasserted themselves. His government turned against the Sunnis, and many of the gains of the surge were lost.[34]

THE JUNIOR PARTNER

The shift in US strategy left the United Kingdom – its main partner in the coalition – stranded. The United Kingdom had neither the capacity nor the inclination to follow suit, but was still in charge of an area of southern Iraq, including the city of Basra, over which it had lost effective control quite early in the occupation. The advice to ministers was that the surge would fail, and that the best course would be to continue with their current plan, that is, hand over to Iraqi forces as soon as possible and withdraw. Although this was in line with Casey's strategy, the divergence from the new American strategy was stark.

This was even more striking because the original British rationale for joining in the invasion of Iraq had been to confirm that the United Kingdom was standing shoulder-to-shoulder with its US allies. This was the commitment that Tony Blair had made after 9/11, followed through in Afghanistan, and then applied to the war in Iraq. He shared concerns about Saddam Hussein's regime in Iraq and its apparent commitment to developing weapons of mass destruction in violation of numerous UN resolutions. But if Bush had not made Iraq a priority, Blair would not have urged him to do so. He did, however, hope that by actively supporting the president he could influence his strategy. From his perspective, therefore, the nature of the United Kingdom's military contribution to the war was secondary to the fact that it was being made.

The idea that the United Kingdom could influence the United States' policy and military strategy did not seem preposterous, at least not to Blair. He had been in constant discussions with Bush's predecessor, Bill Clinton, during the 1999 Kosovo War, when he argued strongly for a bolder strategy than the one being pursued, leading to some tense moments with Clinton.[35] By the time the Serbian leader Milosevic capitulated, NATO was moving closer to the use of land forces, and Blair's position appeared to have been vindicated.

This case, however, was different. Unlike in Kosovo, Blair was not trying to push Bush into taking a tougher line. Instead, he sought to moderate the tough line upon which Bush had already decided, reframing it so that it became more acceptable to international opinion, as well as being easier to sell at home. In particular, this meant stressing the danger posed by Iraq's weapons of mass destruction, rather than simply a desire to topple an evil and disruptive dictator, and to get the backing of the UN Security Council. Also, unlike in Kosovo, here the United States was taking a clear military lead. The United Kingdom had to fit in with its plans. The issue therefore became one of how to find the best fit.

Blair had worked closely with Bush after 9/11, and had the advantage to Bush of being an articulate supporter of his 'global war on terror', despite coming from a completely different political tradition to that of his own Republican Party. Blair's foreign policy adviser, Sir David Manning, had a good relationship with Rice, then national security advisor, British Foreign Secretary Jack Straw and Secretary of State Colin Powell also worked well together. But Blair's deputy, John Prescott, did not begin to play a role equivalent to Vice President Cheney, while British Defence Secretary Geoff Hoon was no more likely to be consulted on the big issues of military strategy by US Defense Secretary Rumsfeld as was anyone else.

There was also an imbalance in the military relationship. The chief of the defence staff (CDS), then Admiral Michael Boyce, was in overall command of UK forces, with operational command delegated to the chief of joint operations (CJO) at the Permanent Joint Headquarters (PJHQ) at Northwood. This had developed out of the naval HQ that commanded the Falklands campaign in 1982. It dealt directly with CENTCOM. However, while the CJO reported through Boyce to the prime minister, potentially sidelining the secretary of defence, in the United States, CENTCOM reported to the president through the secretary of defense, potentially sidelining the chairman of the Joint Chiefs. Only PJHQ therefore was in a good position to report on American operational views. From the start, Manning complained that this led to 'ventriloquism' from the UK military as they presented their preferences as if they came from CENTCOM.[36] There was no equivalent to General Sir John Dill, who was based in Washington during the Second World War and attended meetings of the US chiefs of staff, helping to make the military relationship work.

Blair saw the UK military contribution as the entrance fee into American decision-making, and was not too concerned about the form it took. A naval and air contribution was never much in doubt, because of forces already in the region. The main issue was whether to despatch a substantial land force. The army did not want to be left out of a major operation. Blair never saw this as essential. Indeed, he achieved his main objective – that Bush should take the issue to the UN Security Council – in September 2002, when it was still uncertain whether the United Kingdom could even have a land contribution ready to meet the American timetable. He was not even keen to have military options discussed too openly when the focus was on diplomatic solutions.

After the United Kingdom gained access to the planning cell at CENT-COM during the summer of 2002, Blair asked whether the Americans had a 'winning concept', and, assuming they did, how, if at all, should the United Kingdom contribute. After studying the early American plans, the military advice was that they were flawed in two respects. First, they depended on attacking Iraq from Kuwait in the south, without introducing any potential threat from the north. Coalition forces based in Turkey might draw Iraqi units and attention away from the south. The second flaw was the apparent lack of interest in the aftermath. Once Saddam had been defeated, there would be a move from combat to maintaining local law and order, thereby facilitating economic and political reconstruction. In September 2002, a Strategic Planning Group concluded: 'Reasons for not participating in the US plan included the absence of a clear post-conflict strategy, which would make it likely that the UK military commitment would become open-ended.'[37]

The UK military sought to address the first flaw but not the second. The northern option appeared as the only land role of any consequence likely to be available for the army, on the assumption that Kuwait was going to be very crowded with the bulk of the US invading force. The second flaw – inadequate preparations for the aftermath – was an area in which the UK military had the experience to help, but it did not wish to do so. Such missions had a habit of dragging on. The objective, therefore, was to acquire a role in the invasion of Iraq but not in the aftermath – to help prepare the main meal, while avoiding the washing up.

The United Kingdom's first problem was that the government did not want to make any overt preparations for war at a time of active diplomacy in the Security Council. Officers working with CENTCOM were under instruction not to make any definite promises about the UK contribution. In September 2002, the Ministry of Defence began to press for a decision on the UK contribution, fearing that delay would lead CENT-COM to assume that none would ever be forthcoming. The pressure became increasingly more urgent. If land forces were not offered soon, the prime minister was warned, this option would be lost by default. The Americans would be disappointed, their strategic concept weakened, British influence jeopardized, and the United Kingdom would end up being stuck with a long-term peacekeeping role. The Ministry of Defence explained that offering a land contribution 'could significantly reduce our vulnerability to US requests to provide a substantial (and costly) contribution to post-conflict stabilisation operations'.[38]

The advice was based on a false prospectus. The aspiration reflected institutional preferences more than political realities. The core proposal, to base a divisional headquarters and an armoured brigade in Turkey, had not been seriously explored with the Americans, nor, more importantly, with the Turks. It was never likely that the Turkish government would agree. Equally, it was unlikely that the United Kingdom could play a leading role in invading a country and then avoid a commensurate role in the subsequent occupation. All this soon became clear. Whatever the strategic merits of putting pressure on Iraq from the north, the Turks did not want any coalition troops on their soil, and in particular British troops. The possibility of a substantial UK land role was only rescued because the Americans saw value for one in the south. The plan was for British forces to enter Iraq from Kuwait with US forces, but then hold the area close to Basra as the Americans passed through en route to Baghdad. This would also be the area for which the United Kingdom would end up being responsible once Iraq had been occupied.

During the first months of 2003, Blair was fully engaged, with Straw, in a desperate and ultimately unsuccessful effort to get the Security Council to authorize the invasion. At the time, UN inspectors were searching unavailingly for weapons of mass destruction in Iraq. The prime minister therefore paid little attention to the military strategy. Few doubted that any Iraqi resistance would be overpowered. The question of how to handle the aftermath was played down in military presentations as something to be dealt with when the moment came rather than planned for in advance. This was even though US planning had, if anything, worsened once responsibility had passed from the State Department to the Pentagon. When Blair had a high-level briefing on the military plans on 17 January, the discussion focused on the main combat phases of the operation. This meant not only evading questions about US preparedness, but also that insufficient attention was paid to the strategic implications of the commitments made by the United

Kingdom. The prime minister was largely concerned about the potential impact of air strikes on Iraq's civilian population, and how that might effect domestic and international support for the war. Air Marshal Sir Brian Burridge, the UK national contingent commander, who was based with CENTCOM in Qatar, would be able to use his 'red card' to object to specific operations, and in particular air strikes with a high risk of civilian casualties.[39]

STRANDED IN BASRA

The land invasion of Iraq, which began on 20 March, went more or less to plan. UK forces entered the relatively benign, largely Shi'ite, south, surrounding the city of Basra but not seizing it, while US troops moved to Baghdad, to complete the main business of the war.[40] Initially, resistance was fiercer than expected, including from Iraq's Fedayeen militias. Blair developed a view that it would make more sense for the United States to join the United Kingdom in making an early push to take Basra, thereby giving the campaign more momentum, rather than press on for what could turn into a bitter fight for the Iraqi capital. This effort prompted no interest from the Americans, who were not about to make such a drastic change to a developed strategy, and was opposed by the British commanders, who, if anything, were more interested in leaving Basra behind and joining the Americans in the fight for Baghdad.[41] British forces eventually took Basra on the night of 7/8 April, just before US forces entered Baghdad on 9 April. As they were now occupying southern Iraq, this became a UK area of responsibility and there they stayed once the war was over. The United Kingdom had not wanted a major post-war role, and had failed to prepare for one, as we have seen, looking forward instead to getting its land forces out of Iraq as soon as possible. It had soon become evident during the weeks of fighting that there was no one else in a position to take over this responsibility. The UK operation, known as TELIC, was not going to end quickly but would go through 13 stages until it concluded in 2009.

A defined area of responsibility had advantages. The command arrangements were straightforward and there would be a focus for British efforts on political and economic reconstruction, which Blair insisted should be 'exemplary'. Most importantly, the south was assumed to have a more benign security situation than the rest of the country, as this was a Shi'ite and anti-Ba'ath area. The UK commitment took the form of a brigade in Multi-National Division South-East (MND–SE), which included a number of other national contingents.[42] The United Kingdom provided the general officer commanding (GOC), MND–SE, who in principle was acting under the tactical command of the US commander of the Multi-National Force–Iraq (MNF–I) and Multi-National Corps–Iraq (MNC–I), headquartered in Baghdad. In practice, the GOC was most responsive to the UK Permanent Joint Headquarters (PJHQ). In addition, as this command was on a six-month rotation, it was difficult for a single individual to put their stamp on the campaign. Indeed, if they tried to do so, they could aggravate further the problems caused by discontinuity.

Having decided from the start to concentrate on its own sector, where for the moment things seemed quiet, the United Kingdom decided to keep clear of the trouble developing in the rest of the country, where the United States was coping badly with a restless Sunni population. There was concern in London from the start that the Americans had not thought through how to reconstruct Iraq's security structures. Although it was not part of his responsibilities, General David Richards, assistant chief of the general staff, was asked by Hoon to go and bring some of the United Kingdom's 'post-conflict experience to bear'. Few in the command structure were pleased by this initiative. When he got to Baghdad, Richards was alarmed by a 'slackness of attitude', a lack of enthusiasm on both American and British sides for the next stage, and insensitivity to the developing resentments among Iraqis at the lack of law and order and shortages of food and electricity. Richards became concerned that the American troops did not know how to get a feel for local attitudes and concerns.

> Their idea of getting out and about was to drive around in their tanks and armoured personnel carriers with their guns at the ready and their dark glasses firmly clamped across their eyes. It is a detail but an important one – there was no eye contact, something we knew was critical in building trust. If they did get out of their noisy vehicles, the American idea of patrol or even a checkpoint was to pick a spot, a so-called 'strong point' surround it with barbed wire and stand there doing very little.

Richards came up with proposals for the 16 Air Assault Brigade to deploy to Baghdad to work with the Americans on various aspects of security sector reform. He got some buy-in from senior American officers, from the prime minister's staff and from Mike Jackson, now chief of the general staff. Yet, when he went to brief all the chiefs of staff about the plan, the response was negative. PJHQ wanted to get 16 Air Assault Brigade out, and argued that the Americans had enough capacity to do what was necessary. Richards suspected that they did not like to be dealing with a proposal from

> an officer on a non-operational appointment who had been sent out by the Defence Secretary outside the normal chain of command ... They were going to assert their authority over those who were responsible for the conduct of the war, irrespective of the sense of the recommendations.[43]

This left the British making condescending comments about the US Army's tactics, without doing anything to improve the situation, and staying clear of the American effort. Eventually, in October 2004, as American irritation with the United Kingdom's reluctance to help became evident, the government agreed to deploy the Black Watch to North Babil for 30 days to backfill US forces needed for operations in Fallujah. As the deployment led to casualties and controversy, it reinforced the view that it was best to stick to the south. The 'boundary between MND–SE and the rest of the force was more like an international border than a tactical divisional boundary'.[44] On either side of the border, separate campaigns were being conducted.

This separation was reflected in the command arrangements.[45] The United Kingdom was well represented in Baghdad, providing a three-star as the deputy to the commander of MNF–I as deputy commanding general (DCG), as well as senior British military representative Iraq (SBMRI), and a two-star to the corps commander. But these senior figures spent barely 10 per cent of their time on the south-east and tried to stay neutral when issues connected to MND–SE came up. Nor did they have any direct line responsibility for MND–SE. By and large, the GOCs MND–SE rarely looked to Baghdad for advice or resources. They held the national 'red card' and were mostly responsive to the British PJHQ at Northwood. PJHQ's own engagement with Baghdad was limited, neither fully explaining their priorities, nor paying close attention to the campaign plan being followed there, in with which the British were supposed to fit. All this aggravated the problems of discontinuity as each new GOC developed his own tactical plan with limited reference to the Corps' tactical plan. For its part the Corps HQ in Baghdad was preoccupied with the Sunni–Shi'ite dynamic and tended to ignore the intra-Sh'ite politics of the south, assuming that unless they heard otherwise all was well.

While being left to their own devices in the south might have had some advantages in terms of security, it also came with disadvantages. The region's infrastructure needs had been neglected under Saddam. After the war, Baghdad and central Iraq still had the first call on resources, especially as the funds for reconstruction were largely provided by the Americans. The British Foreign Office and Department for International Development had been opposed to the war and were reluctant supporters of the post-war reconstruction effort. A generally risk-averse and low-cost approach was also reflected in the efforts to rebuild the Iraqi army and police. This was done more by training programmes than by having UK personnel embedded with the forces.

The challenge in the south presented itself as lawlessness in a predominantly Shi'ite area. The most prominent of the local militias was the Jaysh al-Mahdi (JAM), which had backing from Iran and links to Muqtada al-Sadr. Its death squads made life miserable for the Basrawi population. The police were too infiltrated by the militias to be susceptible to reform. For the first couple of years of the occupation, violence was only occasionally directed against UK forces, which led to claims that the situation was largely under control. But, the more the British took an active interest in the affairs of Basra, the more JAM was likely to target them with indirect fire from mortars and rockets.

Until well into 2006, the core UK strategy was presented as following that of the Americans. The aim was to strengthen Iraq's political institutions and build up its army and police forces to provide security sufficiently for transition to Provincial Iraqi Control (PIC) and the subsequent withdrawal of UK forces. This was a conditions-based approach, so in principle the forces were not going to be able to leave until the level of threat was down, the capabilities of the Iraqi security forces and the local and national governments were up, and coalition forces were in a position to re-intervene, if necessary. But, though these offered some criteria for judging, there was always going to be a subjective element. The approach also begged two other possibilities. The first was that in practice the conditions could not be met, and so, at some point, it might just be best to cut losses and leave. The second went further, arguing that the reason the conditions might not be met was the presence of foreign troops, which made the security situation worse. In this case, rather than waiting for the conditions to be reached before leaving, leaving might help create the conditions. Senior officers in both the United States and United Kingdom were thinking along these lines during 2006. The UK chiefs of staff found these arguments compelling. Bush's decision in early 2007 in favour of the surge in effect rejected them, accepting that there had to be a continuing responsibility for improving both the security situation and the quality of the Iraqi security forces.

To the UK chiefs, the belief that the insurgency was kept going rather than dampened down by the presence of foreign troops argued for an accelerated reduction of the commitment to Iraq. It was a welcome argument, because the army was at the same time preparing to expand its role in Afghanistan. In September 2005, when the situation in Basra was relatively calm, Secretary of Defence John Reid asked the chief of the defence staff for an assurance that the two operations could be managed, even if there was some slippage in the drawdown in Iraq, and was satisfied by a confident answer. Reid later told the Iraq Inquiry that he was not concerned about 'a diminution of our resources in Iraq, personnel or otherwise. Why? Because I had asked that specific question and been told, "No".'[46]

Over time, however, there was an unavoidable tension between the two commitments, if only in the allocation of scarce resources such as helicopters and surveillance assets. A wider strategic assessment might have concluded that Basra was of greater strategic importance, by virtue of its geography and oil reserves. The institutional preference, however, was to shift the main effort from Iraq to Afghanistan, a war for which there was much more popular support, and which provided opportunities for soldiering in wide open spaces instead of cramped urban areas, as well as a chance to redeem a reputation tarnished by Iraq.

But a hurried departure from Iraq without anything to show for the effort would result in reputational damage. In October 2005, the chiefs observed, 'Ministers needed to be clear that the campaign could potentially be heading for "strategic failure", with grave national and international consequences if the appropriate actions were not taken.'[47] Little action was taken. No extra resources were found to cope with the demands of the operation. The sums devoted to reconstruction were miserly.

The next May, Jackson, who had been consistently candid about the failings of the Iraqi operation, reported:

> The perception, right or wrong, in some – if not all – US military circles is that the UK is motivated more by the short-term political gain of early withdrawal than by the long-term importance of mission accomplishment; and that, as a result, MND–SE's operational posture is too laissez faire and lacks initiative . . .[48]

That month the new chief of the defence staff, Air Marshal Sir Jock Stirrup, also visited Iraq. Compared with his predecessor, General Sir Michael Walker, who had a collegiate approach to his role and was inclined to follow staff advice as it reached him, Stirrup was a more decisive and ruthless figure, disinclined to be diverted from a chosen course of action. He advised Reid that there were 'compelling reasons' why the United Kingdom should 'press on' with handing over security to Iraq, even though the conditions required by the established policy might not be met. The obstacles to meeting the conditions were the militias and Iraqi governance.

> Neither is substantially in our hands, and we need firm action by the government in Baghdad. But as consent continues to reduce (as we have always foreseen it would), so too does our ability to effect further (significant) improvement. The law of diminishing returns is now firmly in play, and there is an increasing risk that we become part of the problem, rather than of the solution.[49]

The implication was that, without the provocation of foreign troops, the situation in Basra might calm down. He acknowledged the risk of a perception of strategic failure. He suggested that 'astute conditioning of the UK public may be necessary' to avoid that. The problem was now seen to be one of managing the transition from Iraq to Afghanistan, as much as the transition within Iraq to what was described as Provisional Iraqi Control (PIC).

Later that year, in a controversial interview with a newspaper, Jackson's replacement as chief of the general staff, General Sir Richard Dannatt, following Stirrup's line, said that UK forces were part of the problem as much as the solution and argued for a switch from Iraq to Afghanistan.

> The hope that we might have been able to get out of Iraq in 12, 18, 24 months after the initial start in 2003 has proved fallacious. Now hostile

elements have got a hold it has made our life much more difficult in Baghdad and in Basra . . . [We should] get ourselves out sometime soon because our presence exacerbates the security problems.

He expressed 'much more optimism that we can get it right in Afghanistan'.[50] The chiefs of staff were getting ahead of the politicians. 'As you can imagine,' recalled Blair, 'I wasn't best pleased.'[51] But the course had been set. The response to Dannatt's remarks confirmed the unpopularity of the Iraq War.

Stirrup's successor as chief of the air staff, who had previously been CJO, Air Marshal Glenn Torpy, explained that the need was to 'force the pace of transition, but in a controlled manner'. The 'view collectively' was that 'we had provided the Iraqis with the wherewithal to manage their own security and it was now time for them to take responsibility for their own future'. The aim was now 'playing for a draw in Iraq and playing to win in Afghanistan'.[52] Torpy's successor as CJO, General Sir Nick Houghton, recalled the 'imperative' coming down from his 'superior headquarters' to draw down in Iraq to support the coming deployment in Afghanistan.[53]

In May 2006, General Richard Shirreff, on a reconnaissance visit to Basra before he took command of MND–SE in July, developed a different view. Shirreff, 'a dynamic cavalry officer with a taste for action, and supreme confidence in his ability to use the force of his personality to shape events', was unimpressed.[54] He was told by a battalion commander, responsible for a city of 1.3 million people, that he could put no more than 200 soldiers on the ground. This resulted in a cycle of insecurity. Shirreff did not wish to be associated with failure. His complaint, which he shared widely, was that the United Kingdom was following an 'an exit strategy rather than a winning strategy'.[55] He recalled that 'an awful lot of the citation awards for gallantry coming through were all about rescuing people rather than taking the fight to the enemy'.[56] He also believed that Iraq should continue to be the 'main effort' and not Afghanistan. To rectify the situation, he developed a plan, in the first instance known as Operation SALAMANCA, which would involve a series of consecutive operations in areas of the city, clearing them of the militias and the death squads as they did so, to be followed up with reconstruction projects.

The issue, however, was not whether there should be an 'exit strategy', but the form it should take. UK strategy at this stage was still aligned with the American strategy of getting the Iraqis to 'stand up', so that they could 'stand down'. Houghton believed that he was following an instruction from Casey 'to get out of the cities so that the Iraqis could be the face of the security in their own cities'.[57] CENTCOM as well as PJHQ was still attracted to the view that foreign troops were increasingly adding to the security problem rather than solving it. The implication was defeatist.

This was not how Operation TELIC was meant to end. The conditions for a transition to Provisional Iraqi Control would not be met, and, in the light of early claims about how well the British knew how to cope with restless populations, this was embarrassing. It created, as Houghton acknowledged, 'issues of reputation and self-worth', but acknowledging that as a problem could not set strategy. It would certainly be better to leave Basra with heads held high, but given the obstacles faced, what was the price worth paying for some measure of reputational gain? In this respect, while Shirreff might have viewed SALAMANCA as part of a winning strategy, the higher levels of command were more sceptical. It might create conditions for exit in terms of more security in Basra, though further advances would still have to be taken forward by the Iraqi security forces. The best argument was that it might help the exit by reducing the adverse impact on the reputation of UK armed forces. Thus, Houghton supported Shirreff's plan, as did Stirrup, as a way of demonstrating what could be done in Basra before getting out of the city. Some extra forces – about 360 troops – were found to boost numbers for the duration of the operation. But their support could not extend beyond the limits of increasingly stretched resources. While this operation was under way, Houghton was preparing the next stage – Operation ZENITH – which was about continuing with the drawdown.

Shirreff saw things differently. In his message to his brigade and battalion commanders, he proclaimed: 'The time has come to take the offensive against the enemy and challenge the defeatists who seem to pervade Whitehall and much of Northwood.' Only if properly resourced, with 'clout' rather than 'dribble', would it be possible to 'avoid disastrous failure in Iraq'. For this reason, Houghton's conditional support appeared to those close to Shirreff as 'more about creating a credible *narrative* for exit rather than creating credible results'.[58] Relations between the two were 'tense'. Shirreff was instructed to avoid 'any unnecessary displays of military testosterone' and situations which exceeded British capacity. Houghton remained concerned that Shirreff would 'push the envelope of his delegated authority' and derail the withdrawal plans.[59]

Shirreff got more sympathy from his US Corps headquarters, presenting SALAMANCA as part of a Corps strategy. Lieutenant General Peter Chiarelli, commanding MNC-I, offered him resources, including a battalion from his operational reserve. This meant crossing the border between the British sector and the rest. Stirrup was not interested. He wanted to reinforce the separation, and was opposed to using American forces to reinforce UK forces, as he was to sending UK forces in the other direction. This would, he noted, cross a clear 'red line'.[60] Shirreff did, however, get some surveillance assets from the US, and some money to spend on economic and social projects in those areas that had been cleared of militias.

The main challenge, however, came on the Iraqi side. In June, Maliki had declared a state of emergency in Basra, and established a 'Basra security plan'.[61] Although it had ambitious objectives, in practice it was largely a committee to oversee security in the city, led by General Hamadi who was beholden to Sadrists in both Baghdad and Basra. This suited Maliki because it bypassed the governor of Basra, Mohammed al-Waeli, one of his opponents. Shirreff made progress with Hamadi, but then the Sadrists 'got at him'. Casey and Chiarelli tried to make the case directly to Maliki for a major commitment of Iraqi forces to take on the militias, but, at this time, Maliki still depended on Sadrist support. Only later did he feel that the moment had come to take them on.

In his weekly report of 16 September 2006, Shirreff was still looking forward to Operation SALAMANCA. Through 'decisive action', his force would improve 'the lot of Basrawis', while making it possible to have police stations 'capable of providing basic security in their local areas'. Five days later, he reported that over the weekend 'Maliki told Casey that the political situation in Basra needs to be dealt with quietly and that the security situation in Basra was not bad enough to warrant an operation that would upset the political balance.'[62]

The operation, now renamed SINBAD, went ahead, but only in a watered-down form. Instead of a security operation backed by reconstruction efforts, it was now a reconstruction programme supported by efforts to improve security, shifting the balance between the so-called 'kinetic' and 'non-kinetic' elements. It was still a substantial operation, but not substantial enough. Units moved into particular areas, assessed the state of police stations, and undertook straightforward reconstruction projects. The idea had been for the UK forces to move from one area on to the next, with the Iraqi army holding the area just cleared. But this was an army locally recruited, which was 'not prepared to fight the militia, because they knew that, if they did, they would come off worst'.[63] In his final report, after the operation, Shirreff pointed out that, unlike the Americans, the United Kingdom had 'not lived, trained and fought alongside' the Iraqi units they were supposed to be training. 'The result has been a lacklustre, inadequately trained and supported division that failed the test when it came.'[64]

He did have one final defiant gesture, which he saved for Christmas Day 2006. He blew up the al-Jamaat police station, the home of the Serious Crimes Unit, a vicious group responsible for abductions, torture and murders, with which British special forces had clashed a year earlier. This was achieved 'with an exaggerated amount of explosives'. By Shirreff's account, the action was extremely popular with the local Basrawis, but less so with the local Iraqi government, and Maliki, who denounced it as an infringement of sovereignty.

In MND–SE, the operation was still seen to have had a positive effect, raising the morale of troops and the Basrawis, and providing valuable experience for the Iraqi army.[65] But whatever the beneifts of the operation, which cost the lives of 11 British, 17 Iraqi and one Danish soldiers, they were fleeting because success could not be reinforced. The militia suffered some losses but it made no difference to the indirect fire using rockets and mortars, with which the militias were regularly battering the British garrison. Dealing with this required artillery and attack helicopters, capabilities where the competing demands of Afghanistan were keenly felt. Shirreff warned of the prospect ahead: 'Unable to draw down completely until the US effectively declare game over, we could find ourselves laagered up in Basra Air Station and effectively fixed outside a city in hostile hands.'[66]

GETTING OUT OF BASRA

In December, the objectives for Operation ZENITH were set at withdrawing most UK troops from bases in Basra City to Basra Air Station, once Operation SINBAD was completed. This aim was to reduce troop numbers from 7,100 to 4,500 by May 2007. Just as the British put in their last big effort and were preparing to pull away, Bush was deciding to order a surge in US forces.

Blair was told of this when preparing for an end of year call with Bush on 29 December. This would be 'awkward' for the UK as 'our plans in Basra go in the opposite direction'.[67] There was no reason to suppose that the surge would succeed – the advice Blair was given was that it probably would not – but it would now be necessary to explain to the Americans why the United Kingdom would not follow its example. Blair had been aware since the previous year of a 'pretty acute sense among the senior command in the Army that we had done all we could in Basra', and that UK forces had come to be more of a provocation than a support. Although he was 'deeply sceptical about the notion that Iraqis or indeed anyone else wanted to live like this', and was impressed by Shirreff when he visited Basra in December 2006 ('seemed to have the required mettle'), he was also frustrated by Maliki's attitude, and accepted Stirrup's view that, without more political support from the Iraqi government, it was now best to move on.[68]

The six-month rotation of the GOC MND–SE meant that there was little opportunity for generals to learn on the job and almost guaranteed disruptive handovers. When Shirreff moved on, the change in strategy had already been decided. His replacement, Major General Jonathan Shaw, was tasked with implementing Operation ZENITH. He was described as 'more cerebral, more political' than Shirreff, though 'just as tough-minded'.[69] When he asked Stirrup about the relevance of the surge, he was told that 'the surge has nothing to do with us'. Although Stirrup also told him that he had cleared the plan with Casey and he was 'very happy', this soon turned out not to be the case. When Shaw met Casey in January 2007, he was told, 'I am not happy with your plans.' As Shaw later observed, at the 'very top-level our countries were now on different paths, and asking military people to ... contrive military justifications for stuff that fundamentally is underwritten by different political directions'.[70]

In late 2006, Operation ZENITH had been approved at Corps level, although with some doubts about whether the southern provinces were really ready to hand over to the Iraqis. So, it could be claimed that the troop reductions had been endorsed by the US. By 27 January 2007, however, when Secretary of Defence Des Browne briefed the cabinet that the two countries did not disagree on force levels, this was no longer the case. In February 2007, Sir David Manning, now British ambassador to the US, reported that Secretary Rice had asked him 'to tell her honestly whether the UK was now making for the exit as fast as possible'. The same month, the new US secretary of defense, Robert Gates, came away with this conclusion after meeting Blair.[71] Not only was the United Kingdom not following the United States into a surge, but it was rushing for the exit.[72]

In January 2007, the British embassy in Washington reported significant concerns in the United States that 'lawlessness was rife in Basra and that the UK military were doing little to confront it', and that 'an early UK drawdown would leave a security vacuum'. After seeing this, Blair commented: 'Either this is correct in which case we have a real problem, or it isn't in which case we must correct it. But what is going on in Basra?'[73] The concern on the military side was that in the first instance the US moves were going to lead to a deterioration in security, as there could be a Shi'ite backlash in Basra to any crackdown in Baghdad.[74] But while he urged that the implementation of the plan be slowed down, Blair was not prepared to reverse direction. When he announced the new policy to parliament on 21 February, he followed the line that, as the Multi-National Force attracted the attacks, once it was gone, the violence would naturally decrease, especially as the Iraqi security forces were ready to take over Basra's security. UK force levels would now be reduced from 7,100 to about 5,500. The aim was for PIC, the handover to the Iraqi authorities, to occur at the end of the year.[75]

In Basra, Shaw pushed back against American complaints. He dismissed a negative response from US Ambassador Crocker to his plans, as 'more to do with US aspirations to tie us to remaining in Iraq than they do with objective assessment'. An example he gave to underline his point was revealing about the British approach to security. Crocker had raised the issue of Basra's port, which was being run by the militias, and suggested military action to take it back, a prospect Shaw found 'depressing'. The port, he noted, 'may be corrupt, but is also stable and functions. Upsetting the balance of power would not advance stability in Basra by a single step and would not be the best use of Iraqi Army assets . . .'[76] He debated with Petraeus his proposition that the problem in the south was closer to 'Palermo and not Beirut', that is, more one of criminality than insurgency. If it was not a civil war, then there should be a possibility of some sort of accommodation among the key factions. Outsiders could not 'fight the soil'. He argued that an 'outright victory for one side is likely to prove a goad to revenge'. The alternative to continuing with 'blood feuds' would be an accommodation that gave 'honour to all reconcilable sides'. This would prove more enduring.[77] While Petraeus was aware of the political climate in London, and so was polite in his discussions with British politicians and generals, he was unconvinced. As Shaw reported back to London, Petraeus did not 'consider that we are even close' for PIC.[78]

The awkward logic of the position was for the British to reach their own accommodation with JAM, the Shi'ite militia group, which they did. A truce was negotiated in the summer. There would be no attacks on the UK positions in return for the gradual release of prisoners. This was seen as an opportunity to extract forces from their vulnerable base in Basra palace, even though this would mean a further loss of 'situational awareness'. The result was immediate, with mortar and rocket attacks on UK forces dropping by some 90 per cent, and the relocation of a battalion from its city base in Basra palace to the main base by the airport being achieved without incident. With force protection no longer such an issue, more could be done to train the Iraqi army as well as undertake some redevelopment work at the airport. But this came at a cost. The militia was able to take over the city and imposed a hardline Islamist regime.[79] And, as they were still fighting JAM elsewhere, the Americans were unimpressed. Desmond Bowen, a senior MoD official, observed that there was a 'risk of undermining our trustworthiness as a close ally with the permanent organs of the US state and armed forces'. This could do 'lasting damage' to UK security interests.[80]

Shaw's view was not simplistic. He had researched the local society and politics. But, whatever the merits of his argument, it just appeared to the Americans as an attempt to rationalize the UK's disengagement in Basra. It was treated with scepticism. Within the British Army, even many who accepted the logic of the deal with JAM were embarrassed, and aware of the limits of the 'Palermo more than Beirut' narrative. This overstated financial motives and understated the ideological motives among the militias.[81] One example was provided by Colonel Richard Iron, then serving as mentor to General Mohan al-Furayji, in charge of the Iraqi forces in Basra. He observed how, in December 2007, a report of 40 women raped and murdered was interpreted from the British base as 'immoral criminality', rather than punishment for women considered 'inappropriately dressed'.[82] The issue, therefore, was not whether there might be value in talking to JAM, to explore possibilities to calm the conflict, but that this was being done from such an evident position of weakness.

When Gordon Brown took over as prime minister, in the summer of 2007, he had no idea about the dealings with JAM ('It took me months to get to the bottom of what was happening'), but this, along with the growing number of casualties, convinced him that there was indeed a 'law of diminishing returns' in play and that the United Kingdom should get out. Petraeus urged that the position should be 'in together, out together', but he replied that the United Kingdom would do no more than create enough stability to depart.[83] Even that, of course, was easier said than done. In October 2007, Brown announced that UK forces would be reduced further, from 5,000 to 2,500 personnel, by spring 2008. The assumption behind this drawdown was that the security situation was now better because UK forces were not being attacked. General Binns, who took over from Shaw as GOC MND–SE that summer, observed that extracting UK forces from the centre of the city had a 'dramatic effect on the metrics that we used to measure the violence'.[84] Unfortunately, if the metrics had measured the security of the local population, they would not look so healthy. 'I'm not pretending the security situation significantly improved for Basrawis; it wouldn't and I knew it wouldn't until the Iraqi security forces got back in there.'[85] This was the second part of the rationale for the drawdown: the Iraqi security forces would step up, once they were obliged to take responsibility, building on the advice and training they had received. This logic led to the proposition that any help to the Iraqi forces (even releasing materials to help them build their own fortifications) would mean that they would never learn to look after themselves and so should not be granted.

The theory behind the American surge – that more troops working closely with Iraqi forces could help the people become more secure – appeared vindicated by early 2008. The same was not true for the British theory – that without foreign troops the Iraqis would sort themselves out. The militias in Basra were stronger than ever. They had capabilities well beyond gangsters, with sophisticated IEDs and backing from Iran. Far from finding a new equilibrium, the situation was unstable. As Maliki belatedly turned his attention to Basra, as he no longer needed the Sadrists, he was alarmed by the breakdown in law and order in Iraq's third largest city, and the strength of his political opponents.

If something was going to be done about Basra, it was now doubtful whether the British would have a role. They would be left watching from the sidelines, stuck in their base, as the Americans came in to help the Iraqis fight for the city. Faced with this prospect, Brigadier Julian Free, in charge of 4 Brigade; Colonel Iron; General Mohan; and Daniel Marston, an American academic who was a regular visitor to MND–SE, worked up an outline plan as to how Free's brigade could work more effectively with Mohan's 14th Division. To bypass both chains of command, Marston took the plan to Baghdad, so that at Corps level they were aware of the possibility that, when push came to shove, British forces could embed with the 14th Division.[86] Iron and Mohan then followed up with a visit to Baghdad.

Planning was still in its relatively early stages when Maliki became impatient. After ordering more of his own army and police forces to Basra, he launched what became known as the 'Charge of the Knights' on 25 March 2008. All coalition commanders, in Baghdad as well as Basra, were taken by surprise. Neither American General Lloyd Austin, the new commander of MNC–I, nor General Barney White-Spunner, the new GOC MND–SE, had anticipated an imminent battle and neither relished the prospect.[87] As the operation had not been properly prepared, it soon ran into trouble. The first Iraqi brigade fled. Maliki and his HQ came under heavy fire, while a JAM counter-attack seized Iraqi army and police bases and vehicles. Petraeus immediately determined that Maliki could not be allowed to fail. The Americans began to move forces into MND–SE, ending the past geographical separation between the US and UK areas, which Stirrup had been so keen to sustain.

As they arrived, they set up their own HQ, judging that MND–SE had lost situational awareness and lacked the drones, helicopters and aircraft necessary to take the fight to the enemy. Unlike the British, the Americans were able to fight alongside the Iraqis. The worry in London was not only that this Maliki-led effort might well fail, or at best lead to a bloody stalemate, but also that this was would reflect badly on the United Kingdom. Maliki was already openly blaming the United Kingdom for the state of affairs. In London, this was assessed as an awkward crisis to be managed, after which it would be even more important than before to accelerate the drawdown of UK forces.

In Basra itself, there was a different take. There was early evidence that the Basrawis welcomed the sight of Iraqi forces working closely with Americans to take on the militias. Prior to the battle, Free had planned to form mentoring teams with the 14th Division, similar to those used by the Americans. He now took the opportunity do so, explaining to Austin that he did not have the authority but would do it nonetheless.[88] Approval from PJHQ was received in retrospect. The developing battle had not been anticipated, reported White-Spunner, but Basra was now part of the US main effort, and there was an

> opportunity that we must enable the Iraqis to capitalise on. A coalition-led, but Iraqi-faced surge over the coming month would build on the Basrawi consent and optimism and has the potential to dramatically reshape the security environment.[89]

On 10 April, he urged that should the 'next phase of the ISF security operation' be successful then 'we must be prepared to exploit that success more quickly'.[90] Dannatt went to visit during this phase and 'found everyone in the Division in an extremely positive, but cautious mood about the potential for delivering success on the ground'. As a result, he accepted that there was '*another* opportunity to be successful in Basra – we must not let this one go'. This would require putting more resources into MND–SE, with a message that was 'proactive, aggressive and co-ordinated'.[91]

By 7 May, the JAM militants had been defeated by the revived Iraqi forces backed by US and UK units. In the end, White-Spunner was surprised at 'how quickly the Shi'a militia crumbled'. While the UK role was welcomed in London, it was not part of any approved operational concept and resulted from local initiatives. For now, British force levels would remain at 4,100, and British Forces would work closely with Iraq's 14th Division. The de facto border that had separated MND–SE from the rest of Iraq was no longer there. The idea that the United States had no part to play in the UK area of responsibility was over. The determination not to get too engaged with Iraqi forces had reversed. When UK forces concluded their mission in June 2009, Basra was enjoying a degree of security.

CONCLUSION: ALLIES OUT OF STEP

In the build-up to the war in Iraq and its long aftermath, British armed forces were given a substantial but subordinate role in a coalition in which the United States would always set the strategic direction. Within the framework set by the United States, they therefore worked to achieve institutional goals, which at first meant seeking a prominent role in the military campaign to overthrow Saddam Hussein's regime. As this involved a large contribution but a secondary purpose, holding the south as US forces advanced to Baghdad, they then explored how they might also get involved in the battle for Baghdad. But the south was where they stayed. They would have preferred to leave once the war was over, but the United Kingdom had responsibilities as an occupying power, a role that had not been sought but was now unavoidable.

The south was not the most challenging part of the country to occupy, just as it had not been the most challenging to invade. This encouraged complacency. As the insurgency developed during the summer of 2003, it was concentrated in and around Baghdad. The instinct of the UK high command was to stay clear of American counter-insurgency operations, as if instability and insecurity in Baghdad would not affect the south. Their allies were left unimpressed, especially as the British then found it progressively harder to impose law and order in Basra.

By the middle of 2006, both the Americans and British saw the danger of failure in their areas of responsibility. In both cases, the senior commanders saw no option other than to wait for the Iraqi security forces to improve until they could take over, but the accumulating evidence was that this would be a long wait. By the end of the year, President Bush had decided that he did not wish to preside over a failure and was prepared to make one last push to remedy the situation. Instead of directly demanding that his secretary of defense and senior commanders come up with a new strategy, the new strategy was developed outside the chain of command. The British, politicians and military alike, had no idea that US strategy was about to change in this way – the military because their main interlocutors were not in the loop, and the politicians because their interlocutors were not telling and were not sure themselves until late in the day. This was in large part because the success of the surge depended on Maliki's cooperation, and this was not forthcoming until well into December 2006.

The later British claim that Operation SINBAD was their 'surge' was treated with some derision because of its limited scale and duration, but Shirreff's plan required raising extra forces for the effort and was informed by a similar tactical philosophy. What was lacking was Maliki's support and cooperation. In this respect, the operation was too little too early. If it had been synchronized with the wider coalition effort and begun a few months later, with more Iraqi cooperation, it might have made more of a difference on the ground, and with less a sense of the parting of the ways with the United States during the course of 2007. Had the American and British efforts been more closely inte-grated at an early stage, this might have been avoided. Had JAM been better contained in the years after the invasion, it would not have become so much of a challenge to take it on, especially when the Iraqi government was reluctant to do so. A change in the political context in 2008 provided a late opportunity to make amends. This was taken, largely, because of local initiatives.

While the chairman of the US Joint Chiefs judged in December 2006 that he had to follow the president and make the new strategy work, the chief of the defence staff in the United Kingdom had a clear strategy that went in a different direction to that of the Americans, and he was determined to follow it. This led him to play down the extent of Ameri-can unease and talk up the readiness of the Iraqi security forces. 'Both the US HQs in Baghdad and the British in Basra had drifted by mutual consent into a situation where each HQ paid insufficient attention to the other's operations.'[92] The situations in the two areas were different, but their differences were aggravated by this enforced separation. The United Kingdom took on a commitment to Iraq out of solidarity with its closest ally, following intense discussions between Blair and Bush. But as Blair approached the end of his premiership, he was ready to accept that not much more could be done in Iraq, and that it was time to do more in Afghanistan. The US Army history laments that British policymakers failed to discuss the implications of the Afghan commit-ment for Iraq with their US counterparts. This required a conversation between Blair and Bush that never took place.[93]

Blair gave determined political direction when getting Britain into the war, but not so much on its later conduct. He recognized, before

President Bush, the emerging difficulties in the aftermath and sought to put his government on a 'war-footing' to meet them, but this never really happened. Blair attempted to influence American decision-making, but he could not do as much once the war had begun as he had done in the pre-war diplomacy. He set ambitious objectives for an 'exemplary' occupation of southern Iraq, but it was never backed up with sufficient resources and personnel, and eventually the United Kingdom found itself left alone with its area of responsibility and increasingly unable to cope. The commitment was never there. Government departments were unwilling to invest people or resources in Iraq, and the UK reconstruction effort was never properly coordinated or funded. By the mid-2000s, there was an extraordinary turnover in the civilian leadership of the Ministry of Defence. The senior military leadership, therefore, acted in a way that reflected its own frustrations with the course the war had taken and the competing demands of Afghanistan. Strategy was left to develop out of an uneasy conversation between the field commanders and their superiors in London. The politicians ended up following the military lead.

There was an inherent equivocation around the UK commitment to Iraq. The government worked hard to make a case for toppling Saddam Hussein's regime, but put less effort into working out what to do with its replacement. As a result, the military set its own course to serve its own institutional requirements. It sought a large and active role in the invasion, and then, once stuck with its own area of responsibility in southern Iraq, sought first to stay out of trouble and then to leave as soon as possible. This was not that different to the American position in 2006. While in the United States the president worked to realign the military strategy with his political priorities, in the United Kingdom the military, in the end, set the policy.

15

War among the People:
Fighting the Taliban and Isis

We fight amongst the people. Literally, figuratively and virtually (through the media) in the 'theatre' of operations. In streets and fields, in hospitals and schools, in airports and theatres, on the ground, in the air, and across cyberspace.

Rupert Smith[1]

For the historian John Keegan, 'heroic leaders' are 'champions of display, of skill-at-arms, of bold speech but, above all, of exemplary risk-taking.'[2] Alexander the Great represents the classic ideal of such a leader – the complete commander, combining in his person the political and military strands of generalship, leading from the front, accepting the dangers of close combat, looking and acting the part, creating his own theatre of war with pre-battle rituals, oratorical appeals, magnificence in dress, and riding on his special horse, Bucephalus. The other figures Keegan studies for his book *The Mask of Command* are not so heroic. They accepted personal risk as they move back and forth across the battlefield, keeping an eye on the developing situation, but warfare had become much more complex, with large and cumbersome armies. Thus, the severe Wellington is 'anti-heroic' as he takes on the Emperor Napoleon, with a restricted and apolitical view of his role, while Ulysses Grant, in the American Civil War, is 'un-heroic', democratic in his instincts and wholly professional in managing his battles. Neither has much flair for theatricality. Adolf Hitler, by contrast, presents himself as a truly heroic leader, his bravery validated through his intense experience of combat in the First World War. Like Alexander, he brings together in one person the political and military strands of leadership,

I S I S Areas of Control, 2015–18

N

TURKEY

Aleppo
Idlib

Raqqa

Mediterranean
Sea

SYRIA

Deir al-Zou

Palmyra

Albu k

LEBANON

Damascus

ISRAEL

JORDAN

SAUDI ARABIA

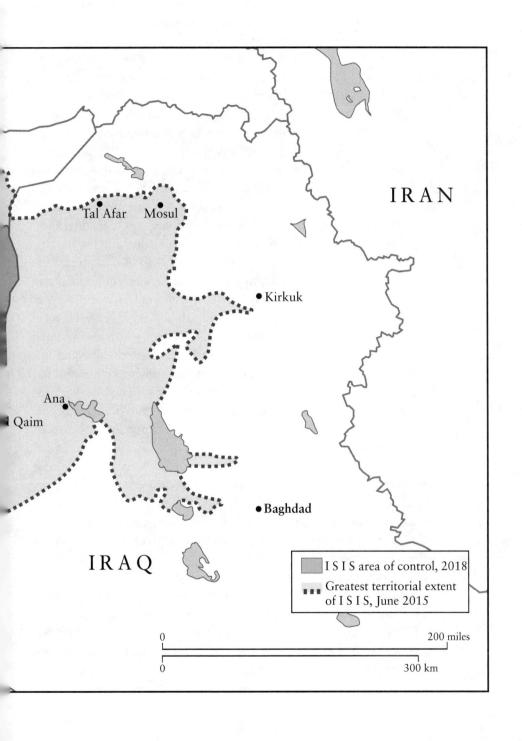

IRAN

Tal Afar   Mosul

• Kirkuk

Ana

Qaim

• Baghdad

IRAQ

ISIS area of control, 2018

Greatest territorial extent
of ISIS, June 2015

0   200 miles

0   300 km

urging his armies forward as expressions of his will. Keegan considers this 'fake-heroism', as the Nazi leader did not share the suffering of his men. In the conclusion to his book, in recognition of the predicaments of the nuclear age, he looks forward to a 'post-heroic' commanders, who understand the importance of restraint and modest ambition.

Brian Linn identifies the 'heroes' as one of the US Army's three intellectual/martial traditions (the other two are 'guardians', preoccupied with defending the homeland, and 'managers', mobilizing all resources for a titanic struggle). The heroes view warfare as 'chaotic, violent, and emotional, which puts a premium on 'the human element' – 'personal intangibles such as military genius, experience, courage, morale, and discipline'.[3] The great wars of the twentieth century were industrial in scale, and, while there were certainly opportunities for acts of individual heroism, they were decided as wars of numbers, production and logistics.

By contrast, for the West the wars of the twenty-first century were fought against radical groups, mounting insurgencies and committing acts of terrorism, often leading to small-scale encounters. For the senior levels of command, these were post-heroic, though at lower levels there were opportunities for true heroism. They required tough and inspired leadership, including an ability to work with local fighters from quite different cultures, and to operate in harsh and unforgiving conditions. But Keegan's hopes for restraint also came into play, not in holding back for fear of nuclear escalation, but holding back so as not to harm the people supposedly being helped. The success of counter-insurgency operations has been seen to depend on restraint. This is heroic because it means acting with moderation at times of extreme provocation and against uncertain hidden dangers. The approach found in the 2007 US Army *Counterinsurgency Field Manual* spoke of being 'population-centric' rather than 'enemy-centric'.[4] This provided the strategic logic behind the 2007 surge in Iraq. The aim was to bring security to people who were being threatened and intimidated by the insurgents. That meant the troops had to be visible and active away from their bases. This contrasted with the approach of the British in Basra, who were stuck in their bases, taking shelter from incoming fire and unable to do much to fight back.

To use Rupert Smith's terminology these are not 'industrial wars' but 'wars among the people'. The mark of victory is that the people feel sufficiently supported to reject the rebels and insurgents, but they in turn need to provide support if there is to be a hope of victory. 'People',

Smith notes, 'are the main reason we, the international coalitions, find it difficult to win.'[5] Restraint is required to show the people who their friends are, that working with the army is a way to a better future. Every move has to convey this message, because the media is always alert to signs of misdeeds and mishaps. Every encounter can feed into the narrative wars that are a vital feature of such conflicts. Most of all, civilian casualties have to be kept as low as possible. It is unlikely that the people will show confidence in a force that is also threatening their security with careless strikes and ill-disciplined operations.

One commander who fitted the bill of the heroic leader who understood the unique needs of this type of war was General Stanley McChrystal. Unusually for those who joined the American army as the Vietnam War ended, when the focus was moving sharply to preparations for a big war with the Soviet bloc, McChrystal was intrigued by the demands of counter-insurgency. During the 2000s he made his reputation as a celebrated commander of special operations in both Iraq and Afghanistan. One of his notable achievements was leading the long effort to find and kill Abu Musab al-Zarqawi, the al Qaeda leader in Iraq.

His interest in this form of warfare had been piqued while at high school, when he studied the French colonial wars in Indochina and Algeria and became fascinated with the 'outsized personalities and human flaws' of the key characters, including Marcel Bigeard, one of the models for Lartéguy's Raspéguy.[6] McChrystal recalls in his foreword to Lartéguy's *The Praetorians* how the author had portrayed the French paratroopers as 'rough men . . . from the society they defend and yet detached from it'. Their role as warriors shaped their physiques and mental states and provided them with their moral compass. As a young paratrooper, he was drawn to emulate them with their 'sinewy physique, steady nerves and nonchalant demeanour'.[7] When his time came to lead men in war, McChrystal did so by example, with his own punishing exercise regime. President Obama was struck when he met him by a man whose 'whole manner was that of someone who's burned away frivolity and distractions from his life'.[8]

In 2003, he was given command of TF 714, known as 'The Green', modelled on the British SAS and made up largely of Rangers and Green Berets. He described these men as matching this idealized image. With faces that were 'leathery but not grizzled', they tended to be 'hyperfit, opinionated, iconoclastic, fearless, intelligent, type A problem solvers who thrived without guidance'. Far from being 'hardened, cynical soldiers for pay who floated from one battlefield to the next, without regard for the cause for which they employed their skills', they were intensely patriotic. 'Belief in our cause, and their leaders, was critically important to them.' [9]

In command, McChrystal remained convinced of the relevance of the French experience of the 1950s. He showed his men Pontecorvo's film *The Battle of Algiers*, in which the paratrooper commander, Lieutenant Colonel Mathieu, was said to be a composite of Massu, Bigeard and Massu's deputy, Roger Trinquier.[10] McChrystal also asked his men to read and comment upon Trinquier's 1964 treatise *Modern Warfare*, which included a justification for torture. McChrystal noted, somewhat coyly, that he 'disagreed with many of the hard-edged solutions', but thought the 'analysis of the challenge was instructive'. He insisted that the lesson he drew for his men was that the use of torture was counterproductive.[11] The French also understood the need for popular support, but the indiscriminate, rough and often cruel methods they employed were likely to alienate.

General David Petraeus, the prime promoter of the new American counter-insurgency doctrine, was also drawn to the Algerian example, and the role played by Bigeard. He first came across him in 1976 as a portrait on the wall of a French army mess hall in the Pyrenees, and was soon intrigued by the French Algerian campaigns and their theorists, until he inevitably came across Lartéguy's novels and the compelling figure of Colonel Raspéguy. According to Kaplan, Petraeus was particularly taken by a passage in *The Centurions* in which a French officer explains the advantage the Viet Minh have over the French in Indochina, by comparing playing bridge, with 52 cards in the pack, to the similar French game of belote, with 32 cards.

> Those twenty cards short will always prevent us from getting the better of them. They've got nothing to do with traditional warfare, they're marked with the sign of politics, propaganda, faith, agrarian reform . . .

This encouraged the conviction that successful counter-insurgency required paying attention to how the conflict looked to the people caught up in it, in order to try to address their needs.[12]

McChrystal embraced this logic, but he could see how it raised issues of motivation for his own troops. He wrote that the French had taught him that it was not enough to be opposed to something. There also had to be something positive to fight for. In addition, the French approach to counter-insurgency was that fighting in a way sure to lead to defeat was stupid, and so immoral. The only way to fight was with the tactics or measures that would lead to victory. And he recognized the desire to win was as much 'visceral' as 'logical'. In a war of heroic restraint, when it was necessary to hold back if an enemy was hiding in the villages and urban streets, coming out for the occasional ambush, the efforts to avoid alienating the people risked alienating the troops. It was easier to urge restraint when you were not in the line of fire. When directives and guidance sent from afar, even though informed by the most impeccable logic, failed to grasp the needs of the moment, they were likely to be dismissed and treated with disdain by those caught up with the emotions of combat. In this way, local commanders could become detached from the civilian authorities and their senior commanders.

SURGING IN AFGHANISTAN

In June 2009, McChrystal was appointed commander of the multinational International Security Assistance Force (ISAF) in Afghanistan. He got this job because Robert Gates, who had been asked by President Barack Obama to stay on as secretary of defense, concluded that General David McKiernan, then commanding the force, needed to be replaced. McKiernan was the first senior commander since MacArthur in 1951 to be relieved of his post while fighting a war, although in this case there was neither insubordination nor any spectacular failure.

There were undoubted problems. The attention demanded by Iraq under Bush had led to neglect of Afghanistan. The Taliban, having been routed in 2001, were back as an effective guerrilla force, while the government in Kabul was ineffectual and riddled with corruption. The Pakistani government was still hedging its bets, working with Washington while providing the Taliban with training, assistance and sanctuary. Distinctive and not always compatible strategies were being pursued at the same time, involving a variety of agencies, including the CIA and special forces, along with conventional forces from not only the United States, but also allied countries, as well as Afghanistan. This had led to tensions in the command arrangements. The Afghan government lacked a single point of contact when it needed to discuss military policy. The international contributors were wary about being under an American command, when they had no say in some of the operations that the Americans conducted, and the large civilian contingent in Afghanistan struggled to find ways of communicating with the military.

McKiernan had the unified command he had sought, and was now looking for 30,000 more troops. But Gates considered the campaign stalled, and he was being pressed on the regular and embarrassing incidents that led to civilian casualties. McKiernan was a Damon rather than a Massengale. He had been a successful armoured commander, and had not made his career in Washington or worked on his political profile. He also disagreed with Petraeus, who was now at CENTCOM, about how to take the campaign forward. He saw Afghanistan as a long haul, requiring a sustained commitment from the United States and a focus on governance in Kabul. To get popular support, they needed to be governed well by individuals who had earned their trust. Petraeus, he judged, was too inclined to follow the Iraq model, as if the success of the surge in Iraq could be replicated in Afghanistan. But he also understood that 'a new administration wanted a new general for a new policy'.[13]

Obama, then in his first months in office, was unable to draw on any military experience of his own. He had made his name as an opponent of the Iraq War. In doing so, he had compared Iraq, a poor war of choice, unfavourably with Afghanistan, which he considered to be a more noble and necessary war. But while Iraq seemed to be largely sorted out by 2009 (an impression that also turned out to be illusory), this was not the case with Afghanistan. One of the first acts of the administration was to send 17,000 more troops, plus 4,000 military trainers, to stabilize the situation in Afghanistan. McChrystal soon concluded he needed more. Even if there was to be a political solution at some point, the security situation would first need to be addressed. And he was after a lot more troops – some 40,000. Gates recalled 'almost falling off his chair' when he was told of the request, because he knew how badly this would go down with an administration that had only just approved more troops.[14] McChrystal persisted, coming back with detailed proposals at the end of August. The extra troops would bring the total commitment to Afghanistan to 100,000.

As Obama believed his predecessor had been far too willing to accept military advice without question, he was determined to subject this new proposal to proper scrutiny, and so asked the NSC staff to look over the proposals and settle on a way forward. 'As it turned out,' he recalled in his memoir, 'the generals had other ideas.'[15] He was soon suspicious that he had been subjected to a 'bait and switch': the Pentagon had accepted the first modest tranche of extra troops as 'merely a temporary, tactical retreat on the path to getting more'.[16] A political offensive was under way. In response to an article in the *Washington Post* on 2 September expressing doubts about the wisdom of the plan, Petraeus came back in the same paper insisting that a 'fully resourced, comprehensive' strategy was required. Admiral Mullen, chairman of the Joint Chiefs, used very similar language before the Senate Armed Services Committee. More seriously, a member of McChrystal's staff passed on the plan to Bob Woodward of the *Post*. A synopsis appeared on 21 September, under the headline 'McChrystal: More Forces or "Mission Failure"'. On 1 October, McChrystal spoke of his plan in a television interview and then in a speech in London. Soon Republican senators were demanding that Obama follow the advice of the commanders on the ground. Commentators spoke of 'dithering'.

Obama was irritated that he was being bounced into a decision. Vice President Joe Biden, who was opposed to the plan, described the media onslaught as 'fucking outrageous'.[17] Even if the commanders intended to do no more than prepare the ground for a decision that was eventually bound to go their way, they were taking the president for granted. For Obama, this 'was the first instance during my presidency when I felt as if an entire agency under my charge was working its own agenda'. After Mullen's testimony he called him into the Oval Office, with Gates. The reprimand began with the president observing that he had created an environment in which all views could be heard. He continued:

> So, when I set up a process that's going to decide whether I send tens of thousands more troops into a deadly war zone at the cost of hundreds of billions of dollars, and I see my top military leaders short-circuiting that process to argue their position in public, I have to wonder.
>
> Is it because they figure they know better and don't want to be bothered answering my questions? Is it because I'm young and didn't serve in the military? Is it because they don't like my politics?

Mullen replied:

> I think I speak for all your flag officers, Mr. President, when I say we have the highest respect for you and the office.

After promising to take a careful decision based on what best served the interests of the country, Obama added, 'I'd sure like to stop having my military advisors telling me what I have to do on the front page of the morning paper. Is that fair?'[18]

Biden was most opposed to the Pentagon's plan, pushing his own alternative of a substantial force dedicated more to counter-terrorism than counter-insurgency, geared to preventing further al Qaeda attacks against the United States. Biden had no confidence that the Afghani military and police force could be turned into an effective force. The effort to turn them into one had yet to show much progress even with tens of thousands of troops on the ground. The problem was the lack of 'a reliable partner in the Afghanistan government', and, if that was the case, then simply adding more troops was just prolonging the agony. ('If the government's a criminal syndicate a year from now, how will troops make a difference?') Nor was he convinced that the Taliban had any interest in relaunching terrorist attacks against the United States. Biden was prepared for the Afghan government to fall. Obama demurred: 'the downside was too great.'[19]

Obama was in a difficult position, although largely one of his own making. By calling Afghanistan a good war, he was unable to take the risk of an early failure. As Bush did in Iraq, he was confronting the possibility that doing nothing would mean presiding over defeat. His opponents would condemn him for disregarding his top commanders. 'I couldn't ignore the unanimous recommendation of experienced generals who'd managed to salvage some measure of stability in Iraq and were already in the thick of the fight in Afghanistan.' If a similar result was on offer it was tempting to take the risk. But many of his staff did not share this inclination.

The arguments went on for weeks, with long and often bad-tempered meetings. As Obama recalled, by the 'third or fourth go-round of Power-Point slides, battlefield maps, and balky video feeds, along with the ever-present fluorescent lighting, bad coffee, and stale air, everyone was sick of Afghanistan, sick of meetings, and sick of one another'.[20] The decision-making process almost buckled under the strain. By presenting a united front with McChrystal and Petraeus, Mullen was not well placed to find some way to align the conflicting perspectives of the commanders and the White House. Instead of ensuring that Obama could assess a range of options, the chairman had worked to marginalize alternatives, such as Biden's proposal. He ordered his staff not to provide analytical support, although his deputy, General John Cart-wright, who agreed with Biden, did just that. Mullen was irritated, but constitutionally Cartwright had the right to offer his own advice to the president and vice president. The national security advisor, James Jones, another retired general, was less committed to a particular policy, but lacked the authority to manage the process. He was not an insider, and his deputy, Tom Donilon, supported Biden's position. At the State Department, Hillary Clinton supported the commanders, but her dep-uty, Jim Steinberg, was lukewarm, while Obama's representative in the region, the former general Karl Eikenberry, doubted it could be made to work.[21] This was not a simple civilian–military split.

It took until the ninth meeting in late November for a compromise position to be reached. It reflected more the balance of power within Washington than that in Afghanistan. McChrystal acknowledged that his proposed campaign would erode but not eliminate the capabilities of the Taliban. His critics accepted that little could be done about al Qaeda if the Taliban were rampant. Both agreed that the only way out was to train local forces to cope. While there were limits to what could be done to improve the country's government, within those limits there were sig-nificant reforms to be made. McChrystal did not get his 40,000 extra troops, but instead had to settle for 30,000, and only for a limited period.

The most important aspect of the final decision was Obama's deter-mination that, while the numbers would be allowed to spike up, they must then spike down. The length of the deployment would be gov-erned by an agreed departure date, to begin in 2011, and not by success against the agreed objectives. Indeed, there was more definition of the timeline than of objectives. In these circumstances, it was unclear what victory could mean. There was as much talk about disrupting and degrading the enemy as about defeating it, and ambiguity about how much the focus on al Qaeda should extend to the Taliban. When the decision was made, McChrystal was provided with a six-page docu-ment setting out the agreed plan – in effect, his orders from Obama. Having been played once, Obama did not intend to be played again.[22]

Strategically this was odd. Obama wanted to reassure the American people that this was not an indefinite commitment. It also, however, greatly reassured the Taliban. There might be short-term gains, but there could now be no guarantee that they would be sustained. While the campaign would need to be conducted with restraint, to gain the trust of the Afghan people, a different sort of restraint was required to convince the American people that this was a worthwhile effort and not an open-ended commitment. In his memoir, Gates commented unfavourably on Biden worrying about how the Democratic Party base would react to McChrystal's proposal.[23] Obama did not see the problem. Gates was one of 'Washington's savviest operators' and well understood 'congressional pressure, public opinion, and budgetary constraints'. The difference was that he seemed to see them as 'obstacles to navigate around, not legitimate factors that should inform our decisions', whereas Obama accepted them as part of the process. This was how democracy should work. He could not avoid questions of priorities, why billions should be spent on these matters rather than health and education. He went further:

> As much as any specific differences over strategy or tactics, such fundamental issues – the civilian control of policy making, the respective roles of the president and his military advisors in our constitutional system, and the considerations each brought to bear in deciding about war – became the subtext of the Afghan debate.[24]

Obama's point was underlined in June 2010, just over six months after the decision had been announced, when McChrystal offered his resignation, on publication of disparaging remarks he had made to a reporter from *Rolling Stone* magazine about Biden, Eikenberry and others, including the president. When explaining why McChrystal had to go, Obama stressed this was not about differences over strategy but because his remarks had undermined 'the civilian control of the military that's at the core of our democratic system'.[25]

Yet, while it was the excessive frankness about his civilian masters that got McChrystal fired, the article is revealing in another sense. On the one hand, it paints a portrait of a super-smart and hard commander. His team prided themselves 'on their can-do attitude and their disdain for authority'. He set them a 'manic pace' – 'sleeping four hours a night, running seven miles each morning, and eating one meal a day'. On the other hand, Michael Hastings, the reporter, noted a lack of progress. More deaths and bombings, and a population that had yet to be won over. Hastings had noted how McChrystal's team were 'in indisputable command of all military aspects of the war'. There was 'no equivalent position on the diplomatic or political side'. The team could frame the issues, as they did with Obama over Afghanistan, in ways that shaped the policy debate, by underplaying the political and strategic factors likely to limit the benefits of the counter-insurgency campaign, and other options that might have gone some way to meeting US objectives without such a large and costly commitment.[26] McChrystal understood the need to work closely with the Afghan government, but, on the military side, his team, largely with backgrounds in special operations, did not always work well in a multinational headquarters. He could not direct the war as he wanted, as members of the coalition were committed to particular regions, while the Marine Corps, to his frustration, insisted that they would work to their own Lieutenant General in CENTCOM and not to McChrystal.

McChrystal was adamant that avoiding civilian casualties was a key to popular support. This was 'insurgent math'. For every innocent person killed, ten new enemies were created. Strict directives were issued, restricting reckless driving by convoys, the use of air power and night raids. Hastings picked up the resentment the restrictions imposed by McChrystal were causing among his own troops. They were not sold on the idea of heroic restraint. 'Being told to hold their fire, soldiers complain, puts them in greater danger.' They wanted to fight, but were held back from doing so. He reported an intense conversation the general had with some soldiers. McChrystal asked, 'Anybody feel like you're losing?' There was no encouraging answer. In this area, the insurgency still had momentum. 'The more we pull back, the more we restrain ourselves, the stronger it's getting.'

The answers underlined the strategic dilemma of Afghanistan. Fighting harder might hurt the enemy, but might still increase their support. 'What do you want to do? You want to wipe the population out here and resettle it?' Against various measures of success, McChrystal could offer progress, but he could not offer a conclusive victory.[27] As he explained the need for heroic restraint, his troops knew that they would pay the price.

CUTTING AND RUNNING

By the time Donald Trump became president, at the start of 2017, the surge was over, and the United States was doing what it could to help the Afghan government and forces cope with a resurgent Taliban. Donald Trump's relations with his national security advisors were volatile. His approach to policy, and policymaking, was intuitive and idiosyncratic. He preferred loyalty to constructive criticism, and was suspicious of claims to expertise if they contradicted his convictions. During a meeting in the Pentagon, in July 2017, he became increasingly restless as the top civilian and military members of the national security establishment tried to school him on current policy. When the conversation turned to Afghanistan, he exploded. 'I want to win . . . We don't win any wars anymore . . . We spend $7 trillion, everybody else got the oil and we're not winning anymore.' Trump, who had never seen combat, told the astonished officers in front of him, 'I wouldn't go to war with you people . . . You're a bunch of dopes and babies.'[28] He was persuaded to give more support to the Afghan forces, but his patience would not last. He later complained, 'I should have followed my instincts, not my generals!'[29]

He had no interest in putting more effort into winning in Afghanistan. He considered the country corrupt and the 'people are not worth fighting for'.[30] The next year, he pushed for an effort to get an agreement with the Taliban. Formal negotiations began on 22 January 2019. The Afghan government was not part of the talks, and, though consulted, their misgivings carried little weight. A deal was reached in Qatar on 29 February 2020. According to its terms, the United States would immediately start cutting back the numbers of troops, then another 12,000, and withdraw completely by late April 2021. In return, the Taliban promised that they would not aid or harbour terrorists, would exchange prisoners and would engage in talks with the Afghan government, though they did not consider the government legitimate. Nor were there any commitments on human rights, especially women's rights.

With his customary boastfulness, Trump claimed that he was sure that 'the Taliban wants to do something to show that we're not all wasting time', suggesting that they might even be unlikely new allies in the war on terror. He told the press:

> I'll be meeting personally with Taliban leaders in the not-too-distant future, and will be very much hoping that they will be doing what they say. They will be killing terrorists. They will be killing some very bad people. They will keep that fight going.

The Taliban take was somewhat different. 'From here, the defeat of the arrogance of the White House in the face of the white turban will be announced,' wrote the Taliban's media chief on Twitter.[31] In July 2020, Trump decided to cut troop levels by half – to about 4,000 – without waiting for a review of how well the Taliban were complying with the agreement. Later, he pressed for troop numbers to be cut to 2,500 by Christmas.

This was the situation Joe Biden inherited when he became president in January 2021. He had opposed Obama's surge in 2009, and he could now feel vindicated. He had campaigned to end what had come to be known as the 'forever wars'. It was evident to the US military that he was not going to budge from this position. But with the American command in Kabul now worried about the Taliban moving into a position to overthrow the government, they hoped the new president could be persuaded to delay the final withdrawal.

Under Trump's agreement with the Taliban, all US troops should be withdrawn by 1 May. A bipartisan panel led by a former chairman of the Joint Chiefs, General Dunford, who had commanded the Afghanistan force, recommended at the start of February that the 1 May deadline should be abandoned, more peace talks encouraged and American forces pushed back up to 4,500. Numbers should be reduced further only as security conditions improved, rather than according to a strict deadline.[32] This was the recommendation from the commander of US forces in Afghanistan and from CENTCOM.[33]

Biden's dilemma was that, without an American promise to leave, the Taliban would resume the war, and the United States would have to boost its troop numbers to be able to cope. Withdrawal, on the other hand, would require the Afghan government to cope, and it was unclear how long it could withstand a Taliban offensive. Talks between the Taliban and the Afghan government had unsurprisingly broken down. Should the government collapse, could al Qaeda then return and mount new acts of terrorism? His generals, like Obama's and Trump's, warned him that the denouement could be unpleasant and bloody. The intelligence, however, suggested that the Afghan security forces could keep going for some time.

The president, recalling how sure the Pentagon was at the start of the Obama administration that tens of thousands more troops were essential, was unconvinced. In the event of a Taliban push, what could such a small force achieve, other than provide another reason for the Afghan government not to become self-reliant?[34] A government that could only be propped up by US efforts did not have good long-term prospects. Although there were newspaper reports that he was moving to agree to a residual force in Kabul, Biden told his national security staff on 6 April 2021 that he wanted all American troops out of Afghanistan. Defense Secretary Lloyd Austin and chairman of the Joint Chiefs, General Mark A. Milley, asked if this was his final decision. He said it was. They had hoped to persuade him to keep a more modest troop presence, to continue to work as necessary with Afghan forces, and to require the Taliban to agree to conditions. In one meeting, Milley, who had served three tours in Afghanistan, warned of the consequences of a Taliban takeover and was said to have become 'emotional'. He warned that women's rights would go 'back to the Stone Age', and that so much 'blood and treasure' would have been wasted.[35]

Biden was unmoved. He was aware that the consequences of the US withdrawal might be dire for those Afghanis who would be seen as anti-Taliban, and who had served US forces. He was reluctant to accept any responsibility for their fate, a judgement tempered by his expectation that the Afghan government would survive long enough for evacuations to be achieved in an orderly fashion. Biden wanted an unconditional withdrawal before 11 September 2021, the 20th anniversary of the al Qaeda attacks on New York and Washington. Austin warned him, 'We've seen this movie before.'[36] When he announced the withdrawal, Biden recalled that he had been asked by Obama to visit Afghanistan after the 2008 election, and had come to the conclusion then that 'more and endless American military force could not create or sustain a durable Afghan government'. The objective for which the United States had entered Afghanistan – to defeat al Qaeda – had been achieved. In his speech, he explicitly rejected the idea that the US exit should be linked to conditions on the ground. What would the conditions be? 'By what means and how long would it take to achieve them, if they could be achieved at all? And at what additional cost in lives and treasure?'[37]

Yet still the working assumption was that somehow the government in Kabul would survive. A senior White House official was reported saying:

I can tell you, having sat through every single meeting that took place on this topic and having read every single intelligence assessment, military document, State Department cable, there was nobody anywhere in our government, even up until a day or two before Kabul fell, that foresaw the collapse of the government and army before the end of our troop withdrawal at the end of August, and most of the projections were that there would still be weeks to months before we would face the very real prospect of the collapse of Kabul.

A more realistic assessment might have resulted in better preparations for what was to come when Kabul did fall, and begun to identify potentially vulnerable Afghanis and start to move them out of the country on commercial flights from the spring.[38]

As the withdrawal began, Austin was asked if Afghan forces were ready. He replied: 'They must be ready.'[39] But they were not. Trump's deal had undermined the Afghan government, as it had been negotiated without their participation, and anyway the government itself did not inspire great loyalty. The Taliban's offensives had pushed Afghan forces back, and they had already taken casualties in a hard winter's fighting. As the final departure drew close in August, the Taliban pushed hard, taking one provincial capital after another until they reached Kabul. The US military had managed an orderly and early withdrawal, so by that time they controlled few assets in the country. Instead of beginning an evacuation in good time, the Biden administration had worried about the 'optics' of moving people out while still proclaiming confidence in the durability of the government. Then, as the Taliban drew closer, the panic began, and with it new concerns about the 'optics'. Now the worry was of the spectacle of people scrambling to get out of the country without any assistance from their supposed protectors. At the last minute, 5,000 troops were sent to Kabul to do what they could with the evacuation to rescue their own personnel and Afghans who had worked with them through the war years. Eventually – in chaotic scenes – they managed to evacuate 124,000 people by the end of August.[40]

Many got out, but many were left stuck in Afghanistan facing a new Taliban regime. The chaotic and painful withdrawal, reminiscent of the hurried departure from Saigon in 1975, something Biden had promised would not happen,[41] left behind many Afghans who had supported the war against the Taliban, in the hope of a more prosperous and freer future. They were now stuck in a country that remained violent, and was closing down opportunities for women and girls, insisting on uniformity of thought and experiencing a crashing economy. A journalist commenting on this desperate conclusion to the war observed:

> In the United States, historians and analysts will look back on the failed solutions and the misguided strategies and general officers who assured victory even though in off-the-record briefings and closed-door sessions they acknowledged that the United States was losing.[42]

Motivating troops, reassuring the public and calming friendly governments can require an ingrained optimism about the prospects for success. Once it is acknowledged openly that a mission is bound to fail, then it becomes harder to sustain morale. Why would front-line troops die for a cause that their commanders consider already lost? That is why the moment when the narrative turns from being one of long-term resolve to short-term retreat is apt to be one of maximum chaos.

RESTRAINT FROM THE AIR

On 26 August 2021, with Afghans seeking to escape the Taliban crowding into Kabul airport, desperate to get on a flight to safety, 13 US troops and more than 170 Afghan civilians were killed in an Islamic State (ISIS) suicide attack. Fearful of yet another attack, senior American commanders delegated authority to those who could act quickly, should they see suspicious terrorist activity. Three days later, drone operators believed they had spotted an imminent threat. An individual who they thought worked for ISIS had visited a compound that might have been used by ISIS, and was seen, with others, loading what appeared to be explosives into his white Toyota Corolla. Back at his home, they saw him talking to another man, and so decided to take the chance and unleashed a Hellfire missile, which crashed into the car, followed by secondary explosions, which seemed to confirm that explosives had been present. The chairman of the Joint Chiefs declared this to be 'a righteous strike'. Unfortunately, this was not true. The individual had no connection to ISIS. Nor did the site he attended. It was owned by an NGO. He was doing a variety of errands, and what were assumed to be explosives were in fact water canisters, which later provided the secondary explosions. And there were not just two adults present as the missile struck. It killed three adults and seven children. The next day a similar white Toyota, driving through the same neighbourhood, launched rockets at the airport.

This episode was far from unique – there had been similar ones in the air campaigns of the previous decade. The problems lay in fuzzy images, which were not quite sharp enough, and 'confirmation bias', leading those operating the drones to see what fitted in with their preconceptions. They were viewing behaviour they could not fully understand, without any guidance from anyone on the ground who might have done, fearful they had insufficient time to act to stop an atrocity. There was also a familiar pattern in an initial denial that anything had gone wrong, followed by a grudging admission without anybody held accountable. John F. Kirby, the Pentagon's chief spokesman, explained that there had been 'a breakdown in process, in execution and procedural events', but this was 'not the result of negligence, not the result of misconduct, not the result of poor leadership'.[43]

After Kosovo, a war in which Western aircraft operated without fear of being shot down, Michael Ignatieff wrote of 'virtual war' – 'waged with death removed, waged in conditions of impunity'.[44] In the decades following Kosovo, especially with fewer troops on the ground to confirm the validity of particular targets, decisions on what to attack were often taken by people far from the action, in no personal danger themselves; at times, apparently compelling evidence, on closer inspection, proved at best ambiguous and at worst downright wrong. Yet reliance on air power was the preferred way of war for the West.

The image of air power left over from the Second World War was of combat that required undoubted bravery, whether the fighter pilots duelling in the sky or the bomber crews relentlessly pressing forward through anti-aircraft fire. In subsequent wars, pilots continued to take intense personal risks to complete their missions, for example the UK Harrier pilots during the Falklands trying to protect those unloading supplies at San Carlos, and the Argentine pilots facing a barrage of air defence systems as they tried to hit them. At the same time, there was also a moral unease around the unrestricted use of air power. The mass air raids of the Second World War caused tremendous civilian suffering without any proportionate strategic effect. The practice of bombing centres of population continued, largely as a form of intimidation. Recall Nixon's greater interest in the spectacle of B-52s bearing down on Hanoi than in the new smart weapons that were just starting to demonstrate their extraordinary efficiency.

Smart weapons displayed their capabilities to the full during the 1991 Persian Gulf War. It was now possible to consider air campaigns that concentrated on important targets with far less loss of innocent life. Thereafter it became increasingly possible to attack targets without risking the pilots. This was because the enemy had no serious air defences, or those that they had were soon destroyed in the first attacks. Manned aircraft were not even essential. In the Gulf War, cruise missiles were launched from submarines. Recall also the qualms at the end of this war about the 'turkey shoot' of Iraqi troops fleeing Kuwait, reflecting concerns about causing unwarranted casualties, which led the president to decide it was time to stop the war. From the start of this century, unmanned aerial vehicles (drones) became in many cases the weapons of choice. The expectation grew that whatever needed to be hit could be hit; whatever did not need to be hit could be avoided. All this transformed the image of air power. It could be employed without great danger to attack whatever needed to be attacked.

These developments challenged the self-image of the airman. The fighter pilots had always nurtured a heroic image, equivalent to the tough and resourceful paratrooper. The image, first forged during the pioneering days of the First World War, was of 'knights of the air', aggressive individuals who engaged in thrilling aerial combat. Even more so than army warriors, their success depended on being able to manipulate the machines in which they flew and fought. The test of any aircraft was performance in a 'dogfight', as pilots circled and manoeuvred around each other, until one moved in for the kill.

To recapture this glory in the 1960s and 1970s, the so-called 'fighter mafia' in the US Air Force pushed for aircraft that were simple and agile, unencumbered with technology included for what they considered superfluous roles, notably ground attack. The influence of this group, with an essentially nostalgic view, could be seen in the design and production of two fighter aircraft – the F-15 and F-16. When the first major test of the USAF came after Vietnam in the 1991 Persian Gulf War, there were few dogfights but many ground attack missions.[45] Thereafter, that became the norm.

In subsequent decades, more roles were found for drones, in both gathering intelligence and striking discrete targets. All the new sensor and communications technologies came together to allow the president to receive and act upon recommendations, complete with legal and strategic opinions, to authorize the assassination of foreign fighters. The targets were watched by a drone loitering above them being flown by an operator thousands of miles away. The MQ-9 Reaper drone, combined with laser-guided Hellfire missiles, became the preferred vehicle for both surveillance and strikes. Their use carried few of the downsides associated with occupying foreign countries – if it had been possible after 9/11 to take out the al Qaeda leadership directly in this way, rather than worry about the Taliban, the grief of subsequent years might have been avoided. A remarkable feature of Barack Obama's presidency was the extent to which he became actively engaged in decisions on whether to assassinate terrorist leaders. He approved strikes against numerous suspected terrorists. While he worried about their extra-judicial quality, this was not to the extent that he abandoned the methodology.[46] One author wondered whether the increasing reliance on drones heralded a new form of warfare, which was too easy to undertake because the human costs had been reduced so significantly.[47]

There were still limits on what drones could achieve. They could not dislodge enemy units from entrenched positions. If the United States wanted to concentrate on air power when supporting friendly governments in their fights against insurgents, then they would need to work closely with indigenous forces. As these forces moved against the enemy, then air support, whether from drones or manned aircraft, had to be agreed quickly, to keep up with the developing battle. This way of warfare became a feature of the 2010s – in the post-surge fighting in Afghanistan, and a brief war supporting rebels in Libya in 2011, which led to the overthrow of its dictator, Muammar Gaddafi. The most important and intense tests came in the campaigns against ISIS, a successor terror group to al Qaeda, that took large swathes of territory in Iraq and Syria in 2014.

The origins of this war lay in the largely peaceful protests directed against Syria's President Bashar al-Assad in 2011. They were dealt with harshly and so turned violent. Rebel groups, many populated by deserters from the Syrian army, sought to overthrow the regime by force. Western countries willed Assad's departure but not the means to make this happen. Although Obama declared in 2012 that any chemical weapons use against civilians would be a 'red line', when the evidence for that came the next summer, he held back. As he did so, he took pride in rejecting the Washington 'playbook' despite heavy criticism.[48] He was prepared to assist some of the many competing groups fighting Assad's forces, but it proved hard to choose which ones. Attempts to establish umbrella organizations to coordinate their activities were generally unsuccessful, leaving individual cells of fighters to work out their own tactics and keep themselves supplied.[49] The choices became more difficult as large numbers of Islamic extremists were attracted to the fight.

ISIS (or the 'Islamic State' or 'Daesh') was the most effective of the Islamist groups. Its roots lay in the Iraqi branch of al Qaeda led by Abu Musab al-Zarqawi, whose methods were more vicious than bin Laden's and his anti-Shia convictions more intense. After he was caught by an American air strike in June 2006 (one of McChrystal's more celebrated operations), his depleted group moved into Syria, where the conditions contributed to its revival. Its new leader, Abu Bakr al-Baghdadi (a *nom de guerre*), another Iraqi, used extreme tactics to give his group its distinctive character and prominence. After ISIS took the Syrian city of Raqqa, which became its de facto capital, it then swept back into Iraq, and by June 2014 had taken Mosul, Iraq's second largest city, from where al-Baghdadi declared a new caliphate. In the face of this advance, the much stronger and far better equipped Iraqi army had fled, as the Afghan army would do in 2021 as the Taliban advanced. The methods adopted by ISIS were brutal, marked by executions and massacres, including thousands of Yazidi Kurds

Obama had little choice but to re-engage with Iraq, at first in the form of limited air strikes in support of the forces, initially largely Kurdish, seeking to hold back ISIS. This was very much a war among the people, but not really like the earlier counter-insurgency campaigns in Afghanistan and Iraq. This enemy was even more ruthless and vicious, and, instead of using guerrilla warfare, was occupying towns and cities. Its militants were apparently prepared to fight to the death, with no regard for civilian life. Civilians were executed for failing to give support or for lacking the appropriate faith. This was a war in which the people were caught in situations from which they could not escape, used as human shields, vulnerable to booby traps and in constant danger, as fighting raged in and around their streets and buildings.

The campaign against ISIS was initially framed as a return to those of the previous decade, requiring central control and demanding rules of engagement, largely to avoid civilian casualties. That depended on those commanding the air strikes to discriminate in their targeting and reduce the 'collateral' damage, that is the innocents who might lose their homes and their lives, because they were in the wrong place at the wrong time. The issue of how well such a war could be conducted largely from the air had been raised in Kosovo, although in that case the targets were not geared to an ongoing fight on the ground. They were more about undermining the government in Belgrade. Even then, there were a number of tragic mishits.

The Americans eventually realized that ISIS was a different sort of enemy – not so much a 'reenergized regional insurgency' and more an 'emerging proto-state'.[50] In early 2015, a new secretary of defense, Ash Carter, became concerned that CENTCOM 'lacked a comprehensive, achievable plan for success'.[51] With General Joseph Dunford, the new chairman of the Joint Chiefs, gradually the approach changed. Instead of concentrating on preventing ISIS gaining or holding bits of land (so-called 'terrain denial'), which often meant using expensive munitions for little effect, the objective shifted to undermining ISIS's support structures and revenue streams, including its weapons factories, banks and oil refineries.

By the start of October 2016, ISIS had lost 45 per cent of areas once held in Iraq and 20 per cent of those in Syria. It now began its defence of Mosul.[52] The Iraqi government, supported by an international co-alition, had some 100,000 troops, including 40,000 Kurdish Peshmerga, backed by Western air power. They had a numerical advantage against up to 5,000 ISIS combatants inside the city, but nonetheless had to anticipate some fearsome urban warfare as the enemy was equipped with machine guns, rocket-propelled grenade launchers, mortars and rockets. There were reports of suicide bombers being sent from Syria to support these fighters, and civilians being used as human shields.

Government forces moved cautiously, first taking surrounding villages, before the eastern part of the city was entered. This had largely been taken by the end of the year. Western Mosul was much more difficult, with block-to-block fighting. At the start of 2017, the team advising incoming President Donald Trump concluded that Obama had been too cautious and risk-averse. Trump wanted ISIS utterly destroyed. Trump, no micromanager, left it to his secretary of defense, retired General James Mattis, to develop the plan. Mattis explained:

> We have already shifted from attrition tactics where we shove them from one position to another in Iraq and Syria, to annihilation tactics where we surround them. Our intention is that the foreign fighters do not survive

the fight to return home to North Africa, to Europe, to America, to Asia, to Africa. We're not going to allow them to do so. We're going to stop them there and take apart the caliphate.[53]

He also said that he would not relax those rules of engagement intended 'to protect the innocent'. The Pentagon had already developed options for expanding the fight.[54]

By mid-May 2017, some 90 per cent of western Mosul had been captured, putting ISIS close to total defeat. Their fighters were unable to abandon their positions. They had only two options: 'Die and go to hell or raise the white flag.'[55] By June there were some 350 left, mingling with Iraqi civilians in the old city. They were eventually dislodged from the Mosque from which al-Baghdadi had proclaimed his caliphate in 2014.

During the campaign against ISIS, US command practice changed. The pressures for delegation grew with the need to respond to the exigencies of urban warfare. In October 2014, CENTCOM established the Combined Joint Task Force–Inherent Resolve (CJTF–IR) to serve as the HQ for all anti-ISIS operations. Operations in individual theatres were delegated to rotating divisional HQs. For Iraq, at the time of the battle for Mosul, the land component commander was Major General Joseph Martin of 1st Infantry Division. Because of the concern with civilian casualties, any high-risk strikes had to be authorized by CENTCOM in Tampa.

When Ash Carter had become secretary of defense, he found the campaign moving at a ponderous pace. To speed things up, he loosened the rules of engagement and delegation of the Target Engagement Authority (TEA). As a first move, in October 2015, TEA was passed to CJTF–IR. Then it went to the brigadier generals running the strike cells in the Combined Joint Operations Center in Baghdad. Eventually, in August 2016, just before the battle for Mosul, it reached the colonels in these cells. This was a significant extension of the number of officers who could approve strikes. It ensured a 24-hour presence, avoiding 'don't wake the generals' delays. As the fighting became more intense, it became necessary for the local ground forces commander – an Iraqi or a Kurdish Peshmerga general – to authorize strikes, which required that the US battalion commanders serving as their advisers had to have the Target Engagement Authority. Until March 2017, some 90 per cent of air strikes were predetermined, with the rest authorized to support forces in direct contact with ISIS fighters. Once the battle for West Mosul began in earnest, this ratio was reversed.[56]

Key to their operations was the quality of the incoming intelligence. Lambeth describes 'heavy use of overhead full-motion video platforms that constantly monitored the dense, complex urban battlespace below'. Weapon-carrying Predator and Reaper drones loitered over the city, should opportunities arise for strikes. At any given time, there could be more than 40 platforms flying above Mosul, including these remotely piloted vehicles, strike aircraft, helicopters and reconnaissance aircraft.[57] According to General Martin, 'When we had relevant real time intelligence and the ability to strike, we had to be decisive.' In circumstances where there was need to act quickly but there could be risks in doing so, Martin stressed the importance of mutual trust between the advisers and the Iraqi units, as well as ensuring that there was sufficient capacity available to act as the local commanders wished.[58] However, the multitude of intelligence gatherers meant that there was often confusing duplication. Not all levels of the chain of command would be looking at the same imagery, or treating it in the same way.

The 'strike cells', considered a valuable innovation, brought together many players – 'pilots, sensor operators, intelligence experts, ground forces, weaponeering specialists, civilian-casualty-mitigation analysts, lawyers, even weather officers'. They were said to have boasted that 'with their video feeds and surveillance aircraft, they could understand what was happening on the battlefield as well as if they were there themselves'.[59] With delegated authority and a fast-moving battle, the cells conducted 'dynamic strikes', requested and implemented within hours or even minutes. Those authorizing the strikes were still asked to consider whether the target had been properly identified and the risks to civilians. But there was no expectation that all civilian deaths could be avoided, only that they had to be proportional to the 'expected military advantage gained'. This required knowledge of how the targets were being used by the enemy, as well as by civilians, so that the risk to both could be assessed.[60]

To what extent were the efforts to minimize casualties successful? By the time the Battle of Mosul concluded, the city contained some eight million tons of rubble (three times the mass of the Great Pyramid of Giza). The US-led coalition had carried out more than 1,250 strikes in the city, hitting thousands of targets with over 29,000 munitions. What was less clear was how many had died in the process. Official figures suggested around 1,000 civilian dead: independent investigations concluded that the number could be up to ten times higher, with about a third of the deaths the result of coalition or Iraqi bombardments.[61] Although the Pentagon acknowledged 1,417 civilian deaths in air strikes in the overall campaign against ISIS in Iraq and Syria, an investigation by the *New York Times* concluded that there were many more. As more evidence emerged of how the air strikes had been conducted, it became apparent not only that civilian deaths were higher than official estimates, but that little effort had been put into checking the numbers or explaining the causes, let alone holding anybody accountable. The information used to pick targets was faulty, often disastrously so, with suspicions aroused by activities those watching simply did not understand.

Why did those in the strike cells underestimate the risks of civilian deaths? Confirmation bias appears to be a major culprit. Information was interpreted in the light of a pre-existing belief, so that, for example, if people could be seen moving towards a fresh bomb site, they were assumed to be fighters and not civilian rescuers. If surveillance did not pick up people moving as normal in and out of their houses, it did not occur to the analysts that during the fast of Ramadan they were sleeping during the day. The quality of the footage was often poor, with insufficient on view to assess whether civilians were present or not. In some instances, a wider view would have shown civilians about to walk into a target. If there had been more time, as there was with the more deliberative strikes, these things might have been checked and more care taken. With dynamic strikes, there was not enough time to do a proper assessment of the risks to civilians. And, of course, ISIS was not inclined to make it any easier to assess these risks. Yet there were still few efforts made to assess the impact of individual strikes. Instead, reports of casualties were dismissed, or the death toll undercounted, so that no lessons were learned.[62] Perhaps that was not surprising when units were allowed to assess their own performance.

Furthermore, there was a readily available get-out clause when there was a desire to attack a target without bothering with the elaborate processes designed to protect civilians. This was to report an urgent need for self-defence. This might be fair when facing direct enemy fire, but it could also be invoked when observing individuals displaying 'hostile intent'. Interpreted broadly, this could give the strike cell considerable latitude. Hostile intent could be inferred from anything out of the ordinary. Invoking this clause to justify strikes was particularly favoured by a special forces unit known as Task Force 9 in charge of ground operations in Syria. By late 2018, self-defence accounted for about 80 per cent of the air strikes they called in. The American Air Force command in Qatar observed this with some concern, noting that details were added to justify strikes, for example by stating that an individual was carrying a gun, even though it was not visible in the drone footage. Task Force 9, however, was acting independently, and was not coordinating its activities with the operations centre in Qatar.

By early 2019, ISIS fighters were gathered in a farm by the Euphrates River near Baghuz in Syria as the setting for their last stand. Many civilians got away from the camp, but thousands remained. Some supported ISIS: most did not. Drones passed over the site regularly, building up a picture of the layout of the camp and the patterns of life of the residents. On 18 March 2019, ISIS launched an early morning counter-offensive. The fighters pressed forward firing rifles and launching grenades. Some of their forward fighters wore suicide vests. In response, numerous missiles were launched from drones, so many that they were all used. Still ISIS advanced. Local Syrian forces feared that they were about to be overrun and called for an air strike. There was one remaining, unarmed, drone. This tracked fighters moving through the camp to the area where women and children sheltered. The drone's camera did not have a particularly high definition. As the officer looking at the footage did not see any civilians, he gave the order to fire. This was done on grounds of self-defence. As no precision missiles were left, an F-15E dropped a 500-pound bomb on the target. Soon, as people fled the blast site, it dropped two 2,000-pound bombs. All this took 12 minutes.

As this was going on, a team in Qatar were watching the same area, only they had access to a stream of footage from a high-definition drone and, instead of seeing committed fighters moving into position, they saw a few men engaging with the many civilians around them. They were, however, unaware that an air strike was being planned and they had not been asked by Task Force 9 to check the site for civilians. They saw the bombs being dropped and their impact with 'stunned disbelief'. An initial damage assessment quickly found that there were about 70 dead. A legal officer immediately flagged the strike as a possible war crime that required an investigation, but then moves were made to conceal the extent of the strike, sanitizing reports, and not informing senior leaders. An official investigation was begun, but got nowhere. [63]

RUSSIA IN SYRIA

There is a pertinent point of comparison for the American campaign against ISIS. As it was going on, the Russians were working with Syrian forces to push rebels out of the key cities. In 2015, President Putin had decided to join the war by backing Syrian President Assad, whose position was then desperate, with his army suffering from casualties, desertions and defections, and rebels gearing up to cut off his capital, Damascus, from the Mediterranean coast. In eastern Syria, ISIS was well established. Aleppo, which had seen intense fighting since July 2012, was not yet lost to the rebels, but the only road in for government forces was vulnerable to interdiction.[64] Assad's regime was propped up by Iran and Shi'ite groups, such as Hezbollah. In the early summer of 2015, Major General Qassim Soleimani, commander of the Iranian Revolutionary Guards Corps Quds Force, visited Moscow to seek help.[65] He found a willing audience. Putin had just seen Ukraine turn away from Russia. Now he faced losing one of his few remaining overseas partners. Russia already had a naval facility in Tartus, which would be useful should an intervention be agreed. Assad's survival would deal a blow to the United States and its allies. Yet Putin also shared their fear of ISIS, because of its potential influence in Russia and neighbouring states with large Muslim populations. Compared with Ukraine there was no issue with international law, because Russia would be supporting an established government. There would be no need for pretence. This would be a display of Russian power, about which Putin could boast rather than dissemble.

There were some similarities between the American and Russian responses. Putin also had no intention of risking unpopularity at home by inserting a substantial number of ground forces into Syria. He agreed to provide air power and arms supplies, while the Iranians promised to provide fighters to bolster Assad's flagging army. The air commitment was not large. The deployment varied from 30 to 50 combat aircraft and 16 to 40 helicopters. In August 2015, it was agreed that the Russian aviation group would use the Hmeimim airbase in Latakia Province.[66] By the end of September, Russian air assets were in place, along with some 5,000 personnel. There were artillery and rocket contingents from the Rocket Ground Forces.[67]

It was telling too that the sort of pressure for delegated authority that had shaped the American-led campaign against ISIS also influenced the Russian. At first, as the chief of the Russian general staff, Army General Valery Gerasimov, recalled, collaboration between all the various detachments and Russian aerospace forces, and sorting out the logistics, were difficult.[68] The Russians effectively provided the leadership for the Syrian army. There were military advisers in every Syrian unit, whether battalion, brigade, regiment or division, planning operations. They also served as forward air controllers, though the more strategic weapons, such as air-launched cruise missiles, heavy bombers, land attack missiles and carrier-launched strike aircraft, were coordinated by the National Defence Command Centre in Moscow.[69] From December 2015, the Russians began to use Israeli Forpost drones to provide real-time imagery, which had an almost immediate impact on operational effectiveness.[70] By streamlining the command arrangements, the Russians were able to increase the tempo of combat management between 20 and 30 per cent. Although they did not use many precision-guided munitions, better intelligence, including the real-time information provided by drones, enabled them to use unguided munitions more effectively, although still with heavy civilian casualties.[71] The difference with the American campaign was that this was not necessarily seen as a failure.

According to the Syrian Observatory on Human Rights, Russian airstrikes in Syria had killed 20,697 people by January 2022, of whom 8,683 were civilians, including 2,108 children under the age of 18.[72] The tempo of the American campaign led to the processes intended to prevent civilian losses being circumvented or rushed. In the Russian campaign, not only were there fewer concerns over collateral damage, but there was deliberate targeting of civilian facilities, notably hospitals. This had been a feature of the Syrian regime's strategy from early in the war, as they sought to make life miserable for populations supporting the rebels. The practice did not stop when the Russians came to support Assad's campaign.[73] In June 2021, Physicians for Human Rights, one of a number of NGOs monitoring the situation, reported that from the start of the conflict there had been 600 attacks on at least 350 health facilities, leading to the deaths of 930 medical personnel, in addition to patients and other civilians.[74] Of these, 540 could be shown to have been carried out by the Syrian government and its allies, including the Russians.

These attacks were not random but closely connected to offensives against rebel-held areas, designed to encourage populations to abandon strongholds. In the spring of 2019, the Russian-backed Syrian government campaign focused on Idlib, one of the last rebel-controlled areas. In June 2019, it was reported that 25 medical facilities had been bombed. One disturbing feature was that, in nine cases, the medical staff had shared the coordinates of the facilities with the United Nations, in the hope that this would mean that they were not attacked. In turn these coordinates were shared with the Russians. As a result, they were all attacked. One hospital had already been hit twice and so had been moved into a mountain cave. It was still bombed.[75] The *New York Times* used Russian Air Force radio recordings, plane-spotter logs and witness accounts to demonstrate that Russian pilots were responsible for attacks against four hospitals on 5 May 2019.[76] By mid-September, 54 hospitals and clinics in opposition territory had been attacked. As we have seen, the readiness to attack civilian life in this way had been a feature of the war in Chechnya, and presaged what was to happen to Ukraine in 2022.

It, of course, made little difference to the victims or their families whether they were killed because of a tragic error or a deliberate strategy, or whether others would have died in even greater numbers if ISIS had not been defeated. It does, however, illustrate the operational choices facing commanders fighting 'wars among the people', according to whether the aim is to win over a suspicious population or to intimidate and even expel a population deemed to be irredeemably hostile. The counter-insurgency model adopted by the Americans assumed that, with the right combination of methods, populations could be won over, although the field manual also cautioned that: 'Eventually all foreign armies are seen as interlopers or occupiers.'[77] Either way, once these campaigns were conducted by the interloping power largely using air power, against which their opponents could do little, they were a long way from the heroics of 'exemplary risk-taking'.

16

Past, Present and Future of Command

He who wishes to be obeyed must know how to command.
Niccolo Machiavelli, *The Prince*

The years since the Korean War have seen transformational changes in the international system and the theory and practice of war. These have had a major impact on command.

In 1950, the memories of the great wars of the first half of the twentieth century were fresh. The stockpile of atomic bombs available to the United States was small and thermonuclear weapons were still a few years away; the Korean War was therefore fought with the systems and tactics of the Second World War. But, over time, the links with this war were broken. Periods of antagonism came and went without the major powers fighting each other directly. A third in a sequence of world wars was avoided for a number of compelling reasons, including memories of the death, destruction and suffering caused by past wars. But, after 1945, there was an added ingredient – the prospect of massive nuclear exchanges. Plans to fight a major war without using them required keeping these weapons in reserve, their only role to deter the enemy's nuclear arsenal. It was not hard to imagine the mechanisms of escalation: a state refusing to accept defeat when it could still conjure up a nuclear threat; one of those terrible misjudgements that were a staple of Cold War literature, in which a cataclysm was triggered inadvertently; a deluded confidence that a credible way to 'win' a nuclear war had been found. It was optimistic to assume that any conflict presented as a cataclysmic struggle for regional or world domination could end with the most powerful weapons left in storage. The speed with which these issues rushed to the fore during the high-intensity Russo-Ukrainian War of 2022, launched by the obsessive leader of a nuclear power, serves as a disturbing reminder of the potential fragility of restraints.

In Korea, Truman was determined to keep the war limited, and this led to his clash with MacArthur and his belief that all means should be employed in the pursuit of victory. During the Cuban Missile Crisis, Kennedy insisted that US moves must be controlled and measured, and this led to a clash with the Joint Chiefs of Staff, who were sure he was missing a chance to get rid of communism in Cuba. Later wars saw other limits imposed. When intervening in distant conflicts, high and persistent casualties increasingly came to be seen as domestically intolerable. Once it became possible to hit targets more precisely with 'smart' weapons, then there were even fewer excuses for hurting non-combatants while seeking out combatants, as in Kosovo. The rough and often cruel methods used when flushing out enemy fighters hiding among their people adopted during the colonial and post-colonial wars of the 1950s and 1960s came to be recognized, at least in the West, as being both unacceptable and counterproductive. An acknowledgement of the importance – military as well as moral – of the 'hearts and minds' of the people set limits on counter insurgency campaigns, although, as we saw in the previous chapter, the practice often fell short of the principle, and in other cases (East Pakistan and Syria) the principle was explicitly rejected. Sometimes limitation in means followed from strictly limited war aims, as with the liberation of Kuwait in 1991. Often the UN Security Council stepped in, pushing ceasefires on reluctant belligerents to stop further bloodshed, as in the Arab-Israeli and Indo-Pakistani wars. Sometimes geography made the difference. Stretched supply lines restricted what was available to front-line commanders, as in the 1982 Falklands War.

These limits faced by commanders, whether the result of politically determined boundaries or simply a scarcity of resources, created many of the tensions explored in this book. They led to awkward choices: whether to consolidate a defensive position or rush into a risky offensive, reinforcing some divisions at the expense of others; giving priority to air strikes against the enemy's advancing troops or disrupting its supply lines to the rear; insisting on keeping vital assets safe, even though this meant sacrificing others; leaving one's own troops more exposed, to reduce the risk of civilian casualties; pushing hard against the enemy, even though this made allies uneasy, and generally trying to get the military and diplomatic strategies to align.

How these choices were made by commanders depended on many factors. An obvious one was the interests at stake. Choices that might go one way when the existence of the state was threatened might go another away when engaged in a more discretionary intervention away from home. Another was the whether the decisions were being taken in a dictatorship or a democracy. A third was the quality of the command arrangements, including the communications networks. And then, of course, the characters and perspectives of individuals mattered. In this book, we have come across dictators who denied themselves critical advice as they made reckless gambles; political leaders furious with unresponsive field commanders, and field commanders stunned that senior policymakers would not recognize their predicaments; egotistical generals, convinced they knew better than anyone else what was good for their country, who harassed subordinates trying to do the right thing in deteriorating conditions; earnest revolutionaries on an ideological mission; unruly militia leaders unsure who would respond to their orders; CIA agents calling in air strikes; and presidents checking targets to minimize civilian casualties. There is no simple pattern. The varieties of choices discussed in this book and how they were made reflect the great variety of conflicts and command decisions between Korea and the present.

THE CHANGING CHARACTER
OF COMMAND

Yet we can also see how the practice of command has evolved in response to the changing character of war. Conventional campaigns have become more complex to manage. There have been substantial technological advances affecting the familiar components of air, sea and land warfare, but also the introduction of new elements. American preparations for a major war against a 'peer competitor', that is, another great power, now involve separate provisions for space, cyber and information. The challenges of command have moved beyond collecting information, organizing logistics, and planning and then executing campaigns, to synchronizing many disparate activities – while under pressure to make quick decisions to keep up with the pace of battle. Meanwhile, complex counter-insurgencies have required commanders to direct and motivate their own units, while working with allies, building up the capacity of friendly indigenous forces, and keeping the population on side. International and non-governmental organizations have sought to complement the military effort by improving both governance and social and economic conditions. In addition, private military companies have been assigned tasks once handled by regular forces. All these developments have raised their own problems of coordination.

Anthony King argues that the increasing demands of command have made it progressively more 'collective'. Decision-making authority has had to be more widely distributed 'to empowered subordinates, forming executive teams, closely united around a common understanding of the mission'.[1] British General David Richards observed that the modern commander must be an 'entrepreneurial networker and communicator rather than a dictator',[2] Stanley McChrystal has written about the importance of teamwork[3] and Eitan Shamir has spoken of command as a 'collaborative effort'.[4] For this reason, staffs have grown and the senior commander has become more dependent on their quality. Yet military organizations remain hierarchical, and, at the heart of the exercise of command, personal responsibility and accountability are still essential. In the end, at each level, one individual is answerable for the decisions taken. As David Petraeus, one of the more successful American generals of recent times, observed to King: 'There is one commander. He is the guy. Everyone else is in support of him.'[5]

King's example of the modern form of collective command is the command headquarters set up by UK Major General Nick Carter in Afghanistan for operations in and around Kandahar City in 2009–2010. It covered an area of 78,000 square miles, where some 4.2 million people lived. His Combined Joint Task Force involved 60,000 soldiers, organized in eight brigade teams, from 11 different nationalities. There were 800 personnel in the headquarters staff. Carter developed a strong group of deputies around him to smooth what might have otherwise been troubled relations among the component parts of his Task Force. He still spent much of his time negotiating, with not only the corps command above him and six one-star brigadiers below, but also the heads of the national contingents, the various organizations dealing with aid and development, and the local Afghan population. In this respect, he was more 'than a purely military commander'. Carter 'also assumed the role of a pro-consul, influencing military, political and civil domains. Indeed, many of his decisions were purely political.'[6]

The complex politics of these operations was not the only reason for the size of the headquarters. A quarter of Carter's staff were on the intelligence side, because of the sheer volume of information coming in. In the past, when information was scarce, commanders would be forming judgements with only scraps of hard intelligence on enemy positions, while they waited anxiously for messages from the front. They are now inundated with information from all directions. This must be processed, assessed and presented in a form that provides a useful appreciation of an unfolding situation, rather than as a mass of incomprehensible data. All this must be done sufficiently quickly to be still current by the time it reaches the commander. With information always coming in, this requires shift work. There are also incentives for people to take time away from other duties to keep themselves abreast of the latest information. At the height of operations in Iraq, about 7,000 people watched the Operations and Intelligence Briefing on the Joint Special Operations Command video teleconference (VTC) for up to two hours each day.[7]

This combination of political complexity and information overload explains much of the growth of command headquarters over recent decades, but the sheer extent of the growth suggests that other factors are at work too. The great battles of the Second World War were waged by headquarters that would now seem ridiculously small. The size of staff did not grow markedly through the 1970s. It was only after the end of the Cold War that serious growth began. By the late 2010s, at 400 staff officers, a typical American divisional headquarters was ten times the size of a 1940s headquarters, and at least four times the size of its Cold War equivalent.[8]

Jim Storr, a former senior British officer, argues that this growth in the size of command headquarters has been pushed up by bureaucratic and doctrinal considerations and has come at the cost of effectiveness and responsiveness. He assesses them to be top heavy in senior officers. Analyses of the performance of the commands in the wars against Iraq in 1991 and 2003 found that the bulk of the useful work was done by captains and majors; the multiple layers above them added little of value, and contributed to duplication and inefficiency.

With large staffs come the bureaucratic problems that are familiar in any organization – awkward characters as well as trusted colleagues, and a multiplication of personnel issues. Once planning for operations follows set procedures it becomes dominated by the necessity to have all the right inputs, rather than focusing on the quality and timeliness of the outputs. Once planning becomes separate from the conduct of operations, it tends to neglect the problems those executing the plans are likely to face, so that the operators can come to distrust the planners. The commander's ability to keep track of what is going on is reduced, including what subordinates are being asked to accomplish and their success in doing so. Requiring headquarters to work round the clock can be another cause of incoherent and disjointed planning.[9]

That headquarters have been able to grow so noticeably is in part a function of their static nature. When headquarters had to be on the move, following the ebb and flow of battle, and when communications were less reliable, so commanders had to stay in close touch with their subordinates, there were incentives to keep staff numbers down. Limits on the size of their command posts were set by the number that could be transported at a time. Also, in fast-moving situations, there might be no time for written orders. It would all be done through direct communications. But in the post-Cold War interventions, the headquarters had fixed locations. With improved mobility and communications, armies have spread out. In Afghanistan, a company of fewer than 100 soldiers held territory that would have been held by two Civil War armies of 200,000 men in 1863, or been controlled by a reinforced mechanized battalion some 1,000 strong during the 1991 war against Iraq.[10] With their networked communications, junior officers could check with their superiors before acting, and their superiors could expect to be involved. There was no longer the excuse that it was pointless consulting superior officers, or even the highest political authorities, because they would be inadequately briefed and it would take too long to wait for their advice.

Yet, even though it has become increasingly easy to keep senior commanders in the loop, there has been pressure to delegate decision-making when engaged in high-tempo operations. Interest in 'mission command' developed in the United States during the later stages of the Cold War, when there was a growing enthusiasm for manoeuvre warfare, on the assumption that speed of movement and decision was essential to victory.[11] This led to proposals to streamline the chain of command, so that key decisions did not have to be taken by a disputatious committee, hampered by interservice rivalries or a bureaucratic determination to be sure that the right people had been consulted or informed. Both the United States and United Kingdom established chains of command that bypassed the chiefs of staff, and, in the US case, the chairman of the Chiefs, to strengthen the line with the civilian leadership. In the United Kingdom, the Permanent Joint Headquarters came to deal with all operations. In the United States, the combatant commanders focused on specific regions. The Russians also reformed their command structure to reduce the number of echelons in command operations, cutting decision-time and improving the flow of analyses and information between them.[12]

The American system was more streamlined in terms of the relations between civilian policymakers, but less so once the combatant commanders took over. There were new problems of coordination when a conflict needed to be managed by, for example, both European and Central commands. For reasons already shown, for example in the Battle of Tora Bora in 2001, these commands could become muscle-bound, with too many layers, and key components spread too wide geographically. They reproduced the problems they were supposed to solve. These regional commands were supposed to be able to formulate plans and conduct operations without having to worry about management and budgetary issues. In practice, their performance was at best mixed, with cumbersome organizations that struggled to focus.[13] Meanwhile, the pace of operations encouraged decentralization. As we have seen, the growing importance of air power as a factor in land battles added to the importance of the forward air controllers, who called in strikes, and had to do so when the targets might soon escape and there was a risk of hitting civilians.

The American-led campaigns against the Taliban and ISIS both demonstrate that, however much the political imperatives of contemporary warfare favour restraint and limitation, once the pace of combat picks up and tactical decisions have to be made at great speed, there are counter-imperatives favouring delegation down the chain of command. Until 2016, not only were plans formed at the top, but all the supporting functions were also coordinated there, including intelligence, surveillance, cyber and information operations. This was too slow and cumbersome. Instead of relying on the senior commander to synchronize the different activities, individual units had to 'self-synchronize'. The higher commands set the terms for operations, but still needed 'to encourage and regulate the actions of other organizations' over which they had 'little or no direct control'. Information-sharing across organizational and national boundaries remained challenging. Unavoidably, more responsibility had to be pushed onto the front line to get them to cooperate and talk to each other. Junior commanders made the most of the tactical freedom this gave them, often resisting restrictions imposed from above on planned action and finding ways to get round procedures that were seen as inhibiting and constraining. Only activities which were more obviously political in nature continued to be held by the centre. One colonel observed of the fight against ISIS: 'It is far easier to drop a bomb in this theater than it is to send a tweet.'[14]

DELEGATED DECISION-MAKING

The need to delegate decision-making because of the imperatives of a demanding campaign reinforces the mission command approach. The underlying principle is that subordinate commanders invariably have a better grasp of their own situation. This was Sharon's rationale for regularly disregarding orders from his superiors. By this argument, instead of front-line commanders being encumbered with unhelpful detail, they should be encouraged to work out their own plans and tactics, so long as they are in line with the overall campaign's objectives, to facilitate speedier responses to changing situations. Significant advantages can be gained by making decisions faster than the opponent.

Moreover, when there is potential for cyberattacks (or just direct hits) on command headquarters, there is a risk of junior officers finding themselves on their own, cut off from their superiors. Communications can get disrupted or information flows clogged up by the sheer volume of messages. In such circumstances, subordinate commands must be empowered at the very least to 'carry out last mission orders' as best they can, adapting to the circumstances in which they find themselves.

There are other arguments for delegation. There can be difficulties passing on new orders regularly to units of another country with a different language. David Richards explained why he put in a lot of effort framing orders based on his intent for a multinational command:

> On the military side, I had to get my subordinates, from whatever country, to get accustomed to working to the Commander's Intent, a formal

498

written summary of my objectives, what was required of them and why. I had to accept that every country would probably interpret their orders differently and do things in ways that I had not anticipated. I quickly began to see that. So I put a lot of effort into my Intent. I then told my commanders: 'You do it as you wish, but that's what you've got to achieve.'[15]

Lastly, this sort of delegation should provide the senior commander with more time to worry about the bigger picture. Even without having to think about a particular subordinate's situation, the tempo of any future large-scale war might well leave senior commanders scrambling to make sense of what is going on around the theatre of operations and to work out how they should allocate what may be increasingly scarce reserve forces and direct their firepower.

Yet some very human factors at work in the decision-making process provide grounds for caution when considering just how much delegation will take place in future operations. Individual commanders, at whatever level, are apt to believe that they are best placed to take the key decisions. Mission command requires senior officers to trust juniors, relying on their grasp of the objectives, the local political sensitivities and the rules of engagement. Conrad Crane has reported how his students at the US Army War College, when asked what mission command means, 'usually come up with a somewhat contradictory definition that basically allows them to do whatever they wish within loose guidelines from their superiors, while their subordinates do exactly what they are supposed to do'.[16]

With the decentralization of military decision-making comes the decentralization of political decision-making. During the 1990s, there was talk of a 'strategic corporal', able to 'make well-reasoned and *independent* decisions under extreme stress – decisions that will likely be subject to the harsh scrutiny of both the media and the court of public opinion'. The strategic corporal's actions would 'potentially influence not only the immediate tactical situation, but the operational and strategic levels as well', and so the 'outcome of the larger operation'.[17] There are a number of ways in which an apparently tactical decision can have large political consequences, especially if it is in some way 'deviant', that is, goes against the claimed purposes of an operation, for example the use of torture.[18] There can be a greater awareness now of what units are up to because of the ease with which soldiers can post on social media, allowing for activities to be tracked and reported. Whatever has been communicated about the commander's intent, there will always be a possibility of units that have gone 'rogue' or simply come up against situations for which they have no guidance. Their superiors will need to know about these events, and, where necessary, deal with any local and international political fallout.

So long as the communications networks are working, operational decisions can easily be passed up to superiors to the highest level, especially those decisions that might have large political implications. It is now possible for political leaders to feel part of the action, and engaged in operational decisions, in ways that would have been in practice impossible, but also considered inappropriate interference, in earlier times. Senior commanders, and even presidents, can spend hours looking at images coming back from drones, consulting with legal advisers on whether an individual, perhaps a suspected terrorist, should be killed. They can also look over the shoulders of field commanders as they are making critical choices while fulfilling a mission. Think of the images of President Obama and his national security team watching the special forces raid to take out Osama bin Laden in Pakistan in 2011. Richards, when UK chief of the defence staff, and despite his own preference for delegating decisions, observed the National Security Council discuss the redeployment of 120 men in Afghanistan, and wondered whether that was the best use of time for busy ministers. Governments, he noted, tend to focus on the 'near-term and the tactical as opposed to the big foreign policy and strategic issues'.[19]

The more self-sufficient the unit the more it should be able to cope without central support, but it will always be dependent upon its headquarters for some capabilities, including intelligence, surveillance and reconnaissance, as well as supporting firepower and, where necessary, reserves should it get into trouble. Not all these needs will be met. What happens when a local initiative has the effect of substituting new operational goals for those originally assigned? Or when the initiatives cannot be taken unless more resources are released from the centre? A force designed to be self-sufficient might find itself in difficulties facing an unexpectedly formidable opponent. In the early days on Israel's southern front in the October War of 1973, confused information from the front led to unrealistic guidance from the centre, leading to commanders working at cross purposes and unable to provide mutual support.

In practice, in a conflict of any complexity and intensity, the command arrangements will not follow a neat organizational diagram. There will be decisions that have to be hauled back to the centre because that is the only place that priorities can be decided and strategic direction determined; yet, if junior officers are left waiting for new orders, or must seek approval for every move, operations may grind to a halt. New communications technologies offer the prospect of a much smoother relationship between senior commanders and all subordinate commanders, but their value means that the enemy will seek to disrupt them, replacing active conversations with silence, able to listen in to messages that disclose too much. The test of war can soon show up rigidities in command relationships and technological dependencies. As B. A. Friedman observes, the best arrangement will be one that 'is most appropriate for the mission, situation, and forces available'. Centralized command suits situations that require tight coordination and involve relatively inexperienced troops and junior leaders, while 'highly trained, cohesive troops, led by experienced commanders who are well known and trusted by subordinates and each other can operate in a more decentralised manner'.[20] The problems come when operations that require decentralized forms of command must be conducted by forces that are more suited to centralized forms.

This is what happened to Russian forces when they went to war against Ukraine. As noted in chapter 12, the Russian command systems were poor and easily disrupted. This was despite expectations that Russian investment in reforms of their command and control systems, overseen by Defence Minister Shoigu and Chief of the General Staff Gerasimov, meant that they would be fit for purpose. The reforms had followed the US pattern of flattening the command structure, removing the individual services from an operational role, and improving coordination among combat arms. They had already paid dividends when it came to the annexation of Crimea and the campaign in Syria.[21] But these were limited operations against weak opponents. The 2022 campaign was far larger and more complex and against a capable and astute opponent, and this time the command system failed.

This failure, along with the Russian army's problems, from the ambition of the early offensive moves to the problems with logistics, communications and poor morale, was a consequence of underestimating the Ukrainians. The senior commanders had not appreciated the situation they were about to enter and so had not designed a plan of campaign appropriate to the capabilities of their forces. Ordinary soldiers had little idea of why they were in Ukraine and what they were supposed to do.

Because of the decision to invade from four directions, the headquarters of four military districts were involved. Each was required to coordinate air, army aviation, airborne, missile and special forces, with the Southern Military District also in charge of naval and amphibious forces. The strategic integration of the operation took place at the National Defence Control Centre inside the Russian Ministry of Defence building in Moscow, presided over by Defence Minister Sergei Shoigu. In April the Southern Military District, which had run the separatist operations from 2014, was assigned responsibility for coordinating operations in Ukraine.

This was an operation on a scale beyond anything attempted recently, and against an enemy that was stronger than expected. Nor could the Russians use all their assets as they would wish. Because the Ukrainian air force was still operating, Russian airborne command and early warning systems had to stay out of range.[22] The lack of secure communications on the Russian side meant that commanders ended up talking to their units using cell phones and other unsecure channels. All this helped Ukraine gather intelligence and intercept key targets. Meanwhile social media enabled Ukrainians to acquire intelligence from civilian sources, keep track of Russian movements, record engagements and destroyed equipment, and wage an effective information campaign to garner international support. NATO countries provided Ukrainian forces with electronic warfare equipment capable of interrupting Russian transmissions and allowing them to target Russian command posts. As a result of these problems, different units ended up competing for resources rather than coordinating their efforts, Senior officers had to move up the line as their forward units hit problems. This led to a number of generals being killed.[23]

The last time the Russian military had been seriously challenged had been during the First Chechen War, and in the end they had found a way to prevail, without having to care about the costs being imposed on civilians. In Syria, officers could use radios and cell phones with no concerns about interference or tracking.[24] They were not fighting the land war, and the enemy lacked serious air defences or an air force of its own.

One Ukrainian pilot observed that in this war their Russian counter-parts were complacent and 'absolutely not ready for resistance':

> Syria was just a training range for them. They were working at high altitudes or medium altitudes without real resistance. [In Ukraine] they were prepared for typical missions in good weather conditions and with total dominance of all technologies, like GPS systems and electronic warfare systems. But here in Ukraine, there is an absolutely different situation. We use much more advanced systems than in Syria.[25]

It was also some time since lower-level commanders had needed to think for themselves and adapt to new situations. An American volunteer fighting with the Ukrainians observed: 'The Russians have no imagination. They would shell our positions, attack in large formations, and when their assaults failed, do it all over again. Meanwhile, the Ukrainians would raid the Russian lines in small groups night after night, wearing them down.' When the plan failed, so did the command system.[26]

A classic example in the war with Ukraine was the battle for Chornobayivka airfield near Kherson airport. Having been told to use it as an operating base, Russian troops flew in in helicopters, only for them to be blown up by Ukrainian units close by. Officers kept on ordering troops and heavy equipment in before securing it allowing the Ukrainians to destroy the equipment with direct strikes, leading to the deaths of many troops and two Russian generals. To a Ukrainian officer, this reflected the old Soviet culture of fulfilling orders without question. 'They are more afraid of being punished by commanders than failing their mission or losing their subordinates.' Units had to await orders from their higher commands when they faced unexpected difficulties. As former US Army General Mark Hertling observed, 'Unlike U.S. and other Western militaries, the Russian military does not have noncommissioned officers. Troops are left floundering when their original orders don't pan out.'[27] By contrast, the Ukrainians met the conditions for effective delegated command: mutual trust between the different levels of command; distributed capabilities that could be operated by small, self-sufficient units; strong junior leadership, partly because of the development of NCOs but also because of experienced veterans coming into the ranks on mobilisation; and high motivation and commitment to the core purpose of defending the homeland.

INTELLIGENCE,
HUMAN AND ARTIFICIAL

New technologies will almost certainly change command relationships in the future. In the 1990s, the remarkable improvements in sensing and communications technologies opened up the prospect that the 'fog of war' would be dispelled and that there would be almost perfect situational awareness.[28] As the next set of wars involved enemies who knew how to hide, whether in the country or in cities, merging with the civilian population, the fog of war remained. Concealment, deception and pure confusion were still present. Nonetheless, the ability to track developments on the ground and transmit information to all levels of commands has improved dramatically. Vital intelligence is no longer scarce, and it is easily accessible. The extraordinary capabilities of modern sensor technologies mean that the moves of prospective enemies can be monitored constantly, so that even small changes in deployments and preparations can be noted. While intelligence gathering has been transformed, and should alert civilian and military policymakers to dangers and opportunities, it is still not necessarily predictive – even the best intelligence can be subject to a range of interpretations. This could be seen with the intense speculation surrounding the Russian military build-up around Ukraine from late 2021.

This limitation needs to be kept in mind when considering the claims made for artificial intelligence (AI) as potentially transformational in its influence on the practice of warfare and the exercise of command. It has become more important as vast amounts of data are acquired, stored and processed. AI will enable machines to support human decision-making. Perhaps the machines might make the decisions themselves?

Some types of operations already depend on handing over vital calculations to computers. Contrast how Fighter Command in the United Kingdom managed the Battle of Britain in 1940 with Israel's Iron Dome air defence system. In 1940, radars, the most advanced sensors of their time, backed up by spotters on the ground, provided vital information about incoming attacks to a command centre that would send urgent messages to units to scramble to get aircraft in the air and take on the invaders. With the Iron Dome this is all achieved without human intervention: the trajectory of incoming rockets is tracked; those likely to miss important targets are left alone as interceptor missiles are directed to those that might. Future offensive operations might exploit AI's ability to coordinate and direct numerous distributed units. Swarms of autonomous vehicles could come together, destroying potential targets almost as soon as they are picked up.

The advantage of an AI commander will be in the acquisition and analysis of a mass of information from disparate sources, to make sense of developing situations. It would be possible, albeit worrying for reasons of both prudence and ethics, for an AI commander to launch lethal weapons to manoeuvre and fire on their own, without requiring further human interventions. An AI commander would not need to forge bonds of understanding and comradeship, while developing trust, which is what a human commander must do when exercising mission command. 'You don't need the inspirational NCO with years of experience and a combat ribbon ... And you don't need the senior officer with martial bearing and inspiring pre-battle speeches.'[29] Get the algorithms right and the best way to achieve the commander's intent with the available systems will be computed in a matter of seconds. Robert Work, a former deputy secretary at the Pentagon and enthusiastic promoter of AI, described it as a potential source of *coup d'œil*, the intuitive grasp of what was happening on the battlefield, which, as noted in the introduction, was seen in Napoleon's time as a feature of a great general.[30]

Figures as illustrious as Henry Kissinger and Eric Schmidt, former head of Google, have argued that 'nonhuman logic' will transform strategy. A key theme in their analysis is that AI calculations that disregard the conventional wisdom and established human expectations will generate insights and exert influence in ways that will surprise and occasionally unsettle practitioners – even those who own the systems. They will introduce even more unpredictability:

> How does one develop a strategy – offensive or defensive – for something that perceives aspects of the environment that humans may not, or may not as quickly, and that can learn and change through processes that, in some cases, exceed the pace or range of human thought?[31]

Yet, set against a human commander, an AI commander will still have many drawbacks. Machines cannot lead by their brave example, act on hunches, or explain the rationales for their decisions to humans. They have no moral sense or personal fear. They might be able to manage multiple tasks, but would struggle to switch to a wholly new endeavour. Moreover, because AI is about machine learning, situations with many new features may spook the AI commander. As for a human commander, experience will still inform future expectations. Machines learn through pattern recognition, label matching and data classification, and new data might not match what it has been trained to receive and act upon. Unlike a human commander, an AI commander may fail to attach significance to a few odd points in the incoming data that would attract human curiosity. Instead, anomalous data may lead to perverse decisions. The complexity and confusion of future battlefields, as targets disperse and deceive, could leave an AI commander as baffled as a human commander, but without the ability to reappraise the situation or the restraint to hold back.[32] There will always be questions about whether the systems will work as intended, especially those that have not yet actually been tested in battle conditions, and are up against enemy systems designed to confuse and disrupt their efforts.

We can also assume that human commanders will be reluctant to cede their authority. Operational commanders are already familiar with the automated decision-making that allows weapons systems to pick on targets and attack them in fractions of a second. The developing possibilities of AI may mean that, even while they are being kept in the loop, commanders may be presented with options for managing a situation, which may be counter-intuitive and impossible to interrogate. Few expect to see AI guiding the higher command decisions soon. As Kenneth Payne notes, AI may be tactically brilliant but it is strategically banal.[33] Frank Hoffman offers a similar thought:

> Surely, war's essence as politically directed violence remains its most enduring aspect. The 'Face of Battle' in the future will retain the chaos of close quarter battle, but more destruction may be generated by swarms of unmanned platforms guided by organic algorithms. Yet, at the strategic level, political figures and their military advisors will be responsible for directing war and for electing the time and place of battle.[34]

CHINESE COMMAND: RED OR EXPERT?

One country investing heavily in AI is the People's Republic of China. China has identified AI as a vital technology that should enable it not only to catch up with the United States in information and communication technologies, but even to cut a corner so that it can move ahead. To explain the focus, it is necessary to put it in the context of China's efforts to turn itself into a military power capable of challenging the United States in all domains.

China has barely appeared in this book since the first chapter on the Korean War, when its sudden intervention upended Douglas MacArthur's plans for a quick victory. It fought limited wars against India in 1962 and Vietnam in 1979, but that was before it became an economic superpower and began to build up its armed forces at a remarkable rate. Since Xi Jinping became general secretary of the Chinese Communist Party (CCP) in 2012 and president of the People's Republic of China the next year, the country has become even more assertive and more focused on its military capabilities.

This has extended to command capabilities. Concerns about the lack of operational experience of its senior commanders – described as suffering from a 'peace disease'[35] – led to efforts to improve their quality. These concerns were grouped together as the 'Three Whethers':

(1) Whether our armed forces can constantly maintain the party's absolute leadership;
(2) whether they can fight victoriously when needed by the party and the people; and
(3) whether commanders at all levels are competent to lead forces and command in war.

Reforms to deal with problems 'above the neck', that is political direction and the organization of the higher command, were set in motion in September 2013 and were largely completed by February 2016. The aim, following Western countries, was to streamline the chain of command, so that there was more of a direct link between the political leadership and the theatre commanders. The Central Military Committee of the Communist Party would provide overall management of the armed forces. Theatre commands would focus on operations. The individual services would manage force building. More opportunities for initiatives would be granted to junior officers.[36]

With a move away from preparing for a dogged territorial defence to more offensive operations, the role of the army could be reduced, while those of the navy, air force and strategic rocket divisions were elevated. The service departments, which previously had command responsibilities, were demoted, left to deal with personnel and equipment issues. More emphasis was put on new capabilities, including cyberspace and electronic and information warfare, and the command structure was geared to joint operations. There was to be no cumbersome transition from a peace to a war footing. The slogan for a more simplified chain of command was *Ping Zhan Yi Ti* ('peace and war as one'). Another slogan refers to the 'three modernizations' of mechanization, informatization and intelligentization. This reflected beliefs in the possibility of using disruptive technologies to gain strategic advantage, improving their own decision-making while confusing and paralysing the enemy's.[37]

There was, however, another factor in the reforms, which raised questions about the aspiration for quick decision-making. The reforms were part of a shake-up of the Chinese political system. Xi considered his predecessor Hu Jintao to have been weak and the Politburo Standing Committee slow-moving, with its members cultivating their own power bases. Once President Xi introduced sweeping anti-corruption measures, which he used to purge his enemies as well as the evident crooks, he consolidated his own position, ending the two-term limit on the Chinese presidency intended to prevent a dictatorship. His image as a worthy successor to Mao Zedong and Deng Xiaoping, his most substantial predecessors, was cultivated, notably by demands that his ideological contributions should be studied diligently. Loyalists were put into key party positions. From 2015, he cracked down on dissent, insisting on conformity of thought following lines he set down.

Reining in the army was important to this strategy. Many officers were purged as part of the anti-corruption campaign. The People's Liberation Army (PLA) had always been accountable to the party and not the state, with the Central Military Commission (CMC), a committee of the Communist Party, the key body. As party members, officers were required to study the party's constitution and regulations, and Xi's speeches. There was no straightforward equivalent to the US secretary of defense. The person with that formal position was well outside the formal chain of command.[38] The vice chairman of the CMC, Zhang Youxia, was an old friend of Xi's and reported directly to him. Unusually for China's senior military figures, Zhang had combat experience in the 1979 war with Vietnam. Six of the commission's seven members were career military officers. Xi, the only civilian, chaired the CMC. In April 2016, after the last of the reforms had been announced, Xi visited the People's Liberation Army new joint command centre. Instead of wearing a green suit in the style of Mao Zedong, he put on camouflage fatigues, demonstrating his intention to combine political with military power, and his status as the PLA's 'commander-in-chief'.[39] It was clear who would be giving the orders.

Political imperatives thus now encourage centralization in the Chinese armed forces, even while the operational imperatives point to decentralization. The demand is to be both 'red' (politically loyal and ideologically pure) and 'expert' (professionally competent and combat capable). When the two conflict, loyalty will normally be a safer route than taking the initiative. With few rewards for acting independently of the chain of command, there had long been a culture of risk aversion, and, whatever the encouragement in principle to respond to circumstances, in practice it will be best to get instructions from superiors.

THE POLITICIANS AND THE GENERALS

Issues of political control arise during the course of armed control at all levels. Tactical decisions can cause civilian leaders headaches. The most serious tensions, however, will be felt at the top, where the big issues of war and peace are addressed. In early 2021, American specialists in civil–military relations warned of a deep crisis. It was not one of overt military insubordination but of excessive influence. 'Too often, unelected military leaders limit or engineer civilians' options so that generals can run wars as they see fit.'[40] Those in the Western world reaching power in the 1990s had no relevant military experience. Awkwardly, in the United States they had managed to avoid Vietnam. None of the post-Cold War presidents who might have fought in that war – Clinton, Bush, Trump and Biden – had done so. Obama was too young. Yet they all became the commander-in-chief, occupying the supreme position in the chain of command. They were not entitled to wear uniforms, but they could put on bomber jackets as the next best thing. And they had to salute. Obama recalled the high priority given to a lesson on saluting on the eve of his inauguration.[41] But being able to salute does not make you a commander.

As the presidents became less military, the military became more political. While in uniform, senior commanders avoided a close association with any party, but once retired they saw no need to show restraint. From 1998, when a 'Veterans for Bush' organization was established, endorsements from former military commanders were energetically sought and often willingly given. Time spent in uniform, preferably on the front line, helped anyone running for an elected office. As politicians appeared unqualified to make those choices about war constitutionally reserved for them, they could only 'sell' their policies by demonstrating that they had the enthusiastic backing of the armed forces. There was the conviction, another legacy of Vietnam, that the military had been hampered by incessant civilian interference.

Yet the military is not a single, homogeneous entity with a single world view. Military organizations do develop conceptions of the proper purpose of their role in any operation.[42] But these can be contested within a particular branch of the military (for example, advocates of preparations for major war versus counter-insurgency specialists in the army) and between different branches. It was, if anything, unusual for the military establishment to speak with a single voice. Presidents were often frustrated by disagreements among the Chiefs as interservice rivalries took hold. Moments of unity were comparatively rare. H. R. McMaster's book *Dereliction of Duty*, on the failure of the Joint Chiefs to challenge Lyndon Johnson's Vietnam policy, was often assumed to be about the point at which the military leadership should have been prepared to resign because the president was not following their advice, a point of particular interest when McMaster was serving as Trump's national security advisor. The book's main theme, however, was that disagreements among the Chiefs and a lack of strategic acuity had limited their effectiveness.[43] The 1986 Goldwater–Nichols Act, which discouraged, although by no means eliminated, interservice rivalries, meant that it was more likely that the civilians would be faced with a more united military view.

In practice, as we have seen, determined presidents got their way. The Bush administration decided on the wars in Afghanistan and Iraq, and set expectations for how they should be conducted. Donald Rumsfeld imposed his own ideas on how to fight the 'war on terror'. This led to some bitter resistance from senior generals, but not to his downfall: that came when Bush lost confidence in his strategy. Nixon was frustrated by the pushback he received on his orders to give more priority to strikes against North Vietnam, but, in the end, he got what he wanted. As vice president, Joe Biden opposed a 'surge' of troops into Afghanistan. When he became president, he insisted that the troops be removed. The problem was not usually one of presidential orders being blatantly disobeyed or neglected, though that could happen, but that such a large and complex military organization was unresponsive.

MacArthur remains the classic case of insubordination in the American system. After he was dismissed, as noted in the chapter on Korea, he complained about the dangerous concept that members of the forces owed 'primary allegiance and loyalty to those who temporarily exercise the authority of the executive branch of government rather than to the country and its Constitution which they are sworn to defend'. As we have seen, similar claims have occasionally been made by disgruntled generals in other countries, in some cases leading to coups or attempted coups. The reason this view is still considered unacceptable in democracies is that only elected leaders have the authority to set national policy. This was not a serious issue in the United States until the presidency of Donald Trump.

When he entered office in 2017, Trump presented himself as pro-military. He spoke of the military as almost his own personal force, at least as voters. ('We had a wonderful election, didn't we? And I saw those numbers – and you like me, and I like you.')[44] He appointed former generals to senior political roles – secretary of defense, national security advisor and White House chief of staff – and described them as 'my generals'. It was clear that he saw his designated principal military adviser, the chairman of the Joint Chiefs, as one of his.[45] When addressing troops, he assumed that they were on his side, would relish his tough-talking and welcome relaxed rules of engagement. He backed the warriors, who should not be held back by liberal sentimentality and intrusive civilians. This exhibition of toughness led Trump to interfere with military disciplinary processes. He pardoned individuals who had been called out by their comrades because of their recklessness in the field, and in doing so undermined military discipline.

After Trump was defeated in the November 2020 elections, he refused to accept the result and made allegations of cheating, none of which were substantiated, and all of which were thrown out by courts. On 6 January 2021, his supporters stormed Capitol Hill to attempt to stop the votes being validated. One of his supporters, retired General Michael Flynn, who had briefly been his national security advisor, called for martial law to rerun the election and, once Biden was in the White House, suggested support for a military coup.[46] Through this, senior military figures insisted on their political neutrality, resisting any idea that they could act on Trump's behalf against his domestic opponents. The chairman of the Joint Chiefs, General Mark Milley, later refused to confirm reports he feared that Trump wanted a coup and his relief when the White House was finally vacated. He did insist that the military was an 'apolitical institution'.[47] In remarks at the opening of a new military museum, Milley said:

> We are unique among armies, we are unique among militaries. We do not take an oath to a king or queen, or tyrant or dictator, we do not take an oath to an individual. No, we do not take an oath to a country, a tribe or a religion.
>
> We take an oath to the Constitution, and every soldier that is represented in this museum – every sailor, airman, marine, coastguard – each of us protects and defends that document, regardless of personal price.[48]

The distinction was similar to the one made by MacArthur. The difference was that, while Truman was acting in his constitutionally approved role, Trump was looking to act outside the constitution. In terms of legal and moral obligations this made all the difference. Nonetheless the point remained. Obedience to the commander-in-chief had its limits.

In his introduction to Lartéguy's *The Praetorians*, McChrystal observed a recurring tension in warfare 'between unquestioning obedience and a broader interpretation of responsibility'.[49] The Algerian example showed how the line between 'the civilians who craft a policy for war and the soldiers who fight' could get blurred. He knew from his own experience how difficult it was, when fighting an insurgency, to stick to a model of soldiering confined to mastering and executing the 'mechanics of war' while leaving the politics to others. Soldiers of his generation, he recalled, had been taught to follow Samuel Huntington's advice that 'a military commander should endeavour to operate as independently of political or even policy pressures as possible'. When he became a senior commander, he realized that this was an impossible ideal. The simple division of labour between the civilian policy maker and the military policy-executor did not work in practice. 'The process of formulating, negotiating, articulating, and then prosecuting even a largely military campaign involved politics at multiple levels that were impossible to ignore.'[50]

The unavoidable political nature of operational decisions has provided this book's core theme. That does not mean that the institutional separation of armed forces from governments is either unimportant or irrelevant. It improves the quality of both, even though their agendas are bound to overlap. Governments derive their authority from elections and must consider all issues facing the state, including revenue raising and spending priorities. Senior commanders, who are promoted into their positions, spend much of their time preparing for wars that never come, training their units, keeping their equipment up to date, refining their doctrines, and planning for possible campaigns. When considering the potential use of armed force, governments must work out what interests are at stake, what domestic opinion will bear in their pursuit, the potential of diplomatic alternatives, possible coalition partners and how to sustain support in international organizations. The military will need to come up with credible campaign plans, considering how long it will take to mobilize the requisite forces and then keep them supplied. There is an ever-present question about how much they should speak up, if they feel that a prospective war could be disastrous, or, alternatively, is being rejected too readily.

Should the civilian leadership discourage the military from pushing back, so that dissent becomes career threatening and self-censorship kicks in, then it will not only get poor policy advice, but it is more likely that grumbles and dissent will be expressed in leaks to the media.[51] The best policy is likely to emerge from a readiness by the government to have a vigorous debate. And this is a debate that recognizes distinctive perspectives rather than simply presenting the civilians with the 'best military advice' offering no choice. In modern warfare, there is a complex interplay between political objectives and military options, which requires discussion of a range of possible strategies.[52]

The consequences of institutional separation breaking down tends to be bad government and an incompetent military. Dictators can boost their authority by promoting themselves to field marshal, whatever their actual experience, and develop an exaggerated belief in the military instrument as a means of dealing with popular discontent, as well as awkward neighbours. Uncertain of their own political legitimacy, nervous dictators seek to 'coup-proof' their military. Capable commanders start to appear as threats rather than assets. We have seen many examples in this book – Yahya Khan in Pakistan, Thieu in Vietnam, Mobutu in Zaire, Galtieri in Argentina, Saddam in Iraq – of authoritarian leaders failing. This is the case even if they had worked their way up through the ranks, and so might have been expected to understand the basics of military operations. When military and political power come together in one individual, there might be anticipated advantages in being able to act decisively, but dictatorships, or indeed any excessively rigid command structure, will encourage sycophancy and tolerance of foolish schemes.

Vladimir Putin's decision to embark on a war against Ukraine was a spectacular example of this tendency, a tragic example of how the delusions and illusions of one individual can be allowed to shape events without any critical challenge. Autocrats who put their cronies into key positions, control the media to crowd out discordant voices, have acquired the arrogance and certainty to trust only their own judgements, avoiding contrary advice, are able to command their subordinates to follow the most foolish orders. When the process of command is understood in this way, whether by the leader of a nuclear power or an overbearing colonel, as a rigid sequence of order and obedience, bad decisions will be left unchallenged, and the possibilities for improving strategies and tactics by testing and probing alternative courses of action will be lost.

It is ironic that Putin's nemesis turned out to be a politician with no background in either espionage or the military. As a peace-time president, Volodymyr Zelensky was something of a disappointment, but as a war-time president he rose to the occasion, demonstrating his bravery by staying with his people even as Kyiv was threatened, finding the words to articulate the anger and determination of his people, admonishing European leaders to get them to do more to help his country fight back against the invaders, warning of sacrifices to come, yet never doubting the possibility of eventual victory.

The advantages of democratic systems lie not in their ability to avoid bad decisions, either by governments or commanders. Many poor decisions have been recounted here. The advantage lies in their ability to recognize these mistakes, learn, and adapt. Closed systems, in which subordinates dare not ask awkward questions, and in which independent initiatives risk punishment, will suffer operationally. If there is a lesson from this book, it is not that the civilians and military must stick to their own spheres of influence, and not interfere in the other's, but that they must engage constantly with each other. Even while recognizing the vital importance of civilian primacy, the military must advise on the realism of political objectives. Even while acknowledging the importance of professional judgements, the civilians must check that operational plans support those objectives.

In the introduction, I defined commands as authoritative orders. To make a chain of command work, commanders must depend on not only the formal authority that comes with the position, but also a grasp of the informal networks that ensure that systems work effectively, and develop mutual trust. Senior officers, from the commander-in-chief down, learn to appreciate particular individuals for their loyalty, but also their initiative and intelligence. Equally, subordinates learn to be wary of superiors who show an inadequate understanding of the circumstances in which they are operating, so that they are asked to undertake impossible, illegal, or potentially suicidal missions. Respect for the chain of command, reinforced by the imperatives of military discipline, may not be enough to ensure that orders are followed effectively. Those issuing the orders should have the authority that brings the respect of colleagues and subordinates. Authority is something to be earned, not taken for granted – and that goes for the civilians as well as the generals.

Notes

INTRODUCTION

1. Ministry of Defence, *Joint Doctrine Publication 0-01 – Joint Operations* (Shrivenham: Development, Concepts and Doctrine Centre, 2011), p. 3.
2. Roger H. Nye, *The Challenge of Command: Reading for Military Excellence* (New York: Perigee, 1986).
3. US Army, '11 Timeless Principles of Leadership', *US Army Field Manual* (1951).
4. General Sir John Hackett, *The Profession of Arms* (London: Sidgwick & Jackson, 1983).
5. B. H. Liddell Hart, *Thoughts on War* (London: Faber & Faber, 1943).
6. Andrew Roberts (ed.), *Great Commanders of the Modern World, 1866–Present Day* (London: Quercus, 2011), pp. 3–4.
7. Carl von Clausewitz, *On War*, tr. Michael Howard and Peter Paret (Princeton: Princeton University press, 1976), p. 578.
8. Barbara Tuchman, 'Generalship', Address, U.S. Army War College, April 1972, in *Practicing History: Selected Essays by Barbara W. Tuchman* (New York: Alfred A. Knopf, 1981), pp. 277–8.
9. Norman F. Dixon, *On the Psychology of Military Incompetence* (New York: Vintage, 1976). For an assessment of Dixon and the issue of 'competence', see Christopher Dandeker 'Military Incompetence Revisited: The Dark Side of Professionalism', *Res Militaris* (http://resmilitaris.net), 6:2 (Summer–Autumn/Été–Automne 2016).
10. Robert Pois and Philip Langer, *Command Failure in War: Psychology and Leadership* (Bloomington: Indiana University Press, 2004).
11. Cited in Nye, *op. cit.*, pp. 34–5.
12. See Thomas E. Ricks, *The Generals: American Military Command from World War II to Today* (New York: Penguin Books, 2012), ch. 1. On the relevant experiences, see Mark Ethan Grotelueschen, *The AEF Way of War: The American Army and Combat in World War I* (Cambridge: Cambridge University Press, 2006).

13. Meighen McCrae, *Coalition Strategy and the End of the First World War: The Supreme War Council and War Planning, 1917–1918* (Cambridge: Cambridge University Press, 2019).

14. Ricks, *op.cit.*, p. 86.

15. Field Marshal Lord Alanbrooke, *War Diaries, 1939–1945*, ed. Alex Danchev and Daniel Todman (London: Weidenfeld & Nicholson, 2001), p. 417.

16. Carlo D'Este, 'Dwight D. Eisenhower' in Roberts, *op. cit.*, p. 274. D'Este also wrote a full biography of Eisenhower: *Eisenhower: A Soldier's Life* (New York: Holt, 2002).

17. Roberts, *op. cit.*, p. 2.

18. Maj. Brian Babcock-Lumish, 'Uninformed, Not Uniformed? The Apolitical Myth', *Military Review* (September–October 2013), pp. 48–56. See also Mackubin Thomas Owens, 'Military Officers: Political without Partisanship', *Strategic Studies Quarterly* (Fall 2015), pp. 88–101.

19. Hew Strachan, *The Direction of War: Contemporary Strategy in Historical Perspective* (Cambridge: Cambridge University Press, 2013), p. 219.

20. For a discussion of this issue, and why there can be no politics-free operational level, see B. A. Friedman, *On Operations: Operational Art and Military Disciplines* (Annapolis: Naval Institute Press, 2021).

21. Rupert Smith, *The Utility of Force: The Art of War in the Modern World*, 2nd edn (London: Penguin, 2019), p. xviii. At the same time, Smith has a traditional view of the role of the commander: 'Above all, the commander is the primary source of morale for his command. I define morale as that spirit that triumphs in adversity; it is a product of leadership, discipline, comradeship, confidence in self, and in the commander and his staff' (p. 63).

22. Thomas Waldman, *Vicarious Warfare: American Strategy and the Illusion of War on the Cheap* (Bristol: Bristol University Press, 2021).

CHAPTER I

1. 'Historical Notes: Giving Them More Hell', *Time* (3 December 1973).

2. Peter Feaver, 'The Civil–Military Problematique: Huntington, Janowitz, and the Question of Civilian Control', *Armed Forces and Society*, 23:2 (1996), p. 149.

3. Samuel Huntington, *The Soldier and the State: The Theory and Politics of Civil-Military Relations* (Cambridge, MA: The Belknap Press of Harvard University Press, 1959), p. 84.

4. Eliot A. Cohen, *Supreme Command: Soldiers, Statesmen, and Leadership in Wartime* (New York: The Free Press, 2002).

5. Robert D. Putnam, 'Samuel P. Huntington: An Appreciation', *PS*, 19:4 (Autumn 1986), pp. 837–45.

6. H. W. Brands, *The General vs the President: MacArthur and Truman at the Brink of Nuclear War* (New York: Doubleday, 2016), p. 78.

7. Ricks, 2012, *op. cit.*, p. 126. On the relations between the two men, see David L. Roll, *George Marshall: Defender of the Republic* (New York: Dutton, 2019).

8. David Halberstam, *The Coldest Winter* (New York: Hyperion, 2007).

9. D. Clayton James, 'Command Crisis: MacArthur and the Korean War', USAFA Harmon Memorial *Lecture 24* (12 November 1981), https://www.usafa.edu/app/uploads/Harmon24.pdf

10. 'Oral History Interview with Floyd M. Boring' (21 September 1988), https://www.trumanlibrary.gov/library/oral-histories/boring. See Ricks 2012, *op. cit.*, p. 129.

11. David McCullough, *Truman* (New York: Simon & Schuster, 1992), pp. 800–808.

12. Brands, *op. cit.*, p. 165.

13. The Acting Secretary of State to the United States Mission at the United Nations, September 26, 1950, *Foreign Relations of the United States 1950*, vol. VII, *Korea*, ed. John P. Glennon (Washington, DC: Government Printing Office, 1976), p.781.

14. The Secretary of Defense to the Commander in Chief, Far East, September 29, 1951, *ibid.*, p.826.

15. Brands, *op. cit.*, p. 180.

16. *Ibid.*, p. 183.

17. *Ibid.*, p. 196.

18. *Ibid.*, p. 231.

19. *Ibid.*, p. 237.

20. 'Joint Chiefs of Staff to Douglas MacArthur, attached to copy of letter from Douglas MacArthur to Joe Martin' (1951), https://www.trumanlibrary.gov/node/316936

21. 'Statement and Order by the President on Relieving General MacArthur of His Commands' (11 April 1951), https://www.trumanlibrary.gov/library/public-papers/77/statement-and-order-president-relieving-general-macarthur-his-commands

22. Diary entry by Truman on 6 April 1951. See Harry S. Truman, *Memoirs by Harry S. Truman: Years of Trial and Hope: 1946–1952* (New York: Doubleday, 1956), pp. 441–2.

23. *Ibid.*, p. 444.

24. Halberstam, 2007, *op. cit.*

25. Ricks provides a scathing critique of the generalship in Korea. See: Ricks, 2012, *op. cit.*, p. 142.

26. *Ibid.*, p. 80.

27. On Ridgway's success in Korea, see Carter Malkasian, A *History of Modern Wars of Attrition* (Westport, CT: Praeger, 2002), ch. 7.

28. Col. Chester Clifton, cited in McCullough, *op. cit.*, p. 840.

29. Huntington, *op. cit.*, p. 390.

30. 'Gen. Douglas MacArthur's "Old Soldiers Never Die" Address to Congress, 19 April 1951, https://www.loc.gov/item/mcc.034/

31. Testimony before the Senate Committees on Armed Services and Foreign Relations, 15 May 1951. 'Military Situation in the Far East: Hearings ... Eighty-second Congress, First Session, Part 2' (1951), p. 732.

32. Douglas MacArthur, 'War Cannot Be Controlled, It Must Be Abolished', speech before Massachusetts legislature, Boston, 25 July 1951. Cited in Gen. Sir John Hackett, 'The Military in the Service of the State', in Lt Col. Harry Borowski (ed.), *The Harmon Memorial Lectures in Military History, 1959-1987: A Collection of the First Thirty Harmon Lectures Given at the United States Air Force Academy* (washington, DC: Office of Air Force History, 1988), pp. 518–19.

CHAPTER 2

1. Jean Lartéguy, *The Centurions* (London: Penguin Classics, 2015).

2. https://quoteinvestigator.com/2012/09/23/anger-of-legions/#more-4489

3. Early works on the French position on Indochina and Dien Bien Phu are Jules Roy, *The Battle of Dienbienphu* (New York: Carroll & Graf Publishers, Inc., 1984), Bernard Fall, *Hell in a Very Small Place: The Siege of Dien Bien Phu* (Philadelphia: Lippincott, 1967) and Pierre Rocolle, *Pourquoi Dien Bien Phu?* (Paris: Flammarion, 1968). Two more recent studies are Martin Windrow, *The Last Valley: Dien Bien Phu and the French Defeat in Vietnam* (London: Weidenfeld & Nicolson, 2004) and Kevin Boylan and Luc Olivier, *Valley of the Shadow: The Siege of Dien Bien Phu* (Oxford: Osprey, 2018). For an excellent overall account see Fredrik Logevall, *Embers of War: The Fall of an Empire and the Making of America's Vietnam* (New York: Random House, 2012). Attention to command issues is paid in Phillip B. Davidson, *Vietnam at War: The History, 1946–1975* (Novato, CA: Presidio Press, 1988). On communist strategy and policy see Pierre Asselin, *Vietnam's American War: A History* (Cambridge: Cambridge University Press, 2018). The official account of the battle is Võ Nguyên Giáp with Hữu Mai, tr. Lady Borton, *Điện Biên Phủ: Rendezvous with History* (Hanoi: Thê Giới Publishers, 2004).

4. Logevall, *op. cit.*, p. 445.

5. Windrow, *op. cit.*

6. 'Battle of Indochina', *TIME*, 28 September 1953, p. 21. Cited in Bruce Hupe, *The Generalship of General Henri E. Navarre during the Battle of Dien Bien Phu* (Normanby Press, 2015).

7. Logevall, *op. cit.*, p. 511.

8. Davidson, *op. cit.*, pp. 162, 165.

9. Henri Navarre, *Agonie de l'Indochine* (1953–1954) (Paris: Plon, 1958), p. 303.

10. Fall, *op. cit.*, p. 27.
11. Giáp, *op. cit.*, p. 85.
12. Asselin, *op. cit.*, p. 66.
13. Fall, *op. cit.*, p. 129.
14. Navarre, *op. cit.*, p. 315.
15. Rocolle, *op. cit.*, pp. 242–3.
16. Navarre, *op. cit.*, p. 335.
17. Rocolle, *op. cit.*, p. 178.
18. Windrow, *op. cit.*, p. 199.
19. Lt Gen. John W. O'Daniel, report to Joint Chiefs of Staff, cited in Hupe, *op. cit.*, p. 34.
20. Logevall, *op. cit.*
21. Fall, *op. cit.*, p. 102
22. Boylan and Olivier, *op. cit.*, p. 69.
23. Davidson, *op. cit.*, p. 210.
24. Hupe. *op. cit.*, p. 97.
25. Boylan and Olivier, *op. cit.*, p. 62.
26. *Ibid.*, p. 96.
27. There is little corroboration for Fall's claim that this was a malign putsch. De Castries approved the new arrangements and remained engaged.
28. Windrow, *op. cit.*, p. 275.
29. Boylan and Oliver, *op. cit.*, p. 131.
30. Windrow, *op. cit.*, p. 297.
31. Fall, *op. cit.*, p. 203; Davidson, *op. cit.*, pp. 249.
32. Boylan and Oliver, *op. cit.*, p. 131.
33. *Ibid.*, pp. 152–3
34. *Ibid.*, *op. cit.*, p. 229.
35. Fall, *op. cit.*, p. 257.
36. Roy, *op. cit.*, p. 313.
37. Max Hastings, *Vietnam: An Epic Tragedy, 1945–1975* (New York: Harper-Collins, 2018), pp. 80–81.
38. 'Rapport concernant la conduite des opérations en Indochine sous la direction du général Navarre', in G. Elgey, *Histoire de la IVe République*, vol. 2, annex 1, pp. 641–722.
39. Bernard Fall opens with this case in his 'Post Mortems on Dien-Bien-Phu: Review Article', *Far Eastern Survey*, 27:10 (October 1958), pp. 155–8.
40. The best-known English language account of the war is Alistair Horne, *A Savage War of Peace: Algeria 1954–1962* (London: Macmillan, 1977). Also, John Talbott, *The War Without a Name: France in Algeria, 1954–1962* (London: Faber & Faber, 1981). A more recent account is Martin Evans, *Algeria: France's Undeclared War* (New York: Oxford University Press, 2012). See also Martha Crenshaw Hutchinson, *Revolutionary Terrorism: The FLN in Algeria, 1954–1962* (Stanford, CA: Hoover Institution Press, 1978); Martin

Alexander and J. F. V. Keiger, 'France and the Algerian War: Strategy, Opera-
tions and Diplomacy', *Journal of Strategic Studies*, 25:2 (June 2002);
Matthew Connelly, 'Rethinking the Cold War and Decolonization: The
Grand Strategy of the Algerian War for Independence', *International Journal
of Middle East Studies*, 33:2 (2001), pp. 221–45; Jo McCormack, 'Torture
during the Algerian War', *Modern and Contemporary France*, 10:3 (2002);
Orville D. Menard, 'The French Army above the State', *Military Affairs*, 28:3
(Autumn 1964), pp. 123–9.

41. Constantin Melnik, 'The French Campaign against the FLN', RAND Memorandum RM-5449-ISA (September 1967), pp. 12–13.

42. After the war Roger Trinquier published *Modern Warfare: A French View of
Counterinsurgency* (London: Pall Mall, 1964), a treatise drawing lessons
from his experience as a senior commander. Somewhat retrospectively, David
Galula, who saw service in Algeria, has been celebrated particularly by US
counter-insurgency experts, as the major theorist to emerge from the war,
although his influence at the time was limited. See A. A. Cohen, *Galula: The
Life and Writings of the French Officer Who Defined the Art of Counterin-
surgency* (Santa Barbara, CA: Praeger, 2012). For a contemporary analysis
of the French theorists see Peter Paret, *French Revolutionary Warfare from
Indochina to Algeria: The Analysis of a Political and Military Doctrine* (New
York: Praeger, 1964); Michael P. M. Finch, 'A Total War of the Mind: The
French Theory of *La Guerre Révolutionnaire*, 1954–1958', *War in History*,
25:3 (2018), pp. 410-34; and Christopher Cradock and M. L. R. Smith,
'"No Fixed Values": A Reinterpretation of the Influence of the Theory of
Guerre Révolutionnaire and the Battle of Algiers, 1956–1957', *Journal of
Cold War Studies*, 9:4 (Fall 2007), pp. 68–105.

43. Jacques Soustelle, 'France Looks at Her Alliances', *Foreign Affairs* (October
1956), p. 129.

44. Gillo Pontecorvo, *The Battle of Algiers*, filmed in 1965, released in late 1967.
The part of Col. Mathieu was played by Jean Martin, the only established
actor in the film, who had been a prominent opponent of the war. The film
triggered a debate about the rights and wrongs of the war. It prompted Gen.
Jacques Massu, one of the models for Col. Mathieu, to write his own account.
After Gen. Paul Aussaresses' memoir implicated the French in torture, he
was prosecuted, and state archives were opened to permit a proper explor-
ation of the events. See Jacques Massu, *La Vraie Bataille d'Alger* (Paris: Plon,
1971); Jacques Massu, *Le Torrent et la digue* (Paris: Plon, 1972); Paul Aussaresses, *The Battle of the Casbah: Terrorism and Counter-Terrorism in
Algeria, 1955–1957* (New York: Enigma, 2002); and Neil MacMaster, 'The
Torture Controversy (1998–2002): Towards a "New History" of the Algerian War?', *Modern & Contemporary France*, 10:4 (2002).

45. In late 1956, France and the UK, in collusion with Israel, attempted to
take control of the Suez Canal in Egypt, after it had been nationalized

by President Nasser. Under American pressure they were obliged to back off.

46. Evans, *op.cit.*, p. 301.
47. Trinquier, *op.cit.*, pp. 11–14.
48. Horne, *op.cit.*, pp. 178–80.
49. *Ibid.*, p. 188.
50. Aussaresses, *op.cit.*, p. 217. Trinquier doesn't mention this in his book.
51. Melnik, *op. cit.*, p. 61.
52. Massu, *op.cit.*, p. 49.
53. Trinquier, *op. cit.*, pp. 21–2.
54. *Ibid.*, p. 18.
55. *Ibid.*, pp. 20–22. It should be noted that much of the dialogue in Aussaresses's book appears to be invented.
56. Captain Joseph Estoup on trial, cited by Cradock and Smith, *op.cit.*, p. 105.
57. Cited by Evans, *op. cit.*, p. 206.
58. Aussaresses, *op. cit.*, p. 76.
59. Trinquier, cited by Cradock and Smith, *op. cit.*, p. 95.
60. *Ibid.*, p. 214. The government tried, with varying degrees of success, to suppress first-hand accounts of torture.
61. Horne, *op. cit.*, p. 282. Raoul Salan, *Mémoires: Fin d'un empire* (Paris: Presses de la Cité, 1972), p. 285.
62. For a full account of these events, see Julian Jackson, *A Certain Idea of France: The Life of Charles de Gaulle* (London: Allen Lane, 2018).
63. Harold Callender, 'French View of MacArthur: He Is Much Like de Gaulle: Both Called Audacious, Nationalistic, and Sure of Special Destiny in Affairs of World', *New York Times* (12 May 1951).
64. Julian Jackson, *op.cit.*, p. 487.
65. Horne, *op. cit.*, pp. 311, 331.
66. François-Marie Gougeon, 'The Challe Plan: Vain Yet Indispensable Victory', *Small Wars & Insurgencies*, 16:3 (December 2005), p. 297.
67. Challe cited in *ibid.*, p. 299.
68. Maurice Challe, *Notre Révolte* (Paris : Presses de la Cité, 1968), pp. 93, 101, cited in *ibid.*, p. 305.
69. Melnik, *op. cit.*, pp. 26, 45–6.
70. *Ibid.*, p. 33.
71. Julian Jackson, *op. cit.*, p. 515.
72. *Ibid.*, p. 517.
73. Evans, *op. cit.*, p. 20; Horne, *op. cit.*, pp. 354–8.
74. Julian Jackson, *op. cit.*, 521; Evans, *op. cit.*, pp. 272–4.
75. Horne, *op. cit.*, p. 437.
76. Julian Jackson, *op. cit.*, p. 531.
77. Maurice Vaïsse, *Le Putsch d'Alger* (Paris: Éditions Odile Jacob, 2021).
78. Gougeon, *op. cit.*, p. 312.

79. Bruno Tertrais, 'A "Nuclear Coup"?', in Henry D. Sokolski and Bruno Tertrais (eds.), *Nuclear Weapons Security Crises: What Does History Teach?* (Carlisle: PA Strategic Studies Institute and US Army War College Press, 2013).

80. Julian Jackson, *op. cit.*, pp. 531–2. On the coup, see Pierre Abramovici, *Le Putsch des Généraux* (Paris: Fayard, 2011).

81. Julian Jackson, *op. cit.*, p. 734.

82. Lartéguy, 2015, *op. cit.*, pp. 515–16, 518.

83. Jean Lartéguy, *The Praetorians* (London: Penguin, 2016) p. 354.

84. *Ibid.*, p. 358.

85. *Ibid.*, p. 320.

86. Marshal Alphonse Juin, *Trois siècles d'obéissance militaire* (1650–1963) (Paris: L'esprit du livre, 2009). 'Juin Bids French Army Heed Tradition of Obeying Civilians', *New York Times* (12 January 1964).

87. John Hess, 'French Bar Blind Military Obedience', *New York Times* (9 October 1966).

88. Pauline Shanks Kaurin, *On Obedience: Contrasting Philosophies for the Military, Citizenry, and Community* (Annapolis, Maryland: Naval Institute Press, March 2020).

89. 'Pour un retour de l'honneur de nos gouvernants' (21 April 2021), https://www.valeursactuelles.com/politique/pour-un-retour-de-lhonneur-de-nos-gouvernants-20-generaux-appellent-macron-a-defendre-le-patriotisme/

90. 'Signez la nouvelle tribune des militaires' (11 May 2021), https://www.valeursactuelles.com/societe/exclusif-signez-la-nouvelle-tribune-des-militaires/

91. Steven A. Cook, 'How the French Debacle in Algeria Shaped the Rise of Marine Le Pen – and What America Can Learn From It', Council on Foreign Relations (1 May 2017), https://www.cfr.org/blog/how-french-debacle-algeria-shaped-rise-marine-le-pen-and-what-america-can-learn-it. On the elder Le Pen's role, see Giles Tremlett and Paul Webster, 'Battle of Algiers Returns to Haunt Le Pen as Claims of Torture Focus on Far-Right Leader', *Guardian* (4 June 2002).

CHAPTER 3

1. The occasion was a report that a US aircraft had strayed into Soviet airspace during the missile crisis.

2. Erich Fromm, *On Disobedience and Other Essays* (London: Routledge, 1984).

3. The literature on the crisis is immense. Most of the earlier accounts, although influential in their time, have now been superseded. For what remains the most substantial account of the events surrounding the crisis, see Michael Dobbs,

One Minute to Midnight: Kennedy, Khrushchev and Castro on the Brink of Nuclear War (London: Hutchinson, 2008). More recent books include Theodore Voorhees, Jr, *The Silent Guns of Two Octobers: Kennedy and Khrushchev Play the Double Game* (Ann Arbor: University of Michigan Press, 2020), Martin J. Sherwin, *Gambling with Armageddon: Nuclear Roulette from Hiroshima to the Cuban Missile Crisis, 1945–1962* (New York: Alfred A. Knopf, 2020) and Serhii Plokhy, *Nuclear Folly: A New History of the Cuban Missile Crisis* (London: Allen Lane, 2021). After the end of the Cold War, there were a number of accounts from a Soviet perspective, including Anatoli I. Gribkov and William Y. Smith, *Operation ANADYR: US and Soviet Generals Recount the Cuban Missile Crisis* (Chicago: Edition Q, 1994) and Aleksandr Fursenko and Timothy Naftali, '*One Hell of a Gamble': Khrushchev, Castro, and Kennedy, 1958–1964* (New York: W. W. Norton, 1997). The availability of transcripts of recordings made for Kennedy have also made a big difference to the scholarship. These were first published as Ernest R. May and Philip D. Zelikow, *The Kennedy Tapes: Inside the White House during the Cuban Missile Crisis* (Cambridge, MA: Belknap Press of Harvard University Press, 1997). An improved version of the transcripts was made available in Timothy Naftali, Ernest May and Philip Zelikow (eds.), *The Presidential Recordings: John F. Kennedy: Volumes 1–3, The Great Crises* (New York: W. W. Norton & Company, 2001). See also Sheldon M. Stern, *The Week the World Stood Still: Inside the Secret Cuban Missile Crisis* (Stanford, CA: Stanford University Press, 2005).

4. Statement by President Kennedy on Cuba (13 September 1962), https://www.jfklibrary.org/archives/other-resources/john-f-kennedy-press-conferences/news-conference-43

5. US intelligence did, however, know that the Foxtrots were capable of firing nuclear-armed torpedoes. Dino A. Brugioni, *Eyeball to Eyeball: The Inside Story of the Cuba Missile Crisis* (New York: Random House, 1990), p. 386.

6. Peter Huchthausen, *October Fury* (New York: John Wiley, 2002), pp. 16–18.

7. 'Radio and television address to the American people on the Soviet arms build-up in Cuba' (22 October 1962), https://www.jfklibrary.org/learn/about-jfk/historic-speeches/address-during-the-cuban-missile-crisis

8. I deal with this in Lawrence Freedman, *Kennedy's Wars: Berlin, Cuba, Laos and Vietnam* (New York: OUP, 2000).

9. Naftali et al., *op. cit.*, vol. 2, pp. 597–8.

10. Walter Poole, *The Joint Chiefs of Staff and National Policy, 1961–1964*, vol. VIII (Washington, DC: Office of the Chairman of the Joint Chiefs of Staff, 2011), p. 172.

11. John Correll, 'Eisenhower and the Eight Warlords', *Air Force Magazine* (July 2017), pp. 57–61

12. Joseph F. Bouchard, *Command in Crisis: Four Case Studies* (New York: Columbia University Press, 1990), pp. 94–5.

13. Naftali et al., *op. cit.*, vol. 2, p. 579.

14. Dobbs, *op. cit.*, p. 70.
15. Dan Martins, 'The Cuban Missile Crisis and the Joint Chiefs', *Naval War College Review*, 71:4 (Autumn 2018), p. 102.
16. Bouchard, *op. cit.*, p. 94.
17. Naval History and Heritage Command, *The Naval Quarantine of Cuba, 1962*, https://www.history.navy.mil/research/library/online-reading-room/title-list-alphabetically/n/the-naval-quarantine-of-cuba.html
18. *Ibid.*
19. Bouchard, *op. cit.*, p. 104.
20. *Ibid.*, pp. 166–7.
21. *Ibid.*, p. 168.
22. David Coleman, 'Robert McNamara's Feud with Admiral George Anderson', https://jfk14thday.com/tape-mcnamara-anderson/
23. Bouchard, *op.cit.*, pp. 182–3.
24. Oral History Interview with Mr Robert S. McNamara, Washington, DC, 3 April 1986, OSD Historical Office.
25. 'Roswell L. Gilpatric Oral History Interview, John F. Kennedy Library, JFK #2, 5/27/1970', https://www.jfklibrary.org/asset-viewer/archives/JFKOH/Gilpatric%2C%20Roswell%20L/JFKOH-RLG-02/JFKOH-RLG-02
26. 'George W. Anderson, Jr. Oral History Interview, John F. Kennedy Library, JFK #1, 4/25/1967', https://www.jfklibrary.org/asset-viewer/archives/JFKOH/Anderson%2C%20George%20W/JFKOH-GWA-01/JFKOH-GWA-01. Anderson here was probably responding to the first account of the incident which appeared the previous year in Elie Abel, *The Missile Crisis* (New York: Lippincott, 1966). It was in a later interview with Poole that he denied the Gilpatric account: see Poole, *op. cit.*, p. 337. Abel was the reason that the encounter was for many years dated to 24 October, although this did not fit the sequence of events. Eventually, Dobbs established that it could only have been on 23 October: see Dobbs, *op. cit.*, p. 72.
27. William H. J. Manthorpe Jr, 'The Secretary and CNO on 23–24 October 1962', *Naval War College Review,* 66:1 (2013).
28. Martins, *op. cit.*, p. 105.
29. Coleman, *op. cit.*
30. 'Gilpatric, Roswell L.: Oral History Interview – JFK #2, 5/27/1970', https://www.jfklibrary.org/asset-viewer/archives/JFKOH/Gilpatric%2C%20Roswell%20L/JFKOH-RLG-02/JFKOH-RLG-02
31. CNO report, cited by Manthorpe, *op. cit.*, p. 27.
32. 'Strategic Air Command Operations in the Cuban Crisis of 1962', Historical Study no. 90, vol. 1, https://nsarchive2.gwu.edu/nsa/cuba_mis_cri/dobbs/SAC_history.pdf
33. Poole, *op. cit.*, p. 174.
34. *Ibid.*, p. 176.
35. Lawrence Kaplan et al., *History of the Office of the Secretary of Defense,*

vol. 5: *The McNamara Ascendancy, 1961–1965* (Historical Office, Office of the Secretary of Defense Washington, DC, 2006), p. 212.

36. According to May and Zelikow, *The Kennedy Tapes* p. 347, McNamara approved raising the level of alert, although the relevant document is from the Joint Chiefs: cable JCS 6917 to CINCSAC, 23 October 1962, 'The Pentagon during the Cuban Missile Crisis, Part I, New Documents' (16 October 2012), https://nsarchive2.gwu.edu/NSAEBB/NSAEBB397/

37. 'Strategic Air Command Operations . . . ', *op. cit.*, p. vii.

38. Plokhy, *op. cit.*, p. 194.

39. Naftali et al., *op. cit.*, vol. 3, pp. 190–94.

40. Robert Kennedy, *Thirteen Days: A memoir of the Cuban Missile Crisis,* (New York: W. W. Norton, 1969), pp. 69–71.

41. Alexander Fursenko and Yuri M. Zhukov, 'Night Session of the Presidium of the Central Committee, 22–23 October 1962', *Naval War College Review*, 59:3 (Summer 2006), pp. 128–40; Timothy Naftali, 'The Malin Notes: Glimpses Inside the Kremlin during the Cuban Missile Crisis–Introduction', *Cold War International History Project Bulletin*, Issue 17/18 (2012).

42. Fursenko and Zhukov, *op. cit.*, pp. 135–7; Dobbs, *op. cit.*, p. 5. Huchthausen, *op. cit.*, put this at 15 October, which Plokhy, *op. cit.*, follows. This does not fit in with other evidence. Although the published notes of the Presidium meeting on 22 October only cover the first part, they include a reference to Khrushchev saying that the boats should stay on their approaches, so they cannot have already turned round. See 'October 23, 1962, Central Committee of the Communist Party of the Soviet Union Presidium Protocol 60', Wilson Center Digital Archive, https://digitalarchive.wilsoncenter.org/document/115076.pdf ?v=248ca38859ac69a6fed46a692b0cc280. Ketov's account explicitly states that the order to move to change course came after 22 October.

43. Naftali et al., *op. cit.*, vol. 2, p. 155.

44. Manthorpe, *op. cit.*, p. 29. The author of this article was the designated naval briefer that evening.

45. *Ibid.*, pp. 30–1.

46. *Ibid.*, p. 33.

47. Naftali et al., *op. cit.*, vol. 2, pp. 191–2, 196, 200–201.

48. *Ibid.*, vol. 2, p. 197.

49. *Ibid.*, vol. 3, p. 156.

50. Dobbs, *op. cit.*, p. 88.

51. Naftali et al., *op. cit.*, vol. 2, pp. 234–5.

52. *Ibid.*, vol. 2, p. 256.

53. Brugioni, *op. cit.*, p. 418. British public opinion was already very uncertain on the wisdom of American policy.

54. Naftali et al., *op. cit.*, vol. 2, pp. 497, 505. A. Walter Dorn and Robert Pauk, 'The Closest Brush: How a UN Secretary-General Averted Doomsday', *Bulletin of the Atomic Scientists*, 68:6 (2012), pp. 79–84.

55. Bouchard, *op. cit.*, p. 117.
56. Although the American anti-submarine effort was well covered in the litera-ture on the crisis, the experience of the Soviet submarines was not well known, and the revelation that they were carrying nuclear weapons came as a shock to many Americans. In 2002, relevant documents were published by the National Security Archive: William Burr and Thomas S. Blanton (eds.), *The Submarines of October: U.S. and Soviet Naval Encounters during the Cuban Missile Crisis,* National Security Archive Electronic Briefing Book No. 75 (31 October 2002), https://nsarchive2.gwu.edu/NSAEBB/NSAEBB75/# orlov. Peter Huchthausen, who had been an officer on board one of the US ASW destroyers, pulled together American and Soviet sources for his book *October Fury*. Memoirs from Soviet submariners were published as 'Caribbean crisis. Confrontation. Collection of memoirs of participants in the events of 1962', compiled by Rear Admiral V. V. Naumov. Relevant material occurs in parts 29 to 33. They are online in English at https://flot.com/blog/historyofNVMU/5702.php?print=Y (this is the page for part 29 – subsequent parts are at 5705, 5708 and 5711). The new material is also discussed in Svetlana V. Savranskaya, 'New Sources on the Role of Soviet Submarines in the Cuban Missile Crisis', *Journal of Strategic Studies*, 28:2 (2005), pp. 233–59. At the same time, an important account by one of the submarine captains was published as Ryurik A. Ketov, 'The Cuban Missile Crisis as Seen Through a Periscope', *Journal of Strategic Studies*, 28:2 (2005), pp. 217–31.
57. Huchthausen, *op. cit.*, pp. 16–18.
58. Rear Admiral V. V. Naumov (ed.), 'Caribbean crisis. Confrontation. Collec-tion of memoirs of participants in the events of 1962', part 31, https://flot.com/blog/historyofNVMU/5711.php?print=Y
59. Aleksei F. Dubivko, 'In the Depths of the Sargasso Sea', in *On the Edge of the Nuclear Precipice*, tr. Svetlana Savranskaya (Moscow: Gregory Page, 1998), p. 318, https://nsarchive2.gwu.edu/NSAEBB/NSAEBB75/Dubivko.pdf.
60. Huchthausen, *op. cit.*, pp. 151–3. Rybalko appears to have been a major source for this book.
61. *Ibid.*, p. 209. This is not mentioned in Shumkov's own account.
62. See, for example, Sherwin, *op. cit.*
63. Savranskaya, *op. cit.*, pp. 246–7. She notes that Arkhipov's widow mentioned that his submarine had almost fired a torpedo at an American destroyer.
64. Naumov, *op. cit.*, part 29, https://flot.com/blog/historyofNVMU/5705.php?print=Y
65. *Ibid.*
66. Gary Slaughter, 'A Soviet Nuclear Torpedo, an American Destroyer, and the Cuban Missile Crisis', *Task & Purpose* (4 September 2016).
67. Savranskaya, *op. cit.*, 247
68. Bouchard, *op. cit.*, pp. 98–9.

69. Dobbs, *op. cit.*, pp. 329–30.
70. Fletcher Knebel and Charles W. Bailey II, *Seven Days in May* (New York: Harper & Row, 1962).
71. Theo Zenou, 'John F. Kennedy's Warning to the Republic', *History Today* (8 February 2021).
72. Robert Dallek, 'JFK vs. the Military', *the Atlantic* (10 September 2013).

CHAPTER 4

1. David Landau, *Arik: The Life of Ariel Sharon* (New York: Knopf, 2014), p. 47.
2. Benny Morris, 'The 2005 Time 100: Ariel Sharon', *Time* (18 April 2005); Thomas Mitchell, 'Sharon Was No De Gaulle', +972 *Magazine* (20 January 2014), https://www.972mag.com/sharon-was-no-de-gaulle/.
3. The standard work on the war is Michael B. Oren, *Six Days of War: June 1967 and the Making of the Modern Middle East* (Oxford: OUP, 2002). See also Yossi Goldstein, 'The Six Day War: The War that No One Wanted', *Israel Affairs*, 24:5 (2018), p. 2 (fn 14); Mordechai Bar-On, 'The Generals' "Revolt": Civil–Military Relations in Israel on the Eve of the Six Day War', *Middle Eastern Studies*, 48:1 (2012), pp. 33–50; A. Gluska, *The Israeli Military and the Origins of the 1967 War: Government, Armed Forces and Defence Policy 1963– 1967* (London: Routledge, 2007).
4. Michael B. Oren, *op. cit.*, p. 123.
5. *Ibid.*, p. 136.
6. *Ibid.*, pp. 133–4; Arye Naor, 'Civil–Military Relations and Strategic Goal Setting in the Six Day War', *Israel Affairs*, 12:3 (2006), p. 402.
7. Landau, *op. cit.*, p. 58.
8. Ariel Sharon, with David Chanoff, *Warrior: The Autobiography of Ariel Sharon* (New York: Simon & Schuster, 2001).
9. Michael B. Oren, *op. cit.*, p. 134; Naor, *op. cit.*, p. 400.
10. George W. Gawrych, 'The Egyptian Military Defeat of 1967', *Journal of Contemporary History*, 26:2 (April 1991), pp. 277–305.
11. Landau, *op. cit.*, pp. 62–3.
12. Avraham (Bren) Adan, *On the Banks of the Suez* (London: Arms & Armour, 1980), p. 156.
13. Landau, *op. cit.*, p. 20.
14. Uzi Benziman, *Sharon: An Israeli Caesar* (London: Robson Books, 1987), p. 139.
15. Adan, *op. cit.*, p. 12.
16. Abraham Rabinovich, *The Yom Kippur War: The Epic Encounter that Transformed the Middle East* (New York: Schocken Books, 2017).
17. Adan, *op. cit.*, pp. 126–7.

18. Anna Ahronheim, '"There Is Going to Be a War Tonight" – Israel Opens Yom Kippur War Archive', *The Jerusalem Post* (7 October 2019).
19. Rabinovich, *op. cit.*, p. 328.
20. Adan, *op. cit.*, p. 190.
21. Landau, *op. cit.*, p. 109.
22. Martin Indyk, *Master of the Game: Henry Kissinger and the Art of Middle East Diplomacy* (New York: Knopf, 2021), pp. 137–41.
23. Landau, *op. cit.*, p. 116.
24. Sharon, with Chanoff, *op. cit.*, p. 316.
25. *Ibid.*, p. 317.
26. Moshe Dayan, *Story of My Life* (New York: Morrow, 1976), p. 530.
27. *Ibid.*, p. 529.
28. Sharon, with Chanoff, *op. cit.*, pp. 329.
29. *Ibid.*, p. 330.
30. Cited by Landau, *op. cit.*, p. 132.
31. Dayan, *op. cit.*, p. 524.
32. *Ibid.*, p. 128.
33. Charles Mohr, 'Israeli General Assails Superiors', *New York Times* (9 November 1973). See also Charles Mohr, 'Israeli General Tells How Bridgehead Across the Suez Canal Was Established', *New York Times* (12 November 1973).
34. Amos Perlmutter, 'The Covenant of War: A Dispatch from Israeli-Occupied "Africa"', *Harper's Magazine* (February 1974).
35. Raful Eitan, *A Soldier's Story: The Life and Times of an Israeli War Hero* (New York: Shapolsky, 1991).
36. Ze'ev Schiff and Ehud Ya'ari, *Israel's Lebanon War* (New York: Simon & Schuster, 1984), pp. 104–6; Landau, *op. cit.*, pp. 182–3.
37. Schiff and Ya'ari, *op. cit.*, pp. 163–4.
38. Benny Morris, 'The Israeli Army Papers that Show What Ariel Sharon Hid from the Cabinet in the First Lebanon War', *Haaretz* (March 2018), https://www.haaretz.com/life/books/.premium-the-idf-papers-that-show-what-sharon-hid-in-the-lebanon-war-1.5867371
39. Landau, *op. cit.*, p. 191.
40. Schiff and Ya'ari, *op. cit.*, p. 187.
41. Landau, *op. cit.*, p. 193.
42. Amir Oren, 'With Ariel Sharon Gone, Israel Reveals the Truth about the 1982 Lebanon War', *Haaretz* (17 September 2017), https://www.haaretz.com/israel-news/with-sharon-gone-israel-reveals-the-truth-about-the-lebanon-war-1.5451086
43. Landau, *op. cit.*, p. 196.
44. *Ibid.*, pp. 203–4.
45. *Ibid.*, p. 205.
46. Schiff and Ya'ari, *op. cit.*, p. 39.

47. Kirsten E. Schulze, 'Israeli Crisis Decision-Making in the Lebanon War: Group Madness or Individual Ambition?', *Israel Studies*, 3:2 (Fall 1998), pp. 215–37; Eitan, *op. cit.*

48. Sharon, with Chanoff, *op. cit.*, pp. 463–4.

49. Landau, *op. cit.*, pp. 184–5.

50. Morris, 2018, *op. cit.*

51. Sharon, with Chanoff, *op. cit.*, p. 321.

52. Jacob Even and Simcha B. Maoz, *At the Decisive Point in the Sinai: Generalship in the Yom Kippur War* (Lexington: University of Kentucky Press, 2017), p. 53.

53. Amir Oren, *op. cit.*

54. Rabinovich, *op. cit.*

55. Yoram Peri, *Between Battle and Ballots: Israeli Military in Politics* (Cambridge: Cambridge University Press, 1983), p. 118. Interview in *Maariv*, 25 (January 1974).

56. https://israeled.org/agranat-yom-kippur-war/. See also Ben Hartman, 'Archives Reveal: Commanding Officer Blasted Ariel Sharon's Yom Kippur War "Dereliction of Duty"', *Jerusalem* Post (22 September 2015), https://www.jpost.com/israel-news/letter-from-commanding-officer-blasts-ariel-sharons-dereliction-of-duty-during-yom-kippur-war-417779

57. Landau, *op. cit.*, p. 144.

CHAPTER 5

1. Samuel Finer, *The Man on Horseback: The Role of the Military in Politics* (London: Pall Mall Press, 1962).

2. Lt Gen. Jahan Dad Khan, *Pakistan Leadership Challenges* (Karachi: Oxford University Press, 1999), pp. 36–8.

3. Samuel P. Huntington, *Political Order in Changing Societies* (New Haven, CT: Yale University Press, 1968), pp. 250–51.

4. Richard Sisson and Leo E. Rose, *War and Secession: Pakistan, India, and the Creation of Bangladesh* (Berkeley: University of California Press, 1990), p. 23.

5. *Ibid.*, p. 24.

6. *Ibid.*, p. 81.

7. Srinath Raghavan, *1971: A Global History of the Creation of Bangladesh* (Cambridge, MA: Harvard University Press, 2013), p. 42.

8. Sisson and Rose, *op. cit.*, p. 99.

9. Akbar Ahmed, '1971 Field Notes: Lessons for Pakistan', *Dawn* (26 December 2017).

10. *Ibid.*, p. 29; Shuja Nawaz, *Crossed Swords: Pakistan, Its Army, and the Wars Within* (Oxford: OUP, 2008), p. 266.

11. Sisson and Rose, *op. cit.*, pp. 132–3.

12. See Chandrashekhar Dasgupta, 'The Decision to Intervene: First Steps in India's Grand Strategy in the 1971 War', *Strategic Analysis*, 40:4 (2016), pp. 321–33; Kapil Kak, 'India's Grand Strategy for the 1971 War', *CLAWS Journal* (Summer 2012). https://archive.claws.in/images/journals_doc/13947 90936Kapil%20Kak%20%20CJ%20Sumer%202012.pdf

13. In one account, after this meeting, he tendered his resignation to Gandhi, who declined it. He then promised victory, if he was allowed to set the date for the conflict and handle it on his own terms. The prime minister agreed. See V. K. Singh, *Leadership in the Indian Army: Biographies of Twelve Soldiers* (New Delhi: SAGE, 2005), pp. 204–5. Others treat this story more sceptically. See Raghavan, *op. cit.*, pp. 67–8.

14. Lt Gen. J. F. R. Jacob, *An Odyssey in War and Peace* (New Delhi: Roli Books, 2011).

15. *1971 War: Eastern Theatre,* Command & Staff College Military History Primer: 2011 (Quetta: Command & Staff College, 2011), p. 14.

16. Abdul Qayyum, 'Remembering Lt Gen Gul Hasan', *Defence Journal,* 3 (2000).

17. Hamoodur Rahman Commission, *Supplementary Report to the Commission's Official Inquiry into the 1971 India-Pakistan War* (Rockwille, MD: Arc Manor, 2007).

18. Lt Gen. A. A. K. Niazi, *The Betrayal of East Pakistan* (Karachi: Oxford University Press, 1998).

19. Jahan Dad Khan, *op. cit.*, p. 117.

20. Lt Gen. (retd) Kamal Matinuddin, *Tragedy of Errors: East Pakistan Crisis, 1968–1971* (Lahore: Wajidalis, 1994).

21. Siddiq Salik, *Witness to Surrender* (Karachi: Oxford University Press, 1998).

22. Interview by A. H. Amin, with Brig. (retd) Zahir Alam Khan, 'Remembering Our Warriors', *Defence Journal* (April 2002).

23. Sumit Walia, '1971 War: What Happened before Pakistan's Public Surrender to India' (SIFY, 15 December 2017), https://www.sify.com/news/1971-war-what-happened-before-pakistans-public-surrender-to-india-news-columns-rmpqGydddeajd.html

24. On the scale and impact of sexual violence in East Pakistan, see Christina Lamb, *Our Bodies, Their Battlefields: What War Does to Women* (London: Collins, 2020).

25. Hamoodur Rahman Commission, *op. cit.*, p. 15.

26. Niazi, *op. cit.*, p. 54.

27. Nawaz, *op. cit.*, p. 284.

28. Niazi, *op. cit.*, p. 67.

29. *Ibid.*, p. 80.

30. Maj. Gen. Shaukat Riza, *The Pakistan Army, 1966–1971* (Dehra Dunn: Natraj Publishers, 1990), pp. 103–9; Nawaz, *op. cit.*, p. 289.

31. Walia, *op. cit.*

32. Nawaz, *op. cit.*, pp. 292–5.
33. *Ibid.*, p. 291.
34. Gen. K. K. Singh, director general of military operations, felt 'rather strongly that the Indian Army, with its inherent inhibitions against anything unorthodox and a more speedy type of manoeuvre' was ill suited to capturing Dacca: see Raghavan, *op. cit.*, p. 236.
35. *Ibid.*, pp. 238–9.
36. John H. Gill, *An Atlas of the 1971 India–Pakistan War: The Creation of Bangladesh* (Near East South Asia Center for Strategic Studies, 2003), pp. 54–5.
37. Nawaz, *op. cit.*, p. 239.
38. G-1104, from the Commander to the Chief of General St, 21 November 1971. This and other signals referenced below appear in an appendix to Hanoodur Rahman Commission, *op. cit.*
39. G-1086, from the Chief of Staff to the Commander, 22 November 1971
40. G-0866, for Commander in Chief from Commander, 28 November 1971. This was in reply to signal G-022, of 27 October.
41. G-0338, for COMMANDER from CHIEF OF STAFF, 5 December 1971.
42. G-0235, personal for COMMANDER from CHIEF OF STAFF, 5 December 1971.
43. Gill, *op. cit.*, pp. 54–5.
44. G-1233, Commander to Chief of Staff, 6 December 1971. The reference to China was implicit in this message but explicit in one that followed.
45. G-0907, for COMMANDER from CHIEF OF GENERAL STAFF, 8 December 1971.
46. Gill, *op. cit.*, p. 19.
47. Rao Farman Ali Khan, *How Pakistan Got Divided* (Karachi: Oxford University Press, 2017). The Hamoodur Rahman Commission, having come down hard on Farman in its first report, was more inclined to believe him and disbelieve Niazi in their second, but their explanations were not wholly convincing.
48. A-6905, 7th December from Governor to President, 7 December 1971.
49. A-4555, from PRESIDENT for GOVERNOR, 8 December 1971.
50. A-4660 of 091800. For the President, 9 December 1971.
51. G-0001, President to Governor, 9 December 1971. The next day Niazi was told that the president had 'left the decision to the Governor in close consultation with you'. The signal added that, whatever was done, Niazi 'should attempt to destroy maximum military equipment so that it does not fall into enemy hands'. See G-0237, For Comd from COS Army, 10 December 1971.
52. Raghavan, *op. cit.*, p. 253.
53. Niazi notes that this sentence is left out of the version published by Farman.
54. Hamoodur Rahman Commission, *op. cit.* He says it had his signature only because it was due to be transmitted through army channels.

55. G-0002, President to Governor, 10 December 1971.

56. Raghavan, *op. cit.*, p. 255.

57. Gill, *op. cit.*, p. 28.

58. Col. Khalid M. Zaki, *Through the Lens of Operational Art: 1971 Bangladesh Campaign* (Fort Leavenworth, KS: Army School of Advanced Military Studies, United States Army Command and General Staff College, AY 2011–2012).

59. S. N. Prasad, *Official History of the 1971 War* (New Delhi: Ministry of Defence, 1992), pp. 788–92. Cited in Anit Mukherjee, '"Every Death Matters?" Combat Casualties, Role Conception, and Civilian Control', *European Journal of international Security*, 7:1 (2022), p. 133.

60. G-?, from COMMANDER for CHIEF OF THE GENERAL STAFF, 10 December 1971.

61. G-0002, for GOVERNOR from PRESIDENT, 11 December 1971.

62. G-0011, for COMMANDER FROM chief of staff, 11 December 1971.

63. Niazi, *op. cit.*

64. G-127, COMMANDER FOR CHIEF OF STAFF, 11 December 1971.

65. G-1286, from COMD for COS your G-0011, 12 December 1971.

66. G-1279, from COMD for COS, 12 December 1971.

67. G-1286, from COMD for COS, 13 December 1971.

68. G-012, for COMMANDER from CHIEF OF STAFF, 14 December 1971.

69. Raghavan, *op. cit.*

70. Walia, *op. cit.*

71. Salil Tripathi, *The Colonel Who Would Not Repent: The Bangladesh War and Its Unquiet Legacy* (New Haven: Yale University Press, 2016).

72. Walia, *op. cit.*

73. G-0015, from Chief of Staff to General Niazi, 15 December 1971.

74. Maj. Gen. Sukhwant Singh, *India's Wars since Independence* (New Delhi: Lancer, 2013).

75. Gill, *op. cit.*, p. 65.

76. Nicholas J. Wheeler, *Saving Strangers: Humanitarian Intervention in International Society* (Oxford: OUP, 2002).

77. Ahmad Faruqui, 'Evaluating the Generalship of AAK Niazi', *Daily Times* (19 December 2017).

78. Caitlin Talmadge, *The Dictator's Army: Battlefield Effectiveness in Authoritarian Regimes* (Ithaca, NY: Cornell University Press, 2015).

CHAPTER 6

1. Memorandum from President Nixon to the President's Assistant for National Security Affairs (Kissinger) and the President's Deputy Assistant for National Security Affairs (Haig), *Foreign Relations of the United States, 1969–1976*,

vol. VIII: *Vietnam, January–October 1972*, ed. John M. Carland (Washington, DC: US State Department, 2010), p. 547. Hereinafter referred to as *FRUS 1972*.

2. Cited in Richard H. Kohn, 'The Erosion of Civilian Control of the Military in the United States Today,' *Naval War College Review*, 55:3 (2002), p. 17.

3. Alexander M. Haig, *Inner Circles: How America Changed the World* (New York: Warner, 1992), p. 208.

4. Richard Nixon, *RN: The Memoirs of Richard Nixon* (New York: Grosset & Dunlap, 1978), p. 385.

5. Haig, *op. cit.*, p. 209. On Nixon's inability to confront, see Henry Kissinger, *The White House Years* (New York: Little, Brown & Co., 1979), p. 482.

6. Editorial Note, *FRUS 1972*, *op. cit.*, p. 80.

7. Stephen P. Randolph, *Powerful and Brutal Weapons: Nixon, Kissinger and the Easter Offensive* (Cambridge, MA: Harvard University Press, 2007), p. 82.

8. *Ibid.*, p. 20.

9. Moorer Diary, 1 February and 4 February 1972, *FRUS 1972*, *op. cit.*, p. 81.

10. Memorandum for the Record by the Chairman of the Joint Chiefs of Staff (Moorer), 1972 April 14, *FRUS 1972*, *op. cit.*, p. 252.

11. Davidson, *op. cit.*, p. 640.

12. Gregory Daddis, *Withdrawal: Reassessing America's Final Years in Vietnam* (New York: Oxford University Press, 2017).

13. Randolph, *op. cit.*, p. 98.

14. Graham A. Cosmas, *MACV: The Joint Command in the Years of Withdrawal, 1968–1973*, United States Army in Vietnam (Washington, DC: US Army Center of Military History, 2006), p. 354.

15. Talmadge, *op. cit.*, pp. 54–7.

16. Allan E. Goodman, *An Institutional Profile of the South Vietnamese Officer Corps (U)*, RM-6189-ARPA (June 1970), https://apps.dtic.mil/sti/pdfs/AD0514242.pdf

17. Cited by Talmadge, *op. cit.*, p. 59.

18. Davidson, *op. cit.*, p. 655.

19. Talmadge, *op. cit.*, pp. 105–6.

20. Richard A. Hunt, *Melvin Laird and the Foundation of the Post-Vietnam Military 1969–1973* (Washington, DC: Historical Office, Office of the Secretary of Defense, 2015), pp. 216–17.

21. Mark Clodfelter, *Violating Reality: The Lavelle Affair, Nixon, and the Parsing of the Truth* (Washington, DC: National Defense University Press, 2016), p. 4.

22. *Ibid.*, pp. 4, 14, 18.

23. Cosmas, *op. cit.*, pp. 350–53.

24. When the truth became apparent, the *New York Times* published its own correction to the stories it had published about Lavelle. These had suggested

that he was a rogue officer waging his own 'massive, private air war'. See: 'Correction: The Lavelle Case', *New York Times* (7 August 2010).

25. National Security Council Meeting, 2 February 1972, *FRUS* 1972, *op. cit.*, pp. 66–7.

26. Conversation among Nixon, Kissinger and Bunker, 3 February 1972, *FRUS* 1972, *op. cit.*, pp. 73–75.

27. Clodfelter, *op. cit.*, p. 34.

28. Message attached to Moorer's diary, *FRUS* 1972, *op. cit.*, p. 159.

29. Memorandum for the Record by Moorer, 3 April 1972, *ibid.*, p. 186.

30. Lien-Hang T. Nguyen, *Hanoi's War: An International History of the War for Peace in Vietnam* (Chapel Hill: University of North Carolina Press, 2012); Asselin, *Vietnam's American War*.

31. Randolph, *op. cit.*, p. 93.

32. Conversation among Nixon, Kissinger and Moorer, 3 April 1972, *FRUS* 1972, *op. cit.*, pp. 176, 172, 174.

33. Moorer to McCain and Abrams, 4 April 1972, *ibid.*, p. 185, Fn. 3.

34. Willard J. Webb and Walter S. Poole, *The Joint Chiefs of Staff and the War in Vietnam, 1971–1973* (Washington, DC: Office of Joint History, Office of the Chairman of the Joint Chiefs of Staff, 2007), p. 156.

35. Diary Entry by the Assistant to the President (Haldeman), 6 April 1972, *FRUS* 1972, *op. cit.*, p. 222.

36. Wayne Thompson, *To Hanoi and Back: The U.S. Air Force and North Vietnam, 1966–1973* (Washington, DC: Smithsonian Institution Press, 2000), pp. 116–17.

37. Hunt, *op. cit.*, p. 230.

38. *Ibid.*, pp. 229–30.

39. Randolph, *op. cit.*, p. 120.

40. *Ibid.*, p. 120.

41. *Ibid.*, pp. 65–6.

42. Gerald Turley, *The Easter Offensive: The Last American Advisors, Vietnam, 1972* (Annapolis: Naval Institute Press, 1985), p. 162.

43. *Ibid.*, p. 112.

44. *Ibid.*, pp. 230, 98, 251.

45. Ngo Quang Truong, *The Easter Offensive of 1972* (Washington, DC: US Army Center of Military History, 1980), pp. 37–8.

46. *Ibid.*, pp. 44–6.

47. Memorandum from Kissinger to Nixon, undated, *FRUS* 1972, *op. cit.*, p. 309.

48. Lewis Sorley (ed.), *Vietnam Chronicles: The Abrams Tapes, 1968–1972* (Lubbock, TX: Texas Tech University Press, 2004), p. 841.

49. Webb and Poole, *op. cit.*, pp. 159–60.

50. Hunt, *op. cit.*, p. 239.

51. Editorial Note, *FRUS* 1972, *op. cit.*, pp. 391–2.

52. Kissinger to Nixon, 3 May 1972, *ibid.*, p. 403.
53. Truong, *op. cit.*, p. 53.
54. Message from Moorer to McCain and Abrams, 8 April 1972, *FRUS 1972*, *op. cit.*, p. 232.
55. Webb and Poole, *op. cit.*, p. 159.
56. Diary Entry by Moorer, 12 April 1972, *FRUS 1972*, *op. cit.*, p. 238.
57. Message 38158 from Saigon, 8 April 1972, *ibid.*, p. 238, Fn. 4.
58. One explanation for the poor results is that bombing was controlled by Combat Skyspot, a ground-directed instrument bombing system that worked in the South but lacked the radar sites to make it work well in the North. A further strike on 12/13 April against less sensitive targets went better because the B-52s relied instead on their own internal bombing radar. Marshall L. Michel III, *Operation Linebacker 1 1972: The First High-Tech Air War* (Oxford: Osprey Publishing, 2019), p. 35.
59. Moorer Diary Entry, 15 April 1972, *FRUS 1972*, *op. cit.*, pp. 251–3.
60. Cosmas, *op. cit.*, p. 367.
61. Webb and Poole, *op. cit.*, p. 159.
62. Kissinger to Laird, 28 April 1972, *FRUS 1972*, *op. cit.*, p. 332.
63. Nixon to Kissinger, 30 April 1972, *ibid.*, p. 341.
64. White House Tapes, Oval Office, Conversation, 4 May 1972, *ibid.*, p. 414.
65. Message from the Abrams to Moorer and McCain, 4 May 1972, *ibid.*, pp. 413–14.
66. Kissinger to Bunker, 4 May 1972, *ibid.*, pp. 433–4.
67. Conversation between Nixon and Kissinger, 5 May 1972, *ibid.*, p. 439.
68. Editorial Note, *ibid.*, p. 429.
69. Randolph, *op. cit.*, p. 161.
70. Kissinger, *op. cit.*, p. 1178.
71. Message from Kissinger to Bunker, 7 May 1972, *FRUS 1972*, *op. cit.*, pp. 478–9.
72. Editorial Note, *ibid.*, p. 513.
73. Bunker to Kissinger, 9 May 1972, *ibid.*, pp. 517–18.
74. Davidson, *op. cit.*, p. 705.
75. Douglas M. White, *Rolling Thunder to Linebacker: U.S. Fixed Wing Survivability Over North Vietnam* (Fort Leavenworth, KS: US Army Command and General Staff College, 2000), p. 76.
76. *Ibid.*, p. 3.
77. Michel, *op. cit.*, p. 36.
78. *Ibid.*, pp. 51–2.
79. Telephone Conversation between Moorer and Kissinger, 8 May 1972, *FRUS 1972*, *op. cit.*, p. 508.
80. Nixon to Kissinger and Haig, 19 May 1972, *ibid.*, p. 617.
81. Memorandum from Kissinger to Nixon, 19 May 1972, *ibid.*, p. 610.

82. Gareth Porter, *A Peace Denied: The United States, Vietnam and the Paris Agreement* (Bloomington: Indiana University Press, 1975), p. 118.

83. For the North Vietnamese history of the war, see The Military History Institute of Vietnam, *Victory in Vietnam: The Official History of the People's Army of Vietnam, 1954–1975*, tr. Merle L. Pribbenow (Lawrence, KS: University Press of Kansas, 2002).

84. Hastings, *op. cit.*, p. 637.

85. Talmadge, *op. cit.*

86. Truong, *op. cit.*, p. 172.

87. Sorley, *op. cit.*, pp. 832, 839.

CHAPTER 7

1. Adm. Sandy Woodward, with Patrick Robinson, *One Hundred Days: The Memoirs of the Falklands Battle Group Commander*, 2nd edn (London: HarperCollins, 2003), Preface to the Second Edition.

2. Much of this chapter is drawn from Lawrence Freedman, *The Official History of the Falklands Campaign: Revised and Updated Edition*, two vols. (London: Routledge, 2005). Volume 1 deals with the origins of the conflict. References in this chapter are to volume 2, *War and Diplomacy*. Digitized documents on the war can be found at the website of the Margaret Thatcher Foundation, https://www.margaretthatcher.org/archive.

3. Three women – Susan Whitley, Doreen Bonner and Mary Goodwin – lost their lives as the result of a stray British shell.

4. Adm. of the Fleet Sir Henry Leach, *Endure No Makeshifts* (London: Leo Cooper, 1993), pp. 209–13.

5. Freedman, *op. cit.*, p. 21. It was 'to report as necessary to the Defence and Oversea Policy Committee'. In practice, this committee was superfluous and met only once.

6. Charles Moore, *Margaret Thatcher: The Authorized Biography*, vol. 1: *Not for Turning* (London: Allen Lane, 2013), p. 682.

7. Over Gibraltar and Northern Ireland, respectively.

8. Moore, *op. cit.*, p. 699.

9. *Ibid.*, p. 742.

10. *Ibid.*, p. 698.

11. Richard Hill, *Lewin of Greenwich: The Authorised Biography of Admiral of the Fleet Lord Lewin* (London: Cassell, 2000).

12. In addition to Woodward, Clapp and Thompson wrote accounts of the war from their perspectives: Michael Clapp and Ewen Southby-Tailyour, *Amphibious Assault Falklands: The Battle of San Carlos Water* (London: Leo Cooper, 1996) and Julian Thompson, *No Picnic*, 3rd edn (London: Cassell, 2001).

13. Cited in Geoffrey Till, *Understanding Victory: Naval Operations from Trafalgar to the Falklands* (Santa Barbara: Praeger, 2014), p. 158.
14. Imperial War Museum oral interview with Linley Eric Middleton, 13 October 2011, https://www.iwm.org.uk/collections/item/object/80032610
15. Julian Thompson, *op. cit.*, pp. 17–18.
16. Clapp and South by- Tailyour, *op. cit.*, p. 57.
17. Ewen Southby-Tailyour, *Reasons in Writing: A Commando's View of the Falklands War* (London: Leo Cooper, 1993), pp. 140, 141.
18. Sandy Woodward, *op. cit.*
19. Jorge Boveda, *All for One, One for All: Argentine Naval Operations during the Falklands/Malvinas War* (Warwick: Helion, 2021), p. 45.
20. Alejandro L. Corbacho, 'Argentine Command Structure and Its Impact on Land Operations during the Falklands/Malvinas War (1982)', CEMA Working Papers: Serie Documentos de Trabajo, 338 (Universidad del CEMA, 2006).
21. Boveda, *op. cit.*, pp. 49–50.
22. I have put all timings at the local times of wherever the action was taking place. There was a four-hour time difference between London and the theatre of operations. The task force operated at Zulu time, equivalent to Greenwich Mean Time, so that all, including the Northwood HQ, had their watches set to the same zone. Zulu time was three hours ahead of local time in the South Atlantic and one hour ahead of British Summer Time.
23. Full details of the role of signals intelligence in the Falklands campaign can be found in John Ferris, *Behind the Enigma: The Authorised History of GCHQ, Britain's Secret Cyber-Intelligence Agency* (London: Bloomsbury, 2020).
24. Freedman, *op. cit.*, p. 292.
25. In Michael Bilton and Peter Kosminsky, *Speaking Out: Untold Stories from the Falklands War* (London: André Deutsch, 1989), p. 299.
26. R. L. Wade-Gery, 'Falklands: Military Decisions' (London: Cabinet Office, 2 May 1982), https://c59574e9047e61130f13-3f71d0fe2b653c4f00f32175760e96e7.ssl.cf1.rackcdn.com/3357C50D26884F9791EBC18D522A9C35.pdf. Freedman, *op. cit.*, p. 292.
27. Mariano Sciaroni, *A Carrier at Risk: Argentinean Aircraft Carrier and Anti-Submarine Operations against Royal Navy's Attack Submarines during the Falklands/Malvinas War, 1982* (Warwick: Helion & Co., 2019), pp. 7–8.
28. Boveda, *op. cit.*, pp. 51–2.
29. The subsequent discussion of what was known was confused by a statement by Adm. Anaya, the chief of the Argentine navy, suggesting that the 20.07 order was to withdraw, when in fact it was to go on the offensive. Arthur Gavshon and Desmond Rice, *The Sinking of the Belgrano* (London: Secker & Warburg, 1984).
30. Freedman, *op. cit.*, p. 297.

31. Boveda, *op. cit.*, pp. 52–3.
32. Sandy Woodward, *op. cit.*
33. Boveda, *op. cit.*, p. 54.
34. *Ibid.*
35. Julian Thompson, *op. cit.*, p. 81.
36. Jeremy Moore, oral history (14 November 1988), https://www.iwm.org.uk/collections/item/object/80010260
37. Freedman, *op. cit.*, p. 450.
38. *Ibid.*, p. 557.
39. *Ibid.*, p. 560.
40. Robert Harris, *Gotcha! The Government, Media and the Falklands Crisis* (London: Faber, 1994), p. 117.
41. Bilton and Kosminsky, *op. cit.*, p. 301.
42. Moore, *op. cit.*, p. 741.
43. Julian Thompson, *op. cit.*, p. 81.
44. Freedman, *op. cit.*, p. 563.
45. *Ibid.*, p. 568.
46. Spencer Fitz-Gibbon, *Not Mentioned in Despatches: The History and Mythology of the Battle of Goose Green* (Cambridge: Lutterworth Press, 1995), p. 20.
47. Nicholas van der Bijl, *Nine Battles to Stanley* (London: Leo Cooper, 1999), p. 129. The battle is covered from a soldier's perspective in Helen Parr, *Our Boys: The Story of a Paratrooper* (London: Allen Lane, 2018). See also Mark Adkin, *The Battle of Goose Green* (London: Pen & Sword, 1992), and Freedman, *op. cit.* I discuss some of the operational aspects of the battle in Lawrence Freedman, 'A Theory of Battle or a Theory of War?' *Journal of Strategic Studies*, 28:3 (2005), pp. 425–35.
48. Brig. Hew Pike, 'The Army's Infantry and Armoured Reconnaissance Forces', in Linda Washington (ed.), *Ten Years On: The British Army in the Falklands War* (London: National Army Museum, 1992), p. 40.
49. Julian Thompson, *op. cit.*, p. 25.

CHAPTER 8

1. Adeed Dawisha, *Iraq: A Political History from Independence to Occupation* (Princeton: Princeton University Press, 2009), p. 212.
2. Jessica Weeks, *Dictators at War and Peace* (Ithaca, NY: Cornell University Press, 2014), ch. 4.
3. Talmadge, *op. cit.*
4. Mark Bowden, 'Tales of the Tyrant', *Atlantic Unbound* (May 2002).
5. Efraim Karsh and Inari Rautsi, *Saddam Hussein: A Political Biography* (New York: Free Press, 1991), p. 2.

6. Williamson Murray and Kevin M. Woods, *The Iran–Iraq War: A Military and Strategic History* (Cambridge: Cambridge University Press, 2014), p. 287.

7. Joseph Sassoon, *Saddam Hussein's Ba'th Party: Inside an Authoritarian Regime* (Cambridge: Cambridge University Press, 2011).

8. Jerrold M. Post, 'Saddam Hussein of Iraq: A Political Psychology Profile', *Political Psychology*, 12:2 (June 1991), pp. 279–89.

9. Charles Duelfer, *Comprehensive Report of the Special Advisor to the DCI on Iraq's WMD* (Central Intelligence Agency, 30 September 2004).

10. Bowden, *op. cit.*

11. Kevin M. Woods, Williamson Murray and Thomas Holaday, with Mounir Elkhamri, *Saddam's War: An Iraqi Military Perspective of the Iran–Iraq War*, McNair Paper 70 (Washington, DC: Institute for National Strategic Studies, National Defense University, 2009), pp. 16–17.

12. *Ibid.*

13. Documents and tapes seized by the US after the 2003 invasion help illuminate Saddam's decision-making. They permit a glimpse into Saddam's thought processes and his relationships with his advisers. This material has therefore been drawn upon heavily for this chapter. The material was gathered under the US government's 'Harmony' project. See Lawrence Rubin, 'Research Note: Documenting Saddam Hussein's Iraq', *Contemporary Security Policy*, 32:2 (2011), pp. 458–66. This chapter will refer to a number of books and articles emerging from this project. These include: Kevin M. Woods, David D. Palkki and Mark E. Stout, *The Saddam Tapes: The Inner Workings of a Tyrant's Regime, 1978–2001* (Cambridge: Cambridge University Press, 2011); Murray and Woods, *op. cit.*; Kevin M. Woods, *The Mother of All Battles: Saddam Hussein's Strategic Plan for the Persian Gulf War* (Annapolis: Naval Institute Press, 2008); Kevin Woods, James Lacey and Williamson Murray, 'Saddam's Delusions: The View from the Inside', *Foreign Affairs* (May/June 2006); Kevin M. Woods, with Michael R. Pease, Mark E. Stout, Williamson Murray and James G. Lacey, *Iraqi Perspectives Project: A View of Operation Iraqi Freedom from Saddam's Senior Leadership* (Washington, DC: Joint Center for Operational Analysis, 2006); Kevin M. Woods and Mark E. Stout, 'Saddam's Perceptions and Misperceptions: The Case of "Desert Storm"', *Journal of Strategic Studies*, 33:1 (2010), pp. 5–41. See also Ibrahim Al-Marushi, *Iraq's Armed Forces: An Analytical History* (London: Routledge, 2004).

14. Woods et al., *The Saddam Tapes*, *op. cit.*, pp. 132–8.

15. *Ibid.*, p. 139.

16. Efraim Karsh, *The Iran–Iraq War, 1980–1988* (London: Osprey Publishing, 2002), p. 30.

17. Charles Kurzman, 'Death Tolls of the Iran–Iraq War' (31 October 2013), https://kurzman.unc.edu/death-tolls-of-the-iran-iraq-war/

18. Murray and Woods, *op. cit.*, p. 6.

19. *Ibid.*, pp. 61, 64.

20. *Ibid.*, pp. 300–301.

21. Karsh, *op. cit.*, p. 70.

22. Anthony Cordesman, *The Lessons of Modern War*, vol. II: *The Iran–Iraq War* (London: Routledge, 1990), ch. 5.

23. Woods et al., *The Saddam Tapes*, *op. cit.*, pp. 148, 146, 147.

24. Con Coughlin, *Saddam: His Rise and Fall* (New York: Harpers, 2005).

25. Woods et al., *The Saddam Tapes*, *op. cit.*, p. 158.

26. F. Gregory Gause III, 'Iraq's Decisions to Go to War, 1980 and 1990', *Middle East Journal*, 56:1 (Winter 2002), p. 56.

27. 'An Interview with Tariq Aziz', PBS-Frontline, https://www.pbs.org/wgbh/pages/frontline/shows/saddam/interviews/aziz.html.

28. Woods, 2008, *op. cit.*, p. 60.

29. Sa'd al-Bazzaz, editor of an Iraqi paper in 1990, cited in Gause, *op. cit.*, p. 54.

30. Lawrence Freedman and Efraim Karsh, *The Gulf Conflict, 1990–1991* (London: Faber, 1993), pp. 60–61

31. 'An Interview with Tariq Aziz', *op. cit.*

32. Woods, 2008, *op. cit.*, pp. 62–3. Al-Bazzaz reports that it was only on 29 July 1990 that Saddam decided to implement the second plan, but that seems a bit late. Cited in Gause, *op. cit.*, p. 54.

33. Coughlin, *op. cit.*, p. 252.

34. 'Interview with General Wafic Al Samarrai, Head of Iraqi Military Intelligence', https://www.pbs.org/wgbh/pages/frontline/gulf/oral/samarrai/1.html

35. *Ibid.*

36. Coughlin, *op. cit.*, p. 140.

37. Norman Cigar, 'Iraq's Strategic Mindset and the Gulf War: Blueprint for Defeat', *Journal of Strategic Studies*, 15:1 (1992), p. 3.

38. *Ibid.*, p. 4.

39. Saddam speech on Army Day, *Al-'Iraq*, Baghdad (7 January 1991), in *ibid.*, p. 5.

40. Saddam press conference for Iraqi media, *Al-Thawra* (14 January 1991), in *ibid.*, pp. 7–8.

41. Woods, 2008, *op. cit.*, pp. 162, 185.

42. Saddam speech to the People's International Islamic Conference, *Sawt Al-Sha'b*, Amman (12 January 1991), in Cigar, *op. cit.*, p. 14.

43. Saddam speech of 31 December 1990, reported by Baghdad INA in Arabic, FBIS-NES-91-001 (1 January 1991), p. 23, in *ibid.*, p. 15.

44. Staff Brig. Amjad Al-Zumayri, 'Ru'ya 'askariyya' ['A Military Viewpoint'], *Al-Jumhuriyya* (5 December 1990), in *ibid.*, p. 15.

45. Woods, 2008, *op. cit.*, p. 125. This would work both ways. A meeting held on 20 November is revealing for this assessment process. On that occasion, speaking to his ground force commanders, Saddam reportedly scoffed that for the

Americans to go on the offensive 'it would require that they have guaranteed three times the number of Iraq's defending forces . . . that is three million'.

46. 'Interview with General Wafic Al Samarrai . . .', *op. cit.*

47. Cigar, *op. cit.*, p. 18.

48. Saddam speech while visiting the front, 23 January 1991, reported by Baghdad INA in Arabic, FBIS-NES-91-016 (24 January 1991), p. 22, in *Ibid.*, pp. 18–19.

49. Woods, 2008, *op. cit.*, p. 197.

50. Woods and Stout, *op. cit.*, p. 21.

51. Woods, 2008, *op. cit.*, p. 16. Unless otherwise stated, this account is based on chapter 2 of that book.

52. Norman Schwarzkopf, *It Doesn't Take a Hero: The Autobiography of General Norman Schwarzkopf* (New York: Bantam, 1992), p. 424. Freedman and Karsh, *op. cit.*, p. 365. See also HRH General Khaled bin Sultan, *Desert Warrior: A Personal View of the Gulf War by the Joint Forces Commander* (New York: HarperCollins, 1995), p. 363.

53. Woods, 2008, *op. cit.*

54. *Ibid.*

55. *Ibid.*

56. *Ibid.*

57. *Ibid.*, p. 222.

58. Thomas G. Mahnken, 'A Squandered Opportunity? The Decision to End the Gulf War', in Andrew J. Bacevich and Efraim Inbar (eds.), *The Gulf War of 1991 Reconsidered* (London: Frank Cass, 2003).

59. Toby Dodge, 'Saddam Hussein and US Foreign Policy: Diabolical Enemy Images, Policy Failure and the Administrations of Bush Senior and Junior', in Lawrence Freedman and Jeffrey Michaels (eds.), *Scripting Middle East Leaders: The Impact of Leadership Perceptions on US and UK Foreign Policy* (London: Bloomsbury, 2013), pp. 117–37.

60. Christian Alfonsi, *Circle in the Sand: Why We Went Back to Iraq* (New York: Doubleday, 2006), pp. 154–62.

61. George Bush and Brent Scowcroft, *A World Transformed* (New York: Knopf, 1998), pp. 471, 487. The 20 February quote comes from Alfonsi, *op. cit.*, p. 167. For background, see Freedman and Karsh, *op. cit.*, and Lawrence Freedman, *A Choice of Enemies: America Confronts the Middle East* (London: Weidenfeld & Nicolson, 2008).

62. 'Interview with General Wafic Al Samarrai . . .', *op. cit.*

63. Freedman and Karsh, *op. cit.*, p. 410.

64. Bush and Scowcroft, *op. cit.*, p. 487.

65. Woods, 2008, *op. cit.*, p. 239.

66. *Ibid.*, p. 255.

67. *Ibid.*, p. 242.

68. Michael Gordon and Bernard Trainor, *The Generals' War* (Boston, MA: Little, Brown, 1995), pp. 428–9.

69. Woods and Stout, *op. cit.*, p. 12.

70. Cited in Woods, 2008, *op. cit.*, p. 266.

71. Woods and Stout, *op. cit.*, p. 19.

72. Raad Hamdani, in Woods, with Pease et al., *op. cit.*, p. 13.

73. Kevin M. Woods, Williamson Murray, Elizabeth A. Nathan, Laila Sabara and Ana M. Venegas, *Saddam's Generals: Perspectives of the Iran–Iraq War* (Washington DC: Institute for Defense Analyses, 2011), pp. 37–38, 46, 61–2.

74. Woods and Stout, *op. cit.*, p. 27.

75. Woods, with Pease et al., *op. cit.*, p. 12.

CHAPTER 9

1. Ernesto Che Guevara, *I Embrace You With All My Revolutionary Fervor: Letters 1947–1967* (London: Penguin, 2021), p. 330.

2. See Ludo De Witte, *The Assassination of Lumumba* (London: Verso, 2001), and Emmanuel Gerard and Bruce Kuklick, *Death in the Congo: Murdering Patrice Lumumba* (Cambridge, MA: Harvard University Press, 2015). The US and the UN share culpability.

3. Mike Hoare, *Congo Mercenary* (London: Hale, 1967).

4. Alanna O'Malley, 'The Simba Rebellion, the Cold War, and the Stanleyville Hostages in the Congo', *Journal of Cold War Studies*, 23:2 (Spring 2021), pp. 75–99.

5. Kabila left no autobiographical writing and rarely gave interviews. I have used for his biography Erik Kennes, 'A Road Not Taken? The Biography of Laurent Kabila (1939–2001)', in Klaas van Walraven (ed.), *The Individual in African History: The Importance of Biography in African Historical Studies* (Leiden: Koninklijke Brill NV, 2020); and C. Kabuya-Lumuna Sando, 'Laurent Désiré Kabila', *Review of African Political Economy*, 29: 93–4 (2002), pp. 616–19.

6. On the context, see Ludo De Witte, 'The Suppression of the Congo Rebellions and the Rise of Mobutu, 1963–5', *International History Review*, 39:1 (2017), pp. 107–25, and Jeffrey H. Michaels, 'Breaking the Rules: The CIA and Counterinsurgency in the Congo 1964–1965', *International Journal of Intelligence and CounterIntelligence*, 25:1 (2012), pp. 130–59.

7. Philip Roessler and Harry Verhoeven, *Why Comrades Go to War: Liberation Politics and the Outbreak of Africa's Deadliest Conflict* (London: Hurst & Co., 2016), p. 152.

8. *Ibid.*, p. 193. See also Jon Lee Anderson, *Che Guevara: A Revolutionary Life* (New York: Grove Press, 1997), and Paul Dosal, *Comandante Che: Guerrilla*

Soldier, Commander, and Strategist, 1956–1967 (Pennsylvania: Pennsylvania University Press, 2003).

9. Matt D. Childs, 'An Historical Critique of the Emergence and Evolution of Ernesto Che Guevara's *Foco* Theory', *Journal of Latin American Studies*, 27:3 (October 1995), pp. 593–624.

10. Che Guevara, *Guerrilla Warfare* (Harmondsworth: Penguin, 1967). See also Che Guevara, *The Bolivian Diaries* (London: Penguin, 1968).

11. Dosal, *op. cit.*, p. 313.

12. William Gálvez, *Che in Africa: Che Guevara's Congo Diary* (New York: Ocean Press, 1999), p. 36.

13. *Ibid.*, p. 37; Anderson, *op. cit.*, pp. 622–3.

14. Mohamed Heikal, *Nasserl: The Cairo Documents* (London: New English Library, 1972), p. 349.

15. Gálvez, *op. cit.*, p. 55.

16. *Ibid.*, pp. 92–3.

17. Paco Ignacio Taibo II, *Guevara, Also Known as Che* (New York: St Martin's Press, 1997), p. 421.

18. Anderson, *op. cit.*, p. 648.

19. Taibo, *op. cit.*, p. 426.

20. Anderson, *op. cit.*, pp. 652–3.

21. Gálvez, *op. cit.*, p. 123.

22. Dosal, *op. cit.*, p. 238.

23. Gálvez, *op. cit.*, p. 172.

24. *Ibid.*, p. 183.

25. Guevara, *The Bolivian Diaries, op. cit.*

26. Gálvez, *op. cit.*, p. 45.

27. *Ibid.*, pp. 69–70.

28. Anderson, *op. cit.*, p. 654.

29. In a TV programme, cited by Greg Mills, 'The Boot is Now on the Other Foot: Rwanda's Lessons from Both Sides of Insurgency', *RUSI Journal*, 153:3 (2008).

30. Gálvez, *op. cit.*, pp. 69–70.

31. Jason K. Stearns, *Dancing in the Glory of Monsters: The Collapse of the Congo and the Great War of Africa* (New York: PublicAffairs, 2011), pp. 149–50.

32. The state created in 1960 as the Republic of the Congo, was sometimes known as Congo-Léopoldville (after its capital). To the north-west there was another Republic of the Congo, known as Congo-Brazzaville. In 1964, the official name of the first state became the Democratic Republic of the Congo, and in 1966 Léopoldville became Kinshasa. Mobutu's full name was Mobutu Sese Sekko Kuku Ngbendu Wa Za Banga, meaning 'The all-powerful warrior who, because of his endurance and inflexible will to win, will get from conquest to conquest, leaving fire in his wake.'

33. Tom Cooper, *Great Lakes Holocaust: First Congo War, 1996–1997* (London: Helion, 2013), p. 7.

34. Stearns, *op. cit.*, pp. 85–6.

35. In 2018, magistrates in France dropped charges against nine Rwandan officials investigated over this action, because of insufficient evidence. See 'France Drops Charges Against Rwandan Officials: Judicial Source', *Reuters* (26 December 2018).

36. Stearns, *op. cit.*, pp. 86–7.

37. *Ibid.*, p. 116.

38. *Ibid.*

39. William G. Thom, 'Congo–Zaire's 1996–97 Civil War in the Context of Evolving Patterns of Military Conflict in Africa in the Era of Independence', *Journal of Conflict Studies*, 19:2 (Fall 1999).

40. Roessler and Verhoeven, p. 192.

41. Stearns, *op. cit.*, pp. 112–20.

42. *Ibid.*, p. 118.

43. Thom, *op. cit.*

44. Stearns, *op. cit.*, p. 124.

45. Gérard Prunier, *Africa's World War: Congo, the Rwandan Genocide, and the Making of a Continental Catastrophe* (Oxford: Oxford University Press, 2009), p. 149.

46. *Ibid.*, p. 150.

47. Niko Price, 'Kabila Makes Surprise Visit to Cuba', AP (24 July 1998), https://www.cubanet.org/htdocs/CNews/y98/jul98/24e6.htm

48. Michaela Wrong, *Do Not Disturb: The Story of a Political Murder and an African Regime Gone Bad* (New York: PublicAffairs, 2021), p. 309.

49. Prunier, *op. cit.*, p. 183.

50. *Ibid.*, p. 188. See also François Ngolet, *Crisis in the Congo: The Rise and Fall of Laurent Kabila* (New York: Palgrave Macmillan, 2011).

51. Kennes, *op. cit.*, pp. 292–3.

CHAPTER 10

1. In an interview given towards the end of his life, Grachev gave the impression of being more in sympathy with the coup, but wanting to avoid bloodshed in Moscow and turning against the plotters when they decided that they needed to take out Yeltsin. See 'Pavel Grachev's Last Interview: "Across the White House, Runaway, Fire!"' (19 October 2012), https://en.topwar.ru/20105-poslednee-intervyu-pavla-gracheva-po-belomu-domu-beglymi-ogon.html

2. Vasilii Seliunin, 'On the General's Bass Notes: From a Conversation with Russian Minister of Defence Pavel Grachev', *Russian Politics & Law*, 3:5 (1993), pp. 19–26.

3. Timothy J. Colton, *Yeltsin: A Political Life* (New York: Basic Books, 2008), pp. 277–8.

4. Andrei Raevsky, 'Russian Military Performance in Chechnya: An Initial Evaluation', *Journal of Slavic Military Studies*, 8:4 (1995), pp. 686–7.

5. For a thorough study on the problem of corruption within the Russian armed forces, see Graham H. Turbiville Jr, 'Mafia in Uniform: The Criminalization of the Russian Armed Forces', *Foreign Military Studies Office Blue Book* (July 1995), p. 29.

6. For histories of the conflict, see Mark Galeotti, *Russia's Wars in Chechnya, 1994–2009* (Oxford: Osprey Publishing, 2014): Tracey C. German, *Russia's Chechen War* (London: Routledge, 2003); John B. Dunlop, *Russia Confronts Chechnya* (Cambridge: Cambridge University Press, 1998); Anatol Lieven, *Chechnya: Tombstone of Russian Power* (New Haven: Yale University Press, 1998); O. Oliker, *Russia's Chechen Wars, 1994–2000* (Santa Monica: RAND Corporation, 2001).

7. Andrew Higgins, 'Grachev "Allowed Rebels to Keep Soviet Arms"', *Independent* (11 January 1995).

8. Pavel Felgenhauer, 'The Chechen Campaign', in Mikhail Tsypkin (ed.)., *War in Chechnya: Implications for Russian Security Policy* (Monterey: Naval Postgraduate School, 1996), p. 41.

9. German, *op. cit.*, pp. 119–23.

10. Galeotti, *Russia's Wars in Chechnya, op. cit.*, p. 32; Pjer Simunovic, 'The Russian Military in Chechnya – A Case Study of Morale in War', *Journal of Slavic Military Studies*, 11:1 (January 1998), pp. 63–95, at p. 72.

11. The origin of the 'one paratroop regiment' claim appears to lie in Grachev's attempt to deny Russian military involvement in the failed fiasco of 26 November. His is reported to have said that he would never have sent tanks into Grozny, and that 'if the Army had fought … one airborne regiment within two hours would have been able to handle the whole thing'. See Pavel Litovkin, 'Ministerstvo oborony RF: versiyu ob uchastii rossiiskoi armii v chechenskom konflikte General Grachev nazyvayet bredom' [Ministry of Defence of the Russian Federation: General Grachev calls the version about Russian army participation in the Chechen conflict nonsense], *Izvestiya* (29 November 1994), p. 1.

12. Nikolai V. Grammatikov, 'The Russian Intervention in Chechnya in December 1994: Issues and Decision-Making', *Journal of Slavic Military Studies*, 11:4 (1998), pp. 111–32.

13. Raevsky, *op. cit.*, p. 686.

14. Felgenhauer, *op. cit.*

15. Colton, *op. cit.*, p. 291.

16. Charles J. Dick, 'A Bear without Claws: The Russian Army in the 1990s', *Journal of Slavic Military Studies*, 10:1 (March 1997), pp. 1–10.

17. Simunovic, *op. cit.*, p. 78.
18. Dick, *op. cit.*, pp. 5–8.
19. Benjamin S. Lambeth, 'Russia's Wounded Military', *Foreign Affairs* (March–April 1995). Lambeth not only describes the parlous state of the Russian armed forces but also the low regard for Grachev as someone who owed his position to Yeltsin rather than any professional achievements.
20. Dick, *op. cit.*, p. 9.
21. Timothy Thomas, 'The Russian Armed Forces Confront Chechnya: I. Military-Political Aspects 11–31 December 1994', *Journal of Slavic Military Studies*, 8:2 (1995), sect. 1, fn. 52.
22. 12 December radio interview, cited in *ibid.*
23. David Remnick, 'Letter from Chechnya', *New Yorker* (24 July 1995), pp. 58–9.
24. Raevsky, *op. cit.*, p. 684.
25. Jennifer Mathers, 'The Lessons of Chechnya: Russia's Forgotten War?', *Civil Wars*, 2:1 (1999), pp. 100–116, at pp. 109–10.
26. Simunovic, *op. cit.*
27. Mathers, *op. cit.*
28. Oliker, *op. cit.*, pp. 72–3; Eugene Miakinkov, 'The Agency of Force in Asymmetrical Warfare and Counterinsurgency: The Case of Chechnya', *Journal of Strategic Studies*, 34:5 (2011), pp. 647–80, at pp. 657–8.
29. 'ILYAS AKHMADOV, ADC to Shamil Basaev and later to Aslan Maskhadov, Presently Foreign Minister of the Chechen Republic Ichkeria, Interview' (June 1999), https://smallwarsjournal.com/documents/akhmadovinterview.pdf
30. Maj. Aleksandr Belkin (retd), 'War in Chechnya: The Impact on Civil–Military Relations in Russia', in Tsypkin, *op. cit.*, p. 32.
31. Mathers, *op. cit.*
32. Sebastien Roblin, 'How Vladimir Putin Rose from the Ashes of the First Chechen War: The Muslim Chechens had Clashed with Russia for Centuries', *National Interest* (9 February 2021), https://nationalinterest.org/blog/reboot/how-vladimir-putin-rose-ashes-first-chechen-war-177927
33. Lieven, 1998, *op. cit.*, p. 111.
34. Simunovic, *op. cit.*, p. 65.
35. Mathers, *op. cit.*, p. 108. 'The most striking feature about Russia's performance in this conflict is how few of the problems which plagued the Russian armed forces were created by the Chechens they were fighting.'
36. Timothy L. Thomas, 'The Caucasus Conflict and Russian Security: The Russian Armed Forces Confront Chechnya III. The Battle for Grozny, 1–26 January 1995', *Journal of Slavic Military Studies*, 10:1 (1997), pp. 50–108.
37. Carlotta Gall and Thomas de Waal, *Chechnya: Calamity in the Caucasus* (New York: New York University Press, 1998).
38. Simunovic, *op. cit.*

39. Felgenhauer, *op. cit.*, p. 46.

40. Igor Korotchenko, 'Grachev's Words Backfired on Him, Bloodshed Lifts all Taboos', *Nezavisimaya Gazeta* (21 January 1995).

41. M. J. Orr, 'The Current State of the Russian Armed Forces', Conflict Studies Research Center, D60 (November 1996), p. 11.

42. Anatol Lieven, 'Russia's Military Nadir: The Meaning of the Chechen Debacle', *National Interest*, (Summer 1996), pp. 24–33.

43. 'Letter from Officer X', *Time* (23 January 1995).

44. Simunovic, *op. cit.*

45. Miakinkov, *op. cit.*, pp. 660–61.

46. Roblin, *op. cit.*

47. Catherine Belton, *Putin's People: How the KGB Took Back Russia and Then Took on the West* (London: William Collins, 2020); Lajos F. Szászdi, *Russian Civil–Military Relations and the Origins of the Second Chechen War* (Lanham: University Press of America, 2008).

48. Galeotti, *Russia's Wars in Chechnya, op. cit.*, pp. 52–65; Timothy Thomas, 'Russian Tactical Lessons Learned Fighting Chechen Separatists', *Journal of Slavic Military Studies*, 18:4 (2005), pp. 731–66.

49. Mark Kramer, 'The Perils of Counterinsurgency: Russia's War in Chechnya', *International Security*, 29:3 (Winter 2004/2005), pp. 5–6.

50. Matthew Evangelista, 'Is Putin the New de Gaulle? A Comparison of the Chechen and Algerian Wars', *Post-Soviet Affairs*, 21:4 (2005), p. 360.

CHAPTER 11

1. Ivo Daalder and Michael O'Hanlon, *Winning Ugly: NATO's War to Save Kosovo* (Washington, DC: Brookings Institution, 2000).

2. Smith, *op. cit.*

3. Anton Myrer, *Once an Eagle* (New York: HarperCollins, 1999), p. 845.

4. *Ibid.*, p. 611.

5. Maj. Gen. Robert Scales, US Army (retd), 'O! The Damage "Once an Eagle" Has Done to My Army – And Yes, It Is Partly My Fault', *Foreign Policy* (18 December 2013).

6. Robert Stone, 'Battle Hymn of the Republic', *New York Review of Books* (5 October 2000).

7. Elizabeth Becker, 'Military Goes by the Book, But It's a Novel', *New York Times* (16 August 1999).

8. Mark Perry, *The Pentagon's Wars: The Military's Undeclared War against America's Presidents* (New York: Basic Books, 2017), p. 72.

9. David Halberstam, *War in a Time of Peace: Bush, Clinton, and the Generals* (New York: Scribner, 2001), p. 414. See also Daalder and O'Hanlon, *op. cit.*

10. Perry, *op. cit.*, pp. 63–4.

11. Halberstam, 2001, *op. cit.*, p. 430.

12. Peter Boyer, 'General Clark's Battles', *New Yorker* (17 November 2003).

13. Kohn, *op. cit.*, p. 10.

14. Halberstam, 2001, *op. cit.*, p. 416.

15. *Ibid.*, p. 421.

16. Gen. Wesley K. Clark, *Waging Modern War* (New York: PublicAffairs, 2001), p. 403. For a critique, see Andrew Stigler, 'Hoping for Victory: Coercive Air Power and NATO's Strategy in Kosovo', in Phil M. Haun, Colin F. Jackson and Timothy P. Schultz, *Air Power in the Age of Primacy: Air Warfare since the Cold War* (Cambridge: Cambridge University Press, 2022).

17. Clark, *op. cit.*, p. 201.

18. Halberstam, 2001, *op. cit.*, pp. 444–5.

19. Benjamin S. Lambeth, *NATO's Air War for Kosovo: A Strategic and Operational Assessment* (Santa Monica: RAND Corporation, 2001), p. 181.

20. *Ibid.*, pp. 192, 195.

21. Stigler, *op. cit.*, p. 79.

22. Clark, *op. cit.*, p. 195.

23. Dana Priest, 'Tension Grew with Divide over Strategy', *Washington Post* (21 September 1999); and William M. Arkin, 'How Sausage Is Made', *Washington Post* (17 July 2000). Both cited by Lambeth 2001, *op. cit.*, pp. 199–201.

24. Clark, *op. cit.*, p. 303.

25. Gen. (retd) Hugh Shelton, with Ronald Levinson and Malcolm McConnell, *Without Hesitation: The Odyssey of an American Warrior* (New York: St. Martin's Press, 2010), p. 383; Clark, *op. cit.*, pp. 272, 273.

26. Tony Blair, *A Journey* (London: Hutchinson, 2010), p. 240.

27. Steven Lee Myers, 'U.S. Military Chiefs Firm: No Ground Force for Kosovo', *New York Times* (3 June 1999).

28. Thomas, 1997, *op. cit.*

29. Strobe Talbott, *The Russia Hand: A Memoir of Presidential Diplomacy* (New York: Random House, 2002), pp. 321–3.

30. *Ibid.*, p. 333.

31. Clark, *op. cit.*, p. 377.

32. Clark gave a full account of this episode in his memoir, as did Jackson in his. They do not differ greatly in terms of the description of the events or the dialogue between the two men. See Gen. Sir Mike Jackson, *Soldier: The Autobiography* (London: Bantam, 2007). An account also appears as Mike Jackson, 'Command of the Kosovo Force 1999', in Jonathan Bailey, Richard Iron and Hew Strachan (eds.), *British Generals in Blair's Wars* (Farnham: Ashgate, 2013).

33. Clark, *op. cit.*, pp. 385–6; Mike Jackson, 2007, *op. cit.*, p. 324.

34. Talbott, *op. cit.*, p. 342.

35. *Ibid.*, p. 344.

36. Richard Dannatt, *Leading from the Front: An Autobiography* (London: Bantam, 2010), pp. 251–2.

37. Mike Jackson, 2007, *op. cit.*, p. 242.

38. Blair, *op. cit.*, p. 243.

39. 'Memorandum of Telephone Conversation – Vice President Al Gore and Prime Minister Sergey Stepashin of Russia' (12 June 1999), https://clinton.presidentiallibraries.us/items/show/101594

40. 'Memorandum of Telephone Conversation – President Boris Yeltsin of Russia' (13 June 1999), https://clinton.presidentiallibraries.us/items/show/101608

41. 'Memorandum of Telephone Conversation – Vice President Al Gore and Prime Minister Sergey Stepashin of Russia' (14 June 1999), https://clinton.presidentiallibraries.us/items/show/101595

42. 'Memorandum of Telephone Conversation – President Boris Yeltsin of Russia' (14 June 1999), https://clinton.presidentiallibraries.us/items/show/101607

43. 'Memorandum of Telephone Conversation – National Security Advisor Samuel Berger and Russian FSB Chief and National Security Advisor Vladimir Putin' (15 June 1999), https://clinton.presidentiallibraries.us/items/show/101583

44. Clark, *op. cit.*, p. 396.

45. Mike Jackson, 2007, *op. cit.*, p. 213.

46. *Ibid.*

47. Clark, *op. cit.*, p. 245.

48. Smith, *op. cit.*, p. 89.

49. Boyer, *op. cit.*

50. Scales, 2013, *op. cit.*

CHAPTER 12

1. Vladimir Putin, *First Person: An Astonishingly Frank Self-Portrait by Russia's President Vladimir Putin* (New York: PublicAffairs, 2000).

2. I deal with the conflict in Lawrence Freedman, *Ukraine and the Art of Strategy* (New York: OUP, 2019).

3. This was a speech of late January 2013 to the annual general meeting of the Russian Academy of Military Science on 'The Role of the General Staff in the Organization of the Defense of the Country in Correspondence with the New Statute about the General Staff Confirmed by the President of the Russian Federation.' Sam Jones, 'Ukraine: Russia's New Art of War', *Financial Times* (28 August 2014); and Paul Goble, 'Putin's Actions in Ukraine Following Script by Russian General Staff a Year Ago', *The Interpreter* (20 June 2014), http://www.interpretermag.com/putins-actions-in-ukraine-following-script-by-russian-general-staff-a-year-ago/.

4. Seth Jones, *Three Dangerous Men: Russia, China, Iran and the Rise of Irregular Warfare* (New York: Norton, 2021), p. 57.

5. M. Galeotti, 'The "Gerasimov Doctrine" and Russian Non-Linear War' (6 July 2014), https://inmoscowsshadows.wordpress.com/2014/07/06/the-gerasimov-doctrine-and-russian-non-linear-war; Mark Galeotti, *Russian Political War: Moving Beyond the Hybrid* (London: Routledge, 2019); and Daniel Triesman, 'Why Putin Took Crimea: The Gambler in the Kremlin', *Foreign Affairs* (May/June 2006).

6. As with many figures in this drama, his emails were hacked. 'Who is Strelkov-Girkin according to the Hackers of the Anonymous International' (5 October 2014), http://lj.rossia.org/users/anticompromat/2379137.html

7. Noah Sneider, 'Shadowy Rebel Wields Iron Fist in Ukraine Fight', *New York Times* (10 July 2014).

8. Anna Matveeva, *Through Times of Trouble: Conflict in Southeastern Ukraine Explained from Within* (Lanham, MD: Lexington Books, 2018).

9. 'Who is Strelkov-Girkin according to the Hackers of Anonymous International', *op. cit.*; and 'The Most Dangerous Man in Ukraine is an Obsessive War Reenactor Playing Now with Real Weapons', *New Republic* (23 July 2014), https://newrepublic.com/article/118813/igor-strelkov-russian-war-reenactor-fights-real-war-ukraine

10. Courtney Weaver, 'Malofeev: The Russian Billionaire Linking Moscow to the Rebels', *Financial Times* (24 July 2014). Malofeev denied any political ambitions for himself: 'I want the Russian Empire back,' he says. 'I don't want to be head of it.'

11. Marlene Laruelle, 'The Three Colors of Novorossiya, or the Russian Nationalist Mythmaking of the Ukrainian Crisis', *Post-Soviet Affairs*, 32:1 (2016), pp. 55–74.

12. Alexander Boroday, 'We Are Not Ready to Make Peace on the Terms of Surrender', *Novaya Gazeta*, 89 (13 August 2014).

13. Max Delany, 'Mysterious Russian Fixer Heads Ukraine Rebel State', *Times of Israel* (18 May 2014), https://www.timesofisrael.com/mysterious-russian-fixer-heads-ukraine-rebel-state/

14. Anatoly Stepanov, 'The Word Novorossiya Caresses My Ears', *Russian Folk Line: Orthodoxy. Autocracy. Nationality* (8 August 2014), https://ruskline.ru/analitika/2014/08/8/slovo_novorossiya_laskaet_mne_sluh/

15. Komov to Frolov, 12 September 2013, in 'FrolovLeaks VI: Tomorrow Was the War', InformNapalm (7 November 2018), https://informnapalm.org/en/frolovleaks-vi-tomorrow-was-the-war/

16. Serhiy Halchenko, 'Russian Orthodox Church Supporting War in Ukraine', EuroMaidan Press (19 May 2014), https://euromaidanpress.com/2014/05/20/russian-orthodox-church-supporting-war-in-ukraine/

17. This was denied by Malofeev, who by the time it was published was already being sanctioned by the EU for his role in Ukraine. 'Council Implementing Regulation (EU) No 826/2014' (30 July 2014), https://eur-lex.europa.eu/legal-content/EN/TXT/?uri=CELEX:32014R0826; and Neil MacFarquhar,

'Early Memo Urged Moscow to Annex Crimea, Report Says', *New York Times* (25 February 2015).

18. 'Novaya Gazeta's "Kremlin Papers" Article' (25 February 2015), https://www.unian.info/politics/1048525-novaya-gazetas-kremlin-papers-article-full-text-in-english.html

19. Charles Clover, *Black Wind, White Snow: The Rise of Russia's New Nationalism* (New Haven: Yale University Press, 2016), p. 326.

20. Cited by Mikhail Zygar, *All the Kremlin's Men: Inside the Court of Vladimir Putin* (London: Perseus, 2016).

21. Mark Galeotti, *Armies of Russia's War in Ukraine* (Oxford: Osprey, 2019), p. 11.

22. Peter Hobson, 'Battle for Sevastopol: How a Crimean Romantic Fought the Kremlin's Bureaucrat', *Moscow Times* (8 April 2016), https://www.themoscow-times.com/2016/04/08/battle-for-sevastopol-how-a-crimean-romantic-fought-the-kremlins-bureaucrat-a52439

23. 'Transcript: Vladimir Putin's April 17 Q&A', *Washington Post* (17 April 2014), https://www.washingtonpost.com/world/transcript-vladimir-putins-april-17-qanda/2014/04/17/ff77b4a2-c635-11e3-8b9a-8e0977a24aeb_story.html

24. Quoted in Carl Bildt, 'Is Peace in Donbas Possible?', European Council on Foreign Relations (12 October 2017).

25. Galeotti, *Armies of Russia's War*, *op. cit.*, p. 11.

26. Matveeva, *op. cit.*

27. 'Vladimir Putin Answered Journalists' Questions on the Situation in Ukraine' (4 March 2014), http://eng.kremlin.ru/news/6763

28. 'Address by President of the Russian Federation' (18 March 2014), http://eng.kremlin.ru/news/6889

29. Sergei Loiko, 'The Unraveling of Moscow's "Novorossia" Dream' (1 June 2016), https://www.rferl.org/a/unraveling-moscow-novorossia-dream/27772641.html

30. 'The Most Dangerous Man in Ukraine . . .', op. cit.

31. '"Who Are You, the Shooter?" – Interview with Igor Strelkov' (20 November 2014), https://igorstrelkov.wordpress.com/2014/11/20/who-are-you-the-shooter-interview-with-igor-strelkov/

32. International Crisis Group, 'Rebels without a Cause: Russia's Proxies in Eastern Ukraine', Report No. 254 (16 July 2019), https://www.crisisgroup.org/europe-central-asia/eastern-europe/ukraine/254-rebels-without-cause-russias-proxies-eastern-ukraine

33. 'English Translation of Audio Evidence of Putin's Adviser Glasyev and Other Russian Politicians Involvement in War in Ukraine' (29 August 2016), http://uaposition.com/analysis-opinion/english-translation-audio-evidence-putins-adviser-glazyev-russian-politicians-involvement-war-ukraine/

34. Interview with *Zavtra* in November 2014. Anna Dolgov, 'Russia's Igor Strelkov: I Am Responsible for War in Eastern Ukraine', *Moscow Times* (21 November 2014).

35. Matveeva, *op. cit.*, p. 107.

36. Mark Rachkevych, 'Armed Pro-Russian Extremists Launch Coordinated Attacks in Donetsk Oblast, Seize Regional Police Headquarters, Set Up Checkpoints', *Kyiv Post* (12 April 2014).

37. At Russian urging, the OSCE hostages were later released. Instructions to do so came in early May from one of Putin's envoys, Vladimir Lukin.

38. '"Who Are You, the Shooter?" – Interview with Igor Strelkov', *op. cit.*

39. Halya Coynash, 'Key Insurgent Admits There Was No Civil War, Just Russian Aggression', Kharkiv Human Rights Protection Group (11 January 2021), https://khpg.org/en/1608808721

40. International Crisis Group, *op. cit.*

41. Gerard Toal, *Near Abroad: Putin, the West, and the Contest over Ukraine and the Caucasus* (Oxford: Oxford University Press, 2019), p. 264.

42. Zygar, *op. cit.*, p. 287.

43. Strelkov interview, quoted in Dolgov, *op. cit.*

44. '"Who Are You, the Shooter?" – Interview with Igor Strelkov', *op. cit.*

45. Griff Witte, 'Pro-Russian Separatists in Eastern Ukraine Were "Nobodies" – Until Now', *Washington Post* (30 April 2014).

46. 'The Saboteur "Shooter" Declared War on Kyiv after the Coup and Asked the Kremlin for Help' (12 May 2014), https://www.pravda.com.ua/news/2014/05/12/7025115/

47. Matveeva, *op. cit.*, p. 130.

48. Anna Shamanska, 'Former Commander of Pro-Russian Separatists Says He Executed People Based on Stalin-Era Laws', Radio Free Europe (19 January 2016), https://www.rferl.org/a/ukraine-girkin-strelkov-executions-stalin-era/27497491.html

49. A photo of the order appeared on the Web signed by the commander of the militia of the DNR Igor Strelkov. 'Igor Strelkov Shot Two Militias for Looting' (26 May 2014), https://life.ru/p/133903

50. '"Murdered" Ukraine Politician Faced Hostile Mob, Video Shows' (23 April 2014), https://www.reuters.com/article/us-ukraine-crisis-politician-video/murdered-ukraine-politician-faced-hostile-mob-video-shows-idUSBREA3M0EX20140423. Bezler was a Russian citizen with extensive military experience and links with the GRU. He had been living in Crimea, where he had worked with Girkin. Later he established his own base in Horlivka, and they fell out.

51. Matveeva, *op. cit.*, p. 129.

52. Alexander Nagorny, 'Sergey Glazyev: "Decisively, Harshly and Precisely"', *Zavtra* (19 June 2014), http://zavtra.ru/content/view/sergej-glazev-reshitelno-zhestko-i-tochno/. This interview conveys the full flavour of Glazyev's nationalism and conviction that the US was behind all of Russia's troubles.

53. Gert-Jan Dennekamp, 'Audio Tapes of Thousands of Overheard Conversations, a Reconstruction of the MH17 Disaster', *Nieuwsuur* (11 April 2021),

https://nos.nl/nieuwsuur/artikel/2376246-audio-tapes-of-thousands-of-overheard-conversations-a-reconstruction-of-the-mh17-disaster.html. This is based largely on intercepts of Dubinsky's conversations.

54. 'Ukraine President Poroshenko Hails "Turning Point"', BBC (6 July 2014), http://www.bbc.co.uk/news/world-europe-28180907

55. Jaroslav Koshiw, 'Donetsk Separatists in Dispute – Khodakovsky vs Strelkov', *OpenDemocracy.net* (11 August 2014).

56. For a later list of the various groups, see Galeotti, *Armies of Russia's War*, *op. cit.*, pp. 19–26. See also Michael Kofman, Katya Migacheva, Brian Nichiporuk, Andrew Radin, Olesya Tkacheva and Jenny Oberholtzer, *Lessons from Russia's Operations in Crimea and Eastern Ukraine* (Santa Monica, CA: RAND Corporation, 2017), p. 53.

57. Sabrina Tavernise and David M. Herszenhorn, 'Patchwork Makeup of Rebels Fighting Ukraine Makes Peace Talks Elusive', *New York Times* (9 July 2014).

58. 'Battles in Social Networks – Is the Kremlin Leaking Strelkov?', BBC (7 July 2014), https://www.bbc.com/russian/international/2014/07/140707_tr_donbass_social_media_debate

59. Interview for the Moscow-based publication *Insider*. 'Igor "Strelkov" Girkin's Revealing Interview', DFRLab (28 December 2017), https://medium.com/dfrlab/igor-strelkov-girkins-revealing-interview-acf44b22b48

60. 'Where Are They Now?' *Meduza* (31 May 2019), https://meduza.io/en/feature/2019/06/01/where-are-they-now

61. Koshiw, *op. cit.*

62. Matveeva, *op. cit.*

63. Glazyer's alarm at the developing situation can be seen in a June 2014 analysis: 'US is Militarizing Ukraine to Invade Russia' (20 June 2014), https://wikispooks.com/wiki/Document:US_is_militarizing_Ukraine_to_invade_Russia

64. Alya Shandra and Robert Seely, 'The Surkov Leaks: The Inner Workings of Russia's Hybrid War in Ukraine', RUSI Occasional Paper (July 2019), https://rusi.org/explore-our-research/publications/occasional-papers/surkov-leaks-inner-workings-russias-hybrid-war-ukraine

65. 'MH17 Witness Appeal November 2019', Politie (Netherlands) (November 2019),https://www.politie.nl/en/information/witness-appeal-crash-mh17-nov-19.html

66. *Ibid.*

67. Official, Bellingcat 'Senior Russian Official Uncovered as MH17 Suspect', BBC (29 April 2020), https://www.bbc.co.uk/news/world-europe-52472142

68. 'Key MH17 Figure Identified as Senior FSB Official: Colonel General Andrey Burlaka', *op. cit.*,

69. Dennekamp, *op. cit.*

70. 'Russian Colonel General Identified as Key MH17 Figure', Bellingcat (8 December 2017), https://www.bellingcat.com/news/uk-and-europe/2017/12/08/russian-colonel-general-delfin/; 'Igor "Strelkov" Girkin's Revealing Interview', *op. cit.*

71. This paragraph is based on Dennekamp, *op. cit.*

72. *Ibid.*

73. This has not been fully confirmed. 'MH17 Trial Part 2: The Bezler Tapes, a Case of Red Herrings?', Bellingcat (17 October 2020), https://www.bellingcat.com/news/2020/10/17/the-mh17-trial-part-2-the-bezler-tapes-a-case-of-red-herrings/

74. Nationals of ten countries were killed, with the largest number Dutch (193), followed by Malaysian (43) and Australian (27).

75. Dennekamp, *op. cit.*

76. See https://www.prosecutionservice.nl/topics/mh17-plane-crash. Much of what we now know about the organization and conversations of the separatist groups is a result of the work of a Dutch-led Joint Investigation Team (JIT).

77. Marc Bennetts, 'Russian Ex-Spy Igor Girkin Takes "Moral Responsibility" for Downing of MH17', *The Times* (20 May 2020).

78. This was soon taken down. As an example of how much was known at the time, see Alec Luhn, 'Three Pro-Russia Rebel Leaders at the Centre of Suspicions over Downed MH17', *Guardian* (20 July 2014).

79. Matveeva, *op. cit.*

80. Denis Kazansky, 'Zhuchkovsky's "85 Days of Slavyansk": Guilty Plea', Liga.net (10 March 2019), http://www.liga.net/politics/opinion/85-dney-slavyanska-juchkovskogo-yavka-s-povinnoy

81. Anton Zverev, 'Ex-Rebel Leaders Detail Role Played by Putin Aide in East Ukraine' (11 May 2017), https://www.reuters.com/article/us-ukraine-crisis-russia-surkov-insight/ex-rebel-leaders-detail-role-played-by-putin-aide-in-east-ukraine-idUSKBN1870TJ

82. International Crisis Group, *op. cit.*

83. 'Igor "Strelkov" Girkin's Revealing Interview', *op. cit.*

84. International Crisis Group, *op. cit.*

85. 'Battles in Social Networks – Is the Kremlin Leaking Strelkov?', *op. cit.*

86. 'Are the Kremlin Hardliners Winning?' (1 October 2014) IMR, https://imrussia.org/en/analysis/world/2041-are-the-kremlin-hardliners-winning

87. Marlene Laruelle, 'Back from Utopia: How Donbas Fighters Reinvent Themselves in a Post-Novorossiya Russia', *Nationalities Papers*, 47:5 (September 2019), pp. 719–33.

88. Franklin Holcomb, *The Kremlin's Irregular Army: Ukrainian Separatist Order of Battle* (Washington, DC: Institute for the Study of War, 2017), p. 10.

89. Ron Synovitz, 'Onetime Russian Hero Selling Gold Crimea Medal Bearing "Despised" Putin' (11 March 2019), https://www.rferl.org/a/onetime-russian-hero-selling-gold-crimea-medal-bearing-despised-putin/29815575.html

90. Lennart Maschmeyer, 'The Subversive Trilemma: Why Cyber Operations Fall Short of Expectations', *International Security*, 46:2 (Fall 2021), pp. 51–90.

91. Halya Coynash, 'Russian Who Brought War to Donbas Admits It Has Turned Into "a Dump" Worse than Ukraine or Russia', Kharkiv Human Rights Protection Group (11 October 2021), https://khpg.org/en/1608809608

92. Vladimir Putin, 'On the Historical Unity of Russians and Ukrainians' (12 July 2021), http://en.kremlin.ru/events/president/news/66181

93. Natasha Bertrand, Oren Liebermann and Matthew Chance, 'US Officials: Indications Russia Has Moved Blood Supplies to Ukraine Border', *CNN* (29 January 2022), https://edition.cnn.com/2022/01/29/politics/us-official-russia-ukraine-blood-supplies/index.html; Michael Kofman, 'Putin's Wager in Russia's Standoff with the West', *War on the Rocks* (24 January 2022), https://warontherocks.com/2022/01/putins-wager-in-russias-standoff-with-the-west/

94. David M. Herszenhorn, 'US Warns War Could Be "Imminent" in Ukraine', *Politico* (11 February 2022), https://www.politico.eu/article/ukraine-russia-european-union-diplomats-leave/

95. Isabelle Khurshudyan, Missy Ryan and Paul Sonne, 'Russia–U.S. Talks Hit Impasse over NATO Expansion as Moscow Denies Plans to Invade Ukraine', Washington Post (10 January 2022), http://www.washingtonpost.com/world/2022/01/10/us-russia-delegations-meet-geneva/

96. Shaun Walker, 'Don't Panic: Why Ukraine Doesn't Like Western Talk of Imminent Attack', *Guardian* (2 February 2022), https://www.theguardian.com/world/2022/feb/02/ukraine-western-talk-of-imminent-attack-putin

97. 'If Vladimir Putin Does Decide on War in Ukraine, Few Russians Will Be Expecting It', *The Economist* (7 February 2022), https://www.economist.com/europe/2022/02/07/if-vladimir-putin-does-decide-on-war-in-ukraine-few-russians-will-be-expecting-it

98. Sebastien Roblin, 'Alleged Captured Documents Imply Ukraine Invasion Planned in January', *Forbes* (3 March 2022), https://www.forbes.com/sites/sebastienroblin/2022/03/03/alleged-captured-documents-imply-ukraine-invasion-planned-in-january/?sh=5ee49ab51b96

99. James Risen, 'U.S. Intelligence Says Putin Made a Last-Minute Decision to Invade Ukraine', *The Intercept* (11 March 2022), https://theintercept.com/2022/03/11/russia-putin-ukraine-invasion-us-intelligence/

100. Tatiana Stanovaya, '3 Things the World Should Know about Putin', *Foreign Policy* (27 January 2022), http://foreignpolicy.com/2022/01/27/putin-russia-ukraine-crisis-invasion/; Paul Kirby, 'Ukraine Conflict: Who's in Putin's Inner Circle and Running the War?', BBC (3 March 2022), https://www.bbc.co.uk/news/world-europe-60573261

101. 'East Ukraine Separatist Regions to Evacuate Civilians to Russia', *Moscow Times* (18 February 2022), https://www.themoscowtimes.com/2022/02/18/east-ukraine-separatist-regions-to-evacuate-civilians-to-russia-a76452

102. Kirby, *op. cit*

103. 'Address by the President of the Russian Federation', (21 February 2022), http://en.kremlin.ru/events/president/news/67828

104. Nick Waters, '"Exploiting Cadavers" and "Faked IEDs": Experts Debunk Staged Pre-War "Provocation" in the Donbas', *Bellingcat* (28 February 2022), https://www.bellingcat.com/news/2022/02/28/exploiting-cadavers-and-faked-ieds-experts-debunk-staged-pre-war-provocation-in-the-donbas/

105. 'Transcript: Vladimir Putin's Televised Address on Ukraine', *Bloomberg News* (24 February 2022), https://www.bloomberg.com/news/articles/2022-02-24/full-transcript-vladimir-putin-s-televised-address-to-russia-on-ukraine-feb-24

106. 'Ukraine Invasion: Putin Urges Ukrainian Military to Overthrow Country's Leaders', Sky News (25 February 2022), https://news.sky.com/story/ukraine-invasion-putin-urges-ukraine-military-to-overthrow-countrys-leaders-12551317

107. Lawrence Freedman, 'A Reckless Gamble' (25 February 2022), https://samf.substack.com/p/a-reckless-gamble?s=w

108. Julian Borger, 'The Drone Operators Who Halted Russian Convoy Headed for Kyiv', *The Guardian* (28 March 2022), https://www.theguardian.com/world/2022/mar/28/the-drone-operators-who-halted-the-russian-armoured-vehicles-heading-for-kyiv. The most informed account of where and how the Russian invasion went wrong is Jack Watling and Nick Reynolds, *Operation Z: The Death Throes of an Imperial Delusion*, (London: RUSI, April 2022), https://static.rusi.org/special-report-202204-operation-z-web.pdf

109. Timothy Snyder, 'Russia's Genocide Handbook: The Evidence of Atrocity and of Intent Mounts', *Thinking About . . .*, (8 April 2022), https://snyder.substack.com/p/russias-genocide-handbook?s=r. For an analysis of the development of anti-Ukrainian ideology in Ukraine see Taras Kuzio, *Russian Nationalism and the Russian-Ukrainian War*, (London: Routledge, 2022).

110. 'Refugees Fleeing Ukraine', UNHCR, https://data2.unhcr.org/en/situations/ukraine

111. See polling by Rating Group Ukraine: 'The Fifth National Poll: Ukraine during the War' (18 March 2022), https://ratinggroup.ua/en/research/ukraine/pyatyy_obschenacionalnyy_opros_ukraina_v_usloviyah_voyny_18_marta_2022.html

112. 'Ukraine Invasion: Putin Puts Russia's Nuclear Forces on "Special Alert"', *BBC* (27 February 2022), https://www.bbc.co.uk/news/world-europe-60547473

113. Tristan Bove, 'How Likely Is It That Putin Will Unleash a Nuclear War?', *Fortune* (27 March 2022), https://fortune-com.cdn.ampproject.org/c/s/fortune.com/2022/03/26/putin-nuclear-war-russia-ukraine/amp/

114. Anton Troianovski and Michael Schwirtz, 'As Russia Stalls in Ukraine, Dissent Brews over Putin's Leadership', *New York Times* (22 March 2022), https://www.nytimes.com/2022/03/22/world/europe/putin-russia-military-planning.html; Nexta TV, Twitter (25 March 2022), https://twitter.com/nexta_tv/status/1507319434121256964

115. Anton Razmakhnin, 'Strelkov Gave Four Tips for Russia to Win in the Operation in Ukraine', *Moskovskij Komsomolets* (27 March 2022), https://www.mk.ru/politics/2022/03/27/strelkov-dal-chetyre-soveta-kak-rossii-pobedit-v-operacii-na-ukraine.html

116. Mark Trevelyan and Alexander Winning, 'Russia States More Limited War Goal to "Liberate" Donbass', *Reuters* (25 March 2022), https://www.reuters.com/world/europe/russia-says-first-phase-ukraine-operation-mostly-complete-focus-now-donbass-2022-03-25/

117. https://www.oryxspioenkop.com/2022/02/attack-on-europe-documenting-ukrainian.html

118. https://en.wikipedia.org/wiki/Casualties_of_the_Russo-Ukrainian_War

119. For a detailed critique of Russia's military performance see Speech by UK Defence Secretary Ben Wallace on Russia's invasion of Ukraine, 9 May 2022, https://www.gov.uk/government/speeches/speech-by-defence-secretary-on-russias-invasion-of-ukraine.

120. Lawrence Freedman, 'A Victory Parade Without Victories', (10 May 2022), https://samf.substack.com/p/a-victory-parade-without-victories?s=w

121. Tim Lister and Taras Zadorozhnyy, 'Setbacks in Ukraine trigger rare criticism of Russia's war effort by Russian bloggers', CNN, 18 May 2022, https://edition.cnn.com/2022/05/18/europe/russia-bloggers-ukraine-criticism-intl-cmd/index.html

122. 'Ukraine Invasion: Kremlin Policy Adviser Reveals His Shock over Vladimir Putin's Decision to Invade', *Sky News* (2 March 2022), http://news.sky.com/story/ukraine-invasion-kremlin-policy-adviser-reveals-his-shock-over-vladimir-putins-decision-to-invade-12555163; Mike Eckel, 'Russian Officials Predicted a Quick Triumph In Ukraine: Did Bad Intelligence Skew Kremlin Decision-Making?' *Fletcher School* (11 March 2022), https://sites.tufts.edu/fletcherrussia/russian-officials-predicted-a-quick-triumph-in-ukraine-did-bad-intelligence-skew-kremlin-decision-making/

123. Michael Schwirtz and Eric Schmitt, 'Russia's top officer visited the front line to change the offensive's course, U.S. and Ukraine officials say.' *New York Times*, 1 May 2022, https://www.nytimes.com/2022/05/01/world/europe/russian-general-dead-valery-gerasimov.html

124. Dan Sabbagh, 'Putin involved in war 'at level of colonel or brigadier', say western sources', *The Guardian*, 16 May 2022, https://www.theguardian.com/world/2022/may/16/putin-involved-russia-ukraine-war-western-sources

CHAPTER 13

1. 'Rumsfeld Snowflakes Come in from the Cold', National Security Archive (24 January 2018), https://nsarchive.gwu.edu/briefing-book/foia/2018-01-24/rumsfeld-snowflakes-come-cold

2. George W. Bush, *Decision Points* (New York: Crown, 2010), p. 193.

3. Shelton, *Without Hesitation, op. cit.*, pp. 406–9.

4. Donald Rumsfeld, *Known and Unknown: A Memoir* (New York: Penguin, 2011), p. 374.

5. Gen. Hugh Shelton, 'Inside the War Room the Final Days', History Reader (12 October 2010), https://www.thehistoryreader.com/military-history/inside-war-room-final-days/

6. Donald Rumsfeld, '2001-10-10 to Myers Pace re What Will Be the Military Role in the War on Terrorism?', Rumsfeld Papers, www.rumsfeld.com, cited by Yaniv Barzilai, *102 Days of War: How Osama bin Laden, al Qaeda and the Taliban Survived 2001* (Washington, DC: Potomac Books, 2013), pp. 50–51.

7. Robert Grenier, *88 Days to Kandahar* (New York: Simon & Schuster, 2016), pp. 8, 90.

8. Michael DeLong, *Inside CentCom: The Unvarnished Truth about the Wars in Afghanistan and Iraq* (Chicago: Regnery Publishing, 2004), p. 28.

9. Shelton, *Without Hesitation, op. cit.*, p. 447.

10. Tommy Franks, *American Soldier* (New York: Regan Books, 2004), p. 276; Perry, *op. cit.*, p. 130; Shelton, 'Inside the War Room . . .', *op. cit.*

11. DeLong, *Inside CentCom, op. cit.*, p. 28.

12. Perry, *op. cit.*, p. 130.

13. Interview with Doug Feith: see Barzilai, *op. cit.*, p. 109.

14. Bob Woodward, *Bush at War* (New York: Simon & Schuster, 2002), pp. 58–9.

15. Franks, *American Soldier, op. cit.*, pp. 296–300.

16. Bob Woodward, *Bush at War, op. cit.*, p. 251.

17. Thomas Ricks, 'Rumsfeld's Hands-On War', *Washington Post* (9 December 2001).

18. Grenier, *op. cit.*, pp. 82–5.

19. George Tenet, with Bill Harlow, *At the Center of the Storm: My Years at the CIA* (New York: HarperCollins, 2007).

20. Bob Woodward, *Bush at War, op. cit.*, p. 34.

21. Richard Myers, *Eyes on the Horizon: Serving on the Front Lines of National Security* (New York: Threshold, 2009), p. 164.

22. Bob Woodward, *Bush at War, op. cit.*, p. 311.

23. Franks, *American Soldier, op. cit.*, p. 315.

24. Interview with Gen. Tommy Franks, conducted on 12 June 2002, PBS Front-line, https://www.pbs.org/wgbh/pages/frontline/shows/campaign/interviews/franks.html
    Tommy Franks, 'War of Words', *New York Times* (19 October 2004).
25. Donald Wright et al., *A Different Kind of War: The United States Army in OPERATION ENDURING FREEDOM (OEF) October 2001– September 2005* (Fort Leavenworth, KS: Combat Studies Institute Press, US Army Combined Arms Center, 2010), p. 116.
26. Jim Mattis and Bing West, *Call Sign Chaos: Learning to Lead* (New York: Random House, 2019), pp. 75–6.
27. *Ibid.*, p. 76.
28. Gary Berntsen and Ralph Pezzullo, *Jawbreaker* (New York: Crown Publishing, 2005).
29. Gary C. Schroen, *First In: An Insider's Account of How the CIA Spearheaded the War on Terror in Afahanistan* (New York: Ballantine Books, 2005), p. 38.
30. Interview in Barzilai, *op. cit.*, p. 46.
31. Chris Woolf, 'Remembering the Battle of Tora Bora in 2001', *The World* (22 December 2015), https://www.pri.org/stories/2015-12-22/remembering-battle-tora-bora-2001
32. Interview in Barzilai, *op. cit.*, p. 71.
33. *Ibid.*, p. 57.
34. Berntsen and Pezzullo, *op. cit.*, p. 266.
35. Woolf, *op. cit.*
36. Bob Woodward, *Bush at War*, *op. cit.*, p. 112.
37. Henry Crumpton, *The Art of Intelligence: Lessons from a Life in the CIA's Clandestine Service* (New York: Penguin, 2012), p. 259.
38. *United States Special Operations Command History*, 6th edn (March 2008), pp. 90, 99, https://irp.fas.org/agency/dod/socom/2007history.pdf
39. Berntsen and Pezzullo, *op. cit.*, p. 214.
40. Dalton Fury, *Kill Bin Laden: A Delta Force Commander's Account of the Hunt for the World's Most Wanted Man* (New York: St. Martin's Press, 2008).
41. Peter Bergen, 'The Account of How We Nearly Caught Osama bin Laden in 2001', *New Republic* (30 December 2009).
42. Wright et al., *op. cit.*, p. 115, describes them as being 'busy with security tasks'.
43. *United States Special Operations Command History*, *op. cit.*, p. 99.
44. Mary Anne Weaver, 'Lost at Tora Bora', *New York Times Magazine* (11 September 2005).
45. Wright et al., *op. cit.*, p. 118.
46. Interview with Gen. Tommy Franks, *op. cit.*
47. Franks, 'War of Words', *op. cit.*
48. John F. Kerry, *Tora Bora Revisited: How We Failed to Get Bin Laden and Why It Matters Today: A Report to Members of the Committee on Foreign*

Relations, United States Senate (Washington, DC: U.S. Government Printing Office, 2009). On the confirmation of bin Laden's presence, see Wright et al., *op. cit.*, p. 115. Although the consensus is that bin Laden left Tora Bora on 14 December, one account has him leaving by 10 December. See Mustafa Hamid and Leah Farrall, *The Arabs at War in Afghanistan* (London: Hurst, 2015), pp. 9, 210, 283–9.

49. Michael DeLong, 'Setting the Record Straight on Tora Bora', *Wall Street Journal* (1 November 2004).
50. DeLong, *Inside CentCom, op. cit.*, p. 56
51. Ricks, 'Rumsfeld's Hands-On War', *op. cit.*
52. Bush, *op. cit.*, p. 202.
53. Mattis and West, *op. cit.*, p. 76.
54. Crumpton cited by Barzilai, *op. cit.*, p. 113.
55. Bob Woodward, 'Secret CIA Units Playing a Central Combat Role', *Washington Post* (18 November 2001).
56. Rumsfeld, 2011, *op. cit.*, p. 402.
57. *Ibid.*, p. 403.
58. Bergen, *op. cit.*
59. Barzilai, *op. cit.*
60. Michael E. O'Hanlon, 'A Flawed Masterpiece', *Foreign Affairs* (May/June 2002).
61. Benjamin Runkle, 'Tora Bora Reconsidered: Lessons from 125 Years of Strategic Manhunts', *Joint Forces Quarterly*, issue 70 (2013), pp. 40–46; and Peter John Paul Krause, 'The Last Good Chance: A Reassessment of U.S. Operations at Tora Bora', *Security Studies*, 17:4 (2008), pp. 644–84.
62. Tenet and Harlow, *op. cit.*, pp. 139–140.
63. Ricks, 2012, *op. cit.*, pp. 398, 402–3. Franks features in a list of the five worst generals in American history: see Michael Peck, 'Take Your Pick: Who Are the 5 Worst Generals in American History?', *National Interest* (6 November 2019), https://nationalinterest.org/blog/buzz/take-your-pick-who-are-5-worst-generals-american-history-94271

CHAPTER 14

1. Blair, *op. cit.*, p. 471.
2. 'National Strategy for Victory in Iraq' (Annapolis, November 2005), https://georgewbush-whitehouse.archives.gov/infocus/iraq/iraq_strategy_nov2005.html; Thomas E. Ricks, *The Gamble: General David Petraeus and the American Military Adventure in Iraq, 2006–2008* (New York: Penguin Press, 2009), p. 14.

3. Timothy Andrews Sayle, Jeffrey A. Engel, Hal Brands and William Inboden (eds.), *The Last Card: Inside George W. Bush's Decision to Surge in Iraq* (Ithaca, NY: Cornell University Press, 2019), p. 41.

4. Ricks, 2009, *op. cit.*, pp. 11–12.

5. *Ibid.*, p. 56.

6. Sayle et al., *op. cit.*, p. 329.

7. *Ibid.*, p. 264.

8. Ricks, 2009, *op. cit.*, p. 77.

9. Kori Schake, 'Civil–Military Relations and the 2006 Iraqi Surge', in Sayle et al., *op. cit.*, p. 318.

10. Greg Newbold, 'Why Iraq Was a Mistake', *Time* (9 April 2006); David S. Cloud, Eric Schmitt and Thom Shanker, 'Rumsfeld Faces Growing Revolt by Retired Generals', *New York Times* (13 April 2006).

11. Sayle et al., *op. cit.*, p. 253.

12. Schake, *op. cit.*, p. 314.

13. Bob Woodward, *State of Denial* (New York: Simon & Schuster, 2002), pp. 145–6.

14. Schake, *op. cit.*, p. 325.

15. Stephen Benedict Dyson, *Leaders in Conflict: Bush and Rumsfeld in Iraq* (Manchester: Manchester University Press, 2014), p. 90.

16. Sayle et al., *op. cit.*, p. 248.

17. *Ibid.*, p. 280.

18. Andrew Preston, 'Iraq, Vietnam, and the Meaning of Victory', in Sayle et al., *op. cit.*, p. 257.

19. Frederick W. Kagan, 'Choosing Victory: A Plan for Success in Iraq' (Washington, DC: American Enterprise Institute, 5 January 2007).

20. James A. Baker, III, and Lee H. Hamilton et al., *The Iraq Study Group Report: The Way Forward – A New Approach* (New York: Vintage Books, 2006).

21. Ricks, 2009, *op. cit.*, p. 281.

22. Bob Woodward, *The War Within: A Secret White House History (2006–2008)* (New York: Simon & Schuster, 2008), p. 289.

23. Peter D. Feaver, 'The Right to Be Right: Civil–Military Relations and the Iraq Surge Decision', *International Security*, 35:4 (Spring 2011), p. 108.

24. Ricks, 2009, *op. cit.*, pp. 99–100.

25. Bob Woodward, 2008, *op. cit.*, p. 282.

26. Sayle et al., *op. cit.*, p. 53.

27. Fred Kaplan, *The Insurgents: David Petraeus and the Plot to Change the American Way of War* (New York: Simon & Schuster, 2013).

28. Peter Mansoor, *Surge: My Journey with General David Petraeus and the Remaking of the Iraq War* (New Haven: Yale University Press, 2013).

29. Michael Gordon, 'Bush Aide's Memo Doubts Iraqi Leader', *New York Times* (29 November 2006), https://www.nytimes.com/2006/11/29/world/middle-east/29cnd-military.html

30. Linda Robinson, *Tell Me How This Ends: General David Petraeus and the Search for a Way Out of Iraq* (New York: PublicAffairs, 2009), p. 24.

31. Dyson, *op. cit.*, pp. 120–21.

32. 'President's Address to the Nation' (10 January 2007), https://georgewbushwhitehouse.archives.gov/news/releases/2007/01/20070110-7.html

33. Part of Fallon's difficulty was that he had publicly warned about starting yet another war, with Iran, proposing diplomacy instead. Elaine Sciolino, 'Push for New Direction Leads to Sudden Dead End for a 40-Year Naval Career', *New York Times* (31 May 2008).

34. Carter Malkasian, *Illusions of Victory: The Anbar Awakening and the Rise of the Islamic State* (New York: Oxford University Press, 2017).

35. Blair, *op. cit.*, p. 227.

36. *The Report of the Iraq Inquiry* (6 July 2016), vol. V, 'Section 6.1: Development of the Military Options for an Invasion of Iraq', p. 254.

37. *Ibid.*, vol. VI, 'Section 6.4: Planning and Preparation for a Post-Saddam Hussein Iraq, Mid-2001 to January 2003', p. 185.

38. *Ibid.*, vol. V, 'Section 6.1', p. 308.

39. He told the Iraq Inquiry that he had done this. See *ibid.*, vol. VII, 'Section 8', p. 7.

40. *Ibid.*, vol. V, 'Section 6.2', p. 398.

41. I deal with this episode in Lawrence Freedman, 'Political Impatience and Military Caution', *Journal of Strategic Studies*, 44:1 (2021), pp. 91–116.

42. During the early days of the occupation, there were troops from Holland, Norway, Italy, Japan, Australia, New Zealand, Romania, Denmark, Portugal, the Czech Republic and Lithuania.

43. Gen. David Richards, *Taking Command* (London: Headline, 2014), pp. 172–80.

44. Justin Maciejewski, ' "Best Effort": Operation Sinbad and the Iraq Campaign', in Bailey et al., *British Generals in Blair's Wars*, p. 158.

45. U K Ministry of Defence, 'Operations in Iraq, January 2005–May 2009 (Op TELIC 5–13): An Analysis from the Land Perspective' (29 November 2010), ch. 3, https://assets.publishing.service.gov.uk/government/uploads/system/uploads/attachment_data/file/557326/20160831-FOI07003_77396_Redacted.pdf

46. *The Report of the Iraq Inquiry, op. cit.*, vol. VII, 'Section 9.4, June 2005 to May 2006', p. 522.

47. *Ibid.*, p. 550.

48. *Ibid.*, p. 608.

49. *Ibid.*, p. 605.

50. Dannatt, *op. cit.*, pp. 253–7; 'A Very Honest General', *Daily Mail* (12 October 2006); *The Report of the Iraq Inquiry, op. cit.*, vol. VIII, 'Section 9.5, June 2006 to 27 June 2007', p. 43.

51. Blair, *op. cit.*, p. 117.

52. Tim Ripley, *Operation Telic: The British Campaign in Iraq, 2003–2009* (Lancaster: Telic-Herrick Publications, 2016), p. 316.

53. Evidence to the Iraq Inquiry, Houghton transcript, p. 22. See https://webarchive.nationalarchives.gov.uk/ukgwa/20171123122801/http://www.iraqinquiry.org.uk/the-evidence/

54. Ripley, 2016, *op. cit.*, p. 320.

55. *The Report of the Iraq Inquiry, op. cit.*, vol. VIII, 'Section 9.5', p. 82.

56. Simon Akam, *The Changing of the Guard: The British Army since 9/11* (London: Scribe, 2021), p. 240.

57. Evidence to the Iraq Inquiry, Houghton transcript, *op. cit.*, p. 22.

58. Maciejewski, *op. cit.*, p. 161.

59. Ripley, 2016, *op. cit.*, p. 320.

60. *The Report of the Iraq Inquiry, op. cit.*, vol. VIII, 'Section 9.5', p. 494.

61. *Ibid.*, p. 493.

62. *Ibid.*, pp. 36–7.

63. Evidence to the Iraq Inquiry, Shirreff transcript. See https://webarchive.nationalarchives.gov.uk/ukgwa/20171123122801/http://www.iraqinquiry.org.uk/the-evidence/

64. 'Post-Operational Report MND SE' (19 January 2007), cited by Daniel Patrick Marston, 'Operation TELIC VIII to XI: Difficulties of Twenty-First-Century Command', *Journal of Strategic Studies*, 44:1 (2021), pp.63–90.

65. Maciejewski, *op. cit.*, p. 171

66. *The Report of the Iraq Inquiry, op. cit.*, vol. VIII, 'Section 9.5', p. 37.

67. *Ibid.*, p. 68.

68. Blair, *op. cit.*, pp. 470–71.

69. Christopher Elliott, *High Command: British Military Leadership in the Iraq and Afghanistan Wars* (Oxford: Oxford University Press, 2015).

70. Evidence to the Iraq Inquiry, Shaw testimony (private session), pp. 32–3. See https://webarchive.nationalarchives.gov.uk/ukgwa/20171123122801/http://www.iraqinquiry.org.uk/the-evidence/. Shaw's chapter, 'Basra 2007: The Requirements of a Modern Major General', in Bailey et al., *op. cit.*, p. 178, claims that the US and UK approaches were aligned and Petraeus and Odierno gave their approval 'to everything we did'. This is not inconsistent with unhappiness about the speed of the drawdown.

71. *The Report of the Iraq Inquiry, op. cit.*, vol. VIII, 'Section 9.5', pp. 99, 492, 80.

72. *Ibid.*

73. *Ibid.*, p. 89.

74. Dannatt, *op. cit.*, p. 296.

75. *The Report of the Iraq Inquiry, op. cit.*, vol. VIII, 'Section 9.5', p. 114.

76. *Ibid.*, p. 153.

77. Col. Joel D. Rayburn and Col. Frank K. Sobchak (eds.), *The U.S. Army in the Iraq War*, vol. 2: *Surge and Withdrawal, 2007–2011* (Washington, DC: Strategic Studies Institute and US Army War College Press, 2019), p. 122.

78. *The Report of the Iraq Inquiry*, *op. cit.*, vol. VIII, 'Section 9.6, 27 June 2007 to April 2008', p. 203.

79. Ben Barry, *Blood, Metal and Dust: How Victory Turned into Defeat in Afghanistan and Iraq* (Oxford: Osprey, 2020), p. 331.

80. *The Report of the Iraq Inquiry*, *op. cit.*, vol. VIII, 'Section 9.6', p. 196.

81. See Marston, *op. cit.*

82. Richard Iron, 'Basra 2008: Operation Charge of the Knights', in Bailey et al., *op. cit.*, p. 188.

83. Gordon Brown, *My Life, Our Times* (London: The Bodley Head, 2017), p. 262.

84. Rayburn and Sobchak, *op. cit.*, p. 355.

85. *The Report of the Iraq Inquiry*, *op. cit.*, vol. VIII, 'Section 9.6', pp. 355–6.

86. Marston describes the episode in 'Operation TELIC VIII to XI', *op. cit.*, and Iron in 'Basra 2008: Operation Charge of the Knights', *op. cit.*, pp. 187–99.

87. *The Report of the Iraq Inquiry*, *op. cit.*, vol. VIII, 'Section 9.6', p. 338.

88. Akam, *op. cit.*, p. 231.

89. *The Report of the Iraq Inquiry*, *op. cit.*, vol. VIII, 'Section 9.6', p. 357.

90. *The Report of the Iraq Inquiry*, *op. cit.*, vol. VIII, 'Section 9.5', p. 366.

91. *Ibid.*, p. 374. In his autobiography, he accepted responsibility for the failure to embed earlier with Iraqi forces. See Dannatt, *op. cit.*, p. 304.

92. Barry, *op. cit.*, p. 341.

93. Rayburn and Sobchak, *op. cit.*, p. 617.

CHAPTER 15

1. Smith, *op. cit.*, p. 423.

2. John Keegan, *The Mask of Command* (London: Pimlico, 1999), p. 11.

3. Brian McAllister Linn, *The Echo of Battle: The Army's Way of War* (Cambridge, MA: Harvard University Press, 2007), pp. 6–7.

4. *The US Army/Marine Corps Counterinsurgency Field Manual (FM-24)* (Chicago: University of Chicago Press, 2007).

5. Smith, *op. cit.*, p. 423.

6. Gen. Stanley McChrystal, *My Share of the Task: A Memoir* (New York: Penguin, 2014), p. 17.

7. Gen. Stanley McChrystal, Foreword to Lartéguy, 2016, *op. cit.*, p. vii.

8. Bob Woodward, *Obama's Wars* (New York: Simon & Schuster, 2010).

9. McChrystal, 2014, *op. cit.*, p. 98.

10. Trinquier was also said to be the model for Julien Boisfeuras in *The Praetorians*.

11. McChrystal, 2014, *op. cit.*, pp. 121–2.

12. Fred Kaplan, *The Insurgents*

13. David Loyn, *The Long War: The Inside Story of America and Afghanistan since 9/11* (New York: St. Martin's Press, 2021), p. 179.

14. Robert Gates, *Duty: Memoirs of a Secretary at War* (New York: Alfred A. Knopf, 2014), p. 353. On the Afghanistan decision, see in addition Barack Obama, *A Promised Land* (New York: 2020); Penguin, Perry, *op. cit.*, and Bob Woodward, 2010, *op. cit.*

15. Obama, *op. cit.*, p. 433.

16. *Ibid.*, p. 432.

17. *Ibid.*, p. 434.

18. *Ibid.*, pp. 434–5.

19. Andrew Prokop, 'Why Biden Was So Set on Withdrawing from Afghanistan', *vox* (18 August 2021), https://www.vox.com/2021/8/18/22629135/biden-afghanistan-withdrawal-reasons

20. Obama, *op. cit.*, p. 438.

21. On Eikenberry's concerns, see: Eric Schmitt, 'U.S. Envoy's Cables Show Worries on Afghan Plans', *New York Times* (25 January 2010).

22. Loyn, *op. cit.*, p. 195.

23. Gates, *op. cit.*

24. Obama, *op. cit.*

25. President Obama on Gen. McChrystal's resignation, Office of the Press Secretary, 23 June 2010.

26. Risa Brooks, 'Paradoxes of Professionalism', *International Security*, 44:4 (Spring 2020), p. 7.

27. Michael Hastings, 'The Runaway General', *Rolling Stone* (8–22 July 2010).

28. Philip Rucker and Carol Leonnig, *A Very Stable Genius: Donald J. Trump's Testing of America* (New York: Penguin, 2020).

29. Steve Coll and Adam Entous, 'The Secret History of the U.S. Diplomatic Failure in Afghanistan', *New Yorker* (29 December 2021).

30. Bob Woodward, *Fear: Trump in the White House* (New York: Simon & Schuster, 2018), p. 124.

31. Mujib Mashal, 'Taliban and U.S. Strike Deal to Withdraw American Troops from Afghanistan', *New York Times* (29 February 2020).

32. *Afghanistan Study Group Final Report: A Pathway for Peace in Afghanistan* (Washington, DC: United States Institute of Peace, February 2021), https://www.usip.org/publications/2021/02/afghanistan-study-group-final-report-pathway-peace-afghanistan

33. Helene Cooper, Eric Schmitt and David E. Sanger, 'Debating Exit from Afghanistan, Biden Rejected Generals' Views', *New York Times* (19 April 2021).

34. There were about 7,000 from other allied forces then in Afghanistan, and about 18,000 private contractors from the US.

35. Alex Ward, 'An "Emotional" Moment at an NSC Meeting Shows Why Withdrawing from Afghanistan is So Hard', Vox (4 March 2021).

36. Cooper, Schmitt and Sanger, *op. cit.*

37. 'Remarks by President Biden on the Way Forward in Afghanistan' (14 April 2021), https://www.whitehouse.gov/briefing-room/speeches-remarks/2021/04/14/remarks-by-president-biden-on-the-way-forward-in-afghanistan/

38. George Packer, 'The Betrayal', *The Atlantic* (31 January 2022).

39. Thomas Gibbons-Neff, 'U.S. Military Begins Task of Leaving Afghanistan', *New York Times* (26 April 2021).

40. Packer, *op. cit.*

41. 'There's going to be no circumstance where you see people being lifted off the roof of a embassy in the – of the United States from Afghanistan. It is not at all comparable.' See 'Remarks by President Biden on the Drawdown of U.S. Forces in Afghanistan' (8 July 2021), https://www.whitehouse.gov/briefing-room/speeches-remarks/2021/07/08/remarks-by-president-biden-on-the-drawdown-of-u-s-forces-in-afghanistan/. Packer notes that at the time of the withdrawal from Saigon, Biden, then a very junior senator, had refused to authorize expenditure to evacuate Vietnamese allies. He did not believe the US had 'an obligation, moral or otherwise, to evacuate foreign nationals' other than diplomats. That was the job of private organizations. See Packer, *op. cit.*

42. Thomas Gibbons-Neff, 'A Solemn Pullout in the Last Hours of a Lost Fight', *New York Times* (31 August 2021).

43. Eric Schmitt, 'No U.S. Troops Will Be Punished for Deadly Kabul Strike, Pentagon Chief Decides', *New York Times* (13 December 2021).

44. Michael Ignatieff, *Virtual War: Kosovo and Beyond* (New York: Henry Holt, 2000).

45. Michael W. Hankins, *Flying Camelot: The F-15, the F-16, and the Weaponization of Fighter Pilot Nostalgia* (Ithaca, NY: Cornell University Press, 2021),

46. Jack McDonald, *Enemies Known and Unknown: Targeted Killings in America's Transnational War* (Oxford: Oxford University Press, 2017).

47. Samuel Moyn, *Humane: How the United States Abandoned Peace and Reinvented War* (London: Verso, 2022).

48. Jeffrey Goldberg, 'The Obama Doctrine', *The Atlantic* (April 2016).

49. Keith Grant and Bernd Kaussler, 'The Battle of Aleppo: External Patrons and the Victimization of Civilians in Civil War', *Small Wars & Insurgencies*, 31:1 (2020), p. 6.

50. Benjamin S. Lambeth, *Airpower in the War against ISIS* (Annapolis: Naval Institute Press, 2021), p. 12.

51. Ash Carter, *A Lasting Defeat: The Campaign to Destroy ISIS*, Belfer Special Report (2017), https://www.belfercenter.org/publication/lasting-defeat-campaign-destroy-isis

52. On ISIS's military organization and its approach to the Battle of Mosul, see Ahmed S. Hashim, *The Caliphate at War: Operational Realities and Innovations of the Islamic State* (Oxford: OUP, 2018), pp. 228–33.

53. 'Transcript: Defense Secretary James Mattis on "Face the Nation"', CBS (28 May 2017), https://www.cbsnews.com/news/transcript-defense-secretary-james-mattis-on-face-the-nation-may-28-2017/

54. Lambeth, 2021, *op. cit.*, p. 111.

55. *Ibid.*, p. 101.

56. *Ibid.*

57. *Ibid.*, p. 99.

58. 'Commander's Perspective: CJFLCC Operations in Iraq, Insights from MG Joseph M. Martin, Commanding General 1st Infantry Division', Center for Army Lessons Learned (26 October 2017), https://usacac.army.mil/sites/default/files/publications/17567.pdf

59. Azmat Khan, 'Hidden Pentagon Records Reveal Patterns of Failure in Deadly Airstrikes', *New York Times* (18 December 2021).

60. *Ibid.*

61. Susannah George, Qassim Abdul-Zahra, Maggie Michael and Lori Hinnant, 'Mosul is a Graveyard: Final IS Battle Kills 9,000 Civilians', *AP News* (21 December 2017). Another report, based on death certificates, suggested that nearly 5,000 civilians had died between October 2016 and July 2017: Jane Arraf, 'More Civilians than ISIS Fighters Are Believed Killed in Mosul Battle', NPR (19 December 2017), https://www.npr.org/sections/parallels/2017/12/19/570483824/more-civilians-than-isis-fighters-are-believed-killed-in-mosul-battle. In one conservative estimate, 1,066 and 1,579 civilians likely died from coalition air and artillery strikes, though the details were unavoidably difficult to establish: Samuel Oakford, 'Counting the Dead in Mosul: The Civilian Death Toll in the Fight against ISIS is Far Higher than Official Estimates', *The Atlantic* (5 April 2018).

62. Azmat Khan, *op. cit.*

63. Dave Phillips and Eric Schmitt, 'How the U.S. Hid an Airstrike that Killed Dozens of Civilians in Syria', *New York Times* (13 November 2021).

64. For a full account of the Russian war in Syria, see Tim Ripley, *Operation Aleppo: Russia's War in Syria. The Inside Story of Putin's Military Intervention in the Syrian War* (Lancaster: Telic-Herrick Publications, 2018).

65. On Soleimani, see Seth Jones, *Three Dangerous Men*.

66. Michael Birnbaum, 'The Secret Pact between Russia and Syria that Gives Moscow Carte Blanche', *Washington Post* (15 January 2016), https://www.washingtonpost.com/news/worldviews/wp/2016/01/15/the-secret-pact-between-russia-and-syria-that-gives-moscow-carte-blanche/

67. Ripley, 2018, *op. cit.*

68. Samuel Charap, Elina Treyger and Edward Geist, 'Understanding Russia's Intervention in Syria', RAND (2019), p. 10.

69. Ripley, 2018, *op. cit.*, p. 89.

70. *Ibid.*, p. 55.

71. Dmitry (Dima) Adamsky, 'Russian Lessons from the Syrian Operation and the Culture of Military Innovation', The Marshall Center Security Insights (February 2020), no. 47, https://www.marshallcenter.org/en/publications/security-insights/russian-lessons-syrian-operation-and-culture-military-innovation. See also: Michael Kofman, 'Syria and the Russian Armed Forces: An Evaluation of Moscow's Military Strategy and Operational Performance' in Robert E. Hamilton, Chris Miller and Aaron Stein (eds.), *Russia's War in Syria: Assessing Russian Military Capabilities and Lessons Learned* (Philadelphia: Foreign Policy Research Institute, 2020).

72. 'Russian Intervention in Syria 76 Months On', Syrian Observatory For Human Rights (30 January 2022), https://www.syriahr.com/en/236975/ Overall casualties in the Syrian civil war have been assessed by the UN as at least 350,209 people, although this is almost certainly an underestimate. See 'Syria: 10 Years of War Has Left at Least 350,000 Dead', UN News (24 September 2021), https://news.un.org/en/story/2021/09/1101162

73. Ralph Shield, 'Russia's Air War Win in Syria: A Kinetic Approach to Counterinsurgency', in Haun et al., *Air Power in the Age of Primacy*, pp. 231, 241. Grant and Kaussler, *op. cit.*, pp. 1–33.

74. 'Physicians for Human Rights' Findings of Attacks on Health Care in Syria', Physicians for Human Rights (findings of June 2021), http://syriamap.phr.org/#/en/findings

75. Richard Hall and Barzou Daragahi, 'Doctors in Idlib Will No Longer Share Coordinates of Hospitals with UN after Repeated Attacks from Russian and Syrian Forces', *Independent* (3 June 2019). The UN secretary general was sufficiently disturbed by the 'destruction of, or damage to, facilities on the deconfliction list and UN-supported facilities in the area' that he ordered an investigation. See 'Secretary-General Establishes Board to Investigate Events in North-West Syria since Signing of Russian Federation–Turkey Memorandum on Idlib', UN (1 August 2019).

76. Evan Hill and Christiaan Triebert, '12 Hours. 4 Syrian Hospitals Bombed. One Culprit: Russia', *New York Times* (13 October 2019), https://www.nytimes.com/2019/10/13/world/middleeast/russia-bombing-syrian-hospitals.html

77. *US Army/Marine Corps Counterinsurgency Field Manual, op. cit.*

CHAPTER 16

1. Anthony King, *Command: The Twenty-First-Century General* (Cambridge: Cambridge University Press, 2019), p. 18.

2. David Richards, 'The Art of Command in the Twenty-First Century', in Julian Lindley-French and Yves Boyer (eds.), *The Oxford Handbook of War* (Oxford: OUP, 2012), pp. 382–4.

3. Stanley McChrystal, *Team of Teams* (London: Penguin, 2015), p. 57.

4. Eitan Shamir, *Transforming Command: The Pursuit of Mission Command in the U.S., British, and Israeli Armies* (Stanford: Stanford University Press, 2011).

5. King, 2019, *op. cit.*, p. 21.

6. Anthony King, 'Operation Moshtarak: Counter-Insurgency Command in Kandahar 2009–10', *Journal of Strategic Studies*, 44:1 (2021), p. 50. This is also covered in King, 2019, *op. cit.*

7. King, 2019, *op. cit.*, p. 418.

8. *Ibid.*, p. 302.

9. Jim Storr, *Something Rotten: Land Command in the 21st Century* (Havant: Howgate Publishing, 2022), pp. 14, 9.

10. Maj. Gen. Bob Scales, *Scales on War* (Annapolis: Naval Institute Press, 2016), p. 113.

11. Andrew Hill and Heath Niemi, 'The Trouble with Mission Command: *Flexive Command* and the Future of Command and Control', *Joint Forces Quarterly*, 86 (3rd quarter, 2017), pp. 94–100.

12. Michael Kofman, 'Syria and the Russian Armed Forces: An Evaluation of Moscow's Military Strategy and Operational Performance', in Robert E. Hamilton, Chris Miller and Aaron Stein (eds.), *Russia's War in Syria: Assessing Russia's Military Capabilities and Lessons Learned* (Philadelphia: Foreign Policy Research Institute, 2020), pp. 47–9.

13. Thomas-Durell Young, 'The United States: Planning and Managing Control and Effectiveness', in Thomas Bruneau and Aurel Croissant (eds.), *Civil–Military Relations: Control and Effectiveness across Regimes* (Boulder: Lynne Rienner, 2019).

14. Lt. Gen. Gary Volesky and Maj. Gen. Roger Noble, 'Theater Land Operations: Relevant Observations and Lessons from the Combined Joint Land Force Experience in Iraq', *Military Review* (June 2017).

15. Richards, 2012, *op. cit.*, p. 192.

16. Conrad Crane, 'Mission Command and Multi-Domain Battle Don't Mix', *War on the Rocks* (23 August 2017), https://warontherocks.com/2017/08/mission-command-and-multi-domain-battle-dont-mix/

17. Gen. Charles C. Krulak, 'The Strategic Corporal: Leadership in the Three Block War', *Marines Magazine* (January 1999).

18. Chiara Ruffa, Christopher Dandeker and Pascal Vennesson, 'Soldiers Drawn into Politics? The Influence of Tactics in Civil–Military Relations', *Small Wars & Insurgencies*, 24:2 (2013), pp. 322–34.

19. Richards, 2014, *op. cit.*, p. 308.

20. Friedman, *op. cit.*, p. 111.

21. For a detailed analysis of the efforts to reform the Russian command systems see Greg Whisler, 'Strategic Command and Control in the Russian Armed Forces: Untangling the General Staff, Military Districts, and Service Main Commands (Part Three)', *Journal of Slavic Military Studies*, 33:2 (2020), pp. 237–58. But note his conclusion: 'Western observers who dismissed the Russian military for two decades as a slow, bloated, and inefficient replica of its Soviet predecessor, and now marvel at how it has been able to operate effectively in Ukraine and Syria, should first look to Moscow's new strategic planning and command and control architecture to understand the advancement of Russian military capabilities more broadly.'

22. Tim Ripley, 'Ukraine Conflict: Russian Military Adapts Command-and-Control for Ukraine Operations', *Janes* (7 March 2022), https://www.janes.com/defence-news/news-detail/ukraine-conflict-russian-military-adapts-command-and-control-for-ukraine-operations

23. The quality of actionable intelligence from the US helped in this, although the need to sort out problems at the front and general lack of operational security added to the vulnerability of senior officers. Julian E. Barnes, Helene Cooper and Eric Schmitt, 'U.S. Intelligence Is Helping Ukraine Kill Russian Generals, Officials Say', New York Times, 4 May 2022, https://www.nytimes.com/2022/05/04/us/politics/russia-generals-killed-ukraine.html; Katie Bo Lillis and Zachary Cohen, 'Who is Russia's Top Field Commander in Ukraine? The US Isn't Sure', *CNN* (21 March 2022).

24. Alex Horton and Shane Harris, 'Russian Troops' Tendency to Talk on Unsecured Lines is Proving Costly', *Washington Post* (27 March 2022), https://www.washingtonpost.com/national-security/2022/03/27/russian-military-unsecured-communications/

25. Nolan Peterson, 'Dispatch: Interview with a Ukrainian Mig-29 Pilot' *Coffee or Die Magazine* (27 March 2022), https://coffeeordie.com/ukrainian-mig-29-pilot-interview/

26. Elliot Ackerman, 'Ukraine's Three-to-One Advantage', *The Atlantic* (24 March 2022), https://www.theatlantic.com/ideas/archive/2022/03/american-volunteer-foreign-fighters-ukraine-russia-war/627604/

27. Liz Sly, 'Nine Ways Russia Botched Its Invasion of Ukraine', *Washington Post* (8 April 2022), https://www.washingtonpost.com/world/2022/04/08/how-russia-botched-ukraine-invasion/; Maxim Tucker, 'Ukrainians Watch Astonished at Groundhog Day Blunders', *Sunday Times* (27 March 2022).

28. Admiral Bill Owens, with Ed Offley, *Lifting the Fog of War* (Baltimore: Johns Hopkins University Press, 2000).

29. Kenneth Payne, *I, Warbot: The Dawn of Artificially Intelligent Conflict* (New York: OUP, 2021).

30. Sydney Freedberg Jr, 'War Without Fear: DepSecDef Work on How AI Changes Conflict', *Breaking Defense* (31 May 2017), https://breakingdefense.com/2017/05/killer-robots-arent-the-problem-its-unpredictable-ai/

31. Henry A. Kissinger, Eric Schmidt and Daniel Huttenlocher, with Schuyler Schouten, *The Age of AI: And Our Human Future* (London: Allen Lane, 2021).

32. Paddy Walker, 'Leadership Challenges from the Deployment of Lethal Autonomous Weapons Systems', *The RUSI Journal*, 166:1 (2021), pp. 10–21.

33. Payne, *op. cit.*; and Elsa Kania, 'Artificial Intelligence in Future Chinese Command Decision Making', in Nicholas D. Wright (ed.), *Artificial Intelligence, China, Russia, and the Global Order* (Maxwell AFB, AL: Air University Press, 2019).

34. Frank Hoffman, *Squaring Clausewitz's Trinity in the Age of Autonomous Weapons* (Foreign Policy Research Institute, 2018), p. 61.

35. Seth Jones, *Three Dangerous Men*, p. 154.

36. Sources on the Chinese reforms: Yasuyuki Sugiura, 'The Joint Operation Structure of the Chinese People's Liberation Army with Focus on the Reorganization of the Chain of Command and Control under the Xi Jinping Administration', originally published in Japanese in *Boei Kenkyusho Kiyo* [NIDS Security Studies], 19:1 (March 2017); Dennis J. Blasko, 'The PLA Army after "Below the Neck" Reforms: Contributing to China's Joint Warfighting, Deterrence and MOOTW Posture', *Journal of Strategic Studies*, 44:2 (2021), pp. 149–183; and Phillip C. Saunders et al. (eds.), *Chairman Xi Remakes the PLA: Assessing Chinese Military Reforms* (Washington, DC: National Defense University Press, 2019).

37. Yuan-Chou Jing, 'How Does China Aim to Use AI in Warfare?', *The Diplomat* (28 December 2021), https://thediplomat.com/2021/12/how-does-china-aim-to-use-ai-in-warfare/

38. This became apparent in May 2021, when US Secretary of Defense Lloyd Austin sought to make contact with his Chinese counterpart. See Tom Fox, *Washington Post* (24 June 2021).

39. Charles Clover, 'Xi's China: Command and Control', *Financial Times* (26 July 2016).

40. Risa Brooks, Jim Golby and Heidi Urben, 'Crisis of Command: America's Broken Civil–Military Relationship Imperils National Security', *Foreign Affairs* (May/June 2021). See also Brooks, *op. cit.*, pp. 7–44.

41. Obama, *op. cit.*, pp. 307–8.

42. Christoph Harig, Nicole Jenne and Chiara Ruffa, 'Operational Experiences, Military Role Conceptions, and Their Influence on Civil–Military Relations', *European Journal of International Security*, 7:1 (2022), p. 9.

43. H. R. McMaster, *Dereliction of Duty: Lyndon Johnson, Robert McNamara, the Joint Chiefs of Staff and the Lies that Led to Vietnam* (New York: HarperPerennial, 1997).

44. 'President Trump Remarks at MacDill Air Force Base' (6 February 2017), https://www.c-span.org/video/?423618-1/president-trump-accuses-very-dishonest-press-not-reporting-isis-attacks

45. Peter Feaver and Richard Kohn, 'Civil–Military Relations in the United States: What Senior Leaders Need to Know (and Usually Don't)', *Strategic Studies Quarterly* (Summer 2021), p. 24.

46. Maggie Astor, 'Michael Flynn Suggested at a QAnon-Affiliated Event that a Coup Should Happen in the U.S.', *New York Times* (1 June 2021); and Nicholas Schmidle, 'Michael Flynn, General Chaos', *New Yorker* (18 February 2017).

47. Dan Lamothe, 'Pentagon's Top General Defends Military as "Apolitical" after Reported Comments About Trump', *Washington Post* (21 July 2021). The revelations about Milley's concerns appeared in Philip Rucker and Carol D. Leonnig, *I Alone Can Fix It: Donald J. Trump's Catastrophic Final Year* (New York: Penguin, 2021).

48. James Walker, 'Top General Says Military Doesn't Take Oath to Any Individual amid Pentagon Shakeup', *Newsweek* (13 November 2020). Milley was opening the new National Museum of the United States Army.

49. McChrystal, Foreword to Lartéguy, 2016, *op. cit.*, p. x.

50. McChrystal, 2014, *op. cit.*, p. 17.

51. See the discussion in Mackubin Thomas Owens, *US Civil–Military Relations after 9/11* (New York: Continuum, 2011), pp. 112–13.

52. Feaver and Kohn, *op. cit.*

Index

Page references in *italics* indicate images.